Reference

Reference

THE NEW
ATLAS

of the United States, Canada, and the World

Maps created by
GeoSystems Global Corporation

Gareth Stevens Publishing
MILWAUKEE

K-III Reference Corporation Staff

Director of Editorial Production
Andrea J. Pitluk

Director–Purchasing and Production
Edward A. Thomas

Deputy Editor
William A. McGeveran, Jr.

Managing Editor
Eileen O'Reilly

Associate Editors
Ileana Parvulescu
Lori Wiesenfeld

Vice President & Editorial Director
Robert Famighetti

GeoSystems Staff

Project Manager
Keith Winters

Project Coordinator
(Encyclopedia map set) Nancy Hamme
Associate Project Coordinator
(Encyclopedia map set) Andrew DeWitt

Project Coordinator
(Atlas) Andrew Green
Associate Project Coordinator
(Atlas) Matt Tharp

Layout & Design
Jeannine Schonta, Andy Skinner

Research & Compilation
Marley Amstutz, John Clements, Ron Haag,
Laura Hartwig, Bill Truninger

Research Librarian Luis Freile

GIS
John Fix, Mark Leitzell, Mike Marino,
Brad Sauder, Dave Folk, Larry Meyers,
Darrin Smith

Cartographers
Kumar Chaudhari, Wendy Crumbaugh,
Sherri Cumberledge, Zach Davis,
Linda Dows-Byers, Nicole Emmich,
Michael Gadd, Brian Goudreau, Chris Gruber,
Marc Hershey, Kendall Marten, Todd Martin,
Jeff Martz, Tara McCoy, Justin Morrill,
Tracey Morrill, Linda Peters, Hylon Plumb,
Robert Rizzutti, West Rowles

Editors
Robert Harding, Dana Wolf

Production Support
Jill Luettgens, Nina Luettgens,
Shawna Roberts, Brenda Stackler

Imagesetting/Proofing
Fred Hofferth, Ron Rittenhouse, Robin White

Copyright © 1998
GeoSystems Global Corporation

For a free color catalog describing Gareth
Stevens' list of high-quality books and
multimedia programs, call 1-800-542-2595
(USA) or 1-800-461-9120 (Canada).
Gareth Stevens Publishing's Fax:
(414) 225-0377.
See our catalog, too, on the World Wide Web:
http://gsinc.com

Library of Congress Cataloging-in-Publication
Data available upon request from publisher.
Fax: (414) 225-0377 for the attention of the
Publishing Records Department.

ISBN 0-8368-2092-4

This edition first published in 1998 by
Gareth Stevens Publishing
1555 North RiverCenter Drive, Suite 201
Milwaukee, Wisconsin 53212 USA

Printed in the United States of America

1 2 3 4 5 6 7 8 9 02 01 00 99 98

TABLE OF CONTENTS

4 WORLD

ASIA and OCEANIA

6 ASIA
8 Japan
9 North Korea, South Korea, Taiwan
10 China
11 Vietnam, Laos, Cambodia, Mongolia
12 Thailand, Burma (Myanmar), Philippines
13 Indonesia, Brunei, Singapore, Malaysia
14 Australia
15 Papua New Guinea, New Zealand,
   Federated States of Micronesia
16 Marshall Is., Nauru, Solomon Is., Tuvalu
17 Kiribati, Fiji, Palau, Tonga
18 Vanuatu, New Caledonia &
   Dependencies, Samoa, American Samoa
19 Nepal, Maldives, Bhutan, Sri Lanka
20 India
21 Bangladesh, Pakistan
22 Afghanistan, Iran, Turkmenistan
23 Kazakhstan, Uzbekistan, Kyrgyzstan,
   Tajikistan
24 Iraq, Kuwait, Saudi Arabia
25 Bahrain, Qatar,
   United Arab Emirates, Yemen, Oman
26 Lebanon, Israel, Jordan
27 Turkey, Cyprus, Syria

EUROPE

30 Great Britain & Northern Ireland
31 Republic of Ireland
32 Denmark, Netherlands
33 Belgium, Luxembourg, Liechtenstein
34 France
35 Monaco, Switzerland
36 Portugal, Malta, Gibraltar, Andorra
37 Spain
38 Italy
39 Austria, Vatican City, San Marino
40 Germany
41 Poland
42 Czech Republic, Slovakia
43 Hungary, Romania
44 Russia
45 Georgia, Armenia, Azerbaijan
46 Estonia, Latvia, Lithuania
47 Belarus, Ukraine
48 Slovenia, Croatia,
   Bosnia & Hercegovina,
   F.Y.R. Macedonia
49 Albania, Yugoslavia
50 Moldova, Bulgaria
51 Greece
52 Iceland, Norway
53 Sweden, Finland

54 AFRICA

56 Egypt, Libya
57 Algeria, Tunisia, Morocco
58 Western Sahara, Cape Verde,
   Mali, Mauritania
59 Chad, Niger, Sudan
60 Eritrea, Djibouti, Ethiopia, Somalia
61 Kenya, Uganda, Rwanda, Burundi
62 Senegal, The Gambia, Guinea,
   Guinea-Bissau
63 Sierra Leone, Côte d'Ivoire,
   São Tomé & Príncipe, Liberia
64 Ghana, Burkina Faso, Benin, Togo
65 Nigeria, Cameroon
66 Equatorial Guinea, Republic of the
   Congo, Gabon, Central African Republic
67 Comoros, Democratic Republic of the
   Congo, Zambia
68 Tanzania, Malawi, Mozambique
69 Mauritius, Zimbabwe, Botswana,
   Madagascar
70 Angola, Namibia, Seychelles
71 South Africa, Swaziland, Lesotho

72 SOUTH AMERICA

74 Argentina
75 Paraguay, Uruguay
76 Chile
77 Peru, Bolivia
78 Colombia
79 Ecuador, Venezuela
80 Guyana, Suriname, French Guiana
81 Brazil

82 NORTH AMERICA

84 Mexico
85 Belize, Guatemala
86 Honduras, El Salvador, Costa Rica
87 Nicaragua, Panama
88 Cuba, Jamaica
89 Dominican Republic, Haiti, Bahamas,
   Turks & Caicos Is.
90 Puerto Rico, Antigua & Barbuda,
   St. Kitts & Nevis, Dominica
91 St. Lucia, Barbados,
   St. Vincent & the Grenadines,
   Grenada, Trinidad & Tobago
92 Canada
93 Canadian Provincial & Territorial Flags
94 Alberta
95 British Columbia
96 Manitoba
97 New Brunswick
98 Newfoundland
99 Northwest Territories
100 Nova Scotia, Prince Edward Island
101 Ontario, Québec
102 Southern Ontario
103 Southern Québec
104 Saskatchewan
105 Yukon Territory

LEGEND

POLAR REGIONS

106 Arctic Regions, Greenland
107 Antarctica

108 WORLD INDEX

UNITED STATES

126 U.S. Political
127 U.S. Physical
128 Alabama
129 Alaska
130 Arizona
131 Arkansas
132 California
133 Colorado
134 Connecticut
135 Delaware
136 Florida
137 Georgia
138 Hawaii
139 Idaho
140 Illinois
141 Indiana
142 Iowa
143 Kansas
144 Kentucky
145 Louisiana
146 Maine
147 Maryland
148 Massachusetts
149 Michigan
150 Minnesota
151 Mississippi
152 Missouri
153 Montana
154 Nebraska
155 Nevada
156 New Hampshire
157 New Jersey
158 New Mexico
159 New York
160 North Carolina
161 North Dakota
162 Ohio
163 Oklahoma
164 Oregon
165 Pennsylvania
166 Rhode Island
167 South Carolina
168 South Dakota
169 Tennessee
170 Texas
171 Utah
172 Vermont
173 Virginia
174 Washington
175 West Virginia
176 Wisconsin
177 Wyoming

178 STATE INDEXES

General

- ⊛ National Capital
- ★ Territorial Capital
- • Other City
- International Boundary (subject area)
- International Boundary (non-subject)
- Internal Boundary (state, province, etc.)
- Disputed Boundary
- Perennial River
- Intermittent River
- Canal
- Dam

U.S. States, Canadian Provinces & Territories
(additions and changes to general legend)

- ★ State Capital
- ◎ County Seat
- Built Up Area
- State Boundary
- County Boundary
- National Park
- Other Park, Forest, Grassland
- Indian, Other Reservation
- ■ Point of Interest
- ▲ Mountain Peak
- Continental Divide
- Time Zone Boundary
- Limited Access Highway
- Other Major Road
- 90 Highway Shield

PROJECTION

The only true representation of the earth, free of distortion, is a globe. Maps are flat, and the process by which the geographic locations (latitude and longitude) are transformed from a three-dimensional sphere to a two-dimensional flat map is called a Projection.

For a detailed explanation of Projections, see *MapScope* in Volume 2 of *Funk & Wagnalls New Encyclopedia.*

This example is used on pages 20, 21 for India, Bangladesh, and Pakistan.

The Globe is centered on the continent of Asia, as shown on pages 6, 7.

The subject countries are shown in a stronger red/brown color.

LOCATOR

TYPES OF SCALE

VISUAL SCALE

Every map has a bar scale, or a Visual Scale, that can be used for measuring. It shows graphically the relationship between map distance and ground distance.

Miles

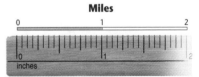

One inch represents 1 mile

Kilometers

One centimeter represents 10 kilometers

REPRESENTATIVE FRACTION

The scale of a map, expressed as a numerical ratio of map distance to ground distance, is called a Representative Fraction (or RF). It is usually written as 1/50,000 or 1:50,000, meaning that one unit of measurement on the map represents 50,000 of the same units on the ground.

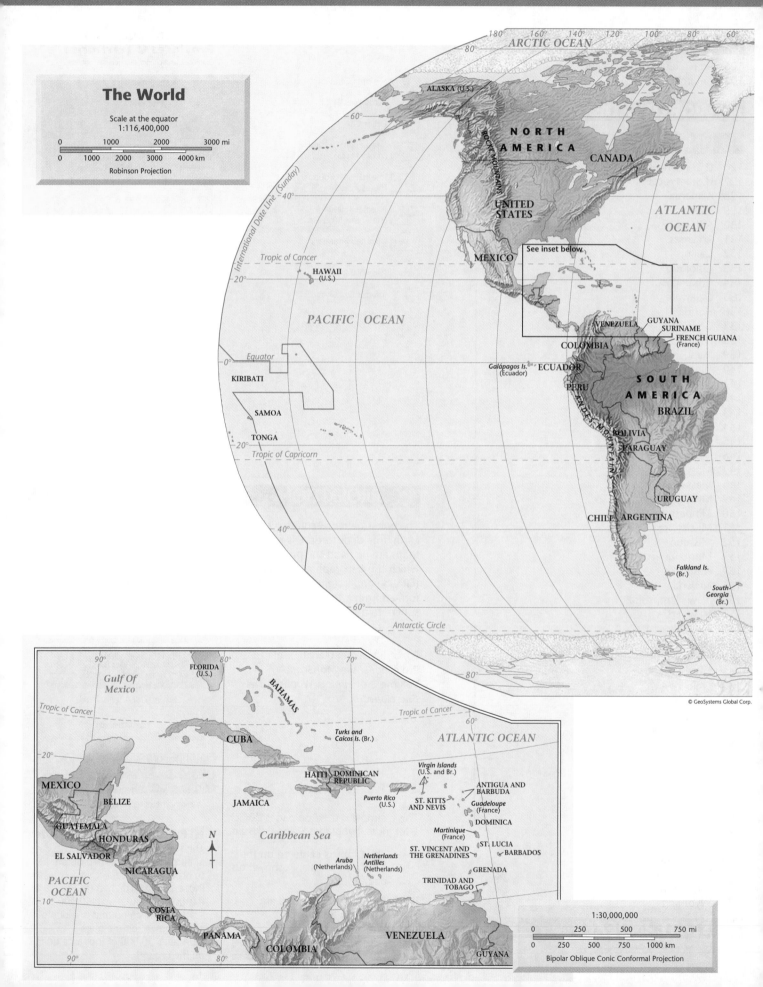

The World

Scale at the equator
1:116,400,000

| 0 | 1000 | 2000 | 3000 mi |
| 0 | 1000 | 2000 | 3000 | 4000 km |

Robinson Projection

ARCTIC OCEAN

ALASKA (U.S.)

NORTH AMERICA

CANADA

UNITED STATES

ATLANTIC OCEAN

ROCKY MOUNTAINS

International Date Line (Sunday)

Tropic of Cancer

HAWAII (U.S.)

MEXICO

See inset below

PACIFIC OCEAN

Equator

KIRIBATI

Galápagos Is. (Ecuador)

VENEZUELA

GUYANA

SURINAME

FRENCH GUIANA (France)

COLOMBIA

ECUADOR

PERU

SOUTH AMERICA

BRAZIL

SAMOA

BOLIVIA

PARAGUAY

ANDES MOUNTAINS

TONGA

Tropic of Capricorn

URUGUAY

CHILE ARGENTINA

Falkland Is. (Br.)

South Georgia (Br.)

Antarctic Circle

© GeoSystems Global Corp.

Inset map

Gulf Of Mexico

FLORIDA (U.S.)

BAHAMAS

Tropic of Cancer

CUBA

Turks and Caicos Is. (Br.)

ATLANTIC OCEAN

MEXICO

HAITI DOMINICAN REPUBLIC

Virgin Islands (U.S. and Br.)

ANTIGUA AND BARBUDA

BELIZE

JAMAICA

Puerto Rico (U.S.)

ST. KITTS AND NEVIS

Guadeloupe (France)

DOMINICA

GUATEMALA

Caribbean Sea

Martinique (France)

ST. LUCIA

HONDURAS

N

ST. VINCENT AND THE GRENADINES

BARBADOS

EL SALVADOR

NICARAGUA

Aruba (Netherlands)

Netherlands Antilles (Netherlands)

GRENADA

PACIFIC OCEAN

TRINIDAD AND TOBAGO

COSTA RICA

PANAMA

VENEZUELA

COLOMBIA

GUYANA

1:30,000,000

| 0 | 250 | 500 | 750 mi |
| 0 | 250 | 500 | 750 | 1000 km |

Bipolar Oblique Conic Conformal Projection

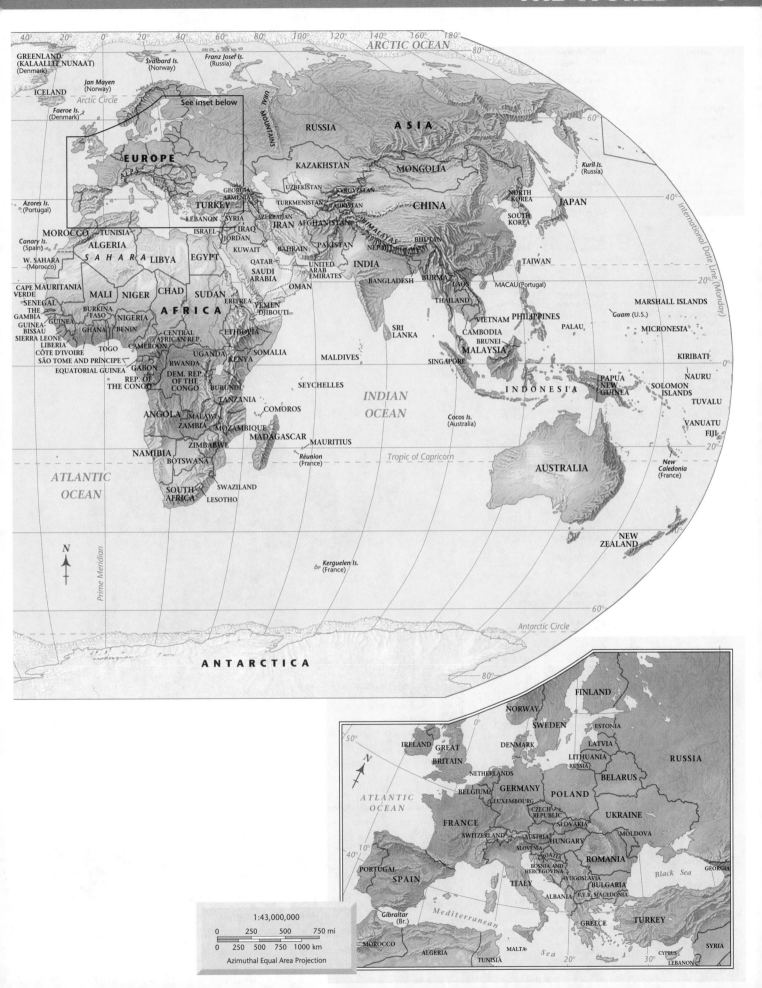

ARCTIC OCEAN

GREENLAND
(KALAALLIT NUNAAT)
(Denmark)

Svalbard Is.
(Norway)

Franz Josef Is.
(Russia)

ICELAND

Jan Mayen
(Norway)

Arctic Circle

Faeroe Is.
(Denmark)

See inset below

RUSSIA

ASIA

URAL MOUNTAINS

Kuril Is.
(Russia)

EUROPE

ALPS

KAZAKHSTAN

MONGOLIA

Azores Is.
(Portugal)

GEORGIA
ARMENIA

UZBEKISTAN

KYRGYZSTAN

NORTH
KOREA

JAPAN

TURKEY

TURKMENISTAN

TAJIKISTAN

CHINA

SOUTH
KOREA

LEBANON

SYRIA

AZERBAIJAN

MOROCCO

ISRAEL

IRAQ

IRAN

AFGHANISTAN

HIMALAYAS

TAIWAN

Canary Is.
(Spain)

JORDAN

KUWAIT

PAKISTAN

NEPAL

BHUTAN

TUNISIA

BAHRAIN

MARSHALL ISLANDS

ALGERIA

LIBYA

EGYPT

QATAR
SAUDI
ARABIA

UNITED
ARAB
EMIRATES

INDIA

BANGLADESH

BURMA

MACAU (Portugal)

W. SAHARA
(Morocco)

SAHARA

OMAN

LAOS

Guam (U.S.)

CAPE
VERDE

MAURITANIA

MALI

NIGER

CHAD

SUDAN

ERITREA

YEMEN

THAILAND

VIETNAM

PHILIPPINES

PALAU

MICRONESIA

SENEGAL
THE
GAMBIA
GUINEA-
BISSAU

BURKINA
FASO

NIGERIA

DJIBOUTI

AFRICA

ETHIOPIA

CAMBODIA

BRUNEI

KIRIBATI

GUINEA

BENIN

SRI
LANKA

MALAYSIA

NAURU

SIERRA LEONE
LIBERIA
CÔTE D'IVOIRE

GHANA

CENTRAL
AFRICAN REP.

UGANDA

SOMALIA

MALDIVES

SINGAPORE

TOGO
SÃO TOME AND PRÍNCIPE

CAMEROON

KENYA

SOLOMON
ISLANDS

EQUATORIAL GUINEA

GABON
REP. OF
THE CONGO

RWANDA
DEM. REP.
OF THE
CONGO

BURUNDI

SEYCHELLES

INDONESIA

PAPUA
NEW
GUINEA

TUVALU

TANZANIA

INDIAN
OCEAN

VANUATU

ANGOLA

MALAWI
ZAMBIA

COMOROS

FIJI

ZIMBABWE

MOZAMBIQUE

MADAGASCAR

MAURITIUS

Cocos Is.
(Australia)

Tropic of Capricorn

New
Caledonia
(France)

NAMIBIA

BOTSWANA

Réunion
(France)

ATLANTIC
OCEAN

SOUTH
AFRICA

SWAZILAND

LESOTHO

AUSTRALIA

N

Prime Meridian

NEW
ZEALAND

Kerguelen Is.
(France)

International Date Line (Monday)

ANTARCTICA

Antarctic Circle

Antarctic Circle

1:43,000,000

0   250   500   750 mi

0 250 500 750 1000 km

Azimuthal Equal Area Projection

FINLAND

NORWAY

SWEDEN

ESTONIA

IRELAND

GREAT
BRITAIN

DENMARK

LATVIA

LITHUANIA

RUSSIA

RUSSIA

BELARUS

NETHERLANDS

N

ATLANTIC
OCEAN

BELGIUM

GERMANY

POLAND

LUXEMBOURG

UKRAINE

FRANCE

CZECH
REPUBLIC

SLOVAKIA

SWITZERLAND

AUSTRIA

MOLDOVA

SLOVENIA

HUNGARY

CROATIA

ROMANIA

PORTUGAL

SPAIN

BOSNIA AND
HERCEGOVINA

YUGOSLAVIA

GEORGIA

Black Sea

ITALY

BULGARIA

ALBANIA

F.Y.R. MACEDONIA

Gibraltar
(Br.)

GREECE

TURKEY

Mediterranean

MOROCCO

ALGERIA

TUNISIA

MALTA

Sea

CYPRUS

SYRIA

LEBANON

MAJOR CITIES

Afghanistan
Kabul 1,424,000

Bahrain
Manama 151,000

Bangladesh (metro)
Dhaka 3,459,000

Bhutan
Thimphu 8,900

Brunei
Band. Seri Begawan 51,000

Burma (Myanmar)
Rangoon 2,513,000

Cambodia
Phnom Penh 800,000

China
Shanghai 7,500,000
Beijing 5,700,000
Tianjin 4,500,000
Shenyang 3,600,000
Wuhan 3,200,000
Guangzhou 2,900,000
Chongqing 2,700,000
Harbin 2,500,000
Chengdu 2,500,000
Zibo 2,200,000
Xi'an 2,200,000
Nanjing 2,091,000

Cyprus (metro)
Nicosia 167,000

India (metro)
Bombay 12,572,000
Calcutta 10,916,000
Delhi 8,375,000
Madras 5,361,000
Hyderabad 4,280,000
Bangalore 4,087,000

Indonesia
Jakarta 8,200,000
Surabaya 2,400,000
Bandung 2,000,000
Medan 1,700,000

Iran
Tehran 6,043,000
Mashhad 1,464,000

Iraq
Baghdad 3,841,000

Israel
Jerusalem 544,000

Japan
Tokyo 8,164,000
Yokohama 3,220,000
Osaka 2,624,000
Nagoya 2,155,000
Sapporo 1,672,000
Kobe 1,477,000
Kyoto 1,461,000
Fukuoka 1,237,000
Kawasaki 1,174,000
Hiroshima 1,086,000

Jordan
Amman 936,000

Kazakhstan
Almaty 1,147,000

North Korea
P'yŏngyang 2,300,000

South Korea
Seoul 10,628,000
Pusan 3,798,000
Taegu 2,229,000

Kuwait
Kuwait 78,000

Kyrgyzstan
Bishkek 628,000

Laos
Vientiane 377,000

Lebanon
Beirut 475,000

Malaysia
Kuala Lumpur 920,000

Maldives
Male 55,000

Mongolia
Ulan Bator 536,000

Nepal
Kathmandu 419,000

Oman
Masqat 85,000

Pakistan (metro)
Karachi 5,181,000
Lahore 2,953,000
Faisalabad 1,104,000
Islamabad 204,000

Philippines (metro)
Manila 1,895,000

Qatar
Doha 236,000

Russia (Asian)
Novosibirsk 1,442,000
Yekaterinburg 1,371,000
Omsk 1,169,000
Chelyabinsk 1,143,000
Krasnoyarsk 925,000

Saudi Arabia
Riyadh 1,300,000
Jiddah 1,200,000

Singapore
Singapore 2,818,000

Sri Lanka
Colombo 615,000

Syria
Damascus 1,451,000
Halab (Aleppo) 1,445,000

Taiwan
Taipei 1,770,000

Tajikistan
Dushanbe 602,000

Thailand
Bangkok 5,876,000

Turkey (Asian)
Ankara 2,559,000
İzmir 1,757,000

Turkmenistan
Ashgabat 407,000

United Arab Emirates
Abu Dhabi 722,000

Uzbekistan
Tashkent 2,094,000

Vietnam
Ho Chi Minh City 2,900,000
Hanoi 1,090,000

Yemen (metro)
Sana 427,000

International comparability of city population data is limited by various data inconsistencies.

© GeoSystems Global Corp.

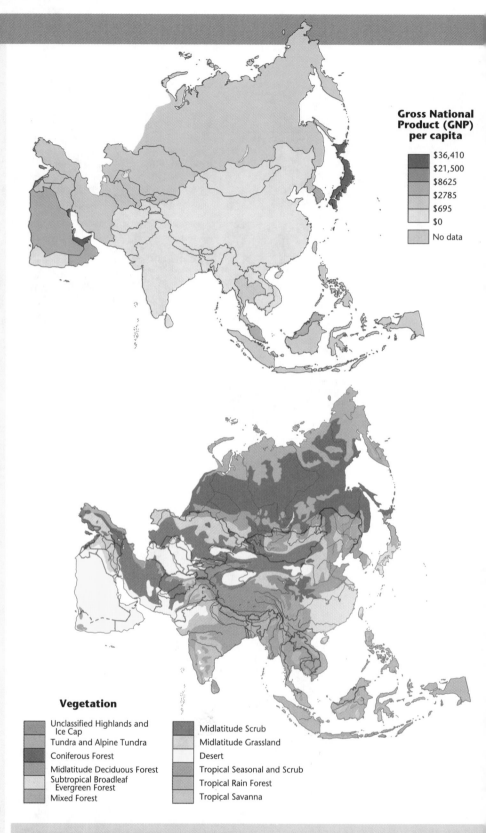

Gross National Product (GNP) per capita

- $36,410
- $21,500
- $8625
- $2785
- $695
- $0
- No data

Vegetation

- Unclassified Highlands and Ice Cap
- Tundra and Alpine Tundra
- Coniferous Forest
- Midlatitude Deciduous Forest
- Subtropical Broadleaf Evergreen Forest
- Mixed Forest
- Midlatitude Scrub
- Midlatitude Grassland
- Desert
- Tropical Seasonal and Scrub
- Tropical Rain Forest
- Tropical Savanna

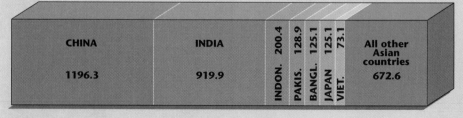

Asia: Population, by nation (in millions)

CHINA	INDIA	INDON.	PAKIS.	BANGL.	JAPAN	VIET.	All other Asian countries
1196.3	919.9	200.4	128.9	125.1	125.1	73.1	672.6

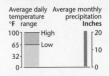

CLIMATE

Average daily temperature °F range
Average monthly precipitation Inches

ALMATY, Kazakhstan

BEIRUT, Lebanon

COLOMBO, Sri Lanka

DHAKA, Bangladesh

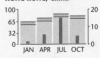

HONG KONG, China

JAKARTA, Indonesia

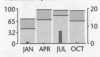

NEW DELHI, India

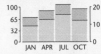

RIYADH, Saudi Arabia

TEHRAN, Iran

TIANJIN, China

TOKYO, Japan

YAKUTSK, Russia

Temp. Range −53 to −45

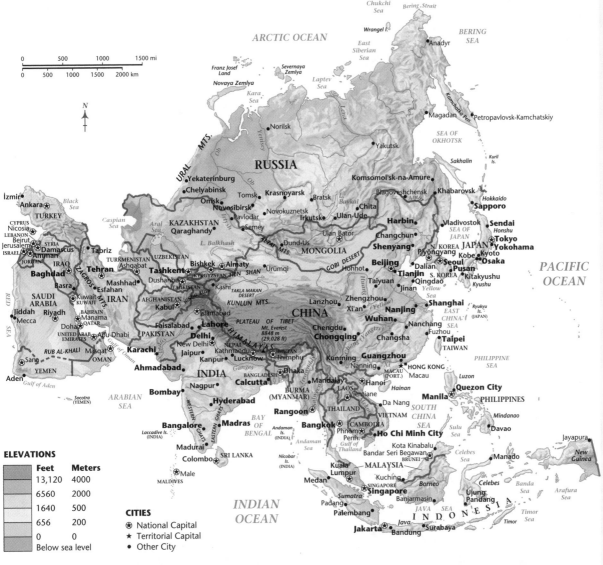

ELEVATIONS

Feet	Meters
13,120	4000
6560	2000
1640	500
656	200
0	0
Below sea level	

CITIES

⊛ National Capital
★ Territorial Capital
• Other City

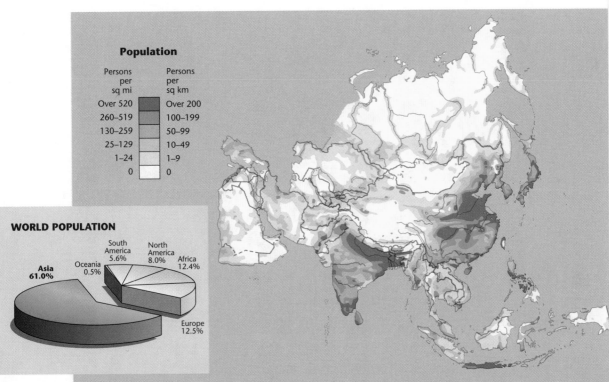

Population

Persons per sq mi	Persons per sq km
Over 520	Over 200
260–519	100–199
130–259	50–99
25–129	10–49
1–24	1–9
0	0

WORLD POPULATION

Asia 61.0%
Oceania 0.5%
South America 5.6%
North America 8.0%
Africa 12.4%
Europe 12.5%

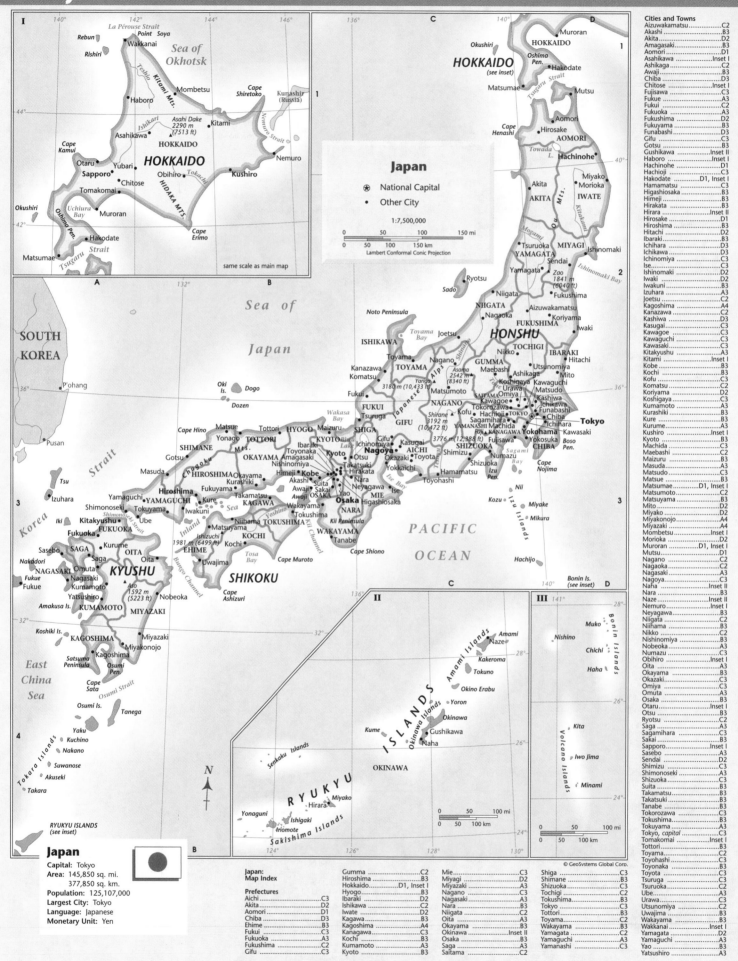

North Korea and South Korea

- ⊛ National Capital
- ● Other City

1:6,625,000

0　　50　　100 mi
0　50　100 km
Lambert Conformal Conic Projection

CHINA

RUSSIA

NORTH KOREA

Paektu-san 2744 m (9003 ft)

NORTH HAMGYŎNG

YANGGANG

CHAGANG

NORTH P'YŎNGAN

Korea Bay

SOUTH HAMGYŎNG

SOUTH P'YŎNGAN

P'yŏngyang NAMP'O

Yellow Sea

SOUTH HWANGHAE

NORTH HWANGHAE

KAESŎNG

KANGWŎN

Sea of Japan

Ullŭng-do

Seoul INCH'ŎN

KYŎNGGI

KANGWŎN

TAEBAEK-SANMAEK

NORTH CH'UNGCH'ŎNG

SOUTH CH'UNGCH'ŎNG

SOUTH KOREA

NORTH KYŎNGSANG

TAEGU

NORTH CHŎLLA

SOUTH KYŎNGSANG

KWANGJU

SOUTH CHŎLLA

PUSAN

Koje-do

Western Channel

Korea Strait

Tsu

Cheju Strait

CHEJU

Cheju
Halla-san 1950 m (6398 ft)

same scale as main map

© GeoSystems Global Corp.

Japan: Map Index

Yokkaichi C3
Yokohama C3
Yokosuka C3
Yonago B3
Yubari ....Inset I

Other Features
Akuseki, island A4
Amakusa, island A3
Amami, island ....Inset II
Amami, islands ....Inset II
Asahi Dake, mt. ....Inset I
Asama, mt. C2
Ashizuri, cape B3
Aso, mt. A3
Awaji, island B3
Biwa, lake B3
Bonin, islands ....Inset III
Boso, peninsula D3
Bungo, channel B3
Chichi, island ....Inset III
Chugoku, mts. B3
Dogo, island B2
Dozen, island B2
East China, sea A4
Erimo, cape ....Inset I
Fuji, mt. C3
Fukue, island A3
Hachijo, island C3
Haha, island ....Inset III
Henashi, cape C1
Hidaka, mts. ....Inset I
Hino, cape B3
Hokkaido, island ...D1, Inset I
Honshu, island C2
Iki, island A3
Inland, sea B3
Iriomote, island ....Inset II
Ise, bay C3
Ishigaki, island ....Inset II
Ishikari, river ....Inset I
Ishinomaki, bay D2
Ishizuchi, mt. B3
Iwo Jima, island ....Inset III
Izu, islands C3
Izu, peninsula C3
Japan, sea B2
Japanese Alps, mts. C3
Kakeroma, island ....Inset II
Kamui, cape ....Inset I
Kii, channel B3
Kii, peninsula B3
Kita, island ....Inset III
Kitakami, river D2
Kitami, mts. ....Inset I
Korea, strait A3
Koshiki, islands A4
Kozu, island C3
Kuchino, island A4
Kume, island ....Inset II
Kyushu, island A3
La Pérouse, strait ....Inset I
Mikura, island C3
Minami, island ....Inset III
Miyake, island C3
Miyako, island ....Inset II
Mogami, river D2
Muko, island ....Inset III
Muroto, cape B3
Nakadori, island A3
Nakano, island A4
Nemuro, strait ....Inset I
Nii, island C3
Nishino, island ....Inset III
Nojima, cape D3
Noto, peninsula C2
Okhotsk, sea ....Inset I
Oki, islands B2
Okinawa, island ....Inset II
Okinawa, islands ....Inset II
Okino Erabu, island ....Inset II
Okushiri, island ....C1, Inset I
Oshima, peninsula ..D1, Inset I
Osumi, islands A4
Osumi, peninsula A4
Osumi, strait A4
Ou, mts. D2
Rebun, island ....Inset I
Rishiri, island ....Inset I
Ryukyu, islands ......A4, Inset II
Sado, island C2
Sagami, bay C3
Sakishima, islands ....Inset II
Sata, cape A4
Satsuma, peninsula A4
Senkaku, islands ....Inset II
Shikoku, island B3
Shimonoseki, strait A3
Shinano, river C2
Shiono, cape B3
Shirane, mt. C3
Shiretoko, cape ....Inset I
Soya, point ....Inset I
Suwanose, island A4
Takara, island A4
Tanega, island A4
Tenryu, river C3
Teshio, river ....Inset I
Tokachi, river ....Inset I
Tokara, islands A4
Tokuno, island ....Inset II
Tone, river C2
Tosa, bay B3
Towada, lake D1
Toyama, bay C2
Tsu, island A3
Tsugaru, strait ...D1, Inset I
Uchiura, bay ....Inset I
Volcano, islands ....Inset III
Wakasa, bay B3
Yaku, island A4
Yariga, mt. C2
Yonaguni, island ....Inset II
Yoron, island ....Inset II
Yoshino, river B3
Zao, mt. D2

North Korea: Map Index

Provinces
Chagang B2
Kaesŏng B3
Kangwŏn B3
Namp'o A3
North Hamgyŏng C1
North Hwanghae A3
North P'yŏngan A2
P'yŏngyang A3
South Hamgyŏng B2
South Hwanghae A3
South P'yŏngan A3
Yanggang B2

Cities and Towns
Anju A3
Changjin B2
Changyŏn A3
Ch'ŏngjin A3
Chŏngju A3
Haeju A3
Hamhŭng B2
Hoeryŏng C1
Hŭich'ŏn B2
Hŭngnam B2
Hyesan C2
Ich'ŏn B3
Kaesŏng B4
Kanggye B2
Kilchu C2
Kimch'aek C2
Kosŏng C3
Kowŏn B2
Kusŏng B2
Manp'o B2
Musan C1
Najin D1
Namp'o A3
Ongjin A4
Onsŏng C1
P'anmunjŏm B4
Pukch'ŏng B2
P'ungsan B2
P'yŏnggang B3
P'yŏngyang B3
P'yŏngsŏng A3
P'yŏngyang, capital A3
Sariwŏn A3
Sinp'o C2
Sinŭiju A3
Songnim A3
Tanch'ŏn B2
Wŏnsan B3
Yangdŏk B3

Other Features
Chaeryŏng, river A3
Changjin, river B2
Ch'ongch'ŏn, river A3
Hamgyŏng, mts. C2
Imjin, river B3
Kanghwa, bay A4
Korea, bay A3
Musu-dan, point C2
Nangnim-sanmaek, mts. B3
Paektu-san, mt. C2
Sŏjosŏn, bay A3
Sup'ung, reservoir A2
Taedong, river A3
Tongjosŏn, bay B2
Tumen, river C1
Yalu, river B2

South Korea: Map Index

Provinces
Cheju ....Inset
Inch'ŏn B4
Kangwŏn B5
Kwangju B5
Kyŏnggi B4
North Chŏlla B5
North Ch'ungch'ŏng B4
North Kyŏngsang C4
Pusan C5
Seoul B4
South Chŏlla B5
South Ch'ungch'ŏng B4
South Kyŏngsang C5
Taegu C5
Taejŏn B4

Cities and Towns
Andong C4
Anyang B4
Chech'ŏn C4
Cheju ....Inset
Chinhae C5
Chinju C5
Chŏnju B5
Ch'ŏnan B4
Ch'ŏngju B4
Ch'ungju C4
Inch'ŏn B4
Iri B5
Kangnŭng C4
Kimch'ŏn C4
Kunsan B5
Kwangju B5
Kyŏngju C5
Masan C5
Mokp'o B5
Munsan B4
Nonsan B4
P'ohang C4
Pusan C5
Samch'ŏk C4
Seoul, capital B4
Sokch'o C3
Sŏngnam B4
Sunch'ŏn B5
Suwŏn B4
Taegu C5
Taejŏn B4
Ulchin C4
Ulsan C5
Wŏnju C4
Wando B5
Yŏngju C4
Yŏsu B5

Other Features
Cheju, island ....Inset
Cheju, strait ....Inset
Halla-san, mt. ....Inset
Han, river B4
Hŭksan Chedo, islands A5
Kanghwa, bay A4
Koje-do, island C5
Korea, strait C5
Kum, river B4
Naktong, river C5
Soan-kundo, islands B5
Sobaek, mts. C5
Taebaek-Sanmaek, mts. C3
Tŏkchŏk-kundo, islands A4
Ullŭng-do, island D4
Western, channel C5

North Korea

Capital: P'yŏngyang
Area: 47,399 sq. mi.
　122,795 sq. km.
Population: 23,067,000
Largest City: P'yŏngyang
Language: Korean
Monetary Unit: Won

South Korea

Capital: Seoul
Area: 38,330 sq. mi.
　99,301 sq. km.
Population: 45,083,000
Largest City: Seoul
Language: Korean
Monetary Unit: Won

Taiwan

- ⊛ National Capital
- ● Other City

1:10,292,000

0　30　60 mi
0　30　60 km
Lambert Conformal Conic Projection

CHINA

East China Sea

Tanshui
Chilung
Hsinchuang
T'aoyüan
Taipei
Chungli
Yungho
Panch'iao
Hsintien
Hsinchu
Chungho
Ilan
Chunan
Miaoli
Tan shui
Fengyüan
Shanchung
Changhua
T'aichung
Hualien
Nant'ou
CHUNG-YANG RANGE
P'enghu Is. (Pescadores)
Touliu
Yü Shan 3997 m (13,113 ft)
Choshui
Makung
Pescadores Channel
Chiai
Hsinying
T'ainan
Kangshan
P'ingtung
T'aitung
Kaohsiung
Fengshan
Fang-liao
Hengch'un
Lü I.
South China Sea
Philippine Sea
Luzon Strait
Lan I.

© GeoSystems Global Corp.

Taiwan

Capital: Taipei
Area: 13,969 sq. mi.
　36,189 sq. km.
Population: 21,299,000
Largest City: Taipei
Language: Mandarin Chinese
Monetary Unit: New Taiwan dollar

Taiwan: Map Index

Cities and Towns
Changhua B1
Chiai B2
Chilung B1
Chunan B1
Chungho B1
Chungli B1
Fangliao B2
Fengshan B2
Fengyüan B1
Hengch'un B2
Hsinchu B1
Hsinchuang B1
Hsintien B1
Hsinying B2
Hualien B2
Ilan B1
Kangshan B2
Kaohsiung B2
Makung A2
Miaoli B1
Nant'ou B1
Panch'iao B1
P'ingtung B2

Shanchung B1
T'aichung B1
T'ainan B2
Taipei, capital B1
T'aitung B2
Tanshui B1
T'aoyüan B1
Touliu B2
Yungho B1

Other Features
Choshui, river B2
Chungyang, range B2
East China, sea B1
Kaop'ing, river B2
Lan, island B2
Lü, island B2
Luzon, strait A2
P'enghu (Pescadores), islands A2
Pescadores, channel A2
Philippine, sea B2
South China, sea A2
Taiwan, strait A1
Tanshui, river B1
Tsengwen, river B2
Yü Shan, mt. B2

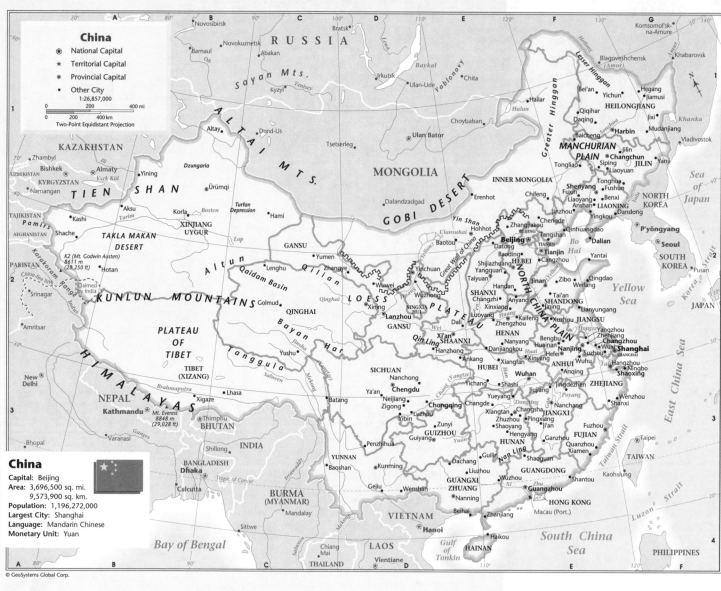

China

- ⊛ National Capital
- ★ Territorial Capital
- ◉ Provincial Capital
- • Other City

1:26,857,000

0   200   400 mi
0 200 400 km
Two-Point Equidistant Projection

China

Capital: Beijing
Area: 3,696,500 sq. mi.
9,573,900 sq. km.
Population: 1,196,272,000
Largest City: Shanghai
Language: Mandarin Chinese
Monetary Unit: Yuan

© GeoSystems Global Corp.

Hong Kong S.A.R.

Population: 5,841,000
• City

1:1,800,000

0   10   20 mi
0 10 20 km
Transverse Mercator Projection

© GeoSystems Global Corp.

China: Map Index

Internal Divisions
Provinces
Anhui E2
Fujian E3
Gansu C1, D2
Guangdong E3
Guizhou D3
Hainan D4
Hebei E2
Heilongjiang F1
Henan E2
Hubei E2
Hunan E3
Jiangsu E2
Jiangxi E3
Jilin F1
Liaoning F1
Qinghai C2
Shaanxi D2
Shandong E2
Shanxi E2
Sichuan D2
Yunnan C3
Zhejiang E3

Autonomous Regions
Guangxi Zhuang D3
Inner Mongolia E1
Ningxia Hui D2
Tibet (Xizang) B2
Xinjiang Uygur B1

Independent Municipalities
Beijing E1
Shanghai E2
Tianjin E2

Special Administrative Region (S.A.R.)
Hong Kong ....E3, Inset

Cities and Towns
Aksu B1
Aberdeen ....Inset
Altay B1
Ankang E2
Anqing E2
Anshan F1
Anyang E2

Baicheng F1
Baoding E2
Baoshan C3
Baotou E1
Batang C3
Bei'an F1
Beihai D3
Beijing, capital E2
Bengbu E2
Benxi F1
Cangzhou E2
Changchun F1
Changde E3
Changsha E3
Changzhi E2
Changzhou F2
Chek Keng ....Inset
Chengde E1
Chengdu D2
Chifeng E1
Chongqing D3
Chung Hau ....Inset
Dachang D3
Dali D2
Dalian F2
Dandong F1
Danjiangkou E2
Daqing F1
Datong E1
Erenhot E1
Fushun F1
Fuxin F1
Fuzhou E3
Ganzhou E3
Gejiu D3
Golmud C2
Guangzhou E3
Guilin D3
Guiyang D3
Haikou E4
Hailar E1
Hami C1
Handan E2
Hangzhou F2
Hanzhong D2
Harbin F1
Hefei E2
Hegang G1
Hengyang E3
Hohhot E1
Hotan A2
Huainan E2

Jiamusi G1
Ji'an E3
Jilin F1
Jinan E2
Jingdezhen E3
Jining E2
Jinzhou F1
Jiujiang E3
Jixi G1
Kaifeng E2
Kashi A2
Korla B1
Kowloon ....Inset
Kunming D3
Lanzhou D2
Lenghu C2
Lhasa C3
Lianyungang E2
Liaoyang F1
Liaoyuan F1
Liuzhou D3
Lo Wu ....Inset
Luoyang E2
Luzhou D3
Mudanjiang F1
Nanchang E3
Nanchong D2
Nanjing E2
Nanning D3
Nanyang E2
Neijiang D3
New Kowloon ....Inset
Ningbo F3
Penzhihua D3
Pingxiang E3
Qingdao E2
Qinhuangdao E2
Qiqihar F1
Quanzhou E3
Sai Kung ....Inset
Sha Tin ....Inset
Shache A2
Shanghai F2
Shantou E3
Shanxi E2
Shaoguan E3
Shaoxing F3
Shaoyang E3
Shashi E2
Shek Pik ....Inset
Shenyang F1
Shijiazhuang E2

Siping F1
Suzhou F2
Tai'an E2
Taiyuan E2
Tangshan E2
Tianjin E2
Tonghua F1
Tongliao F1
Tsuen Wan ....Inset
Tuen Mun ....Inset
Ürümqi B1
Weifang E2
Wenshan D3
Wenzhou F3
Wuhan E2
Wuhu E2
Wuwei D2
Wuxi F2
Wuzhong D2
Wuzhou E3
Xiamen E3
Xi'an D2
Xiangfan E2
Xiangtan E3
Xigaze B3
Xining D2
Xinxiang E2
Xinyang E2
Xuzhou E2
Ya'an D2
Yangquan E2
Yangzhou E2
Yanji F1
Yantai E2
Yibin D3
Yichang E2
Yichun F1
Yinchuan D2
Yingkou F1
Yining B1
Yuen Long ....Inset
Yueyang E3
Yumen C2
Zhangjiakou E2
Zhangye D2
Zhanjiang D3
Zhengzhou E2
Zhenjiang E3
Zhuzhou E3
Zibo E2
Zigong D3

Zunyi D3

Other Features
Altai, mts. B1
Altun, range B2
Bayan Har, range C2
Bo Hai, gulf E2
Bosten, lake B1
Brahmaputra, river B3
Chang (Yangtze), river .D2, E2
Deep, bay ....Inset
Dongting, lake E3
Dzungaria, desert basin B1
East China, sea F2
Fen, river E2
Gan, river E3
Gobi, desert D1
Greater Hinggan, range F1
Great Wall of China D2
Han, river E3
Heilong (Amur), river F1
Himalayas, mts. B3
Hong Kong, island ....Inset
Hongze, lake E2
Huai, river E2
Huang (Yellow), river ..D2, E2
Hulun, lake E1
Indus, river A2
Jinsha (Yangtze), river C2
Khanka, lake G1
Kunlun, mts. B2
K2 (Godwin Austen), mt. ..A2
Lantau, island ....Inset
Lesser Hinggan, range F1
Liao, river E1
Loess, plateau E2
Lop, lake C1
Manchurian, plain F1
Mekong, river C2
Nan Ling, mts. E3
New Territories, island ....Inset
North China, plain E2
Pamirs, region A2
Poyang, lake E3
Qaidam, basin C2
Qilian, range C2
Qinghai, lake C2
Qin Ling, mts. D2
Salween, river C3
Songhua, river F1
South China, sea ....E4, Inset
StoneCutters (S.I.), island ....Inset

Tai, lake F2
Taiwan, strait E3
Takla Makan, desert B2
Tanggula, range C2
Tarim, river B1
Tibet, plateau B2
Tien Shan, range A1
Tonkin, gulf D4
Turfan, depression C1
Ulansuhai, lake D1
Wei, river D2
Xi, river D3
Yalu, river F1
Yangtze, river C2, D2
Yellow, sea F2
Yin Shan, mts. D1
Yuan, river D3
Zhu, river E3

Vietnam: Map Index

Cities and Towns

Bac Lieu	A5
Bien Hoa	B4
Buon Me Thuot	B4
Ca Mau	A5
Cam Ranh	B4
Can Tho	A4
Cao Bang	B1
Chau Doc	A4
Da Lat	B4
Da Nang	B3
Dien Bien Phu	A2
Dong Hoi	B3
Ha Giang	A1
Haiphong	B2
Hanoi, capital	A2
Hoa Binh	A2
Ho Chi Minh City	B4
Hon Gai	B2
Hue	B3
Khe Sanh	B3
Kontum	B3
Lang Son	B2
Lao Cai	A1
Long Xuyen	A4
My Tho	B4
Nam Dinh	B2
Nha Trang	B4
Phan Rang	B4
Phan Thiet	B4
Pleiku	B4
Quang Ngai	B3
Quang Tri	B3
Qui Nhon	B4
Rach Gia	A4
Soc Trang	A5
Son La	A2
Tay Ninh	B4
Thai Nguyen	A2
Thanh Hoa	A2
Tuy Hoa	B4
Viet Tri	A2
Vinh	A2
Vung Tau- Con Dao	B4
Yen Bai	A2

Other Features

Annam, mts.	A2
Ba, river	B3
Black (Da), river	A2
Ca, river	A2
Central, highlands	B4
Con Son, islands	B5
Cu Lao Thu, island	B4
Dao Phu Quoc, island	A4
Dong Nai, river	B4
Fan Si Pan, mt.	A1
Gam, river	A1
Lo, river	A1
Ma, river	A2
Mekong, delta	B5
Mekong, river	A4
Mui Bai Bung, point	A5
Ngoc Linh, mt.	B3
Red (Hong), river	A2
Tonkin, gulf	B2

Vietnam

Capital: Hanoi
Area: 127,246 sq. mi.
    329,653 sq. km.
Population: 73,104,000
Largest City: Ho Chi Minh City
Language: Vietnamese
Monetary Unit: Dong

Vietnam
⊛ National Capital
• Other City
1:14,333,000
0 50 100 150 200 mi
0 50 100 150 200 km
Lambert Conformal Conic Projection

© GeoSystems Global Corp.

Laos: Map Index

Cities and Towns

Attapu	D4
Ban Houayxay	A1
Champasak	C4
Louang Namtha	A1
Luang Prabang	B2
Muang Khammouan	C3
Muang Không	C4
Muang Khôngxédôn	C4
Muang Paklay	A2
Muang Pakxan	B2
Muang Vangviang	B2
Muang Xaignabouri	A2
Muang Xay	A1
Muang Xépôn	D3
Muang Xon	B1
Pakse	C4
Phôngsali	B1
Saravan	D4
Savannakhet	C3
Vientiane, capital	B3
Xam Nua	C1
Xiangkhoang	B2

Other Features

Annam, range	C3
Banghiang, river	C3
Bolovens, plateau	D4
Kong, river	D4
Luang Prabang, range	A3
Mekong, river	A1, C3
Nam Ngum, reservoir	B2
Ou, river	B1
Phou Bia, mt.	B2
Xiangkhoang, plateau	B2

Laos

Capital: Vientiane
Area: 91,429 sq. mi.
    236,085 sq. km.
Population: 4,702,000
Largest City: Vientiane
Language: Lao
Monetary Unit: New kip

Laos
⊛ National Capital
• Other City
1:14,533,000
0   50   100 mi
0 50 100 km
Lambert Conformal Conic Projection

© GeoSystems Global Corp.

Cambodia

⊛ National Capital
• Other City
• Ruins
1:8,573,000
0   50   100 mi
0 50 100 km
Conic Projection

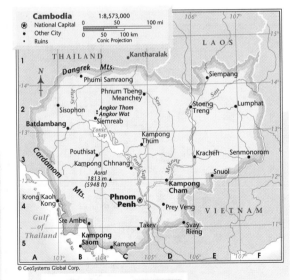

© GeoSystems Global Corp.

Mongolia: Map Index

Cities and Towns

Altay	B2
Arvayheer	C2
Baruun-Urt	D2
Bayanhongor	C2
Bulgan	C2
Buyant-Uhaa	D3
Choybalsan	D2
Dalandzadgad	C3
Darhan	C2
Dund-Us	B2
Erdenet	C2
Mandalgovĭ	C2
Mörön	C2
Ölgiy	A2
Ondörhaan	D2
Sühbaatar	C2
Tamsagbulag	D2
Tsetserleg	C2
Ulaangom	B2
Ulaan-Uul	B2
Ulan Bator, capital	C2
Uliastay	B2

Other Features

Altai, mts.	B2
Bööntsagaan, lake	B2
Dörgön, lake	B2
Dzavhan, river	B2
Gobi, desert	C3
Hangayn, mts.	B2
Har Us, lake	B2
Hovd, river	B2
Hövsgöl, lake	C1
Hyargas, lake	B2
Ih Bogd Uul, mt.	C3
Kerulen, river	D2
Mongolian, plateau	D2
Onon, river	D2
Orhon, river	C2
Selenge Mörön, river	C2
Tavan Bogd Uul, mt.	A2
Tesiyn, river	B2
Tuul, river	C2
Uvs, lake	B1

Mongolia

Capital: Ulan Bator
Area: 604,800 sq. mi.
    1,566,839 sq. km.
Population: 2,430,000
Largest City: Ulan Bator
Language: Mongolian
Monetary Unit: Tughrik

Mongolia
⊛ National Capital
• Other City
1:2,857,000
0   125   250 mi
0 125 250 km
Lambert Conformal Conic Projection

© GeoSystems Global Corp.

Cambodia

Capital: Phnom Penh
Area: 70,238 sq. mi.
    181,964 sq. km.
Population: 10,265,000
Largest City: Phnom Penh
Language: Khmer
Monetary Unit: New riel

Cambodia: Map Index

Cities and Towns

Batdambang	B2
Kampong Cham	D4
Kampong Chhnang	C3
Kampong Saom	B5
Kampong Thum	C3
Kampot	C5
Kracheh	E3
Krong Kaoh Kong	A4
Lumphat	F2
Phnom Penh, capital	C4
Phnum Tbeng Meanchey	C2
Phumi Samraong	B1
Pouthisat	B3
Prey Veng	D4
Senmonorom	F3
Siempang	E1
Siemreab	B2
Sisophon	B2
Snuol	E3
Sre Ambel	B4
Stoeng Treng	D2
Svay Rieng	D4
Takev	C5

Other Features

Angkor Thom, ruins	B2
Angkor Wat, ruins	B2
Aoral, mt.	C3
Cardamom, mts.	A3
Dangrek, mts.	B1
Mekong, river	D3
San, river	E2
Sen, river	D2
Sreng, river	B2
Thailand, gulf	A4
Tonle Sap, lake	B2, C3
Tonle Sap, river	B2

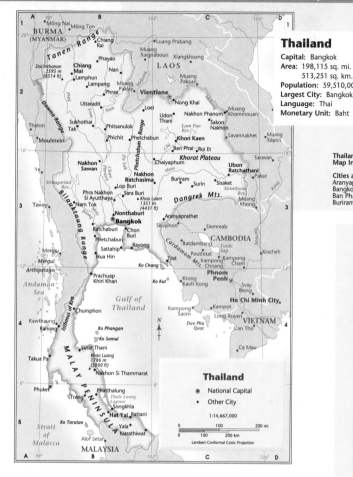

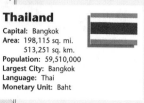

Thailand

Capital: Bangkok
Area: 198,115 sq. mi.
   513,251 sq. km.
Population: 59,510,000
Largest City: Bangkok
Language: Thai
Monetary Unit: Baht

Thailand:
Map Index

Cities and Towns
Aranyaprathet	C3
Bangkok, capital	C3
Ban Phai	C2
Buriram	C3
Chaiyaphum	C3
Chiang Mai	B2
Chiang Rai	B2
Chon Buri	B3
Chumphon	B4
Hat Yai	B5
Hua Hin	B3
Khon Kaen	B2
Lampang	B2
Lamphun	B2
Loei	B2
Lop Buri	B3
Nakhon Phanom	C2
Nakhon Ratchasima	B3
Nakhon Sawan	B3
Nakhon Si Thammarat	B4
Nam Tok	B3
Nan	B2
Narathiwat	B5
Nong Khai	B2
Nonthaburi	B3
Pattani	B5
Phatthalung	B5
Phayao	B2
Phetchaburi	B3
Phichit	B2
Phitsanulok	B2
Phrae	B2
Phra Nakhon Si Ayutthaya	B3
Phuket	B5
Prachuap Khiri Khan	B4
Ranong	B4
Ratchaburi	B3
Rayong	B3
Roi Et	C2
Sakon Nakhon	C2
Sara Buri	B3
Sattahip	B3
Sisaket	C3
Songkhla	B5
Sukhothai	B2
Surat Thani	B4
Surin	C3
Tak	B2
Takua Pa	B4
Trang	B5
Trat	C3
Ubon Ratchathani	C3
Udon Thani	B2
Uttaradit	B2
Yala	B5

Other Features
Bilauktaung, range	B3
Chao Phraya, river	B3
Chi, river	C2
Dangrek, mts.	C3
Dawna, range	B2
Inthanon, mt.	B2
Khorat, plateau	C3
Ko Chang, island	B3
Ko Kut, island	C4
Ko Phangan, island	B4
Ko Samui, island	B4
Ko Tarutao, island	B5
Kra, isthmus	B4
Laem, mt.	B3
Lam Pao, reservoir	C2
Luang, mt.	B4
Mae Klong, river	B3
Malacca, strait	B5
Malay, peninsula	B4
Mekong, river	C2
Mun, river	C3
Nan, river	B2
Pa Sak, river	B3
Phetchabun, range	B3
Ping, river	B2
Salween, river	A2
Sirinthorn, reservoir	C3
Srinagarind, reservoir	B3
Tanen, range	B2
Thailand, gulf	B4
Thale Luang, lagoon	B5
Yom, river	B2

Burma:
Map Index

States and Divisions
Chin, state	B2
Irrawaddy, division	B3
Kachin, state	C1
Karen, state	C3
Kayah, state	C2
Magwe, division	B2
Mandalay, division	B2
Mon, state	C3
Pegu, division	B3
Rakhine, state	B2
Rangoon, division	C3
Sagaing, division	B2
Shan, state	C2
Tenasserim, division	C3

Cities and Towns
Bassein	B3
Bhamo	C1
Haka	B2
Henzada	B3
Kawthaung	C4
Keng Tung	C2
Kyaukpyu	B2
Lashio	C2
Loi-kaw	C2
Mandalay	C2
Maymyo	C2
Meiktila	B2
Mergui	C3
Monywa	B2
Moulmein	C3
Myingyan	B2
Myitkyina	C1
Pa-an	C3
Pegu	C3
Prome	B2
Putao	C1
Rangoon, capital	C3
Sagaing	B2
Shwebo	B2
Sittwe	B2
Tamu	B1
Taunggyi	C2
Tavoy	C3
Toungoo	C2
Ye	C3

Other Features
Andaman, sea	B3
Arakan Yoma, mts.	B2
Bengal, bay	B3
Bilauktaung, range	C3
Cheduba, island	B2
Chin, hills	B2
Chindwin, river	B1
Coco, islands	B3
Hkakabo Razi, mt.	C1
Irrawaddy, river	B2
Martaban, gulf	C3
Mekong, river	C2
Mergui, archipelago	C4
Mouths of the Irrawaddy, delta	B3
Preparis, island	B3
Ramree, island	B2
Salween, river	C2
Shan, plateau	C2
Sittang, river	C2
Tavoy, point	C3
Thailand, gulf	C4

Thailand

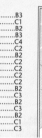

⊛ National Capital
• Other City

1:14,667,000

0   100   200 mi

0 100 200 km

Lambert Conformal Conic Projection

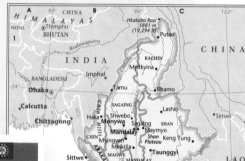

Burma (Myanmar)

Capital: Rangoon
Area: 261,228 sq. mi.
   676,756 sq. km.
Population: 44,277,000
Largest City: Rangoon
Language: Burmese
Monetary Unit: Kyat

Burma (Myanmar)

⊛ National Capital
• Other City

1:24,054,000

0 100 200 mi

0 100 200 km

Lambert Conformal Conic Projection

© GeoSystems Global Corp.

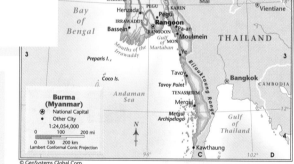

Philipines

⊛ National Capital
• Other City

1:16,000,000

0   100   200 mi

0 100 200 km

Lambert Conformal Conic Projection

Philippines

Capital: Manila
Area: 115,860 sq. mi.
   300,155 sq. km.
Population: 69,809,000
Largest City: Manila
Languages: Pilipino, English
Monetary Unit: Philippine peso

Philippines:
Map Index

Regions
Bicol	B3
Cagayan Valley	B2
Central Luzon	A3
Central Mindanao	C5
Central Visayas	B4
*Cordillera Autonomous Region	B2
Eastern Visayas	C4
Ilocos	B2
*Moslem Mindanao Autonomous Region	B5
National Capital Region	B3
Northern Mindanao	C4
Southern Mindanao	C5
Southern Tagalog	B3
Western Mindanao	B5
Western Visayas	B4

Cities and Towns
Angeles	B3
Bacolod	B4
Baguio	B2
Basilan	B5
Batangas	B3
Bislig	C4
Butuan	C4
Cabanatuan	B3
Cadiz	B4
Cagayan de Oro	C4
Calapan	B3
Calbayog	C3
Cebu	B4
Cotabato	C5
Dagupan	B2
Davao	C5
Dipolog	B4
Dumaguete	B4
General Santos	C5
Iligan	C4
Iloilo	B4
Jolo	B5
Laoag	B2
Laoang	C3
Legazpi	B3
Lipa	B3
Lucena	B3
Mamburao	B3
Mandaue	B4
Manila, capital	B3
Masbate	B3
Naga	B3
Olongapo	B3
Ormoc	C4
Pagadian	B5
Puerto Princesa	A4
Quezon City	B3
Roxas	B4
San Carlos	B4
San Fernando	B3
San Pablo	B3
Silay	B4
Surigao	C4
Tacloban	C4
Tuguegarao	B2
Vigan	B2
Zamboanga	B5

Other Features
Agusan, river	C4
Apo, volcano	C5
Babuyan, channel	B2
Babuyan, islands	B1
Balabac, island	A5
Balabac, strait	A5
Bashi, channel	B1
Basilan, island	B5
Bataan, peninsula	B3
Batan, islands	B1
Bohol, island	C4
Bohol, sea	C4
Cagayan, islands	B4
Cagayan, river	B2
Cagayan Sulu, island	A5
Calamian, islands	A3
Caramoan, peninsula	B3
Catanduanes, island	C3
Cebu, island	B4
Celebes, sea	B5
Cordillera Central, mts.	B2
Corregidor, island	B3
Cuyo, islands	B4
Davao, gulf	C5
Dinagat, island	C4
Diuata, mts.	C4
Jolo, island	B5
Laguna de Bay, lake	B3
Lamon, bay	B3
Leyte, island	C4
Lingayen, gulf	B2
Luzon, island	B3
Luzon, strait	B1
Manila, bay	B3
Marinduque, island	B3
Masbate, island	B3
Mayon, volcano	B3
Mindanao, island	C5
Mindoro, island	B3
Mindoro, strait	B3
Moro, gulf	B5
Negros, island	B4
Palawan, island	A4
Panay, gulf	B4
Panay, island	B4
Philippine, sea	C3
Pulangi, river	C5
Samar, island	C3
Samar, sea	C3
Siargao, island	C4
Sibuyan, island	B3
Sibuyan, sea	B3
Sierra Madre, mts.	B2
South China, sea	A3
Sulu, archipelago	B5
Sulu, sea	A5
Tablas, island	B3
Tawi Tawi, island	A5
Visayan, islands	B4
Visayan, sea	B4
Zambales, mts.	B3
Zamboanga, peninsula	B5
*Not on map	

© GeoSystems Global Corp.

Indonesia:
Map Index

Cities and Towns
Amahai	D2
Ambon	D2
Balikpapan	C2
Banda Aceh	A1
Bandar Lampung	B2
Bandung	C2
Banjarmasin	C2
Baubau	D2
Bengkulu	B2
Bogor	C2
Cilacap	C2
Cirebon	B2
Denpasar	C2
Dili	D2
Ende	D2
Fakfak	E2
Gorontalo	D1
Jakarta, capital	B2
Jambi	B2
Jayapura	F2
Kediri	C2
Kendari	D2
Kupang	D3
Madiun	C2
Magelang	C2
Malang	C2
Manado	D1
Manokwari	E2
Mataram	C2
Medan	A1
Merauke	F2
Padang	B2
Palangkaraya	C2
Palembang	B2
Palu	C2
Pangkalpinang	B2
Parepare	C2
Pekalongan	B2
Pekanbaru	B1
Pematangsiantar	A1

Pontianak	B2
Raba	C2
Samarinda	C2
Semarang	C2
Sorong	E2
Sukabumi	B2
Surabaya	C2
Surakarta	C2
Tanjungpinang	B1
Tarakan	C1
Tasikmalaya	C2
Tegal	C2
Ternate	D1
Ujung Pandang	D2
Waingapu	D2
Yogyakarta	C2

Other Features
Agung, mt.	C2
Alor, island	D2

Arafura, sea	E2
Aru, islands	E2
Babar, island	D2
Bali, island	C2
Banda, sea	D2
Bangka, island	B2
Belitung, island	B2
Biak, island	E2
Borneo, island	C1
Buru, island	D2
Celebes (Sulawesi), island	D2
Celebes, sea	D1
Ceram, island	D2
Ceram, sea	D2
Digul, river	E2
Enggano, island	B2
Flores, island	D2
Flores, sea	C2
Greater Sunda, islands	B2
Halmahera, island	D1

Irian Jaya, region	E2
Java, island	C2
Java, sea	C2
Jaya, mt.	E2
Kahayan, river	C2
Kai, island	E2
Kalimantan, region	C2
Kerinci, mt.	B2
Krakatau, island	B2
Lesser Sunda, islands	C2
Lingga, island	B2
Lombok, island	C2
Madura, island	C2
Makassar, strait	C2
Malacca, strait	A1
Mentawai, islands	A2
Misool, island	E2
Moa, island	D2
Molucca, sea	D2
Moluccas, islands	D2

Morotai, island	D1
Muna, island	D2
Natuna Besar, island	B1
New Guinea, island	E2
Nias, island	A1
Obi, island	D2
Peleng, island	D2
Savu, sea	D2
Semeru, mt.	C2
Siberut, island	A2
Simeulue, island	A1
South China, sea	C1
Sudirman, range	E2
Sula, islands	D2
Sulu, sea	D1

Sumatra, island	B2
Sumba, island	C2
Sumbawa, island	C2
Talaud, islands	D1

Indonesia

Capital: Jakarta
Area: 741,052 sq. mi.
1,919,824 sq. km.
Population: 200,410,000
Largest City: Jakarta
Language: Bahasa Indonesian
Monetary Unit: New rupiah

Timor, island	D2
Timor, sea	D3
Waigeo, island	E2
Wetar, island	D2
Yapen, island	E2

Singapore:
Map Index

Cities and Towns
Bedok	B1
Bukit Panjang	B1
Bukit Timah	B1
Changi	B1
Choa Chu Kang	A1
Jurong	A1
Kranji	B1
Nee Soon	B1
Punggol	B1
Queenstown	B1
Sembawang	B1
Serangoon	B1
Singapore, capital	B1
Tampines	B1
Thong Hoe	A1
Toa Payoh	B1
Tuas	A1
Woodlands	B1

Other Features
Ayer Chawan, island	A1
Bukum, island	B2
Johor, strait	B1

Singapore

Capital: Singapore
Area: 247 sq. mi.
640 sq. km.
Population: 2,859,000
Largest City: Singapore
Languages: Mandarin Chinese, English,
Malay, Tamil
Monetary Unit: Singapore dollar

Keppel, harbor	B2
Pandan, strait	A2
Semakau, island	B2
Senang, island	A2
Sentosa, island	B2
Singapore, island	B1
Singapore, strait	B2
Tekong, island	C1
Timah, hill	B1
Ubin, island	B1

Brunei

Capital: Bandar Seri
Begawan
Area: 2,226 sq. mi.
5,767 sq. km.
Population: 285,000
Largest City: Bandar Seri Begawan
Language: Malay
Monetary Unit: Brunei dollar

Brunei: Map Index

Cities and Towns
Badas	A2
Bandar Seri Begawan, capital	B2
Bangar	B2
Batang Duri	B2
Jerudong	B2
Kerangan Nyatan	B3
Kuala Abang	B2
Kuala Belait	A2
Labi	A3
Labu	B2
Lumut	A2
Medit	C1
Muara	C1
Seria	A2
Sukang	B3
Tutong	B2

Other Features
Belait, river	B3
Brunei, bay	C1
Brunei, river	B2
Bukit Pagon, mt.	C3
Pandaruan, river	C2
South China, sea	A2
Temburong, river	C2
Tutong, river	B2

Malaysia:
Map Index

Cities and Towns
Alor Setar	A1
Batu Pahat	B2
George Town	A2
Ipoh	A2
Johor Baharu	B2
Kelang	A2
Keluang	B2
Kota Baharu	B1
Kota Kinabalu	D2
Kuala Lumpur, capital	A2
Kuala Terengganu	B1

Kuantan	B2
Kuching	C2
Melaka	B2
Miri	D1
Muar	B2
Sandakan	D2
Seremban	A2
Sibu	C2
Tawau	D2
Telok Anson	A2

Other Features
Banggi, island	D1
Baram, river	D2
Crocker, range	D2
Kinabalu, mt.	D1
Kinabatangan, river	D2
Labuan, island	D2
Langkawi, island	A1
Malacca, strait	A2
Malay, peninsula	A1
Pahang, river	B2
Peninsular Malaysia, region	B2
Perak, river	A2
Pinang, island	A2
Rajang, river	C2
Sabah, state	D2
Sarawak, state	C2
Tahan, mt.	B2

Malaysia

Capital: Kuala Lumpur
Area: 127,584 sq. mi.
330,529 sq. km.
Population: 19,283,000
Largest City: Kuala Lumpur
Language: Bahasa Malaysia
Monetary Unit: Ringgit

Australia: Map Index

States and Territories

Australian Capital Territory D3
New South Wales D3
Northern Territory C2
Queensland D2
South Australia C2
Tasmania D4
Victoria D3
Western Australia B2

Aboriginal Lands

Alawa-Ngandji C1
Balwina B2
Central Australia B2
Central Desert C2
Daly River B1
Haasts Bluff C2
Lake Mackay B2
Nganyatjara B2
Petermann B2
Pitjantjatjara C2
Waani/Garawa C1
Yandeyarra A2
Unnamed B2
Unnamed C1
Unnamed D1

Cities and Towns

Adelaide, S.A., *capital* .. C3, Inset II
Albany, W.A. A3
Albury, N.S.W. D3
Alice Springs, N.T. C2
Altona, Vic. ...... Inset V
Armadale, W.A. ...... Inset I
Armidale, N.S.W. E3
Asquith, N.S.W. ...... Inset IV
Auburn, N.S.W. ...... Inset IV
Balcatta, W.A. ...... Inset I
Bald Hills, Qld. ...... Inset III
Ballarat, Vic. D3
Bankstown, N.S.W. ...... Inset IV
Bayswater, W.A. ...... Inset I
Beenleigh, Qld. ...... Inset III
Belmont, W.A. ...... Inset I
Bendigo, Vic. D3
Berwick, Vic. ...... Inset V
Blacktown, N.S.W. ...... Inset IV
Botany, N.S.W. ...... Inset IV
Bourke, N.S.W. D3
Bowen, Qld. D2
Box Hill, Vic. ...... Inset V
Brighton, S.A. ...... Inset II
Brighton, Qld. ...... Inset III
Brighton, Vic. ...... Inset V
Brisbane, Qld., *capital* ...... E2, Inset III
Broadmeadows, Vic. ...... Inset V
Broken Hill, N.S.W. D3
Broome, W.A. B1
Brown Plains, Qld. ...... Inset III
Bunbury, W.A. A3
Bundaberg, Qld. E2
Burnside, S.A. ...... Inset II
Byford, W.A. ...... Inset I
Cairns, Qld. D1
Campbelltown, S.A. ...... Inset II
Campbelltown, N.S.W. ...... Inset IV
Canberra, A.C.T., *national capital* D3
Cannington, W.A. ...... Inset I
Canterbury, N.S.W. ...... Inset IV
Carnarvon, W.A. A2
Castle Hill, N.S.W. ...... Inset IV
Caulfield, Vic. ...... Inset V
Ceduna, S.A. C3
Charleville, Qld. D2
Charters Towers, Qld. D2
Chelsea, Vic. ...... Inset V
Chermside, Qld. ...... Inset III
City Beach, W.A. ...... Inset I
Cleveland, Qld. ...... Inset III
Cloncurry, Qld. D2
Coburg, Vic. ...... Inset V
Coober Pedy, S.A. C2
Coopers Plains, Qld. ...... Inset III
Cranbourne, Vic. ...... Inset V
Cronulla, N.S.W. ...... Inset IV
Dampier, W.A. A2
Dandenong, Vic. ...... Inset V
Darwin, N.T., *capital* C1
Dee Why, N.S.W. ...... Inset IV
Devonport, Tas. D4
Doncaster, Vic. ...... Inset V
Dubbo, N.S.W. D3
Elizabeth, S.A. ...... Inset II
Eltham, Vic. ...... Inset V
Emerald, Qld. D2
Enfield, S.A. ...... Inset II
Epping, N.S.W. ...... Inset IV
Esperance, W.A. B3
Essendon, Vic. ...... Inset V
Fairfield, N.S.W. ...... Inset IV
Ferntree Gully, Vic. ...... Inset V
Ferny Grove, Qld. ...... Inset III
Frankston, Vic. ...... Inset V
Fremantle, W.A. ...... A3, Inset I
Geelong, Vic. D3
Geraldton, W.A. A2
Gladstone, Qld. E2
Glenelg, S.A. ...... Inset II
Glen Forrest, W.A. ...... Inset I
Gold Coast, Qld. E2
Goodna, Qld. ...... Inset III
Gosford, N.S.W. E3
Gosnells, W.A. ...... Inset I
Grafton, N.S.W. E2
Grange, S.A. ...... Inset II
Greenslopes, Qld. ...... Inset III
Griffith, N.S.W. D3
Gympie, Qld. E2
Heidelberg, Vic. ...... Inset V
Hobart, Tas., *capital* D4
Holland Park, Qld. ...... Inset III
Holroyd, N.S.W. ...... Inset IV
Hornsby, N.S.W. ...... Inset IV
Hurstville, N.S.W. ...... Inset IV
Inala, Qld. ...... Inset III
Ipswich, Qld. ...... Inset III
Kalamunda, W.A. ...... Inset I
Kalgoorlie, W.A. B3
Katherine, N.T. C1
Keilor, Vic. ...... Inset V
Kelmscott, W.A. ...... Inset I
Kersbrook, S.A. ...... Inset II
Kwinana, W.A. ...... Inset I
Kwinana Beach, W.A. ...... Inset I
La Perouse, N.S.W. ...... Inset IV
Launceston, Tas. D4
Leichhardt, N.S.W. ...... Inset IV
Lilydale, Vic. ...... Inset V
Lismore, N.S.W. E2
Liverpool, N.S.W. ...... Inset IV
Lobethal, S.A. ...... Inset II
Logan, Qld. ...... Inset III
Longreach, Qld. D2
Mackay, Qld. D2
Mandurah, W.A. A3
Manly, Qld. ...... Inset III
Manly, N.S.W. ...... Inset IV
Marion, S.A. ...... Inset II
Maryborough, Qld. E2
Melbourne, Vic., *capital* ...... D3, Inset V
Melville, W.A. ...... Inset I
Merredin, W.A. A3
Midland, W.A. ...... Inset I
Mildura, Vic. D3
Mitcham, S.A. ...... Inset II
Mona Vale, N.S.W. ...... Inset IV
Moorabbin, Vic. ...... Inset V
Mordialloc, Vic. ...... Inset V
Moree, N.S.W. D2
Morningside, Qld. ...... Inset III
Mosman Park, W.A. ...... Inset I
Mount Barker, S.A. ...... Inset II
Mount Gambier, S.A. D3
Mount Gravatt, Qld. ...... Inset III
Mount Isa, Qld. C2
Mount Nebo, Qld. ...... Inset III
Mullaloo, W.A. ...... Inset I
Narrogin, W.A. A3
Nedlands, W.A. ...... Inset I
Newcastle, N.S.W. E3
Newman, W.A. A2
Newmarket, Qld. ...... Inset III
Noarlunga, S.A. ...... Inset II
North Adelaide, S.A. ...... Inset II
Northcote, Vic. ...... Inset V
North Sydney, N.S.W. ...... Inset IV
Nunawading, Vic. ...... Inset V
Oakleigh, Vic. ...... Inset V
Orange, N.S.W. D3
Parramatta, N.S.W. ...... Inset IV
Perth, W.A., *capital* ...... A3, Inset I
Petrie, Qld. ...... Inset III
Pickering Brook, W.A. ...... Inset I
Port Adelaide, S.A. ...... Inset II
Port Augusta, S.A. C3
Port Hedland, W.A. A2
Port Lincoln, S.A. C3
Port Macquarie, N.S.W. E3
Port Pirie, S.A. C3
Prahran, Vic. ...... Inset V
Preston, Vic. ...... Inset V
Queenstown, Tas. D4
Randwick, N.S.W. ...... Inset IV
Redcliffe, Qld. ...... Inset III
Redland Bay, Qld. ...... Inset III
Reynella, S.A. ...... Inset II
Ringwood, Vic. ...... Inset V
Rockdale, N.S.W. ...... Inset IV
Rockhampton, Qld. E2
Roma, Qld. D2
Ryde, N.S.W. ...... Inset IV
St. Ives, N.S.W. ...... Inset IV
St. Kilda, S.A. ...... Inset II
St. Kilda, Vic. ...... Inset V
Salisbury, S.A. ...... Inset II
Samford, Qld. ...... Inset III
Sandgate, Qld. ...... Inset III
Scarborough, W.A. ...... Inset I
Spearwood, W.A. ...... Inset I
Springvale, Vic. ...... Inset V
Stirling, W.A. ...... Inset I
Stirling, S.A. ...... Inset II
Sunshine, Vic. ...... Inset V
Sutherland, N.S.W. ...... Inset IV
Sydney, N.S.W., *capital* ...... E3, Inset IV
Tamworth, N.S.W. E3
Taree, N.S.W. E3
Tea Tree Gully, S.A. ...... Inset II
Tennant Creek, N.T. C1
Tom Price, W.A. A2
Toowoomba, Qld. E2
Townsville, Qld. D1
Unley, S.A. ...... Inset II
Victoria Park, W.A. ...... Inset I
Victoria Point, Qld. ...... Inset III
Wagga Wagga, N.S.W. D3
Wanneroo, W.A. ...... Inset I
Warrnambool, Vic. D3
Waverley, Vic. ...... Inset V
Weipa, Qld. D1
Whyalla, S.A. C3
Willoughby, N.S.W. ...... Inset IV
Wollongong, N.S.W. E3
Woodside, S.A. ...... Inset II
Woodville, S.A. ...... Inset II
Woomera, S.A. C3
Wyndham, W.A. B1
Wynnum, Qld. ...... Inset III

Other Features

Arafura, *sea* C1
Arnhem, *cape* C1
Arnhem Land, *region* C1
Ashburton, *river* A2
Ashmore and Cartier, *islands* B1
Australian Alps, *mts.* D3
Barkly, *tableland* C1
Bass, *strait* D3
Bate, *bay* ...... Inset IV
Blue, *mts.* E3
Botany, *bay* ...... Inset IV
Brisbane, *river* ...... Inset III
Burdekin, *river* D1
Canning, *river* ...... Inset I
Cape York, *peninsula* D1
Carpentaria, *gulf* C1
Coral, *sea* E1
Daly, *river* C1
Darling, *range* A3
Darling, *river* D3
Drysdale River Natl. Park B1
Eyre, *lake* C2
Eyre, *peninsula* C3
Fitzroy, *river* B1
Flinders, *range* C3
Flinders, *river* D1
Frome, *lake* D2
Gairdner, *lake* C3
Garden, *island* ...... Inset I
Gascoyne *river* A2
Gibson, *desert* B2
Gilbert, *river* D1
Great Artesian, *basin* D2
Great Australian, *bight* B3
Great Barrier, *reef* D1
Great Dividing, *range* D1, D3
Great Sandy, *desert* B2
Great Victoria, *desert* B2
Gregory Natl. Park C1
Grey, *range* D2
Groote Eylandt, *island* C1
Hamersley, *range* A2
Hobsons, *bay* ...... Inset V
Jackson, *port* ...... Inset IV
Kakadu Natl. Park C1
Kangaroo, *island* C3
Kimberley, *plateau* B1
King Leopold, *range* B1
Kosciusko, *mt.* D3
Lakefield Natl. Park D1
Leeuwin, *cape* A3
Leichhardt, *river* D1
Leveque, *cape* B1
Logan, *river* ...... Inset III
Macdonnell, *ranges* C2
Melville, *island* C1
Mitchell, *river* D1
Moreton, *bay* ...... Inset III
Murchison, *river* A2
Murray, *river* D3
Murrumbidgee, *river* D3
Musgrave, *ranges* C2
New England, *range* E3
North West, *cape* A2
Nullarbor, *plain* B3
Port Phillip, *bay* ...... Inset V
Roper, *river* C1
Rudall River Natl. Park B2
St. Vincent, *gulf* ...... Inset II
Samsonvale, *lake* ...... Inset III
Simpson, *desert* C2
Simpson Desert Natl. Park C2
Spencer, *gulf* C3
Swan, *river* ...... Inset I
Tasman, *sea* E3
Timor, *sea* B1
Torrens, *lake* C2
Torrens, *river* ...... Inset II
Torres, *strait* D1
Uluru (Ayers Rock) C2
Victoria, *river* C1
Witjira Natl. Park C2
Yampi, *sound* B1
York, *cape* D1

Australia

Capital: Canberra
Area: 2,966,200 sq. mi.
7,684,456 sq. km.
Population: 18,077,000
Largest City: Sydney
Language: English
Monetary Unit: Australian dollar

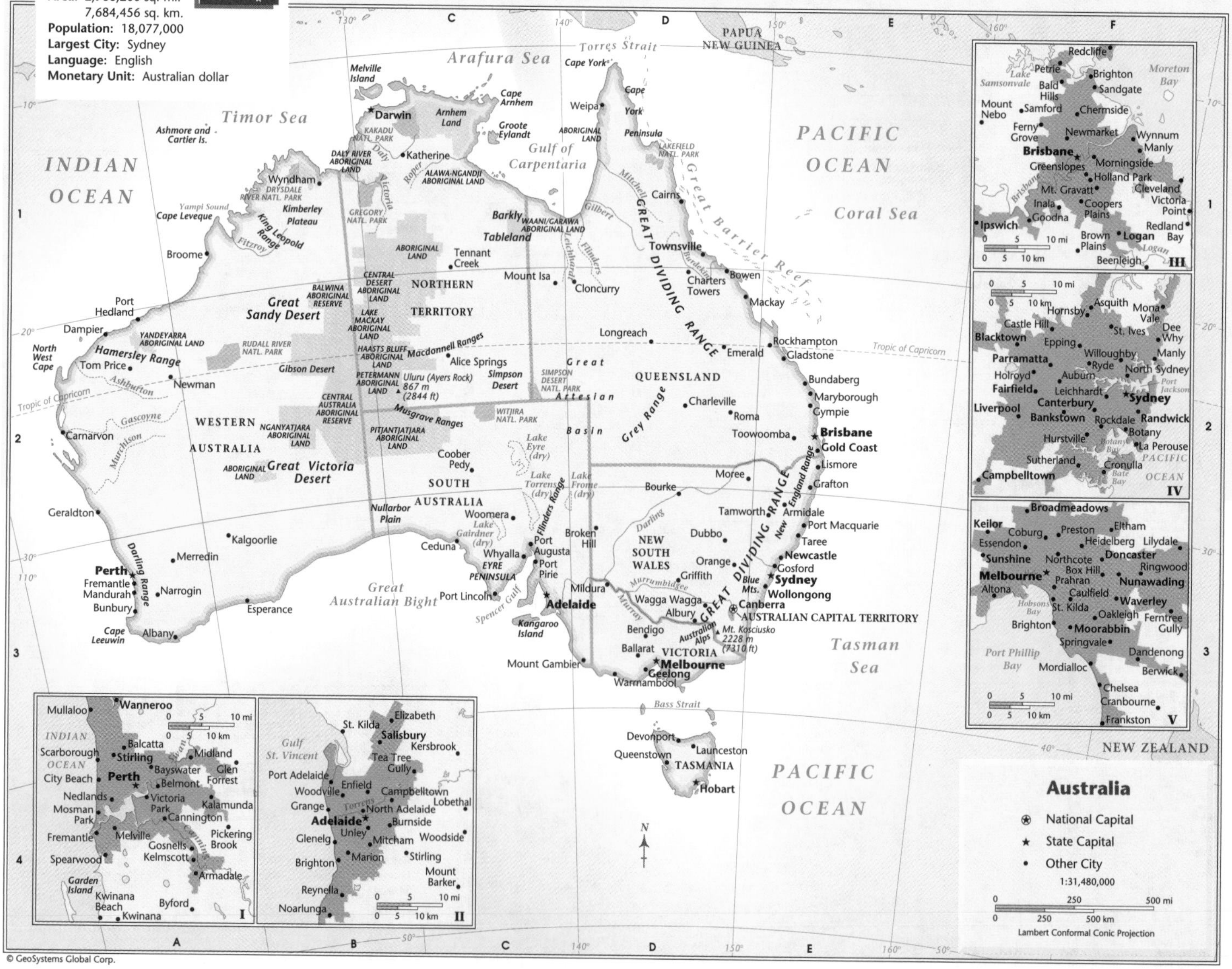

Arafura Sea
Timor Sea
INDIAN OCEAN
PACIFIC OCEAN
Coral Sea
Tasman Sea
Gulf of Carpentaria
Great Australian Bight
Torres Strait
PAPUA NEW GUINEA
NEW ZEALAND
NORTHERN TERRITORY
WESTERN AUSTRALIA
SOUTH AUSTRALIA
QUEENSLAND
NEW SOUTH WALES
VICTORIA
TASMANIA
AUSTRALIAN CAPITAL TERRITORY
Great Sandy Desert
Gibson Desert
Great Victoria Desert
Simpson Desert
Nullarbor Plain
Great Artesian Basin
GREAT DIVIDING RANGE
Great Barrier Reef
Uluru (Ayers Rock) 867 m (2844 ft)
Mt. Kosciusko 2228 m (7310 ft)
Tropic of Capricorn
Darwin
Perth
Adelaide
Melbourne
Sydney
Brisbane
Hobart
Canberra
Inset I
Inset II
Inset III
Inset IV
Inset V
Australia
National Capital
State Capital
Other City
1:31,480,000
Lambert Conformal Conic Projection

© GeoSystems Global Corp.

Papua New Guinea: Map Index

Cities and Towns
Alotau B3
Arawa B2
Daru A2
Goroka A2
Kavieng B2
Kerema A2
Kimbe B2
Lae A2
Lorengau A2
Madang A2
Morehead A2
Mount Hagen A2
Popondetta A2
Port Moresby, *capital* B2
Rabaul A2
Vanimo A2
Wabag A2
Wau A2
Wewak A1

Other Features
Admiralty, *islands* A2
Bismarck, *archipelago* A2
Bismarck, *range* A2
Bismarck, *sea* A2
Bougainville, *island* B2
Buka, *island* B2
Central, *range* A2
Coral, *sea* A3
D'Entrecasteaux, *islands* B2
Feni, *islands* B2
Fly, *river* A2
Gazelle, *peninsula* B2
Green, *islands* B2
Huon, *peninsula* A2
Karkar, *island* A2
Lihir, *group* B2
Louisiade, *archipelago* B3
Manus, *island* A2
Markham, *river* A2
Milne, *bay* B3
Murray, *lake* A2
Mussau, *island* A2
New Britain, *island* B2
New Guinea, *island* A2
New Hanover, *island* B2
New Ireland, *island* B2
Ninigo, *group* A2
Nuguria, *islands* B2
Owen Stanley, *range* A2
Papua, *gulf* A2
Purari, *river* A2
Ramu, *river* A2
Rossel, *island* B3
St. George's, *channel* B2
Sepik, *river* A2
Solomon, *sea* B2
Tabar, *island* B2
Tagula, *island* B3
Tanga, *islands* B2
Tauu, *islands* B3
Torres, *strait* A2
Trobriand, *islands* B2
Umboi, *island* A2
Whiteman, *range* A2
Wilhelm, *mt.* A2
Witu, *islands* A2
Woodlark (Muyua), *island* B2

Papua New Guinea

Capital: Port Moresby
Area: 178,704 sq. mi.
          462,964 sq. km.
Population: 4,197,000
Largest City: Port Moresby
Language: English
Monetary Unit: Kina

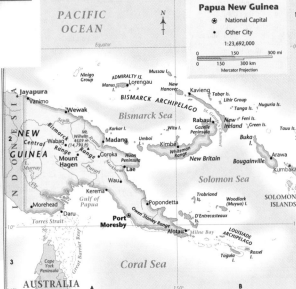

© GeoSystems Global Corp.

New Zealand

Capital: Wellington
Area: 104,454 sq. mi.
          270,606 sq. km.
Population: 3,389,000
Largest City: Auckland
Language: English
Monetary Unit: New Zealand dollar

New Zealand: Map Index

Cities and Towns
Alexandra A4
Ashburton B3
Auckland B2
Blenheim B3
Christchurch B3
Collingwood B3
Dunedin B4
East Coast Bays B2
Gisborne C2
Greymouth B3
Hamilton C2
Hastings C2
Hicks Bay C2
Invercargill A4
Kaeo B2
Kaikoura B3
Kaitaia B2
Kawhia B2
Lower Hutt B3
Manukau B2
Milford Sound A3
Napier C2
Nelson B3
New Plymouth B2
Oamaru B4
Palmerston North C3
Queenstown A3
Rotorua C2
Taumarunui C2
Taupo C2
Tauranga C2
Timaru B3
Waimamaku B2
Wanganui C2
Wellington, *capital* B3
Westport B3
Whakatane C2
Whangarei B2

Other Features
Aspiring, *mt.* A3
Banks, *peninsula* B3
Canterbury, *bight* B3
Canterbury, *plains* B3
Clutha, *river* A4
Cook, *mt.* B3
Cook, *strait* B3
Coromandel, *peninsula* C2
East, *cape* B2
Egmont, *cape* B2
Egmont, *mt.* B2
Farewell, *cape* B3
Foveaux, *strait* A4
Great Barrier, *island* C2
Hawea, *lake* A3
Hawke, *bay* C2
Ngauruhoe, *mt.* C2
North, *cape* B1
North, *island* B2
North Taranaki, *bight* B2
Palliser, *cape* C3
Pegasus, *bay* B3
Plenty, *bay* C2
Puysegur, *point* A4
Rangitikei, *river* C2
Raukumara, *range* C2
Ruahine, *range* C2
Ruapehu, *mt.* C2
South, *island* A3
Southern Alps, *mts.* A3
Southland, *plains* A4
South Taranaki, *bight* B2
South West, *cape* A4
Stewart, *island* A4
Tararua, *range* C3
Tasman, *bay* B3
Tasman, *sea* A2
Taupo, *lake* C2
Te Anau, *lake* A4
Tekapo, *lake* B3
Three Kings, *islands* B1
Tongariro, *mt.* C2
Waikato, *river* C2
Wairau, *river* B3
Waitaki, *river* B3
Wanaka, *lake* A3

New Zealand

⊛ National Capital
• Other City

1:16,077,000

0   150   300 mi
0   150   300 km
Lambert Conformal Conic Projection

© GeoSystems Global Corp.

Micronesia: Map Index

Cities and Towns
Colonia A2
Kosrae D2
Palikir, *capital* C2
Weno C2

Other Features
Caroline, *islands* B2
Chuuk, *islands* C2
Eauripik, *atoll* B2
Faraulep, *atoll* B2
Kapingamarangi, *atoll* C2
Kosrae, *island* D2
Mortlock, *islands* C2
Murilo, *atoll* C2
Namoluk, *atoll* C2
Namonuito, *atoll* C2
Ngulu, *atoll* A2
Nukuoro, *atoll* C2
Oroluk, *atoll* C2
Pohnpei, *island* D2
Pulusuk, *island* B2
Ulithi, *atoll* B2
Weno, *island* C2
Yap, *islands* A2

Micronesia

Capital: Palikir
Area: 271 sq. mi.
          702 sq. km.
Population: 120,000
Largest City: Palikir
Language: English
Monetary Unit: U.S. dollar

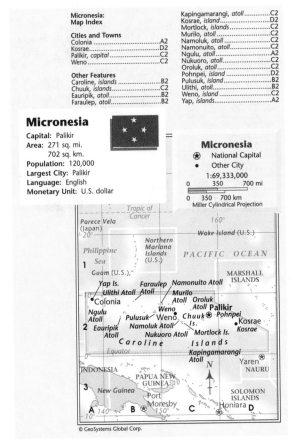

Micronesia

⊛ National Capital
• Other City

1:69,333,000

0   350   700 mi
0   350   700 km
Miller Cylindrical Projection

© GeoSystems Global Corp.

Marshall Islands

- ⊛ National Capital
- • Other City

1:25,750,000

0   150   300 mi

0   150   300 km

Mercator Projection

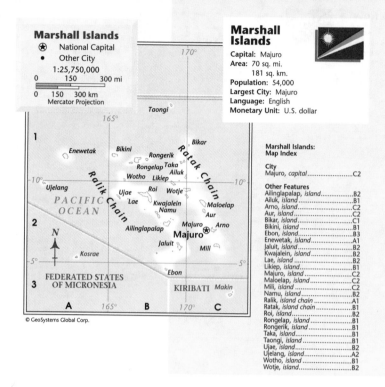

Marshall Islands

Capital: Majuro
Area: 70 sq. mi.
     181 sq. km.
Population: 54,000
Largest City: Majuro
Language: English
Monetary Unit: U.S. dollar

Marshall Islands:
Map Index

City
Majuro, capital C2

Other Features
Ailinglapalap, island B2
Ailuk, island B1
Arno, island C2
Aur, island C2
Bikar, island C1
Bikini, island B1
Ebon, island B3
Enewetak, island A1
Jaluit, island B2
Kwajalein, island B2
Lae, island B2
Likiep, island B1
Majuro, island C2
Maloelap, island C2
Mili, island C2
Namu, island B2
Ralik, island chain A1
Ratak, island chain B1
Roi, island B2
Rongelap, island B1
Rongerik, island B1
Taka, island B1
Taongi, island B1
Ujae, island B2
Ujelang, island A2
Wotho, island B1
Wotje, island B2

Nauru

- ⊛ National Capital
- • Other City

1:135,000

0   1   2 mi

0   1   2 km

Lambert Conformal Conic Projection

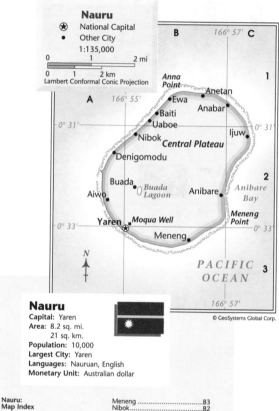

Nauru

Capital: Yaren
Area: 8.2 sq. mi.
     21 sq. km.
Population: 10,000
Largest City: Yaren
Languages: Nauruan, English
Monetary Unit: Australian dollar

Nauru:
Map Index

Cities and Towns
Aiwo A2
Anabar C1
Anetan B1
Anibare B2
Baiti B1
Buada B2
Denigomodu A2
Ewa B1
Ijuw C2

Other Features
Anibare, bay C2
Anna, point B1
Buada, lagoon B2
Central, plateau B2
Meneng, point C2
Moqua, well B2

Meneng B3
Nibok B2
Uaboe B1
Yaren, capital B3

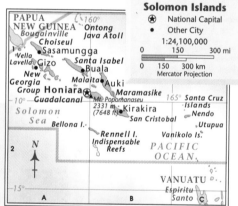

Solomon Islands:
Map Index

Cities and Towns
Auki B1
Buala A1
Gizo A1
Honiara, capital A1
Kirakira B2
Sasamungga A1

Other Features
Bellona, island A2
Choiseul, island A1
Guadalcanal, island A1
Indispensable, reefs B2
Malaita, island B1
Maramasike, island B1
Nendo, island C2
New Georgia Group,
   islands A1
Ontong Java, island A1
Popomanaseu, mt. B1
Rennell, island B2
San Cristobal, island B2
Santa Cruz, islands C2
Santa Isabel, island A1
Solomon, sea A2
Utupua, island C2
Vanikolo, islands C2
Vella Lavella, island A1

Solomon Islands

- ⊛ National Capital
- • Other City

1:24,100,000

0   150   300 mi

0   150   300 km

Mercator Projection

Solomon Islands

Capital: Honiara
Area: 10,954 sq. mi.
     28,378 sq. km.
Population: 386,000
Largest City: Honiara
Language: English
Monetary Unit: Dollar

Tuvalu

Capital: Funafuti
Area: 9.4 sq. mi.
     24.4 sq. km.
Population: 10,000
Largest City: Funafuti
Languages: Tuvaluan, English
Monetary Unit: Tuvalu dollar,
     Australian dollar

Tuvalu:
Map Index

City
Funafuti, capital C3

Other Features
Funafuti, island C3
Nanumanga, island B2
Nanumea, island B1
Niulakita, island C4
Niutao, island B2
Nui, island B2
Nukufetau, island C2
Nukulaelae, island C3
Vaitupu, island C2

Tuvalu

- ⊛ National Capital
- • Other City

1:12,500,000

0   75   150 mi

0   75   150 km

Mercator Projection

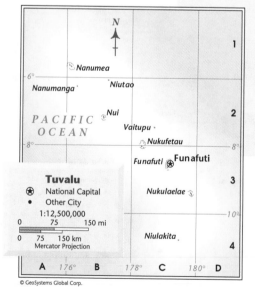

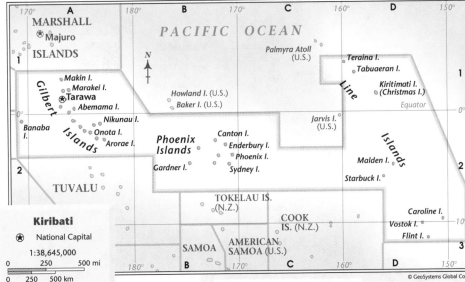

MARSHALL
Majuro
ISLANDS

PACIFIC OCEAN

Palmyra Atoll (U.S.)

Teraina I.

Tabuaeran I.

Makin I.
Marakei I.
Tarawa
Abemama I.

Howland I. (U.S.)
Baker I. (U.S.)

Line

Kiritimati I.
(Christmas I.)

Gilbert Islands

Nikunau I.

Banaba I.

Onota I.
Arorae I.

Phoenix Islands

Jarvis I. (U.S.)

Equator

Canton I.
Enderbury I.
Phoenix I.

Islands

Malden I.

Gardner I.
Sydney I.

Starbuck I.

Caroline I.

TOKELAU IS. (N.Z.)

TUVALU

COOK IS. (N.Z.)

Vostok I.

Flint I.

SAMOA

AMERICAN SAMOA (U.S.)

© GeoSystems Global Corp.

Fiji: Map Index

Cities and Towns
Galoa B3
Labasa B2
Lami B3
Lautoka A2
Lomawai A3
Nabouwalu B2
Nadi A2
Naduri B2
Nakodu B2
Navua B3
Suva, *capital* B3
Vunisea B3

Other Features
Beqa, *island* B3
Bligh Water, *sound* B2
Cicia, *island* C2
Cikobia, *island* C1
Gau, *island* B1
Great Sea, *reef* A2
Kadavu, *island* B3
Kadavu, *passage* A3
Kioa, *island* C2

Koro, *island* B2
Koro, *sea* B2
Lakeba, *island* C3
Lakeba, *passage* C3
Lau, *island group* C2
Laucala, *island* C2
Moala, *island group* B3
Nadi, *bay* A2
Navua, *river* A3
Ono, *island* B3
Ovalau, *island* B2
Qamea, *island* C2
Qelelevu, *island* C2
Rabi, *island* C2
Soso, *bay* B3
Taveuni, *island* C2
Tomanivi, *mt.* B2
Udu, *point* C2
Vanua Balavu, *island* ...C2
Vanua Levu, *island* B2
Vatu Lele, *island* A3
Vetauua, *island* C1
Viti Levu, *island* A2
Vunaniu, *bay* A3
Washington, *cape* A3
Yasawa, *island group* ...A2

Kiribati

National Capital

1:38,645,000

0 250 500 mi

0 250 500 km

Mercator Projection

Kiribati

Capital: Tarawa
Area: 313 sq. mi.
     811 sq. km.
Population: 78,000
Largest City: Tarawa
Languages: I-Kiribati (Gilbertese), English
Monetary Unit: Australian dollar

Kiribati: Map Index

City
Tarawa, *capital* A1

Other Features
Abemama, *island* A1
Arorae, *island* A2

Banaba, *island* A2
Canton, *island* B2
Caroline, *island* D2
Enderbury, *island* B2
Flint, *island* D3
Gardner, *island* B2
Gilbert, *islands* A1
Kiritimati (Christmas), *island* ..D1
Line, *islands* D1
Makin, *island* A1
Malden, *island* D2
Marakei, *island* A1
Nikunau, *island* A2
Onota, *island* A2
Phoenix, *island* B2
Phoenix, *islands* B2
Starbuck, *island* D2
Sydney, *island* B2
Tabuaeran, *island* D1
Teraina, *island* D1
Vostok, *island* D3

Fiji

National Capital
• Other City

1:8,900,000

0 50 100 mi

0 50 100 km

Azimuthal Equal Area Projection

Capital: Suva
Area: 7,056 sq. mi.
     18,280 sq. km.
Population: 764,000
Largest City: Suva
Languages: Fijian, Hindi, English
Monetary Unit: Fiji dollar

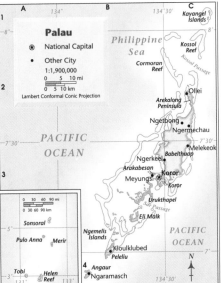

Cikobia

Great Sea Reef

Udu Point

Vetauua

Qelelevu

Vanua Levu Labasa
Naduri
Rabi
Kioa

Yasawa Group

Bligh Water

Laucala
Qamea
Taveuni

Viti Levu

Koro
Nakodu

Vanua Balavu

Lautoka
Tomanivi 1323 m (4340 ft)

Nadi Bay

Ovalau

Lau Group

Nadi Lami

Lomawai Navua Suva
Vunaniu Bay Galoa
Beqa

Gau

Koro Sea

Cicia

Lakeba Passage

Lakeba

Vatu Lele

Kadavu Passage
Kadavu

Vunisea Ono
Cape Washington Soso Bay

Moala Group

© GeoSystems Global Corp.

Tonga

National Capital
• Other City

1:11,000,000

0 75 150 mi

0 75 150 km

Mercator Projection

Niuafo'ou I.

Niuatoputapu I.
Tafahi I.

Niuatoputapu Group

PACIFIC OCEAN

Vava'u Group

Fonualei I.
Toku I.

Late I.

Vava'u I.
Neiafu

Tofua I.
Lifuka I.

Ha'apai Group

Fonuafo'ou I. (Falcon I.)

Tongatapu I.
Tongatapu Group

Nuku'alofa
Fua'amotu
Ohonua
'Eua I.

© GeoSystems Global Corp.

Palau: Map Index

Cities and Towns
Kloulklubed B3
Koror, *capital* B3
Melekeok C3
Meyungs B3
Ngaramasch B4
Ngerkeel B3
Ngermechau C2
Ngetbong C2
Ollei C2

Other Features
Angaur, *island* B4
Arakabesan, *island* B3
Arekalong, *peninsula* C2

Babelthuap, *island* C3
Cormoran, *reef* B2
Eli Malk, *island* B3
Helen, *reef* ....Inset
Kayangel, *islands* C1
Koror, *island* C3
Kossol, *passage* C2
Kossol, *reef* C2
Merir, *island* ....Inset
Ngemelis, *islands* B4
Peleliu, *island* B4
Philippine, *sea* B2
Pulo Anna, *island* ....Inset
Sar, *passage* B3
Sonsoral, *island* ....Inset
Tobi, *island* ....Inset
Urukthapel, *island* B3

Palau

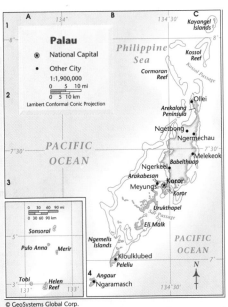

Palau

National Capital
• Other City

1:1,900,000

0 5 10 mi

Lambert Conformal Conic Projection

Kayangel Islands

Philippine Sea

Kossol Reef
Cormoran Reef

Kossol Passage

PACIFIC OCEAN

Ollei

Arekalong Peninsula

Ngetbong

Ngermechau

Ngerkeel Melekeok

Babelthuap

Arakabesan

Meyungs Koror
Koror

Urukthapel

Sar Passage

Eli Malk

0 30 60 90 mi

0 30 60 90 km

Sonsoral

Pulo Anna Merir

Ngemelis Islands

Kloulklubed
Peleliu

Tobi Helen Reef

Angaur
Ngaramasch

PACIFIC OCEAN

© GeoSystems Global Corp.

Palau

Capital: Koror
Area: 177 sq. mi.
     458 sq. km.
Population: 16,661
Largest City: Koror
Languages: English, Sonsorolese, Angaur, Japanese, Tobi, Palauan
Monetary Unit: U.S. dollar

Tonga

Capital: Nuku'alofa
Area: 301 sq. mi.
     780 sq. km.
Population: 105,000
Largest City: Nuku'alofa
Languages: Tongan, English
Monetary Unit: Pa'anga

Tonga: Map Index

Cities and Towns
Fua'amotu B4
Neiafu C2
Nuku'alofa, *capital* B4
Ohonua C4

Other Features
'Eua, *island* C4
Fonuafo'ou (Falcon), *island* ..B3
Fonualei, *island* C2

Ha'apai, *island group* B3
Late, *island* C2
Lifuka, *island* C3
Niuafo'ou, *island* B1
Niuatoputapu, *island* C1
Niuatoputapu, *island group* ..C1
Tafahi, *island* C1
Toku, *island* C2
Tongatapu, *island* B4
Tongatapu, *island group* ...B4
Vava'u, *island* C2
Vava'u, *island group* C2

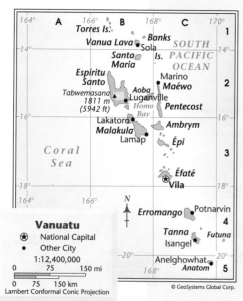

Vanuatu

Capital: Vila
Area: 4,707 sq. mi.
　　　　12,194 sq. km.
Population: 170,000
Largest City: Vila
Languages: French, English, Bislama
Monetary Unit: Vatu

Vanuatu: Map Index

Cities and Towns
Anelghowhat............C5
Isangel................C4
Lakatoro...............B3
Lamap.................B3
Luganville..............B2
Marino.................C2
Potnarvin...............C4
Sola..................B1
Vila, *capital*.............C3

Other Features
Ambrym, *island*..........C3
Anatom, *island*..........C5
Aoba, *island*............B2
Banks, *islands*...........B1
Coral, *sea*..............C3
Éfaté, *island*............C3
Épi, *island*.............C3
Erromango, *island*........C4
Espiritu Santo, *island*......B2
Futuna, *island*...........C4
Homo, *bay*.............B2
Maéwo, *island*...........C2
Malakula, *island*.........B3
Pentecost, *island*.........C2
Santa Maria, *island*.......B2
Tabwemasana, *mt.*........B2
Tanna, *island*...........C4
Torres, *islands*...........B1
Vanua Lava, *island*.......B1

Vanuatu
⊛ National Capital
● Other City
1:12,400,000
0　　75　　150 mi
0　　75　　150 km
Lambert Conformal Conic Projection

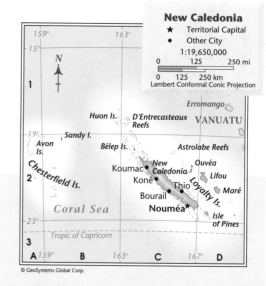

New Caledonia
★ Territorial Capital
● Other City
1:19,650,000
0　125　250 mi
0　125　250 km
Lambert Conformal Conic Projection

New Caledonia: Map Index

Cities and Towns
Bourail................C2
Koné..................C2
Koumac................C2
Nouméa, *capital*.........C2
Thio...................C2

Other Features
Astrolabe, *reefs*..........C2
Avon, *islands*...........A2
Bélep, *islands*...........C2
Chesterfield, *islands*.......A2
Coral, *sea*.............B2
D'Entrecasteaux, *reefs*.....C1
Huon, *islands*...........B1
Lifou, *island*............D2
Loyalty, *islands*..........C2
Maré, *island*............D2
New Caledonia, *island*.....C2
Ouvéa, *island*...........C2
Pines, *island*...........D2
Sandy, *island*...........B2

New Caledonia

Capital: Nouméa
Area: 8,548 sq. mi.
　　　　21,912 sq. km.
Population: 172,000
Largest City: Nouméa
Language: French
Monetary Unit: CFA Franc

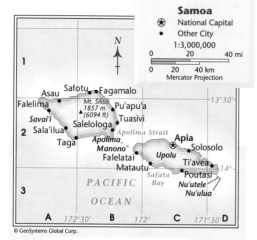

Samoa
⊛ National Capital
● Other City
1:3,000,000
0　　20　　40 mi
0　20　40 km
Mercator Projection

Samoa

Capital: Apia
Area: 1,093 sq. mi.
　　　　2,832 sq. km.
Population: 204,000
Largest City: Apia
Languages: Samoan, English
Monetary Unit: Tala

Samoa: Map Index

Cities and Towns
Apia, *capital*............C2
Asau..................A2
Fagamalo...............B1
Falelatai................C2
Falelima................A2
Matautu................C2
Poutasi.................C3
Pu'apu'a...............B2
Safotu.................B1
Sala'ilua................A2
Salelologa...............B2
Solosolo................C2
Taga..................A2
Ti'avea.................D2
Tuasivi.................B2

Other Features
Apolima, *island*..........B2
Apolima, *strait*..........B2
Manono, *island*.........B2
Nu'ulua, *island*..........D3
Nu'utele, *island*.........D3
Safata, *bay*............C3
Savai'i, *island*...........A2
Silisili, *mt.*.............B2
Upolu, *island*...........C2

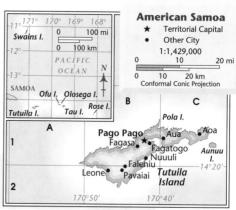

American Samoa
★ Territorial Capital
● Other City
1:1,429,000
0　　10　　20 mi
0　10　20 km
Conformal Conic Projection

American Samoa: Map Index

Cities and Towns
Aoa...................C1
Aua...................C1
Fagasa.................B1
Fagatogo................B1
Faleniu.................B1
Leone..................B2
Nuuuli.................B1
Pago Pago, *capital*.......B1
Pavaiai.................B2

Other Features
Aunuu, *island*..........C1
Ofu, *island*............A1
Olosega, *island*.........A1
Pola, *island*............C1
Rose, *island*............A1
Swains, *island*..........A1
Tau, *island*.............A1
Tutuila, *island*..........A1, C2

American Samoa

Capital: Pago Pago
Area: 77 sq. mi.
　　　　199 sq. km.
Population: 46,773
Largest City: Pago Pago
Language: English
Monetary Unit: U.S. dollar

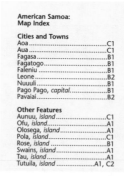

© GeoSystems Global Corp.

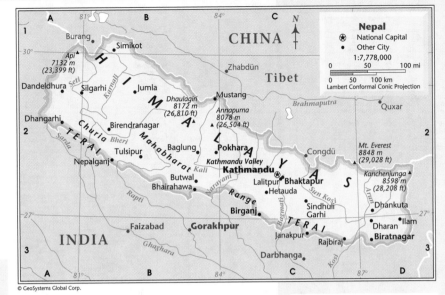

CHINA

Tibet

Api 7132 m (23,399 ft)

Dhaulagiri 8172 m (26,810 ft)

Annapurna 8078 m (26,504 ft)

Mt. Everest 8848 m (29,028 ft)

Kanchenjunga 8598 m (28,208 ft)

Brahmaputra

Quxar

Zhabdün

Mustang

Congdü

Burang

Simikot

Jumla

Dandeldhura

Silgarhi

Dhangarhi

Birendranagar

Tulsipur

Nepalganj

Baglung

Pokhara

Kathmandu Valley

Kathmandu

Lalitpur

Bhaktapur

Hetauda

Butwal

Bhairahawa

Sindhuli Garhi

Birganj

Dhankuta

Dharan

Ilam

Biratnagar

Rajbiraj

Janakpur

Darbhanga

Gorakhpur

Faizabad

INDIA

HIMALAYAS Range

TERAI

Churia Mahabharat

Seti Kali Bheri Sarda Narayani Rapti Ghaghara Bagmati Sun Kosi Arun Kosi

© GeoSystems Global Corp.

Nepal

 National Capital
• Other City

1:7,778,000

0   50   100 mi
0   50   100 km
Lambert Conformal Conic Projection

Nepal: Map Index

Cities and Towns

Baglung	B2
Bhairahawa	B2
Bhaktapur	C2
Biratnagar	D3
Birendranagar	B2
Birganj	C2
Butwal	B2
Dandeldhura	A2
Dhangarhi	A2
Dhankuta	D3
Dharan	D3
Hetauda	C2
Ilam	D3
Janakpur	C3
Jumla	B2
Kathmandu, *capital*	C2
Lalitpur	C2
Mustang	B2
Nepalganj	B2
Pokhara	B2
Rajbiraj	C3
Silgarhi	B2
Simikot	B1
Sindhuli Garhi	C2
Tulsipur	B2

Other Features

Annapurna, *mt.*	B2
Api, *mt.*	A2
Arun, *river*	D2
Bagmati, *river*	C2
Bheri, *river*	B2
Churia, *mts.*	B2
Dhaulagiri, *mt.*	B2
Everest, *mt.*	C2
Himalayas, *mts.*	B2
Kali, *river*	B2
Kanchenjunga, *mt.*	D2
Karnali, *river*	B2
Kathmandu, *valley*	C2
Mahabharat, *range*	B2
Narayani, *river*	B2
Rapti, *river*	B2
Sarda, *river*	A2
Seti, *river*	A2
Sun Kosi, *river*	C2
Terai, *region*	A2, C3

Maldives

Capital: Male
Area: 115 sq. mi.
298 sq. km.
Population: 252,000
Largest City: Male
Language: Divehi
Monetary Unit: Rufiyaa

Nepal

Capital: Kathmandu
Area: 56,827 sq. mi.
147,220 sq. km.
Population: 21,042,000
Largest City: Kathmandu
Language: Nepali
Monetary Unit: Rupee

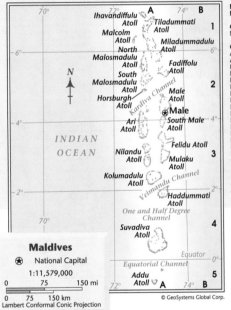

Ihavandiffulu Atoll
Tiladummati Atoll
Malcolm Atoll
Miladummadulu Atoll
North Malosmadulu Atoll
Fadiffolu Atoll
South Malosmadulu Atoll
Horsburgh Atoll
Male Atoll
Male
South Male Atoll
Ari Atoll
Felidu Atoll
Nilandu Atoll
Mulaku Atoll
Kolumadulu Atoll
Haddummati Atoll
Suvadiva Atoll
Addu Atoll

INDIAN OCEAN

Kardiva Channel
Veimandu Channel
One and Half Degree Channel
Equator
Equatorial Channel

© GeoSystems Global Corp.

Maldives: Map Index

City

Male, *capital*	A2

Other Features

Addu, *atoll*	A5
Ari, *atoll*	A3
Equatorial, *channel*	A5
Fadiffolu, *atoll*	A2
Felidu, *atoll*	A3
Haddummati, *atoll*	A4
Horsburgh, *atoll*	A2
Ihavandiffulu, *atoll*	A1
Kardiva, *channel*	A2
Kolumadulu, *atoll*	A3
Malcolm, *atoll*	A1
Male, *atoll*	A2
Miladummadulu, *atoll*	A1
Mulaku, *atoll*	A3
Nilandu, *atoll*	A3
North Malosmadulu, *atoll*	A2
One and Half Degree, *channel*	A4
South Male, *atoll*	A3
South Malosmadulu, *atoll*	A2
Suvadiva, *atoll*	A4
Tiladummati, *atoll*	A1
Veimandu, *channel*	A3

Maldives

 National Capital

1:11,579,000

0   75   150 mi
0   75   150 km
Lambert Conformal Conic Projection

Sri Lanka: Map Index

Provinces

Central	B4
Eastern	C4
North Central	B3
Northern	B2
North Western	B4
Sabaragamuwa	B5
Southern	B5
Uva	C5
Western	A4

Cities and Towns

Amparai	C4
Anuradhapura	B3
Batticaloa	C4
Colombo, *capital*	A5
Dehiwala-Mt. Lavinia	A5
Galle	B5

Hambantota	C5
Jaffna	B2
Kalutara	A5
Kandy	B4
Kilinochchi	A5
Kotte	A5
Kurunegala	B4
Mankulam	B2
Mannar	A2
Matale	B4
Matara	A5
Moratuwa	A5
Mullaittivu	B2
Negombo	A4
Nuwara Eliya	B5
Point Pedro	B2
Polonnaruwa	C4
Pottuvil	C5
Puttalam	A3
Ratnapura	B5

Trincomalee	C3
Vavuniya	B3

Other Features

Adam's, *peak*	B4
Adam's Bridge, *shoal*	A3
Aruvi, *river*	B3
Bengal, *bay*	C3
Delft, *island*	A2
Dondra Head, *cape*	B6
Jaffna, *lagoon*	B2
Kalu, *river*	B5
Kelani, *river*	B4
Mahaweli Ganga, *river*	C4
Mannar, *gulf*	A3
Mannar, *island*	A2
Palk, *strait*	A2
Pidurutalagala, *mt.*	B4
Trincomalee, *harbor*	C3
Yan, *river*	B3

Sri Lanka

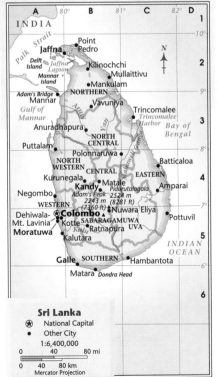

INDIA

Palk Strait

Jaffna
Point Pedro
Delft Island
Jaffna Lagoon
Kilinochchi
Mannar Island
Mullaittivu
Mankulam
Adam's Bridge
Mannar
Vavuniya
NORTHERN
Gulf of Mannar
Trincomalee
Trincomalee Harbor
Bay of Bengal
Anuradhapura
NORTH CENTRAL
Polonnaruwa
Puttalam
Batticaloa
NORTH WESTERN
CENTRAL
EASTERN
Kurunegala
Matale
Amparai
Negombo
Kandy
Pidurutalagala 2524 m (8281 ft)
Adam's Peak 2243 m (7360 ft)
Nuwara Eliya
WESTERN
Dehiwala-Mt. Lavinia
Colombo
Kotte
SABARAGAMUWA
Ratnapura
UVA
Moratuwa
Kalutara
Pottuvil
SOUTHERN
Galle
Hambantota
INDIAN OCEAN
Matara Dondra Head

Aruvi Yan Mahaweli Ganga Kelani Kalu

Capital: Colombo
Area: 25,332 sq. mi.
65,627 sq. km.
Population: 18,033,000
Largest City: Colombo
Language: Sinhalese
Monetary Unit: Rupee

Bhutan

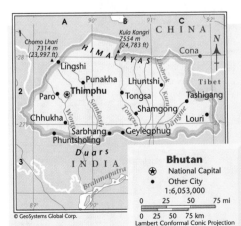

Chomo Lhari 7314 m (23,997 ft)
Kula Kangri 7554 m (24,783 ft)
CHINA
Cona
HIMALAYAS
Lingshi
Punakha
Lhuntshi
Tongsa
Tashigang
Paro
Thimphu
Shamgong
Louri
Chhukha
Sarbhang
Geylegphug
Phuntsholing
Duars
INDIA
Brahmaputra
Tibet

Amo Wong Sankosh Tongsa Mangde Kuru Dangme

© GeoSystems Global Corp.

Bhutan

Capital: Thimphu
Area: 18,147 sq. mi.
47,013 sq. km.
Population: 1,739,000
Largest City: Thimphu
Language: Dzongkha
Monetary Unit: Ngultrum

Bhutan: Map Index

Cities and Towns

Chhukha	A2
Geylegphug	B3
Lhuntshi	A2
Lingshi	A2
Louri	C2
Paro	A2
Phuntsholing	A3
Punakha	A2
Sarbhang	B3
Shamgong	B2
Tashigang	C2

Thimphu, *capital*	A2
Tongsa	B2

Other Features

Chomo Lhari, *mt.*	A1
Dangme, *river*	C2
Duars, *plain*	A3
Himalayas, *mts.*	B1
Kula Kangri, *mt.*	B1
Kuru, *river*	C2
Lhobrak, *river*	B1
Sankosh, *river*	B2
Tongsa, *river*	B2
Wong, *river*	A2

Bhutan

 National Capital
• Other City

1:6,053,000

0   25   50   75 mi
0   25   50   75 km
Lambert Conformal Conic Projection

Sri Lanka

 National Capital
• Other City

1:6,400,000

0   40   80 mi
0   40   80 km
Mercator Projection

© GeoSystems Global Corp.

India:
Map Index

Internal Divisions

Andaman and Nicobar
Islands (territory) F6
Andhra Pradesh (state) C5
Arunachal Pradesh (state) F3
Assam (state) F3
Bihar (state) E4
Chandigarh (territory) C2
Dadra and Nagar
Haveli (territory) B4
Daman and Diu (territory) B4
Delhi (territory) C3
Goa (state) B5
Gujarat (state) B4
Haryana (state) C3
Himachal Pradesh (state) C2
Jammu and Kashmir (state) C2
Karnataka (state) C6

Kerala (state) C6
Lakshadweep (territory) B6
Madhya Pradesh (state) C4
Maharashtra (state) B5
Manipur (state) F4
Meghalaya (state) F3
Mizoram (state) F4
Nagaland (state) F3
Orissa (state) D4
Pondicherry (territory) C6
Punjab (state) C2
Rajasthan (state) B3
Sikkim (state) E3
Tamil Nadu (state) C6
Tripura (state) F4
Uttar Pradesh (state) C3
West Bengal (state) E4

Cities and Towns

Agartala F4
Agra C3

Ahmadabad B4
Aizawl F4
Ajmer B3
Akola C4
Alampur ....Inset II
Aligarh C3
Allahabad D3
Alleppey (Alappuzha) C7
Amdanga ....Inset II
Amravati C4
Amritsar B2
Andheri ....Inset I
Ara D3
Asansol E4
Aurangabad C5
Babu Bheri ....Inset II
Baidyabati ....Inset II
Bally ....Inset II
Bamangachi ....Inset II
Bananga F7
Bandra ....Inset I

Bangalore C6
Bansaria ....Inset II
Barakpur ....Inset II
Baranagar ....Inset II
Barasat ....Inset II
Bareilly C3
Bargachia ....Inset II
Bauria ....Inset II
Behala ....Inset II
Belapurpada ....Inset I
Belgaum B5
Bellary C5
Bhadrakh E4
Bhadreswar ....Inset II
Bhagalpur E3
Bhamapur D5
Bhandup ....Inset I
Bharatpur C3
Bhatapara D4
Bhatpara ....Inset II
Bhavnagar B4

Bhayandar ....Inset I
Bhimpur ....Inset II
Bhiwandi ....Inset I
Bhopal C4
Bhubaneshwar E4
Bhuj A4
Bihar E3
Bijapur C5
Bikaner B3
Bilaspur D4
Bishnupur ....Inset II
Bombay ....B5, Inset I
Borivli ....Inset I
Buj-Buj ....Inset II
Burdwan E4
Burhanpur C4
Calcutta ....E4, Inset II
Chandannagar ....Inset II
Chandigarh C2
Chandrapur C5
Chembur ....Inset I

Chene ....Inset I
Cherrapunji F3
Chirner ....Inset I
Cochin (Kochi) C7
Coimbatore C6
Cuddalore C6
Cuttack E4
Daman B4
Darbhanga E3
Darjiling E3
Dehra Dun C2
Delhi C3
Dhulagarh ....Inset II
Dibrugarh F3
Dispur F3
Diu B4
Dum-Dum ....Inset II
Dumjor ....Inset II
Faizabad D3
Gandhinagar B4
Ganganagar B3
Gangtok E3
Garden Reach ....Inset II
Garulia ....Inset II
Gauhati F3
Gaya E4
Ghatkopar ....Inset I
Gorakhpur D3
Gulbarga C5
Guntur D5
Gwalior C3
Halisahar ....Inset II
Haora ....E4, Inset II
Hisabpur ....Inset II
Hubli-Dharwar C5
Hugli-Chunchura ....Inset II
Hyderabad C5
Imphal F4
Indore C4
Itanagar F3
Jabalpur C4
Jadabpur ....Inset II
Jagdalpur D5
Jaipur C3
Jammu B2
Jamnagar B4
Jampur ....Inset II
Jamshedpur E4
Janai ....Inset II
Jhansi C3
Jodhpur B3
Joka ....Inset II
Jullundur C2
Junagadh B4
Kakinada D5
Kalwa ....Inset I
Kaman ....Inset I
Kamarhati ....Inset II
Kanchipuram C6
Kanchrapara ....Inset II
Kanpur D3
Kansaripara ....Inset II
Kasinathpur ....Inset II
Kathgodam C3
Kharagpur E4
Kohima F3
Kolhapur B5
Kolshet ....Inset I
Konnagar ....Inset II
Kota C3
Kozhikode C6
Kurla ....Inset I
Kurnool C5
Lakhpat A4
Lucknow D3
Ludhiana C2
Madras D6
Madurai C7
Malad ....Inset I
Malegaon B4
Mangalore B6
Mathura C3
Meerut C3
Moradabad C3
Mulund ....Inset I
Mumbra ....Inset I
Mysore C6
Nagpur C4
Naihati ....Inset II
Nalikut ....Inset II
Nanded C5
Nangi ....Inset I
Nanole ....Inset I
Nasik B4
Nellore C6
New Delhi, capital C3
Nizamabad C5
Ongole C5
Panaji B5
Panihati ....Inset II
Patiala C2
Patna E3
Paye ....Inset I
Polba ....Inset I
Pondicherry C6
Port Blair F6
Pune B5
Raipur D4
Rajkot B4
Rajpur ....Inset II
Ranmabati ....Inset II
Ranchi E4
Raurkela D4
Rishra ....Inset II
Saharanpur Panipat C3
Salem C6
Sambalpur D4
Sankrail ....Inset II
Sasaram D4
Sheva ....Inset I
Shillong F3
Sholapur C5
Shrirampur ....Inset II
Silvassi B4
Simla C2
Singur ....Inset II
Sonarpur ....Inset II
South Dum-Dum ....Inset II
Srinagar B2
Surat B4
Thane ....Inset I
Thanjavur C6
Tiruchchirappalli C6
Titagarh ....Inset II
Trivandrum
(Thiruvananthapuram) C7
Trombay ....Inset I
Tuticorin C7
Udaipur B4

India

⊛ National Capital

• Other City

1:20,000,000

0 100 200 300 400 mi

0 100 200 300 400 km

Lambert Conformal Conic Projection

India

Capital: New Delhi
Area: 1,222,559 sq. mi.
    3,167,251 sq. km.
Population: 919,903,000
Largest City: Bombay
Languages: Hindi, English
Monetary Unit: Rupee

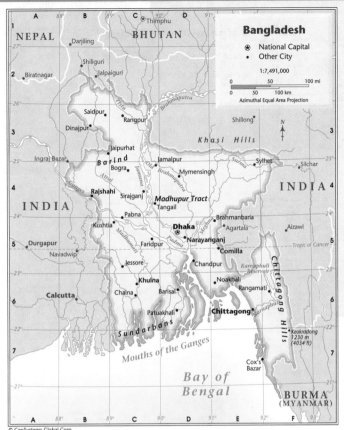

Bangladesh

Capital: Dhaka
Area: 57,295 sq. mi.
  148,433 sq. km.
Population: 125,149,000
Largest City: Dhaka
Language: Bengali
Monetary Unit: Taka

Bangladesh:
Map Index

Cities and Towns

Barisal D6
Bogra C4
Brahmanbaria E5
Chalna C6
Chandpur D5
Chittagong E5
Comilla E5
Cox's Bazar E7
Dhaka, *capital* D5
Dinajpur B3
Faridpur C5
Jaipurhat B3
Jamalpur C4
Jessore C6
Khulna C6
Kushtia C5
Mymensingh D4
Narayanganj D5
Noakhali E6
Pabna C4
Patuakhali D6
Rajshahi B4
Rangamati F6
Rangpur C3
Saidpur B3
Sirajganj C4
Sylhet E4
Tangail C4

Other Features

Atrai, *river* B4
Barind, *region* B4
Bengal, *bay* D7
Brahmaputra, *river* D3
Chittagong Hills, *region* F5
Ganges, *river* B4
Jamuna, *river* C4
Karnaphuli, *reservoir* F6
Karnaphuli, *river* E6
Keokradong, *mt.* F7
Madhumati, *river* C5
Madhupur Tract, *region* D4
Meghna, *river* D5
Mouths of the Ganges,
  delta C7
Old Brahmaputra, *river* C4
Padma, *river* C5
Sundarbans, *region* C7
Surma, *river* E3
Tista, *river* C2

India: Map Index

Ujjain C4
Ulubaria ....Inset II
Uran ....Inset I
Utan ....Inset I
Vadodara B4
Varanasi D3
Vasai ....Inset I
Vellore C6
Vijayawada D5
Vishakhapatnam D5
Warangal C5

Other Features

Amindivi, *islands* B6
Andaman, *islands* F6
Androth, *island* B6
Arabian, *sea* ....AS, Inset I
Aravalli, *range* B3
Bengal, *bay* E5
Bhima, *river* C5
Bombay, *harbor* ....Inset I
Brahmaputra, *river* F3
Car Nicobar, *island* F7
Cauvery, *river* C6
Chambal, *river* C3
Chata Nagpur, *plateau* D4
Comorin, *cape* C7
Coromandel, *coast* D6
Deccan, *plateau* C5
Eastern Ghats, *mts.* C5
Elephanta, *island* ....Inset I
False Divi, *point* D5
Ganges, *river* E3
Ghaghara, *river* D3
Godavari, *river* C5
Great Indian, *desert* B3
Great Nicobar, *island* F7
Himalayas, *mts.* C2, E3
Hirakud, *reservoir* D4
Hugli, *river* ....Inset II
Indus, *river* C2
Kalpeni, *island* B7
Kamet, *mt.* C2
Kanchenjunga, *mt.* E3
Karakoram, *range* C1
Kathiawar, *peninsula* B4
Kavaratti, *island* B6
Khambhat, *gulf* B4
Khasi, *hills* F3
Kolar, *gold fields* C6
Krishna, *river* C5
Kutch, *gulf* A4
Laccadive, *islands* B6
Little Andaman, *island* F6
Mahanadi, *river* D4
Mahim, *bay* ....Inset I
Malabar, *coast* B6
Malabar, *point* ....Inset I
Mannar, *gulf* C7
Manori, *point* ....Inset I
Middle Andaman, *island* F6
Minicoy, *island* B7
Mizo, *hills* F4
Mouths of the Ganges, *delta* ..E4
Naga, *hills* F3
Nanda Devi, *mt.* C2
Narmada, *river* C4
Nicobar, *islands* F7
Nilgiri, *hills* C6
North Andaman, *island* F6
Palk, *strait* C7
Rann of Kutch, *mud flat* B4
Ritchies, *archipelago* F6
Salsette, *island* ....Inset I
Salt Water, *lake* ....Inset II
Satpura, *range* C4
Son, *river* D4
South Andaman, *island* F6
Sutlej, *river* C2
Ten Degree, *channel* F7
Ulhas, *river* ....Inset I
Vasai, *creek* ....Inset I
Vindhya, *range* C4
Western Ghats, *mts.* B5
Yamuna, *river* C3

Pakistan

Capital: Islamabad
Area: 339,697 sq. mi.
  880,044 sq. km.
Population: 121,856,000
Largest City: Karachi
Languages: Urdu, English
Monetary Unit: Pakistani rupee

Pakistan:
Map Index

Internal Divisions

Azad Kashmir Province........D2
Baluchistan Province............B4
Federally Administrated
  Tribal Areas C3
Islamabad Capital Territory ...D3
Northern Areas D2
North-West Frontier Province..D2
Punjab Province D3
Sind Province C5

Cities and Towns

Bahawalpur...........................D4
Bela C4
Chiniot D3
Chitral D2
Dadu C4
Dera Ghazi Khan D3
Dera Ismail Khan D3
Faisalabad D3
Gilgit E2
Gujranwala E3
Gujrat E3
Gwadar B5
Hyderabad C5
Islamabad, *capital* D3
Jhang Sadar D3
Jhelum D3
Karachi..................................C5
Kasur E3
Khuzdar C4
Lahore E3
Larkana C4
Mardan D2
Mianwali D3
Mirpur Khas C5
Multan D3
Muzaffarabad D2
Nawabshah C4
Nok Kundi B4

Okara D3
Panjgur B4
Peshawar D3
Quetta C3
Rahimyar Khan D4
Rawalpindi D3
Sahiwal D3
Sargodha D3
Shikarpur C4
Sialkot E3
Sukkur C4
Surab C4

Other Features

Arabian, *sea* B6
Central Makran, *range* B4
Chagai, *hills* B4
Chenab, *river* D3
Hindu Kush, *mts.* D2
Indus, *river* C4, E2
Jhelum, *river* D3
Karakoram, *range* E2
Khojak, *pass* C3
Khyber, *pass* D2
Kirthar, *range* C4
Konar, *river* D2
K2 (Godwin Austen), *mt.*......E2
Makran Coast, *range* B5
Mouths of the Indus, *delta* ...C5
Nal, *river* B4
Nanga Parbat, *mt.* E2
Nara, *canal* C4
Nowshak, *mt.* D2
Rakaposhi, *mt.* E2
Ravi, *river* D3
Safed Koh, *range* B4
Siahan, *range* B4
Sulaiman, *range* C4
Sutlej, *river* D4
Thar, *desert* C4
Tirich Mir, *mt.* D2
Toba Kakar, *range* C3
Zhob, *river* C3

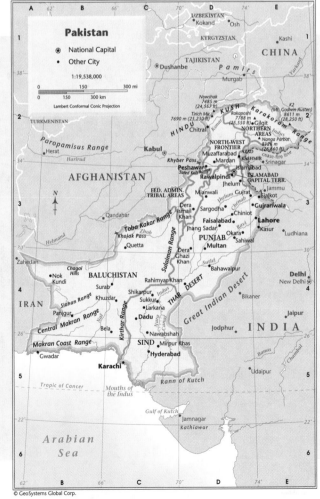

Afghanistan: Map Index

Cities and Towns
Asadabad	C2
Baghlan	B1
Balkh	B1
Bamian	B2
Baraki Barak	B2
Chaghcharan	B2
Charikar	B1
Farah	A2
Feyzabad	C1
Gardez	B2
Ghazni	B2
Herat	A2
Jalalabad	B2
Kabul, capital	B2
Khowst	B2
Konduz	B1

Kowt-e Ashrow	B2
Lashkar Gah	B2
Mazar-e Sharif	B1
Meymaneh	A1
Qalat	B2
Qaleh-ye Now	A2
Qaleh-ye Panjeh	C1
Qandahar	B2
Samangan	B2
Sar-e Pol	B1
Sheberghan	B1
Shindand	A2
Taloqan	B1
Tarin Kowt	B2
Zaranj	A2
Zareh Sharan	B2

Other Features
Amu Darya, river	B1
Arghandab, river	B2

Farah, river	A2
Fuladi, mt.	B2
Gowd-e Zereh, lake	A3
Hamun-e Saberi, lake	A2
Harirud, river	A2
Helmand, river	A2
Hindu Kush, range	B1
Kabul, river	B2
Khojak, pass	B2
Khyber, pass	C2
Konar, river	C1
Konduz, river	B1
Morghab, river	A1
Nowshak, mt.	C1
Panj, river	B1
Paropamisus, range	A2
Registan, region	A2
Shibar, pass	B2
Vakhan, region	C1

Afghanistan

Capital: Kabul
Area: 251,825 sq. mi.
652,396 sq. km.
Population: 16,903,000
Largest City: Kabul
Languages: Pashto, Dari Persian
Monetary Unit: Afghani

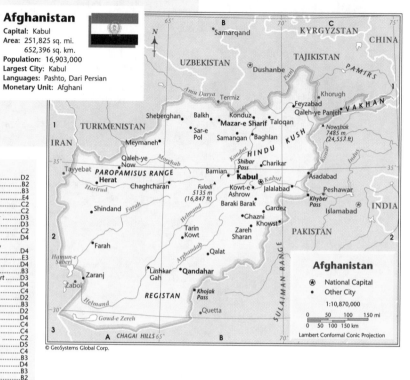

Afghanistan
- ⊛ National Capital
- • Other City

1:10,870,000

0 50 100 150 mi
0 50 100 150 km
Lambert Conformal Conic Projection

© GeoSystems Global Corp.

Iran

Capital: Tehran
Area: 632,457 sq. mi.
1,638,490 sq. km.
Population: 65,612,000
Largest City: Tehran
Languages: Persian, Turkic, Luri, Kurdish
Monetary Unit: Rial

Iran: Map Index

Cities and Towns
Abadan	B3
Ahvaz	B3
Arak	B3
Ardabil	B2
Bakhtaran	B3
Bam	D4
Bandar Beheshti	E4
Bandar-e Abbas	D4
Bandar-e Anzali	B2
Bandar-e Busehr	C4
Bandar-e Khomeyni	B3
Bandar-e Torkeman	C2
Birjand	D3
Dezful	B3

Esfahan	C3
Hamadan	B3
Ilam	B3
Iranshahr	E4
Jask	E4
Karaj	C2
Kashan	C3
Khorramabad	B3
Khorramshahr	B3
Khvoy	A2
Mashhad	D2
Neyshabur	D2
Orumiyeh (Urmia)	A2
Qazvin	B2
Qom	C3
Rasht	B2
Sabzevar	D2
Sanandaj	B2
Sari	C2
Shahr-e Kord	C3
Shiraz	C4
Sirjan	D4
Tabriz	A2
Tehran, capital	C3
Yasuj	C3
Yazd	D3
Zabol	E3
Zahedan	E4
Zanjan	B2

Other Features
Aras, river	B2

Atrak, river	D2
Azerbaijan, region	B2
Bakhtiari, region	B3
Baluchistan, region	E4
Caspian, sea	C2
Damavand, mt.	C2
Dasht-e Kavir, desert	D3
Dasht-e Lut, desert	D3
Elburz, mts.	C2
Halil, river	D4
Hamun-e Jaz Murian, lake	D4
Hashtadan, region	E3
Hormuz, strait	D4
Karun, river	B3
Kavir-e Namak, desert	D3
Kerman, region	D4
Kharg, island	C4
Khorasan, region	D2
Khuzestan, region	B3
Kopet, mts.	D2
Kul, river	D4
Larestan, region	C4
Mand, river	C4
Mazandaran, region	C2
Oman, gulf	D5
Persian, gulf	C4
Qareh, river	B2
Qeshm, island	D4
Shatt al-Arab, river	B3
Urmia, lake	B2
Yazd, region	C3
Zagros, mts.	B3

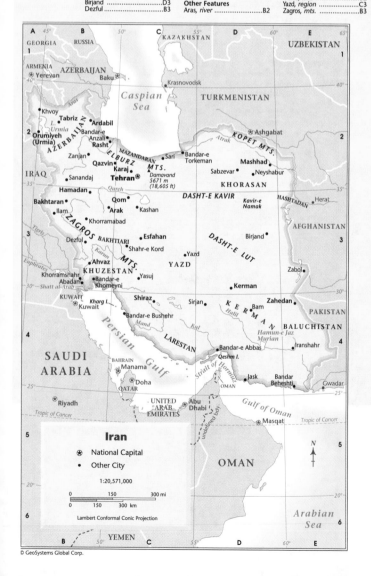

Iran
- ⊛ National Capital
- • Other City

1:20,571,000

0 150 300 mi
0 150 300 km
Lambert Conformal Conic Projection

© GeoSystems Global Corp.

Turkmenistan: Map Index

Cities and Towns
Ashgabat, capital	C3
Bakhardok	C2
Bayramaly	D3
Büzmeyin	C2
Chardzhou	D2
Cheleken	A2
Dashhowuz	C2
Ensenguly	A3
Gazanjyk	B2
Gumdag	B2
Gushgy	D3
Gyzylarbat	B2
Kerki	D3
Krasnovodsk	A2
Mary	C3

Other Features
Amu Darya, river	D2
Caspian, sea	A2
Etrek, river	B3
Garabil, plateau	D3
Garabogazköl, lake	A2
Gushgy, river	D3
Kara-Kum, canal	D3
Kara-Kum, desert	C2
Kopet, mts.	B2
Murgab, river	D3
Sarygamysh Koli, lake	B2
Sumbar, river	A3
Tedzhen, river	C3
Turan, lowland	C2
Nebitdag	B2
Tedzhen	C3

Turkmenistan

Capital: Ashgabat
Area: 188,417 sq. mi.
488,127 sq. km.
Population: 3,995,000
Largest City: Ashgabat
Languages: Turkmen, Russian, Uzbek
Monetary Unit: Ruble

Turkmenistan
- ⊛ National Capital
- • Other City

1:16,929,000

0 100 200 mi
0 100 200 km
Lambert Conformal Conic Projection

© GeoSystems Global Corp.

Balkhash	D2
Beyneu	B2
Ekibastuz	D1
Embi	B2
Esil	C1
Kokshetau	C1
Leninsk	C2
Lepsi	D2
Oral	B1
Öskemen	
(Ust-Kamenogorsk)	E1
Pavlodar	D1
Petropavl	C1
Qaraghandy (Karaganda)	D2
Qostanay	C1
Qyzylorda	C2
Rudnyy	C1
Saryshaghan	D2
Semey (Semipalatinsk)	E1
Shalqar	B2
Shymkent (Chimkent)	C2
Taldyqorghan	D2
Temirtau	D1
Zaysan	E2
Zhambyl (Dzhambul)	D2
Zhezqazghan	C2

Other Features

Alakol, lake	E2
Aral, sea	B2
Balkhash, lake	D2
Betpak Dala, plain	C2
Caspian, depression	B2
Caspian, sea	A2
Ili, river	D2
Irtysh, river	D1
Ishim, river	C1
Kazakh Upland, region	C2
Khan-Tengri, mt.	E2
Muyun Kum, desert	D2
Syrdarya, river	C2
Tengiz, lake	C1
Tobol, river	C1
Torghay, plateau	C1
Ural, river	B2
Ustyurt, plateau	B2
Zaysan, lake	E2

Kazakhstan

Capital: Almaty
Area: 1,049,200 sq. mi.
2,718,135 sq. km.
Population: 17,268,000
Largest City: Almaty
Language: Kazakh
Monetary Unit: Tenge

Kazakhstan: Map Index

Cities and Towns
Akmola (Tselinograd)	D1
Almaty (Alma-Ata), capital	D2
Aqtau	B2
Aqtobe	B1
Aral	C2
Arqalyq	C1
Atbasar	C1
Atyrau	B2
Ayagöz	E2

Kazakhstan
⊛ National Capital
• Other City
1:26,667,000
0 125 250 mi
0 125 250 km
Lambert Conformal Conic Projection

© GeoSystems Global Corp.

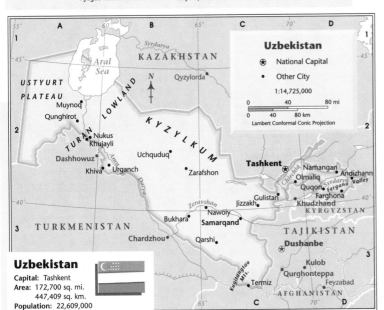

Uzbekistan

⊛ National Capital
• Other City
1:14,725,000
0 40 80 mi
0 40 80 km
Lambert Conformal Conic Projection

© GeoSystems Global Corp.

Uzbekistan

Capital: Tashkent
Area: 172,700 sq. mi.
447,409 sq. km.
Population: 22,609,000
Largest City: Tashkent
Languages: Uzbek, Russian
Monetary Unit: Ruble

Uzbekistan: Map Index

Cities and Towns
Andizhan	D2
Bukhara	B3
Farghona	D2
Gulistan	C2
Jizzakh	C2
Khujayli	A2
Muynoq	A2
Namangan	D2
Nawoiy	C2
Nukus	A2
Olmaliq	C2
Qarshi	C3
Qunghirot	A2
Quqon	D2
Samarqand	C3
Tashkent, capital	C2
Termiz	C3
Uchquduq	B2
Urganch	B2
Zarafshon	B2

Other Features
Amu Darya, river	B2
Aral, sea	A2
Chirchiq, river	C2
Fergana, valley	D2
Kyzylkum, desert	B2
Syrdarya, river	D2
Turan, lowland	A2
Ustyurt, plateau	A2
Zeravshan, river	B2

Kyrgyzstan: Map Index

Cities and Towns
At-Bashy	D2
Balykchy	E1
Bishkek, capital	D1
Cholpon-Ata	E1
Jalal-Abad	C2
Jangy-Bazar	B2
Karakol	F1
Kara-Say	F2
Kyzyl-Kyya	C2
Naryn	E2
Osh	C2
Özgön	C2
Sary Tash	C3
Songköl	D2
Sülüktü	A3
Talas	C1
Tash Kömür	C2

Tokmok	D1
Toktogul	C2

Other Features
Alay, mts.	C3
Chatkal, river	B2
Chu, river	D1

Jengish Chokusu, mt.	G1
Kyzyl-Suu, river	C3
Naryn, river	E2
Tien Shan, mts.	E2
Toxkan, river	E2
Ysyk-Köl, lake	E1

Kyrgyzstan

Capital: Bishkek
Area: 76,642 sq. mi.
198,554 sq. km.
Population: 4,698,000
Largest City: Bishkek
Language: Kirghiz
Monetary Unit: Som

Kyrgyzstan
⊛ National Capital
• Other City
1:14,286,000
0 75 150 mi
0 75 150 km
Lambert Conformal Conic Projection

© GeoSystems Global Corp.

Tajikistan

Capital: Dushanbe
Area: 55,300 sq. mi.
143,264 sq. km.
Population: 5,995,000
Largest City: Dushanbe
Language: Tajik
Monetary Unit: Ruble

Tajikistan: Map Index

Cities and Towns
Dangara	A1
Dushanbe, capital	A1
Jirgatol	B1
Kalai Khum	B1
Kansay	A1
Khorugh	B2
Khudzhand	A1
Konibodom	A1
Kulob	A2
Morghob	B1
Navabad	A2
Norak	A2
Panj	A2
Panjakent	A1
Qurghonteppa	A2
Tursunzoda	A1
Uroteppa	A1
Zarafobod	A1

Other Features
Alay, mts.	B1
Bartang, river	B1

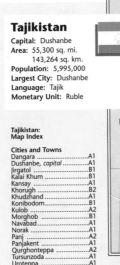

Tajikistan
⊛ National Capital
• Other City
1:7,622,000
0 40 80 mi
0 40 80 km
Lambert Conformal Conic Projection

© GeoSystems Global Corp.

Communisim, mt.	B1
Darya, river	A2
Kofarnihon, river	A2
Morghob, river	B1
Oqsu, river	B1

Pamirs, mts.	B2
Panj, river	A2
Pyandzh, river	B1
Qarokul, lake	B1
Surkhob, river	B1

Syrdarya, river	A1, B1
Turkestan, mts.	A1
Vahsh, river	A1
Zeravshan, mts.	A1
Zeravshan, river	A1

Iraq:
Map Index

Cities and Towns
Amarah, al- C2
Baghdad, *capital* B2
Baqubah B2
Basra B2
Dahuk B1
Diwaniyah, ad- B2
Fallujah, al- B2
Hadithah, al- B2
Hillah, al- B2
Irbil B1
Karbala B2
Khanaqin C2
Kirkuk C2
Kut, al- C2
Mosul B1
Najaf, an- B2
Nasiriyah, an- C2
Qayyarah, al- B1
Ramadi, ar- B2
Rutbah, ar- B2

Samarra B2
Samawah, as- C2
Sulaymaniyah, as- C1
Tall Afar B1
Tikrit B2
Umm Qasr C2

Other Features
Babylon, *ruins* B2
Diyala, *river* C2

Euphrates, *river* C2
Great Zab, *river* B1
Haji Ibrahim, *mt.* B1
Little Zab, *river* B1
Mesopotamia, *region* B2
Milh, *lake* B2
Persian, *gulf* C3
Shatt al-Arab, *river* C2
Syrian, *desert* B2
Tigris, *river* B1

Iraq
Capital: Baghdad
Area: 167,975 sq. mi.
  435,169 sq. km.
Population: 19,890,000
Largest City: Baghdad
Language: Arabic
Monetary Unit: Dinar

Kuwait
Capital: Kuwait
Area: 6,880 sq. mi.
  17,924 sq. km.
Population: 1,819,000
Largest City: Kuwait
Language: Arabic
Monetary Unit: Dinar

Kuwait:
Map Index

Cities and Towns
Abdali B1
Ahmadi, al- C2
Fuhayhil, al- C2
Hawalli C2
Jahrah, al- B2
Khiran, al- C3
Kuwait, *capital* B2
Qasr as-Sabiyah C2
Rawdatayn, ar- B2
Sulaybikhat, as- B2
Wafrah, al- B3

Other Features
Bubiyan, *island* C2
Faylakah, *island* C2
Kuwait, *bay* B2
Persian, *gulf* C2
Wadi al-Batin, *river* A2
Warbah, *island* C1

Saudi Arabia
Capital: Riyadh
Area: 865,000 sq. mi.
  2,240,933 sq. km.
Population: 18,197,000
Largest City: Riyadh
Language: Arabic
Monetary Unit: Riyal

Saudi Arabia:
Map Index

Cities and Towns
Abha B2
Badanah B1
Buqayq C1
Buraydah B1
Dammam, ad- C1
Dhahran C1
Hail B1
Harad C1
Hillah, al- C1
Hufuf, al- C1
Jawf, al- A1
Jiddah A2
Jizan B2
Jubayl, al- C1

Khamis Mushayt B2
Kharj, al- B1
Mecca A2
Medina A1
Najran B2
Qalat Bishah B2
Qunfudhah, al- A2
Rafha B1
Ras al-Khafji C1
Ras Tanura C1
Riyadh, *capital* B2
Sulayyil, as- B2
Tabuk A1
Taif, at- A2
Turayf A1
Unayzah B1
Wajh, al- A1
Yanbu al-Bahr A1

Other Features
Asir, *region* B2
Dahna, ad-, *desert* B1
Farasan, *islands* B2
Hasa, al-, *region* C1
Hijaz, al-, *region* A1
Jabal Tuwayq, *mts.* B2
Nafud, an-, *desert* B1
Najd, *region* B1
Persian, *gulf* C1
Red, *sea* A1
Rub al-Khali
  (Empty Quarter), *desert* C2
Sabkhat Matti, *salt flat* C2
Sawda, *mt.* B2
Syrian, *desert* B1
Umm as-Samim, *salt flat* C2
Wadi al-Hamd, *river* A1

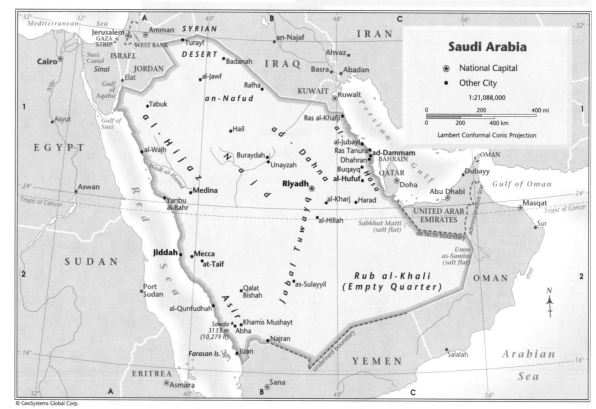

© GeoSystems Global Corp.

Bahrain and Qatar: Map Index

Bahrain
Cities and Towns
Askar	B1
Mamtalah, al-	B2
Manama, capital	B1
Mina Salman	B1

Other Features
Bahrain, gulf	A2
Hawar, islands	B2
Jiddah, island	A1
Muharraq, al-, island	B1
Ras al-Barr, cape	B2
Sitrah, island	B1
Umm an-Nasan, island	A1

Qatar
Cities and Towns
Doha, capital	D3
Dukhan	B3
Jumayliyah, al-	C2
Khawr, al-	D2
Ruways, ar-	C1
Umm Bab	B3
Umm Said (Musayid)	D4
Wakrah, al-	D3

Other Features
Dawhat as-Salwa, bay	B3
Ras Laffan, cape	D2
Ras Rakan, cape	C1
Tuwayyir al-Hamir, hill	C4

Bahrain
Capital: Manama
Area: 268 sq. mi.
694 sq. km.
Population: 586,000
Largest City: Manama
Language: Arabic
Monetary Unit: Dinar

Qatar
Capital: Doha
Area: 4,412 sq. mi.
11,430 sq. km.
Population: 513,000
Largest City: Doha
Language: Arabic
Monetary Unit: Riyal

Bahrain and Qatar
⊛ National Capital
• Other City
1:2,842,000
0 10 20 mi
0 10 20 km
Transverse Mercator Projection

United Arab Emirates
⊛ National Capital
• Other City
1:11,579,000
0 50 100 150 mi
0 50 100 150 km
Lambert Conformal Conic Projection

© GeoSystems Global Corp.

United Arab Emirates (U.A.E.)
Capital: Abu Dhabi
Area: 30,000 sq. mi.
77,720 sq. km.
Population: 2,791,000
Largest City: Abu Dhabi
Language: Arabic
Monetary Unit: Dirham

United Arab Emirates: Map Index
Cities and Towns
Abu Dhabi, capital	C2	Ruways, ar-	B2
Ajman	C2	Sham, ash-	D1
Aradah	B3	Sharjah	C2
Ayn, al-	C2	Tarif	B2
Dubayy	C2	Umm al-Qaywayn	C2
Fujayrah, al-	D2		
Masfut	D2	**Other Features**	
Nashshash, an-	C3	Hormuz, strait	D1
Ras al-Khaymah	C2	Matti, salt flat	B3
		Oman, gulf	D2
		Persian, gulf	B1
		Salamiyah, salt flat	C3

Yemen: Map Index
Cities and Towns
Aden	B2	Mocha (Mukha, al-)	A2
Ahwar	B2	Mukalla, al-	B2
Amran	A1	Qalansiyah	C2
Ataq	B2	Qishn	C1
Balhaf	B2	Rida	B2
Bayda, al-	B2	Sadah	A1
Dhamar	A2	Sana, capital	A1
Ghaydah, al-	C1	Sanaw	C1
Habarut	C1	Sayhut	C1
Hadiboh	C2	Saywun	B1
Hajjah	A1	Shabwah	B1
Hawf	C1	Taizz	A2
Hazm, al-	A1	Zabid	A2
Hudaydah, al-	A2		
Ibb	A2	**Other Features**	
Lahij	A2	Abd al-Kuri, island	C2
Madinat ash-Shab	A2	Aden, gulf	B2
Marib	B1	Arabian, sea	C2
Maydi	A1	Bab al-Mandab, strait	A2
		Hadhramaut, district	B1
		Jabal an-Nabi Shuayb, mt	A1
		Jabal Zuqar, island	A2
		Kamaran, island	A1

Perim, island	A2
Ras al-Kalb, cape	B2
Ras Fartak, cape	C1
Red, sea	A2
Socotra, island	C2
The Brothers, islands	C2
Wadi al-Masilah, river	B1

Yemen
Capital: Sana
Area: 205,356 sq. mi.
532,010 sq. km.
Population: 11,105,000
Largest City: Sana
Language: Arabic
Monetary Unit: Riyal

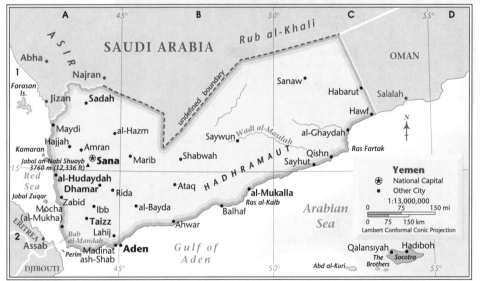

Yemen
⊛ National Capital
• Other City
1:13,000,000
0 75 150 mi
0 75 150 km
Lambert Conformal Conic Projection

© GeoSystems Global Corp.

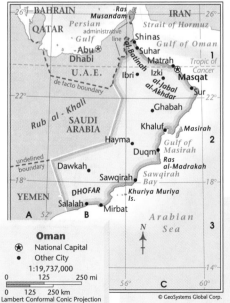

Oman
⊛ National Capital
• Other City
1:19,737,000
0 125 250 mi
0 125 250 km
Lambert Conformal Conic Projection

© GeoSystems Global Corp.

Oman: Map Index
Cities and Towns
Dawkah	B2	Matrah	C1
Duqm	C2	Mirbat	B3
Ghabah	C2	Salalah	B3
Hayma	C2	Sawqirah	B3
Ibri	C1	Shinas	C1
Izki	C1	Suhar	C1
Khaluf	C2	Sur	C1
Masqat, capital	C1		

Other Features
Arabian, sea	C3	Hormuz, strait	C1
Batinah, al-, region	C1	Jabal al-Akhdar, al-, mts.	C1
Dhofar, region	B3	Khuriya Muriya, islands	C3
		Masirah, gulf	C2
		Masirah, island	C2
		Oman, gulf	C1
		Persian, gulf	B1
		Ras al-Madrakah, cape	C2
		Ras Musandam, cape	C1
		Sawqirah, bay	C2

Oman
Capital: Masqat
Area: 118,150 sq. mi.
305,829 sq. km.
Population: 1,701,000
Largest City: Masqat
Language: Arabic
Monetary Unit: Rial Omani

Lebanon

Capital: Beirut
Area: 3,950 sq. mi.
  10,233 sq. km.
Population: 3,620,000
Largest City: Beirut
Languages: Arabic, French
Monetary Unit: Pound

Lebanon: Map Index

Cities and Towns

Amyun	A1
Baalbek	B1
Babda	A2
Batrun, al-	A1
Beirut, capital	A2
Bint Jubayl	A2
Bsharri	B1
Damur, ad-	A2
Duma	B1
Halba	B1
Hirmil, al-	B1
Jazzin	A2
Jubayl	A1
Juniyah	A2
Marj Uyun	A2
Nabatiyah at-Tahta, an-	A2
Qubayyat, al-	B1
Rashayya	A2
Riyaq	B2
Sidon (Sayda)	A2
Sur (Tyre)	A2
Tripoli (Tarabulus)	A1
Zahlah	A2

Other Features

Anti-Lebanon, mts.	B1
Awwali, river	A2
Bekaa, valley	A2
Byblos, ruins	A1
Hermon, mt.	B1
Ibrahim, river	A1
Kebir, river	B1
Lebanon, mts.	B1
Litani, river	A2
Orontes, river	B1
Qurnat as-Sawda, mt.	B1

[Lebanon map]

© GeoSystems Global Corp.

Lebanon
⊛ National Capital
• Other City
1:3,613,000
0 20 40 mi
0 20 40 km
Lambert Conformal Conic Projection

Jordan

Capital: Amman
Area: 34,342 sq. mi.
  88,969 sq. km.
Population: 3,961,000
Largest City: Amman
Language: Arabic
Monetary Unit: Dinar

Jordan: Map Index

Cities and Towns

Amman, capital	A2
Aqabah, al-	A3
Azraq ash-Shishan	B2
Bair	B2
Irbid	A1
Jafr, al-	B2
Jarash	A1
Karak, al-	A2
Maan	A2
Madaba	A2
Mafraq, al-	B1
Mudawwarah, al-	B3
Qatranah, al-	B2
Ramtha, ar-	B1
Ras an-Naqb	A2
Salt, as-	A1
Tafilah, at-	A2
Zarqa, az-	B1

Other Features

Aqaba, gulf	A3
Arabah, al-, river	A2
Dead Sea, lake	A2
Jabal Ramm, mt.	A3
Jordan, river	A2
Petra, ruins	A2
Syrian, desert	B1
Tiberias, lake	A1
Wadi as-Sirhan, depression	B2

[Jordan map]

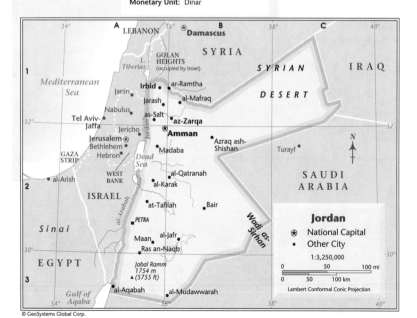

Jordan
⊛ National Capital
• Other City
1:3,250,000
0 50 100 mi
0 50 100 km
Lambert Conformal Conic Projection

© GeoSystems Global Corp.

Israel

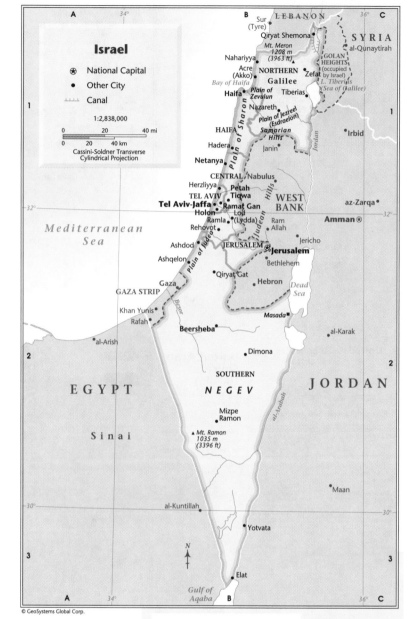

Israel
⊛ National Capital
• Other City
⊢⊣ Canal
1:2,838,000
0 20 40 mi
0 20 40 km
Cassini-Soldner Transverse Cylindrical Projection

© GeoSystems Global Corp.

Capital: Jerusalem
Area: 7,992 sq. mi.
  20,705 sq. km.
Population: 5,051,000
Largest City: Jerusalem
Languages: Hebrew, Arabic
Monetary Unit: New Shekel

Israel: Map Index

Districts

Central	B1
Haifa	B1
Jerusalem	B2
Northern	B1
Southern	B2
Tel Aviv	B1

Cities and Towns

Acre (Akko)	B1
Ashdod	B2
Ashqelon	B2
Beersheba	B2
Dimona	B2
Elat	B3
Hadera	B1
Haifa	B1
Herzliyya	B1
Holon	B1
Jerusalem, capital	B2
Lod (Lydda)	B2
Mizpe Ramon	B2
Nahariyya	B1
Nazareth	B1
Netanya	B1
Petah Tiqwa	B2
Qiryat Gat	B2
Qiryat Shemona	B1
Ramat Gan	B2
Ramla	B2
Rehovot	B2
Tel Aviv-Jaffa	B1
Tiberias	B1
Yotvata	B3
Zefat	B1

Other Features

Aqaba, gulf	B3
Arabah, al-, river	B2
Besor, river	B2
Dead, sea	B2
Galilee, region	B1
Haifa, bay	B1
Jezreel (Esdraelon), plain	B1
Jordan, river	B1
Judea, plain	B2
Masada, ruins	B2
Meron, mt.	B1
Negev, region	B2
Ramon, mt.	B2
Samarian, hills	B1
Sharon, plain	B1
Tiberias (Galilee), lake	B1
Zevulun, plain	B1

Turkey: Map Index

Cities and Towns

Adana	C3
Adapazarı	B2
Afyon	B2
Ağrı	E2
Aksaray	C2
Alanya	C3
Amasya	C2
Ankara, capital	C2
Antalya	B3
Antioch (Antakya)	D3
Artvin	A3
Aydın	A3
Balıkesir	A2
Batman	E3
Bolu	B2
Bursa	A2
Çanakkale	A2
Çankırı	C2
Çorum	C2
Denizli	B3
Divriği	D2
Diyarbakır	E3
Edirne	A2
Elâzığ	D2
Erzincan	D2
Erzurum	E2
Eskişehir	B2
Eyüp	B2
Fethiye	B3
Gaziantep	D3
Gelibolu (Gallipoli)	A2
Giresun	D2
İskenderun	D3
Isparta	B3
İstanbul	B2
İzmir	A2
İzmit	B2
Kadıköy	B2
Karaman	C3
Kars	E2
Kastamonu	C2
Kayseri	C2
Kırıkkale	C2
Kırşehir	C2
Konya	C3
Kütahya	B2
Malatya	D2

Manisa	A2	Silifke	C3	Üsküdar	B2
Maraş	D3	Sinope	C2	Van	E2
Mardin	E3	Sivas	D2	Zonguldak	B2
Mersin	C3	Tarsus	C3		
Muğla	B3	Tekirdağ	A2	**Other Features**	
Muş	E2	Thrace	A2	Aegean, sea	A3
Niğde	C3	Tokat	D2	Anatolia, region	C2
Ordu	D2	Trabzon	D2	Antalya, gulf	B3
Samsun	D2	Urfa	D3	Ararat (Ağrı Dağı), mt.	F2
Siirt	E3	Usak	B2	Aras, river	E2
				Atatürk, reservoir	D3
				Beyşehir, lake	B3
				Black, sea	C1
				Bosporus, strait	B2
				Burdur, lake	B3
				Büyük Menderes, rivers	A3
				Ceyhan, river	D3
				Cilician Gates, pass	C3
				Coruh, river	E2
				Cukorova, region	C3
				Mediterranean, sea	B4
				Eğridir, lake	B2
				Erciyas Daği, mt.	C2
				Euphrates, river	D2
				Great Zab, river	E3
				Iskenderum, gulf	C3
				Keban, reservoir	D2
				Kızıl Irmak, river	C2
				Kura, river	E2
				Marmara, sea	B2
				Murat, river	E2
				Pontic, mts.	C2
				Sakarya, river	B2
				Seyhan, river	C3
				Taurus, mts.	B3
				Tigris, river	E2
				Ulu Daǧ (Mt. Olympus), mt.	B2
				Van, lake	E2
				Yesilirmak, river	D2

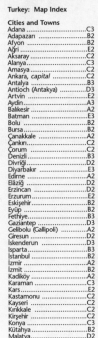

Cyprus

Cyprus: Map Index

Cities and Towns

Episkopi	A2
Famagusta	B1
Kokkina	A1
Kyrenia	B1
Lapithos	B1
Larnaca	B2
Lefka	A1
Lefkoniko	B1
Limassol	B2
Morphou	A1
Nicosia, capital	B1
Paphos	A2
Peyia	A2
Polis	A1

Yialousa	C1

Other Features | |
Akrotiri, bay	B2
Andreas, cape	C1
Arnauti, cape	A1
British Sovereign Base Area	A2, B2
Famagusta, bay	B1
Gata, cape	B2
Greco, cape	C2
Karpas, peninsula	C1
Kormakiti, cape	A1
Kyrenia, range	B1
Mesaoria, plain	B1
Morphou, bay	A1
Olympus, mt.	A2
Troödos, mts.	A2

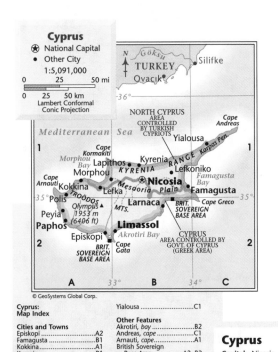

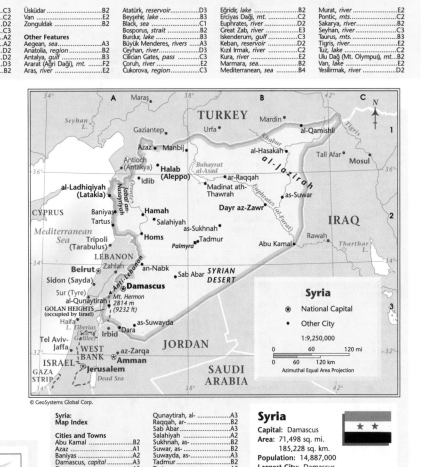

Cyprus

Capital: Nicosia
Area: 3,572 sq. mi.
9,254 sq. km.
Population: 730,000
Largest City: Nicosia
Languages: Greek, Turkish
Monetary Unit: Pound

Syria: Map Index

Cities and Towns

Abu Kamal	B2
Azaz	A1
Baniyas	A2
Damascus, capital	A3
Dara	A3
Dayr az-Zawr	B2
Halab (Aleppo)	A1
Hamah	A2
Hasakah, al-	B1
Homs	A2
Idlib	A2
Ladhiqiyah, al- (Latakia)	A2
Madinat ath-Thawrah	B2
Manbij	B1
Nabk, an-	A3
Qamishli, al-	B1

Qunaytirah, al-	A3
Raqqah, ar-	B2
Sab Abar	A3
Salahiyah	A2
Sukhnah, as-	B2
Suwar, as-	B2
Suwayda, as-	B2
Tadmor	B2
Tartus	A2

Other Features | |
Anti-Lebanon, mts.	A3
Buhayrat al-Asad, lake	B2
Euphrates (al-Furat), river	B2
Golan Heights, occupied territory	A3
Hermon, mt.	A3
Jabal an-Nusayriyah, mts.	A2
Jazirah, al-, region	B1
Khabur, river	B1
Mediterranean, sea	A2
Orontes, river	A2
Palmyra, ruins	B2
Syrian, desert	B3
Tigris, river	C1

Turkey

Capital: Ankara
Area: 300,948 sq. mi.
779,658 sq. km.
Population: 62,154,000
Largest City: İstanbul
Language: Turkish
Monetary Unit: Lira

Turkey
⊛ National Capital
• Other City
1:11,125,000
0   75   150 mi
0   75   150 km
Lambert Conformal Conic Projection

Syria

Capital: Damascus
Area: 71,498 sq. mi.
185,228 sq. km.
Population: 14,887,000
Largest City: Damascus
Language: Arabic
Monetary Unit: Pound

Syria
⊛ National Capital
• Other City
1:9,250,000
0   60   120 mi
0   60   120 km
Azimuthal Equal Area Projection

Cyprus
⊛ National Capital
• Other City
1:5,091,000
0   25   50 mi
0   25   50 km
Lambert Conformal Conic Projection

© GeoSystems Global Corp.

MAJOR CITIES

Albania
Tiranë — 244,000

Andorra
Andorra la Vella — 16,000

Armenia
Yerevan — 1,254,000

Austria
Vienna — 1,539,000

Azerbaijan
Baku — 1,149,000

Belarus
Minsk — 1,613,000

Belgium (metro)
Brussels — 951,000
Antwerp — 465,000

Bosnia and Hercegovina
Sarajevo — 416,000

Bulgaria
Sofia — 1,141,000

Croatia
Zagreb — 704,000

Czech Republic
Prague — 1,212,000

Denmark
Copenhagen — 617,000

Estonia
Tallinn — 478,000

Finland
Helsinki — 495,000

France
Paris — 2,152,000
Marseille — 800,000
Lyon — 416,000

Georgia
Tbilisi — 1,268,000

Germany
Berlin — 3,438,000
Hamburg — 1,661,000
Munich — 1,237,000
Cologne — 956,000
Frankfurt — 647,000
Essen — 626,000
Dortmund — 600,000
Stuttgart — 584,000
Düsseldorf — 577,000
Leipzig — 508,000

Great Britain
London — 6,803,000
Birmingham — 995,000
Leeds — 706,000
Glasgow — 688,000
Sheffield — 520,000
Liverpool — 475,000
Edinburgh — 439,000
Manchester — 433,000

Greece
Athens — 748,000

Hungary
Budapest — 2,017,000

Iceland
Reykjavík — 97,000

Ireland
Dublin — 478,000

Italy
Rome — 2,829,000
Milan — 1,549,000
Naples — 1,208,000
Turin — 1,060,000
Genoa — 742,000
Palermo — 714,000

Latvia
Riga — 909,000

Liechtenstein
Vaduz — 5,000

Lithuania
Vilnius — 591,000

Luxembourg
Luxembourg — 75,000

F.Y.R. Macedonia
Skopje — 393,000

Malta
Valletta — 9,000

Moldova
Chişinău — 667,000

Monaco
Monaco — 27,000

Netherlands
Amsterdam — 713,000
Rotterdam — 590,000

Norway
Oslo — 465,000

Poland
Warsaw — 1,654,000
Łódź — 847,000
Kraków — 751,000
Wrocław — 643,000

Portugal
Lisbon — 678,000

Romania
Bucharest — 2,064,000

Russia (European)
Moscow — 8,747,000
St. Petersburg — 4,437,000
Nizh. Novgorod — 1,441,000
Samara — 1,239,000
Kazan — 1,104,000
Perm — 1,099,000
Ufa — 1,097,000
Rostov-na-Donu — 1,027,000
Volgograd — 1,006,000

San Marino
San Marino — 3,000

Slovakia
Bratislava — 441,000

Slovenia
Ljubljana — 277,000

Spain
Madrid — 2,991,000
Barcelona — 1,668,000
Valencia — 719,000
Seville — 654,000

Sweden
Stockholm — 679,000

Switzerland
Zürich — 342,000
Bern — 135,000

Turkey (European)
İstanbul — 6,620,000

Ukraine
Kiev — 2,643,000
Kharkov — 1,622,000
Dnepropetrovsk — 1,190,000
Donetsk — 1,121,000
Odessa — 1,096,000

Yugoslavia
Belgrade — 1,137,000

International comparability of city population data is limited by various data inconsistencies.

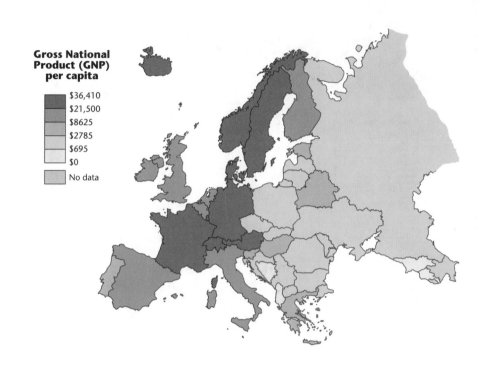

Gross National Product (GNP) per capita

- $36,410
- $21,500
- $8625
- $2785
- $695
- $0
- No data

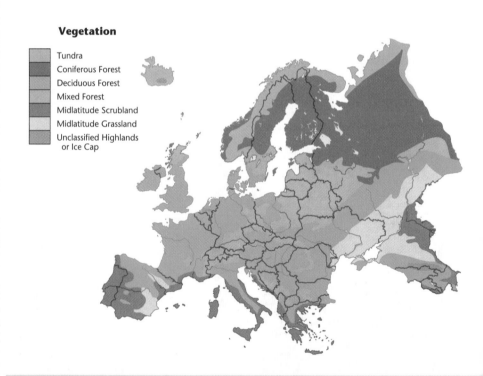

Vegetation

- Tundra
- Coniferous Forest
- Deciduous Forest
- Mixed Forest
- Midlatitude Scrubland
- Midlatitude Grassland
- Unclassified Highlands or Ice Cap

Europe: Population, by nation (in millions)

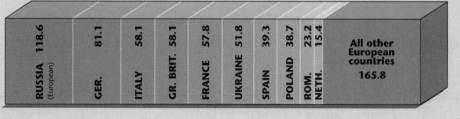

RUSSIA (European)	GER.	ITALY	GR. BRIT.	FRANCE	UKRAINE	SPAIN	POLAND	ROM.	NETH.	All other European countries
118.6	81.1	58.1	58.1	57.8	51.8	39.3	38.7	23.2	15.4	165.8

CITIES

⊗ National Capital
★ Territorial Capital
• Other City

ELEVATIONS

Feet	Meters
13,120	4000
6560	2000
1640	500
656	200
0	0
Below sea level	

CLIMATE

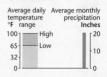

Average daily temperature °F range   Average monthly precipitation Inches

ARKHANGELSK, Russia

ATHENS, Greece

COPENHAGEN, Denmark

DUBLIN, Ireland

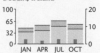

LISBON, Portugal

MOSCOW, Russia

NAPLES, Italy

ODESSA, Ukraine

PARIS, France

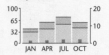

REYKJAVÍK, Iceland

TROMSØ, Norway

VIENNA, Austria

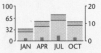

Population

Persons per sq mi	Persons per sq km
Over 520	Over 200
260–519	100–199
130–259	50–99
25–129	10–49
1–24	1–9
0	0

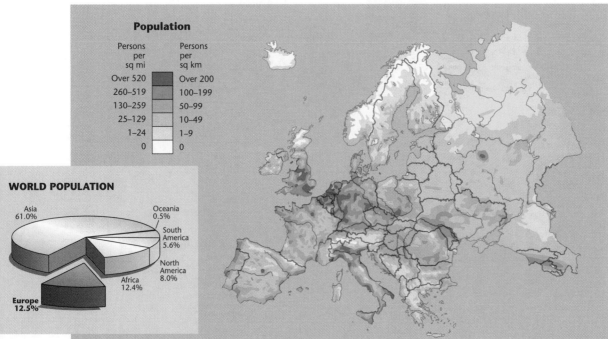

WORLD POPULATION

Asia 61.0%
Oceania 0.5%
South America 5.6%
North America 8.0%
Africa 12.4%
Europe 12.5%

© GeoSystems Global Corp.

Great Britain

⊛ National Capital
• Other City

1:4,375,000

0 25 50 75 100 mi
0 25 50 75 100 125 150 km

Lambert Conformal Conic Projection

Great Britain
Capital: London
Area: 94,251 sq. mi.
244,174 sq. km.
Population: 58,135,000
Largest City: London
Language: English
Monetary Unit: Pound

Great Britain:
Map Index

CHANNEL ISLANDS
Features
Alderney, island............Inset II
Guernsey, island ....Inset II
Jersey, island ....Inset II
St. Malo, gulf ....Inset II
Sark, island ....Inset II

ENGLAND
Cities and Towns
Aylesbury ....Inset III
Banbury C3
Barnsley C3
Barnstaple B3
Barrow-in-Furness B2
Basildon ....Inset III
Bath C3
Bedford C3
Berwick-upon-Tweed C2
Birkenhead B3
Birmingham C3
Blackburn C3
Blackpool C3
Bolton C3
Boston C3
Bournemouth C4
Bradford C3
Braintree ....Inset III
Brentwood ....Inset III
Brighton C4
Bristol C3
Burnley C3
Bury C3
Bury St. Edmunds D3
Buxton C3
Camberley ....Inset III
Cambridge D3
Canterbury D3
Carlisle C2
Chatham ....Inset III
Chelmsford ....D3, Inset III
Cheltenham C3
Chester C3
Chesterfield C3
Chichester C4
Colchester D3
Coventry C3
Cowes C4
Crawley ....Inset III
Crewe C3
Darlington C3
Derby C3
Doncaster C3
Dorchester C4
Dorking ....Inset III
Dover D3
Dudley C3
Dunstable ....Inset III
Durham C2
Eastbourne D4
Ely D3
Epsom ....Inset III
Ewell ....Inset III
Exeter B4
Farnham ....Inset III
Felixstowe D3
Fleetwood C3
Folkestone D3
Gateshead C2
Gillingham D3
Glastonbury C3
Gloucester C3
Gosport C4
Grantham C3
Gravesend ....Inset III
Great Yarmouth D3
Grimsby C3
Guildford C3
Halifax C3
Harlow ....Inset III
Harrogate C2
Haslemere ....Inset III
Hastings D4
Hereford C3
Hertford ....Inset III
High Wycombe ....Inset III
Hove C4
Huddersfield C3
Ipswich D3
Kendal C2
Kenilworth C3
Kidderminster C3
King's Lynn D3
Kingston upon Hull C3
Kingston upon Thames Inset III
Lancaster C2
Launceston B4
Leeds C3
Leicester C3
Lewes D4
Lichfield C3
Lincoln C3
Liverpool C3
London, capital ....C3, Inset III
Lowestoft D3
Luton C3
Maidstone D3
Manchester C3
Margate D3
Matlock C3
Middlesbrough C2
Newcastle-under-Lyme C3
Newcastle upon Tyne C2
Newmarket D3
Newquay B4
Northallerton C2
Northampton C3
North Shields C2
Norwich D3
Nottingham C3
Oldham C3
Oxford C3
Penrith C2
Penzance B4
Peterborough C3
Plymouth B4
Poole C4
Portsmouth C4
Preston C3
Reading C3
Reigate ....Inset III
Rochdale C3
Rotherham C3
St. Albans ....C3, Inset III

Republic of Ireland

Capital: Dublin
Area: 27,137 sq. mi.
70,303 sq. km.
Population: 3,539,000
Largest City: Dublin
Languages: English, Irish
Monetary Unit: Punt

Ireland

⊛ National Capital
• Other City

1:3,960,000

| 0 | 30 | 60 mi |
| 0 | 30 | 60 km |

Lambert Conformal Conic Projection

© GeoSystems Global Corp.

Republic of Ireland:
Map Index

Counties
Carlow C2
Cavan C2
Clare B2
Cork B3
Donegal B1
Dublin C2
Galway B2
Kerry B2
Kildare C2
Kilkenny C2
Laois C2
Leitrim B1
Limerick B2
Longford C2
Louth C2
Mayo B2
Meath C2
Monaghan C1
Offaly C2
Roscommon B2
Sligo B1
Tipperary North Riding ...B2
Tipperary South Riding ...B2
Waterford C2
Westmeath C2
Wexford C2
Wicklow C2

Cities and Towns
Ardara B1
Arklow C2
Athlone C2
Ballina B1
Bantry B3
Blarney B3
Carlingford C1
Carlow C2
Carrick-on-Shannon B2
Cashel C2
Castlebar B2
Cavan C2
Clara C2
Clifden A2
Clonmel C2
Cóbh B3
Cork B3
Dingle A2
Donegal B1
Drogheda C2
Dublin, capital C2
Dundalk C2
Dungarvan C2
Dún Laoghaire C2
Ennis B2
Ennistymon B2
Galway B2
Kildare C2
Kilkee B2
Kilkenny C2
Killarney B2
Letterkenny C1
Lifford C1
Limerick B2
Longford C2
Mallow B2
Maynooth C2
Monaghan C1
Mullingar C2

Naas C2
Nenagh B2
Port Laoise C2
Roscommon B2
Roscrea C2
Rosslare C2
Shannon B2
Sligo B1
Swords C2
Tipperary B2
Tralee B2
Trim C2
Tuam B2
Tullamore C2
Waterford C2
Westport B2
Wexford C2
Wicklow C2
Youghal C3

Other Features
Achill, island A2
Allen, lake B1
Aran, islands B2
Bantry, bay B3
Barrow, river C2
Benwee Head, cape B1
Blackwater, river B2
Blackwater, river C1
Boggeragh, mts. B2
Boyne, river C2
Caha, mts. B3
Carlingford, lake C1
Carnsore, point C2
Carrantuohill, mt. B3
Celtic, sea B3
Clear, cape B3
Conn, lake B1
Connaught, province B2
Connemara, region B2
Corrib, lake B2
Derg, lake B2
Dingle, bay A2
Donegal, bay B1
Erne, river B1
Errigal, mt. B1
Finn, river C1
Foyle, inlet C1
Galway, bay B2
Grand, canal C2
Irish, sea D2
Killala, bay B1
Knockboy, mt. B3
Lee, river B3
Leinster, province C2
Loop Head, cape B2
Malin Head, cape C1
Mask, lake B2
Maumturk, mts. B2
Mizen Head, cape B3
Moher, cliffs B2
Munster, province B2
Ree, lake B2
Royal, canal C2
Saint George's, channel ...C3
Shannon, river B2
Suir, river C2
Twelve Pins, mt. B2
Ulster, province C1
Wicklow, mts. C2
Wicklow Head, cape D2

Great Britain: Map Index
St. Austell B4
St. Helens C3
Salford C3
Salisbury C3
Scarborough C2
Scunthorpe C3
Sheffield C3
Shrewsbury C3
Slough ....Inset III
Solihull C3
Southampton C4
Southend-on-Sea D3
Southport C2
South Shields C3
Stafford C3
Stevenage ....Inset III
Stoke-on-Trent C3
Stratford-upon-Avon C3
Sunderland C2
Swindon C3
Taunton C3
Telford C3
Tewkesbury C3
Thetford D3
Tiverton B4
Tonbridge ....Inset III
Torbay B4
Trowbridge C3
Truro B4
Tunbridge Wells D3
Wakefield C3
Walsall C3
Warrington C3
Warwick C3
Watford ....Inset III
Westminster ....Inset III
Whitehaven B2
Wigan C3
Wimbledon ....Inset III
Winchester C3
Windsor ....Inset III
Wolverhampton C3
Worcester C3
Yeovil C4
York C3

Other Features
Avon, river C3
Black Country, region C3
Bristol, channel B3
Cheviot, hills C2
Cotswold, hills C3
Cumbrian, mts. B2
Dartmoor, plateau B4
Dee, river B3
Dover, strait D4
English, channel C4
Exmoor, plateau B3
Fens, region D3
Flodden Field, plain C2
Humber, river D3
Irish, sea B3
Lake, district B2
Land's End, promontory ...B4
Liverpool, bay B3
Lyme, bay C3
Mersey, river C3
Midlands, region C3
North, sea D2
North Downs, hills C3
North Foreland,
promontory D3
Ouse, river C2, D3
Pennines, mts. C2
Scafell Pike, mt. B2
Scilly, islands A4
Severn, river C3
South Downs, hills C3
Spithead, channel C4
Start, point B4
Tees, river C2
Thames, river ....C3, Inset III
Trent, river C3
Tweed, river C2
Tyne, river C2
Wash, bay D3
Wight, island C3
Wye, river C3
Yare, river D3

ISLE OF MAN
City
Douglas B2

NORTHERN IRELAND
Cities and Towns
Armagh A2
Ballymena A2
Bangor B2
Belfast B2
Coleraine A2
Holywood B2
Larne B2
Londonderry A2
Newry A2
Omagh A2
Portadown A2
Strangford B2

Other Features
Antrim, mts. A2

Bann, river A2
Erne, river A2
Foyle, lake A2
Foyle, river A2
Giant's Causeway,
headland A2
Irish, sea B3
Lough Erne, lake A2
Mourne, mts. A2
Neagh, lake A2
North, channel A2
Rathlin, island A2
Slieve Donard, mt. B2
Sperrin, mts. A2
Upper Lough Erne, lake ...A2

SCOTLAND
Cities and Towns
Aberdeen C1
Aviemore B1
Ayr B2
Campbeltown B2
Clydebank B2
Cupar B2
Dornoch B1
Dumfries B2
Dundee C2
Dunfermline B2
Edinburgh B2
Elgin B1
Fort William B2
Fraserburgh C1
Glasgow B2
Greenock B2
Hamilton B2
Hawick C2
Inverness B1
Kilmarnock B2
Kirkcaldy B2
Kirkwall ....Inset I
Kyle of Lochalsh B1
Lairg B1

Lerwick ....Inset I
Mallaig B1
Montrose C2
Motherwell B2
Newtown St. Boswells C2
Oban B2
Paisley B2
Perth B2
Peterhead C1
Pitlochry B2
Portree A1
St. Andrews C2
Scone B2
Sconser A1
Stirling B2
Stornoway A1
Stranraer B2
Thurso B1
Ullapool B1
Wick B1

Other Features
Arran, island B2
Barra, island A2
Bass Rock, islet C2
Bell Rock (Inchcape),
reef C2
Ben Nevis, mt. B2
Bute, island B2
Cheviot, hills C2
Clyde, estuary B2
Clyde, river B2
Coll, island A2
Colonsay, island A2
Dee, river C1
Dornoch, estuary B1
Duncansby, cape B1
Dunsinane, mt. B2
Eigg, island A2
Fair, island ....Inset I
Forth, estuary C2
Forth, river B2

Grampian, mts. B2
Hebrides, sea A1
Hoy, island ....Inset I
Inner Hebrides, islands ...A2
Islay, island A2
Jura, island B2
Katrine, lake B2
Kinnairds, cape C1
Lammermuir, hills C2
Lewis, island A1
Linnhe, lake A2
Lomond, lake B2
Lorne, estuary A2
Mainland, island ....Inset I
Merrick, mt. B2
Minch, strait B1
Moray, estuary B1
Mull, island A2
Ness, lake B1
North Uist, island A1
Ochil, hills B2
Orkney, islands ....Inset I
Outer Hebrides, islands ...A1
Rhum, island A1
Sanday, island ....Inset I
Shetland, islands ....Inset I
Sidlaw, hills B2
Skye, island A1
Solway, estuary B2
Southern Uplands, mts. ...B2
South Ronaldsay,
island ....Inset I
South Uist, island A1
Spey, river B1
Stronsay, island ....Inset I
Tay, estuary C2
Tay, lake B2
Tay, river B2
Tiree, island A2
Tweed, river C2
Unst, island ....Inset I
Westray, island ....Inset I

Wrath, cape B1
Yell, island ....Inset I

WALES
Cities and Towns
Aberystwyth B3
Bangor B3
Caerleon C3
Caernarfon B3
Cardiff B3
Carmarthen B3
Conwy B3
Fishguard B3
Holyhead B3
Lampeter B3
Llandrindod Wells B3
Merthyr Tydfil B3
Milford Haven B3
Mold B3
Newport C3
Pembroke B3
Port Talbot B3
Rhondda B3
St. David's B3
Swansea B3
Welshpool B3

Other Features
Anglesey, island B3
Bala, lake B3
Brecon Beacons, mts. B3
Bristol, channel B3
Cambrian, mts. B3
Cardigan, bay B3
Dee, river B3
Lleyn, peninsula B3
Menai, strait B3
Snowdon, mt. B3
Teifi, river B3
Tywi, river B3
Usk, river C3
Wye, river C3

Denmark

Capital: Copenhagen
Area: 16,639 sq. mi.
43,080 sq. km.
Population: 5,188,000
Largest City: Copenhagen
Language: Danish
Monetary Unit: Krone

Denmark:
Map Index

Counties
Århus C2
Bornholm E3
Frederiksborg D2
Fyn C3
København D3
Nordjylland B2
Ribe B3
Ringkøbing B2
Roskilde D3
Sønderjylland B3
Storstrøm C4
Vejle B3
Vestsjælland C3
Viborg B2

Cities and Towns
Åbenrå B3
Ålborg B1
Århus C2
Ballerup D3
Copenhagen, *capital* ..D3
Esbjerg B3
Fredericia B3
Frederiksberg D3
Frederikshavn C1
Gentofte D3
Grenå C2
Greve D3
Haderslev B3
Helsingør D2
Herning B2
Hillerød D3
Hirtshals B1
Hjørring B1
Holbæk C3
Holstebro B2
Horsens B3
Kalundborg C3
Kastrup D3
Køge D3
Kolding B3
Næstved C3
Nakskov C4
Nyborg C3
Nykøbing C4
Odense C3
Randers C2
Ribe B3
Ringkøbing B2
Rønne E3
Roskilde D3
Sandur ....Inset
Silkeborg B2
Skagen C1
Skive B2
Slagelse C3
Sønderborg B4
Sorø C3
Svendborg C3
Thisted B2
Tórshavn ....Inset
Trongisvágur ....Inset
Vejle B3
Vestmanna ....Inset
Viborg B2

Other Features
Ærø, *island* C4
Ålborg, *bay* B2
Anholt, *island* C2
Baltic, *sea* D3
Bordoy, *island* .....Inset
Bornholm, *island* ...E3
Eysturoy, *island* ...Inset
Faeroe, *islands* ....Inset
Falster, *island* D4
Fanø, *island* B3
Fehmarn, *strait* C4
Fyn, *island* C3
Gudenå, *river* B2
Jutland, *peninsula* ..B3
Kattegat, *strait* ...C2
Læsø, *island* C1
Langeland, *island* ..C4
Lille, *strait* B3
Limfjorden, *channel* ..B2
Lolland, *island* C4
Møn, *island* D4
Mors, *island* B2
North, *sea* A3
North Frisian, *islands* ..B4
Norwegian, *sea* .....Inset
Odense, *fjord* C3
Øresund, *sound* D3
Rømø, *island* B3
Samsø, *island* C3
Samsø, *strait* C3
Sandoy, *island* .....Inset
Sjælland, *island* ...C3
Skagerrak, *strait* ..B1
Skaw, *cape* C1
Skjern, *river* B3
Storå, *river* B2
Store, *strait* C3
Streymoy, *island* ...Inset
Suduroy, *island* ....Inset
Vágar, *island* ......Inset
Varde, *river* B3
Yding Skovhøj, *hill* ..B2

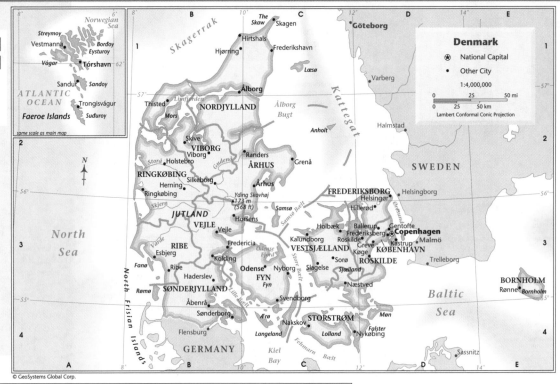

Netherlands:
Map Index

Provinces
Drenthe D2
Flevoland C2
Friesland C1
Gelderland D2
Groningen D1
Limburg C3
North Brabant C3
North Holland B2
Overijssel D2
South Holland B2
Utrecht C2
Zeeland A3

Cities and Towns
Alkmaar B2
Almelo D2
Amersfoort C2
Amsterdam, *capital* ..B2
Apeldoorn C3
Arnhem C3
Assen D2
Bergen op Zoom B3
Breda B3
Delft B2
Delfzijl D1
Den Helder B2
Deventer D2
Doetinchem D3
Dordrecht B3
Edam C2
Ede C3
Eindhoven C3
Emmeloord C2
Emmen D2
Enschede D2
Gouda B2
Groningen D1
Haarlem B2
Heerenveen C2
Heerlen D2
Hengelo D2
Hilversum C2
Hoogeveen D2
Hoorn C2
Leeuwarden C1
Leiden B2
Lelystad C2
Maastricht C4

Meppel D2
Middelburg A3
Nijmegen C3
Oss C3
Otterlo C2
Roermond D3
Rotterdam B3
Scheveningen B2
Schiedam B3
's Hertogenbosch C3
Sittard C4
Sneek C1
The Hague B2
Tilburg C3
Utrecht C3
Venlo D3
Vlaardingen B3
Vlissingen A3
Weert C3
Zaanstad B2
Zwolle D2

Other Features
Ameland, *island* C1
Eems, *river* D1
Flevoland, *polder* ..C2
IJssel, *river* D2
IJsselmeer, *sea* C2
Maas, *river* C3, D3
Neder Rijn, *river* ..C3
New Waterway, *channel* ..B3
Northeast, *polder* ..C2
North Holland, *canal* ..B2
North Sea, *canal* ...B2
Oosterschelde, *channel* ..A3
Overflakkee, *island* ..B3
Princess Margriet, *canal* ..C1
Schiermonnikoog, *island* ..D1
Schouwen, *island* ...A3
Terschelling, *island* ..C1
Texel, *island* B1
Tholen, *island* B3
Vaalserberg, *mt.* ...D4
Vlieland, *island* ...B1
Waal, *river* C3
Waddenzee, *sound* ...C1
Walcheren, *island* ..A3
Westerschelde, *channel* ..A3
West Frisian, *islands* ..B1
Wilhelmina, *canal* ..B3
Zuid-Willemsvaart, *canal* ..C3

Netherlands

Capital: Amsterdam
Area: 16,033 sq. mi.
41,536 sq. km.
Population: 15,368,000
Largest City: Amsterdam
Language: Dutch
Monetary Unit: Guilder

© GeoSystems Global Corp.

North Sea

Middleburg

Breda

NETHERLANDS

Eindhoven

Venlo

Knokke

Turnhout

Antwerp

GERMANY

Zeebrugge

Oostende

Brugge

Sint-Niklaas

ANTWERP

KEMPENLAND

Albert Canal

LIMBURG

Dunkirk

WEST FLANDERS

Ghent

Schelde

Mechelen

Genk

Maas

Cologne

Roeselare

Brugge-Ghent Canal

EAST FLANDERS

Aalst

Schaerbeek

Hasselt

Maastricht

Aachen

Ypres

Kortrijk

Anderlecht

Brussels

Louvain

Sint-Truiden

Bonn

Poperinge

Leie

Ixelles

Uccle

BRABANT

Liège

Limbourg

Lille

Mouscron

Halle

Senne

Verviers

Tournai

Ath

Dender

LIÈGE

Spa

Botrange 694 m (2277 ft)

Lys

HAINAUT

Gembloux

Maas

Malmédy

Valenciennes

Mons

Binche

La Louvière

Namur

NAMUR

Charleroi

Sambre

Dinant

N

FRANCE

Chimay

Bastogne

ARDENNES

Fumay

Oise

LUXEMBOURG

Neufchâteau

Mosel

LUXEMBOURG

Charleville Mézières

Semois

Arlon

Luxembourg

Trier

Belgium
- ⊛ National Capital
- • Other City
- ⊥⊥⊥⊥ Canal

1:2,381,000

0   20   40 mi
0   20   40 km

Lambert Conformal Conic Projection

© GeoSystems Global Corp.

Belgium: Map Index

Provinces

Antwerp	C1
Brabant	C2
East Flanders	B2
Hainaut	B2
Liège	D2
Limburg	D1
Luxembourg	D3
Namur	C2
West Flanders	B1

Cities and Towns

Aalst	C2
Anderlecht	C2
Antwerp	C1
Arlon	D3
Ath	B2
Bastogne	D2
Binche	C2
Brugge	B1
Brussels, capital	C2
Charleroi	C2
Chimay	C2
Dinant	C2
Gembloux	C2
Genk	D2
Ghent	B1
Halle	C2
Hasselt	D2
Ixelles	C2
Knokke	B1
Kortrijk	B2
La Louvière	C2
Liège	D2
Limbourg	D2
Louvain	C2
Malmédy	E2
Mechelen	C1
Mons	B2
Mouscron	B2
Namur	C2
Neufchâteau	D3
Oostende	A1
Poperinge	A2
Roeselare	B2
Schaerbeek	C2
Sint-Niklaas	C1
Sint-Truiden	D2
Spa	D2
Tournai	B2
Turnhout	C1
Uccle	C2
Verviers	D2
Ypres	A2
Zeebrugge	B1

Other Features

Albert, canal	C1
Ardennes, plateau	D2
Botrange, mt.	E2
Brugge-Ghent, canal	B1
Dender, river	B2
Kempenland, region	D1
Leie, river	B2
Maas, river	D2
Meuse, river	D2
Oostende-Brugge, canal	B1
Ourthe, river	D2
Rupel, river	C1
Sambre, river	C2
Schelde, river	B2
Semois, river	D3
Senne, river	C2

Belgium

Capital: Brussels
Area: 11,787 sq. mi.
    30,536 sq. km.
Population: 10,063,000
Largest City: Brussels
Languages: Flemish, French, German
Monetary Unit: Belgian franc

Luxembourg
- ⊛ National Capital
- • Other City

1:1,700,000

0   10   20 mi
0   10   20 km

Azimuthal Equal Area Projection

BELGIUM

Ardennes

Buurgplaatz 559 m (1835 ft)

Troisvierges

Clervaux

Our

Wiltz

Clerve

Sûre

Vianden

Diekirch

Ettelbruck

Sûre

Echternach

Mersch

Larochette

Redange

Bon Pays

Alzette

Grevenmacher

Luxembourg

Mosel

GERMANY

Differdange

Remich

Esch-sur-Alzette

Dudelange

FRANCE

N

© GeoSystems Global Corp.

Luxembourg: Map Index

Cities and Towns

Clervaux	B1
Diekirch	B2
Differdange	A2
Dudelange	B2
Echternach	B2
Esch-sur-Alzette	A2
Ettelbruck	B2
Grevenmacher	B2
Larochette	B2
Luxembourg, capital	B2
Mersch	B2
Redange	A2
Remich	B2
Troisvierges	B1
Vianden	B2
Wiltz	A2

Other Features

Alzette, river	B2
Ardennes, plateau	A1
Bon Pays, region	B2
Buurgplaatz, mt.	B1
Clerve, river	B1
Mosel, river	B2
Our, river	B1
Sûre, river	A2, B2

Luxembourg

Capital: Luxembourg
Area: 999 sq. mi.
    2,588 sq. km.
Population: 402,000
Largest City: Luxembourg
Languages: French, German
Monetary Unit: Luxembourg franc

Liechtenstein

Capital: Vaduz
Area: 62 sq. mi.
    161 sq. km.
Population: 30,000
Largest City: Vaduz
Language: German
Monetary Unit: Swiss franc

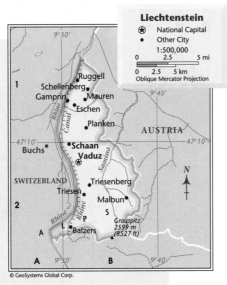

Liechtenstein
- ⊛ National Capital
- • Other City

1:500,000

0   2.5   5 mi
0   2.5   5 km

Oblique Mercator Projection

Ruggell

Schellenberg

Gamprin

Mauren

Rhine Canal

Eschen

Planken

AUSTRIA

Rhine

Buchs

Schaan

Vaduz

Samina

SWITZERLAND

Triesenberg

Triesen

Malbun

Rhine

Grauspitz 2599 m (8527 ft)

ALPS

Balzers

N

© GeoSystems Global Corp.

Liechtenstein: Map Index

Cities and Towns

Balzers	B2
Eschen	B1
Gamprin	B1
Malbun	B2
Mauren	B1
Planken	B1
Ruggell	B1
Schaan	B2
Schellenberg	B1
Triesen	B2
Triesenberg	B2
Vaduz, capital	B2

Other Features

Alps, range	A2
Grauspitz, mt.	B2
Rhine, canal	B1, B2
Rhine, river	A1, A2
Samina, river	B2

France

⊛ National Capital

• Other City

1:5,625,000

0   50   100 mi

0   50   100 km

Lambert Conformal Conic Projection

Same scale as main map

© GeoSystems Global Corp.

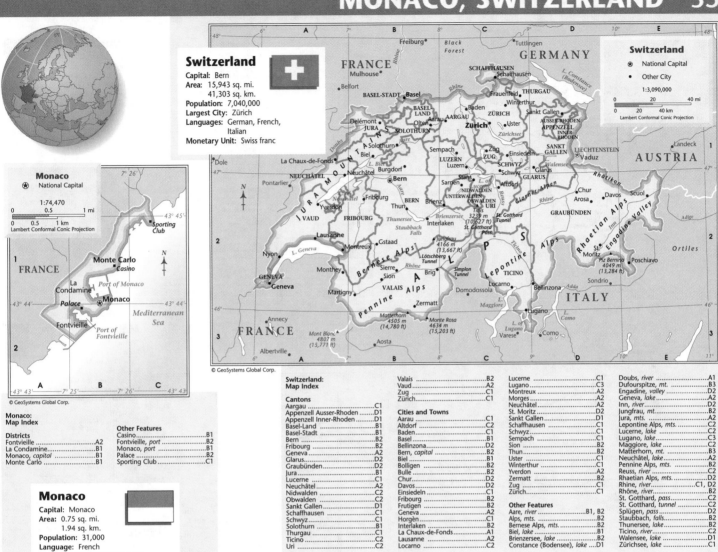

Switzerland

Capital: Bern
Area: 15,943 sq. mi.
41,303 sq. km.
Population: 7,040,000
Largest City: Zürich
Languages: German, French, Italian
Monetary Unit: Swiss franc

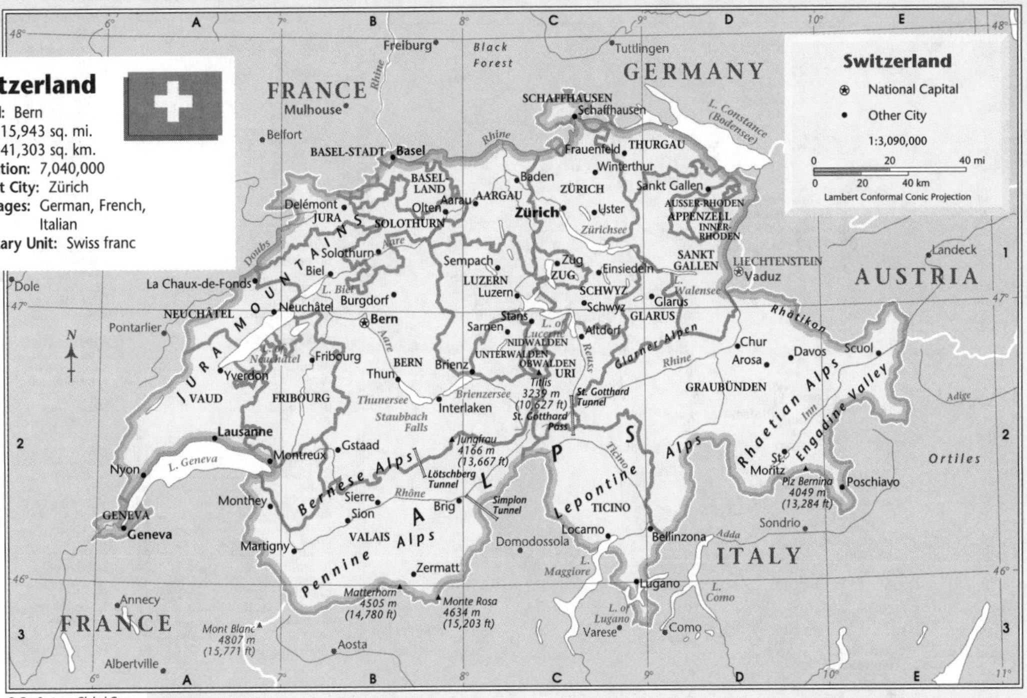
Switzerland
National Capital
Other City
1:3,090,000
0 20 40 mi
0 20 40 km
Lambert Conformal Conic Projection
GERMANY
FRANCE
AUSTRIA
ITALY
LIECHTENSTEIN
Vaduz
Freiburg
Black Forest
Tuttlingen
Mulhouse
Belfort
SCHAFFHAUSEN
Schaffhausen
L. Constance (Bodensee)
BASEL-STADT
Basel
BASEL-LAND
Frauenfeld
THURGAU
Winterthur
Baden
AARGAU
Aarau
Olten
ZÜRICH
Zürich
Uster
Zürichsee
Sankt Gallen
AUSSER-RHODEN
APPENZELL
INNER-RHODEN
SANKT GALLEN
Delémont
JURA
SOLOTHURN
Solothurn
Biel
L. Biel
Burgdorf
Sempach
LUZERN
Luzern
Zug
ZUG
Einsiedeln
SCHWYZ
Schwyz
Glarus
GLARUS
Walensee
Landeck
La Chaux-de-Fonds
NEUCHÂTEL
Neuchâtel
Bern
Pontarlier
Dole
JURA MOUNTAINS
Doubs
L. Neuchâtel
Yverdon
VAUD
Fribourg
FRIBOURG
Thun
BERN
Brienz
Sarnen
Stans
L. of Lucerne
NIDWALDEN
OBWALDEN
UNTERWALDEN
URI
Altdorf
Titlis 3239 m (10,627 ft)
St. Gotthard Pass
St. Gotthard Tunnel
Glarner Alpen
Rhätikon
Chur
Davos
Arosa
Scuol
GRAUBÜNDEN
Rhine
Inn
Rhaetian Alps
Engadine Valley
St. Moritz
Piz Bernina 4049 m (13,284 ft)
Poschiavo
Ortiles
Adige
Thunersee
Brienzersee
Interlaken
Staubbach Falls
Jungfrau 4166 m (13,667 ft)
Lötschberg Tunnel
Simplon Tunnel
Lausanne
Montreux
Gstaad
L. Geneva
Nyon
GENEVA
Geneva
Monthey
Bernese Alps
Sierre
Sion
Rhône
Brig
VALAIS
Alps
Pennine Alps
Martigny
Zermatt
Domodossola
Lepontine Alps
TICINO
Ticino
Locarno
Bellinzona
Adda
Maggiore
Lugano
L. of Lugano
L. Como
Varese
Como
Sondrio
Matterhorn 4505 m (14,780 ft)
Monte Rosa 4634 m (15,203 ft)
Mont Blanc 4807 m (15,771 ft)
Annecy
Aosta
Albertville
FRANCE
A B C D E
1 2 3
6° 7° 8° 9° 10° 11°
48° 47° 46°
N

© GeoSystems Global Corp.

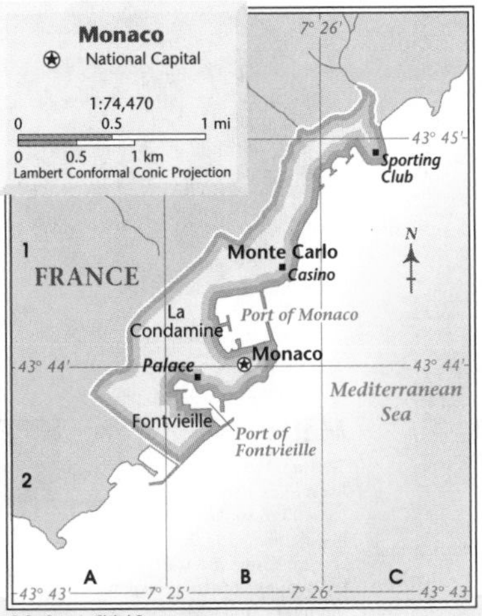
Monaco
National Capital
1:74,470
0 0.5 1 mi
0 0.5 1 km
Lambert Conformal Conic Projection
FRANCE
Sporting Club
Monte Carlo
Casino
Port of Monaco
La Condamine
Monaco
Palace
Mediterranean Sea
Fontvieille
Port of Fontvieille
N
7° 26'
7° 25'
43° 45'
43° 44'
43° 43'
A B C
1 2

© GeoSystems Global Corp.

Monaco:
Map Index

Districts
Fontvieille ... A2
La Condamine ... B1
Monaco, *capital* ... B1
Monte Carlo ... B1

Other Features
Casino ... B1
Fontvieille, *port* ... B2
Monaco, *port* ... B1
Palace ... B2
Sporting Club ... C1

Switzerland:
Map Index

Cantons
Aargau ... C1
Appenzell Ausser-Rhoden ... D1
Appenzell Inner-Rhoden ... D1
Basel-Land ... B1
Basel-Stadt ... B1
Bern ... B2
Fribourg ... B2
Geneva ... A2
Glarus ... D2
Graubünden ... D2
Jura ... B1
Lucerne ... C1
Neuchâtel ... A2
Nidwalden ... C2
Obwalden ... C2
Sankt Gallen ... D1
Schaffhausen ... C1
Schwyz ... C1
Solothurn ... B1
Thurgau ... C1
Ticino ... C2
Uri ... C2
Valais ... B2
Vaud ... A2
Zug ... C1
Zürich ... C1

Cities and Towns
Aarau ... C1
Altdorf ... C2
Baden ... C1
Basel ... B1
Bellinzona ... D2
Bern, *capital* ... B2
Biel ... B1
Bolligen ... B2
Bulle ... B2
Chur ... D2
Davos ... D2
Einsiedeln ... C1
Fribourg ... B2
Frutigen ... B2
Geneva ... A2
Horgèn ... C1
Interlaken ... B2
La Chaux-de-Fonds ... A1
Lausanne ... A2
Locarno ... C2
Lucerne ... C1
Lugano ... C3
Montreux ... A2
Morges ... A2
Neuchâtel ... A2
St. Moritz ... D2
Sankt Gallen ... D1
Schaffhausen ... C1
Schwyz ... C1
Sempach ... C1
Sion ... B2
Thun ... B2
Uster ... C1
Winterthur ... C1
Yverdon ... A2
Zermatt ... B2
Zug ... C1
Zürich ... C1

Other Features
Aare, *river* ... B1, B2
Alps, *mts.* ... B2
Bernese Alps, *mts.* ... B2
Biel, *lake* ... B1
Brienzersee, *lake* ... B2
Constance (Bodensee), *lake* ... D1
Doubs, *river* ... A1
Dufourspitze, *mt.* ... B3
Engadine, *valley* ... D2
Geneva, *lake* ... A2
Inn, *river* ... D2
Jungfrau, *mt.* ... B2
Jura, *mts.* ... A2
Lepontine Alps, *mts.* ... C2
Lucerne, *lake* ... C2
Lugano, *lake* ... C3
Maggiore, *lake* ... C2
Matterhorn, *mt.* ... B3
Neuchâtel, *lake* ... A2
Pennine Alps, *mts.* ... B2
Reuss, *river* ... C2
Rhaetian Alps, *mts.* ... D2
Rhine, *river* ... C1, D2
Rhône, *river* ... B2
St. Gotthard, *pass* ... C2
St. Gotthard, *tunnel* ... C2
Splügen, *pass* ... D2
Staubbach, *falls* ... B2
Thunersee, *lake* ... B2
Ticino, *river* ... C2
Walensee, *lake* ... D1
Zürichsee, *lake* ... C1

Monaco

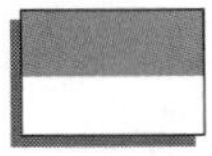

Capital: Monaco
Area: 0.75 sq. mi.
1.94 sq. km.
Population: 31,000
Language: French
Monetary Unit: French franc or Monégasque franc

France

Capital: Paris
Area: 210,026 sq. mi.
544,109 sq. km.
Population: 57,840,000
Largest City: Paris
Language: French
Monetary Unit: Franc

France:
Map Index

Regions
Alsace ... D2
Aquitaine ... B4
Auvergne ... C4
Basse-Normandie ... B2
Bourgogne ... C3
Bretagne ... B2
Centre ... C3
Champagne-Ardenne ... D2
Corse ... Inset I
Franche-Comté ... D3
Haute-Normandie ... C2
Île-de-France ... C2
Languedoc-Roussillon ... C5
Limousin ... C4
Lorraine ... D2
Midi-Pyrénées ... C5
Nord-Pas-de-Calais ... C1
Pays De La Loire ... B3
Picardie ... C2
Poitou-Charentes ... C3
Provence-Alpes-Côte-d'Azur ... D4
Rhône-Alpes ... D4

Cities and Towns
Abbeville ... C1
Agen ... C4
Aix-en-Provence ... D5
Aix-les-Bains ... D4
Ajaccio ... Inset I
Albi ... C5
Alençon ... C2
Alès ... D4
Amiens ... C2
Angers ... B3
Angoulême ... C4
Annecy ... D4
Arachon ... B4
Argenteuil ... Inset II
Arles ... D5
Arpajon ... Inset II
Arras ... C1
Auch ... C5
Aurillac ... C4
Auxerre ... C3
Avignon ... D5
Ballancourt-sur-Essonne ... Inset II
Bar-le-Duc ... D2
Bastia ... Inset I
Bayeux ... B2
Bayonne ... B5
Beauvais ... C2
Belfort ... D3
Bergerac ... C4
Besançon ... D3
Béziers ... C5
Biarritz ... B5
Blois ... C3
Bondy ... Inset II
Bordeaux ... B4
Boulogne-Billancourt ... Inset II
Boulogne-sur-Mer ... C1
Bourg-en-Bresse ... D3
Bourges ... C3
Brest ... A2
Briançon ... D4
Brive-la-Gallarde ... C4
Caen ... B2
Cahors ... C4
Calais ... C1
Calvi ... Inset I
Cambrai ... C1
Cannes ... D5
Carcassonne ... C5
Carnac ... B3
Châlons-sur-Marne ... D2
Chambéry ... D4
Chamonix-Mont-Blanc ... D4
Chantilly ... C2
Charleville Mézières ... D2
Chartres ... C2
Châteauroux ... C3
Châtellerault ... C3
Chaumont ... D2
Chelles ... Inset II
Cherbourg ... B2
Chevreuse ... Inset II
Choisy-le Roi ... Inset II
Cholet ... B3
Clermont-Ferrand ... C4
Clichy ... Inset II
Cluny ... D3
Cognac ... B4
Colmar ... D2
Compiègne ... C2
Conflans-Sainte-Honorine ... Inset II
Corbeil-Essonnes ... Inset II
Coubert ... Inset II
Créteil ... Inset II
Dammartin-en-Goële ... Inset II
Deauville ... C2
Dieppe ... C2
Digne ... D4
Dijon ... D3
Dôle ... D3
Domont ... Inset II
Douai ... C1
Draguignan ... D5
Dreux ... C2
Dunkirk (Dunkerque) ... C1
Épinal ... D2
Etrechy ... Inset II
Évreux ... C2
Évry ... Inset II
Foix ... C5
Fontainebleau ... C2
Fréjus ... D5
Gap ... D4
Gentilly ... Inset II
Grenoble ... D4
Guéret ... C3
Laon ... C2
La Rochelle ... B3
La-Roche-sur-Yon ... B3
Laval ... B2
Le Creusot ... D3
Le Havre ... C2
Le Mans ... C2
Lens ... C1
Le Puy ... C4
Les Ulis ... Inset II
Levallois-Perret ... Inset II
Lille ... C1
Limoges ... C4
Limours ... Inset II
L'Isle-Adam ... Inset II
Lorient ... B3
Lourdes ... B5
Louvres ... Inset II
Luzarches ... Inset II
Lyon ... D4
Mâcon ... D3
Maisons-Laffitte ... Inset II
Marseille ... D5
Massy ... Inset II
Maurepas ... Inset II
Melun ... Inset II
Mende ... C4
Mennecy ... Inset II
Metz ... D2
Meulan ... Inset II
Montargis ... C2
Montauban ... C4
Montélimar ... D4
Montluçon ... C3
Montpellier ... C5
Montreuil ... Inset II
Mont-Saint-Michel ... B2
Morlaix ... B2
Mulhouse ... D3
Nancy ... D2
Nanterre ... Inset II
Nantes ... B3
Narbonne ... C5
Nevers ... C3
Nice ... D5
Nîmes ... D5
Niort ... B3
Orléans ... C3
Ozoir-la-Ferrière ... Inset II
Palaiseau ... Inset II
Paris, *capital* ... C2, Inset II
Pau ... B5
Périgueux ... C4
Perpignan ... C5
Poissy ... Inset II
Poitiers ... C3
Pontchartrain ... Inset II
Pontoise ... Inset II
Porto-Vecchio ... Inset I
Privas ... D4
Quimper ... A2
Reims ... D2
Rennes ... B2
Roanne ... D3
Rochefort ... B4
Rodez ... C4
Roubaix ... C1
Rouen ... C2
Saint-Brieuc ... B2
Saint-Cloud ... Inset II
Saint-Denis ... Inset II
Saint-Dizier ... D2
Saintes ... B4
Saint-Étienne ... D4
Saint-Germain-en-Laye ... Inset II
Saint-Lô ... B2
Saint-Malo ... B2
Saint-Nazaire ... B3
Saint-Tropez ... D5
Sarcelles ... Inset II
Saumur ... B3
Savigny-sur-Orge ... Inset II
Sedan ... D2
Sevran ... Inset II
Sèvres ... Inset II
Soissons ... C2
Strasbourg ... D2
Tarbes ... C5
Taverny ... Inset II
Toulon ... D5
Toulouse ... C5
Tourcoing ... C1
Tours ... C3
Trouville ... C2
Troyes ... D2
Valence ... D4
Valenciennes ... C1
Vannes ... B3
Verdun ... D2
Versailles ... C2, Inset II
Vesoul ... D3
Vichy ... C3
Vierzon ... C3
Villeneuve-Saint-Georges ... Inset II
Vincennes ... Inset II

Other Features
Adour, *river* ... B5
Aisne, *river* ... D2
Allier, *river* ... C3
Alps, *range* ... D4
Ardennes, *region* ... D1
Argonne, *forest* ... D2
Aube, *river* ... D3
Belfort, *gap* ... D3
Belle, *island* ... B3
Biscay, *bay* ... B4
Blanc, *mt.* ... D4
Cévennes, *mts.* ... C4
Charente, *river* ... B4
Corsica, *island* ... Inset I
Cotentin, *peninsula* ... B2
Dordogne, *river* ... C4
Dover, *strait* ... C1
Durance, *river* ... D5
English, *channel* ... B2
Garonne, *river* ... C4
Geneva, *lake* ... D3
Gironde, *river* ... B4
Hague, *cape* ... B2
Isère, *river* ... D4
Jura, *mts.* ... D3
Landes, *region* ... B5
Lion, *gulf* ... D5
Little St. Bernard, *pass* ... D4
Loire, *river* ... C3
Lot, *river* ... C4
Maritime Alps, *range* ... D4
Marne, *river* ... C2, Inset II
Massif Central, *plateau* ... C4
Meuse, *river* ... D2
Moselle, *river* ... D2
Oise, *river* ... C2, Inset II
Oléron, *island* ... B4
Omaha, *beach* ... B2
Orne, *river* ... B2
Pyrenees, *range* ... C5
Rance, *river* ... B2
Raz, *point* ... A3
Ré, *island* ... B3
Rhine, *river* ... D2
Rhône, *river* ... D4
Saint-Malo, *gulf* ... B2
Sambre, *river* ... C1
Saône, *river* ... D3
Seine, *river* ... C2, Inset II
Somme, *river* ... C2
Utah, *beach* ... B2
Vienne, *river* ... C3
Vignemale, *mt.* ... B5
Vilaine, *river* ... B3
Vosges, *mts.* ... D2
Yeu, *island* ... B3
Yonne, *river* ... C2

Portugal: Map Index

Districts

Aveiro	A2
Beja	A4
Braga	A2
Bragança	B2
Castelo Branco	B2
Coimbra	A2
Évora	B3
Faro	A4
Guarda	B2
Leiria	A3
Lisbon	A3
Oporto (Porto)	A2
Portalegre	B3
Santarém	A3
Setúbal	A3
Viana do Castelo	A2
Vila Real	B2
Viseu	B2

Cities and Towns

Abrantes	A3
Almada	A3
Amadora	A3
Aveiro	A2
Barreiro	A3
Beja	B3
Braga	A2
Bragança	B2
Caidasm da Rainha	A3
Castelo Branco	B3
Chaves	B2
Coimbra	A2
Covilhã	B2
Elvas	B3
Estoril	A3
Évora	B3
Faro	B4
Figueira da Foz	A2
Grândola	B3
Guarda	B2
Guimarães	A2
Lagos	A4
Leiria	A3

Leixões	A2
Lisbon, capital	A3
Mafra	A3
Moura	B3
Odemira	A4
Oeiras	A3
Oporto (Porto)	A2
Peniche	A3
Portalegre	B3
Portimão	B4
Queluz	A3
Santarém	A3
Setúbal	A3
Sines	A3
Valença	A1
Viana do Castelo	A2
Vila do Conde	A2
Vila Nova de Gaia	A2
Vila Real	B2
Vila Real de Santo Antonio	B4
Viseu	B2

Other Features

Algarve, region	A4
Cádiz, gulf	B4
Carvoeiro, cape	A3
Chança, river	B4
Douro, river	B2
Espichel, cape	A3
Estrela, mt.	B2
Estrela, mts.	B2
Guadiana, river	B3
Lima, river	A2
Minho, river	A1
Mondego, cape	A2
Mondego, river	A2
Roca, cape	A3
Sado, river	A3
São Vicente, cape	A4
Seda, river	B3
Setúbal, bay	A3
Sor, river	B3
Sorraia, river	A3
Tagus, river	B3
Tâmega, river	B2
Zêzere, river	B2

Portugal

Capital: Lisbon
Area: 35,672 sq. mi.
92,415 sq. km.
Population: 10,524,000
Largest City: Lisbon
Language: Portuguese
Monetary Unit: Escudo

Malta

Capital: Valletta
Area: 122 sq. mi.
316 sq. km.
Population: 367,000
Largest City: Valletta
Languages: Maltese, English
Monetary Unit: Maltese lira

Malta: Map Index

Cities and Towns

Birkirkara	B2
Birzebbuga	C3
Dingli	B2
Mellieha	B1
Nadur	B1
Qormi	B2
Rabat	B2
San Pawl il-Bahar	B2
Siggiewi	B2
Sliema	C2
Valletta, capital	C2
Victoria	A1
Zabbar	C2
Zebbug	A1
Zurrieq	B2

Other Features

Comino, island	B1
Cominotto, island	B1
Filfla, island	B3
Gozo, island	A1
Grand, harbor	C2
Malta, island	B2
Marsaxlokk, bay	C3
Mellieha, bay	B2
North Comino, channel	B1
Saint Paul's, bay	B2
South Comino, channel	B2

Gibraltar

Area: 2.25 sq. mi.
5.83 sq. km.
Population: 30,000
Language: English
Monetary Unit: British Pound

Gibraltar: Map Index

Features

Catalan, bay	A2
Detached, mole	A2
Eastern, beach	A2
Fortress Headquarters	A3
Gibraltar, bay	A2
Gibraltar, harbor	A2
Gibraltar, strait	A4
Governor's Residence	A2
Great Europa, point	A4
Highest point	A3
Little, bay	A4
Mediterranean, sea	A3
North, bay	A2
North Front, airfield	A1
Rosia, bay	A3
Saint Michael's, cave	A3
Sandy, bay	A3
Signal, hill	A2
South, mole	A3
The Rock, prom.	A2

Andorra

Capital: Andorra la Vella
Area: 181 sq. mi.
469 sq. km.
Population: 64,000
Largest City: Andorra la Vella
Language: Catalan
Monetary Unit: French franc

Andorra: Map Index

Cities and Towns

Andorra la Vella, capital	B2
Anyos	B2
Arinsal	B2
El Serrat	B1
Les Escaldes	B2
Llorts	B1
Ordino	B2
Pas de la Casa	C2
Sant Julià de Lòria	A3
Soldeu	B2

Other Features

Coma Pedrosa, mt.	A1
Estany d'Engolasters, lake	B2
Incles, river	C1
La Coma, river	B1
Madriu, river	B3
Os, river	A3
Pyrenees, range	A1
Valira, river	B2
Valira d'Orient, river	B2

© GeoSystems Global Corp.

Spain: Map Index

Regions

Andalusia D4
Aragón F2
Asturias D1
Balearic Islands G3
Basque Country E1
Canary Islands ....Inset I
Cantabria D1
Castile-La Mancha E3
Castile-León D1, E1
Catalonia G2
Estremadura C3
Galicia C1
La Rioja E1
Madrid E2
Murcia F4
Navarra F1
Valencia F2, F3

Cities and Towns

Aguilas F4
Albacete F3
Alcalá de Henares ....Inset II
Alcañiz F2
Alcázar de San Juan E3
Alcira F3
Alcobendas ....Inset II
Alcorcón ....E2, Inset II
Alcoy F3
Algeciras D4
Alicante F3
Almadén D3
Almansa F3
Almendralejo C3
Almería E4
Antequera D4
Aranda de Duero E2
Aranjuez E2
Astorga C1
Ávila D2
Avilés D1
Badajoz C3
Badalona H2
Baracaldo E1
Barcelona H2
Baza E4
Béjar D2
Benavente D1
Benidorm F3
Bilbao E1
Burgos E1
Cáceres C3
Cádiz C4
Calatayud F2
Cartagena F4
Castellón de la Plana F3
Ceuta D5
Cieza F3
Ciudadela H3
Ciudad Real E3
Ciudad Rodrigo C2
Córdoba D4
Cornellá de Llogregat G2
Coslada ....Inset II
Cuenca E2
Don Benito D3
Dos Hermanas D4
Écija D4
Elche F3
El Ferrol B1
Figueras H1
Fuenlabrada ....Inset II
Gerona H2
Getafe ....E2, Inset II
Gijón D1
Granada E4
Guadalajara E2
Guecho E1
Guernica y Luno E1
Hellín E3
Hospitalet H2
Huelva C4
Huesca F1
Ibiza G3
Jaén E4
Jerez de la Frontera C4
La Coruña B1
La Laguna ....Inset I
La Roda E3
Las Palmas ....Inset I
Leganés ....Inset II
León D1
Lérida G2

Linares E3
Logroño E1
Loja D4
Lorca E4
Lucena D4
Lugo C1
Madrid, capital ......E2, Inset II
Mahón J3
Málaga D4
Marbella D4
Mataró H2
Medina del Campo D2
Mérida C3
Mieres D1
Miranda de Ebro E1
Monforte C1
Morón de la Frontera D4
Móstoles ....Inset II
Murcia F4
Orense C1
Oviedo D1
Palencia D1
Palma H3
Pamplona F1
Plasencia C2
Ponferrada C1
Pontevedra B1
Puertollano D3
Reinosa D1
Reus G2
Sabadell H2
Sagunto F3
Salamanca D2
San Baudilio de Llobregat G2
San Fernando C4
San Sebastián F1
Santa Coloma de
  Gramanet H2
Santander D1
Santiago de Compostela B1
Saragossa F2
Segovia D2
Seville D4
Soria E2
Talavera de la Reina D3
Tarragona G2
Tarrasa H2

Telde ....Inset I
Teruel F3
Toledo D3
Tomelloso E3
Torrejón de Ardoz ....Inset II
Torrelavega D1
Torrente G2
Tortosa G2
Úbeda E3
Valdepeñas E3
Valencia F3
Valladolid D2
Vich H2
Vigo B1
Villarreal de los Infantes F3
Vitoria E1
Yecla F3
Zafra C3
Zamora D2

Other Features

Alarcón, reservoir E3
Alboran, sea E4
Alcántara, reservoir C3
Almendra, reservoir C2
Aneto, mt. G1
Balearic, islands G3
Balearic, sea G3
Béticos, mts. D4
Biscay, bay D1
Brava, coast H2
Buendía, reservoir E2
Cabrera, island H3
Cádiz, gulf C4
Canaray, islands ....Inset I
Cantábrica, mts. C1
Cijara, reservoir D3
Duero, river D2
Ebro, river F1
Esla, river D2
Finisterre, cape B1
Formentera, island G3
Fuerteventura, island ......Inset I
Gata, cape E4
Gibraltar, strait D5
Gomera, island ....Inset I
Gran Canaria, island ....Inset I
Gredos, mts. D2

Guadalquivir, river D4
Guadarrama, mts. D2
Guadiana, river C3
Hierro, island ....Inset I
Ibérico, mts. E1
Ibiza, island G3
Jarama, river ....Inset II
Júcar, river F3
Lanzarote, island ....Inset I
La Palma, island ....Inset I
Majorca, island H3
Mediterranean, sea E4
Mequinenza, reservoir F2
Meseta, plateau D3
Miño, river B1
Minorca, island J3
Morena, mts. D3
Mulhacén, mt. E4
Nao, cape G3
Nevada, mts. E4
Orellana, reservoir D3
Ortegal, cape C1
Palos, cape F4
Pyrenees, mts. F1
Ricobayo, reservoir D2
Segura, river E3
Sol, coast D4
Tagus, river D3
Tenerife, island ....Inset I
Toledo, mts. D3
Tormes, river D2
Tortosa, cape D3
Valdecañas, reservoir D3
Valencia, gulf D3
Zújar, reservoir D3

Spain

Capital: Madrid
Area: 194,898 sq. mi.
  504,917 sq. km.
Population: 39,303,000
Largest City: Madrid
Language: Spanish
Monetary Unit: Peseta

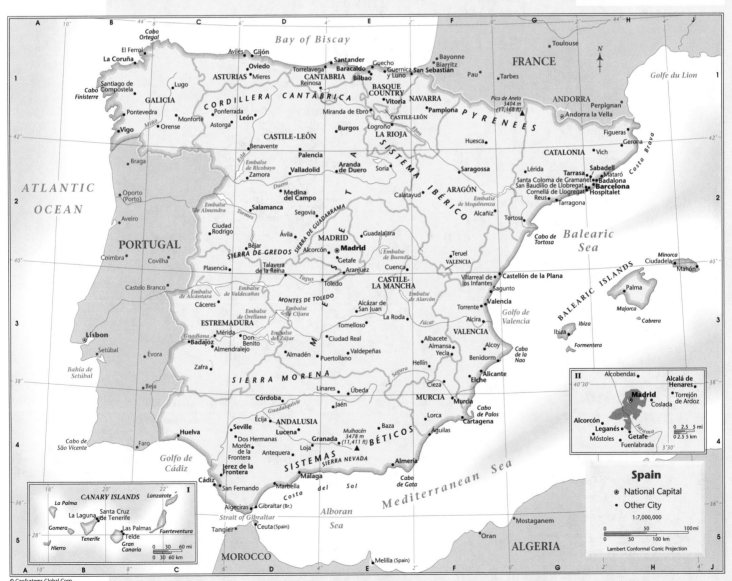

Italy

⊛ National Capital

• Other City

1:5,614,000

0   50   100   150 mi

0   50   100   150 km

Lambert Conformal Conic Projection

Italy

Capital: Rome
Area: 116,333 sq. mi.
    301,381 sq. km.
Population: 58,138,000
Largest City: Rome
Language: Italian
Monetary Unit: Lira

© GeoSystems Global Corp.

Austria
- ⊛ National Capital
- • Other City
1:4,714,000

0   25   50 mi
0   25   50 km
Lambert Conformal Conic Projection

© GeoSystems Global Corp.

Austria

Capital: Vienna
Area: 32,378 sq. mi.
83,881 sq. km.
Population: 7,955,000
Largest City: Vienna
Language: German
Monetary Unit: Schilling

Austria:
Map Index

Provinces

Burgenland	E3
Carinthia	C4
Lower Austria	D2
Salzburg	C3
Styria	D3
Tirol	B3, C4
Upper Austria	C2
Vienna	E2
Vorarlberg	A3

Cities and Towns

Amstetten	D2
Baden	E2
Bad Ischl	C3
Braunau	C2
Feldkirch	A3
Fürstenfeld	E3
Gmünd	D2
Graz	D3
Hieflau	D3
Innsbruck	B3
Kapfenberg	D3
Klagenfurt	D4
Köflach	D3
Kufstein	C3
Lech	B3
Leoben	D3
Lienz	C4
Linz	D2
Mistelbach	E2
Salzburg	C3

Other Features

Sankt Pölten	D2
Steyr	D2
Stockerau	E2
Vienna, capital	E2
Villach	C4
Vöcklabruck	C2
Wels	C2
Wiener Neustadt	E3
Wolfsberg	D4

Other Features

Alps, range	B3
Bavarian Alps, range	B3
Brenner, pass	B3
Carnic Alps, range	C4
Constance, lake	A3
Danube, river	D2
Drava, river	C4
Enns, river	D3
Grossglockner, mt.	C3
Hohe Tauern, mts.	C3
Inn, river	B3, C2
Karawanken, range	D4
Mur, river	D3
Mürz, river	D3
Neusiedler, lake	E3
Niedere Tauern, range	D3
Ötztal Alps, range	B4
Salzach, river	C3
Salzburg Alps, range	C3
Semmering, pass	D3
Traun, river	D2
Ybbs, river	D2
Zillertal Alps, range	B3

Vatican City

Area: 108.7 acres
Population: 811
Languages: Italian, Latin
Monetary Unit: Lira

Vatican City
1:24,000

0   .15   .3 mi
0   .15   .3 km
Transverse Mercator Projection

© GeoSystems Global Corp.

Vatican City:
Map Index

Features

Academy of Sciences	B1
Apostolic Palace	B2
Art Gallery	B2
Audience Hall	B2
Barracks of the Swiss Guard	B1
Church of St. Anne	B1
Civil Administration Building	A2
Entrance to Museums	B1
Ethiopian Seminary	A2
New Gardens	A2
Old Gardens	A1
Palace of Holy Office	B2
St. Charles Palace	B2
St. Martha Palace	B2
St. Peter's Basilica	B2
St. Peter's Square	B2
Sistine Chapel	B2
Vatican Museums	B1

Italy:
Map Index

Regions

Abruzzi	C2
Apulia	C2
Basilicata	C2
Calabria	D3
Campania	C2
Emilia-Romagna	B1
Friuli-Venezia Giulia	C1
Latium	C2
Liguria	B2
Lombardy	B1
Marche	C2
Molise	C2
Piedmont	A1
Puglia	C2
Sardinia	B3
Sicily	C3
Trentino-Alto Adige	B1
Tuscany	B2
Umbria	C2
Valle d'Aosta	A1
Veneto	B1

Cities and Towns

Agrigento	C3
Alessandria	B1
Alghero	B2
Ancona	C2
Aosta	A1
Aquileia	C1
Arezzo	B2
Ascoli Piceno	C2
Asti	B1
Avellino	C2
Bari	C2
Barletta	D2
Belluno	C1
Benevento	C2
Bergamo	B1
Bologna	B1
Bolzano	B1
Brescia	B1
Brindisi	D2
Cagliari	B3
Caltanissetta	C3
Campobasso	C2
Canossa	B1
Capua	C2
Carbonia	B3
Caserta	C2
Castel Gandolfo	C2
Catania	C3
Catanzaro	D3
Cefalù	C3
Chieti	C2
Chioggia	C1
Civitavecchia	B2
Como	B1
Cortina d'Ampezzo	C1
Cortona	B2
Cosenza	D3
Cremona	B1
Crotone	D3
Cuneo	A1
Enna	C3
Faenza	B1
Ferrara	B1
Florence	B2
Foggia	C2
Forlì	C1
Frosinone	C2
Gaeta	C2
Gela	C3

Genoa	B1
Gorizia	C1
Grosseto	B2
Isernia	C2
L'Aquila	C2
La Spezia	B1
Latina	C2
Lecce	D2
Livorno	B2
Lucca	B2
Macerata	C2
Manfredonia	C2
Mantova	B1
Mantua (Mantova)	B1
Marsala	C3
Matera	D2
Merano	B1
Messina	C3
Milan	B1
Modena	B1
Monopoli	D2
Montepulciano	B2
Naples	C2
Novara	B1
Nuoro	B2
Olbia	B2
Oristano	B3
Otranto	D2
Padova	B1
Padua (Padova)	B1
Palermo	C3
Parma	B1
Pavia	B1
Perugia	C2
Pesaro	C2
Pescara	C2
Pisa	B2
Pistoia	B2
Placenza	B1
Potenza	C2
Prato	B2
Ragusa	C3
Ravenna	C1
Reggio di Calabria	C3
Reggio nell'Emilia	B1
Rieti	C2
Rimini	C1
Rome, capital	C2
Rovigo	B1
Salerno	C2
San Gimignano	B2
San Remo	A2
San Severo	C2
Sassari	B2
Savona	B2
Siena	B2
Siracusa	C3
Sondrio	B1
Sorrento	C2
Spoleto	C2
Syracuse (Siracusa)	C3
Taranto	D2
Teramo	C2
Termoli	C2
Terni	C2
Torre del Greco	C2
Trapani	C3
Trento	B1
Treviso	C1
Trieste	C1
Turin	A1
Udine	C1
Venice	C1
Ventimiglia	A2
Vercelli	B1

Verona	B1
Vicenza	B1
Viterbo	C2

Other Features

Adige, river	B1
Adriatic, sea	C2
Alps, mts.	A1, B1
Apennines, range	B1
Arno, river	B2
Asinara, island	B2
Blanc, mt.	A1
Bolsena, lake	C2
Botte Donato, mt.	D3
Bracciano, lake	C2
Brenner, pass	B1
Cagliari, gulf	B3
Campagna di Roma, region	C2
Caprara, point	B2
Capri, island	C2
Carbonara, cape	B3
Cervati, mt.	C2
Cimone, mt.	B1
Como, lake	B1
Corno, mt.	C2
Dolomites, range	B1
Egadi, islands	C3
Elba, island	B2
Etna, mt.	C3
Garda, lake	B1
Gennargentu, mts.	B2
Genoa, gulf	B1
Giglio, island	B2
Ionian, sea	D3
Ischia, island	C2
Ligurian, sea	B2
Lipari, islands	C3
Lombardy, plain	B1
Lugano, lake	B1
Maggiore, lake	B1
Maremma, region	B2
Mediterranean, sea	C3
Messina, strait	C3
Montalto, mt.	C3
Montecristo, island	B2
Naples, bay	C2
Oglio, river	B1
Pantelleria, island	C3
Passero, cape	C3
Pianosa, island	B2
Piave, river	C2
Po, river	A1, B1
Pontine, islands	C2
Pontine, marshes	C2
Rosa, mt.	A1
Salerno, gulf	C2
Sangro, river	C2
San Pietro, island	B3
Santa Maria di Leuca, cape	D3
Sant'Antioco, island	B3
San Vito, cape	C3
Sardinia, island	B2
Sicily, island	C3
Sicily, strait	B3
Spartivento, cape	D3
Stromboli, island	C3
Taranto, gulf	D2
Testa del Gargano, point	D2
Teulada, cape	B3
Tiber, river	C2
Tirso, river	B2
Trasimeno, lake	C2
Tyrrhenian, sea	B2
Ustica, island	C3
Venice, gulf	C1
Vesuvius, volcano	C2

San Marino

Capital: San Marino
Area: 24 sq. mi.
62 sq. km.
Population: 24,000
Largest City: San Marino
Language: Italian
Monetary Unit: Italian lira

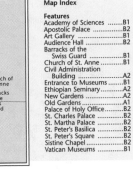

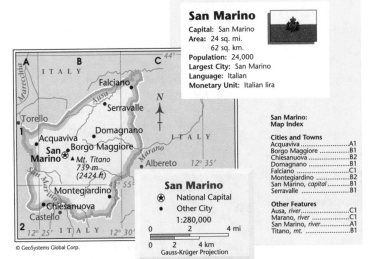

San Marino
- ⊛ National Capital
- • Other City
1:280,000

0   2   4 mi
0   2   4 km
Gauss-Krüger Projection

© GeoSystems Global Corp.

San Marino:
Map Index

Cities and Towns

Acquaviva	A1
Borgo Maggiore	B1
Chiesanuova	B1
Domagnano	B1
Falciano	C1
Montegiardino	B1
San Marino, capital	B1
Serravalle	B1

Other Features

Ausa, river	C1
Marano, river	C1
San Marino, river	B1
Titano, mt.	B1

A B C

North Sea

DENMARK

Sønderborg
Flensburg
Schleswig
Rødby Havn
Kiel Bay
Fehmarn
Puttgarden

Baltic Sea

Bornholm (Den.)

Rügen
Sassnitz

North Frisian Is.

Helgoland

Kiel
Neumünster
SCHLESWIG-HOLSTEIN

Mecklenburg Bay

Stralsund
Rostock
Greifswald
Swinoujście

East Frisian Is.

Cuxhaven
Wilhelmshaven
Emden
Nordenham
Bremerhaven

BREMEN
HAMBURG
Hamburg
Lübeck
Schwerin
Wismar
Güstrow

Schweriner See
Müritz

MECKLENBURG-WESTERN POMERANIA

Neubrandenburg
Neustrelitz
Szczecin

Oderhaff

Groningen
Oldenburg
Bremen

Lüneburger Heide
Lüneburg

Elbe

Wittenberge

P L A I N

Oder

Schwedt

POLAND

Gorzów Wielkopolski

NETHERLANDS

Nordhorn
Nienburg

LOWER SAXONY
N O R T H E R N

Mittelland Canal

Stendal
Brandenburg

BRANDENBURG
Eberswalde

Warta

Arnhem
Bocholt
Kleve

Hannover
Osnabrück
Brunswick
Wolfsburg

Mittelland Canal

Magdeburg
Luckenwalde
Eisenhüttenstadt

BERLIN
Berlin
Spandau
Potsdam
Frankfurt an der Oder

Odra

Münster
Bielefeld
Detmold
Hameln
Hildesheim
Salzgitter

Goslar
Halberstadt
Bernburg
Dessau
Wittenberg

Guben
Zielona Góra

NORTH RHINE-WESTPHALIA
Recklinghausen
Hamm
Paderborn
Northeim
Göttingen

Gelsenkirchen
Marl
Herne
Lippstadt
Büren

Bottrop
Oberhausen
Duisburg
Moers
Lünen
Dortmund
Bochum
Witten
Hagen
Arnsberg

H a r z

Eisleben
Nordhausen
Mühlhausen

SAXONY-ANHALT
Halle
Leipzig
Riesa
Meissen

Bautzen
Görlitz

Mülheim an der Ruhr
Krefeld
Essen
Ratingen

Düsseldorf
Neuss
Wuppertal
Remscheid
Solingen

Ruhr

Kassel

Werra

SAXONY
Dresden
Freiberg

Zittau
Liberec

Mönchengladbach
Leverkusen
Cologne
Bergisch Gladbach
Siegen

Marburg
Giessen
Wetzlar
Fulda

Fulda

Göttingen
Eisenach
Gotha
Erfurt
Weimar
Jena
Gera

Chemnitz
Zwickau

Freiberg

Aachen
Bonn
Remagen

HESSE

Lahn

Saale

Naumburg

THURINGIA
Suhl

Rhine

Maastricht
Liège

BELGIUM

Koblenz
Bad Ems

Thuringian Forest
Coburg

Plauen
Hof

ERZGEBIRGE

Fichtelberg 1214 m (3983 ft)

Karlovy Vary

Labe

Eifel

Taunus

Frankfurt am Main
Hanau
Offenbach

Schweinfurt
Kulmbach

Frankenwald

Prague

LUXEMBOURG
Trier
Luxembourg

Wiesbaden
Bingen
Mainz

Hünsruck
Mosel

Bad Kreuznach
Darmstadt
Worms

Odenwald
Spessart

Bayreuth
Fichtelgebirge
Weiden

Oberpfälzer Wald

CZECH REPUBLIC

Plzeň

RHINELAND-PALATINATE
SAARLAND

Ludwigshafen am Rhein
Mannheim

Würzburg
Bamberg
Erlangen
Fürth

Amberg

Kaiserslautern
Saarbrücken
Neunkirchen
Pirmasens
Speyer
Heidelberg

Nuremberg
Ansbach

Franconian Jura

Weiden

Bohemian Forest Wald

Metz
Nancy

Mosel

Karlsruhe
Heilbronn
Ludwigsburg
Pforzheim

Main-Danube Canal

Regensburg
Straubing

Bayerischer Wald

Strasbourg

Baden-Baden

Schwäbisch Gmünd
Ingolstadt

FRANCE

Black Forest

Stuttgart
Esslingen
Göppingen
Tübingen
Reutlingen
Heidenheim

BAVARIA
Landshut
Passau

Isar

Mulhouse
Freiburg

Swabian Jura

Neckar

Ulm
Augsburg
Dachau

Lech

Inn

Munich

Singen
Constance
Memmingen
Kaufbeuren
Ravensburg
Kempten
Friedrichshafen
Lindau
Hindelang

Starnberg See
Rosenheim

Chiem See

Bad Reichenhall
Salzburg

AUSTRIA

V o s g e s

Basel
L. Constance
Zürich

BAVARIAN ALPS
Oberammergau
Garmisch-Partenkirchen

Zugspitze 2962 m (9718 ft)

Innsbruck

Lucerne
Vaduz
LIECHTENSTEIN

SWITZERLAND

Aare

Chur

ITALY
Bolzano

Germany

Capital: Berlin
Area: 137,735 sq. mi.
356,826 sq. km.
Population: 81,088,000
Largest City: Berlin
Language: German
Monetary Unit: Mark

Germany

⊛ National Capital
• Other City

1:4,066,000

0   25   50   75 mi
0 25 50 75 km

Lambert Conformal Conic Projection

© GeoSystems Global Corp.

Poland

Capital: Warsaw
Area: 120,727 sq. mi.
312,764 sq. km.
Population: 38,655,000
Largest City: Warsaw
Language: Polish
Monetary Unit: Zloty

Poland:
Map Index

Cities and Towns
Biała Podlaska	F2
Białystok	F2
Bielsko-Biała	D4
Bydgoszcz	C2
Bytom	D3
Chełm	F3
Chojnice	C2
Chorzów	D3
Ciechanów	E2
Częstochowa	D3
Darłowo	C1
Elbląg	D1
Ełk	F2
Gdańsk	D1
Gdynia	D1
Gliwice	D3
Głogów	C3
Gorzów Wielkopolski	B2
Grudziądz	D2
Hel	D1
Jelenia Góra	B3
Katowice	D3
Kielce	E3
Kołobrzeg	B1
Konin	D2
Koszalin	C1
Kraków	D3
Krosnow	E4
Kutno	D2
Legnica	C3
Leszno	C3
Łódź	D3
Łomża	F2
Lublin	E3
Nowy Sącz	E4
Nysa	C3
Olsztyn	E2
Opole	C3
Ostrołęka	E2
Piła	C2
Piotrków Trybunalski	D3
Płock	D2
Poznań	C2
Przemyśl	F4
Puck	D1
Puławy	E3
Radom	E3
Ruda Śląka	D3
Rybnik	D3
Rzeszów	F3
Sczcecinek	C2
Siedlce	F2
Sieradz	D3
Skierniewice	E3
Słupsk	C1
Sosnowiec	D3
Suwałki	F1
Świnoujście	B2
Szczecin	B2
Tarnobrzeg	E3
Tarnów	E3
Toruń	D2
Tychy	D3
Ustka	C1
Wałbrzych	C3
Warsaw, capital	E2
Władysławowo	D1
Włocławek	D2
Wodzisław Śląski	D3
Wrocław	C3
Zabrze	D3
Zakopane	D4
Zamość	F3
Zielona Góra	B3

Other Features
Baltic, sea	B1
Beskid, mts.	D4
Bug, river	E2, F3
Carpathian, mts.	E4
Frisches Haff, bay	D1
Gdańsk, gulf	D1
High Tatra, mts.	D4
Mamry, lake	E1
Narew, river	E2
Neisse, river	B3
Noteć, river	C2, D2
Oder, river	B2, C3
Pilica, river	E3
Pomeranian, bay	B1
Rysy, mt.	E4
San, river	F3
Silesia, region	C3
Śniardwy, lake	E2
Sudeten, mts.	B3
Vistula, river	D2, E3
Warta, river	B2, C2
Wieprz, river	F3

Map

BALTIC SEA · Rügen · Darłowo · Ustka · Władysławowo · Hel · Gulf of Gdańsk · Kaliningrad · Kaunas · Vilnius

Pomeranian Bay · Słupsk · Gdynia · Puck · Frisches Haff · RUSSIA · LITHUANIA

Koszalin · Gdańsk · Elbląg · L. Mamry · Suwałki · Hrodna · Nyoman · Baranavichy

Świnoujście · Kołobrzeg · Olsztyn · L. Śniardwy · Ełk

GERMANY · Sczcecinek · Chojnice · Grudziądz · Łomża · Białystok

Szczecin · Piła · Noteć · Vistula · Toruń · Ciechanów · Narew · Ostrołęka · BELARUS

Berlin · Gorzów Wielkopolski · Bydgoszcz · Noteć · Włocławek · Płock · Bug

Poznań · Warta · Konin · Kutno · Warsaw · Siedlce · Brest · Pripyats

Zielona Góra · Leszno · Łódź · Skierniewice · Biała Podlaska

Leipzig · Głogów · Sieradz · Pilica · Radom · Puławy · Wieprz · Bug

Dresden · Legnica · Jelenia Góra · Silesia · Wrocław · Piotrków Trybunalski · Lublin · Chełm · Lutsk

Hradec Králové · Wałbrzych · Nysa · Częstochowa · Opole · Kielce · Zamość

Ruda Śląka · Bytom · Chorzów · Sosnowiec · Tarnobrzeg · Rzeszów · Lviv

Sudeten · Zabrze · Gliwice · Katowice · Tarnów · Przemyśl · UKRAINE

Wodzisław Śląski · Rybnik · Tychy · Kraków · Vistula · San · Krosnow · Dnestr

CZECH REPUBLIC · Ostrava · Bielsko-Biała · CARPATHIAN MOUNTAINS

Olomouc · Beskid Mts. · Nowy Sącz · High Tatra · Zakopane · Rysy 2499 m (8199 ft) · SLOVAKIA · Dnestr

© GeoSystems Global Corp.

Poland

⊛ National Capital
• Other City
⊣⊢ Canal

1:6,687,500

0 — 50 — 100 mi
0 — 50 — 100 km

Lambert Conformal Conic Projection

Germany:
Map Index

States
Baden-Württemberg	B4
Bavaria	B4
Berlin	C2
Brandenburg	C2
Bremen	B2
Hamburg	B2
Hesse	B3
Lower Saxony	B2
Mecklenburg-Western Pomerania	C2
North Rhine-Westphalia	A3
Rhineland-Palatinate	A4
Saarland	A4
Saxony	C3
Saxony-Anhalt	B3
Schleswig-Holstein	B1
Thuringia	B3

Cities and Towns
Aachen	A3
Amberg	B4
Ansbach	B4
Arnsberg	A3
Augsburg	B4
Bad Ems	A3
Baden-Baden	A4
Bad Kreuznach	A4
Bad Reichenhall	C5
Bamberg	B4
Bautzen	C3
Bayreuth	B4
Bergisch Gladbach	A3
Berlin, capital	C2
Bernburg	B3
Bielefeld	B2
Bingen	A4
Bocholt	A3
Bochum	A3
Bonn	A3
Bottrop	A3
Brandenburg	B2
Bremen	B2
Bremerhaven	B2
Brunswick	B2
Büren	B3
Chemnitz	C3
Coburg	B3
Cologne	A3
Constance	B5
Cottbus	C3
Cuxhaven	B2
Dachau	B4
Darmstadt	B4
Dessau	C3
Detmold	B2
Dortmund	A3
Dresden	C3
Duisburg	A3
Düsseldorf	A3
Eberswalde	C2
Eisenach	B3
Eisenhüttenstadt	C2
Eisleben	B3
Emden	A2
Erfurt	B3
Erlangen	B4
Essen	A3
Esslingen	B4
Flensburg	B1
Frankfurt am Main	B3
Frankfurt an der Oder	C2
Freiberg	C3
Freiburg	A5
Friedrichshafen	B5
Fulda	B3
Fürth	B4
Garmisch-Partenkirchen	B5
Gelsenkirchen	A3
Gera	C3
Giessen	B3
Göppingen	B4
Görlitz	C3
Goslar	B3
Gotha	B3
Göttingen	B3
Greifswald	C1
Guben	C2
Güstrow	B2
Hagen	A3
Halberstadt	B3
Halle	B3
Hamburg	B2
Hameln	B2
Hamm	A3
Hanau	B3
Hannover	B2
Heidelberg	B4
Heidenheim	B4
Heilbronn	B4
Herne	A3
Hildesheim	B2
Hindelang	B5
Hof	B3
Ingolstadt	B4
Jena	B3
Kaiserslautern	A4
Karlsruhe	B4
Kassel	B3
Kaufbeuren	B5
Kempten	B5
Kiel	B1
Kleve	A3
Koblenz	A3
Krefeld	A3
Kulmbach	B3
Landshut	C4
Leipzig	C3
Leverkusen	A3
Lindau	B5
Lippstadt	B2
Lübeck	B2
Luckenwalde	C2
Ludwigsburg	B4
Ludwigshafen am Rhein	B4
Lüneburg	B2
Lünen	A3
Magdeburg	B2
Mainz	B4
Mannheim	B4
Marburg	B3
Marl	A3
Meissen	C3
Memmingen	B5
Moers	A3
Mönchengladbach	A3
Mühlhausen	B3
Mülheim an der Ruhr	A3
Munich	B4
Münster	A3
Naumburg	B3
Neubrandenburg	C2
Neumünster	B1
Neunkirchen	A4
Neuss	A3
Neustrelitz	C2
Nienburg	B2
Nordenham	B2
Nordhausen	B3
Nordhorn	A2
Northeim	B3
Nuremberg	B4
Oberammergau	B5
Oberhausen	A3
Offenbach	B3
Oldenburg	B2
Osnabrück	B2
Paderborn	B3
Passau	C4
Pforzheim	B4
Pirmasens	A4
Plauen	C3
Potsdam	C2
Puttgarden	B1
Ratingen	A3
Ravensburg	B5
Recklinghausen	A3
Regensburg	C4
Remagen	A3
Remscheid	A3
Reutlingen	B4
Riesa	C3
Rosenheim	C5
Rostock	C1
Saarbrücken	A4
Salzgitter	B2
Sassnitz	C1
Schleswig	B1
Schwäbisch Gmünd	B4
Schwedt	C2
Schweinfurt	B3
Schwerin	B2
Siegen	B3
Singen	B5
Solingen	A3
Spandau	C2
Speyer	B4
Stendal	B2
Stralsund	C1
Straubing	C4
Stuttgart	B4
Suhl	B3
Trier	A4
Tübingen	B4
Uelzen	B2
Ulm	B4
Weiden	C4
Weimar	B3
Wetzlar	B3
Wiesbaden	B3
Wilhelmshaven	B2
Wismar	B2
Witten	A3
Wittenberg	C3
Wittenberge	B2
Wolfsburg	B2
Worms	B4
Wuppertal	A3
Würzburg	B4
Zittau	C3
Zwickau	C3

Other Features
Ammersee, lake	B4
Baltic, sea	C1
Bavarian Alps, mts.	B5
Bayerischer Wald, mts.	C4
Black, forest	A4
Bohemian, forest	C4
Chiem, lake	C5
Constance, lake	B5
Danube, river	A2
East Frisian, islands	A2
Eifel, plateau	A3
Elbe, river	B2, C3
Ems, river	A3
Erzgebirge, mts.	C3
Fehmarn, island	B1
Fichtelberg, mt.	C3
Fichtelgebirge, mts.	B4
Franconian Jura, mts	B4
Frankenwald, mts.	B3
Fulda, river	B3
Harz, mts.	B3
Havel, river	C2
Helgoland, island	A1
Hünsruck, mts.	A4
Inn, river	C4
Isar, river	C4
Kiel, bay	B1
Lahn, river	B3
Lech, river	B4
Lüneburger Heide, region	B2
Main, river	B4
Main-Danube, canal	B4
Mecklenburg, bay	B1
Mittelland, canal	B2
Mosel, river	A4
Mulde, river	C3
Müritz, lake	C2
Neckar, river	B4
Neisse, river	C3
Nord-Ostsee, canal	B1
North, sea	A1
Northern European, plain	B2
North Frisian, islands	B1
Oberpfälzer Wald, mts.	C4
Odenwald, forest	B4
Oder, river	C2
Oderhaff, lake	C1
Pomeranian, bay	C1
Rhine, river	A3, A4
Rügen, island	C1
Ruhr, river	B3
Saale, river	B3
Saar, river	A4
Salzach, river	C4
Schweriner, lake	B2
Spessart, mts.	B4
Spree, river	C3
Starnberg, lake	B5
Swabian Jura, mts.	B4
Taunus, mts.	B3
Thuringian, forest	B3
Werra, river	B3
Weser, river	B2
Zugspitze, mt.	B5

© GeoSystems Global Corp.

Czech Republic

⊛ National Capital

• Other City

1:3,637,000

0 — 25 — 50 mi
0 — 25 — 50 km
Lambert Conformal Conic Projection

Czech Republic

Capital: Prague
Area: 30,449 sq. mi.
  78,883 sq. km.
Population: 10,408,000
Largest City: Prague
Language: Czech
Monetary Unit: Koruna

Czech Republic:
Map Index

Administrative Regions
Jihočeský B3
Jihomoravský C3
Praha B2
Severočeský A2
Severomoravský C3
Středočeský B3
Východočeský B3
Západočeský A3

Cities and Towns
Břeclav C4
Brno C3
České Budějovice B4
Cheb A2
Děčín A2
Frýdek-Místek D3
Havířov D3
Hradec Králové B2
Jihlava B3
Karlovy Vary A2
Karviná D3
Kladno B2
Klatovy A3
Kolín B2
Liberec C2
Most A2
Olomouc C3
Opava C3
Ostrava D3
Pardubice B2
Plzeň A3
Prague, capital B2
Přerov C3
Prostějov C3
Strakonice A3
Šumperk C3
Svitavy C3
Tábor B3
Trutnov B2
Ústí nad Labem B2
Zlín C3
Znojmo C4

Other Features
Berounka, river A3
Bohemia, region A3
Bohemian, forest A3
Bohemian-Moravian, heights ..B3
Carpathian, mts. D3
Dyje, river B4
Erzgebirge, mts. A2
Labe, Elbe, river B2
Morava, river C3
Moravia, region C3
Odra, Oder, river C2
Sázava, river B3
Silesia, region B2
Sněžka, mt. B2
Šudeten, mts. B2
Šumava, mts. A3
Vltava, river B3

Slovakia

Capital: Bratislava
Area: 18,933 sq. mi.
  49,049 sq. km.
Population: 5,404,000
Largest City: Bratislava
Language: Slovak
Monetary Unit: New Koruna

Slovakia:
Map Index

Regions
Bratislava A2
Stredoslovenský B2
Východoslovenský C2
Západoslovenský A3

Cities and Towns
Banská Bystrica B2
Bardejov C2
Bratislava, capital A2
Humenné C2
Komárno B3
Košice C2
Levice B2
Liptovský Mikuláš B2
Lučenec B2
Martin B2
Michalovce C2
Nitra B2
Nové Zámky B3
Piešťany A2
Poprad C2
Považská Bystrica B2
Prešov C2
Prievidza B2
Ružomberok B2
Spišská Nová Ves C2
Trenčín A2
Trnava A2
Žilina B2
Zvolen B2

Other Features
Biele Karpaty, mts. A2
Carpathian, mts. A2
Danube, river A3
Gerlachovka, mt. C2
Hornád, river B2
Hron, river B2
Ipeľ, river B2
Laborec, river C2
Male Karpaty, mts A2
Morava, river A2
Ondava, river C2
Slaná, river B2
Slovenskérudohorie, mts. B2
Tatra, range B2
Váh, river A2

© GeoSystems Global Corp.

Slovakia

⊛ National Capital

• Other City

1:4,353,000

0 — 25 — 50 — 75 mi
0 — 25 — 50 — 75 km
Lambert Conformal Conic Projection

Romania:
Map Index

Cities and Towns
Alba Iulia B2
Alexandria C4
Arad A2
Bacău D2
Baia Mare B2
Bîrlad D2
Bistrița C2
Botoșani D2
Brăila D3
Brașov C3
Bucharest, capital D3
Buzău D3
Călărași D3
Cernavodă E3
Cluj-Napoca B2
Constanța E3
Craiova B3
Dej B2
Deva B3
Dorohoi D2
Drobeta-Turnu Severin B3
Făgăras C3
Fetești D3
Focșani D3
Galați E3
Giurgiu C4
Hunedoara B3
Iași D2
Lugoj A3
Lupeni B3
Medgidia E3
Mediaș C2
Miercurea Ciuc C2
Oltenița D3
Onești D2
Oradea A2
Petrila B3
Petroșani B3
Piatra Neamț D2
Pitești C3
Ploiești D3
Rădăuți C2
Reghin C2
Reșita A3
Rîmnicu Vîlcea C3
Roman D2
Salonta A2
Satu Mare B2
Sfîntu Gheorghe C3
Sibiu C3
Sighetul Marmației B2

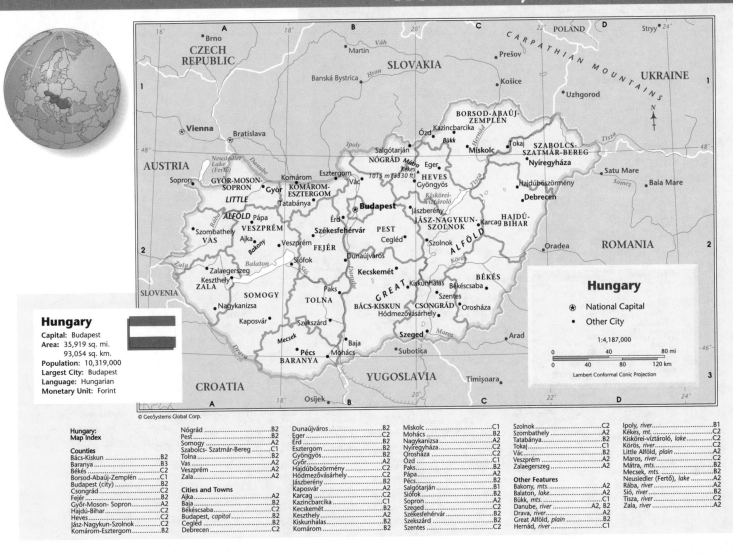

Hungary

Capital: Budapest
Area: 35,919 sq. mi.
93,054 sq. km.
Population: 10,319,000
Largest City: Budapest
Language: Hungarian
Monetary Unit: Forint

Hungary

⊛ National Capital
• Other City

1:4,187,000

0   40   80 mi
0 40 80 120 km

Lambert Conformal Conic Projection

Hungary:
Map Index

Counties
Bács-Kiskun B2
Baranya B3
Békés C2
Borsod-Abaúj-Zemplén C1
Budapest (city) B2
Csongrád C2
Fejér B2
Győr-Moson- Sopron A2
Hajdú-Bihar C2
Heves C2
Jász-Nagykun-Szolnok C2
Komárom-Esztergom B2

Nógrád B2
Pest B2
Somogy B2
Szabolcs- Szatmár-Bereg C1
Tolna B2
Vas A2
Veszprém A2
Zala A2

Cities and Towns
Ajka A2
Baja B2
Békéscsaba C2
Budapest, capital B2
Cegléd B2
Debrecen C2

Dunaújváros B2
Eger C2
Érd B2
Esztergom B2
Gyöngyös B2
Győr A2
Hajdúböszörmény C2
Hódmezővásárhely C2
Jászberény B2
Kaposvár A2
Karcag C2
Kazincbarcika C1
Kecskemét B2
Keszthely A2
Kiskunhalas B2
Komárom B2

Miskolc C1
Mohács B2
Nagykanizsa A2
Nyíregyháza C2
Oroszháza C2
Ózd C1
Paks B2
Pápa A2
Pécs B2
Salgótarján B1
Siófok B2
Sopron A2
Szeged C2
Székesfehérvár B2
Szekszárd B2
Szentes C2

Szolnok C2
Szombathely A2
Tatabánya B2
Tokaj C1
Vác B2
Veszprém A2
Zalaegerszeg A2

Other Features
Bakony, mts. A2
Balaton, lake A2
Bükk, mts. C1
Danube, river A2, B2
Drava, river A2
Great Alföld, plain B2
Hernád, river C1

Ipoly, river B1
Kékes, mt. C2
Kiskörei-víztároló, lake C2
Körös, river C2
Little Alföld, plain A2
Maros, river C2
Mátra, mts. B2
Mecsek, mts. B2
Neusiedler (Fertő), lake A2
Rába, river A2
Sió, river B2
Tisza, river C2
Zala, river A2

Romania

Capital: Bucharest
Area: 91,699 sq. mi.
267,174 sq. km.
Population: 23,181,000
Largest City: Bucharest
Language: Romanian
Monetary Unit: Leu

Romania

⊛ National Capital
• Other City

1:5,750,000

0   40   80 mi
0 40 80 km

Lambert Conformal Conic Projection

Sighișoara C2
Siret D2
Slatina C3
Slobozia D3
Suceava D2
Tecuci D3
Timișoara A3
Tîrgoviște C3
Tîrgu Jiu B3
Tîrgu-Mureș C2
Tîrgu Neamț D2
Tirgu Ocna D2
Tulcea E3
Turda B2
Turnu Măgurele C4
Vaslui D2
Zalău B2

Other Features
Apuseni, mts. B2
Argeș, river C3
Banat, region A3
Bicaz, reservoir D2
Bihor, mts. B2
Bistrița, river C2
Carpathian, mts. B1
Danube, river B3, D3, E3
Dobruja, region E4
Ialomița, river D3
Iron Gate, reservoir B3
Jiu, river B3
Moldavia, region D2
Moldoveanu, mt. B3
Mouths of the Danube, delta ..E3
Mureș, river B2
Olt, river B3
Prut, river E2
Razelm, lake D3
Siret, river D2
Someș, river B2
Transylvanian Alps, mts. B3
Walachia, region B3

Part of Russia extends onto the continent of Asia.

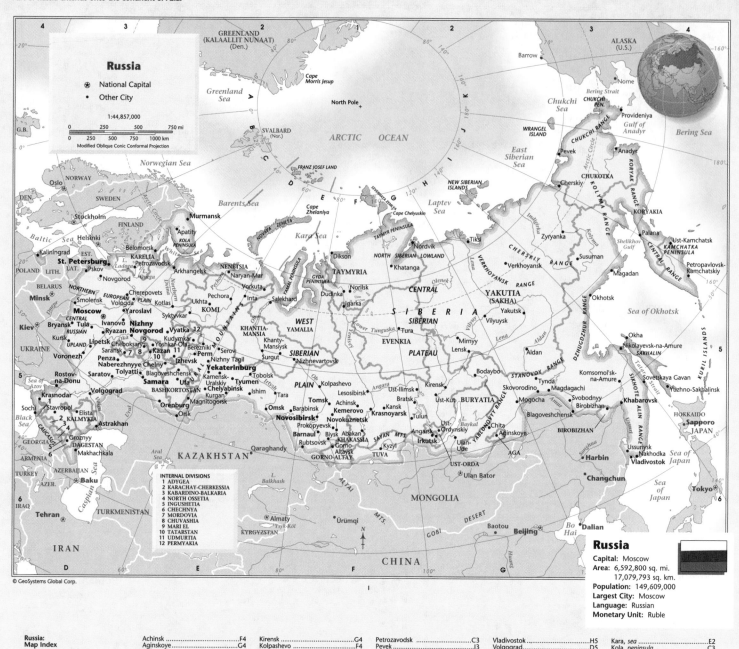

Russia

⊛ National Capital
• Other City

1:44,857,000

0   250   500   750 mi
0 250 500 750 1000 km
Modified Oblique Conic Conformal Projection

Russia
Capital: Moscow
Area: 6,592,800 sq. mi.
     17,079,793 sq. km.
Population: 149,609,000
Largest City: Moscow
Language: Russian
Monetary Unit: Ruble

© GeoSystems Global Corp.

INTERNAL DIVISIONS
1 ADYGEA
2 KARACHAY-CHERKESSIA
3 KABARDINO-BALKARIA
4 NORTH OSSETIA
5 INGUSHETIA
6 CHECHNYA
7 MORDOVIA
8 CHUVASHIA
9 MARI EL
10 TATARSTAN
11 UDMURTIA
12 PERMYAKIA

Russia:
Map Index

Internal Divisions
Adygea (republic) D5
Aga (autonomous okrug) ...G4
Bashkortostan (republic) ...D4
Birobizhan (autonomous
  oblast) H5
Buryatia (republic) G4
Chechnya (republic) D5
Chukotka (autonomous
  okrug) J3
Chuvashia (republic) D4
Dagestan (republic) D5
Evenkia (autonomous okrug) ..F3
Gorno-Altay (republic) E4
Ingushetia (republic) D5
Kabardino-Balkaria (republic) ..D5
Kalmykia (republic) D5
Karachay-Cherkessia (republic) ..C5
Karelia (republic) C3
Khakassia (republic) F4
Khantia-Mansia
  (autonomous okrug) E3
Komi (republic) D3
Koryakia (autonomous okrug) ..J3
Mari El (republic) D4
Mordovia (republic) D4
Nenetsia (autonomous okrug) ..D3
North Ossetia (republic) D5
Permyakia (autonomous okrug) ..D3
Tatarstan (republic) D4
Taymyria (autonomous okrug) ..F2
Tuva (republic) F4
Udmurtia (republic) D4
Ust-Orda (autonomous
  okrug) G4
Yakutia (Sakha) (republic) ..H3
Yamalia (autonomous okrug) ..E3

Cities and Towns
Abakan F4

Achinsk F4
Aginskoye G4
Aldan H4
Anadyr J3
Angarsk G4
Apatity C3
Arkhangelsk D3
Astrakhan D5
Barabinsk E4
Barnaul F4
Belomorsk C3
Berezniki D4
Birobizhan H5
Biysk F4
Blagoveshchensk D4
Blagoveshchensk H4
Bodaybo G4
Bratsk G4
Bryansk C4
Cheboksary D4
Chelyabinsk E4
Cherepovets C4
Cherskiy J3
Chita G4
Dikson F2
Dudinka F3
Elista D5
Gorno-Altaysk F4
Groznyy D5
Igarka F3
Inta D3
Irkutsk G4
Ishim E4
Ivanovo D4
Izhevsk D4
Kaliningrad B4
Kamensk-Uralskiy E4
Kazan D4
Kemerovo F4
Khabarovsk H5
Khanty-Mansiysk E3
Khatanga G2

Kirensk G4
Kolpashevo F4
Komsomol'sk-na-Amure ...H4
Kotlas D3
Krasnodar C5
Krasnoyarsk F4
Kudymkar D4
Kurgan E4
Kursk C4
Kyzyl F4
Lensk G3
Lesosibirsk F4
Lipetsk C4
Magadan I4
Magdagachi H4
Magnitogorsk D4
Makhachkala D5
Mirnyy G3
Mogocha H4
Moscow, capital C4
Murmansk C3
Naberezhnyye Chelny D4
Nakhodka H5
Naryan-Mar D3
Nikolayevsk-na-Amure I4
Nizhnevartovsk E3
Nizhny Novgorod D4
Nizhny Tagil D4
Nordvik G2
Norilsk F3
Novgorod C4
Novokuznetsk F4
Novosibirsk F4
Okha I4
Okhotsk I4
Omsk E4
Orenburg D4
Orsk D4
Palana J4
Penza D4
Pechora D3
Perm D4
Petropavlovsk-Kamchatskiy ..I4

Petrozavodsk C3
Pevek J3
Prokopyevsk F4
Providenya K3
Pskov C4
Rostov-na-Donu C5
Rubtsovsk F4
Ryazan C4
St. Petersburg C4
Salekhard E3
Samara D4
Saransk D4
Saratov D4
Serov E4
Skovorodino H4
Smolensk C4
Sochi C5
Stavropol D5
Surgut E3
Susuman I3
Svobodnyy H4
Syktyvkar D3
Tara E4
Tiksi H2
Tobolsk E4
Tolyatti D4
Tomsk F4
Tula C4
Tulun G4
Tura G3
Tynda H4
Tyumen E4
Ufa D4
Ukhta D3
Ulan-Ude G4
Ussuriysk H5
Ust-Ilimsk G4
Ust-Kamchatsk J4
Ust-Kut G4
Ust-Ordynskiy G4
Verkhoyansk H3
Vilyuysk H3

Vladivostok H5
Volgograd D5
Vologda C4
Vorkuta E3
Voronezh C4
Vyatka D4
Yakutsk H3
Yaroslavl C4
Yekaterinburg D4
Yoshkar-Ola D4
Yuzhno-Sakhalinsk I5
Zyryanka I3

Other Features
Aldan, river H4
Amur, river H4
Anadyr, gulf K3
Angara, river F4
Azov, sea C5
Baltic, sea B4
Barents, sea C2
Baykal, lake G4
Bering, sea K4
Bering, strait K3
Black, sea C5
Caspian, sea D6
Caucasus, mts. D5
Central Russian, upland C4
Central Siberian, plateau ..G3
Central, range I4
Chelyuskin, cape G2
Cherskiy, range H3
Chukchi, peninsula K3
Chukchi, sea K2
Dnepr, river C4
Dzhugdzhur, range H4
East Siberian, sea J2
Franz Josef Land, islands ..D1
Gyda, peninsula E2
Indigirka, river I3
Irtysh, river E3
Kamchatka, peninsula J4

Kara, sea E2
Kola, peninsula C3
Kolyma, range J3
Kolyma, river I3
Koryak, range J3
Kuril, islands I5
Ladoga, lake C3
Laptev, sea H2
Lena, river H3
Lower Tunguska, river F3
New Siberian, islands I2
North Siberian, lowland ...G2
Northern Divina, river C3
Northern European, plain ..C4
Novaya Zemlya, islands ...D2
Ob, river E3
Oka, river D4
Okhotsk, sea I4
Olenek, river G3
Onega, lake C3
Pechora, river D3
Sakhalin, island I4
Sayan, mts. F4
Severnaya Zemlya, islands ..F1
Shelikhov, gulf I3
Siberia, region G3
Sikhote Alin, range H5
Stanovoy, range H4
Tatar, strait I4
Taymyr, peninsula G2
Ural, mts. D4
Ural, river D4
Ussuri, river H5
Verkhoyansk, range H3
Vilyuy, river G3
Volga, river D5
West Siberian, plain E3
White, sea C3
Wrangel, island J2
Yablonovyy, range G4
Yamal, peninsula E3
Yenisey, river F3
Zhelaniya, cape E2

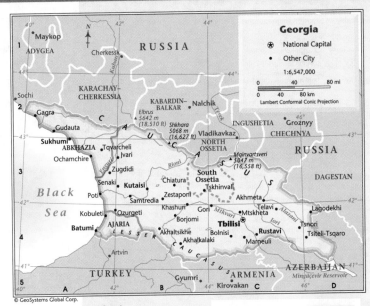

© GeoSystems Global Corp.

Armenia

Capital: Yerevan
Area: 11,500 sq. mi.
29,793 sq. km.
Population: 3,522,000
Largest City: Yerevan
Language: Armenian
Monetary Unit: Dram

Armenia:
Map Index

Cities and Towns

Alaverdi	B1
Ararat	B3
Artashat	B3
Artik	A2
Artsvashen	C2
Dilijan	B2
Echmiadzin	B2
Goris	D3
Gyumri	A2
Hoktemberyan	B2
Hrazdan	B2
Ijevan	C2
Kafan	D3
Kamo	C2
Kirovakan	B2
Martuni	C2
Meghri	D4
Sisian	D3
Sotk	C2
Stepanavan	B2
Tashir	B1
Vardenis	C2
Vayk	C3
Yerevan, *capital*	B2

Other Features

Akhuryan, *river*	A2
Aragats, *mt.*	B2
Aras, *river*	B2
Arpa, *river*	C3
Debed, *river*	B2
Hrazdan, *river*	B2
Lesser Caucasus, *mts.*	B1
Sevan, *lake*	C2
Vorotan, *river*	C3

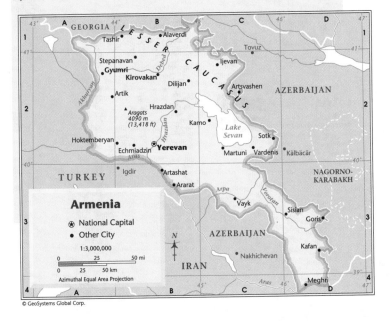

Georgia:
Map Index

Cities and Towns

Akhalkalaki	B4
Akhaltsikhe	B4
Akhmeta	C3
Batumi	A4
Bolnisi	C4
Borjomi	B4
Chiatura	B3
Gagra	A2
Gori	B4
Gudauta	A2
Jvari	B3
Khashuri	B4
Kobuleti	A4
Kutaisi	B3
Lagodekhi	D4
Marneuli	C4
Mtskheta	C4
Ochamchire	A3
Ozurgeti	A4
Poti	A3
Rustavi	C4
Samtredia	B3
Senaki	B3
Sukhumi	A3
Tbilisi, *capital*	C4
Telavi	C4
Tqvarcheli	A3
Tsiteli-Tsqaro	D4
Tskhinvali	B3
Tsnori	C4
Zestaponi	B3
Zugdidi	A3

Other Features

Abkhazia, *autonomous republic*	A3
Ajaria, *autonomous republic*	A4
Alazani, *river*	C4
Caucasus, *mts.*	A2
Enguri, *river*	A3
Iori, *river*	C4
Lesser Caucasus, *mts.*	B4
Mqinvartsveri, *mt.*	C3
Mtkvari, *river*	C4
Rioni, *river*	B3
Shkhara, *mt.*	B3
South Ossetia, *region*	B3

Georgia

Capital: Tbilisi
Area: 26,900 sq. mi.
69,689 sq. km.
Population: 5,681,000
Largest City: Tbilisi
Language: Georgian
Monetary Unit: Lari

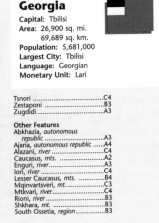

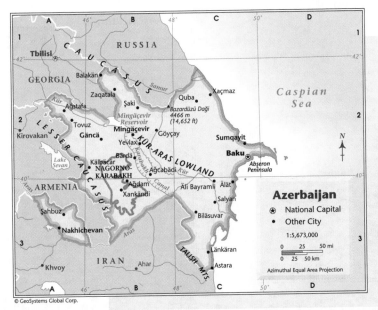

Azerbaijan

Capital: Baku
Area: 33,400 sq. mi.
86,528 sq. km.
Population: 7,684,000
Largest City: Baku
Language: Azerbaijani
Monetary Unit: Manat

Azerbaijan:
Map Index

Cities and Towns

Ağcabädi	B2
Ağdam	B3
Ağstafa	A2
Älät	C3
Äli Bayramli	C3
Astara	C3
Baku, *capital*	C2
Balakän	B2
Bärdä	B2
Biläsuvar	C3
Gäncä	B2
Göyçay	B2
Kälbäcär	A3
Länkäran	C3
Mingäcevir	B2
Nakhichevan	A3
Quba	C2
Şahbuz	A3
Şäki	B2
Salyan	C3
Sumqayit	C2
Tovuz	A2
Xaçmaz	C2
Xankändi	B3
Yevlax	B2
Zaqatala	B2

Other Features

Abşeron, *peninsula*	C2
Aras, *river*	B3
Bazardüzü Daği, *mt.*	B2
Caucasus, *range*	A1
Karabakh, *canal*	B2
Kür, *river*	A2, C2
Kür-Aras, *lowland*	B2
Lesser Caucasus, *range*	A2
Mingäcevir, *reservoir*	B2
Nagorno-Karabakh, *autonomous region*	B2
Samur, *river*	B1
Talish, *mts.*	C3

© GeoSystems Global Corp.

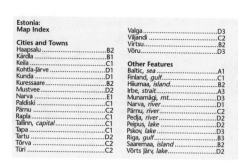

Estonia:
Map Index

Cities and Towns
Haapsalu.............................B2
Kärdla................................B1
Keila.................................C1
Kohtla-Järve........................D1
Kunda................................D1
Kuressaare..........................B2
Mustvee.............................D2
Narva................................E1
Paldiski.............................C1
Pärnu................................C2
Rapla................................C1
Tallinn, capital....................C1
Tapa.................................C1
Tartu................................D2
Tõrva................................C2
Türi.................................C2

Valga................................D3
Viljandi.............................C2
Virtsu...............................B2
Võru.................................D3

Other Features
Baltic, sea..........................A1
Finland, gulf........................C1
Hiiumaa, island.....................B2
Irbe, strait.........................A3
Munamägi, mt.......................D3
Narva, river........................D1
Pärnu, river........................C2
Pedja, river.........................D2
Peipus, lake.........................D2
Pskov, lake..........................D3
Riga, gulf...........................B3
Saaremaa, island...................B2
Võrts Järv, lake....................D2

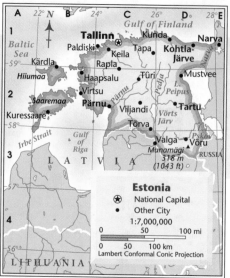

Estonia
National Capital (star symbol)
Other City (dot symbol)
1:7,000,000
0   50   100 mi
0   50   100 km
Lambert Conformal Conic Projection

© GeoSystems Global Corp.

Estonia
Capital: Tallinn
Area: 17,413 sq. mi.
45,111 sq. km.
Population: 1,617,000
Largest City: Tallinn
Language: Estonian
Monetary Unit: Kroon

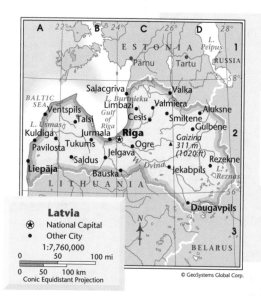

Latvia
National Capital (star symbol)
Other City (dot symbol)
1:7,760,000
0   50   100 mi
0   50   100 km
Conic Equidistant Projection

© GeoSystems Global Corp.

Latvia
Capital: Riga
Area: 24,900 sq. mi.
64,508 sq. km.
Population: 2,749,000
Largest City: Riga
Language: Latvian
Monetary Unit: Lat

Latvia:
Map Index

Cities and Towns
Aluksne.............................D2
Bauska..............................C2
Cesis...............................C2
Daugavpils..........................D3
Gulbene.............................D2
Jekabpils...........................C2
Jelgava.............................B2
Jurmala.............................B2
Kuldiga.............................A2
Liepāja.............................A2
Limbazi.............................C2
Ogre................................C2
Pavilosta...........................A2
Rezekne.............................D2
Riga, capital.......................C2
Salacgriva..........................B2
Saldus..............................B2
Smiltene............................C2
Talsi...............................B2
Tukums..............................B2
Valka...............................C2
Valmiera............................C2
Ventspils...........................A2

Other Features
Baltic, sea.........................A2
Burtnieku, lake.....................C2
Gaizina, mt.........................C2
Reznas, lake........................D2
Riga, gulf..........................B2
Usmas, lake.........................B2
Western Dvina, river................C2

Lithuania
National Capital (star symbol)
Other City (dot symbol)
1:4,600,000
0   30   60 mi
0   30   60 km
Conic Equidistant Projection

© GeoSystems Global Corp.

Lithuania
Capital: Vilnius
Area: 25,213 sq. mi.
65,319 sq. km.
Population: 3,848,000
Largest City: Vilnius
Language: Lithuanian
Monetary Unit: Lit

Lithuania:
Map Index

Cities and Towns
Alytus..............................C2
Biržai..............................C1
Druskininkai........................B2
Jonava..............................C2
Jurbarkas...........................B2
Kaunas..............................B2
Kėdainiai...........................B2
Klaipėda............................A2
Kretinga............................A2
Kuršėnai............................B1
Marijampolė.........................B2
Mažeikiai...........................B1
Naujoji Akmenė......................B1
Palanga.............................A2
Panevėžys...........................C2
Radviliškis.........................B2
Šiauliai............................B2
Šilalė..............................B2

Šilutė..............................A2
Tauragė.............................B2
Telšiai.............................B2
Ukmergė.............................C2
Utena...............................C2
Vilkaviškis.........................B2
Vilnius, capital....................C2

Other Features
Baltic, sea.........................A2
Courland, lagoon....................A2
Dubysa, river.......................B2
Juozapines, mt......................C2
Jura, river.........................A2
Merkys, river.......................C2
Minija, river.......................A2
Mūša, river.........................B1
Nemunas, river..................A2, C2
Neris, river........................C2
Nevėžis, river......................B2
Šventoji, river.....................C2
Venta, river........................B1

© GeoSystems Global Corp.

Belarus

⊛ National Capital
• Other City

1:8,000,000

0 · 75 · 150 mi
0 · 75 · 150 km
Lambert Conformal Conic Projection

© GeoSystems Global Corp.

Belarus

Capital: Minsk
Area: 80,134 sq. mi.
207,601 sq. km.
Population: 10,405,000
Largest City: Minsk
Languages: Belarussian, Russian
Monetary Unit: Belarus ruble

Belarus:
Map Index

Cities and Towns
Asipovichy..................D3
Babruysk..................D3
Baranavichy..............C3
Brest.......................A3
Homyel....................E3
Hrodna....................A3
Krychaw...................E3
Lida........................B3
Mahilyow.................E3
Maladzyechna..........C2
Mazyr.....................D3
Minsk, *capital*.........C3
Orsha.....................E2
Pastavy...................C2
Pinsk......................C3
Polotsk...................D2
Rechytsa.................E3

Salihorsk.................C3
Smilovichi................D3
Smolevichi...............D2
Vawkavysk...............B3
Vitsyebsk................E2
Zhlobin...................D3

Other Features
Bug, *river*...............A3
Byarezina, *river*.......D3
Byelaruskaya Hrada, *range*......C3
Dnepr, *river*............E3
Dnepr-Bug, *canal*......B3
Dzyarzhynskaya Hara, *mt.*...C3
Nyoman, *river*..........B3
Pripyats, *marshes*.....C4
Pripyats, *river*.........C3
Ptsich, *river*...........D3
Sozh, *river*.............E3
Western Dvina, *river*....D2

Ukraine:
Map Index

Cities and Towns
Balaklava..................C4
Belaya Tserkov...........C2
Berdyansk................D3
Cherkassy................C2
Chernigov.................C1
Chernobyl................C1
Chernovtsi...............B2
Dneprodzerzhinsk.......C2
Dnepropetrovsk.........D2
Donetsk..................D2
Feodosiya................D3

Gorlovka.................D2
Ivano-Frankovsk........A2
Izmail.....................B3
Kachovka................C3
Kerch.....................D3
Kharkov..................D1
Kherson..................C3
Khmelnytskyy...........B2
Khust.....................A2
Kiev, *capital*...........C1
Kirovograd...............C2
Konotop.................C1
Korosten.................B1
Kotovsk..................B2
Kovel.....................A1

Kramatorsk..............D2
Kremenchug............C2
Krivoy Rog...............C2
Lisichansk...............D2
Lugansk..................D2
Lutsk.....................B1
Lviv.......................A2
Makeyevka..............D2
Mariupol.................D3
Melitopol................D3
Mogilev Podolskiy......B2
Nikolayev................C2
Nikopol..................C2
Odessa..................C3
Pervomaysk............C2

Poltava..................C2
Priluki...................C1
Rovno...................B1
Sevastopol.............C4
Shostka.................C1
Simferopol.............C4
Sumy....................C1
Ternopol................B2
Uman....................C2
Uzhgorod...............A2
Vinnitsa.................C2
Yalta....................C3
Yevpatoriya............C4
Zaporozhye............D2
Zhitomir.................B1

Other Features
Azov, *sea*..............D3
Black, *sea*.............C3
Bug, *river*..............A1
Carpathian, *mts.*......A2
Crimean, *mts.*.........C4
Crimean, *peninsula*....C4
Desna, *river*...........C1
Dnepr, *river*........C1,C3
Dneprodzerzhinsk, *reservoir*...C2
Dnestr, *river*..........B2
Donets, *basin*.........D2
Donets, *river*..........D2
Hoverla, *mt.*...........A2
Kakhovka, *reservoir*...C3

Karkinit, *bay*...........C3
Kerch, *strait*...........D3
Kiev, *reservoir*........C1
Kremenchug, *reservoir*...C2
Pripyat, *river*..........A1
Prut, *river*..............B2
Psel, *river*.............C1
Sluch, *river*............B1
Southern Bug, *river*....B2
Taganrog, *gulf*.........D3
Tisza, *river*............A2
Volyno-Podol'skaya
Vozvyshennost, *uplands*......B2
Vorskla, *river*..........C1

Ukraine

⊛ National Capital
• Other City

1:9,625,000

0 · 75 · 150 mi
0 · 75 · 150 km
Lambert Conformal Conic Projection

Ukraine

Capital: Kiev
Area: 233,100 sq. mi.
603,886 sq. km.
Population: 51,847,000
Largest City: Kiev
Languages: Ukrainian, Russian
Monetary Unit: Karbovanets

© GeoSystems Global Corp.

Slovenia

Capital: Ljubljana
Area: 7,821 sq. mi.
20,262 sq. km.
Population: 1,972,000
Largest City: Ljubljana
Languages: Slovenian, Serbo-Croatian
Monetary Unit: Tolar

**Slovenia:
Map Index**

Cities and Towns
Celje C2
Idrija B2
Jesenice B2
Kočevje B3
Koper A3
Kranj B2
Krško C3
Ljubljana, *capital* B2
Maribor C2
Murska Sobota D2
Nova Gorica A3
Novo Mesto B3
Postojna B3
Ptuj C2

Other Features
Adriatic, *sea* A3
Drava, *river* C2
Julian Alps, *mts.* A2
Krka, *river* B3
Kupa, *river* B3
Mura, *river* C2
Sava, *river* B2
Savinja, *river* B2
Trieste, *gulf* A3
Triglav, *mt.* A2

Slovenia
★ National Capital
• Other City
1:5,100,000
0   25   50 mi
0   25   50 km
Lambert Conformal Conic Projection

© GeoSystems Global Corp.

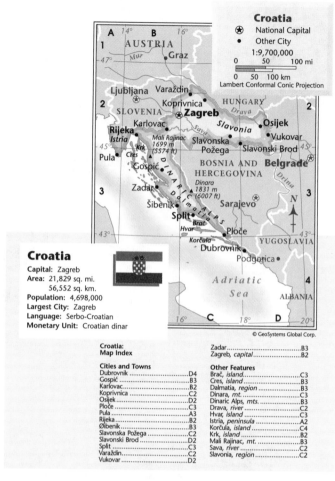

Croatia
✪ National Capital
• Other City
1:9,700,000
0   50   100 mi
0   50   100 km
Lambert Conformal Conic Projection

© GeoSystems Global Corp.

Croatia

Capital: Zagreb
Area: 21,829 sq. mi.
56,552 sq. km.
Population: 4,698,000
Largest City: Zagreb
Language: Serbo-Croatian
Monetary Unit: Croatian dinar

**Croatia:
Map Index**

Cities and Towns
Dubrovnik D4
Gospić B3
Karlovac B2
Koprivnica C2
Osijek D2
Ploče C3
Pula A3
Rijeka B2
Ølbenik B3
Slavonska Požega C2
Slavonski Brod D2
Split C3
Varaždin C2
Vukovar D2

Zadar B3
Zagreb, *capital* B2

Other Features
Brač, *island* C3
Cres, *island* B3
Dalmatia, *region* B3
Dinara, *mt.* C3
Dinaric Alps, *mts.* B3
Drava, *river* C2
Hvar, *island* C3
Istria, *peninsula* A2
Korčula, *island* C4
Krk, *island* B2
Mali Rajinac, *mt.* B3
Sava, *river* C2
Slavonia, *region* C2

**Bosnia and Hercegovina:
Map Index**

Cities and Towns
Banja Luka B1
Bihać A1
Bijeljina C1
Bosanska Gradiška B1
Bosanska Krupa A1
Brčko B1
Bugojno B1
Derventa B1
Doboj B1
Foča B2
Gacko B2
Goražde B2
Gračanica B1
Jajce B2
Livno B2
Mostar B2
Pale B2
Prijedor A1
Sanski Most A1
Sarajevo, *capital* B2
Srebrenica C1
Teslić B1
Trebinje B2
Tuzla B1
Zavidovići B1
Zenica B1
Zvornik C1

Other Features
Bosna, *river* B1
Dinara, *mt.* A2
Dinaric Alps, *mts.* A1
Drina, *river* C1
Neretva, *river* B2
Sava, *river* B1
Una, *river* A1
Vrbas, *river* B1

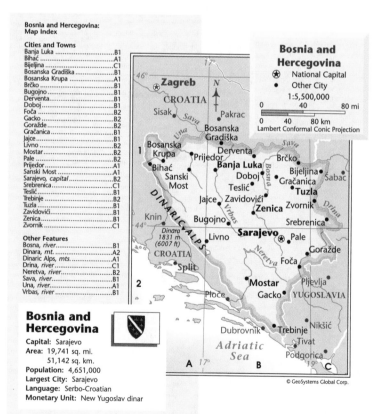

Bosnia and Hercegovina
✪ National Capital
• Other City
1:5,500,000
0   40   80 mi
0   40   80 km
Lambert Conformal Conic Projection

© GeoSystems Global Corp.

Bosnia and Hercegovina

Capital: Sarajevo
Area: 19,741 sq. mi.
51,142 sq. km.
Population: 4,651,000
Largest City: Sarajevo
Language: Serbo-Croatian
Monetary Unit: New Yugoslav dinar

F.Y.R. Macedonia

Capital: Skopje
Area: 9,928 sq. mi.
25,720 sq. km.
Population: 2,214,000
Largest City: Skopje
Languages: Macedonian, Albanian, Serbo-Croatian, Turkish
Monetary Unit: Denar

**F.Y.R. Macedonia:
Map Index**

Cities and Towns
Bitola B2
Blatec C2
Debar A2
Gevgelija C2
Kavadarci C2
Kičevo A2
Kočani C2
Kruševo B2
Kumanovo B1
Ohrid A2
Prilep B2
Skopje, *capital* B2
Štip C2
Struga A2
Strumica C2
Tetovo A1
Titov Veles B2

Other Features
Belasica, *mts.* C2
Bregalnica, *river* C2
Crna, *river* B2
Crna Gora, *mts.* B1
Doiran, *lake* C2
Jakupica, *mts.* B2
Korab, *mt.* A2
Kožuf, *mts.* C2
Nidže, *mts.* B3
Ogražden, *mts.* C2
Ohrid, *lake* A3
Prespa, *lake* B3
Treska, *river* B2
Vardar, *river* C2

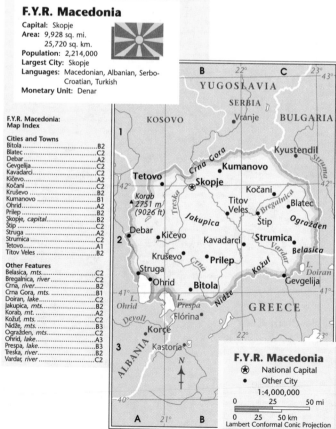

F.Y.R. Macedonia
✪ National Capital
• Other City
1:4,000,000
0   25   50 mi
0   25   50 km
Lambert Conformal Conic Projection

© GeoSystems Global Corp.

Albania

- ⊛ National Capital
- • Other City

1:3,750,000

0   15   30 mi

0   15   30 km

Lambert Conformal
Conic Projection

YUGOSLAVIA
Montenegro
Serbia
NORTH ALBANIAN ALPS
Lake Scutari
Kosovo
Prizren
Bar
Drin
Pukë
Kukës
Shkodër
Korab 2751 m (9026 ft)▲
Skopje
Shëngjin
Peshkopi
Laç
Kruje
Mat
F.Y.R. MACEDONIA
Durrës
Tiranë
Erzen
Lake Ohrid
Kavajë
Elbasan
Shkumbin
Bitola
Lushnjë
Lake Prespa
Devoll
Adriatic Sea
Seman
Fier
Berat
Osum
Pogradec
Flórina
Vijosë
Korçë
Vlorë
Ersekë
Strait of Otranto
Gjirokastër
Erikoússa
Othonoí
Sarandë
Mathrákion
Kérkira
GREECE
Ionian Sea

© GeoSystems Global Corp.

Federal Republic of Yugoslavia

- ⊛ National Capital
- • Other City

1:3,682,000

0   30   60 mi

0   30   60 km

Lambert Conformal Conic Projection

HUNGARY
Békéscsaba
Pécs
Szeged
Mures
Subotica
BANAT
Senta
Tisa
Kikinda
Sombor
Timişoara
Velika
VOJVODINA
Drava
Osijek
Vrbas
Canal
Bečej
Zrenjanin
CROATIA
Bačka Palanka
Novi Sad
Vršac
Fruška Gora
Sremska Mitrovica
Sava
Pančevo
Belgrade ⊛
Šabac
Smederevo
Požarevac
Danube
Drobeta-Turnu Severin
ROMANIA
Tuzla
Drina
Valjevo
SERBIA
Velika Morava
Bor
BOSNIA AND HERCEGOVINA
Kragujevac
Svetozarevo
Vidin
⊛ Sarajevo
Užice
Čačak
Zapandna Morava
Zaječar
Goražde
Zlatibor
Kraljevo
Ibar
Kruševac
Južna
Jastrebac
Niš
Nišava
BALKAN MTS.
Priboj
Pljevlja
Dinaric Alps
Durmitor
Novi Pazar
Kopaonik
Morava
Prokuplje
Pirot
Leskovac
Tara
MONTENEGRO
Nikšić
Zeta
Đaravica 2656 m (8714 ft)▲
Beli Drim
Peć
Kosovska Mitrovica
Pernik
Podgorica
Cetinje
KOSOVO
Priština
Gulf of Kotor
N. Albanian Alps
Đakovica
Uroševac
Vranje
L. Scutari
Drin
Prizren
Bar
Šar Planina
Crna Gora
BULGARIA
Shkodër
Skopje ⊛
ALBANIA
Durrës
Tiranë ⊛
F.Y.R. MACEDONIA
Vardar
Adriatic Sea

© GeoSystems Global Corp.

Albania: Map Index

Cities and Towns

Berat A3
Durrës A2
Elbasan B2
Ersekë B3
Fier A3
Gjirokastër B3
Kavajë A2
Korçë B3
Kruje A2
Kukës B1
Laç A2
Lushnjë A3
Peshkopi B2
Pogradec B3
Puke A1
Sarandë A4
Shëngjin A2
Shkodër A1
Tiranë, capital A2
Vlorë A3

Other Features

Adriatic, sea A2
Buene, river A2
Devoll, river B3

Drin, river A1
Erzen, river A2
Ionian, sea A4
Korab, mt. B2
Mat, river B2
North Albanian Alps, range A1
Ohrid, lake B2
Osum, river A3
Otranto, strait A3
Prespa, lake C3
Scutari, lake A1
Seman, river A3
Shkumbin, river A2
Vijosë, river A3

Albania

Capital: Tiranë
Area: 11,100 sq. mi.
    28,756 sq. km.
Population: 3,374,000
Largest City: Tiranë
Languages: Albanian, Greek
Monetary Unit: Lek

Yugoslavia: Map Index

Internal Divisions

Kosovo (autonomous province)..B3
Montenegro (republic) A3
Serbia (republic) B2
Vojvodina (autonomous province) A2

Cities and Towns

Bačka Palanka A2
Bar A3
Bečej B2
Belgrade, capital B2
Bor C2
Čačak B3
Cetinje A3
Đakovica B3
Kikinda B2
Kosovska Mitrovica B3
Kragujevac B2
Kraljevo B3
Kruševac B3
Leskovac B3
Nikšić A3
Niš B3
Novi Pazar B3
Novi Sad B2
Pančevo B2
Peć B3
Pirot C3
Pljevlja A3

Podgorica A3
Požarevac B2
Priboj A3
Priština B3
Prizren B3
Prokuplje B3
Šabac A2
Senta B2
Smederevo B2
Sombor A2
Sremska Mitrovica A2
Subotica A1
Svetozarevo B3
Uroševac B3
Užice A3
Valjevo A2
Vranje B3
Vrbas A2
Vršac B2
Zaječar C3
Zrenjanin B2

Other Features

Adriatic, sea A4
Balkan, mts. C3
Beli Drim, river B3
Crna Gora, mts. A3
Danube, river A2, B2
Dinaric Alps, mts. A3
Drina, river A3
Durmitor, mts. A3
Fruška Gora, mts. A2

Ibar, river B3
Jastrebac, mts. B3
Južna, river B3
Kopaonik, mts. B3
Kotor, gulf A3
Morava, river B3
Nišava, river C3
North Albanian Alps, mts. B3
Šar Planina, mts. B3
Sava, river A2
Scutari, lake A3
Tara, river A3
Tisa, river B2
Velika Morava, river B2
Veliki, canal A2
Zapandna Morava, river B3
Zeta, river A3
Zlatibor, mts. A3

Yugoslavia

Capital: Belgrade
Area: 39,449 sq. mi.
    102,199 sq. km.
Population: 10,760,000
Largest City: Belgrade
Language: Serbo-Croatian
Monetary Unit: New Yugoslav dinar

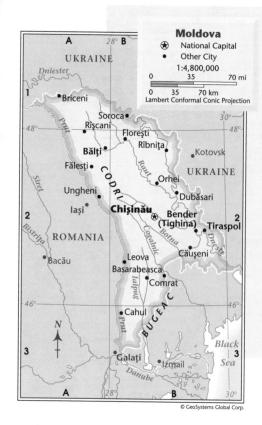

Moldova

Capital: Chişinău
Area: 13,012 sq. mi.
33,710 sq. km.
Population: 4,473,000
Largest City: Chişinău
Languages: Romanian, Russian
Monetary Unit: Moldovan leu

© GeoSystems Global Corp.

Moldova:
Map Index

Cities and Towns
Bălţi	A2
Basarabeasca	B2
Bender (Tighina)	B2
Briceni	A1
Cahul	B3
Căuşeni	B2
Chişinău, *capital*	B2
Comrat	B2
Dubăsari	B2
Făleşti	A2
Floreşti	B2
Leova	B2
Orhei	B2
Rîbniţa	B2
Rîşcani	A2
Soroca	B1
Tiraspol	B2
Ungheni	A2

Other Features
Botna, *river*	B2
Bugeac, *region*	B3
Codri, *region*	A3
Cogalnic, *river*	B2
Dnestr, *river*	B2
Ialpug, *river*	B2
Prut, *river*	A1, B3
Raut, *river*	B2

Bulgaria:
Map Index

Administrative Regions
Burgas	E3
Khaskovo	D4
Lovech	C2
Montana	B2
Plovdiv	C3
Ruse	E2
Sofia City	B3
Sofiya	B3
Varna	F2

Cities and Towns
Asenovgrad	C3
Aytos	F3
Blagoevgrad	B4
Burgas	F3
Dimitrovgrad	D3
Dobrich	F2
Elkhovo	E3
Gabrovo	D3
Kazanlŭk	D3
Khaskovo	D4
Kozloduy	B2
Kŭrdzhali	D4
Kyustendil	A3
Lom	B2
Lovech	C2
Madan	C4
Montana	B2
Oryakhovo	C2
Panagyurishte	C3
Pazardzhik	C3
Pernik	B3
Petrich	B4
Pleven	C2
Plovdiv	C3
Primorsko	F3
Razgrad	E2
Ruse	D2
Samokov	B3
Shumen	E2
Silistra	F1
Sliven	E3
Smolyan	C4
Sofia, *capital*	B3

Stara Zagora	D3
Svilengrad	E4
Svishtov	D2
Tŭrgovishte	E2
Varna	F2
Veliko Tŭrnovo	D2
Vidin	A2
Vratsa	B2
Yambol	E3

Other Features
Arda, *river*	C4
Balkan, *mts.*	
Danube, *river*	
Golyama Kamchiya, *river*	E2
Iskŭr, *river*	C2
Kamchiya, *river*	F2
Luda Kamchiya, *river*	
Ludogorie, *region*	E2
Maritsa, *river*	D3
Mesta, *river*	B4
Musala, *mt.*	B3
Ogosta, *river*	B2
Osŭm, *river*	C3
Rhodope, *mts.*	C4
Rila, *mts.*	B3
Sredna Gora, *mts.*	C3
Struma, *river*	A3
Stryama, *river*	C3
Thrace, *region*	D4
Thracian, *plain*	C3
Tundzha, *river*	E3
Yantra, *river*	D2

Bulgaria

Capital: Sofia
Area: 42,855 sq. mi.
111,023 sq. km.
Population: 8,800,000
Largest City: Sofia
Language: Bulgarian
Monetary Unit: Lev

Bulgaria

⊛ National Capital
• Other City

1:3,210,000

0   25   50   75 mi

0 25 50 75 km

Lambert Conformal Conic Projection

© GeoSystems Global Corp.

Greece

⊛ National Capital

• Other City

1:6,500,000

0 — 75 — 150 mi
0 — 75 — 150 km

Lambert Conformal Conic Projection

© GeoSystems Global Corp.

Greece:
Map Index

Regions

Attica	B2
Central Greece	B2
Central Macedonia	B1
Crete	C4
Eastern Macedonia and Thrace	C1
Epirus	B2
Ionian Islands	A2
Northern Aegean	C2
Peloponnesus	B3
Southern Aegean	C3
Thessaly	B2
Western Greece	B3
Western Macedonia	B1

Cities and Towns

Agrinion	B2
Akharnaí	Inset
Alexandroúpolis	C1
Árgos	B3
Asprópirgos	Inset
Athens, *capital*	B3, Inset
Áyios Dhimítrios	Inset
Corinth	B3
Dháfni	Inset
Elevsís	Inset
Ellinikón	Inset
Glifádha	Inset
Ioánnina	B2
Iráklion	C4
Kalámai	B3
Kalamáki	Inset
Kallithéa	Inset
Kastoría	B1
Kateríni	B1
Kavála	C1
Keratsínion	Inset
Kérkira	A2
Khalándrion	Inset
Khalkís	B2
Khaniá	B4
Kifisiá	Inset
Komotiní	C1
Kozáni	B1
Lamía	B2
Lárisa	B2
Mándra	Inset
Mesolóngion	B2
Mitilíni	C2
Néa Liósia	Inset
Neápolis	B3
Níkaia	Inset
Paianía	B2
Pátrai	B2
Peristéri	Inset
Pílos	B3
Piraiévs	B3, Inset
Préveza	B2
Rhodes	D3
Selínia	Inset
Sérrai	B1
Sparta	B3
Thásos	C1
Thessaloníki	B1
Tríkala	B2
Véroia	B1
Vólos	B2
Xánthi	C1

Other Features

Aegean, *sea*	C2
Aigáleo, *mts.*	Inset
Aíyina, *island*	B3
Akhelóös, *river*	B2
Alfios, *river*	B3
Aliákmon, *river*	B1
Andros, *island*	C3
Astipálaia, *island*	C3
Athos, *mt.*	C1
Corinth, *gulf*	B2
Corinth, *isthmus*	B3
Crete, *island*	C4
Crete, *sea*	C4
Cyclades, *islands*	C3
Delos, *island*	C3
Dodecanese, *islands*	C3
Elevsís, *bay*	Inset
Euboea, *island*	B2
Idhra, *island*	B3
Ikaría, *island*	C3
Ionian, *islands*	B2
Ionian, *sea*	A2
Itháki, *island*	B2
Kárpathos, *island*	C4
Kefallinía, *island*	A2
Kérkira, *island*	A2
Khalkidhikí, *peninsula*	B1
Khíos, *island*	C2
Kifissós, *river*	B2
Kíthira, *island*	B3
Kos, *island*	C3
Lésvos, *island*	C2
Límnos, *island*	C2
Míkonos, *island*	C3
Mílos, *island*	C3
Náxos, *island*	C3
Northern Sporades, *islands*	B2
Olympus, *mt.*	B1
Páros, *island*	C3
Pindus, *mts.*	B2
Piniós, *river*	B2
Prespa, *lake*	B1
Rhodes, *island*	D3
Salamís, *island*	Inset
Sámos, *island*	C3
Samothráki, *island*	C1
Saronic, *gulf*	Inset
Skíros, *island*	C2
Struma, *river*	B1
Thásos, *island*	C1
Thíra, *island*	C3
Zákinthos, *island*	B3

Greece

Capital: Athens
Area: 50,949 sq. mi.
131,992 sq. km.
Population: 10,565,000
Largest City: Athens
Language: Greek
Monetary Unit: Drachma

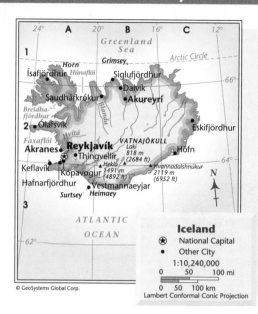

Iceland

Capital: Reykjavík
Area: 36,699 sq. mi.
   95,075 sq. km.
Population: 264,000
Largest City: Reykjavík
Language: Icelandic
Monetary Unit: New Icelandic króna

Iceland:
Map Index

Cities and Towns
Akranes	A2
Akureyrí	B2
Dalvík	B2
Eskifjördhur	C2
Hafnarfjördhur	A3
Höfn	C2
Ísafjördhur	A1
Keflavík	A3
Kópavogur	A2
Ólafsvík	A2
Reykjavík, capital	A2
Saudhárkrókur	B2
Siglufjördhur	B1
Thingvellir	A2
Vestmannaeyjar	A3

Other Features
Blanda, river	B2
Breidhafjördhur, fjord	A2
Faxaflói, bay	A2
Greenland, sea	B1
Grímsey, island	B1
Heimaey, island	A3
Hekla, volcano	B3
Horn, cape	A1
Húnaflói, bay	A2
Hvannadalshnúkur, mt.	B3
Hvítá, river	A2
Laki, volcano	B2
Surtsey, island	A3
Vatnajökull, ice cap	B2

Iceland
⊛ National Capital
• Other City
1:10,240,000
0 — 50 — 100 mi
0 — 50 — 100 km
Lambert Conformal Conic Projection

Norway

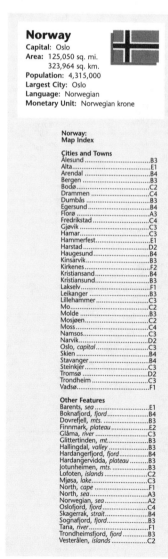

Capital: Oslo
Area: 125,050 sq. mi.
   323,964 sq. km.
Population: 4,315,000
Largest City: Oslo
Language: Norwegian
Monetary Unit: Norwegian krone

Norway:
Map Index

Cities and Towns
Ålesund	B3
Alta	E1
Arendal	B4
Bergen	B3
Bodø	C2
Drammen	C4
Dumbås	B3
Egersund	B4
Florø	A3
Fredrikstad	C4
Gjøvik	C3
Hamar	C3
Hammerfest	E1
Harstad	D2
Haugesund	B4
Kinsarvik	B3
Kirkenes	F2
Kristiansand	B4
Kristiansund	B3
Lakselv	F1
Leikanger	B3
Lillehammer	C3
Mo	C2
Molde	B3
Mosjøen	C2
Moss	C4
Namsos	C3
Narvik	D2
Oslo, capital	C3
Skien	B4
Stavanger	B4
Steinkjer	C3
Tromsø	D2
Trondheim	C3
Vadsø	F1

Other Features
Barents, sea	E1
Boknafjord, fjord	B4
Dovrefjell, mts.	B3
Finnmark, plateau	E2
Glåma, river	C3
Glittertinden, mt.	B3
Hallingdal, valley	B3
Hardangerfjord, fjord	B4
Hardangervidda, plateau	B3
Jotunheimen, mts.	B3
Lofoten, islands	C2
Mjøsa, lake	C3
North, cape	F1
North, sea	A3
Norwegian, sea	A2
Oslofjord, fjord	C4
Skagerrak, strait	B4
Sognafjord, fjord	B3
Tana, river	F1
Trondheimsfjord, fjord	B3
Vesterålen, islands	C2

Norway
⊛ National Capital
• Other City
1:12,075,000
0 — 50 — 100 — 150 — 200 mi
0 — 100 — 200 — 300 km
Lambert Conformal Conic Projection

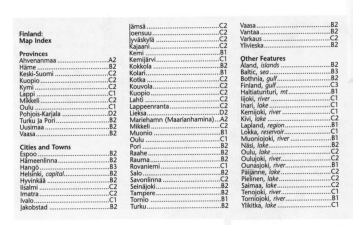

Finland:
Map Index

Provinces
Ahvenanmaa..............................A2
Häme...B2
Keski-Suomi...............................C2
Kuopio......................................C2
Kymi...C2
Lappi..C1
Mikkeli......................................C2
Oulu...C1
Pohjois-Karjala..........................D2
Turku Ja Pori.............................B2
Uusimaa....................................B2
Vaasa.......................................B2

Cities and Towns
Espoo.......................................B2
Hämeenlinna..............................B2
Hangö.......................................B3
Helsinki, capital.........................B2
Hyvinkää....................................B2
Iisalmi.......................................C2
Imatra.......................................C2
Ivalo..C1
Jakobstad..................................B2

Jämsä.......................................C2
Joensuu....................................C2
Jyväskylä...................................C2
Kajaani.....................................C2
Kemi...B1
Kemijärvi...................................C1
Kokkola.....................................B2
Kolari.......................................B1
Kotka.......................................C2
Kouvola.....................................C2
Kuopio......................................C2
Lahti...C2
Lappeenranta.............................C2
Lieksa.......................................D2
Mariehamn (Maarianhamina)...A2
Mikkeli......................................C2
Muonio......................................C1
Oulu...C1
Pori..B2
Raahe.......................................B2
Rauma.......................................B2
Rovaniemi..................................C1
Salo...B2
Savonlinna.................................C2
Seinäjoki...................................B2
Tampere....................................B2
Tornio.......................................B1
Turku.......................................B2

Vaasa.......................................B2
Vantaa......................................B2
Varkaus.....................................C2
Ylivieska....................................B2

Other Features
Åland, islands.............................A2
Baltic, sea.................................B3
Bothnia, gulf..............................B2
Finland, gulf...............................C3
Haltiatunturi, mt.........................B1
Iijoki, river................................C1
Inari, lake.................................C1
Kemijoki, river...........................C1
Kivi, lake..................................C2
Lapland, region..........................C1
Lokka, reservoir..........................C1
Muoniojoki, river.........................B1
Näsi, lake.................................B2
Oulu, lake.................................C1
Oulujoki, river............................C2
Ounasjoki, river..........................B1
Päijänne, lake............................C2
Pielinen, lake.............................C2
Saimaa, lake..............................C2
Tenojoki, river............................B1
Torniojoki, river..........................B1
Ylikitka, lake..............................C1

Sweden:
Map Index

Counties
Alvsborg...................................B3
Blekinge....................................C3
Gävleborg..................................B2
Göteborg och Bohus....................B3
Gotland....................................C3
Halland....................................B3
Jämtland...................................B2
Jönköping..................................B3
Kalmar......................................C3
Kopparberg................................B2
Kristianstad...............................B3
Kronoberg..................................B3
Malmöhus..................................B3
Norrbotten................................C1
Örebro......................................B2
Östergötland..............................B3
Sarjektjakko...............................D2
Skellefteå..................................D2
Skaraborg..................................B3
Södermanland............................C2
Stockholm................................C3
Stockholm, capital.......................C3
Sundsvall..................................B2
Trollhättan.................................B3
Uppsala....................................C2

Värmland...................................B3
Västerbotten..............................C2
Västernorrland............................C2
Västmanland..............................C3

Cities and Towns
Borås.......................................B3
Eskilstuna..................................C3
Falun.......................................C2
Gällivare...................................D1
Gävle.......................................C2
Göteborg..................................B3
Halmstad...................................B3
Haparanda.................................D1
Härnösand.................................C2
Helsingborg...............................B3
Hudiksvall..................................C2
Jönköping..................................B3
Kalmar......................................C3
Karlskrona.................................C3
Karlstad....................................B3
Kiruna......................................D1
Kristianstad...............................B3
Kristinehamn..............................B3
Linköping...................................C3
Luleå.......................................D1
Lund..B3
Malmberget................................D1
Malmö......................................B3
Norrköping.................................C3
Örebro......................................B2
Örnsköldsvik..............................C2
Orrefors....................................C3
Östersund..................................B2
Skellefteå..................................D2
Södertälje..................................C3
Stockholm, capital.......................C3
Sundsvall..................................B2
Trollhättan.................................B3
Uddevalla..................................B3

Umeå.......................................D2
Uppsala....................................C3
Västerås....................................C3
Växjö..B3
Visby..C3

Other Features
Ångermanälven, river...................C2
Baltic, sea.................................C3
Bothnia, gulf..............................D2
Dalälven, river............................C2
Faxälven, river............................C2
Göta, canal................................B3
Gotland, island...........................C3
Hornavan, lake............................C1
Indalsälven, river.........................B2
Kalixälven, river..........................D1
Kattegat, strait...........................B3
Kebnekaise, mt...........................C1
Kjölen, mts................................C1
Klarälven, river............................B2
Ljusnanälven, river.......................C2
Luleälven, river...........................D1
Mälaren, lake.............................C3
Muonioälven, river.......................D1
Norra Storfjället, mt.....................C1
Öland, island..............................C3
Øresund, sound..........................B3
Osterdalälven, river......................B2
Skagerrak, strait.........................A3
Skåne, region.............................B3
Skellefteälven, river......................C1
Småland, region..........................C3
Storavan, lake............................C1
Storsjön, lake.............................B2
Torneälven, river.........................D1
Uddjaur, lake..............................C1
Umeälven, river...........................C2
Vänern, lake..............................B3
Vättern, lake..............................B3
Vindelälven, river.........................C2

MAJOR CITIES

Algeria
Algiers 1,483,000
Oran 590,000
Constantine 483,000

Angola
Luanda 1,100,000

Benin
Cotonou 402,000
Porto-Novo 144,000

Botswana
Gaborone 137,000

Burkina Faso
Ouagadougou 442,000

Burundi
Bujumbura 235,440

Cameroon
Douala 852,000
Yaoundé 700,000

Cape Verde
Praia 61,000

Central African Republic
Bangui 474,000

Chad
N'Djamena 687,000

Comoros (metro)
Moroni 30,000

Congo, Democratic Republic of the
Kinshasa 3,800,000
Lubumbashi 739,000

Congo, Republic of the
Brazzaville 596,000

Côte d'Ivoire
Abidjan 2,700,000
Yamoussoukro 107,000

Djibouti (metro)
Djibouti 450,000

Egypt
Cairo 6,800,000
Alexandria 3,380,000
Port Said 460,000
Suez 388,000

Equatorial Guinea
Malabo 38,000

Eritrea
Asmara 358,000

Ethiopia
Addis Ababa 1,913,000

Gabon
Libreville 275,000

The Gambia
Banjul 40,000

Ghana
Accra 949,000

Guinea
Conakry 705,000

Guinea-Bissau
Bissau 138,000

Kenya
Nairobi 959,000
Mombasa 401,000

Lesotho
Maseru 109,000

Liberia
Monrovia 400,000

Libya
Tripoli 591,000

Madagascar
Antananarivo 802,000

Malawi
Blantyre 332,000
Lilongwe 234,000

Mali
Bamako 658,000

Mauritania
Nouakchott 550,000

Mauritius
Port Louis 142,000

Morocco
Casablanca 2,600,000
Fez 852,000
Rabat 556,000

Mozambique
Maputo 931,000

Namibia
Windhoek 114,000

Niger
Niamey 392,000

Nigeria
Lagos 1,300,000
Ibadan 1,300,000
Abuja 250,000

Rwanda
Kigali 237,000

São Tomé & Príncipe
São Tomé 43,000

Senegal
Dakar 1,700,000

Seychelles (metro)
Victoria 24,000

Sierra Leone
Freetown 470,000

Somalia
Mogadishu 700,000

South Africa (metro)
Johannesburg 1,900,000
Cape Town 1,900,000
Durban 1,100,000
Pretoria 1,000,000
Bloemfontein 270,000

Sudan
Khartoum 476,000

Swaziland
Mbabane 38,000

Tanzania
Dar es-Salaam 1,096,000

Togo
Lomé 600,000

Tunisia
Tunis 620,000

Uganda
Kampala 773,000

Western Sahara
el-Aaiún 90,000

Zambia
Lusaka 982,000

Zimbabwe (metro)
Harare 1,200,000

International comparability of city population data is limited by various data inconsistencies.

© GeoSystems Global Corp.

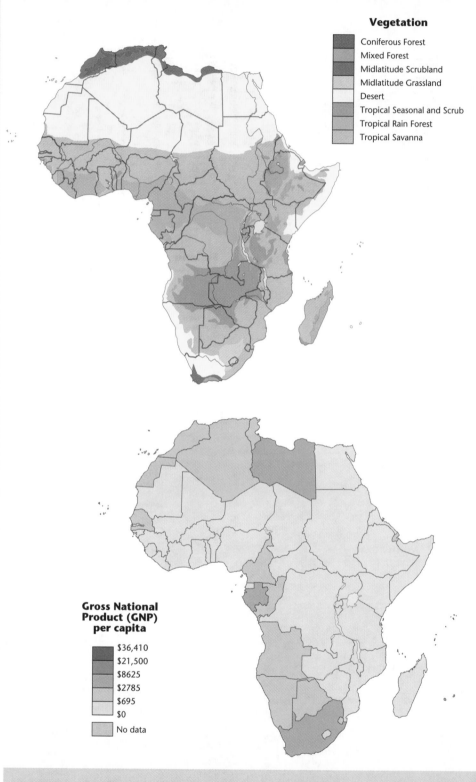

Vegetation

- Coniferous Forest
- Mixed Forest
- Midlatitude Scrubland
- Midlatitude Grassland
- Desert
- Tropical Seasonal and Scrub
- Tropical Rain Forest
- Tropical Savanna

Gross National Product (GNP) per capita

- $36,410
- $21,500
- $8625
- $2785
- $695
- $0
- No data

Africa: Population, by nation (in millions)

Nation	Population
NIGERIA	98.1
EGYPT	59.3
ETHIOPIA	58.7
S. AFR.	43.9
CONGO, DEM.REP.	42.7
SUDAN	29.4
MOROC.	28.6
KENYA	28.2
TANZ.	28.0
ALGERIA	27.9
All other African countries	256.5

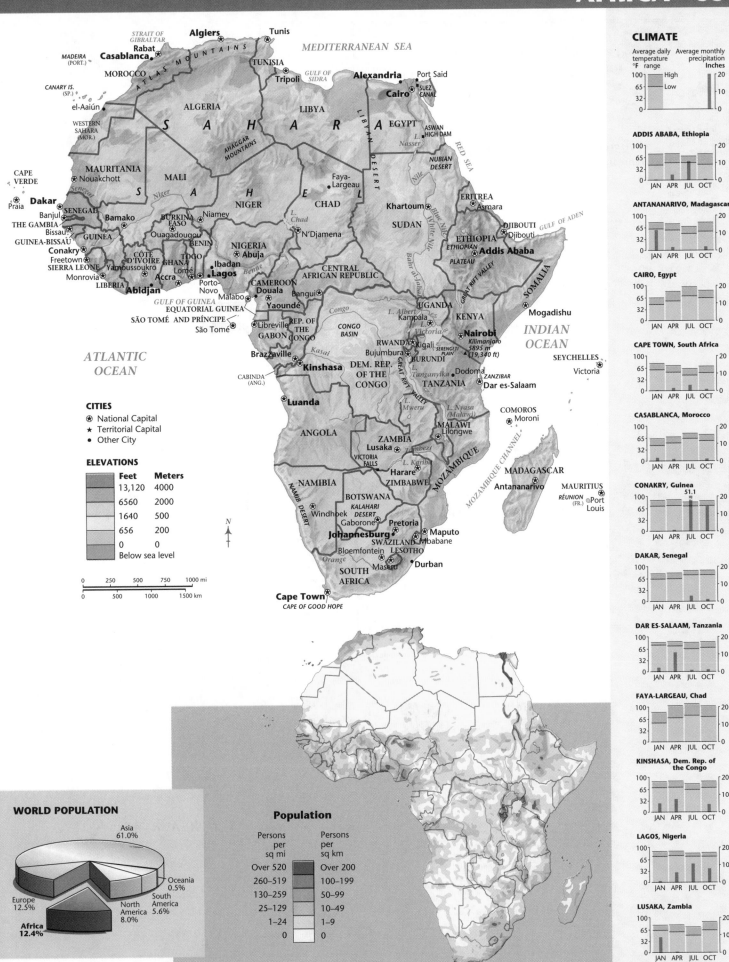

CLIMATE

Average daily temperature °F range
Average monthly precipitation Inches

- 100
- 65 — High
- 32 — Low

ADDIS ABABA, Ethiopia
JAN APR JUL OCT

ANTANANARIVO, Madagascar
JAN APR JUL OCT

CAIRO, Egypt
JAN APR JUL OCT

CAPE TOWN, South Africa
JAN APR JUL OCT

CASABLANCA, Morocco
JAN APR JUL OCT

CONAKRY, Guinea
51.1
JAN APR JUL OCT

DAKAR, Senegal
JAN APR JUL OCT

DAR ES-SALAAM, Tanzania
JAN APR JUL OCT

FAYA-LARGEAU, Chad
JAN APR JUL OCT

KINSHASA, Dem. Rep. of the Congo
JAN APR JUL OCT

LAGOS, Nigeria
JAN APR JUL OCT

LUSAKA, Zambia
JAN APR JUL OCT

CITIES
- ⊛ National Capital
- ★ Territorial Capital
- • Other City

ELEVATIONS

Feet	Meters
13,120	4000
6560	2000
1640	500
656	200
0	0
Below sea level	

0 250 500 750 1000 mi
0 500 1000 1500 km

N ↑

ATLANTIC OCEAN

INDIAN OCEAN

MEDITERRANEAN SEA

STRAIT OF GIBRALTAR
Algiers
Tunis
MADEIRA (PORT.)
Rabat
Casablanca
MOROCCO
ATLAS MOUNTAINS
TUNISIA
Tripoli
GULF OF SIDRA
Alexandria
Port Said
SUEZ CANAL
Cairo
CANARY IS. (SP.)
el-Aaiún
WESTERN SAHARA (MOR.)
ALGERIA
LIBYA
EGYPT
ASWAN HIGH DAM
L. Nasser
AHAGGAR MOUNTAINS
LIBYAN DESERT
NUBIAN DESERT
RED SEA
CAPE VERDE
MAURITANIA
Nouakchott
MALI
NIGER
CHAD
Faya-Largeau
L. Chad
Khartoum
SUDAN
ERITREA
Asmara
GULF OF ADEN
Praia
Dakar
SENEGAL
Senegal
Bamako
Niger
BURKINA FASO
Niamey
N'Djamena
Blue Nile
White Nile
DJIBOUTI
Djibouti
Banjul
THE GAMBIA
Bissau
GUINEA-BISSAU
GUINEA
Ouagadougou
BENIN
NIGERIA
Abuja
CENTRAL AFRICAN REPUBLIC
ETHIOPIA
ETHIOPIAN PLATEAU
Addis Ababa
Conakry
Freetown
SIERRA LEONE
Monrovia
CÔTE D'IVOIRE
Yamoussoukro
GHANA
TOGO
Lomé
Ibadan
Lagos
Accra
Porto-Novo
CAMEROON
Douala
Bangui
Benue
SOMALIA
Mogadishu
LIBERIA
Abidjan
GULF OF GUINEA
EQUATORIAL GUINEA
Malabo
Yaoundé
UGANDA
Kampala
L. Albert
L. Victoria
KENYA
Nairobi
Kilimanjaro 5895 m (19,340 ft)
INDIAN OCEAN
SÃO TOMÉ AND PRÍNCIPE
São Tomé
Libreville
REP. OF THE CONGO
GABON
Congo
CONGO BASIN
RWANDA
Kigali
Bujumbura
BURUNDI
SERENGETI PLAIN
SEYCHELLES
Victoria
ATLANTIC OCEAN
Kasai
Brazzaville
Kinshasa
DEM. REP. OF THE CONGO
GREAT RIFT VALLEY
L. Tanganyika
Dodoma
TANZANIA
Dar es-Salaam
ZANZIBAR
CABINDA (ANG.)
Luanda
L. Mweru
L. Nyasa (Malawi)
COMOROS
Moroni
ANGOLA
ZAMBIA
Lusaka
Zambezi
MALAWI
Lilongwe
MADAGASCAR
Antananarivo
MAURITIUS
RÉUNION (FR.)
Port Louis
VICTORIA FALLS
L. Kariba
Harare
ZIMBABWE
MOZAMBIQUE
MOZAMBIQUE CHANNEL
NAMIBIA
NAMIB DESERT
Windhoek
KALAHARI DESERT
Gaborone
BOTSWANA
Pretoria
Maputo
Johannesburg
SWAZILAND
Mbabane
Bloemfontein
LESOTHO
Maseru
Durban
Orange
SOUTH AFRICA
Cape Town
CAPE OF GOOD HOPE

WORLD POPULATION

Asia 61.0%
Oceania 0.5%
Europe 12.5%
North America 8.0%
South America 5.6%
Africa 12.4%

Population

Persons per sq mi	Persons per sq km
Over 520	Over 200
260–519	100–199
130–259	50–99
25–129	10–49
1–24	1–9
0	0

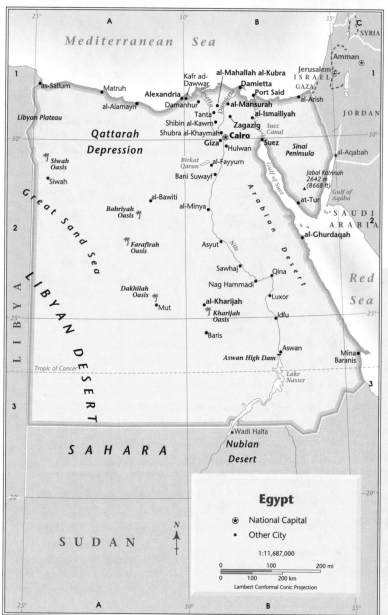

Mediterranean Sea

as-Sallum • Matruh •
al-Alamayn •
Alexandria
Damanhur •
Tanta •
Libyan Plateau
Kafr ad-Dawwar •
al-Mahallah al-Kubra
Damietta
Port Said
al-Arish •
al-Mansurah
Shibin al-Kawm •
al-Ismailiyah
Zagazig
Shubra al-Khaymah •
⊛ **Cairo**
Giza •
Hulwan •
Suez
Suez Canal
Sinai Peninsula
JORDAN
ISRAEL
Jerusalem
GAZA
Amman ⊛
SYRIA

Qattarah Depression

🌴 *Siwah Oasis*
Siwah •

al-Fayyum •
Birkat Qarun
Bani Suwayf •
al-Aqabah •

Great Sand Sea

al-Bawiti •
al-Minya •
🌴 *Bahriyah Oasis*

Arabian Desert
Gulf of Suez
Jabal Katrinah 2642 m (8668 ft) ▲
Gulf of Aqaba
at-Tur •

SAUDI ARABIA

Asyut •
🌴 *Farafirah Oasis*
• **al-Ghurdaqah**

Libyan Plateau

Nile
Sawhaj •
Qina •
Nag Hammadi •
• Luxor
🌴 *Dakhilah Oasis*
• Mut
• **al-Kharijah**
🌴 *Kharijah Oasis*
• Idfu

Red Sea

• Baris

LIBYAN DESERT
LIBYA

Tropic of Cancer
Aswan •
Aswan High Dam
Lake Nasser
Mina Baranis •

• Wadi Halfa
Nubian Desert

SAHARA

SUDAN

Egypt
⊛ National Capital
• Other City

1:11,687,000

0   100   200 mi
0   100   200 km
Lambert Conformal Conic Projection

© GeoSystems Global Corp.

Egypt
Capital: Cairo
Area: 385,229 sq. mi.
    998,003 sq. km.
Population: 59,325,000
Largest City: Cairo
Language: Arabic
Monetary Unit: Pound

Egypt:
Map Index

Cities and Towns
Alamayn, al- A1
Alexandria A1
Arish, al- B1
Aswan B3
Asyut B2
Bani Suwayf B2
Baris B3
Bawiti, al- A2
Cairo, capital B1
Damanhur B1
Damietta B1
Fayyum, al- B2
Ghurdaqah, al- B2
Giza B2
Hulwan B2
Idfu B3
Ismailiyah, al- B1
Kafr ad-Dawwar B1
Kharijah, al- B2
Luxor B2
Mahallah al-Kubra, al- B1
Mansurah, al- A1
Matruh A1
Mina Baranis C3
Minya, al- B2
Mut A2
Nag Hammadi B2
Port Said B1
Qina B2
Sallum, as- A1

Sawhaj B2
Shibin al-Kawm B1
Shubra al-Khaymah B1
Siwah A2
Suez B2
Tanta B1
Tur, at- B2
Zagazig B1

Other Features
Aqaba, gulf B2
Arabian, desert B2
Aswan High, dam B3
Bahriyah, oasis A2
Birkat Qarun, lake B2
Dakhilah, oasis A2
Damietta, river B1
Farafirah, oasis A2
Great Sand Sea, desert A2
Jabal Katrinah, mt. B2
Kharijah, oasis B2
Libyan, desert A2
Libyan, plateau A1
Nasser, lake B3
Nile, river B2
Qattaran, depression A2
Red, sea C2
Rosetta, river B1
Sahara, desert A3
Sinai, peninsula B2
Siwah, oasis A2
Suez, canal B1
Suez, gulf B2

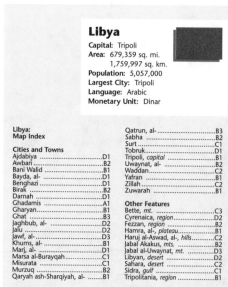

Libya
Capital: Tripoli
Area: 679,359 sq. mi.
    1,759,997 sq. km.
Population: 5,057,000
Largest City: Tripoli
Language: Arabic
Monetary Unit: Dinar

Libya:
Map Index

Cities and Towns
Ajdabiya D1
Awbari B2
Bani Walid B1
Bayda, al- D1
Benghazi D1
Birak B2
Darnah D1
Ghadamis A1
Gharyan B1
Ghat B3
Jaghbub, al- D2
Jalu D2
Jawf, al- D3
Khums, al- B1
Marj, al- D1
Marsa al-Burayqah C1
Misurata C1
Murzuq B2
Qaryah ash-Sharqiyah, al- B1

Qatrun, al- B3
Sabha B2
Surt C1
Tobruk D1
Tripoli, capital B1
Uwaynat, al- B2
Waddan C2
Yafran B1
Zillah C2
Zuwarah B1

Other Features
Bette, mt. C3
Cyrenaica, region D2
Fezzan, region C2
Hamra, al-, plateau B1
Haruj al-Aswad, al-, hills C2
Jabal Akakus, mts. B2
Jabal al-Uwaynat, mt. D3
Libyan, desert C2
Sahara, desert C2
Sidra, gulf C1
Tripolitania, region B1

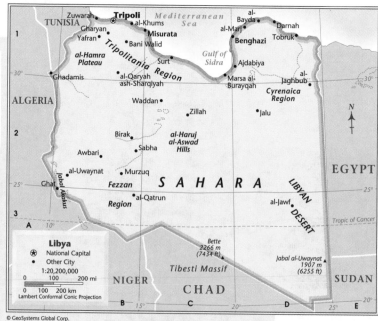

TUNISIA
Zuwarah •
Tripoli ⊛
Mediterranean Sea
al-Bayda •
Gharyan •
• al-Khums
Misurata
Darnah •
Yafran •
Bani Walid •
al-Marj •
Benghazi
Tobruk •
al-Hamra Plateau
Tripolitania Region
Surt •
Gulf of Sidra
Ajdabiya •
ALGERIA
Ghadamis •
• al-Qaryah ash-Sharqiyah
Marsa al-Burayqah •
al-Jaghbub •
Cyrenaica Region
Waddan •
Zillah •
• Jalu
Birak •
al-Haruj al-Aswad Hills
Awbari •
Sabha •
SAHARA
Jabal Akakus
al-Uwaynat •
Murzuq •
EGYPT
Fezzan Region
al-Qatrun •
LIBYAN DESERT
Ghat •
al-Jawf •
Tropic of Cancer
Bette 2266 m (7434 ft) ▲
Jabal al-Uwaynat 1907 m (6255 ft) ▲
Tibesti Massif
NIGER
CHAD
SUDAN

Libya
⊛ National Capital
• Other City

1:20,200,000

0   100   200 mi
0   100   200 km
Lambert Conformal Conic Projection

© GeoSystems Global Corp.

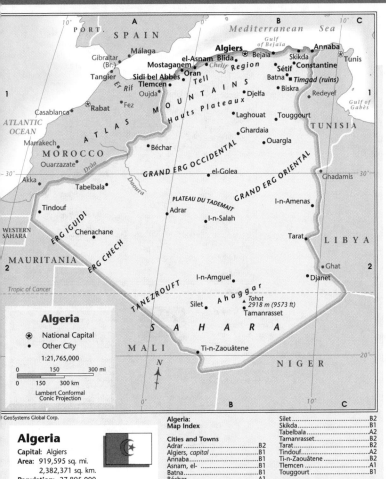

© GeoSystems Global Corp.

Algeria

Capital: Algiers
Area: 919,595 sq. mi.
2,382,371 sq. km.
Population: 27,895,000
Largest City: Algiers
Language: Arabic
Monetary Unit: Dinar

Algeria:
Map Index

Cities and Towns
Adrar B2
Algiers, *capital* B1
Annaba B1
Asnam, el- B1
Batna B1
Béchar A1
Bejaïa B1
Biskra B1
Blida B1
Chenachane A2
Constantine B1
Djanet B2
Djelfa B1
Ghardaia B1
Golea, el- B2
I-n-Amenas B2
I-n-Amguel B2
I-n-Salah B2
Laghouat B1
Mostaganem B1
Oran A1
Ouargla B1
Sétif B1
Sidi bel Abbès A1

Silet B2
Skikda B1
Tabelbala A2
Tamanrasset B2
Tarat B2
Tindouf A2
Ti-n-Zaouâtene A2
Tlemcen A1
Touggourt B1

Other Features
Ahaggar, *mts.* B2
Atlas, *mts.* A1
Bejaïa, *gulf* B1
Chelif, *river* B1
Daoura, *river* A2
Drâa, *river* A1
Erg Chech, *desert* A2
Erg Iguidi, *desert* A2
Grand Erg Occidental, *desert* ...B1
Grand Erg Oriental, *desert* B2
Hauts Plateaux, *plateau* B1
Sahara, *desert* B2
Tademait, *plateau* B2
Tahat, *mt.* B2
Tanezrouft, *mts.* B2
Tell Region, *region* B1
Timgad, *ruins* B1

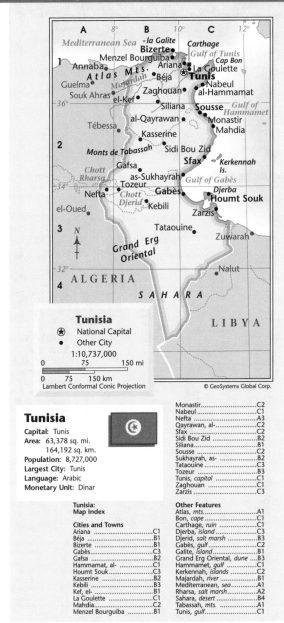

© GeoSystems Global Corp.

Tunisia

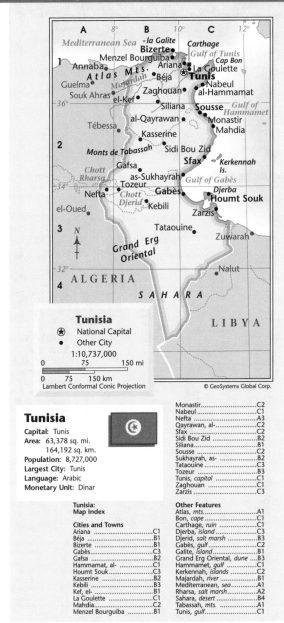

Capital: Tunis
Area: 63,378 sq. mi.
164,192 sq. km.
Population: 8,727,000
Largest City: Tunis
Language: Arabic
Monetary Unit: Dinar

Tunisia:
Map Index

Cities and Towns
Ariana C1
Béja B1
Bizerte B1
Gabès C3
Gafsa B2
Hammamat, al- C1
Houmt Souk C3
Kasserine B2
Kebili B3
Kef, el- B1
La Goulette C1
Mahdia C2
Menzel Bourguiba B1

Monastir C2
Nabeul C1
Nefta A3
Qayrawan, al- C2
Sfax C2
Sidi Bou Zid B2
Siliana B1
Sousse C2
Sukhayrah, as- B2
Tataouine C3
Tozeur B3
Tunis, *capital* C1
Zaghouan C1
Zarzis C3

Other Features
Atlas, *mts.* A1
Bon, *cape* C1
Carthage, *ruin* C1
Djerba, *island* C3
Djerid, *salt marsh* B3
Gabès, *gulf* C2
Galite, *island* B1
Grand Erg Oriental, *dune* ...B3
Hammamet, *gulf* C2
Kerkennah, *islands* C2
Majardah, *river* B1
Mediterranean, *sea* A1
Rharsa, *salt marsh* A2
Sahara, *desert* B4
Tabassah, *mts.* A1
Tunis, *gulf* C1

Morocco

Capital: Rabat
Area: 177,117 sq. mi.
458,852 sq. km.
Population: 28,559,000
Largest City: Casablanca
Language: Arabic
Monetary Unit: Dirham

Morocco:
Map Index

Cities and Towns
Agadir B2
Beni Mellal C1
Casablanca C1
Essaouira C1
Fez C1
Figuig D1
Hoceima, al- D1
Jadida, el- B1
Kenitra C1
Khouribga C1
Larache C1
Marrakech B2
Meknès C1
Mohammedia C1
Ouarzazate C2
Ouezzane C1
Oujda D1
Rabat, *capital* C1
Rachidia, er- C2
Safi B1
Salé C1
Settat C1

Tangier C1
Tan-Tan B2
Taroudant B2
Tata C2
Taza C1
Tétouan C1
Tiznit B2

Other Features
Anti-Atlas, *ranges* B2
Atlas, *mts.* C1
Dades, *river* C2
Drâa, *river* B2, C2
Er Rif, *range* C1
Gibraltar, *strait* C1
High Atlas, *ranges* B2
Jebel Toubkal, *mt.* B2
Mediterranean, *sea* D1
Middle Atlas, *ranges* C1
Moulouya, *river* D1
Oum er-Rbia, *river* B2
Sahara, *desert* B2
Sebou, *river* C1
Sous, *plain* B2
Sous, *river* B2

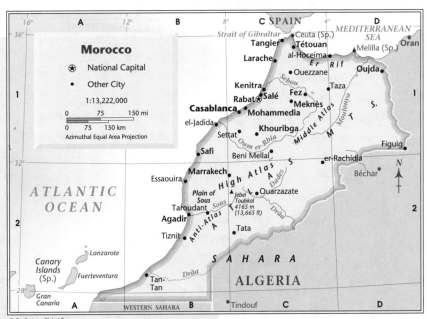

© GeoSystems Global Corp.

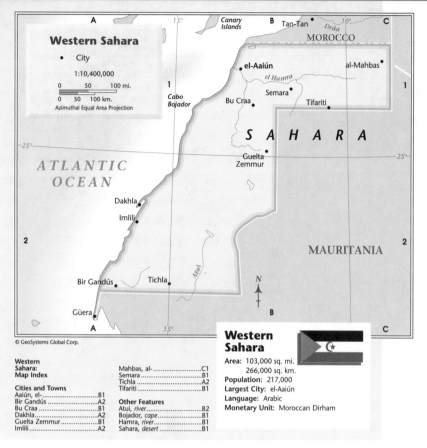

Western Sahara

- City

1:10,400,000

0   50   100 mi.
0   50   100 km.
Azimuthal Equal Area Projection

ATLANTIC OCEAN

MOROCCO

Tan-Tan

Draa

Canary Islands

el-Aaiún
al-Mahbas

el Hamra
Semara
Bu Craa
Tifariti

S A H A R A

Cabo Bojador

Guelta Zemmur

Dakhla
Imlili

MAURITANIA

Atui

Bir Gandús
Tichla

N

Güera

© GeoSystems Global Corp.

Western Sahara: Map Index

Cities and Towns
Aaiún, el- B1
Bir Gandús A2
Bu Craa B1
Dakhla A2
Guelta Zemmur B1
Imlili A2

Mahbas, al- C1
Semara B1
Tichla A2
Tifariti B1

Other Features
Atui, river B2
Bojador, cape B1
Hamra, river B1
Sahara, desert B1

Western Sahara

Area: 103,000 sq. mi.
266,000 sq. km.
Population: 217,000
Largest City: el-Aaiún
Language: Arabic
Monetary Unit: Moroccan Dirham

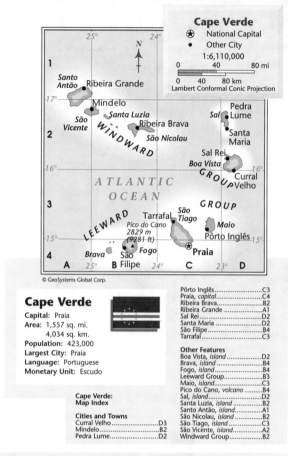

Cape Verde

- (*) National Capital
- Other City

1:6,110,000

0   40   80 mi
0   40   80 km
Lambert Conformal Conic Projection

N

Santo Antão
Ribeira Grande
Mindelo
São Vicente
Santa Luzia
Ribeira Brava
São Nicolau

Sal
Pedra Lume
Santa Maria

Sal Rei
Boa Vista
Curral Velho

WINDWARD GROUP

ATLANTIC OCEAN

GROUP

LEEWARD

Tarrafal
São Tiago
Pico do Cano 2829 m (9281 ft)
Maio
Pôrto Inglês

Brava
São Filipe
Fogo
Praia

© GeoSystems Global Corp.

Cape Verde

Capital: Praia
Area: 1,557 sq. mi.
4,034 sq. km.
Population: 423,000
Largest City: Praia
Language: Portuguese
Monetary Unit: Escudo

Cape Verde: Map Index

Cities and Towns
Curral Velho D3
Mindelo B2
Pedra Lume D2

Pôrto Inglês C3
Praia, capital C4
Ribeira Brava B2
Ribeira Grande A1
Sal Rei D2
Santa Maria D2
São Filipe B4
Tarrafal C3

Other Features
Boa Vista, island D2
Brava, island B4
Fogo, island B4
Leeward Group B3
Maio, island C3
Pico do Cano, volcano ..B4
Sal, island D2
Santa Luzia, island B2
Santo Antão, island A1
São Nicolau, island B2
São Tiago, island C3
São Vicente, island A2
Windward Group B2

Mali: Map Index

Cities and Towns
Ansongo D2
Bafoulabé A3
Bamako, capital B3
Bougouni B3
Bourem C2
Djenné C3
Gao D2
Goundam C2
Kayes A3
Kidal D2
Kita B3
Koulikoro B3
Koutiala B3
Ménaka D2
Mopti C3
Niono B3
Nioro du Sahel B2

San C3
Ségou B3
Sikasso B3
Taoudenni C1
Tessalit D1
Timbuktu C2

Other Features
Adrar des Iforas, massif D2
Azaouâd, region C2
Bani, river B3
Baoulé, river B3
Djouf, el-, desert B1
Erg Chech, desert C1
Hombori, mts. C2
Hombori Tondo, mt. C2
Niger, river B3
Sahara, desert C1
Sahel, region C2
Senegal, river A3

Mali

Capital: Bamako
Area: 482,077 sq. mi.
1,248,904 sq. km.
Population: 9,113,000
Largest City: Bamako
Language: French
Monetary Unit: Franc

Mauritania

Capital: Nouakchott
Area: 398,000 sq. mi.
1,031,088 sq. km.
Population: 2,193,000
Largest City: Nouakchott
Languages: Arabic, Wolof
Monetary Unit: Ouguiya

Mauritania

- (*) National Capital
- Other City

1:2,350,000

0   150   300 mi
0   150   300 km
Lambert Conformal Conic Projection

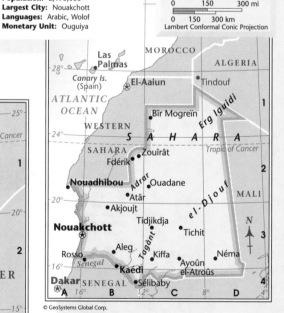

Las Palmas
MOROCCO
ALGERIA
Canary Is. (Spain)
El-Aaiun
Tindouf

ATLANTIC OCEAN

WESTERN SAHARA

S A H A R A

Erg Iguidi
Tropic of Cancer

Bîr Mogrein
Zouîrât
Fdérik
Nouadhibou
Ouadane
Atâr
Akjoujt

Adrar

MALI

el-Djouf

Nouakchott
Tidjikdja
Tichit

Rosso
Aleg
Kiffa
Tagant
Ayoûn el-Atroûs
Néma

Dakar
SENEGAL
Senegal
Kaédi
Sélibaby

© GeoSystems Global Corp.

Mauritania: Map Index

Cities and Towns
Akjoujt B3
Aleg B3
Atâr B2
Ayoûn el-Atroûs C3
Bîr Mogrein C1
Fdérik B2
Kaédi B3
Kiffa C3
Néma D3
Nouadhibou A2
Nouakchott, capital A3

Ouadane C2
Rosso B3
Sélibaby B4
Tichit C3
Tidjikdja C3
Zouîrât B2

Other Features
Adrar, region B2
Djouf, el-, desert C3
Erg Iguidi, desert D1
Sahara, desert C1
Senegal, river B3
Tagânt, region C3

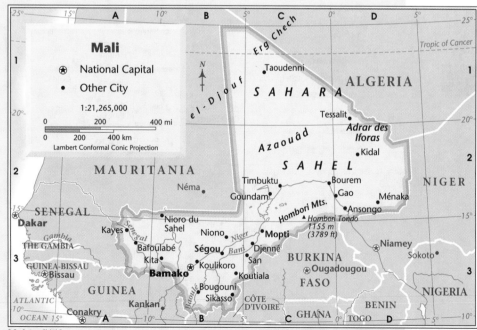

Mali

- (*) National Capital
- Other City

1:21,265,000

0   200   400 mi
0   200   400 km
Lambert Conformal Conic Projection

Tropic of Cancer

Erg Chech
el-Djouf
Taoudenni

SAHARA

ALGERIA

Tessalit

Adrar des Iforas

Azaouâd

SAHEL

Kidal

MAURITANIA

Néma

Timbuktu
Goundam
Bourem
Gao
Ménaka

NIGER

Hombori Mts.
Hombori Tondo
1155 m (3789 ft)
Ansongo

SENEGAL

Dakar

Nioro du Sahel
Niono
Mopti
Djenné
Niamey

Kayes
Senegal
Bani
Sokoto

THE GAMBIA
Gambia

Bafoulabé
Ségou
San

GUINEA-BISSAU

Bissau

Kita
Koulikoro
BURKINA FASO

Bamako
Koutiala
Ouagadougou

GUINEA

Bougouni
Sikasso

NIGERIA

Kankan

CÔTE D'IVOIRE

ATLANTIC OCEAN

Conakry

GHANA
TOGO
BENIN

© GeoSystems Global Corp.

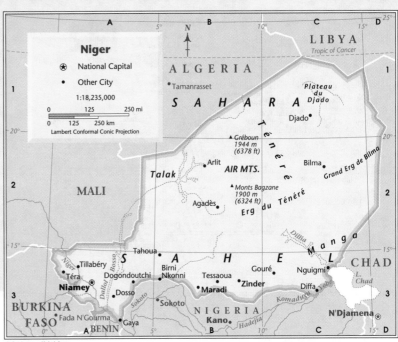

Niger

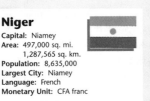

Capital: Niamey
Area: 497,000 sq. mi.
    1,287,565 sq. km.
Population: 8,635,000
Largest City: Niamey
Language: French
Monetary Unit: CFA franc

Niger:
Map Index

Cities and Towns
Agadès B2
Arlit B2
Bilma C2
Birni Nkonni B3
Diffa C3
Djado C1
Dogondoutchi A3
Dosso A3
Gaya A3
Gouré C3
Maradi B3
Nguigmi C3
Niamey, capital A3
Tahoua B3
Téra A3
Tessaoua B3
Tillabéry A3
Zinder B3

Other Features
Air, mts. B2
Bagzane, mt. B2
Chad, lake C3
Dallol Bosso, river A3
Dillia, river C2
Djado, plateau C1
Erg du Ténéré, desert B2
Grand Erg de Bilma,
    desert C2
Gréboun, mt. B1
Komadugu Yobe, river C3
Manga, region C2
Niger, river A3
Sahara, desert A1
Sahel, region A3
Talak, region B2
Ténéré, desert C1

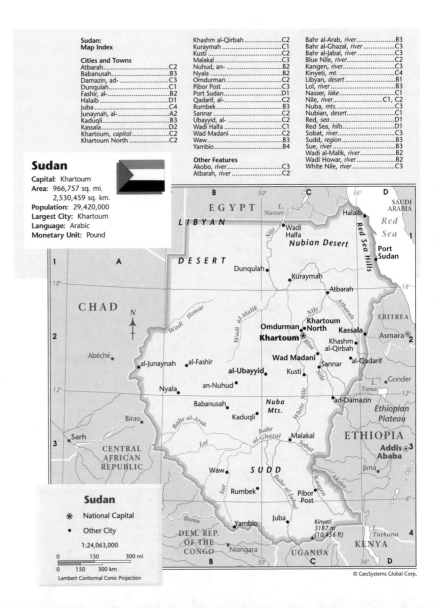

Chad

Capital: N'Djamena
Area: 495,755 sq. mi.
    1,248,339 sq. km.
Population: 5,467,000
Largest City: N'Djamena
Languages: French, Arabic
Monetary Unit: CFA franc

Chad:
Map Index

Cities and Towns
Abéché C4
Abou Deïa B5
Am Timan C5
Aozou B2
Ati B4
Bardaï B2
Berdoba C4
Biltine C4
Bol A4
Bongor A5
Bousso B5
Doba B5
Fada C3
Faya-Largeau B3
Koro Toro B4
Laï B5
Mao A4
Massenya B5
Melfi B4
Mongo B4
Moundou B5
N'Djamena, capital A4
Pala A5
Sarh B5
Zouar B2

Other Features
Bahr Salamat, river B5
Batha, river C4
Bodélé, depression B3
Chad, lake A4
Chari, river A5
Emi Koussi, mt. B3
Ennedi, plateau C3
Enneri Ke, river B3
Ghazal, river B4
Grand Erg de Bilma,
    desert A3
Logone, river A5
Ouadi Maba, river C4
Sahara, desert A2
Tibesti, massif B2

Sudan

Capital: Khartoum
Area: 966,757 sq. mi.
    2,530,459 sq. km.
Population: 29,420,000
Largest City: Khartoum
Language: Arabic
Monetary Unit: Pound

Sudan:
Map Index

Cities and Towns
Atbarah C2
Babanusah B3
Damazin, ad- C3
Dunqulah C1
Fashir, al- B2
Halaib D1
Juba C4
Junaynah, al- A2
Kaduqli B3
Kassala D2
Khartoum, capital C2
Khartoum North C2
Khashm al-Qirbah C2
Kuraymah C1
Kusti C2
Malakal C3
Nuhud, an- B2
Nyala B2
Omdurman C2
Pibor Post C3
Port Sudan D1
Qadarif, al- C2
Rumbek B3
Sannar C2
Ubayyid, al- C2
Wadi Halfa C1
Wad Madani C2
Waw B3
Yambio B4

Other Features
Akobo, river C3
Atbarah, river C2
Bahr al-Arab, river B3
Bahr al-Ghazal, river C3
Bahr al-Jabal, river C3
Blue Nile, river C2
Kangen, river C3
Kinyeti, mt. C4
Libyan, desert B1
Lol, river B3
Nasser, lake C1
Nile, river C1, C2
Nuba, mts. C3
Nubian, desert C1
Red, sea D1
Red Sea, hills D1
Sobat, river C3
Sudd, region B3
Sue, river B3
Wadi al-Malik, river B2
Wadi Howar, river B2
White Nile, river C3

© GeoSystems Global Corp.

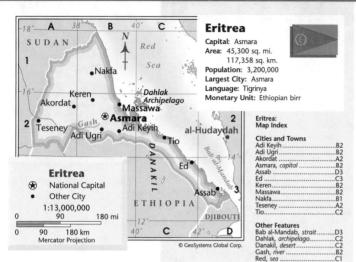

Eritrea

Capital: Asmara
Area: 45,300 sq. mi.
117,358 sq. km.
Population: 3,200,000
Largest City: Asmara
Language: Tigrinya
Monetary Unit: Ethiopian birr

Eritrea

⊛ National Capital
• Other City

1:13,000,000

0   90   180 mi
0   90   180 km
Mercator Projection

Eritrea: Map Index

Cities and Towns
Adi Keyih B2
Adi Ugri B2
Akordat A2
Asmara, capital B2
Assab D3
Ed C3
Keren B2
Massawa B2
Nakfa B1
Teseney A2
Tio C2

Other Features
Bab al-Mandab, strait....D3
Dahlak, archipelago C2
Danakil, desert C2
Gash, river B2
Red, sea C1

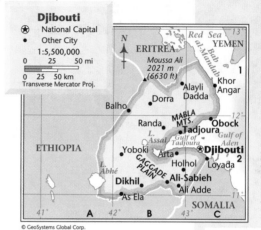

Djibouti

⊛ National Capital
• Other City

1:5,500,000

0   25   50 mi
0   25   50 km
Transverse Mercator Proj.

Djibouti: Map Index

Cities and Towns
Alayli Dadda B2
Ali Adde B2
Ali-Sabieh B2
Arta B2
As Ela B1
Balho B1
Dikhil B2
Djibouti, capital C2
Dorra B1
Holhol B2
Khor Angar C1
Loyada C2
Obock C2
Randa B2
Tadjoura B2
Yoboki B2

Other Features
Abhé, lake A2
Aden, gulf C2
Assal, lake B2
Bab al-Mandab, strait...C1
Gaggade, plain B2
Mabla, mts. B2
Moussa Ali, mt. B1
Red, sea C1
Tadjoura, gulf...............B2

Djibouti

Capital: Djibouti
Area: 8,950 sq. mi.
23,187 sq. km.
Population: 413,000
Largest City: Djibouti
Languages: Cushitic languages
Monetary Unit: Franc

Ethiopia

⊛ National Capital
• Other City

1:15,053,000

0   100   200 mi
0   100   200 km
Lambert Conformal Conic Projection

© GeoSystems Global Corp.

Ethiopia

Capital: Addis Ababa
Area: 437,794 sq. mi.
1,134,181 sq. km.
Population: 58,710,000
Largest City: Addis Ababa
Language: Amharic
Monetary Unit: Birr

Ethiopia: Map Index

Cities and Towns
Addis Ababa, capital C2
Adwa C1
Arba Minch B3
Asela C2
Asosa B2
Awasa C3
Bahir Dar B2
Debre Birhan C2
Debre Markos C2
Degeh Bur D2
Dese C2
Dire Dawa D2
Goba C3
Gonder B1
Gore B2

Harer D2
Imi D3
Jima B3
Mekele C1
Nazret C2
Negele C3
Nekemte B2
Shewa Gimira B3
Weldiya C2
Werder D3

Other Features
Abaya, lake B3
Abhe, lake C2
Akobo, river A3
Atbara, river B1
Awash, river C2
Baro, river B2
Blue Nile, river B2

Choke, mts. B2
Dawa, river C3
Denakil, desert C1
Dinder, river B1
Ethiopian, plateau C2
Genale, river C3
Great Rift, valley C3
Ogaden, region D3
Omo, river B3
Provisional
   Administrative Line ...D1
Ras Dashen, mt. C1
Tana, lake B1
Tekeze, river B1
Turkana, lake B3
Wabe Gestro, river C3
Wabe Shebele, river C3
Ziway, lake C3

Somalia: Map Index

Cities and Towns
Baraawe A3
Baydhabo A3
Beledweyne B3
Benderbeyla C2
Berbera B1
Boosaaso B1

Burco B2
Ceerigaabo B1
Dhuusamareeb B2
Eyl B2
Gaalkacyo B2
Garoowe B2
Hargeysa A2
Hobyo B2
Jamaame A3
Jawhar B3
Jilib A3
Kismayu A3
Luuq A3
Marka A3
Mogadishu, capital B3
Qardho A3
Xuddur A3

Other Features
Aden, gulf B1
Gees Gwardafuy, cape C1
Juba, river A3
Nugaal, valley B2
Raas Xaafun, cape C1
Surud Ad, mt. B1
Webi Shabeelle, river B3

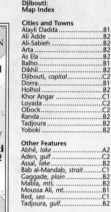

Somalia

Capital: Mogadishu
Area: 246,300 sq. mi.
638,083 sq. km.
Population: 6,667,000
Largest City: Mogadishu
Language: Somali, Arabic
Monetary Unit: Shilling

Somalia

⊛ National Capital
• Other City

1:22,100,000

0   150   300 mi
0   150   300 km
Miller Cylindrical Projection

© GeoSystems Global Corp.

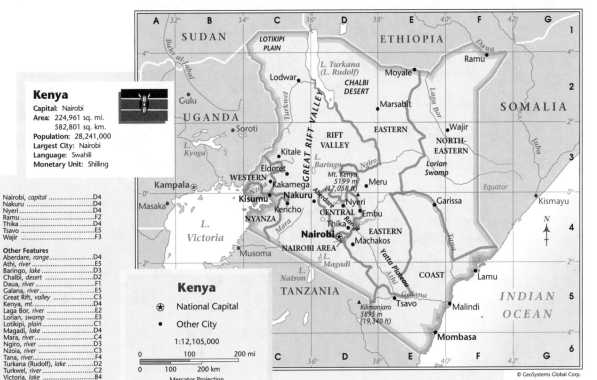

Kenya

Capital: Nairobi
Area: 224,961 sq. mi.
582,801 sq. km.
Population: 28,241,000
Largest City: Nairobi
Language: Swahili
Monetary Unit: Shilling

Kenya:
Map Index

Provinces
Central D4
Coast E5
Eastern E3
Nairobi Area D4
North-Eastern F3
Nyanza C4
Rift Valley D3
Western C3

Cities and Towns
Eldoret C3
Embu D4
Garissa E4
Kakamega C3
Kericho C4
Kisumu C4
Kitale C3
Lamu F5
Lodwar C2
Machakos D4
Malindi F5
Marsabit E2
Meru D3
Mombasa E5
Moyale E2

Nairobi, *capital* D4
Nakuru D4
Nyeri D4
Ramu F2
Thika D4
Tsavo E5
Wajir F3

Other Features
Aberdare, *range* D4
Athi, *river* E5
Baringo, *lake* D3
Chalbi, *desert* D2
Daua, *river* F1
Galana, *river* E5
Great Rift, *valley* C3
Kenya, *mt.* D4
Laga Bor, *river* E2
Lorian, *swamp* E3
Lotikipi, *plain* C1
Magadi, *lake* D4
Mara, *river* C5
Ngiro, *river* D3
Nzoia, *river* C3
Tana, *river* F4
Turkana (Rudolf), *lake* D2
Turkwel, *river* C2
Victoria, *lake* B4
Yatta, *plateau* E5

Kenya

⊛ National Capital
• Other City

1:12,105,000

0 — 100 — 200 mi
0 — 100 — 200 km
Mercator Projection

© GeoSystems Global Corp.

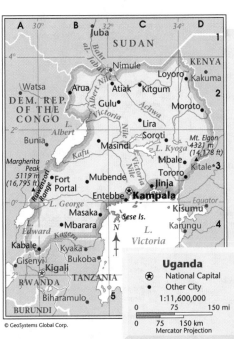

Uganda

Capital: Kampala
Area: 93,070 sq. mi.
241,114 sq. km.
Population: 19,859,000
Largest City: Kampala
Language: English
Monetary Unit: Shilling

Uganda:
Map Index

Cities and Towns
Arua B2
Atiak C2
Entebbe C3
Fort Portal B3
Gulu C2
Jinja C3
Kabale A4
Kampala, *capital* C3
Kitgum C2
Lira C2
Loyoro D2
Masaka B4
Masindi B3
Mbale D3
Mbarara B4
Moroto D2

Mubende B3
Soroti C3
Tororo D3

Other Features
Achwa, *river* C2
Albert, *lake* B3
Albert Nile, *river* B2
Bahr al-Jabal, *river* B2
Edward, *lake* A4
Elgon, *mt.* D3
George, *lake* B4
Kafu, *river* B3
Kagera, *river* B4
Kyoga, *lake* C3
Margherita, *peak* A3
Ruwenzori, *range* B3
Sese, *islands* C4
Victoria, *lake* C4
Victoria Nile, *river* B2,C3

Uganda

⊛ National Capital
• Other City

1:11,600,000

0 — 75 — 150 mi
0 — 75 — 150 km
Mercator Projection

© GeoSystems Global Corp.

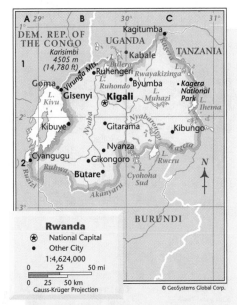

Rwanda

⊛ National Capital
• Other City

1:4,624,000

0 — 25 — 50 mi
0 — 25 — 50 km
Gauss-Krüger Projection

© GeoSystems Global Corp.

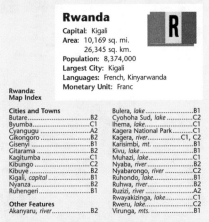

Rwanda

Capital: Kigali
Area: 10,169 sq. mi.
26,345 sq. km.
Population: 8,374,000
Largest City: Kigali
Languages: French, Kinyarwanda
Monetary Unit: Franc

Rwanda:
Map Index

Cities and Towns
Butare B2
Byumba C1
Cyangugu A2
Gikongoro B2
Gisenyi B1
Gitarama B2
Kagitumba C1
Kibungo C2
Kibuye B1
Kigali, *capital* B1
Nyanza B2
Ruhengeri B1

Bulera, *lake* B1
Cyohoha Sud, *lake* C2
Ihema, *lake* C2
Kagera National Park C1
Kagera, *river* C1, C2
Karisimbi, *mt.* B1
Kivu, *lake* B1
Muhazi, *lake* C1
Nyaba, *river* B2
Nyabarongo, *river* B2
Ruhondo, *lake* B1
Ruhwa, *river* A2
Ruzizi, *river* A2
Rwayakizinga, *lake* C1
Rweru, *lake* C2
Virunga, *mts.* B1

Other Features
Akanyaru, *river* B2

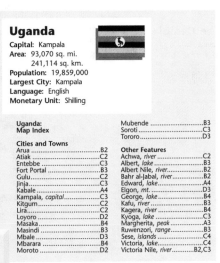

Burundi

⊛ National Capital
• Other City

1:6,548,000

0 — 50 — 100 mi
0 — 50 — 100 km
Conic Equidistant Projection

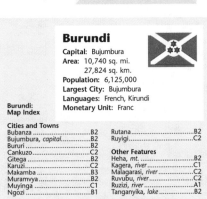

Burundi

Capital: Bujumbura
Area: 10,740 sq. mi.
27,824 sq. km.
Population: 6,125,000
Largest City: Bujumbura
Languages: French, Kirundi
Monetary Unit: Franc

Burundi:
Map Index

Cities and Towns
Bubanza B2
Bujumbura, *capital* B2
Bururi B2
Cankuzo C2
Gitega B2
Karuzi B2
Makamba B3
Muramvya B2
Muyinga C1
Ngozi B1

Rutana B2
Ruyigi C2

Other Features
Heha, *mt.* B2
Kagera, *river* C1
Malagarasi, *river* C2
Ruvubu, *river* C2
Ruzizi, *river* A1
Tanganyika, *lake* B2

© GeoSystems Global Corp.

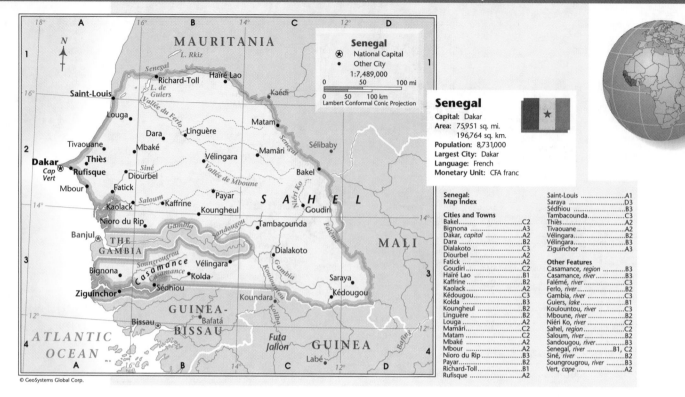

© GeoSystems Global Corp.

Senegal

Capital: Dakar
Area: 75,951 sq. mi.
196,764 sq. km.
Population: 8,731,000
Largest City: Dakar
Language: French
Monetary Unit: CFA franc

Senegal: Map Index

Cities and Towns

Bakel	C2
Bignona	A3
Dakar, *capital*	A2
Dara	B2
Dialakoto	C3
Diourbel	A2
Fatick	A2
Goudiri	C2
Hairé Lao	B1
Kaffrine	B2
Kaolack	A2
Kédougou	C3
Kolda	B3
Koungheul	B2
Linguère	B2
Louga	A2
Mamâri	C2
Matam	C2
Mbaké	A2
Mbour	A2
Nioro du Rip	B3
Payar	B2
Richard-Toll	B1
Rufisque	A2
Saint-Louis	A1
Saraya	D3
Sédhiou	B3
Tambacounda	C3
Thiès	A2
Tivaouane	A2
Vélingara	A2
Vélingara	B2
Ziguinchor	A3

Other Features

Casamance, *region*	B3
Casamance, *river*	B3
Falémé, *river*	C3
Ferlo, *river*	B2
Gambia, *river*	C3
Guiers, *lake*	B1
Kouloutou, *river*	C3
Mboune, *river*	B2
Niéri Ko, *river*	C2
Sahel, *region*	C2
Saloum, *river*	B2
Sandougou, *river*	B3
Senegal, *river*	B1, C2
Siné, *river*	B2
Songrougrou, *river*	B3
Vert, *cape*	A2

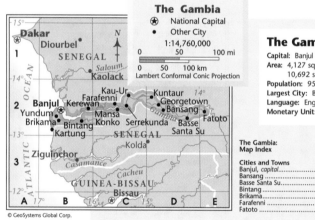

The Gambia

Capital: Banjul
Area: 4,127 sq. mi.
10,692 sq. km.
Population: 959,000
Largest City: Banjul
Language: English
Monetary Unit: Dalasi

The Gambia: Map Index

Cities and Towns

Banjul, *capital*	B2
Bansang	D2
Basse Santa Su	D2
Bintang	B2
Brikama	B2
Farafenni	C2
Fatoto	E2
Georgetown	D2
Kartung	B2
Kau-Ur	C2
Kerewan	C2
Kuntaur	D2
Mansa Konko	C2
Serrekunda	C2
Yundum	B2

Other Feature

Gambia, *river*	D2

© GeoSystems Global Corp.

© GeoSystems Global Corp.

Guinea-Bissau

Capital: Bissau
Area: 13,948 sq. mi.
36,135 sq. km.
Population: 1,098,000
Largest City: Bissau
Language: Portuguese
Monetary Unit: Peso

Guinea-Bissau: Map Index

Cities and Towns

Bafatá	C1
Bambadinca	C1
Barro	B1
Bissau, *capital*	B2
Bissorã	B1
Bolama	B2
Bubo	C2
Bubaque	B2
Bula	B1
Cacheu	A1
Cacine	B2
Canchungo	A1
Catió	B2
Farim	B1
Fulacunda	B2
Gabú	C1
Ondame	B2
Pirada	C1
Quebo	C2
Quinhámel	B2
São Domingos	A1

Other Features

Bijagós, *islands*	A2
Cacheu, *river*	B1
Corubal, *river*	D1
Gêba, *river*	C1

Guinea: Map Index

Cities and Towns

Beyla	D3
Conakry, *capital*	B3
Coyah	B3
Dabola	C2
Fria	B2
Guéckédou	C3
Kailahun	C3
Kali	C1
Kamsar	A2
Kankan	D2
Kérouané	D3
Kindia	B2
Kissidougou	C3
Kouroussa	B2
Labé	B2
Lélouma	B2
Macenta	D3
Mamou	B2
Niagassola	D1
Nzérékoré	D4
Siguiri	D2
Tougué	C2
Yomou	D4

Other Features

Bafing, *river*	C2
Futa Jallon, *plateau*	B1
Gambia, *river*	B2
Los, *islands*	A3
Milo, *river*	D3
Niger, *river*	D2
Nimba, *mts.*	D4
Tinkissa, *river*	C2

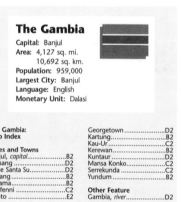

Guinea

Capital: Conakry
Area: 94,926 sq. mi.
245,922 sq. km.
Population: 6,392,000
Largest City: Conakry
Language: French
Monetary Unit: Guinea franc

© GeoSystems Global Corp.

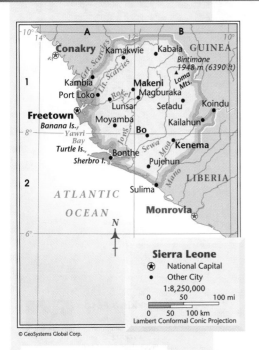

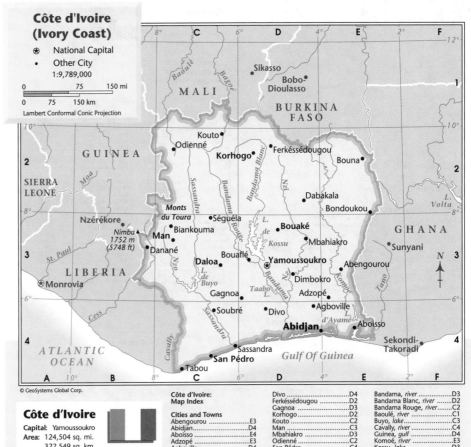

Sierra Leone

National Capital
Other City
1:8,250,000
0   50   100 mi
0   50   100 km
Lambert Conformal Conic Projection

© GeoSystems Global Corp.

Côte d'Ivoire (Ivory Coast)

National Capital
Other City
1:9,789,000
0   75   150 mi
0   75   150 km
Lambert Conformal Conic Projection

© GeoSystems Global Corp.

Sierra Leone

Capital: Freetown
Area: 27,699 sq. mi.
  71,759 sq. km.
Population: 4,630,000
Largest City: Freetown
Language: English
Monetary Unit: Leone

Sierra Leone:
Map Index

Cities and Towns
Bo B2
Bonthe A2
Freetown, *capital* A1
Kabala B1
Kailahun B1
Kamakwie A1
Kambia A1
Kenema B2
Koindu B1
Lunsar A1
Magburaka B1
Makeni B1
Moyamba A1
Port Loko A1

Pujehun B2
Sefadu B1
Sulima B2

Other Features
Banana, *islands* A1
Bintimane, *mt.* B1
Great Scarcies, *river* ...A1
Jong, *river* A2
Little Scarcies, *river* ...A1
Loma, *mts.* B1
Mano, *river* B2
Moa, *river* B2
Rokel, *river* A1
Sewa, *river* B2
Sherbro, *island* A2
Turtle, *islands* A2
Yawri, *bay* A2

Côte d'Ivoire

Capital: Yamoussoukro
Area: 124,504 sq. mi.
  322,549 sq. km.
Population: 14,296,000
Largest City: Abidjan
Language: French
Monetary Unit: CFA franc

Côte d'Ivoire:
Map Index

Cities and Towns
Abengourou E3
Abidjan D4
Aboisso E4
Adzopé E3
Agboville D4
Biankouma C3
Bondoukou E2
Bouaflé D3
Bouaké D3
Bouna E2
Dabakala D2
Daloa C3
Danané B3
Dimbokro D3

Divo D4
Ferkéssédougou D2
Gagnoa D3
Korhogo D2
Kouto C2
Man C3
Mbahiakro D3
Odienné C2
San Pédro C4
Sassandra C4
Séguéla C3
Soubré C3
Tabou C4
Yamoussoukro, *capital* ...D3

Other Features
Ayamé, *lake* E4
Bagoé, *river* C1

Bandama, *river* D3
Bandama Blanc, *river* ...D2
Bandama Rouge, *river* ...C2
Baoulé, *river* C1
Buyo, *lake* C3
Cavally, *river* C4
Guinea, *gulf* D4
Komoé, *river* E3
Kossu, *lake* D3
Nimba, *mt.* B3
Nzi, *river* D3
Nzo, *river* C3
Sassandra, *river* C2, C4
Taabo, *lake* D3
Tano, *river* E3
Toura, *mts.* C2

Liberia

Capital: Monrovia
Area: 38,250 sq. mi.
  99,093 sq. km.
Population: 2,973,000
Largest City: Monrovia
Language: English
Monetary Unit: U.S. dollar

Liberia:
Map Index

Cities and Towns
Buchanan A3
Gbarnga B2
Grand Cess B3
Greenville B3
Harbel A2
Harper C3
Kakata A2
Monrovia, *capital* A2
Nyaake C3
Plibo C3
River Cess B3
Robertsport A2
Tapeta B2
Tubmanburg A2
Voinjama B1
Yekepa B2
Zorzor B2
Zwedru B2

Other Features
Bomi, *hills* A2
Bong, *range* A2
Cavalla, *river* C3
Cess, *river* B3
Dube, *river* C3
Makona, *river* A1
Mano, *river* A2
Mesurado, *cape* A2
Moro, *river* A2
Nimba, *mts.* B2
Palmas, *cape* C3
Putu, *range* B3
St. Paul, *river* B1
Wutivi, *mt.* B1

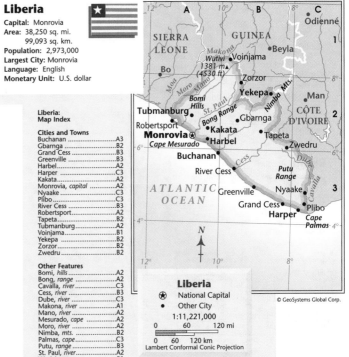

Liberia

National Capital
Other City
1:11,221,000
0   60   120 mi
0   60   120 km
Lambert Conformal Conic Projection

© GeoSystems Global Corp.

São Tomé & Príncipe

Capital: São Tomé
Area: 386 sq. mi.
  1,000 sq. km.
Population: 137,000
Largest City: São Tomé
Language: Portuguese
Monetary Unit: Dobra

São Tomé & Príncipe:
Map Index

Cities and Towns
Jou B4
Neves B4
Porto Alegre B4
São Tomé, *capital* B4
Sundi C1
Terreiro Velho C1

Other Features
Príncipe, *island* C1
São Tomé, *island* B4
São Tomé, *mt.* B4

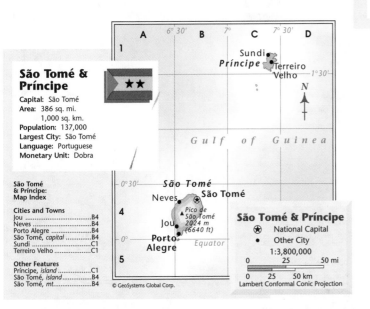

São Tomé & Príncipe

National Capital
Other City
1:3,800,000
0   25   50 mi
0   25   50 km
Lambert Conformal Conic Projection

© GeoSystems Global Corp.

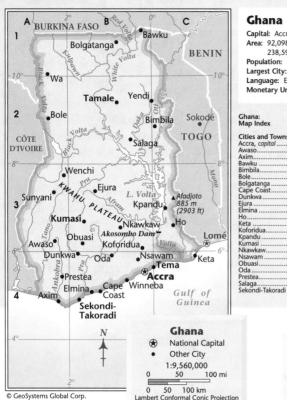

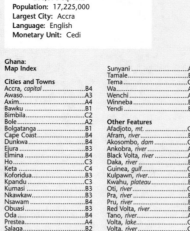

Ghana

Capital: Accra
Area: 92,098 sq. mi.
238,596 sq. km.
Population: 17,225,000
Largest City: Accra
Language: English
Monetary Unit: Cedi

Ghana:
Map Index

Cities and Towns
Accra, *capital*	B4
Awaso	A3
Axim	A4
Bawku	B1
Bimbila	C2
Bole	A2
Bolgatanga	B1
Cape Coast	B4
Dunkwa	B4
Ejura	B3
Elmina	B4
Ho	C3
Keta	C4
Koforidua	B3
Kpandu	C3
Kumasi	B3
Nkawkaw	B3
Nsawam	B3
Obuasi	B3
Oda	B3
Prestea	A4
Salaga	B2
Sekondi-Takoradi	B4
Sunyani	A3
Tamale	B2
Tema	C4
Wa	A1
Wenchi	A3
Winneba	B4
Yendi	B2

Other Features
Afadjoto, *mt.*	C3
Afram, *river*	B3
Akosombo, *dam*	C3
Ankobra, *river*	A4
Black Volta, *river*	A2
Daka, *river*	B2
Guinea, *gulf*	C4
Kulpawn, *river*	B1
Kwahu, *plateau*	B3
Oti, *river*	C2
Pra, *river*	B4
Pru, *river*	B3
Red Volta, *river*	B1
Tano, *river*	A3
Volta, *lake*	C3
Volta, *river*	C3
White Volta, *river*	B1

Ghana
⊛ National Capital
• Other City
1:9,560,000
0   50   100 mi
0   50   100 km
Lambert Conformal Conic Projection

© GeoSystems Global Corp.

Burkina Faso

Capital: Ouagadougou
Area: 105,946 sq. mi.
274,472 sq. km.
Population: 10,135,000
Largest City: Ouagadougou
Language: French
Monetary Unit: CFA franc

Burkina Faso:
Map Index

Cities and Towns
Bobo-Dioulasso	B3
Dédougou	C2
Dori	D1
Gaoua	C3
Koudougou	C2
Léo	C3
Ouagadougou, *capital*	D2
Ouahigouya	D2
Tenkodogo	D3

Other Features
Black Volta, *river*	B3
Red Volta, *river*	D3
Sirba, *river*	D1
Téna Kourou, *mt.*	B3
White Volta, *river*	D2

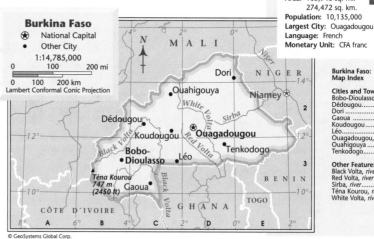

Burkina Faso
⊛ National Capital
• Other City
1:14,785,000
0   100   200 mi
0   100   200 km
Lambert Conformal Conic Projection

© GeoSystems Global Corp.

Benin
⊛ National Capital
• Other City
1:14,800,000
0   100   200 mi
0   100   200 km
Lambert Conformal Conic Projection

© GeoSystems Global Corp.

Benin

Capital: Porto-Novo
Area: 43,500 sq. mi.
112,694 sq. km.
Population: 5,342,000
Largest City: Cotonou
Language: French
Monetary Unit: CFA franc

Benin:
Map Index

Cities and Towns
Abomey	A4
Bassila	A3
Cotonou	B4
Djougou	A3
Kandi	B2
Lokossa	A4
Malanville	B2
Natitingou	A2
Nikki	B3
Ouidah	B4
Parakou	B3
Pobé	B4
Porto-Novo, *capital*	B4
Savalou	A3
Savé	B3
Segbana	B2
Tchaourou	B3

Other Features
Alibori, *river*	B2
Chaîne de l'Atacora, *mts.*	A2
Couffo, *river*	B4
Guinea, *gulf*	A4
Mékrou, *river*	B2
Mono, *river*	A4
Niger, *river*	B1
Ouémé, *river*	B3
Sota, *river*	B2

Togo

Capital: Lomé
Area: 21,925 sq. mi.
56,801 sq. km.
Population: 4,255,000
Largest City: Lomé
Language: French
Monetary Unit: CFA franc

Togo:
Map Index

Cities and Towns
Amlamé	B3
Aného	B3
Anié	B3
Atakpamé	B3
Badou	B3
Bafilo	B2
Bassar	B2
Blitta	B2
Dapaong	B1
Kanté	B2
Kara	B2
Kpalimé	B3
Kpémé	B3
Lomé, *capital*	B3
Mango	B1
Niamtougou	B2
Sokodé	B2
Sotouboua	B2
Tabligbo	B3
Tchamba	B2
Tsévié	B3

Other Features
Agou, *mt.*	B3
Benin, *bight*	B4
Mono, *river*	B2
Oti, *river*	B1

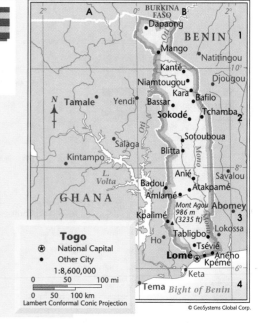

Togo
⊛ National Capital
• Other City
1:8,600,000
0   50   100 mi
0   50   100 km
Lambert Conformal Conic Projection

© GeoSystems Global Corp.

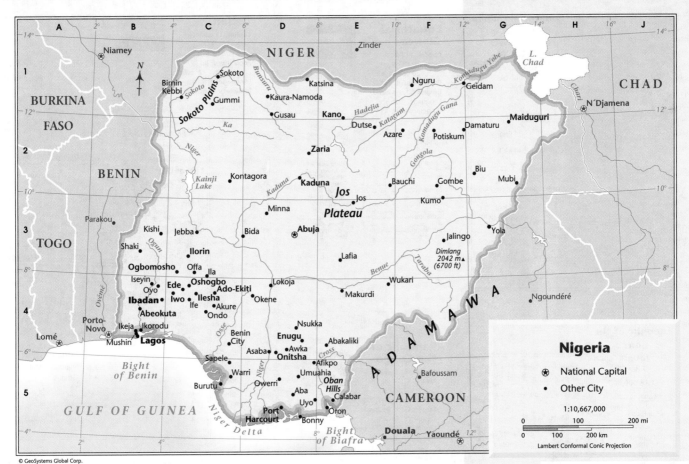

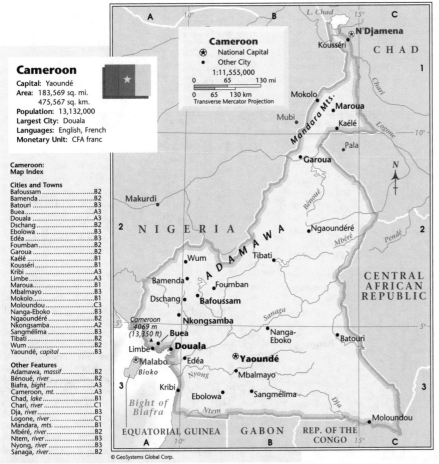

Nigeria

⊛ National Capital

• Other City

1:10,667,000

| 0 | 100 | 200 mi |
| 0 | 100 | 200 km |

Lambert Conformal Conic Projection

© GeoSystems Global Corp.

Nigeria
Capital: Abuja
Area: 356,669 sq. mi.
924,013 sq. km.
Population: 98,091,000
Largest City: Lagos
Language: English
Monetary Unit: Naira

Cameroon
Capital: Yaoundé
Area: 183,569 sq. mi.
475,567 sq. km.
Population: 13,132,000
Languages: English, French
Monetary Unit: CFA franc

Cameroon:
Map Index

Cities and Towns
Bafoussam B2
Bamenda B2
Batouri B3
Buea A3
Douala B2
Dschang B2
Ebolowa B3
Edéa B2
Foumban B2
Garoua B2
Kaélé B1
Kousséri B1
Kribi A3
Limbe A3
Maroua B1
Mbalmayo B3
Mokolo B1
Moloundou C3
Nanga-Eboko B3
Ngaoundéré B2
Nkongsamba A2
Sangmélima B3
Tibati B2
Wum B2
Yaoundé, *capital* B3

Other Features
Adamawa, *massif* B2
Bénoué, *river* B2
Biafra, *bight* A3
Cameroon, *mt.* A3
Chad, *lake* B1
Chari, *river* C1
Dja, *river* B3
Logone, *river* C1
Mandara, *mts.* B1
Mbéré, *river* B2
Ntem, *river* B3
Nyong, *river* B3
Sanaga, *river* B2

Cameroon
⊛ National Capital
• Other City
1:11,555,000
| 0 | 65 | 130 mi |
| 0 | 65 | 130 km |
Transverse Mercator Projection

© GeoSystems Global Corp.

Nigeria:
Map Index

Cities and Towns
Aba D5
Abakaliki E4
Abeokuta B4
Abuja, *capital* D3
Ado-Ekiti C4
Afikpo D5
Akure C4
Asaba D4
Awka D4
Azare F2
Bauchi E2
Benin City C4
Bida D3
Birnin Kebbi C1
Biu G2
Bonny D5
Burutu C5
Calabar E5
Damaturu F2
Dutse E2
Ede C4
Enugu D4
Geidam F1
Gombe F2
Gummi C1
Gusau D1
Ibadan B4
Ife C4
Ikeja B4
Ikorodu B4
Ila C3
Ilesha C4
Ilorin C3
Iseyin C4
Iwo C4
Jalingo F3
Jebba C3
Jos E3
Kaduna D2
Kano E1
Katsina D1
Kaura-Namoda D1
Kishi B3
Kontagora C2
Kumo F2
Lafia E3
Lagos B4
Lokoja D4
Maiduguri G2

Makurdi E4
Minna D3
Mubi G2
Mushin B4
Nguru F1
Nsukka D4
Offa C3
Ogbomosho C3
Okene D4
Ondo C4
Onitsha D4
Oron E5
Oshogbo C4
Owerri D5
Oyo B4
Port Harcourt D5
Potiskum F2
Sapele C5
Shaki B3
Sokoto C1
Umuahia D5
Uyo D5
Warri C5
Wukari E4
Yola G3
Zaria D2

Other Features
Adamawa, *massif* E5
Benin, *bight* B5
Benue, *river* E3
Bunsuru, *river* D1
Chad, *lake* G1
Cross, *river* E4
Dimlang, *mt.* F3
Gongola, *river* F2
Guinea, *gulf* B5
Hadejia, *river* E1
Jos, *plateau* E2
Ka, *river* C2
Kaduna, *river* D2
Kainji, *lake* C2
Katagum, *river* F2
Komadugu Gana, *river* F2
Komadugu Yobe, *river* F1
Niger, *delta* C5
Niger, *river* C2, D5
Oban, *hills* E5
Ogun, *river* B3
Osse, *river* C4
Sokoto, *plains* C1
Sokoto, *river* C1
Taraba, *river* F3

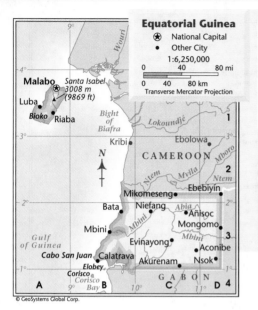

Equatorial Guinea

⊛ National Capital
• Other City

1:6,250,000

0   40   80 mi
0   40   80 km
Transverse Mercator Projection

© GeoSystems Global Corp.

Equatorial Guinea

Capital: Malabo
Area: 10,831 sq. mi.
28,060 sq. km.
Population: 410,000
Largest City: Malabo
Language: Spanish
Monetary Unit: CFA franc

Equatorial Guinea:
Map Index

Cities and Towns
Aconibe	C3
Akurenam	C3
Añisoc	C3
Bata	B3
Calatrava	B3
Ebebiyín	C3
Evinayong	C3
Luba	A1
Malabo, *capital*	A1
Mbini	B3
Mikomeseng	C2
Mongomo	D3

Niefang	C3
Nsok	D3
Riaba	A1

Other Features
Abia, *river*	C3
Biafra, *bight*	B1
Bioko, *island*	A1
Corisco, *bay*	B4
Corisco, *island*	B4
Elobey, *islands*	B3
Guinea, *gulf*	A3
Mbini, *river*	C3
Mboro, *river*	D4
San Juan, *cape*	B3
Santa Isabel, *peak*	A1

Gabon

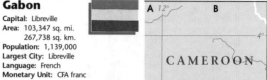

Capital: Libreville
Area: 103,347 sq. mi.
267,738 sq. km.
Population: 1,139,000
Largest City: Libreville
Language: French
Monetary Unit: CFA franc

Gabon

⊛ National Capital
• Other City

1:11,850,000

0   75   150 mi
0   75   150 km
Azimuthal Equal Area Projection

© GeoSystems Global Corp.

Gabon:
Map Index

Cities and Towns
Bélinga	B1
Bitam	A1
Booué	A2
Franceville	B2
Koula-Moutou	B2
Lambaréné	A2
Libreville, *capital*	A1
Makokou	B1
Mayumba	A2
Mékambo	B1
Mitzic	A1
Moanda	B2
Mouila	A2
Ndendé	A2
Ndjolé	A2

Okondja	B2
Omboué	A2
Owendo	A1
Oyem	A1
Port-Gentil	A2
Tchibanga	A2

Other Features
Chaillu, *mts.*	B2
Cristal, *mts.*	A1
Djouah, *river*	B1
Iboundji, *mt.*	A2
Ivindo, *river*	B1
Lopez, *cape*	A2
Ndogo, *lagoon*	A2
Ngounié, *river*	A2
Nyanga, *river*	A2
Ogooué, *river*	A2

Republic of the Congo

⊛ National Capital
• Other City

1:18,000,000

0   100   200 mi
0   100   200 km
Azimuthal Equal Area Projection

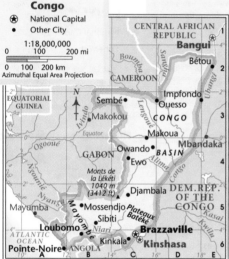

© GeoSystems Global Corp.

Republic of the Congo

Capital: Brazzaville
Area: 132,047 sq. mi.
342,091 sq. km.
Population: 2,447,000
Largest City: Brazzaville
Language: French
Monetary Unit: CFA franc

Republic of the Congo:
Map Index

Cities and Towns
Bétou	E2
Brazzaville, *capital*	C6
Djambala	C5
Ewo	C4
Impfondo	D3
Kinkala	C6
Loubomo	B6
Makoua	C4
Mossendjo	B5
Ouesso	D3
Owando	C4
Pointe-Noire	A6

Sembé	C3
Sibiti	B5

Other Features
Alima, *river*	D4
Batéké, *plateau*	C5
Congo, *basin*	D3
Congo, *river*	D4
Ivindo, *river*	B3
Lékéti, *mts.*	C5
Lengoué, *river*	C3
Mayombé, *massif*	B5
Niari, *river*	B5
Nyanga, *river*	A5
Sangha, *river*	D2
Ubangi, *river*	E2

Central African Republic (C.A.R.)

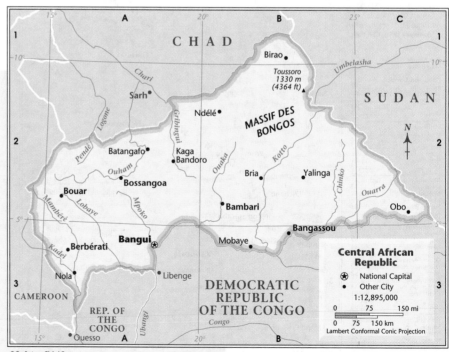

© GeoSystems Global Corp.

Capital: Bangui
Area: 240,324 sq. mi.
622,601 sq. km.
Population: 3,142,000
Largest City: Bangui
Language: French
Monetary Unit: CFA franc

Central African Republic

⊛ National Capital
• Other City

1:12,895,000

0   75   150 mi
0   75   150 km
Lambert Conformal Conic Projection

Central African Republic:
Map Index

Cities and Towns
Bambari	B2
Bangassou	B3
Bangui, *capital*	A3
Batangafo	A2
Berbérati	A3
Birao	B1
Bossangoa	A2
Bouar	A2
Bria	B2
Kaga Bandoro	A2
Mobaye	B3
Ndélé	B2
Nola	A3
Obo	C2
Yalinga	B2

Other Features
Chari, *river*	A2
Chinko, *river*	B2
Gribingui, *river*	A2
Kadei, *river*	A3
Kotto, *river*	B2
Lobaye, *river*	A2
Mambéré, *river*	A2
Massif des Bongos, *range*	B2
Mpoko, *river*	A2
Ouaka, *river*	B2
Ouarra, *river*	C2
Ouham, *river*	A2
Pendé, *river*	A2
Toussoro, *mt.*	B2
Ubangi, *river*	A3

Democratic Republic of the Congo

Capital: Kinshasa
Area: 905,446 sq. mi.
2,345,715 sq. km.
Population: 42,684,000
Largest City: Kinshasa
Language: French
Monetary Unit: New Zaire

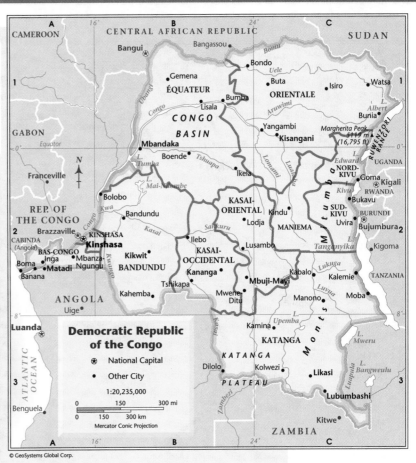

Democratic Republic of the Congo

⊛ National Capital

● Other City

1:20,235,000

0   150   300 mi
0   150   300 km
Mercator Conic Projection

© GeoSystems Global Corp.

Democratic Republic of the Congo: Map Index

Regions

Bandundu	B2
Bas-Congo	A2
Équateur	B1
Kasai-Occidental	B2
Kasai-Oriental	B2
Katanga	C3
Kinshasa	B2
Maniema	C2
Nord-Kivu	C2
Orientale	C1
Sud-Kivu	C2

Cities and Towns

Banana	A2
Bandundu	B2
Boende	B2
Bolobo	A2
Boma	A2
Bondo	B1
Bukavu	C2
Bumba	B1
Bunia	C1
Buta	C1
Dilolo	B3
Gemena	B1
Goma	C2
Ikela	B2
Ilebo	B2
Inga	A2
Isiro	C1
Kabalo	C2
Kahemba	B2
Kalemie	C2
Kamina	C3
Kananga	B2
Kikwit	B2
Kindu	C2
Kinshasa, *capital*	A2
Kisangani	C1
Kolwezi	C3
Likasi	C3
Lisala	B1
Lodja	B2
Lubumbashi	C3
Lusambo	B2
Manono	C2
Matadi	A2
Mbandaka	B2
Mbanza-Ngungu	A2
Mbuji-Mayi	B2
Moba	C2
Mwene-Ditu	B2
Tshikapa	B2
Uvira	C2
Watsa	C1
Yangambi	C1

Other Features

Albert, *lake*	C1
Aruwimi, *river*	C1
Bomu, *river*	C1
Congo, *river*	B1
Congo Basin, *region*	B1
Edward, *lake*	C2
Kasai, *river*	B2
Katanga, *plateau*	B3
Kivu, *lake*	C2
Kwa, *river*	B2
Kwango, *river*	B2
Lomami, *river*	C2
Lualaba, *river*	C2
Luapula, *river*	C3
Lukuga, *river*	C2
Luvua, *river*	C2
Mai-Ndombe, *lake*	B2
Margherita, *peak*	C1
Mitumba, *mts.*	C2
Mweru, *lake*	C3
Sankuru, *river*	B2
Tanganyika, *lake*	C2
Tshuapa, *river*	B2
Tumba, *lake*	B2
Ubangi, *river*	B1
Uele, *river*	C1
Upemba, *lake*	C3

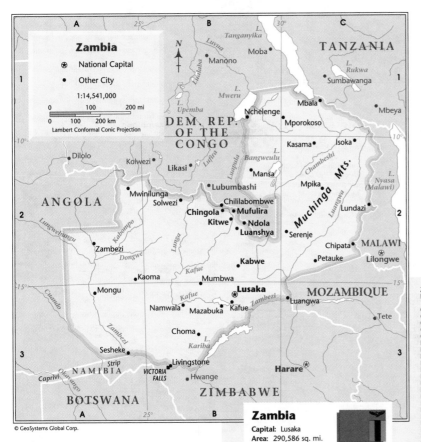

Zambia

⊛ National Capital

● Other City

1:14,541,000

0   100   200 mi
0   100   200 km
Lambert Conformal Conic Projection

© GeoSystems Global Corp.

Zambia

Capital: Lusaka
Area: 290,586 sq. mi.
752,813 sq. km.
Population: 9,188,000
Largest City: Lusaka
Language: English
Monetary Unit: Kwacha

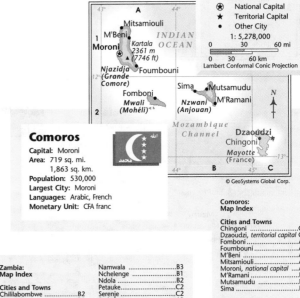

Comoros

⊛ National Capital

★ Territorial Capital

● Other City

1: 5,278,000

0   30   60 mi
0   30   60 km
Lambert Conformal Conic Projection

© GeoSystems Global Corp.

Comoros

Capital: Moroni
Area: 719 sq. mi.
1,863 sq. km.
Population: 530,000
Largest City: Moroni
Languages: Arabic, French
Monetary Unit: CFA franc

Zambia: Map Index

Cities and Towns

Chililabombwe	B2
Chingola	B2
Chipata	C2
Choma	B3
Isoka	C2
Kabwe	B2
Kafue	B3
Kaoma	A2
Kasama	C2
Kitwe	B2
Livingstone	B3
Luangwa	C3
Luanshya	B2
Lundazi	C2
Lusaka, *capital*	B3
Mansa	B2
Mazabuka	B3
Mbala	C1
Mongu	A3
Mpika	C2
Mporokoso	C1
Mufulira	B2
Mumbwa	B3
Mwinilunga	A2
Namwala	B3
Nchelenge	B1
Ndola	B2
Petauke	C2
Serenje	C2
Sesheke	A3
Solwezi	B2
Zambezi	A2

Other Features

Bangweulu, *lake*	B2
Chambeshi, *river*	C2
Cuando, *river*	A3
Dongwe, *river*	A2
Kabompo, *river*	A2
Kafue, *river*	B3
Kariba, *lake*	B3
Luangwa, *river*	C2
Luapula, *river*	B2
Lunga, *river*	A2
Lungwebungu, *river*	A2
Luvua, *river*	B1
Muchinga, *mts.*	C2
Mweru, *lake*	B1
Tanganyika, *lake*	C1
Victoria, *falls*	B3
Zambezi, *river*	A3, B3

Comoros: Map Index

Cities and Towns

Chingoni	C2
Dzaoudzi, *territorial capital*	C2
Fomboni	A2
Foumbouni	A1
M'Beni	A1
Mitsamiouli	A1
Moroni, *national capital*	A1
M'Ramani	B2
Mutsamudu	B2
Sima	B2

Other Features

Kartala, *mt.*	A1
Mayotte, *island*	C2
Mozambique, *channel*	B2
Mwali (Mohéli), *island*	A2
Njazidja (Grande Comore), *island*	A1
Nzwani (Anjouan), *island*	B2

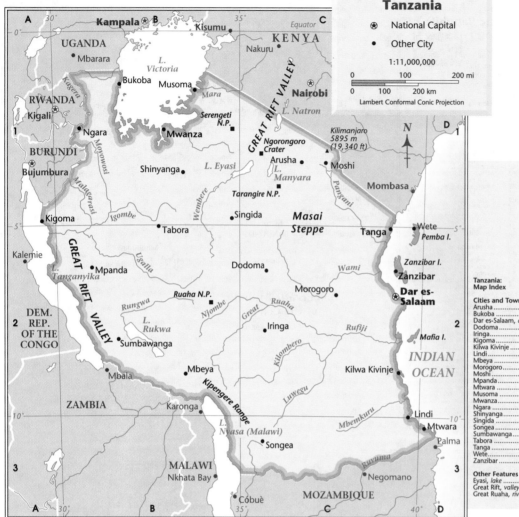

Tanzania

⊛ National Capital

• Other City

1:11,000,000

| 0 | 100 | 200 mi |
| 0 | 100 | 200 km |

Lambert Conformal Conic Projection

Tanzania

Capital: Dar es-Salaam
Area: 364,017 sq. mi.
        943,049 sq. km.
Population: 27,986,000
Largest City: Dar es-Salaam
Languages: Swahili, English
Monetary Unit: Shilling

Tanzania:
Map Index

Cities and Towns
Arusha	C1
Bukoba	B1
Dar es-Salaam, *capital*	C2
Dodoma	C2
Iringa	C2
Kigoma	A1
Kilwa Kivinje	C2
Lindi	C2
Mbeya	B2
Morogoro	C2
Moshi	C1
Mpanda	B2
Mtwara	D3
Musoma	B1
Mwanza	B1
Ngara	B1
Shinyanga	B1
Singida	B1
Songea	C3
Sumbawanga	B2
Tabora	B2
Tanga	C2
Wete	C1
Zanzibar	C2

Other Features
Eyasi, *lake*	B1
Great Rift, *valley*	B2, C1
Great Ruaha, *river*	C2
Igombe, *river*	B1
Kagera, *river*	B1
Kilimanjaro, *mt.*	C1
Kilombero, *river*	C2
Kipengere, *range*	B2
Luwegu, *river*	C2
Mafia, *island*	C2
Malagarasi, *river*	B1
Manyara, *lake*	C1
Mara, *river*	B1
Masai, *steppe*	C1
Mbemkuru, *river*	C2
Moyowosi, *river*	B1
Natron, *lake*	C1
Ngorongoro, *crater*	C1
Njombe, *river*	C2
Nyasa (Malawi), *lake*	B3
Pangani, *river*	C1
Pemba, *island*	C2
Ruaha Natl. Park	B2
Rufiji, *river*	C2
Rukwa, *lake*	B2
Rungwa, *river*	B2
Ruvuma, *river*	C3
Serengeti Natl. Park	B1
Tanganyika, *lake*	A2
Tarangire Natl. Park	C1
Ugalla, *river*	B2
Victoria, *lake*	B1
Wami, *river*	B1
Zanzibar, *island*	C2

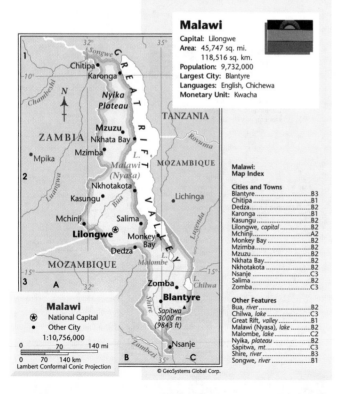

Malawi

Capital: Lilongwe
Area: 45,747 sq. mi.
        118,516 sq. km.
Population: 9,732,000
Largest City: Blantyre
Languages: English, Chichewa
Monetary Unit: Kwacha

Malawi

⊛ National Capital

• Other City

1:10,756,000

| 0 | 70 | 140 mi |
| 0 | 70 | 140 km |

Lambert Conformal Conic Projection

Malawi:
Map Index

Cities and Towns
Blantyre	B3
Chitipa	B1
Dedza	B2
Karonga	B1
Kasungu	B2
Lilongwe, *capital*	B2
Mchinji	A2
Monkey Bay	B2
Mzimba	B2
Mzuzu	B2
Nkhata Bay	B2
Nkhotakota	B2
Nsanje	C3
Salima	B2
Zomba	C3

Other Features
Bua, *river*	B2
Chilwa, *lake*	C3
Great Rift, *valley*	B1
Malawi (Nyasa), *lake*	B2
Malombe, *lake*	B2
Nyika, *plateau*	B2
Sapitwa, *mt.*	C3
Shire, *river*	B3
Songwe, *river*	B1

Mozambique

Capital: Maputo
Area: 313,661 sq. mi.
        812,593 sq. km.
Population: 17,346,000
Largest City: Maputo
Language: Portuguese
Monetary Unit: Metical

Mozambique:
Map Index

Cities and Towns
Angoche	C3
Beira	B3
Chimoio	B3
Chinde	C3
Cuamba	C2
Inhambane	B5
Lichinga	C2
Maputo, *capital*	B5
Moçambique	D2
Mocímboa da Praia	D1
Nacala	C2
Nampula	C2
Pebane	C3
Pemba	D2
Quelimane	C3
Tete	B3
Vilanculos	B4
Xai-Xai	B5

Other Features
Binga, *mt.*	B3
Búzi, *river*	B4
Cabora Bassa, *dam*	B2
Cabora Bassa, *lake*	A2
Changane, *river*	B4
Chilwa, *lake*	B3
Chire, *river*	B3
Lebombo, *mts.*	A4
Limpopo, *river*	B4
Lugenda, *river*	C2
Lúrio, *river*	C2
Mozambique, *channel*	C2
Namuli, *highlands*	C2
Nyasa (Malawi), *lake*	C1
Rovuma, *river*	C1
Save, *river*	B4
Zambezi, *river*	B3

Mozambique

⊛ National Capital

• Other City

1:25,181,000

| 0 | 150 | 300 mi |
| 0 | 150 | 300 km |

Modified Lambert Conformal Conic Projection

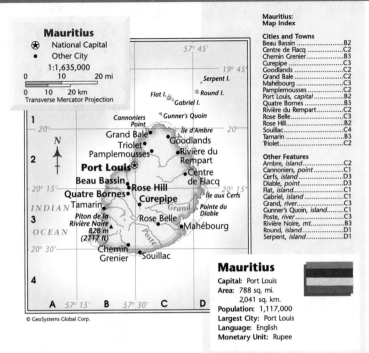

Mauritius

⊛ National Capital
● Other City

1:1,635,000

0   10   20 mi
0   10   20 km
Transverse Mercator Projection

© GeoSystems Global Corp.

**Mauritius:
Map Index**

Cities and Towns
Beau Bassin B2
Centre de Flacq C2
Chemin Grenier B3
Curepipe C3
Goodlands C2
Grand Bale C3
Mahébourg C3
Pamplemousses C2
Port Louis, *capital* B2
Quatre Bornes B3
Rivière du Rempart C2
Rose Belle C3
Rose Hill B2
Souillac C4
Tamarin B3
Triolet C2

Other Features
Ambre, *island* C2
Cannoniers, *point* C1
Cerfs, *island* D3
Diable, *point* D3
Flat, *island* C1
Gabriel, *island* C1
Grand, *river* C1
Gunner's Quoin, *island* ..C1
Poste, *river* C3
Rivière Noire, *mt.* B3
Round, *island* D1
Serpent, *island* D1

Mauritius

Capital: Port Louis
Area: 788 sq. mi.
    2,041 sq. km.
Population: 1,117,000
Largest City: Port Louis
Language: English
Monetary Unit: Rupee

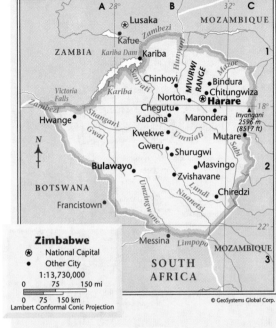

Zimbabwe

⊛ National Capital
● Other City

1:13,730,000

0   75   150 mi
0   75   150 km
Lambert Conformal Conic Projection

© GeoSystems Global Corp.

Zimbabwe

Capital: Harare
Area: 150,872 sq. mi.
    390,860 sq. km.
Population: 10,975,000
Largest City: Harare
Language: English
Monetary Unit: Dollar

**Zimbabwe:
Map Index**

Cities and Towns
Bindura B1
Bulawayo B2
Chegutu B2
Chinhoyi B1
Chiredzi B2
Chitungwiza B1
Gweru B2
Harare, *capital* B1
Hwange A2

Kadoma B2
Kariba B1
Kwekwe B2
Marondera B2
Masvingo B2
Mutare C2
Norton B1
Shurugwi B2
Zvishavane B2

Other Features
Gwai, *river* A2
Hunyani, *river* B1
Inyangani, *mt.* C2
Kariba, *lake* A1
Limpopo, *river* B3
Lundi, *river* B2
Mazoe, *river* B1
Mvurwi, *range* B1
Nuanetsi, *river* B2
Sabi, *river* C2
Sanyati, *river* B1
Shangani, *river* A2
Umniati, *river* B2
Umzingwani, *river* B2
Victoria, *falls* A1
Zambezi, *river* A1, B1

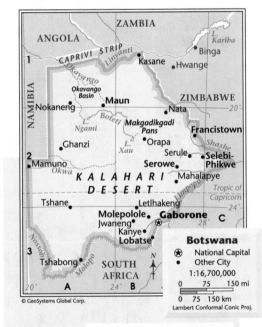

© GeoSystems Global Corp.

Botswana

⊛ National Capital
● Other City

1:16,700,000

0   75   150 mi
0   75   150 km
Lambert Conformal Conic Proj.

Botswana

Capital: Gaborone
Area: 224,607 sq. mi.
    581,883 sq. km.
Population: 1,359,000
Largest City: Gaborone
Language: English
Monetary Unit: Pula

**Botswana:
Map Index**

Cities and Towns
Francistown B2
Gaborone, *capital* B3
Ghanzi A2
Jwaneng B3
Kanye B3
Kasane B1
Letlhakeng B3
Lobatse B3
Mahalapye B2
Mamuno A2
Maun A1
Molepolole B3
Nata B1
Nokaneng A1
Orapa B2
Selebi-Phikwe C2
Serowe B2
Serule B2

Tshabong A3
Tshane A3

Other Features
Boteti, *river* A2
Kalahari, *desert* A2
Limpopo, *river* B2
Linvanti, *river* A1
Makgadikgadi,
  salt pans B2
Molopo, *river* A3
Ngami, *lake* A2
Nossob, *river* A3
Okavango, *basin* A1
Okavango, *river* A1
Okwa, *river* A2
Shashe, *river* B2
Xau, *lake* B2

Madagascar

⊛ National Capital
● Other City

1:17,474,000

0   100   200 mi
0   100   200 km
Lambert Conformal Conic Projection

© GeoSystems Global Corp.

Madagascar

Capital: Antananarivo
Area: 226,658 sq. mi.
    587,197 sq. km.
Population: 13,428,000
Largest City: Antananarivo
Languages: Malagasy, French
Monetary Unit: Malagasy franc

**Madagascar:
Map Index**

Cities and Towns
Ambatolampy B2
Ambatondrazaka B2
Ambositra B3
Ampanihy A3
Andoany B1
Antalaha C1
Antananarivo, *capital* B2
Antsirabe B2
Antsiranana B1
Antsohihy B1
Farafangana B3
Fianarantsoa B3
Ihosy B3
Mahajanga B2
Maintirano A2
Manakara B3
Marovoay B2
Morombe A3
Morondava A3
Toamasina B2
Tôlanaro B3

Toliara A3
Tsiroanomandidy B2

Other Features
Alaotra, *lake* B2
Ambre, *cape* B1
Ankaratra, *mts.* B2
Bemaraha, *plateau* A2
Betsiboka, *river* B2
Kinkony, *lake* B2
L'Isalo, *mts.* B3
Mahajamba, *river* B2
Mangoky, *river* A3
Maromokotro, *mt.* B1
Menarandra, *river* A3
Mozambique, *channel* A2
Nosy Be, *island* B1
Nosy Sainte Marie, *island* ..B2
Onilahy, *river* A3
Saint-André, *cape* A2
Sainte-Marie, *cape* B2
Sofia, *river* B2
Tsaratanana, *mts.* B1
Tsiribihina, *river* B2

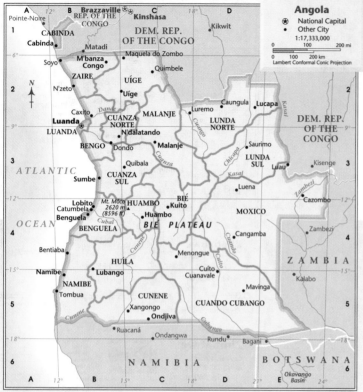

Angola

⊛ National Capital
● Other City

1:17,333,000

0   100   200 mi
0   100   200 km

Lambert Conformal Conic Projection

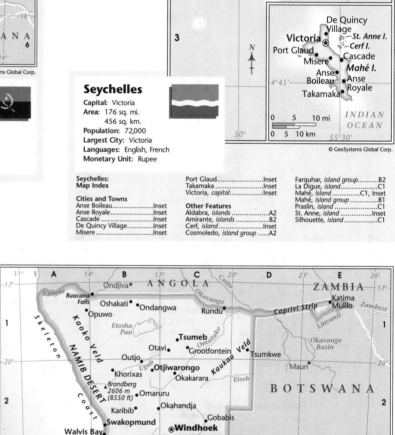

Seychelles

⊛ National Capital
● Other City

1:18,500,000

0   100   200 mi
0   100   200 km

Lambert Conformal Conic Projection

Angola:
Map Index

Provinces
Bengo B3
Benguela B4
Bié C4
Cabinda B1
Cuando Cubango D5
Cuanza Norte B2
Cuanza Sul B3
Cunene C5
Huambo C4
Huíla B4
Luanda B3
Lunda Norte D2
Lunda Sul D3
Malanje C2
Mocico D4
Namibe B5
Uíge B2
Zaire B2

Cities and Towns
Benguela B4
Bentiaba B4
Cabinda B1
Cangamba D4
Catumbela B4
Caungula D2

Caxito B2
Cazombo E3
Cuíto Cuanavale D5
Dondo B3
Huambo C4
Kuito C4
Lobito B4
Luanda, capital B2
Luau E3
Lubango B5
Lucapa D2
Luena D3
Luremo C2
Malanje C3
Maquela do Zombo C2
Mavinga D5
M'banza Congo B2
Menongue C4
Namibe B5
N'dalatando B3
N'zeto B2
Ondjiva C5
Quibala C3
Quimbele C2
Saurimo D3
Soyo B2
Sumbe B3
Tombua B5
Uíge B2
Xangongo C5

Other Features
Bié, plateau C4
Chicapa, river D3
Cuando, river D4
Cuango, river D2
Cuanza, river C3
Cubal, river B4
Cubango, river D5
Cuito, river C4
Cunene, river B5, C4
Dande, river B2
Kasai, river D3
Môco, mt. C4
Zambezi, river E3

Angola

Capital: Luanda
Area: 481,354 sq. mi.
    1,247,031 sq. km.
Population: 9,804,000
Largest City: Luanda
Language: Portuguese
Monetary Unit: Kwanza

Seychelles

Capital: Victoria
Area: 176 sq. mi.
    456 sq. km.
Population: 72,000
Largest City: Victoria
Languages: English, French
Monetary Unit: Rupee

Seychelles:
Map Index

Cities and Towns
Anse Boileau ....Inset
Anse Royale ....Inset
Cascade ....Inset
De Quincy Village ....Inset
Misere ....Inset

Port Glaud..........................Inset
Takamaka............................Inset
Victoria, capital...................Inset

Other Features
Aldabra, islands A2
Amirante, islands B2
Cerf, island ....Inset
Cosmoledo, island group A2

Farquhar, island group...........B2
La Digue, island....................C1
Mahé, island...................C1, Inset
Mahé, island group................B1
Praslin, island C1
St. Anne, island ....Inset
Silhouette, island..................C1

Namibia

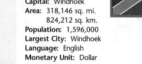

Capital: Windhoek
Area: 318,146 sq. mi.
    824,212 sq. km.
Population: 1,596,000
Largest City: Windhoek
Language: English
Monetary Unit: Dollar

Namibia:
Map Index

Cities and Towns
Bethanien C4
Gobabis C2
Grootfontein C1
Karasburg C4
Karibib B2
Katima Mulilo E1
Keetmanshoop C4
Khorixas B2
Lüderitz B4
Maltahöhe B3
Mariental C3
Okahandja C2
Okakarara C2
Omaruru B2
Ondangwa B1
Opuwo A1
Oranjemund B4
Oshakati B1
Otavi C1
Otjiwarongo B2
Outjo B2
Rehoboth C3
Rundu C1

Swakopmund B2
Tsumeb C1
Tsumkwe D1
Walvis Bay B2
Windhoek, capital C2

Other Features
Auob, river C3
Brandberg, mt. B2
Caprivi, strip D1
Eiseb, river D2
Etosha, pan B1
Fish, river C4
Kalahari, desert C3
Kaoko Veld, mts. A1
Kaukau Veld, region C2
Kunene, river A1
Linyanti, river E1
Namib, desert A1, B3
Nossob, river C3
Okavango, river C1
Omatako, river C1
Orange, river B4
Ruacana, falls B1
Skeleton, coast A1
Ugab, river B2
Zambezi, river E1

Namibia

⊛ National Capital
● Other City

1:16,153,000

0   100   200 mi
0   100   200 km

Lambert Conformal Conic Projection

© GeoSystems Global Corp.

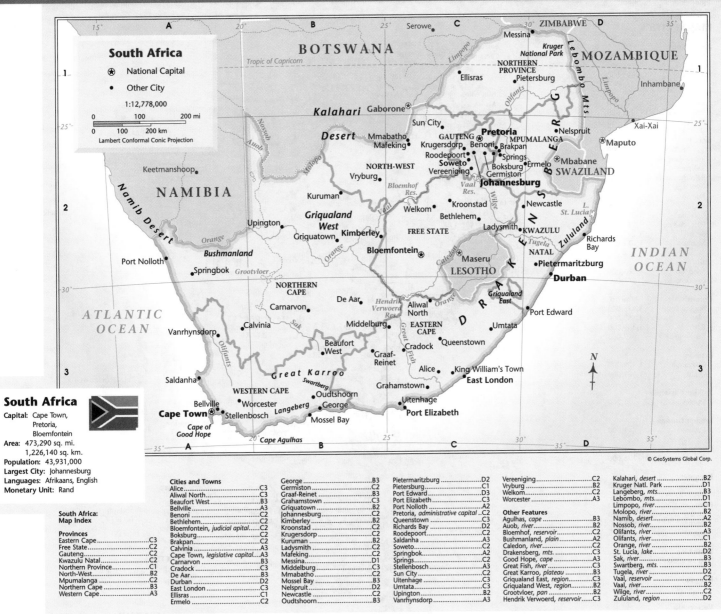

South Africa
- ⊛ National Capital
- • Other City

1:12,778,000

0   100   200 mi
0   100   200 km

Lambert Conformal Conic Projection

South Africa
Capital: Cape Town, Pretoria, Bloemfontein
Area: 473,290 sq. mi.
1,226,140 sq. km.
Population: 43,931,000
Largest City: Johannesburg
Languages: Afrikaans, English
Monetary Unit: Rand

South Africa:
Map Index

Provinces

Eastern Cape	C3
Free State	C2
Gauteng	C2
Kwazulu Natal	C2
Northern Province	C1
North-West	B2
Mpumalanga	C2
Northern Cape	B3
Western Cape	A3

Cities and Towns

Alice	C3
Aliwal North	C3
Beaufort West	B3
Bellville	A3
Benoni	C2
Bethlehem	C2
Bloemfontein, *judicial apital.*	C2
Boksburg	C2
Brakpan	C2
Calvinia	A3
Cape Town, *legislative capital.*	A3
Carnarvon	B3
Cradock	C3
De Aar	B3
Durban	D2
East London	C3
Ellisras	C1
Ermelo	C2

George	B3
Germiston	C2
Graaf-Reinet	B3
Grahamstown	C3
Griquatown	B2
Johannesburg	C2
Kimberley	B2
Kroonstad	C2
Krugersdorp	C2
Kuruman	B2
Ladysmith	C2
Mafeking	C2
Messina	D1
Middelburg	C3
Mmabatho	C2
Mossel Bay	B3
Nelspruit	D2
Newcastle	C2
Oudtshoorn	B3

Pietermaritzburg	D2
Pietersburg	C1
Port Edward	D3
Port Elizabeth	B3
Port Nolloth	A2
Pretoria, *administrative capital*	C2
Queenstown	C3
Richards Bay	D2
Roodepoort	C2
Saldanha	A3
Soweto	C2
Springbok	A3
Springs	C2
Stellenbosch	A3
Sun City	C2
Uitenhage	C3
Umtata	C3
Upington	B2
Vanrhynsdorp	A3

Vereeniging	C2
Vryburg	B2
Welkom	C2
Worcester	A3

Other Features

Agulhas, *cape*	B3
Auob, *river*	B2
Bloemhof, *reservoir*	C2
Bushmanland, *plain*	A2
Caledon, *river*	C2
Drakensberg, *mts.*	C3
Good Hope, *cape*	A3
Great Fish, *river*	C3
Great Karroo, *plateau*	B3
Griqualand East, *region*	C3
Griqualand West, *region*	B2
Grootvloer, *pan*	B2
Hendrik Verwoerd, *reservoir*	C3

Kalahari, *desert*	B2
Kruger Natl. Park	D1
Langeberg, *mts.*	B3
Lebombo, *mts.*	D1
Limpopo, *river*	C1
Molopo, *river*	B2
Namib, *desert*	A2
Nossob, *river*	B2
Olifants, *river*	A3
Olifants, *river*	C1
Orange, *river*	B2
St. Lucia, *lake*	D2
Sak, *river*	B3
Swartberg, *mts.*	B3
Tugela, *river*	D2
Vaal, *reservoir*	C2
Vaal, *river*	B2
Wilge, *river*	C2
Zululand, *region*	D2

© GeoSystems Global Corp.

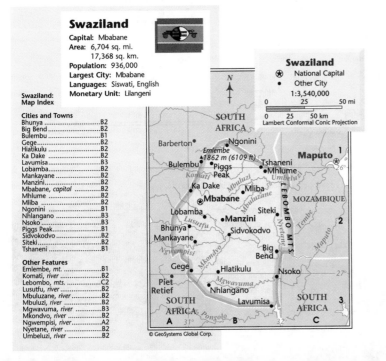

Swaziland
Capital: Mbabane
Area: 6,704 sq. mi.
17,368 sq. km.
Population: 936,000
Largest City: Mbabane
Languages: Siswati, English
Monetary Unit: Lilangeni

Swaziland:
Map Index

Cities and Towns

Bhunya	B2
Big Bend	B2
Bulembu	B1
Gege	B2
Hlatikulu	B2
Ka Dake	B3
Lavumisa	B3
Lobamba	B2
Mankayane	B2
Manzini	B2
Mbabane, *capital*	B2
Mhlume	B2
Mliba	B2
Ngonini	B1
Nhlangano	B3
Nsoko	B3
Piggs Peak	B1
Sidvokodvo	B2
Siteki	B2
Tshaneni	B1

Other Features

Emlembe, *mt.*	B1
Komati, *river*	B2
Lebombo, *mts.*	C2
Lusutfu, *river*	B2
Mbuluzane, *river*	B2
Mbuluzi, *river*	B2
Mgwavuma, *river*	B3
Mkondvo, *river*	B2
Ngwempisi, *river*	A2
Nyetane, *river*	B2
Umbeluzi, *river*	B2

Swaziland
- ⊛ National Capital
- • Other City

1:3,540,000

0   25   50 mi
0   25   50 km
Lambert Conformal Conic Projection

© GeoSystems Global Corp.

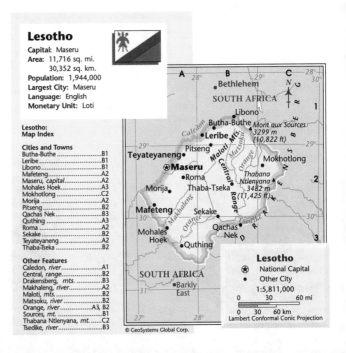

Lesotho
Capital: Maseru
Area: 11,716 sq. mi.
30,352 sq. km.
Population: 1,944,000
Largest City: Maseru
Language: English
Monetary Unit: Loti

Lesotho:
Map Index

Cities and Towns

Butha-Buthe	B1
Leribe	B1
Libono	B1
Mafeteng	A2
Maseru, *capital*	A2
Mohales Hoek	A3
Mokhotlong	C2
Morija	A2
Pitseng	B2
Qachas Nek	B3
Quthing	A3
Roma	A2
Sekake	B2
Teyateyaneng	A2
Thaba-Tseka	B2

Other Features

Caledon, *river*	A1
Central, *range*	B2
Drakensberg, *mts.*	B3
Makhaleng, *river*	A3
Maloti, *mts.*	B2
Matsoku, *river*	B2
Orange, *river*	A3, B2
Sources, *mt.*	B1
Thabana Ntlenyana, *mt.*	C2
Tsedike, *river*	B3

Lesotho
- ⊛ National Capital
- • Other City

1:5,811,000

0   30   60 mi
0   30   60 km
Lambert Conformal Conic Projection

MAJOR CITIES

Argentina
Buenos Aires	2,961,000
Córdoba	1,148,000
Rosario	895,000

Bolivia
La Paz	711,000
Santa Cruz	695,000
Sucre	131,000

Brazil
São Paulo	9,480,000
Rio de Janeiro	5,336,000
Salvador	2,056,000
Belo Horizonte	2,049,000
Fortaleza	1,758,000
Brasília	1,596,000
Recife	1,290,000
Curitiba	1,290,000
Pôrto Alegre	1,263,000
Belém	1,246,000
Manaus	1,011,000

Chile
Santiago	4,385,000
Concepción	306,000

Colombia
Bogotá	(metro)
	3,975,000
Medellín	1,452,000
Cali	1,369,000
Barranquilla	917,000

Ecuador
Guayaquil	1,508,000
Quito	1,101,000

Falkland Islands
Stanley	1,200

French Guiana
Cayenne	41,000

Guyana
Georgetown	195,000

Paraguay
Asunción	502,000

Peru
Lima	(metro)
	6,415,000
Arequipa	635,000
Trujillo	532,000

Suriname
Paramaribo	192,000

Uruguay
Montevideo	1,360,000

Venezuela
Caracas	1,825,000
Maracaibo	1,208,000
Valencia	903,000
Barquisimeto	603,000

International comparability of city population
data is limited by various data inconsistencies.

CITIES
⊗ National Capital
★ Territorial Capital
● Other City

ELEVATIONS
	Feet	Meters
	13,120	4000
	6560	2000
	1640	500
	656	200
	0	0
	Below sea level	

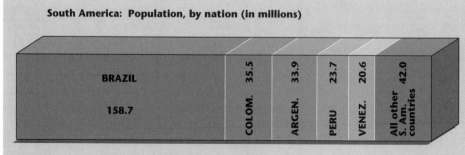

South America: Population, by nation (in millions)

| BRAZIL 158.7 | COLOM. 35.5 | ARGEN. 33.9 | PERU 23.7 | VENEZ. 20.6 | All other S. Am. countries 42.0 |

© GeoSystems Global Corp.

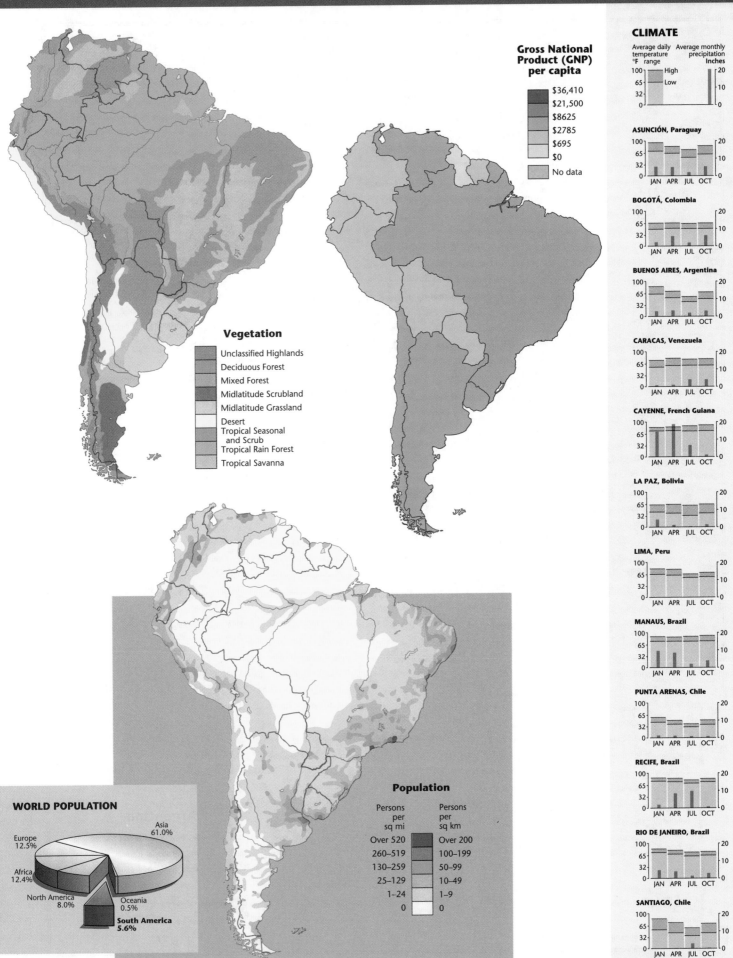

Gross National Product (GNP) per capita

- $36,410
- $21,500
- $8625
- $2785
- $695
- $0
- No data

Vegetation

- Unclassified Highlands
- Deciduous Forest
- Mixed Forest
- Midlatitude Scrubland
- Midlatitude Grassland
- Desert
- Tropical Seasonal and Scrub
- Tropical Rain Forest
- Tropical Savanna

CLIMATE

Average daily temperature °F range / Average monthly precipitation Inches

- ASUNCIÓN, Paraguay
- BOGOTÁ, Colombia
- BUENOS AIRES, Argentina
- CARACAS, Venezuela
- CAYENNE, French Guiana
- LA PAZ, Bolivia
- LIMA, Peru
- MANAUS, Brazil
- PUNTA ARENAS, Chile
- RECIFE, Brazil
- RIO DE JANEIRO, Brazil
- SANTIAGO, Chile

Population

Persons per sq mi	Persons per sq km
Over 520	Over 200
260–519	100–199
130–259	50–99
25–129	10–49
1–24	1–9
0	0

WORLD POPULATION

- Asia 61.0%
- Europe 12.5%
- Africa 12.4%
- North America 8.0%
- Oceania 0.5%
- South America 5.6%

PACIFIC
OCEAN

ATACAMA DESERT

BOLIVIA

PARAGUAY

BRAZIL

Tropic of Capricorn

Chuquicamata

Antofagasta

JUJUY
Embarcación
San Salvador
de Jujuy
Llullaillaco
6723 m
(22,057 ft)
Salta
SALTA

GRAN CHACO

Pilcomayo

Concepción

FORMOSA
Formosa
Asunción

Foz do Iguaçu
Iguaçu Falls
Curitiba

Ojos del Salado
6880 m
(22,572 ft)
CATAMARCA

San Miguel
de Tucumán
TUCUMÁN

SANTIAGO
DEL
ESTERO

CHACO
Presidencia Roque Sáenz Peña
Resistencia
Corrientes
Posadas

MISIONES

La Serena

Desaguadero

Catamarca
Santiago
del Estero

CORRIENTES

Reconquista
Curuzú Cuatiá

Santa Maria

La Rioja

Salado

SANTA FE
Pôrto Alegre
L. dos Patos

Mercedario
6770 m
(22,211 ft)

SAN JUAN
San Juan

LA RIOJA

CÓRDOBA
Córdoba
L. Mar Chiquita
San Francisco

ENTRE RÍOS
Santa Fe
Concordia
Pelotas

Aconcagua
6960 m
(22,834 ft)
Tupungato
6800 m
(22,310 ft)

Mendoza
Godoy Cruz
San Luis

Champaquí
2850 m
(9350 ft)
Villa
María
Río
Cuarto

Paraná
Rosario
San Nicolás

URUGUAY

Negro

Santiago

San
Rafael

SAN
LUIS

DISTRITO FEDERAL
Buenos Aires
Avellaneda
Montevideo

MENDOZA

Atuel

Salado

Lanús
Lomas de
Zamora
La
Plata

Río de la Plata

CHILE

Domuyo
4709 m
(15,450 ft)

LA PAMPA

PAMPAS

Santa Rosa

BUENOS AIRES
Olavarría
Tandil

Cabo
San Antonio

Concepción

Colorado

NEUQUÉN

Mar del Plata

Neuquén

Negro

Bahía Blanca
Necochea

Bahía Blanca

Lanín
3776 m
(12,389 ft)

Puerto Montt

San Antonio
Oeste
Viedma
Punta Rasa

ATLANTIC
OCEAN

RÍO NEGRO

San Carlos
de Bariloche

Golfo
San Matías

Chiloé

ANDES

Chubut

Península Valdés

Esquel

CHUBUT

Rawson

PATAGONIA

Chico

Coihaique

Comodoro Rivadavia
Golfo San Jorge

Península
Taitao

Deseado

Cabo Tres Puntas

L. Buenos
Aires
SANTA CRUZ

Puerto Deseado

Fitzroy
3375 m
(11,073 ft)

L. San
Martín
L. Cardiel

L. Viedma

Santa Cruz

Calafate
L.
Argentino

Puerto Santa Cruz

Bahía
Grande

West
Falkland I.

East
Falkland I.
Stanley

Gallegos

Río Gallegos
Punta Dungeness
Strait of Magellan

Falkland Islands
(Islas Malvinas)
(Br.)
(claimed by Argentina)

N

Punta Arenas

TIERRA
DEL
FUEGO

Ushuaia
Isla de
los Estados

Beagle
Channel
Cape Horn

Argentina

⊛ National Capital

★ Territorial Capital

● Other City

1:17,760,000

0   200   400 mi

0   200   400 km
Modified Chamberlain Trimetric Projection

© GeoSystems Global Corp.

Paraguay

⊛ National Capital

• Other City

1:10,375,000

0   50   100 mi
0   50   100 km
Conic Equidistant Projection

© GeoSystems Global Corp.

Argentina

Capital: Buenos Aires
Area: 1,073,518 sq. mi.
2,781,134 sq. km.
Population: 33,913,000
Largest City: Buenos Aires
Language: Spanish
Monetary Unit: Peso

Argentina: Map Index

Provinces

Buenos Aires	C4
Catamarca	B2
Chaco	C2
Chubut	B5
Córdoba	C3
Corrientes	D2
Distrito Federal	D3
Entre Ríos	D3
Formosa	D1
Jujuy	B1
La Pampa	B4
La Rioja	B2
Mendoza	B3
Misiones	E2
Neuquén	B4
Río Negro	B5
Salta	B2
San Juan	B3
San Luis	B3
Santa Cruz	A6
Santa Fe	C2
Santiago del Estero	C2
Tierra del Fuego	B7
Tucumán	B2

Cities and Towns

Avellaneda	D3
Bahía Blanca	C4
Buenos Aires, *capital*	D3
Calafate	A7
Catamarca	B2
Comodoro Rivadavia	B6
Concordia	D3
Córdoba	C3
Corrientes	D2
Curuzú Cuatiá	D2
Embarcación	C1
Esquel	A5
Formosa	D2
Godoy Cruz	B3
Lanús	D3
La Plata	D4
La Rioja	B2
Lomas de Zamora	D4
Mar del Plata	D4
Mendoza	B3
Necochea	D4
Neuquén	B4
Olavarría	C4
Paraná	C3
Posadas	D2
Presidencia Roque Sáenz Peña	C2
Puerto Deseado	B6
Puerto Santa Cruz	B7
Rawson	B5
Reconquista	D2
Resistencia	D2
Río Cuarto	C3
Río Gallegos	B7
Rosario	C3
Salta	B1
San Antonio Oeste	B5
San Carlos de Bariloche	A5
San Francisco	C3
San Juan	B3
San Luis	B3
San Miguel de Tucumán	B2
San Nicolás	C3
San Rafael	B3
San Salvador de Jujuy	B1
Santa Fe	C3
Santa Rosa	C4
Santiago del Estero	C2
Tandil	D4
Ushuaia	B7
Viedma	C5
Villa María	C3

Other Features

Aconcagua, *mt.*	A3
Andes, *mts.*	A6–B1
Argentino, *lake*	A7
Atuel, *river*	B3
Beagle, *channel*	B7
Bermejo, *river*	C2
Blanca, *bay*	C4
Buenos Aires, *lake*	A6
Cardiel, *lake*	A6
Champaquí, *mt.*	C3
Chico, *river*	B6
Chubut, *river*	A5
Colorado, *river*	B4
Córdoba, *range*	B3
Desaguadero, *river*	B3
Deseado, *river*	B6
Domuyo, *volcano*	A4
Dungeness, *point*	B7
Estados, *island*	C7
Fitzroy, *mt.*	A6
Gallegos, *river*	A7
Gran Chaco, *region*	C1
Grande, *bay*	B7
Iguaçu, *falls*	E2
Iguaçu, *river*	E2
Lanín, *volcano*	A4
Llullaillaco, *volcano*	B1
Magellan, *strait*	B7
Mar Chiquita, *lake*	C3
Mercedario, *mt*	B3
Negro, *river*	B4
Ojos del Salado, *mt.*	B2
Pampas, *plain*	C4
Paraguay, *river*	D2
Paraná, *river*	D2
Patagonia, *region*	A6
Pilcomayo, *river*	C1
Plata, Río de la, *estuary*	D3
Rasa, *point*	C5
Salado, *river*	B3
Salado, *river*	C2
San Antonio, *cape*	D4
San Jorge, *gulf*	B6
San Martín, *lake*	A6
San Matías, *gulf*	C5
Santa Cruz, *river*	A7
Tres Puntas, *cape*	B6
Tupungato, *mt*	B3
Uruguay, *river*	D3
Valdés, *peninsula*	C5
Viedma, *lake*	A6

Paraguay

Capital: Asunción
Area: 157,048 sq. mi.
406,752 sq. km.
Population: 4,007,000
Largest City: Asunción
Language: Spanish
Monetary Unit: Guarani

Paraguay: Map Index

Departments

Alto Paraguay	C2
Alto Paraná	E4
Amambay	E3
Asunción	B3
Boquerón	B3
Caaguazú	D4
Caazapá	D5
Canendiyú	E4
Central	C4
Chaco	C2
Concepción	D3
Cordillera	D4
Guairá	D4
Itapúa	D5
Misiones	D5
Neembucú	C5
Nueva Asunción	B2
Paraguarí	D5
Presidente Hayes	C4
San Pedro	D4

Cities and Towns

Abaí	E4
Asunción, *capital*	C4
Caacupé	D4
Caaguazú	E4
Caazapá	D5
Capitán Pablo Lagerenza	B1
Ciudad del Este	E4
Concepción	D3
Coronel Oviedo	D4
Doctor Pedro P. Peña	A3

General

Encarnación	E5
Filadelfia	B3
Fuerte Olimpo	D2
Eugenio A. Garay	A2
Mariscal Estigarribia	B3
Paraguarí	D4
Pedro Juan Caballero	E3
Pilar	C5
Pozo Colorado	C3
Puerto Bahía	D2
Puerto Pinasco	D3
Salto del Guairá	E4
San Juan Bautista	D5
San Lorenzo	D4
San Pedro	D4
Villa Hayes	D4
Villarrica	D4

Other Features

Acaray, *river*	E4
Amambay, *mts.*	E3
Apa, *river*	D3
Chaco Boreal, *region*	B2
Gran Chaco, *region*	B3
Iguazú, *falls*	E4
Itaipú, *reservoir*	E4
Jejuí-Guazú, *river*	D4
Montelindo, *river*	C3
Paraguay, *river*	C2, C5
Paraná, *river*	C5, E5
Pilcomayo, *river*	B3, C4
Tebicuary, *river*	D5
Verde, *river*	C3
Ypané, *river*	D3
Ypoá, *lake*	D4

Uruguay

⊛ National Capital

• Other City

1:6,625,000

0   40   80 mi
0   40   80 km
Lambert Conformal Conic Projection

© GeoSystems Global Corp.

Uruguay

Capital: Montevideo
Area: 68,037 sq. mi.
176,215 sq. km.
Population: 2,921,798
Largest City: Montevideo
Language: Spanish
Monetary Unit: New peso

Uruguay: Map Index

Cities and Towns

Artigas	B1
Bella Unión	B1
Canelones	B3
Carmelo	A2
Colonia	B3
Durazno	B2
Florida	B3
Fray Bentos	A2
Las Piedras	B3
Melo	C2
Mercedes	A2
Minas	C3
Montevideo, *capital*	B3
Nueva Palmira	A2
Pando	C3
Paso de los Toros	B2
Paysandú	A2
Piedra Sola	B2
Punta del Este	C1
Rivera	C1
Rocha	C3
Salto	B1
San Carlos	C1
San José	B3
Tacuarembó	C1
Treinta y Tres	C2
Trinidad	B2

Other Features

Arapey Grande, *river*	B1
Baygorria, *lake*	B2
Cebollatí, *river*	C2
Cuareim, *river*	B1
Daymán, *river*	B1
Grande, *range*	C2
Haedo, *range*	B2
Merín, *lagoon*	D2
Mirador Nacional, *mt.*	B3
Negra, *lagoon*	D2
Negro, *river*	C2
Paso de Palmar, *lake*	B2
Plata, *river*	B3
Queguay Grande, *river*	B2
Rincón del Bonete, *lake*	B2
Salto Grande, *reservoir*	B1
San José, *river*	A2
San Salvador, *river*	A2
Santa Ana, *range*	C1
Santa Lucía, *river*	B3
Tacuarembó, *river*	C1
Tacuarí, *river*	D2
Uruguay, *river*	A1
Yaguarí, *river*	C1
Yaguarón, *river*	D2
Yi, *river*	C2

Chile

Capital: Santiago
Area: 292,135 sq. mi.
  756,826 sq. km.
Population: 12,951,000
Largest City: Santiago
Language: Spanish
Monetary Unit: Peso

Chile:
Map Index

Regions
Aisén del General Carlos
  Ibáñez del Campo B8
Antofagasta B2
Atacama B3
Bío-Bío B6
Coquimbo B4
El Libertador General
  Bernardo O'Higgins B4
La Araucanía B6

Los Lagos B7
Magallanes y Antártica
  Chilena B9
Maule B5, B6
Región Metropolitana ....B4, Inset
Tarapacá C1
Valparaíso ....B4, Inset

Cities and Towns
Aguada de Cachinal C2
Aguas Blancas C2
Algarrobo ....Inset

Altamira C3
Ancud B7
Angol B6
Antofagasta B2
Arica B1
Balmaceda B8
Calama C2
Casablanca ....Inset
Castro B7
Cerro Castillo B7
Chaitén B7
Chañaral B3
Chiapa C1

Chile Chico B8
Chillán B6
Chuquicamata C2
Cochrane B8
Coihaique B8
Colina ....Inset
Collaguasi C1
Concepción B6
Conchalí ....Inset
Constitución B5
Copiapó B3
Coquimbo B3
Curicó B4

El Tabo ....Inset
El Trebolar ....Inset
Freirina B3
Gatico B2
Illapel B4
Iquique C1
Lampa ....Inset
La Serena B3
La Unión B7
Lebu B6
Linares B5
Los Andes B4
Los Ángeles B6
Maipú ....Inset
Mamiña C2
Melipilla ....Inset
Ñuñoa ....Inset
Osorno B7
Ovalle B4
Parral B6
Pisagua B1
Porvenir B9
Potrerillos C3
Puente Alto ....Inset
Puerto Aisén B8
Puerto Cisnes B8
Puerto Montt B7
Puerto Natales B9
Puerto Varas B7
Puerto Williams C9
Punta Arenas B9
Punta Delgada B9
Putre C1
Quellón B7
Quillota B4
Quilpué ....Inset
Rancagua B4
Rungue ....Inset
San Antonio ....B4, Inset
San Bernardo ....Inset
San Félix B3
San Fernando B4
San Pedro de Atacama ...C2
Santa Inés ....Inset
Santiago, capital ...B4, Inset
Socompa C2
Talagante ....Inset
Talca B5
Talcahuano B6
Taltal B3
Temuco B6
Tilomonte C2
Tocopila B2
Tomé B6
Unión C2
Valdivia B7
Vallenar B3
Valparaíso ....B4, Inset
Victoria B6
Viña del Mar ....B4, Inset

Other Features
Aconcagua, river B4
Ancud, gulf B7
Andes, mts. B8, C4
Atacama, desert C2
Bascuñán, cape B3
Bío-Bío, river B6
Brunswick, peninsula B9
Buenos Aires, lake B8
Campana, island A8
Chiloé, island B7
Chonos, archipelago B7
Cochrane, lake B8
Concepción, bay B6
Copiapó, river B3
Corcovado, gulf B7
Desolación, island B9
Domeyko, mts. C3
Dungeness, point C9
Duque de York, island ...A9
Elqui, river B3
Fitzroy, mt. B8
Galera, point B6
Horn, cape C9
Hoste, island C9
Imperial, river B6
Lanín, volcano B6
Lengua de Vaca, point ...B4
Llanquihue, lake B7
Llullaillaco, volcano C2
Loa, river B2
Madre de Dios, island A9
Magdalena, island B7
Magellan, strait B9
Maipo, river ....B4, Inset
Maule, river B5
Navarino, island C9
Occidental, mts. C1
Ojos del Salado, mt. C3
Ollagüe, volcano C2
Penas, gulf B8
Rapel, river B4
Reina Adelaida, archipelago ...B9
San Martín, lake B8
San Valentín, mt. B8
Santa Inés, island B9
Taitao, peninsula A8
Tierra del Fuego, island ...C9
Toltén, river B6
Wellington, island A8

Peru

Capital: Lima
Area: 496,225 sq. mi.
 1,285,216 sq. km.
Population: 21,256,000
Largest City: Lima
Languages: Spanish, Quechua
Monetary Unit: Nuevo Sol

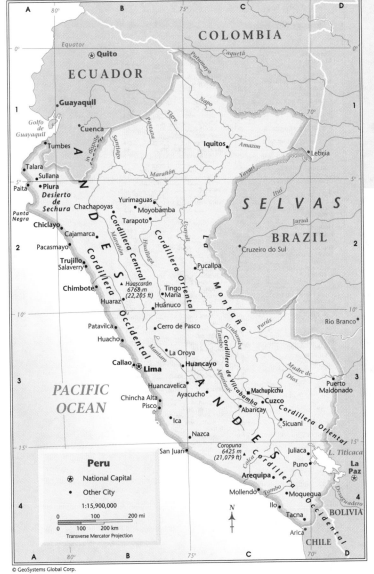

Peru:
Map Index

Cities and Towns

Abancay	C3
Arequipa	C4
Ayacucho	C3
Cajamarca	B2
Callao	B3
Cerro de Pasco	B3
Chachapoyas	B2
Chiclayo	B2
Chimbote	B2
Chincha Alta	B3
Cuzco	B3
Huacho	B3
Huancavelica	B3
Huancayo	B3
Huánuco	B2
Huaraz	B2
Ica	B3
Ilo	C4
Iquitos	C1
Juliaca	C3
La Oroya	B3
Lima, capital	B3
Mollendo	C4
Moquegua	C4
Moyobamba	B2
Nazca	C3
Pacasmayo	B2
Paita	A2
Patavilca	B3
Pisco	B3
Piura	A2
Pucallpa	C2
Puerto Maldonado	D3
Puno	C4
Salaverry	B4
San Juan	B4
Sicuani	C3
Sullana	A1
Tacna	C4
Talara	A1
Tarapoto	B2
Tingo María	B2
Trujillo	B2
Tumbes	A1
Yurimaguas	B2

Other Features

Amazon, river	C1
Andes, mts.	B1, C3
Apurímac, river	C3
Central, mts.	B2
Colca, river	C4
Coropuna, mt.	C4
Guayaquil, gulf	A1
Huallaga, river	B2
Huascarán, mt.	B2
La Montaña, region	C2
Machupicchu, ruins	C3
Madre de Dios, river	C3
Mantaro, river	B3
Marañón, river	B1, B2
Napo, river	C1
Negra, point	A2
Occidental, mts.	B2, C4
Oriental, mts.	B2, C3
Pastaza, river	B1
Purús, river	C3
Putumayo, river	C1
Santiago, river	B1
Sechura, desert	A2
Tambo, river	C3
Tambo, river	C4
Tigre, river	B1
Titicaca, lake	D4
Ucayali, river	C2
Urubamba, river	C3
Vilcabamba, mts.	C3
Yavarí, river	C1

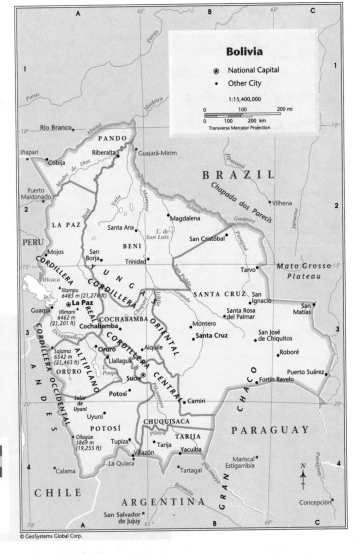

Bolivia:
Map Index

Departments

Beni	A2
Chuquisaca	B4
Cochabamba	A3
La Paz	A3
Oruro	A3
Pando	A4
Potosí	A4
Santa Cruz	B3
Tarija	B4

Cities and Towns

Aiquile	A3
Camiri	B4
Cobija	A2
Cochabamba	A3
Fortín Ravelo	B3
Guaqui	A3
La Paz, capital	A3
Llallagua	A3
Magdalena	B2
Mojos	A2
Montero	A3
Oruro	A3
Potosí	A3
Puerto Suárez	C3
Riberalta	A2
Roboré	C3
San Borja	A2

San Cristóbal	B2
San Ignacio	B3
San José de Chiquitos	B3
San Matías	C3
Santa Ana	A2
Santa Cruz	B3
Santa Rosa del Palmar	A3
Sucre, capital	A3
Tarija	B4
Tarvo	B3
Trinidad	B2
Tupiza	A4
Uyuni	A4
Villazón	A4
Yacuiba	B4

Other Features

Abuná, river	A2
Altiplano, plateau	A3
Beni, river	A3
Chaparé, river	A3
Cordillera Central, mts.	A3
Cordillera Occidental, mts.	A3
Cordillera Oriental, mts.	A3
Cordillera Real, mts.	A3
Desaguadero, river	A3
Gran Chaco, region	B4
Grande, river	B3
Guaporé, river	B2
Ichilo, river	B3
Illampu, mt.	A3
Illimani, mt.	A3

Iténez, river	B2
Madre de Dios, river	A2
Mamoré, river	A2
Ollagüe, volcano.	A4
Paraguá, river	B2
Paraguay, river	C4
Pilaya, river	B4
Pilcomayo, river	B3
Poopó, lake	A3
Sajama, mt.	A3
Salar de Uyuni, salt flat	A4
San Luis, lake	B2
San Pablo, river	B3
Titicaca, lake	A3
Yata, river	A2
Yungas, region	A3

Bolivia

Capital: La Paz, Sucre
Area: 424,164 sq. mi.
 1,098,871 sq. km.
Population: 7,719,000
Largest City: La Paz
Languages: Spanish, Quechua, Aymara
Monetary Unit: Boliviano

© GeoSystems Global Corp.

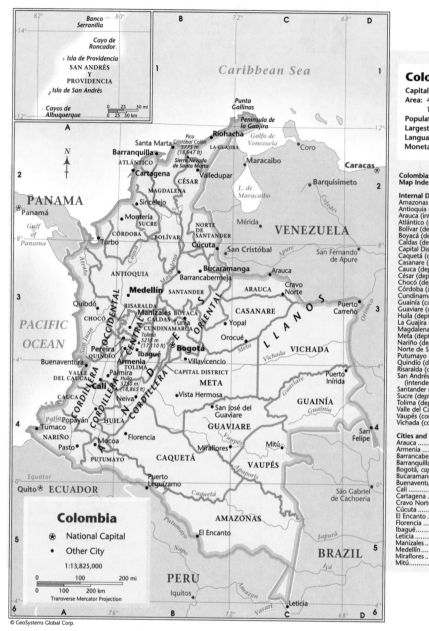

Colombia

Capital: Bogotá
Area: 440,831 sq. mi.
1,142,049 sq. km.
Population: 35,578,000
Largest City: Bogotá
Language: Spanish
Monetary Unit: Peso

Colombia Map

Map Legend
⊛ National Capital
• Other City

1:13,825,000

0 — 100 — 200 mi
0 — 100 — 200 km
Transverse Mercator Projection

© GeoSystems Global Corp.

Colombia: Map Index

Internal Divisions
Amazonas (commissary) B5
Antioquia (dept.) B3
Arauca (intendency) C3
Atlántico (dept.) B2
Bolívar (dept.) B2
Boyacá (dept.) B3
Caldas (dept.) B3
Capital District B4
Caquetá (dept.) B4
Casanare (intendency) C3
Cauca (dept.) A4
César (dept.) B2
Chocó (dept.) A3
Córdoba (dept.) B2
Cundinamarca (dept.) B3
Guainía (commissary) C4
Guaviare (commissary) B4
Huila (dept.) A4
La Guajira (dept.) B2
Magdalena (dept.) B2
Meta (dept.) B4
Nariño (dept.) A4
Norte de Santander (dept.) B2
Putumayo (intendency) A4
Quindío (intendency) B3
Risaralda (dept.) B3
San Andrés y Providencia (intendency) .... Inset
Santander (dept.) B3
Sucre (dept.) B2
Tolima (dept.) B4
Valle del Cauca (dept.) A4
Vaupés (commissary) C4
Vichada (commissary) C3

Cities and Towns
Arauca C3
Armenia B3
Barrancabermeja B3
Barranquilla B2
Bogotá, capital B3
Bucaramanga B3
Buenaventura A4
Cali A4
Cartagena B2
Cravo Norte C3
Cúcuta B2
El Encanto B5
Florencia B4
Ibagué B3
Leticia C6
Manizales B3
Medellín B3
Miraflores B4
Mitú C4

Mocoa A4
Montería B2
Neiva B4
Orocué C3
Palmira A4
Pasto A4
Pereira B3
Popayán A4
Puerto Carreño D3
Puerto Inírida D4
Puerto Leguízamo B5
Quibdó A3
Riohacha B2
San Felipe D4
San José del Guaviare B4
Santa Marta B2
Sincelejo B2
Tumaco A4
Tunja B3
Turbo A2
Valledupar B2
Villavicencio B3
Vista Hermosa B4
Yopal B3

Other Features
Albuquerque, cays .... Inset
Amazon, river C5
Andes, range A4
Apaporis, river C4
Atrato, river A3
Caquetá, river B5
Cauca, river B3
Cordillera Central, range A4
Cordillera Occidental, range A4
Cordillera Oriental, range B4
Cristóbal Colón, peak B2
Gallinas, point C1
Guainía, river C4
Guajira, peninsula C1
Guaviare, river C4
Huila, mt. A4
Llanos, prairie C3
Magdalena, river B3
Meta, river C3
Orinoco, river D3
Patía, river A4
Providencia, island .... Inset
Putumayo, river B5
Roncador, cay .... Inset
San Andrés, island .... Inset
Serranilla, bank .... Inset
Sierra Nevada de Santa Marta, mts. B2
Tolima, mt. B3
Vaupés, river B4
Vichada, river C3

Venezuela: Map Index

Internal Divisions
Amazonas (territory) C3
Anzoátegui (state) D2
Apure (state) C2
Aragua (state) C2
Barinas (state) C2
Bolívar (state) D2
Carabobo (state) C2
Cojedes (state) C1
Delta Amacuro (territory) D2
Dependencias Federales C1
Distrito Federal C1
Falcón (state) B1
Guárico (state) C2
Lara (state) B1
Mérida (state) B2
Miranda (state) C1
Monagas (state) D2
Nueva Esparta (state) D1
Portuguesa (state) C2
Sucre (state) D1
Táchira (state) B2
Trujillo (state) B2
Yaracuy (state) C1
Zulia (state) B2

Cities and Towns
Acarigua C2
Anaco D2
Barcelona D1
Barinas B2
Barquisimeto C1
Baruta C1
Cabimas B1
Calabozo C2
Canaima D2
Caracas, capital C1
Carora C1
Carúpano D1
Ciudad Bolívar D2
Ciudad Guayana D2
Coro C1
Cumaná D1
El Tigre D2
Guanare C2
Güiria D1
La Asunción D1
La Guaira Maiquetía C1
Los Teques C1
Maiquetía C1
Maracaibo B1
Maracay C1
Maturín D2
Mérida B2

Petare C1
Puerto Ayacucho C2
Puerto Cabello C1
Puerto La Cruz D1
Punto Fijo B1
San Cristóbal B2
San Felipe C1
San Fernando de Apure C2
San Juan de Los Morros C2
Santa Elena de Uairén D3
Trujillo B2
Tucupita D2
Valencia C1
Valera B2

Other Features
Angel, falls D2
Apure, river C2
Arauca, river C2
Bolívar, mt. B2
Caroní, river D2
Casiquiare, river C3
Caura, river D2
Cojedes, river C2
Guri, reservoir D2
Guiana, highlands D3
La Tortuga, island C1
Llanos, plain B2

Maracaibo, lake B2
Margarita, island D1
Mérida, mts. B2
Meta, river C2
Neblina, mt. C3
Negro, river B3
Orinoco, river C3, D2
Pacaraima, mts. D3
Paria, gulf D1
Parima, mts. D3
Roraima, mt. D2
Venezuela, gulf B1

Venezuela

Capital: Caracas
Area: 352,144 sq. mi.
912,050 sq. km.
Population: 10,677,000
Largest City: Caracas
Language: Spanish
Monetary Unit: Bolivar

Ecuador

Capital: Quito
Area: 105,037 sq. mi.
272,117 sq. km.
Population: 10,677,000
Largest City: Guayaquil
Language: Spanish
Monetary Unit: Sucre

Ecuador: Map Index

Provinces

Azuay	B4
Bolívar	B3
Cañar	B4
Carchi	C2
Chimborazo	B3
Cotopaxi	B3
El Oro	B4
Esmeraldas	B2
Galápagos	Inset
Guayas	A4
Imbabura	B2
Loja	B5
Los Ríos	B3
Manabí	A3
Morona-Santiago	C4
Napo	C3
Pastaza	B2
Pichincha	C3
Sucumbíos	D3
Tungurahua	B3
Zamora-Chinchipe	B5

Cities and Towns

Ambato	B3
Azogues	B4
Babahoyo	B3
Baquerizo Moreno	Inset
Chone	A3
Cuenca	B4

Esmeraldas	B2
Guaranda	B3
Guayaquil	B4
Ibarra	B2
Jipijapa	A3
La Libertad	A4
Latacunga	B3
Loja	B4
Macas	B4
Machala	A3
Manta	A3
Milagro	B4
Nueva Loja	C2
Nuevo Rocafuerte	D3
Otavalo	B2
Portoviejo	A3
Puerto Bolívar	B4
Puyo	C3
Quevedo	B3
Quito, *capital*	B3
Riobamba	B3
San Lorenzo	B2
Santa Rosa	B4
Santo Domingo de los Colorados	B3
Tena	C3
Tulcán	C2
Zamora	B5

Other Features

Aguarico, *river*	C3
Andes, *mts.*	B4
Cayambe, *mt.*	C3

Chimborazo, *mt.*	B3
Chira, *river*	A5
Cordillera Occidental, *mts.*	B4
Cordillera Oriental, *mts.*	C4
Cotopaxi, *mt.*	B3
Curaray, *river*	C3
Daule, *river*	B3
Española, *island*	Inset
Fernandina, *island*	Inset
Galera, *point*	A2
Guaillabamba, *river*	B2
Guayas, *gulf*	A4
Guayas, *river*	B4
Isabela, *island*	Inset
Manta, *bay*	A3
Marchena, *island*	Inset
Napo, *river*	C3
Pastaza, *river*	C4
Pinta, *island*	Inset
Plata, *island*	A3
Puná, *island*	A4
Putumayo, *river*	D2
San Cristóbal, *island*	Inset
San Lorenzo, *cape*	A3
San Salvador, *island*	Inset
Santa Cruz, *island*	Inset
Santa Elena, *point*	A4
Santa María, *island*	Inset
Santiago, *river*	B4
Tigre, *river*	C3
Vinces, *river*	B3
Wolf, *mt.*	Inset
Zamora, *river*	B4

© GeoSystems Global Corp.

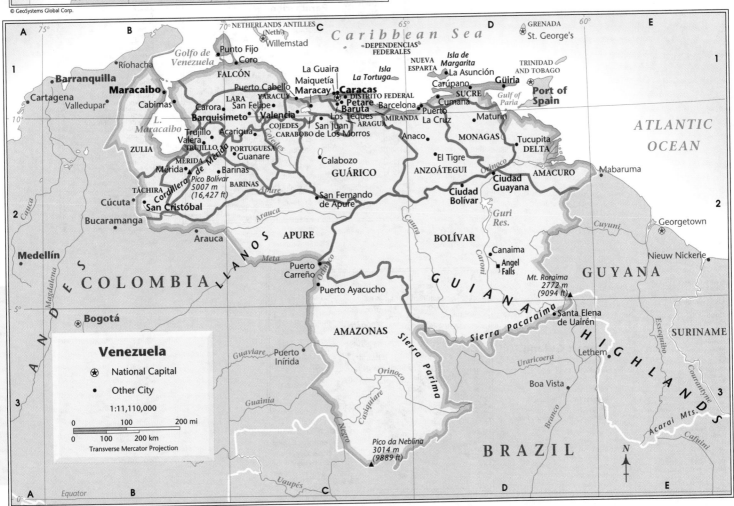

© GeoSystems Global Corp.

Guyana

National Capital ✪
Other City •
1:10,660,000
0   75   150 mi
0   75   150 km
Transverse Mercator Projection

Guyana

Capital: Georgetown
Area: 83,000 sq. mi.
214,969 sq. km.
Population: 754,000
Largest City: Georgetown
Language: English
Monetary Unit: Guyana dollar

Guyana:
Map Index

Cities and Towns
Anna Regina B2
Apoteri B4
Bartica B2
Biloku B5
Charity B2
Georgetown, *capital* B2
Isherton B4
Lethem B4
Linden B3
Mabaruma B1
Mahdia B3
Matthews Ridge A2
New Amsterdam C2
Suddie B2

Other Features
Acarai, *mts.* B5
Barama, *river* B2
Berbice, *river* B3
Courantyne, *river* B3
Cuyuni, *river* A2
Demerara, *river* B3
Essequibo, *river* B3, B5
Kaieteur, *falls* B3
Kanuku, *mts.* B4
Mazaruni, *river* A2
Merume, *mts.* A2
New, *river* C4
Pakaraima, *mts.* B3
Potaro, *river* B3
Rawa, *river* B4
Roraima, *mt.* A3
Takutu, *river* B4

Suriname

Capital: Paramaribo
Area: 63,037 sq. mi.
163,265 sq. km.
Population: 423,000
Largest City: Paramaribo
Language: Dutch
Monetary Unit: Suriname guilder

Suriname

National Capital ✪
Other City •
1:9,840,000
0   60   120 mi
0   60   120 km
Conic Equidistant Projection

Suriname:
Map Index

Cities and Towns
Albina B2
Apetina B3
Apoera A2
Benzdorp B3
Brokopondo B2
Groningen B2
Moengo B2
Nieuw Amsterdam B2
Nieuw Nickerie A2
Paramaribo, *capital* B2
Paranam B2
Sipaliwini A3
Totness A2
Zanderij B2

Other Features
Coeroeni, *river* A3
Coppename, *river* A2
Corantijn, *river* A2
Ellerts de Haan, *mts.* A3
Juliana Top, *mt.* A3
Kabelebo, *river* A2
Kayser, *mts.* A3
Lawa, *river* B2
Litani, *river* B3
Lucie, *river* A3
Marowijne, *river* B2
Nickerie, *river* A2
Oelemari, *river* B3
Oranje, *mts.* B3
Saramacca, *river* B2
Suriname, *river* B3
Tapanahoni, *river* B3
Tumuc-Humac, *mts.* B3
Wilhelmina, *mts.* A2
W.J. van Blommestein, *lake* B2

French Guiana:
Map Index

Cities and Towns
Apatou A1
Cacao B1
Camopi B2
Cayenne, *capital* B1
Grand Santi A1
Iracoubo B1
Kaw B1
Kourou B1
Mana B1
Maripasoula A2
Ouanary C1
Régina B1
Rémire B1
Saint-Élie B1
Saint-Georges C2
Saint-Laurent du Maroni A1
Saül B2

Other Features
Camopi, *river* B2
Devil's, *island* B1
Lawa, *river* A2
Litani, *river* A2
Mana, *river* B1
Maroni, *river* A1
Oyapock, *river* B2
Salut, *islands* B1
Tampok, *river* B2
Tumuc-Humac, *mts.* A2

French Guiana

Capital: Cayenne
Area: 35,135 sq. mi.
91,000 sq. km.
Population: 94,700
Largest City: Cayenne
Language: French
Monetary Unit: French franc

French Guiana

Territorial Capital ★
Other City •
1:8,410,000
0   50   100 mi
0   50   100 km
Conic Equidistant Projection

Brazil: Map Index

States and Federal District

Acre A2
Alagoas E2
Amapá C1
Amazonas B2
Bahia D3
Ceará E2
Espírito Santo D3
Federal District D3
Goiás D3
Maranhão D2
Mato Grosso C3
Mato Grosso do Sul D3
Minas Gerais D3
Pará E2
Paraíba E2
Paraná C4
Pernambuco D2
Piauí D2
Rio de Janeiro .... D4, Inset I
Rio Grande do Norte E2
Rio Grande do Sul B4
Rondônia B3
Roraima .... Inset II
Santa Catarina C4
São Paulo .... C4, Inset II
Sergipe E3
Tocantins D3

Cities and Towns

Alagoinhas E3
Altamira C2
Anápolis D3
Aracaju E3
Bacabal D2
Bauru D2
Belém D2
Belford Roxo .... Inset I
Belo Horizonte D3
Boa Vista B1
Bom Jesus da Lapa D3
Brasília, capital D3

Cáceres C3
Cachimbo C2
Campina Grande E2
Campinas D4
Campo Grande C4
Campos D4
Campos Elísios .... Inset II
Carapicuíba .... Inset II
Corumbá C3
Cotia .... Inset II
Cruzeiro do Sul A2
Cubatão .... Inset II
Cuiabá C3
Curitiba D4
Diadema .... Inset II
Dourados C4
Duque de Caxias .... Inset I
Feira de Santana D2
Floriano D2
Florianópolis D4
Fortaleza E2
Foz do Iguaçu C4
Goiânia D3
Governador Valadares D3
Guajara Mirim B3
Guarujá .... Inset II
Guarulhos .... Inset II
Ilhéus E3
Imbariê .... Inset I
Imperatriz D2
Inhomirim .... Inset I
Ipiíba .... Inset I
Itabira D3
Itabuna E3
Itaipu .... Inset I
Itajaí D4
Itapecerica da Serra ..... Inset II
Itapeva .... Inset II
Itaquaquecetuba .... Inset II
Jaboatão E2
Jacare-Acanga C2
Japeri .... Inset II
Jir Paraná B3
João Pessoa E2
Joinville D4

Juàzeiro D2
Juàzeiro do Norte E2
Juiz de Fora D4
Jundiaí D4
Lajes C4
Londrina C4
Macapá C1
Maceió E2
Majé .... Inset I
Manaus C2
Maraba D3
Mariana D3
Mauá .... Inset II
Mogi das Cruzes .... Inset II
Monjolo .... Inset I
Montes Claros D3
Mozzoro E2
Natal E2
Neves .... Inset I
Nilópolis .... Inset I
Niterói .... D4, Inset I
Nova Iguaçu .... Inset I
Olinda E2
Osasco .... Inset II
Palmas D3
Paranaguá D4
Parnaíba D2
Passo Fundo C4
Paulo Afonso E2
Pelotas C5
Petrolina D3
Petrópolis .... D4, Inset I
Poá .... Inset II
Pôrto Alegre C5
Pôrto Velho B2
Queimados .... Inset I
Randonopolis C3
Recife E2
Ribeirão Pires .... Inset II
Ribeirão Prêto D4
Rio Branco B2
Rio de Janeiro ...... D4, Inset I
Rio Grande C5
Rio Verde C3

Salvador E3
Santa Maria C4
Santana do Livramento C5
Santarém C2
Santo André .... Inset II
Santos .... D4, Inset II
São Bernardo do Campo . Inset II
São Caetano do Sul .... Inset II
São Gonçalo .... Inset I
São João de Meriti .... Inset I
São José do Rio Prêto D2
São Luís D2
São Paulo .... D4, Inset II
São Vicente .... Inset II
Sorocaba D4
Suzano .... Inset II
Tabôa da Serra .... Inset II
Tefé B2
Teresina D2
Tubarão D4
Uberaba D3
Uberlândia D3
Vicente de Carvalho ...... Inset II
Vitória D3
Vitória da Conquista D3
Volta Redonda D4

Other Features

Acaraí, range C1
Amazon, basin B2
Amazon, river B2
Araguaia, river C3
Aripuanã, river C2
Baleia, point E3
Bandeira, mt. D4
Billings, reservoir .... Inset II
Branco, river B1
Brazilian, highlands D3
Caviana, island D1
Chapada dos Parecis, range . C3
Corcovado, mt. .... Inset I
Corumbau, point E3
Furnas, reservoir D4

Geral, range C4
Grande, river D3
Guandu, river .... Inset I
Guaporé, river B3
Guiana, highlands B1
Içá, river B2
Iguaçu, falls C4
Itaipu, reservoir C4
Japurá, river B2
Jari, river C1
Javari, river A2
Juruá, river B2
Juruena, river C3
Madeira, river B2
Mantiqueira, range D4
Mar, range D4
Marajó, island D2
Mato Grosso, plateau C3
Mexiana, island D1
Neblina, mt. B1
Negro, river B2
Orgãos, range .... Inset I
Pantanal, lowland C4
Pará, river C2
Paraguai, river C3
Paraná, river C4
Parima, range B1
Parnaíba, river D2
Patos, lagoon C5
Paulo Afonso, falls E2
Pedra Açú, mt. .... Inset I
Purus, river B2
Roncador, range C3
São Francisco, river D3
Selvas, region B2
Sobradinho, reservoir D3
Tapajós, river C2
Taquari, river C3
Teles Pires, river C2
Tietê, river .... Inset II
Tocantins, river D2
Tucuruí, reservoir D2
Tumucumaque, range C1
Uruguai, river C4
Xingu, river C3

Brazil

Capital: Brasília
Area: 3,286,470 sq. mi.
8,514,171 sq. km.
Population: 158,739,000
Largest City: São Paulo
Language: Portuguese
Monetary Unit: Cruzeiro real

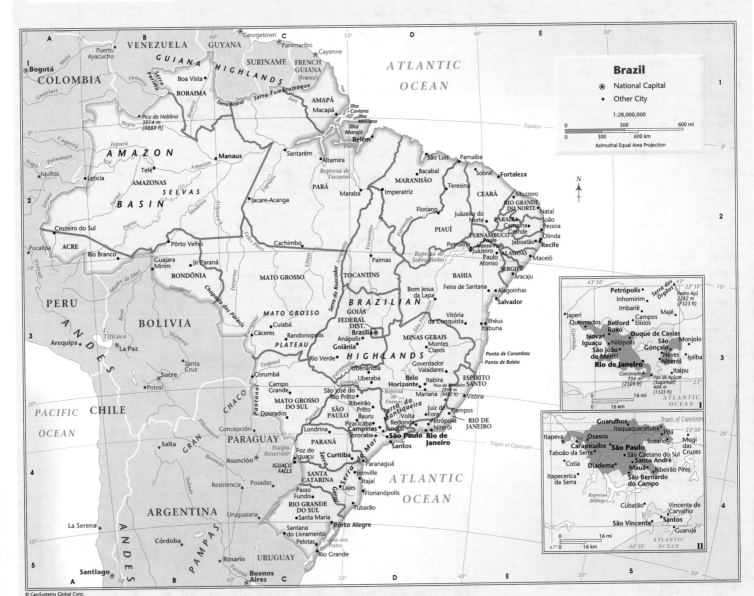

MAJOR CITIES

Antigua & Barbuda
St. Johns — 27,000

Bahamas
Nassau — 172,000

Barbados
Bridgetown — 6,000

Belize
Belize City — 45,000
Belmopan — 4,000

Canada (metro)
Toronto — 3,893,000
Montréal — 3,127,000
Vancouver — 1,603,000
Ottawa — 921,000

Costa Rica (metro)
San José — 1,000,000

Cuba
Havana — 2,119,000

Dominica
Roseau — 16,000

Dominican Republic
Santo Domingo — 2,400,000

El Salvador
San Salvador — 423,000

Grenada
St. George's — 30,000

Guatemala
Guatemala — 1,676,000

Haiti
Port-au-Prince — 690,000

Honduras
Tegucigalpa — 608,000

Jamaica (metro)
Kingston — 587,000

Mexico (metro)
Mexico City — 20,000,000
Guadalajara — 3,000,000
Monterrey — 2,700,000

Nicaragua
Managua — 1,000,000

Panama
Panamá — 447,000

St. Kitts & Nevis
Basseterre — 15,000

St. Lucia
Castries — 45,000

St. Vincent & Grenadines
Kingstown — 15,000

Trinidad & Tobago
Port of Spain — 51,000

United States
New York — 7,323,000
Los Angeles — 3,485,000
Chicago — 2,784,000
Houston — 1,631,000
Philadelphia — 1,586,000
San Diego — 1,111,000
Detroit — 1,028,000
Washington, D.C. — 607,000

International comparability of city population data is limited by various data inconsistencies.

CITIES
⊛ National Capital
★ Territorial Capital
• Other City

ELEVATIONS

Feet	Meters
13,120	4000
6560	2000
1640	500
656	200
0	0
Below sea level	

N

| | 250 | 500 | 750 | 1000 mi |
| | 500 | 1000 | 1500 km |

© GeoSystems Global Corp.

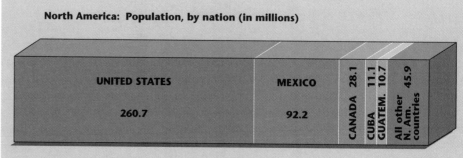

North America: Population, by nation (in millions)

UNITED STATES	MEXICO	CANADA	CUBA	GUATEM.	All other N. Am. countries
260.7	92.2	28.1	11.1	10.7	45.9

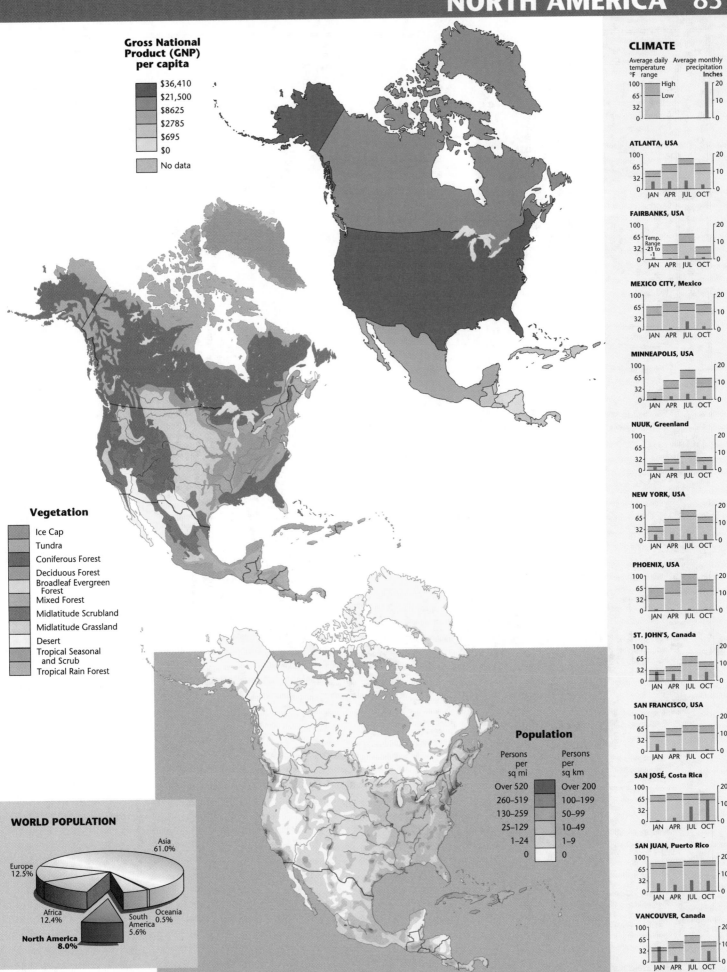

Gross National Product (GNP) per capita

- $36,410
- $21,500
- $8625
- $2785
- $695
- $0
- No data

Vegetation

- Ice Cap
- Tundra
- Coniferous Forest
- Deciduous Forest
- Broadleaf Evergreen Forest
- Mixed Forest
- Midlatitude Scrubland
- Midlatitude Grassland
- Desert
- Tropical Seasonal and Scrub
- Tropical Rain Forest

WORLD POPULATION

- Asia 61.0%
- Europe 12.5%
- Africa 12.4%
- South America 5.6%
- Oceania 0.5%
- North America 8.0%

Population

Persons per sq mi	Persons per sq km
Over 520	Over 200
260–519	100–199
130–259	50–99
25–129	10–49
1–24	1–9
0	0

CLIMATE

Average daily temperature °F range   Average monthly precipitation Inches

- 100 / 65 / 32 / 0   High / Low   20 / 10 / 0

ATLANTA, USA

FAIRBANKS, USA — Temp. Range -21 to -1

MEXICO CITY, Mexico

MINNEAPOLIS, USA

NUUK, Greenland

NEW YORK, USA

PHOENIX, USA

ST. JOHN'S, Canada

SAN FRANCISCO, USA

SAN JOSÉ, Costa Rica

SAN JUAN, Puerto Rico

VANCOUVER, Canada

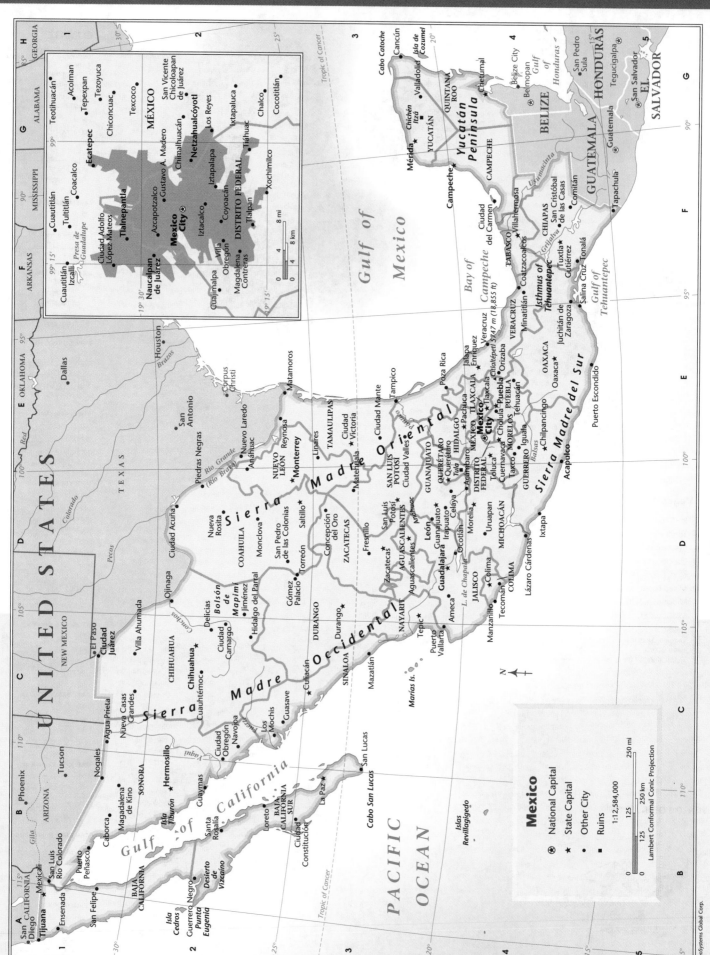

Mexico

⊛ National Capital
★ State Capital
• Other City
■ Ruins

1:12,584,000

Lambert Conformal Conic Projection

© GeoSystems Global Corp.

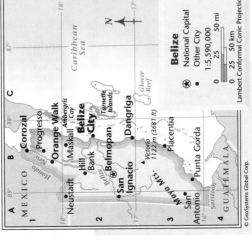

Belize

Capital: Belmopan
Area: 8,867 sq. mi.
22,972 sq. km.
Population: 209,000
Largest City: Belize City
Language: English
Monetary Unit: Belize dollar

Belize:
Map Index

Cities and Towns
Belize City B2
Belmopan, capital B2
Corozal B1
Dangriga B2
Hill Bank B2
Maskall B2
Neustadt B1
Orange Walk B1
Placentia B3
Progresso B1
Punta Gorda B3
San Antonio A3
San Ignacio A2

Other Features
Ambergris Cay, island C2
Belize, river B2
Glover, reef C3
Hondo, river B1
Maya, mts. A3
New, river B1
Sarstoon, river A4
Turneffe, islands C2
Victoria, peak. B3

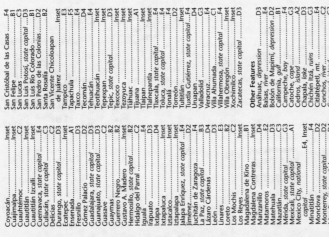

Guatemala

Capital: Guatemala City
Area: 42,042 sq. mi.
108,917 sq. km.
Population: 10,721,000
Largest City: Guatemala City
Language: Spanish
Monetary Unit: Quetzal

Guatemala:
Map Index

Cities and Towns
Antigua C5
Champerico B5
Chinajá C4
Cobán C4
Escuintla C5
Flores D3
Guatemala City, capital ... C5
Huehuetenango B4
Jutiapa D5
La Libertad C3
Mazatenango B5
Paxbán C2
Puerto Barrios D4
Quetzaltenango B5
Salamá C4
San José C5
San Luis D3
Santo Tomás de Castilla .. D4
Tikal D2
Zacapa D5

Other Features
Atitlán, lake B5
Chixoy, river C4
Honduras, gulf E3
Izabal, lake D4
Motagua, river D4
Pasión, river C3
Paz, river C6
Petén-Itzá, lake D2
San Pedro, river D4
Sarstún, river A5
Sierra Madre, mts. A4
Suchiate, river B4
Tajumulco, volcano A4
Usumacinta, river C3

Mexico

Capital: Mexico City
Area: 756,066 sq. mi.
1,958,720 sq. km.
Population: 92,202,000
Largest City: Mexico City
Language: Spanish
Monetary Unit: New peso

Mexico:
Map Index

States
Aguascalientes D3
Baja California A1
Baja California Sur B2
Campeche F4
Chiapas E4
Chihuahua C2
Coahuila D2
Colima D4
Distrito Federal .... E4, Inset
Durango D3
Guanajuato D3
Guerrero E4
Hidalgo E3
Jalisco D4
México .... E4, Inset
Michoacán D4
Morelos .... Inset
Nayarit C3
Nuevo León E3
Oaxaca E4
Puebla E4
Querétaro D3
Quintana Roo G4
Sinaloa C3
Sonora B1
Tabasco F4
Tamaulipas E3
Tlaxcala E4
Veracruz E3
Yucatán G3
Zacatecas D3

Cities and Towns
Acámbaro D4
Acapulco E4
Acolman .... Inset
Agua Prieta C1
Aguascalientes, state capital ... D3
Ameca D3
Anáhuac .... Inset
Atzcapotzalco .... Inset
Caborca B1
Campeche, state capital ... F4
Cancún G3
Chalco .... Inset
Chetumal, state capital G4
Chiconcuac .... Inset
Chihuahua, state capital ... C2
Chilpancingo, state capital . E4
Chimalhuacán .... Inset
Cholula E4
Ciudad Acuña D2
Ciudad Adolfo López Mateos .. Inset
Ciudad Camargo C2
Ciudad Constitución B3
Ciudad del Carmen F4
Ciudad Juárez C1
Ciudad Mante E3
Ciudad Obregón C2
Ciudad Valles E3
Ciudad Victoria, state capital . E3
Coacoalco .... Inset
Coatzacoalcos F4
Cocotitlán .... Inset
Colima, state capital D4
Comitán F4
Concepción del Oro D3

Coyoacán .... Inset
Cuajimalpa .... Inset
Cuauhtémoc C2
Cuautitlán Izcalli .... Inset
Cuernavaca, state capital .. E4
Culiacán, state capital C3
Delicias C2
Durango, state capital D3
Ecatepec .... Inset
Ensenada A1
Fresnillo D3
Gómez Palacio D2
Guadalajara, state capital .. D3
Guanajuato, state capital .. D3
Guasave C3
Guaymas B2
Guerrero Negro B2
Gustavo A. Madero .... Inset
Hermosillo, state capital ... B2
Hidalgo del Parral C2
Iguala E4
Irapuato D3
Ixtapaluca .... Inset
Ixtapalapa .... Inset
Iztacalco .... Inset
Iztapalapa .... Inset
Jalapa Enríquez, state capital . E4
Jiménez D2
Juchitán de Zaragoza F4
La Paz, state capital B3
Lázaro Cárdenas D4
León D3
Linares E3
Loreto B2
Los Mochis C2
Los Reyes .... Inset
Magdalena de Kino B1
Magdalena Contreras .... Inset
Manzanillo D4
Matamoros E2
Matehuala D3
Mazatlán C3
Mérida, state capital G3
Mexicali, state capital A1
Mexico City, national capital ... E4, Inset
Minatitlán F4
Monclova D2
Monterrey, state capital D3
Morelia, state capital D4
Naucalpan de Juárez .... Inset
Navojoa C2
Netzahualcóyotl .... Inset
Nogales B1
Nuevo Casas Grandes C1
Nuevo Laredo E2
Oaxaca, state capital E4
Ocotlán D3
Ojinaga D2
Orizaba E4
Pachuca, state capital E3
Piedras Negras D2
Poza Rica E3
Puebla, state capital E4
Puerto Peñasco B1
Puerto Vallarta C3
Querétaro, state capital E4
Reynosa E2
Salina Cruz E4
Saltillo, state capital D3

San Cristóbal de las Casas .. F4
San Felipe B1
San Lucas C2
San Luis Potosí, state capital . E3
San Pedro de las Colonias .. D2
Santa Rosalía B2
San Vicente Chicoloapan ... Inset
Tampico E3
Tapachula F5
Taxco E4
Tecomán D4
Tehuacán E4
Teotihuacán .... Inset
Tepexpan .... Inset
Tepic, state capital D3
Texcoco .... Inset
Tezoyuca .... Inset
Tláhuac .... Inset
Tijuana A1
Tlalpan .... Inset
Tlalnepantla .... Inset
Tlaxcala, state capital E4
Toluca, state capital E4
Tonalá D2
Torreón D2
Tultitlán .... Inset
Tuxtla Gutiérrez, state capital . F4
Uruapan D4
Valladolid G3
Veracruz E4
Villa Ahumada C1
Villahermosa, state capital . F4
Villa Obregón .... Inset
Xochimilco .... Inset
Zacatecas, state capital D3

Other Features
Anáhuac, depression .... Inset
Balsas, river D4
Bolsón de Mapimí, depression . D2
California, gulf B2
Campeche, bay F4
Catoche, cape G3
Cedros, island A2
Chapala, lake D3
Chichén Itzá, ruins G3
Citlaltépetl, mt. E4
Conchos, river D2
Cozumel, island G3
Eugenia, point A2
Fuerte, river C2
Grijalva, river F4
Guadalupe, island .... Inset
Marías, islands C3
Pánuco, river E3
Revillagigedo, islands B4
Río Grande (Río Bravo), river . D2
San Lucas, cape B3
Sierra Madre del Sur, mts. .. D4
Sierra Madre Occidental, mts. . C2
Sierra Madre Oriental, mts. .. D2
Tehuantepec, gulf E4
Tehuantepec, isthmus F4
Tiburón, island B2
Tula, river D3
Usumacinta, river F4
Vizcaíno, desert B2
Yaqui, river C2
Yucatán, peninsula G4

© GeoSystems Global Corp.

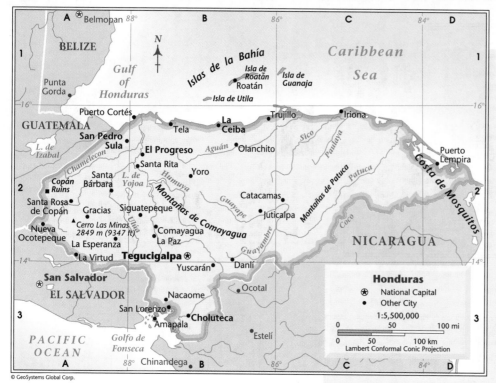

Honduras

Capital: Tegucigalpa
Area: 43,277 sq. mi.
112,117 sq. km.
Population: 5,315,000
Largest City: Tegucigalpa
Language: Spanish
Monetary Unit: Lempira

**Honduras:
Map Index**

Cities and Towns
Amapala	B3
Catacamas	C2
Choluteca	B3
Comayagua	B2
Danlí	B2
El Progreso	B2
Gracias	A2
Iriona	C2
Juticalpa	B2
La Ceiba	B2
La Esperanza	A2
La Paz	B2
La Virtud	A2
Nacaome	B3
Nueva Ocotepeque	A2
Olanchito	B2
Puerto Cortés	B2
Puerto Lempira	D2
Roatán	B1
San Lorenzo	B3
San Pedro Sula	A2
Santa Bárbara	A2
Santa Rita	B2
Santa Rosa de Copán	A2
Siguatepeque	B2
Tegucigalpa, capital	B2
Tela	B2
Trujillo	B2
Yoro	B2
Yuscarán	B3

Other Features
Aguán, river	B2
Bahía, islands	B1
Caribbean, sea	C1
Chamelecon, river	A2
Coco, river	C2
Comayagua, mts.	B2
Copán, ruins	A2
Fonseca, gulf	B3
Guanaja, island	C1
Guayambre, river	B2
Guayape, river	B2
Honduras, gulf	A1
Humuya, river	B2
Las Minas, mt.	A2
Mosquitos, coast	D2
Patuca, mts.	C2
Patuca, river	C2
Paulaya, river	C2
Roatán, island	B1
Sico, river	C2
Ulúa, river	B2
Utila, island	B1
Yojoa, lake	B2

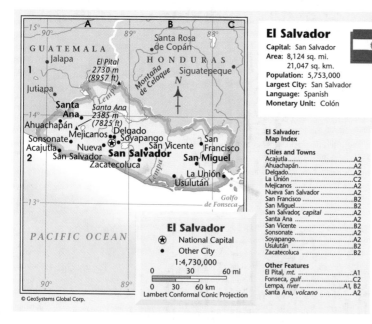

El Salvador

Capital: San Salvador
Area: 8,124 sq. mi.
21,047 sq. km.
Population: 5,753,000
Largest City: San Salvador
Language: Spanish
Monetary Unit: Colón

**El Salvador:
Map Index**

Cities and Towns
Acajutla	A2
Ahuachapán	A2
Delgado	A2
La Unión	C2
Mejicanos	A2
Nueva San Salvador	A2
San Francisco	B2
San Miguel	B2
San Salvador, capital	A2
Santa Ana	A2
San Vicente	B2
Sonsonate	A2
Soyapango	A2
Usulután	B2
Zacatecoluca	B2

Other Features
El Pital, mt.	A1
Fonseca, gulf	C2
Lempa, river	A1, B2
Santa Ana, volcano	A2

**Costa Rica:
Map Index**

Cities and Towns
Alajuela	B2
Cartago	C3
Colorado	C2
Golfito	C4
Heredia	B2
La Cruz	A1
Liberia	A2
Limón	C3
Los Chiles	B1
Puerto Jiménez	C4
Puerto Quepos	B3
Puntarenas	B3
San José, capital	B3
Santa Cruz	A2

Other Features
Arenal, lake	B2
Central, range	B2
Chirripó, mt.	C3
Chirripó, river	C2
Coronado, bay	B3
Dulce, gulf	C4
Frío, river	B2
General, river	C3
Grande, river	B3
Guanacaste, range	A2
Irazú, volcano	C3
Nicoya, gulf	B3
Papagayo, gulf	A2
Pirris, river	B3
Reventazón, river	C3
San Carlos, river	B2
San Juan, river	B2
Sarapiquí, river	B2
Sixaola, river	C3
Talamanca, range	C3
Tempisque, river	A2

Costa Rica

Capital: San José
Area: 19,730 sq. mi.
51,114 sq. km.
Population: 3,342,000
Largest City: San José
Language: Spanish
Monetary Unit: Colón

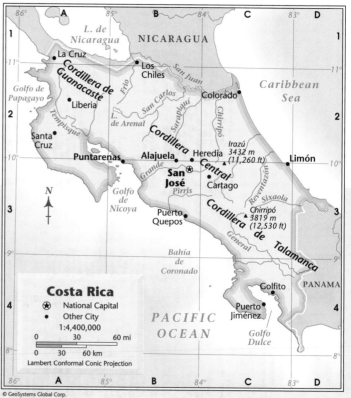

Nicaragua

Capital: Managua
Area: 50,880 sq. mi.
131,813 sq. km.
Population: 4,097,000
Largest City: Managua
Language: Spanish
Monetary Unit: Córdoba

Nicaragua: Map Index

Cities and Towns

Bluefields	C3
Boaco	B2
Bocay	B1
Chinandega	A2
Colonia Nueva Guinea	B3
Corinto	A2
Diriamba	A3
Estelí	A2
Granada	B3
Jinotega	B2
Jinotepe	A3
Juigalpa	B2
La Rosita	B2
León	A2
Managua, *capital*	A3
Masaya	A3
Matagalpa	B2
Nagarote	A2
Ocotal	A2
Prinzapolka	C2
Puerto Cabezas	C1
Puerto Sandino	A2
Rama	B2
Río Blanco	B2
Río Grande	A2
Rivas	B3
San Carlos	B3
San Juan del Norte	C3
San Juan del Sur	B3
Siuna	B2
Somoto	A2
Waspam	C1
Wiwilí	B2

Other Features

Bambana, *river*	B2
Bismuna, *lagoon*	C1
Bluefields, *bay*	C3
Bocay, *river*	B2
Chontaleña, *mts.*	B2
Coco, *river*	A2, C1
Cosigüina, *mt.*	A2
Cosigüina, *point*	A2
Dariense, *mts.*	B2
Escondido, *river*	B2
Fonseca, *gulf*	A2
Gracias a Dios, *cape*	C1
Grande de Matagalpa, *river*	B2
Huapí, *mts.*	B2
Isabelia, *mts.*	B2
Kurinwás, *river*	B2
Maíz, *islands*	C2
Managua, *lake*	A2
Mico, *river*	B2
Miskitos, *cays*	C1
Mogotón, *mt.*	A2
Mosquitos, *coast*	C3
Nicaragua, *lake*	B3
Ometepe, *island*	B3
Perlas, *lagoon*	C2
Perlas, *point*	C2
Prinzapolka, *river*	B2
San Juan, *river*	B3
San Juan del Norte, *bay*	C3
Siquia, *river*	B2
Solentiname, *island*	B3
Tipitapa, *river*	A2
Tuma, *river*	B2
Wawa, *river*	B1
Zapatera, *island*	B3

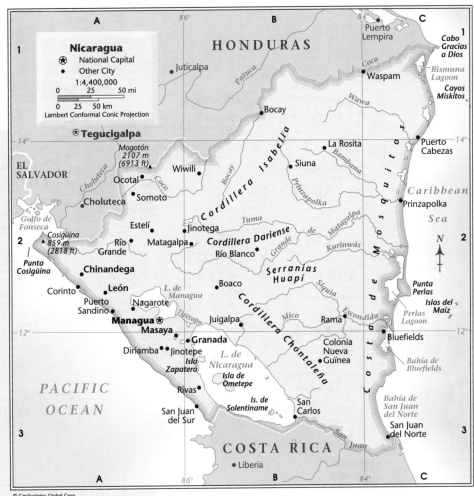

© GeoSystems Global Corp.

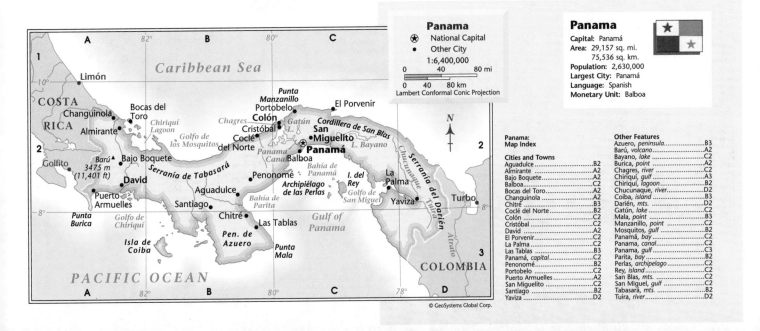

Panama

Capital: Panamá
Area: 29,157 sq. mi.
75,536 sq. km.
Population: 2,630,000
Largest City: Panamá
Language: Spanish
Monetary Unit: Balboa

Panama: Map Index

Cities and Towns

Aguadulce	B2
Almirante	A2
Bajo Boquete	A2
Balboa	C2
Bocas del Toro	A2
Changuinola	B3
Chitré	B3
Coclé del Norte	B2
Colón	C2
Cristóbal	C2
David	A2
El Porvenir	C2
La Palma	C2
Las Tablas	B3
Panamá, *capital*	C2
Penonomé	B2
Portobelo	C2
Puerto Armuelles	A2
San Miguelito	C2
Santiago	B2
Yaviza	D2

Other Features

Azuero, *peninsula*	B3
Barú, *volcano*	A2
Bayano, *lake*	C2
Burica, *point*	A2
Chagres, *river*	C2
Chiriquí, *gulf*	A3
Chiriquí, *lagoon*	B2
Chucunaque, *river*	D2
Coiba, *island*	B3
Darién, *mts.*	D2
Gatún, *lake*	C2
Mala, *point*	B3
Manzanillo, *point*	C2
Mosquitos, *gulf*	C2
Panamá, *bay*	C2
Panama, *canal*	C2
Panama, *gulf*	C3
Parita, *bay*	B2
Perlas, *archipelago*	C2
Rey, *island*	C2
San Blas, *mts.*	C2
San Miguel, *gulf*	C2
Tabasará, *mts.*	B2
Tuira, *river*	D2

© GeoSystems Global Corp.

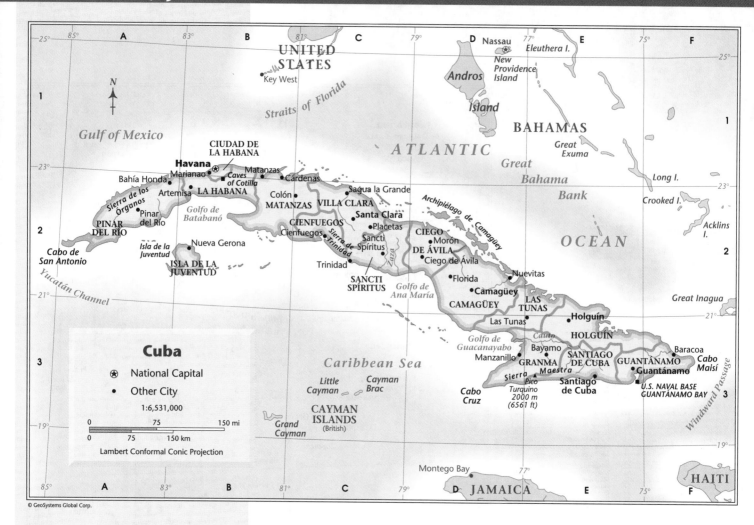

© GeoSystems Global Corp.

Cuba

Capital: Havana
Area: 42,804 sq. mi.
110,890 sq. km.
Population: 11,064,000
Largest City: Havana
Language: Spanish
Monetary Unit: Peso

Cuba:
Map Index

Provinces
Camagüey D2
Ciego de Ávila D2
Cienfuegos C2
Ciudad de La Habana B1
Granma E3
Guantánamo E3
Holguín E3
Isla de la Juventud
(special municipality) B2
La Habana B2
Las Tunas E2
Matanzas B2
Pinar del Río A2
Sancti Spíritus C2
Santiago de Cuba E3
Villa Clara C2

Cities and Towns
Artemisa B2
Bahía Honda A2
Baracoa F3
Bayamo E3
Camagüey D2
Cárdenas B1
Ciego de Ávila D2
Cienfuegos C2
Colón C2
Florida D2
Guantánamo E3
Havana, capital B1
Holguín E3
Las Tunas E3

Manzanillo D3
Marianao B1
Matanzas B1
Morón D2
Nueva Gerona B2
Nuevitas D2
Pinar del Río A2
Placetas C2
Sagua la Grande C2
Sancti Spíritus C2
Santa Clara C2
Santiago de Cuba E3
Trinidad C2

Other Features
Ana María, gulf D2
Batabanó, gulf B2
Camagüey, archipelago D2
Cauto, river E3
Cotilla, caves B2
Cruz, cape D3
Florida, straits B1
Guacanayabo, gulf D3
Juventud, island B2
Maestra, mts. D3
Maisí, cape E3
Mexico, gulf A1
Órganos, mts. A2
San Antonio, cape A2
Trinidad, mts. E3
Turquino, mt. E3
U.S. Naval Base
Guantánamo Bay E3
Windward, passage F3
Yucatán, channel A2
Zaza, river C2

Jamaica

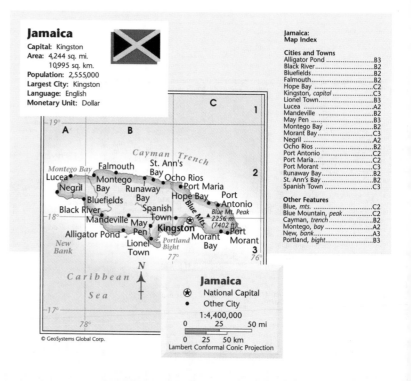

Capital: Kingston
Area: 4,244 sq. mi.
10,995 sq. km.
Population: 2,555,000
Largest City: Kingston
Language: English
Monetary Unit: Dollar

Jamaica:
Map Index

Cities and Towns
Alligator Pond B3
Black River B2
Bluefields B2
Falmouth B2
Hope Bay C2
Kingston, capital C3
Lionel Town B3
Lucea A2
Mandeville B2
May Pen B3
Montego Bay B2
Morant Bay C3
Negril A2
Ocho Rios B2
Port Antonio C2
Port Maria C2
Port Morant C3
Runaway Bay B2
St. Ann's Bay B2
Spanish Town C3

Other Features
Blue, mts. C2
Blue Mountain, peak C2
Cayman, trench B2
Montego, bay A2
New, bank A3
Portland, bight B3

© GeoSystems Global Corp.

Cotuí B1
Dajabón A1
El Macao D2
El Seibo C2
Hato Mayor C2
Higüey D2
Jimaní A2
La Romana D2
La Vega B1
Luperón B1
Mao A1
Miches C2
Moca B1
Monte Cristi A1
Monte Plata C2
Nagua C1
Neiba A2
Oviedo A3
Pedernales A2
Pedro Santana A1
Puerto Plata B1
Sabana de la Mar C1
Sabaneta A1
Salcedo B1
Samaná C1
San Cristóbal B2
San Francisco de Macorís B1
San José de las Matas A1
San Juan A2
San Pedro de Macorís C2
Santiago B1
Santo Domingo, capital C2
Sousúa B1

Dominican Republic:
Map Index

Provinces
Azua B2
Bahoruco A2
Barahona A2
Dajabón A1
Distrito Nacional B2
Duarte C1
El Seibo C2
Espaillat B1
Hato Mayor C2
Independencia A2
La Altagracia D2
La Estrelleta A1
La Romana D2
La Vega B2
María Trinidad Sánchez B1
Monseñor Nouel B2
Monte Cristi A1
Monte Plata C2
Pedernales A3
Peravia B2
Puerto Plata B1
Salcedo B1
Samaná C1
Sánchez Ramírez B1
San Cristóbal B2
San Juan A2
San Pedro de Macorís C2
Santiago B1
Santiago Rodríguez A1
Valverde B1

Cities and Towns
Azua B2
Baní B2
Barahona A2
Bonao B2
Cabrera C1
Comendador A2

Other Features
Bahoruco, mts. A2
Beata, cape A3
Beata, island A3
Calderas, bay B2
Camú, river B1
Central, range B2
Cibao, valley B1
Duarte, mt. B1
Engaño, cape D2
Enriquillo, lake A2
Mona, passage D2
Neiba, mts. A2
Ocoa, bay B2
Oriental, range C2
Ozama, river C1
Samaná, bay C1
Samaná, cape C1
Saona, island D2
Septentrional, range A1
Soco, river C2
Yaque del Norte, river A1
Yaque del Sur, river A2
Yuna, river B2

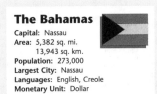

Dominican Republic

Capital: Santo Domingo
Area: 18,704 sq. mi.
  48,456 sq. km.
Population: 88,000
Largest City: Santo Domingo
Language: Spanish
Monetary Unit: Peso

Dominican Republic

⊛ National Capital
• Other City
1:3,778,000
0   20   40 mi
0 20 40 km
Transverse Mercator Projection

© GeoSystems Global Corp.

Haiti

Capital: Port-au-Prince
Area: 10,695 sq. mi.
  27,614 sq. km.
Population: 6,491,000
Largest City: Port-au-Prince
Language: French
Monetary Unit: Gourde

Haiti

⊛ National Capital
• Other City
1:5,593,000
0   30   60 mi
0 30 60 km
Lambert Conformal Conic Projection

© GeoSystems Global Corp.

Haiti:
Map Index

Departments
Artibonite C1
Centre D1
Grand Ande B2
Nord C1
Nord-Est D1
Nord-Ouest B1
Ouest C2
Sud B2
Sud-Est C2

Cities and Towns
Anse-à-Galets C2
Belle-Anse C2
Cap-Haïtien C1
Dame-Marie A2
Ennery C1
Gonaïves C1
Hinche C1
Jacmel C2
Jérémie A2
Léogâne C2
Les Cayes B2
Miragoâne B2
Mirebalais C2
Port-au-Prince, capital C2
Port-de-Paix C1
Port-Salut B2
Saint-Marc C1

Other Features
Artibonite, river C1
Gonâve, gulf B1
Gonâve, island B2
Gravois, point B3
Pic de la Selle, mt. D2
Port-au-Prince, bay C2
Tortuga, island C1
Vache, island B2
Windward, passage B1

Bahamas and
Turks & Caicos Islands:
Map Index

Bahamas

Cities and Towns
Alice Town B2
Arthur's Town B3
Freeport A2
Kemps Bay B3
Marsh Harbour B2
Matthew Town C4
Nassau, capital B2
Nicholls' Town A2
Sandy Point B2

Other Features
Acklins, island C4
Andros, island A3
Cat, island B3
Crooked, island C4
Crooked Island, passage C4
Eleuthera, island B2
Exuma, sound B3
Grand Bahama, island A2
Great Abaco, island B2
Great Bahama, bank A3
Great Exuma, island B3
Great Inagua, island C4
Harbour, island B2
Little Inagua, island C4
Long, island C3
Mayaguana, island C4
Mayaguana, passage C4
New Providence, island B3
Northeast Providence,
  channel B2
Rum, cay C3
Samana, cay C3
San Salvador, island C3
Water, cays A3

Turks & Caicos Islands

Cities and Towns
Cockburn Harbour D4
Grand Turk, capital D4

Other Features
Ambergris, cay D4
Caicos, islands D4
Grand Turk, island D4
Providenciales, island C4
Salt, cay D4
Turks, islands D4

The Bahamas

Capital: Nassau
Area: 5,382 sq. mi.
  13,943 sq. km.
Population: 273,000
Largest City: Nassau
Languages: English, Creole
Monetary Unit: Dollar

Turks and Caicos Is.

Capital: Grand Turk
Area: 193 sq. mi.
  500 sq. km.
Population: 11,700
Largest City: Grand Turk
Language: English
Monetary Unit: U.S. Dollar

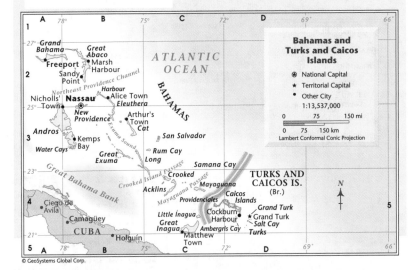

Bahamas and
Turks and Caicos
Islands

⊛ National Capital
★ Territorial Capital
• Other City
1:13,537,000
0   75   150 mi
0 75 150 km
Lambert Conformal Conic Projection

© GeoSystems Global Corp.

ATLANTIC OCEAN

Caribbean Sea

Puerto Rico

Capital: San Juan
Area: 3,492 sq. mi.
9,047 sq. km.
Population: 3,522,037
Largest City: San Juan
Languages: Spanish, English
Monetary Unit: U.S. dollar

Puerto Rico
★ Territorial Capital
— Limited Access Highway
— Other Major Road

1:1,696,000

0   20   40 mi
0 20 40 km

Polyconic Projection

© GeoSystems Global Corp.

Puerto Rico:
Map Index

Cities and Towns
Adjuntas	B2
Aguada	A2
Aguadilla	A2
Aguas Buenas	C2
Aguilita	B2
Aibonito	C2
Añasco	A2
Arecibo	B2
Arroyo	C3
Bajadero	B2
Barceloneta	B2
Barranquitas	C2
Bayamón	C2
Cabo Rojo	A2
Caguas	C2
Camuy	B2
Candelaria	C2
Canóvanas	D2
Carolina	D2
Cataño	C2
Cayey	C2
Ceiba	D2
Celada	D2
Ciales	C2
Cidra	C2
Coamo	C2
Coco	C2
Comerío	C2
Coquí	C3
Corazón	C3
Corozal	C2
Coto Laurel	B2
Dorado	C2
Fajardo	D2
Florida	B2
Guánica	B3
Guayama	C3
Guayanilla	B2
Guaynabo	C2
Gurabo	D2
Hatillo	B2
Hormigueros	A2
Humacao	D2
Imbéry	B2
Isabela	A1
Jayuya	B2
Jobos	C3
Juana Díaz	C2
Juncos	D2
Lajas	A2
Lares	B2
Las Piedras	D2
Levittown	C2
Loíza	D2
Luquillo	D2
Manatí	B2
Martorell	D2
Maunabo	D2
Mayagüez	A2
Moca	A2
Naguabo	D2
Pastillo	C3
Patillas	C2
Peñuelas	B2
Ponce	B2
Puerto Real	A2
Punta Santiago	D2

Quebradillas	B2
Río Grande	D2
Sabana Grande	B2
Salinas	C3
San Antonio	A2
San Germán	A2
San Isidro	D2
San Juan, *capital*	C2
San Lorenzo	D2
San Sebastián	B2
Santa Isabel	C3
Santo Domingo	B2
Trujillo Alto	C2
Utuado	B2
Vega Alta	C2
Vega Baja	C2
Vieques	D2
Villalba	C2
Yabucoa	D2
Yauco	B2

Other Features
Añasco, *beach*	A2
Arenas, *point*	D2
Bayamón, *river*	C2
Brea, *point*	B3
Cabo Rojo Natl. Wildlife Refuge	A3
Caguana Indian Ceremonial Park	B2
Caja de Muertos, *island*	B3
Caña Gorda, *beach*	B3
Caribbean, *sea*	B3
Caribbean Natl. Forest	D2
Carite Forest Reserve	C2
Coamo Hot Springs	C2
Cordillera Central, *mts.*	B2
Culebra, *island*	E2
Culebrinas, *river*	A2
Doña Juana, *mt.*	C2
El Cañuelo, *ruins*	C2
El Toro, *mt.*	D2
Este, *point*	E2
Fortín Conde de Mirasol, *fort*	E2
Grande de Añasco, *river*	A2
Grande de Manatí, *river*	C2
Guajataca Forest Reserve	B2
Guánica Forest Reserve	B3
Guilarte, *mt.*	B2
Guilarte Forest Reserve	B2
Icacos, *key*	D2
La Plata, *river*	C2
Maricao Forest Reserve	A2
Mona, *passage*	A2
Norte, *key*	E2
Puerca, *point*	E2
Punta, *mt.*	B2
Rincón, *bay*	C3
Río Abajo Forest Reserve	B2
Río Camuy Cave Park	B2
Rojo, *point*	A3
Roosevelt Roads Naval Station	D2
San Juan, *passage*	D2
Sierra de Cayey, *mts.*	C2
Sierra de Luquillo, *mts.*	D2
Sombe, *beach*	E2
Susua Forest Reserve	B2
Toro Negro Forest Reserve	C2
Vieques, *island*	D2
Vieques, *passage*	D2
Vieques, *sound*	D2
Yeguas, *point*	D2

Antigua & Barbuda
★ National Capital
• Other City

1:1,480,000

0   10   20 mi
0 10 20 km
Transverse Mercator Projection

Goat Point
Cobb Cove
Codrington Lagoon
Codrington
Palmetto Point
Gravenor Bay
Spanish Point

Barbuda

Caribbean Sea

Antigua
Cedar Grove
St. John's
Bolands
Boggy Pk.
405 m
(1330 ft)
Freetown
Old Road
Falmouth
Willoughby Bay
Cape Shirley

Redonda

© GeoSystems Global Corp.

Antigua and Barbuda

Capital: St. John's
Area: 171 sq. mi.
443 sq. km.
Population: 65,000
Largest City: St. John's
Language: English
Monetary Unit: East Caribbean dollar

Antigua and Barbuda:
Map Index

Cities and Towns
Bolands	D5
Cedar Grove	E5
Codrington	E2
Falmouth	E5
Freetown	E5
Old Road	D5
St. John's, *capital*	D5

Other Features
Antigua, *island*	D4
Barbuda, *island*	E3
Boggy, *peak*	D5
Cobb, *cove*	E1
Codrington, *lagoon*	D1
Goat, *point*	D1
Gravenor, *bay*	E2
Palmetto, *point*	D2
Redonda, *island*	A6
Shirley, *cape*	E6
Spanish, *point*	E2
Willoughby, *bay*	E5

St. Kitts & Nevis
★ National Capital
• Other City

1:670,000

0   4   8 mi
0 4 8 km
Transverse Mercator Projection

Dieppe Bay Town
St. Paul's
Mt. Misery
1315 m
(4314 ft)
Sandy Point Town
Cayon
Old Road Town
Basseterre
St. Kitts
(St. Christopher)
Great Salt Pond
Nag's Head
The Narrows
Newcastle
Nevis
Cotton Ground
Zion
Bath
Charlestown
Fig Tree
Caribbean Sea

St. Kitts & Nevis

Capital: Basseterre
Area: 104 sq. mi.
269 sq. km.
Population: 41,000
Largest City: Basseterre
Language: English
Monetary Unit: East Caribbean dollar

St. Kitts & Nevis:
Map Index

Cities and Towns
Basseterre, *capital*	B2
Bath	C3
Cayon	B1
Charlestown	C3
Cotton Ground	C2
Dieppe Bay Town	B1
Fig Tree	C3
Newcastle	C2
Old Road Town	B2
St. Paul's	A1
Sandy Point Town	A1
Zion	C3

Other Features
Great Salt, *pond*	C2
Nag's Head, *cape*	C2
Narrows, *strait*	C2
Nevis, *island*	C3
St. Kitts (St. Christopher), *island*	B2

Dominica:
Map Index

Cities and Towns
Berekua	B4
Castle Bruce	B2
Colihaut	A2
Glanvillia	A2
La Plaine	B3
Laudat	B3
Marigot	B2
Massacre	B3
Pointe Michel	B3
Pont Cassé	B3
Portsmouth	A2
Rosalie	B3
Roseau, *capital*	B3
Saint Joseph	A3
Salibia	B2
Salisbury	A2
Soufrière	B4
Vieille Case	B1
Wesley	B2

Other Features
Boiling, *lake*	B3
Dominica, *passage*	A1
Grand, *bay*	B4
Layou, *river*	B3
Morne Diablotin, *mt.*	B3
Roseau, *river*	B3
Toulaman, *river*	B2

Dominica

Capital: Roseau
Area: 290 sq. mi.
751 sq. km.
Population: 88,000
Largest City: Roseau
Language: English
Monetary Unit: East Caribbean dollar

Dominica
★ National Capital
• Other City

1:1,076,000

0   6   12 mi
0 6 12 km
Lambert Conformal Conic Projection

Dominica Passage
Caribbean Sea
Vieille Case
Portsmouth
Wesley
Glanvillia
Marigot
Colihaut
Morne Diablotin
1447 m
(4747 ft)
Salibia
Salisbury
Castle Bruce
Saint Joseph
Rosalie
Pont Cassé
Layou
Laudat
Massacre
Roseau
Boiling L.
Roseau
La Plaine
Pointe Michel
Berekua
Soufrière
Grand Bay

© GeoSystems Global Corp.

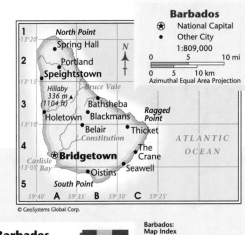

St. Lucia

Capital: Castries
Area: 238 sq. mi.
617 sq. km.
Population: 145,000
Largest City: Castries
Language: English
Monetary Unit: East Caribbean dollar

St. Lucia:
Map Index

Cities and Towns
Canaries A2
Castries, *capital* B1
Choiseul A3
Dauphin B1
Dennery B2
Desruisseau B3
Grand Anse B1
Gros Islet B1
Laborie B3
La Croix Maingot A2
Micoud B3
Mon Repos B2

Other Features
Praslin B2
Soufrière A2
Vieux Fort B3
Canelles, *river* B3
Cul de Sac, *river* B2
Fond d'Or, *river* B2
Gimie, *mt.* A2
Maria, *islands* B3
Moule à Chique, *cape* B3
Point, *cape* B1
Saint Lucia, *channel* B1
Saint Vincent, *passage* B4
Soufrière, *volcano* A2

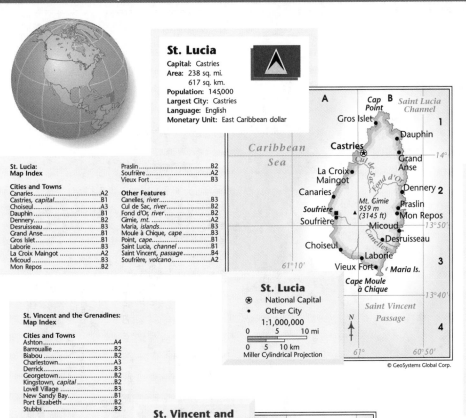

Barbados

Capital: Bridgetown
Area: 166 sq. mi.
430 sq. km.
Population: 256,000
Largest City: Bridgetown
Language: English
Monetary Unit: Dollar

Barbados:
Map Index

Cities and Towns
Bathsheba B3
Belair B4
Blackmans B3
Bridgetown, *capital* A4
Holetown A3
Oistins B5
Portland A2
Seawell C4
Speightstown A2
Spring Hall A2
The Crane C4
Thicket C4

Other Features
Bruce Vale, *river* B3
Carlisle, *bay* A4
Constitution, *river* B4
Hillaby, *mt.* A3
North, *point* A1
Ragged, *point* C3
South, *point* B5

St. Vincent and the Grenadines:
Map Index

Cities and Towns
Ashton A4
Barrouallie B2
Biabou B2
Charlestown A3
Derrick B3
Georgetown B2
Kingstown, *capital* B2
Lovell Village B3
New Sandy Bay B1
Port Elizabeth B2
Stubbs B2

Other Features
Baleine, *bay* B1
Baliceaux, *island* B3
Bequia, *island* B2
Canouan, *island* B3
Grenadines, *islands* A3
Mayreau, *island* A4
Mt. Wynn, *bay* B2
Mustique, *island* B3
North Mayreau, *channel* A3
Palm, *island* A4
Petit Canouan, *island* B3
Petit Mustique, *island* B3
Petit St. Vincent, *island* A4
St. Vincent, *island* B2
Savan, *island* B3
Soufrière, *mt.* B1
Tobago, *cays* A4
Union, *island* A4
Windward, *islands* B4

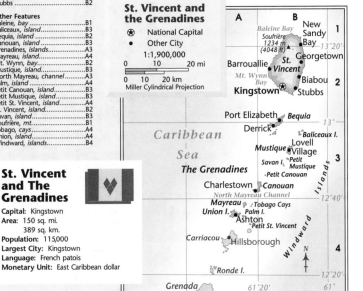

St. Vincent and The Grenadines

Capital: Kingstown
Area: 150 sq. mi.
389 sq. km.
Population: 115,000
Largest City: Kingstown
Language: French patois
Monetary Unit: East Caribbean dollar

Trinidad & Tobago

Capital: Port of Spain
Area: 1,980 sq. mi.
5,130 sq. km.
Population: 1,328,000
Largest City: Port of Spain
Language: English
Monetary Unit: Dollar

Charlotteville B1
Couva A2
Fullarton A2
Guayaguayare A2
Matelot A2
Moruga A2
Pierreville A2
Plymouth B1
Point Fortin A2
Port of Spain, *capital* A2
Princes Town A2
Rio Claro A2
St. Augustine A2
San Fernando A2
San Francique A2
Sangre Grande A2
Scarborough B1
Siparia A2
Toco B2

Trinidad & Tobago:
Map Index

Cities and Towns
Arima A2
Canaan B1
Chaguanas A2

Other Features
El Cerro del Aripo, *mt.* A2
Paria, *gulf* A2
Pitch, *lake* A2
Tobago, *island* B1
Trinidad, *island* A2

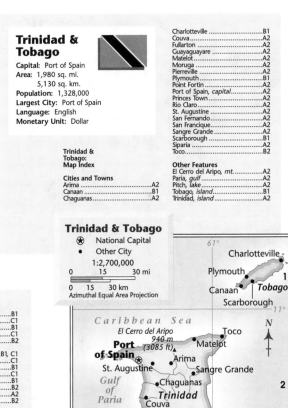

Grenada:
Map Index

Cities and Towns
Grand Bay C1
Grand Roy B2
Hillsborough C1
Marquis B2
St. David's B2
St. George's, *capital* A2
Sauteurs B2
Tivoli B2

Other Features
Bird, *island* B2
Caille, *island* B1
Carriacou, *island* C1
Diamond, *island* B1
Frigate, *island* C1
Grenada, *island* B2
Grenadines, *island group* ..B1, C1
Large, *island* C1
Les Tantes, *island* B1
Petit Martinique, *island* C1
Ronde, *island* B1
St. Catherine, *mt.* B2
Salines, *point* A2
Sandy, *island* B2

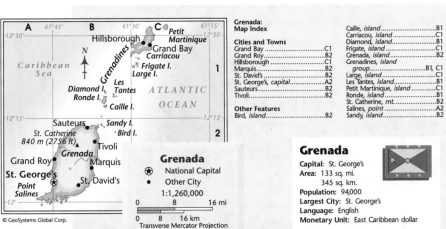

Grenada

Capital: St. George's
Area: 133 sq. mi.
345 sq. km.
Population: 94,000
Largest City: St. George's
Language: English
Monetary Unit: East Caribbean dollar

© GeoSystems Global Corp.

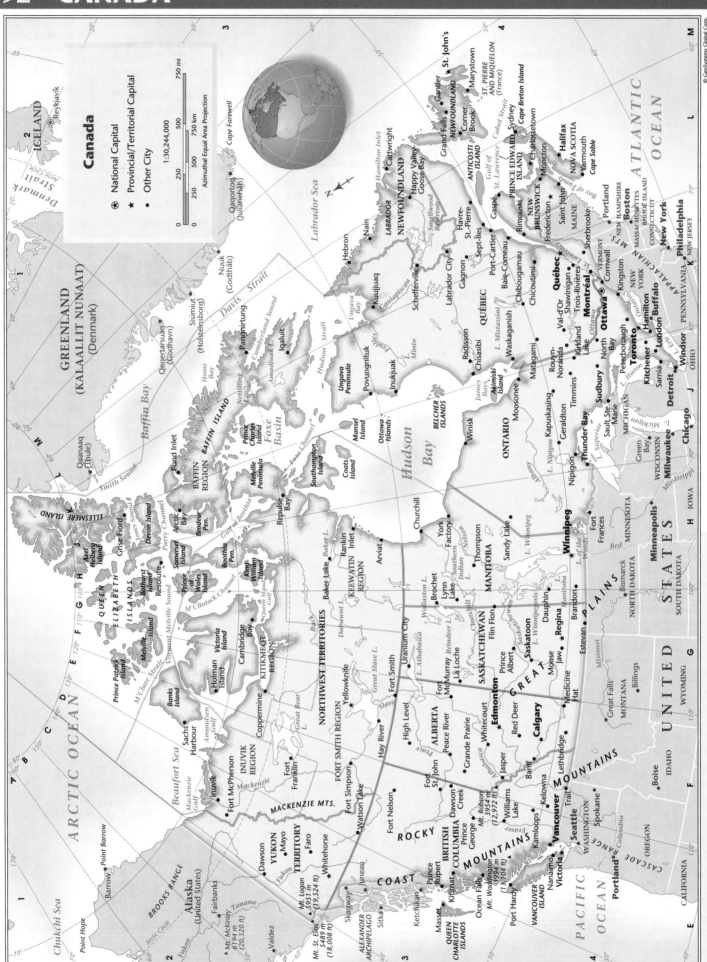

Canada

- ⊛ National Capital
- ★ Provincial/Territorial Capital
- • Other City

1:30,244,000

Azimuthal Equal Area Projection

British Columbia
Capital: Victoria
Area: 365,947 sq. mi.
948,049 sq. km.
Population: 3,282,061
Largest City: Vancouver

New Brunswick
Capital: Fredericton
Area: 28,355 sq. mi.
73,459 sq. km.
Population: 723,900
Largest City: Saint John

Northwest Territories
Capital: Yellowknife
Area: 1,322,909 sq. mi.
3,427,225 sq. km.
Population: 57,649
Largest City: Yellowknife

Ontario
Capital: Toronto
Area: 412,581 sq. mi.
1,068,863 sq. km.
Population: 10,084,885
Largest City: Toronto

Québec
Capital: Québec
Area: 594,860 sq. mi.
1,541,088 sq. km.
Population: 6,895,963
Largest City: Montréal

Yukon Territory
Capital: Whitehorse
Area: 186,661 sq. mi.
483,578 sq. km.
Population: 27,797
Largest City: Whitehorse

Alberta
Capital: Edmonton
Area: 255,287 sq. mi.
661,265 sq. km.
Population: 2,545,553
Largest City: Edmonton

Manitoba
Capital: Winnipeg
Area: 250,947 sq. mi.
650,122 sq. km.
Population: 1,091,942
Largest City: Winnipeg

Newfoundland
Capital: St. John's
Area: 156,949 sq. mi.
406,604 sq. km.
Population: 568,474
Largest City: St. John's

Nova Scotia
Capital: Halifax
Area: 21,425 sq. mi.
55,505 sq. km.
Population: 899,942
Largest City: Halifax

Prince Edward Island
Capital: Charlottetown
Area: 2,185 sq. mi.
5,661 sq. km.
Population: 10,084,885
Largest City: Charlottetown

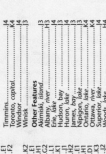

Saskatchewan
Capital: Regina
Area: 251,866 sq. mi.
652,503 sq. km.
Population: 988,928
Largest City: Saskatoon

Canada
Capital: Ottawa
Area: 3,849,674 sq. mi.
9,973,249 sq. km.
Population: 28,114,000
Largest City: Toronto
Languages: English, French
Monetary Unit: Canadian dollar

Canada:
Map Index

ALBERTA
Banff E3
Calgary D3
Edmonton, *capital* D3
Fort McMurray E2
Grande Prairie D3
High Level D2
Jasper D3
Lethbridge E3
Medicine Hat E3
Peace River D2
Red Deer D3
Whitecourt D3
Other Features
Athabasca, *river* E2
Peace, *river* D2

BRITISH COLUMBIA
Cities and Towns
Dawson Creek D2
Fort Nelson D2
Fort St. John D2
Kamloops D3
Kelowna D3
Kitimat C3
Masset C3
Nanaimo D3
Ocean Falls C3
Port Hardy C3
Prince George D3
Prince Rupert C2
Trail D3
Vancouver D3
Victoria, *capital* D3
Williams Lake D3
Other Features
Coast, *mts.* C2
Fraser, *river* D3
Queen Charlotte, *islands* C3
Robson, *mt.* D3
Rocky, *mts.* D3
Vancouver, *island* D3
Waddington, *mt.* C3

MANITOBA
Cities and Towns
Brandon E3
Brochet E2
Churchill F2
Dauphin E3
Flin Flon E2
Lynn Lake E2
Thompson E2
Winnipeg, *capital* F3
York Factory F2
Other Features
Churchill, *river* E2
Hudson, *bay* F2
Manitoba, *lake* E3
Nelson, *river* F2
Saskatchewan, *river* E2
Southern Indian, *lake* E2
Winnipeg, *capital* F3
Winnipegosis, *lake* E3

NEW BRUNSWICK
Cities and Towns
Fredericton, *capital* L4
Moncton L4
Saint John L4

Other Feature
Fundy, *bay* L4

NEWFOUNDLAND
Cities and Towns
Cartwright M3
Corner Brook M4
Gander M4
Grand Falls M4
Happy Valley-Goose Bay L3
Hebron L3
Labrador City L3
Marystown M4
Nain L3
St. John's, *capital* M4
Other Features
Cabot, *strait* M4
Hamilton, *inlet* L3
Labrador, *region* L3
Labrador, *sea* M3
St. Lawrence, *gulf* L3
Smallwood, *reservoir* L3

NORTHWEST TERRITORIES
Cities and Towns
Arctic Bay J1
Arviat H2
Baker Lake G2
Cambridge Bay G2
Coppermine F2

Fort Franklin E2
Fort McPherson D2
Fort Simpson E2
Grise Fiord J1
Hay River F1
Holman Island F1
Inuvik D2
Iqaluit L2
Pangnirtung L2
Pond Inlet K1
Rankin Inlet H2
Repulse Bay J2
Resolute H1
Sachs Harbour E1
Yellowknife, *capital* F2
Other Features
Amadjuak, *lake* K2
Amundsen, *gulf* E1
Axel Heiberg, *island* H1
Back, *river* G2
Baffin, *island* K1
Baffin, *region* K1
Banks, *island* E1
Bathurst, *island* H1
Beaufort, *sea* D1
Belcher, *islands* K3
Boothia, *gulf* H1
Boothia, *peninsula* H1
Brodeur, *peninsula* J1
Coats, *island* J2
Cumberland, *sound* L2
Davis, *strait* M2
Devon, *island* J1
Dubawnt, *lake* F4
Ellesmere, *island* K1
Fort Smith, *region* F2
Foxe, *channel* J2
Foxe, *basin* J2
Great Bear, *lake* E2
Great Slave, *lake* F2
Home, *bay* L2
Hudson, *bay* J3
Hudson, *strait* L2
Inuvik, *region* E2
James, *bay* J3
Jones, *sound* J1
Keewatin, *region* H2
King William, *island* H2
Kitikmeot, *region* G2
Mackenzie, *gulf* D2
Mackenzie, *mts.* D2
Mackenzie, *river* E2
Mansel, *island* J2
M'Clintock, *channel* G1
M'Clure, *strait* F1
Melville, *island* F1
Melville, *peninsula* J2
Nettilling, *lake* K2
Ottawa, *islands* J3
Parry, *channel* F1
Prince Charles, *island* K2
Prince of Wales, *island* H1
Prince Patrick, *island* E1
Queen Elizabeth, *islands* G2
Queen Maud, *gulf* G2
Slave, *river* F2
Smith, *sound* K1
Somerset, *island* H1
Southampton, *island* J2
Victoria, *island* F1
Viscount Melville, *sound* G1

NOVA SCOTIA
Cities and Towns
Halifax, *capital* L4
Sydney M4
Yarmouth L4
Other Features
Cabot, *strait* M4
Cape Breton, *island* M4
Fundy, *bay* L4
Sable, *cape* L4

ONTARIO
Cities and Towns
Cornwall K4
Fort Frances H4
Geraldton J4
Hamilton K4
Kapuskasing J4
Kitchener J4
Kingston K4
Kirkland Lake J4
London J4
Moosonee J3
Nipigon J4
North Bay K4
Peterborough K4
Sandy Lake H3
Sarnia J4
Sault Ste. Marie J4
Sudbury J4
Thunder Bay J4

Timmins J4
Toronto, *capital* K4
Windsor J3
Winisk J3
Other Features
Akimiski, *island* J3
Albany, *river* J3
Erie, *lake* J4
Hudson, *bay* J3
James, *bay* J3
Nipigon, *lake* J3
Ontario, *lake* K4
Ottawa, *river* K4
Superior, *lake* J4
Woods, *lake* H4

PRINCE EDWARD ISLAND
Cities and Towns
Charlottetown, *capital* L4

QUÉBEC
Cities and Towns
Baie-Comeau L4
Chibougamau K4
Chicoutimi K4
Chisasibi K3
Gagnon L4
Gaspé L4
Havre-St-Pierre L3
Inukjuak K3
Kuujjuaq L3
Matagami K4
Montréal K4
Port-Cartier L3
Povungnituk K2
Québec, *capital* K4
Radisson K3
Rimouski L4
Rouyn-Noranda K4
Schefferville L3
Sept-Îles L3
Shawinigan K4
Sherbrooke K4
Trois-Rivières K4
Val-d'Or K4
Waskaganish K3
Other Features
Anticosti, *island* L4
Caniapiscau, *river* L3
Feuilles, *river* K3
Hudson, *bay* J2
Hudson, *strait* K2
James, *bay* K3
Minto, *lake* K3
Mistassini, *lake* K3
Ottawa, *river* K4
St. Lawrence, *gulf* L4
St. Lawrence, *river* L3
Ungava, *bay* L3
Ungava, *peninsula* K2

SASKATCHEWAN
Cities and Towns
Estevan G4
La Loche E2
Moose Jaw G3
Prince Albert F3
Regina, *capital* G3
Saskatoon F3
Uranium City E2
Other Features
Athabasca, *lake* E2
Churchill, *river* F2
Great Plains, *plain* G3
Reindeer, *lake* F2
Saskatchewan, *river* F3
Wollaston, *lake* F2

YUKON TERRITORY
Cities and Towns
Dawson C2
Faro C2
Mayo C2
Watson Lake D2
Whitehorse, *capital* C2
Other Features
Beaufort, *sea* C1
Logan, *mt.* C2
St. Elias, *mts.* C2
Yukon, *river* C2

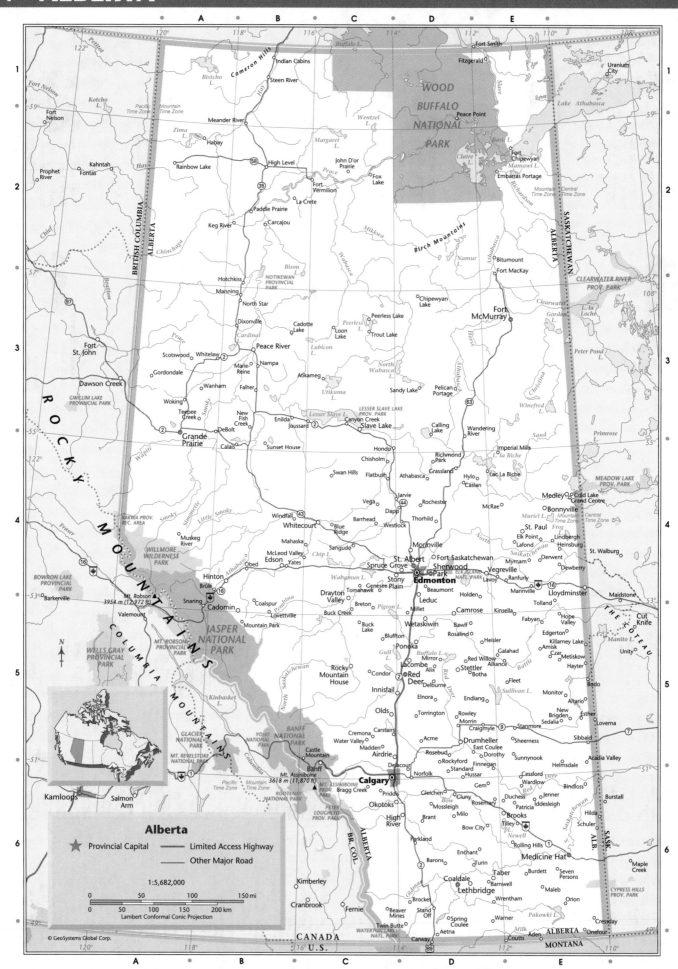

Alberta

★ Provincial Capital — Limited Access Highway
— Other Major Road

1:5,682,000

0   50   100   150 mi

0   50   100   150   200 km

Lambert Conformal Conic Projection

© GeoSystems Global Corp.

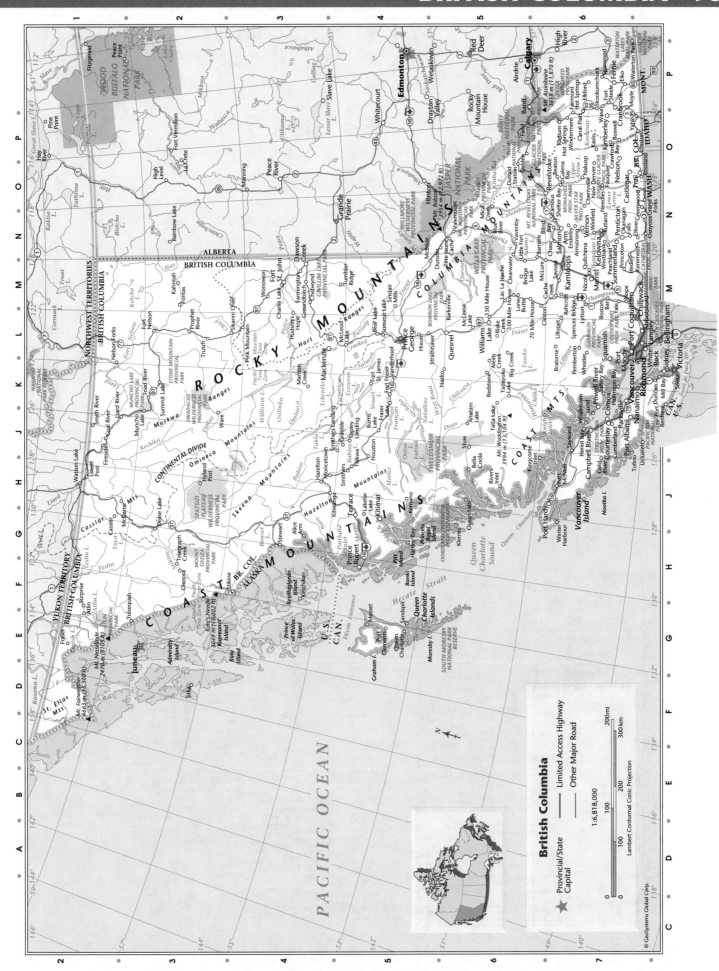

PACIFIC OCEAN

British Columbia

★ Provincial/State
Capital

—— Limited Access Highway
—— Other Major Road

1:6,818,000

Lambert Conformal Conic Projection

© GeoSystems Global Corp.

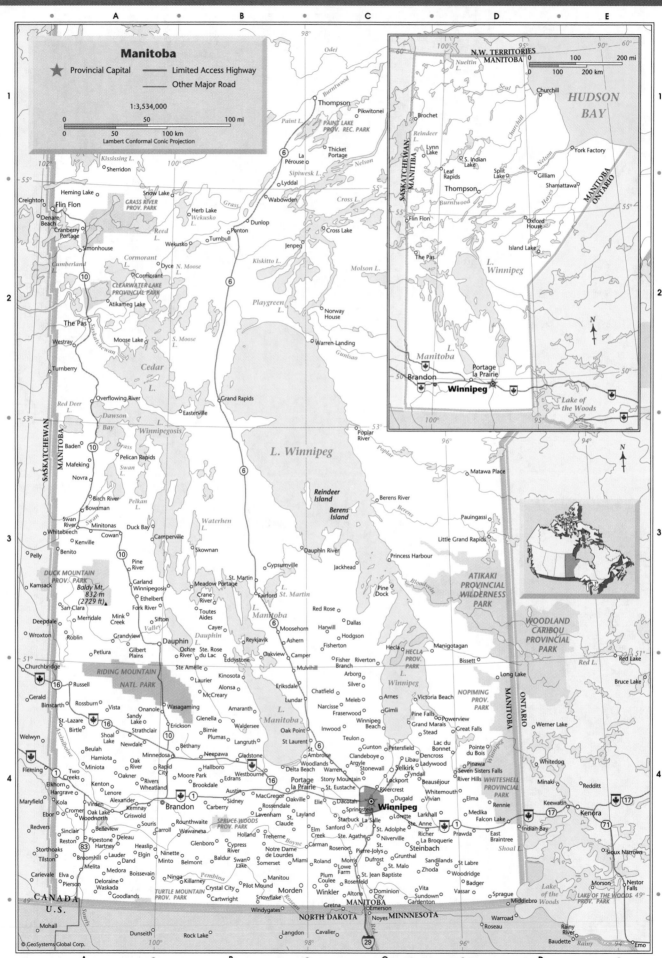

Manitoba

★ Provincial Capital
— Limited Access Highway
— Other Major Road

1:3,534,000

0   50   100 mi
0   50   100 km
Lambert Conformal Conic Projection

© GeoSystems Global Corp.

N.W. TERRITORIES
MANITOBA

0 100 200 mi
0 100 200 km

HUDSON BAY

Churchill
Brochet
Nueltin L.
Reindeer L.
Lynn Lake
S. Indian Lake
Leaf Rapids
Split Lake
Gilliam
York Factory
Thompson
Shamattawa
Flin Flon
Burntwood
Oxford House
The Pas
Island Lake
L. Winnipeg
L. Manitoba
Portage la Prairie
Brandon
Winnipeg
Lake of the Woods

SASKATCHEWAN
MANITOBA
MANITOBA
ONTARIO

Odei
Burntwood
Thompson
Pikwitonei
Paint L.
PAINT LAKE PROV. REC. PARK
La Pérouse
Thicket Portage
Nelson
Sherridon
Kississing L.
Snow Lake
Lyddal
Wabowden
Heming Lake
GRASS RIVER PROV. PARK
Herb Lake
Wekusko L.
Dunlop
Cross L.
Creighton
Flin Flon
Denare Beach
Cranberry Portage
Simonhouse
Reed L.
Wekusko
Turnbull
Ponton
Jenpeg
Cross Lake
Cumberland
Cormorant L.
Dyce
N. Moose L.
Kiskitto L.
Norway House
Clearwater Lake Provincial Park
Atikameg Lake
Playgreen L.
Molson L.
The Pas
Cedar L.
Moose Lake
S. Moose L.
Warren Landing
Gunisao
Westray
Turnberry
Overflowing River
Grand Rapids
Poplar River
Red Deer
Dawson Bay
Easterville
Poplar
Baden
Pelican Rapids
L. Winnipegosis
L. Winnipeg
Matawa Place
Mafeking
Novra
Swan L.
Birch River
Bowsman
Pelkan L.
Reindeer Island
Berens River
Berens
Swan River
Minitonas
Duck Bay
Waterhen L.
Berens Island
Pauingassi
Whitebeech
Cowan
Camperville
Little Grand Rapids
Pelly
Kenville
Benito
Skownan
Dauphin River
Princess Harbour
Pine River
Gypsumville
Jackhead
ATIKAKI PROVINCIAL WILDERNESS PARK
DUCK MOUNTAIN PROV. PARK
Garland
Winnipegosis
Meadow Portage
St. Martin
L. St. Martin
Pine Dock
Baldy Mt. 832 m (2729 ft)
Ethelbert
Crane River
WOODLAND CARIBOU PROVINCIAL PARK
Kamsack
San Clara
Merridale
Fork River
Toutes Aides
Cayer
Red Rose
Bloodvein
Deepdale
Mink Creek
Sifton
Dauphin Valley
Reykjavik
Mooseorn
Harwill
Hodgson
Hecla
Wroxton
Grandview
Dauphin
Ochre River
Ste. Rose du Lac
Ashern
Fisherton
HECLA PROV. PARK
Manigotagan
Roblin
Gilbert Plains
Eddystone
Oakview
Camper
Fisher Branch
Riverton
Bissett
Petlura
Laurier
Fisher River
Red L.
Churchbridge
Ste Amelie
Kinosota
Mulvihill
Arborg
Hecla
Long Lake
Red Lake
RIDING MOUNTAIN NATL. PARK
Silver
L. Winnipeg
Bruce Lake
Russell
Alonsa
Eriksdale
Chatfield
Gerald
McCreary
Lundar
Narcisse
Meleb
Arnes
Victoria Beach
NOPIMING PROV. PARK
Binscarth
Vista
Onanole
Amaranth
Fraserwood
Gimli
Pine Falls
Werner Lake
Rossburn
Wasagaming
L. Manitoba
Winnipeg Beach
Powerview
St.-Lazare
Sandy Lake
Glenella
Waldersee
Oak Point
Inwood
Grand Marais
Great Falls
Birtle
Strathclair
Erickson
Birnie
Plumas
Langruth
St Laurent
Teulon
Stead
Lac du Bonnet
Pointe du Bois
Whitedog
Shoal Lake
Newdale
Bethany
St. Ambroise
Gunton
Petersfield
Dencross
Beulah
Hamiota
Minnedosa
Neepawa
Gladstone
Clandeboye
Libau
Ladywood
Seven Sisters Falls
Minaki
Fleming
Oak River
Rivers
Rapid City
Moore Park
Westbourne
Delta Beach
Warren
Argyle
Stonewall
Selkirk
Tyndall
River Hills
WHITESHELL PROVINCIAL PARK
Redditt
Two Creeks
Miniota
Oakner
Brookdale
Woodlands
Delta Beach
Lockport
Beauséjour
Rennie
Elkhorn
Kenton
Lenore
Alexander
Austin
MacGregor
Sidney
Oakville
Elie
Dacotah
Dugald
Vivian
Elma
Keewatin
Maryfield
Hargrave
Kola
Kemnay
Griswold
Carberry
Rossendale
Layland
Springstein
Winnipeg
Lorette
Larkhall
Medika
Falcon Lake
Minaki
Kenora
Ebor
Cromer
Oak Lake
Souris
Rounthwaite
Wawanesa
Claude
Elm Creek
Sanford
Ste. Agathe
St. Anne
Richer
Prawda
East Braintree
Indian Bay
17
71
Redvers
Sinclair
Belleview
Deleau
Cypress River
Treherne
Carman
Niverville
Rosenort
Pierre-Jolys
La Broquerie
Sioux Narrows
Storthoaks
Reston
Pipestone
Hartney
Heaslip
Elgin
Glenboro
Miami
Roland
Morris
St. Malo
Zhoda
Woodridge
Tilston
Broomhill
Lauder
Ninette
Belmont
Swan Lake
Notre Dame de Lourdes
Somerset
Lowe Farm
St. Jean Baptiste
Dufrost
Grunthal
Sandilands
St Labre
Carievale
Elva
Medora
Boissevain
Ninga
Killarney
Manitou
Plum Coulee
Rosenfeld
Dominion City
Vita
Badger
Sprague
Pierson
Deloraine
Waskada
Goodlands
TURTLE MOUNTAIN PROV. PARK
Crystal City
Pilot Mound
Morden
Winkler
Altona
Gretna
Emerson
Sundown
Vassar
Middlebro
LAKE OF THE WOODS PROV. PARK
CANADA U.S.
Souris
Mohall
Dunseith
Rock Lake
Cartwright
Snowflake
Windygates
NORTH DAKOTA
Langdon
Cavalier
MANITOBA
MINNNESOTA
Noyes
Warroad
Roseau
Rainy River
Baudette
Emo
Rainy

SASKATCHEWAN
MANITOBA

SPRUCE WOODS PROV. PARK
Brandon

Assiniboine
Boyne
Pembina
Red
Shoal L.

MANITOBA
ONTARIO

102°
100°
98°
96°
94°
100°
98°
96°

55°
53°
51°
49°

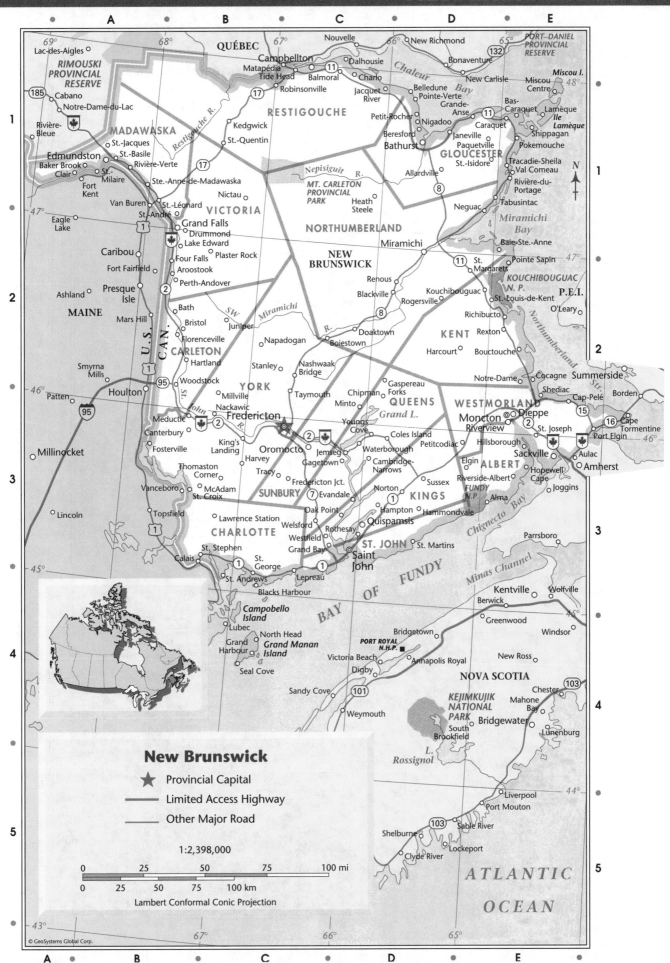

New Brunswick

★ Provincial Capital

━━ Limited Access Highway

── Other Major Road

1:2,398,000

0   25   50   75   100 mi

0   25   50   75   100 km

Lambert Conformal Conic Projection

© GeoSystems Global Corp.

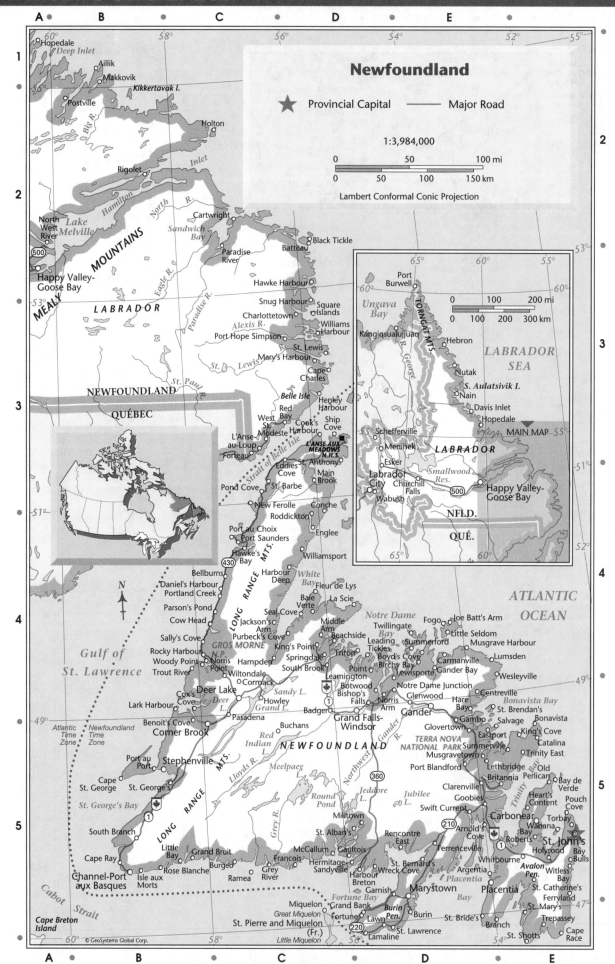

Newfoundland

★ Provincial Capital   ——— Major Road

1:3,984,000

| 0 | 50 | 100 mi |

| 0 | 50 | 100 | 150 km |

Lambert Conformal Conic Projection

Hopedale
Deep Inlet
Aillik
Makkovik
Kikkertavak I.
Postville
Holton
Big R.
Rigolet
Hamilton Inlet
North R.
Cartwright
North West River
Lake Melville
MOUNTAINS
Sandwich Bay
Paradise River
Batteau
Black Tickle
Happy Valley-Goose Bay
MEALY
LABRADOR
Eagle R.
Paradise R.
Hawke Harbour
Snug Harbour
Square Islands
Charlottetown
Williams Harbour
Alexis R.
Port Hope Simpson
St. Lewis
NEWFOUNDLAND
Mary's Harbour
St. Lewis
QUÉBEC
St. Paul R.
Cape Charles
Belle Isle
Henley Harbour
Red Bay
Ship Cove
West St. Cook's Harbour
Modeste
L'Anse-au-Loup
L'ANSE AUX MEADOWS N.H.S.
Forteau
Strait of Belle Isle
St. Anthony
Eddies Cove
Main Brook
Pond Cove
St. Barbe
New Ferolle
Conche
Roddickton
Port au Choix
Englee
Port Saunders
Williamsport
Hawke's Bay
Bellburns
Harbour Deep
White Bay
Fleur de Lys
Daniel's Harbour
La Scie
Portland Creek
Baie Verte
Parson's Pond
Seal Cove
Notre Dame
Twillingate
Fogo
Joe Batt's Arm
Cow Head
Jackson's Arm
Middle Arm
Bay
Little Seldom
Sally's Cove
Purbeck's Cove
Beachside
Leading
Summerford
Musgrave Harbour
LONG RANGE MTS.
King's Point
Tickles
Lumsden
Rocky Harbour
Triton
Boyd's Cove
GROS MORNE N.P.
Hampden
Springdale
Point
Birchy Bay
Carmanville
Woody Point
Norris
South Brook
Leamington
Lewisporte
Gander Bay
Wesleyville
Trout River
Wiltondale
Botwood
Notre Dame Junction
Cormack
Bishop's
Norris
Glenwood
Centreville
Deer Lake
Sandy L.
Falls
Arm
Hare
Bonavista Bay
Howley
Gander
Bay
Lark Harbour
Deer L.
Pasadena
Badger
Glovertown
St. Brendan's
Benoit's Cove
Grand L.
Buchans
Grand Falls-Windsor
Gambo
Salvage
Bonavista
Corner Brook
Red Indian L.
NEWFOUNDLAND
Eastport
King's Cove
Port au Port
Stephenville
Lloyds R.
Summerville
Catalina
LONG RANGE MTS.
Meelpaeg L.
TERRA NOVA NATIONAL PARK
Musgravetown
Trinity East
Cape St. George
Port Blandford
Lethbridge
St. George's
Jeddore L.
Jubilee L.
Clarenville
Britannia
Old Perlican
St. George's Bay
Round Pond
Goobies
Bay de Verde
South Branch
Milltown
Swift Current
Heart's Content
Grey R.
Pouch Cove
Little Bay
Grand Bruit
St. Alban's
Rencontre East
Carbonear
Torbay
Cape Ray
Rose Blanche
Gaultois
Wabana
Channel-Port aux Basques
Burgeo
Francois
Hermitage
Sandyville
St. Bernard's
Arnold's Cove
Conception Bay
St. John's
Isle aux Morts
Ramea
Grey River
Harbour Breton
Wreck Cove
Terrenceville
Roberts
Holyrood
Bay Bulls
Miquelon
Grand Bank
Garnish
Placentia Bay
Whitbourne
Avalon Pen.
Witless Bay
Great Miquelon
Fortune
Lawn
Marystown
Argentia
Placentia
St. Catherine's
Ferryland
St. Pierre and Miquelon
Lamaline
Burin Pen.
Burin
St. Bride's
St. Mary's
(Fr.)
Little Miquelon
St. Lawrence
Fortune Bay
St. Mary's Bay
Branch
Cape Race
Cabot Strait
Cape Breton Island
Gulf of St. Lawrence
Atlantic Time Zone
Newfoundland Time Zone
Atlantic OCEAN

Inset map (upper right)

Port Burwell
TORNGAT MTS.
Ungava Bay
Kangiqsualujjuaq
Hebron
LABRADOR SEA
Nutak
S. Aulatsivik I.
R. George
Nain
Davis Inlet
Schefferville
Hopedale
MAIN MAP
Menihek
LABRADOR
Esker
Smallwood Res.
Labrador City
Churchill Falls
Happy Valley-Goose Bay
Wabush
NFLD.
QUÉ.

© GeoSystems Global Corp.

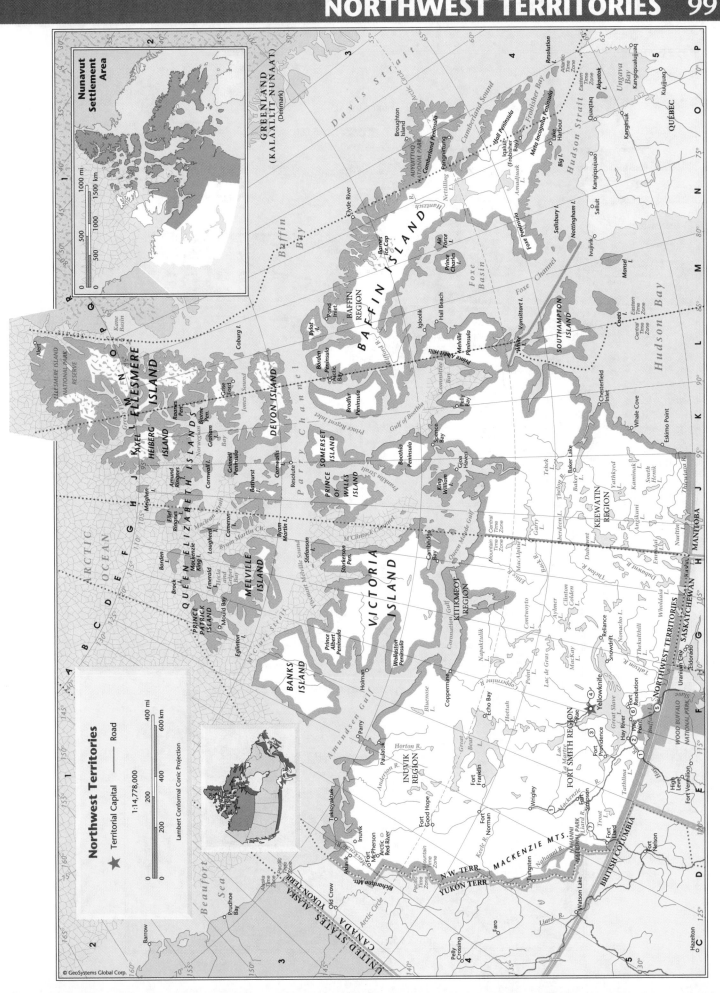

Nunavut Settlement Area

1000 mi
1500 km
500
1000
500

Northwest Territories

★ Territorial Capital — Road

1:14,778,000

0   200   400 mi
0   200   400   600 km

Lambert Conformal Conic Projection

© GeoSystems Global Corp.

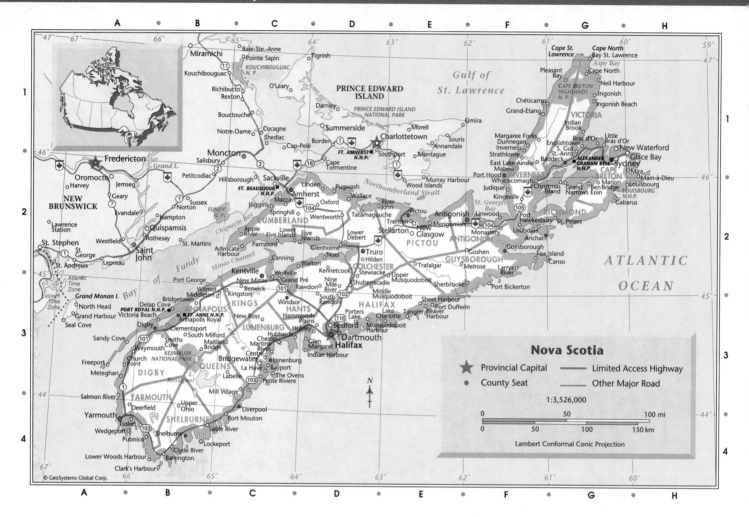

Nova Scotia map showing provinces of New Brunswick, Prince Edward Island, and Nova Scotia with surrounding waters including Gulf of St. Lawrence, Northumberland Strait, Atlantic Ocean, and Bay of Fundy.

Selected place names on the Nova Scotia map:

Miramichi, Baie-Ste.-Anne, Pointe Sapin, Tignish, Cape St. Lawrence, Cape North, Bay St. Lawrence, Neil Harbour, Kouchibouguac, O'Leary, Richibucto, Rexton, Darnley, Pleasant Bay, Chéticamp, Ingonish, Ingonish Beach, Bouctouche, Notre-Dame, Cocagne, Shediac, Summerside, Borden, Charlottetown, Morell, Souris, Elmira, Grand-Étang, Victoria, Indian Brook, Fredericton, Oromocto, Harvey, Salisbury, Sackville, Moncton, Cap-Pelé, Southport, Montague, Annandale, Margaree Forks, Dunnegan, Inverness, Strathlorne, East Lake Ainslie, Mabou, Englishtown, Baddeck, Bras d'Or, Little Bras d'Or, New Waterford, Glace Bay, Sydney, Jemseg, Geary, Petitcodiac, Hillsborough, Amherst, Maccan, Linden, Pugwash, Wallace, Wood Islands, Murray Harbour, Port Hood, Whycocomagh, Judique, Kingsville, Grand Narrows, Ben Eoin, Main-à-Dieu, Marion, Louisbourg, Mira, Gabarus, New Brunswick, Lawrence Station, Quispamsis, Rothesay, Hampton, Norton, Sussex, Apple River, Springhill, Oxford, Joggins, Five Islands, Tatamagouche, Pictou, Antigonish, Merigomish, Linwood, Port Hawkesbury, St. Peters, Louisdale, Arichat, Richmond, St. Stephen, Westfield, Saint John, St. Martins, Advocate Harbour, Parrsboro, Canning, Wentworth, Lower Debert, Stellarton, New Glasgow, Trenton, Monastery, Guysborough, Fox Island, Canso, St. George, Leprea, Digby, Kentville, Wolfville, Grand Pré, Stewiacke, Truro, Hilden, Glenholme, Noel, Walton, Kennetcook, Nine Mile River, Upper Musquodoboit, Trafalgar, Goshen, Melrose, Larrys River, Port George, New Minas, Berwick, Rawdon, South Rawdon, Middle Musquodoboit, Sherbrooke, Port Bickerton, North Head, Grand Harbour, Victoria Beach, Annapolis Royal, Bridgetown, Middleton, Kingston, Windsor, Hammonds Plains, Porters Lake, Charlotte Lake, Sheet Harbour, Port Dufferin, Beaver Harbour, Seal Cove, Clementsport, South Milford, Smiths Cove, New Ross, Hubbards, Chester, Bedford, Musquodoboit Harbour, Tangier, Sandy Cove, Weymouth, Maitland Bridge, Center, Lunenburg, Bayport, Glen Margaret, Halifax, Dartmouth, Indian Harbour, Freeport, Church Point, Bridgewater, La Have, The Ovens, Petite Riviere, Meteghan, Labelle, Mill Village, Upper Ohio, Liverpool, Port Mouton, Salmon River, Deerfield, Yarmouth, Tusket, Wedgeport, Pubnico, Shelburne, Sable River, Lockeport, Lower Woods Harbour, Clyde River, Barrington, Clark's Harbour

Nova Scotia

★ Provincial Capital — Limited Access Highway
● County Seat — Other Major Road

1:3,526,000

0 — 50 — 100 mi
0 — 50 — 100 — 150 km

Lambert Conformal Conic Projection

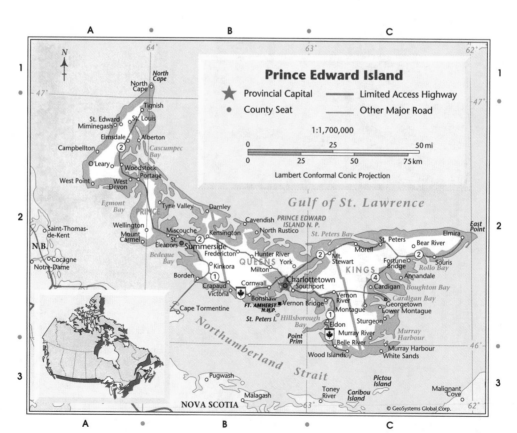

Prince Edward Island

★ Provincial Capital — Limited Access Highway
● County Seat — Other Major Road

1:1,700,000

0 — 25 — 50 mi
0 — 25 — 50 — 75 km

Lambert Conformal Conic Projection

Selected place names on the Prince Edward Island map:

North Cape, Tignish, St. Louis, St. Edward, Mimínegash, Elmsdale, Alberton, Campbellton, O'Leary, Woodstock, Portage, West Point, West Devon, Wellington, Tyne Valley, Darnley, Cavendish, North Rustico, Prince Edward Island N.P., St. Peters Bay, St. Peters, Bear River, Elmira, East Point, Saint-Thomas-de-Kent, Mount Carmel, Miscouche, Kensington, Summerside, St. Eleanors, Fredericton, Hunter River, York, Mt. Stewart, Morell, Fortune Bridge, Souris, Cocagne, Notre-Dame, Milton, Kinkora, Borden, Crapaud, Victoria, Cornwall, Bonshaw, Charlottetown, Southport, Vernon River, Cardigan, Georgetown, Lower Montague, Cape Tormentine, St. Peters I., Vernon Bridge, Montague, Sturgeon, Eldon, Point Prim, Murray River, Belle River, Wood Islands, White Sands, Murray Harbour, Pugwash, Toney River, Caribou Island, Pictou Island, Malagash, Malignant Cove, Gulf of St. Lawrence, Northumberland Strait, N.B., Prince, Queens, Kings, Nova Scotia

© GeoSystems Global Corp.

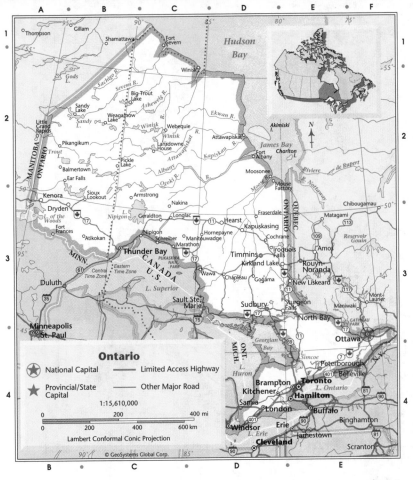

Ontario

★ National Capital   ── Limited Access Highway

★ Provincial/State Capital   ── Other Major Road

1:15,610,000

0   200   400 mi

0   200   400   600 km

Lambert Conformal Conic Projection

© GeoSystems Global Corp.

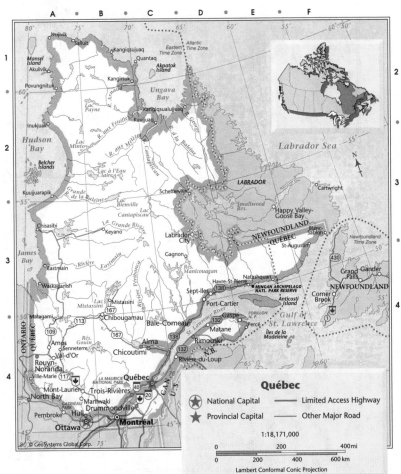

Québec

★ National Capital   ── Limited Access Highway

★ Provincial Capital   ── Other Major Road

1:18,171,000

0   200   400 mi

0   200   400   600 km

Lambert Conformal Conic Projection

© GeoSystems Global Corp.

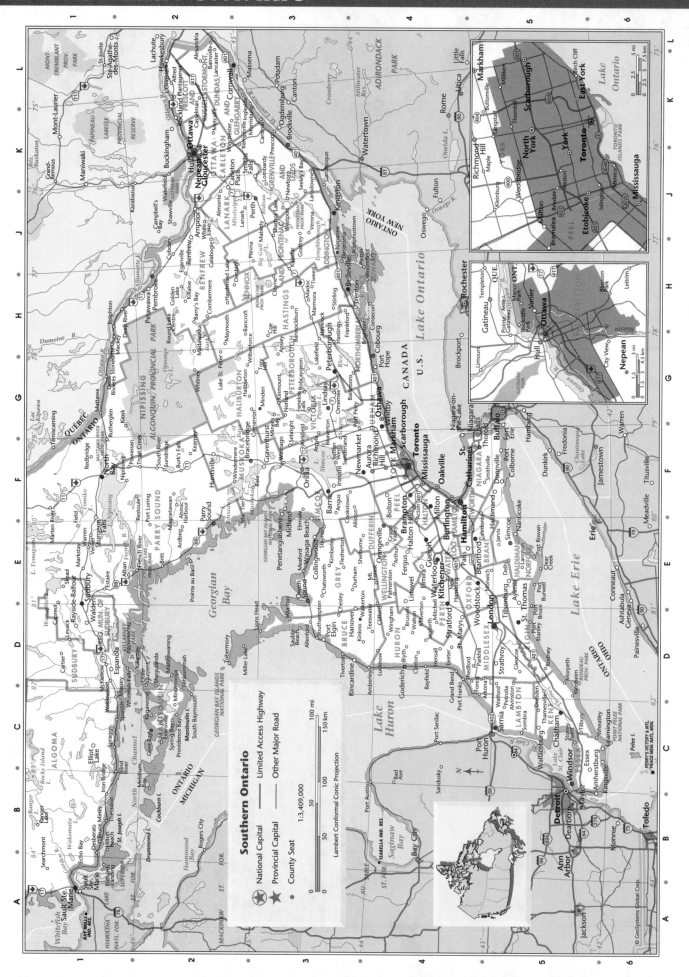

Southern Ontario

National Capital ⊛
Provincial Capital ★
County Seat •

—— Limited Access Highway
—— Other Major Road

1:3,409,000

0   50   100 mi
0   50   100   150 km

Lambert Conformal Conic Projection

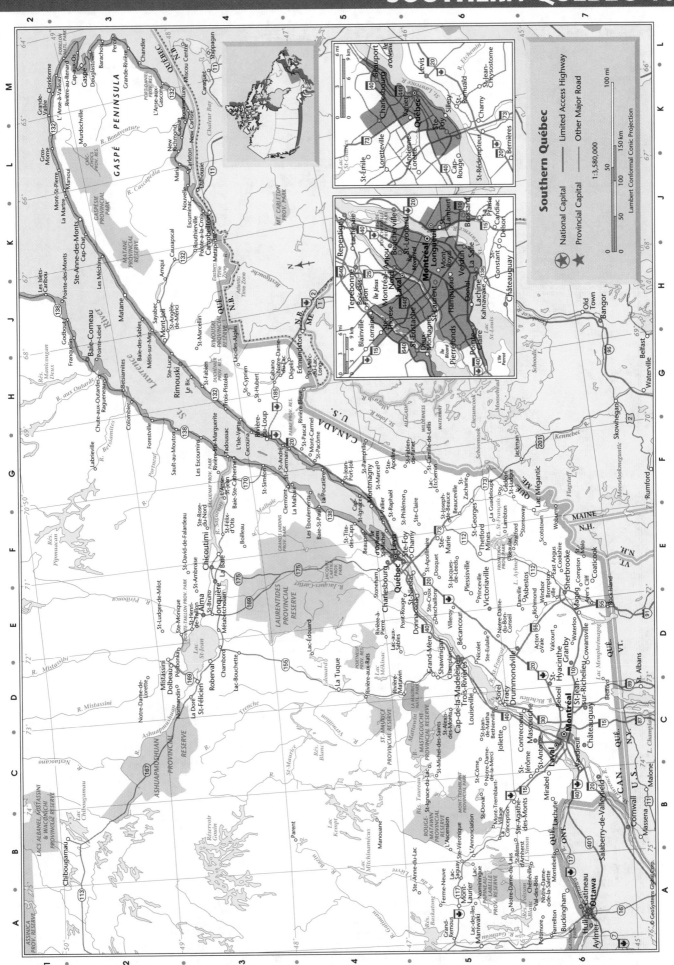

Southern Québec

★ National Capital
★ Provincial Capital

—— Limited Access Highway
—— Other Major Road

1:3,580,000

Lambert Conformal Conic Projection

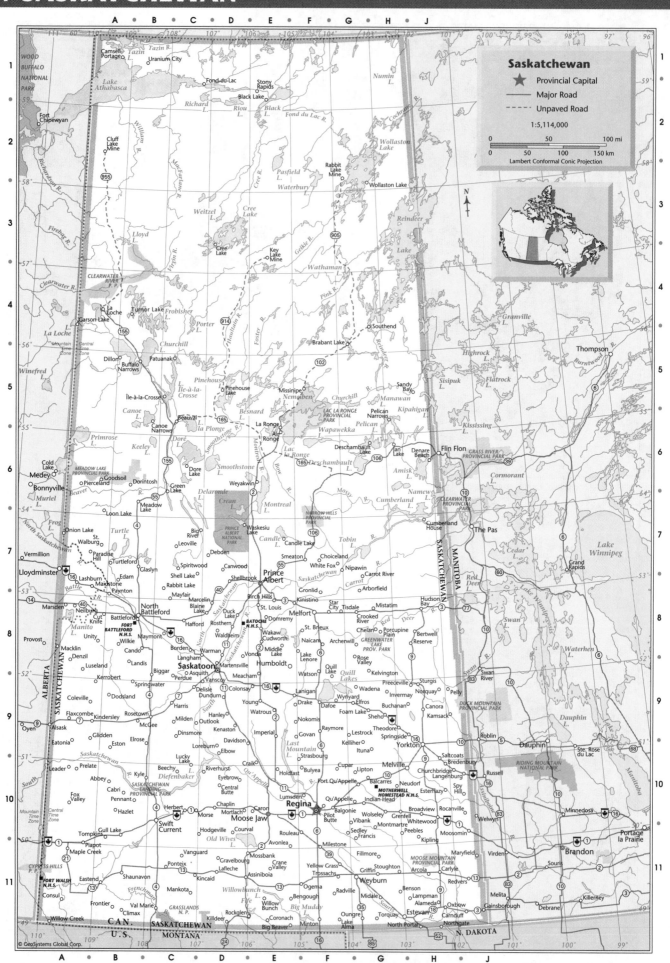

Saskatchewan

★ Provincial Capital
— Major Road
--- Unpaved Road

1:5,114,000

0   50   100 mi
0 50 100 150 km
Lambert Conformal Conic Projection

© GeoSystems Global Corp.

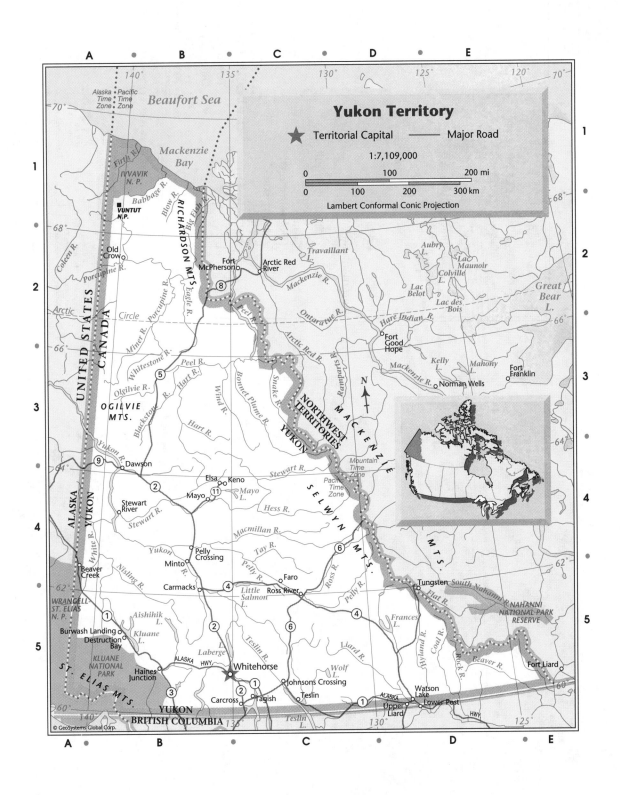

Yukon Territory

★ Territorial Capital ——— Major Road

1:7,109,000

| 0 | 100 | 200 mi |

| 0 | 100 | 200 | 300 km |

Lambert Conformal Conic Projection

Beaufort Sea

Alaska Time Zone · Pacific Time Zone

Mackenzie Bay

Firth R.

IVVAVIK N. P.

VUNTUT N.P.

Babbage R.

Blow R.

Big Fish R.

RICHARDSON MTS.

Coleen R.

Old Crow

Porcupine R.

Eagle R.

Fort McPherson

Arctic Red River

Travaillant L.

Aubry L.

Lac Maunoir

Colville L.

Lac Belot

Lac des Bois

Great Bear L.

UNITED STATES / CANADA

Arctic Circle

Miner R.

Porcupine R.

Peel R.

Mackenzie R.

Ontaratue R.

Hare Indian R.

Fort Good Hope

Mackenzie R.

Kelly L.

Mahony L.

Fort Franklin

Norman Wells

Whitestone R.

Peel R.

Hart R.

Blackstone R.

Olgivie R.

OGILVIE MTS.

Wind R.

Bonnet Plume R.

Snake R.

Arctic Red R.

Ramparts R.

NORTHWEST TERRITORIES

YUKON

M A C K E N Z I E

N

Yukon R.

Hart R.

Dawson

ALASKA / YUKON

Elsa Keno

Mayo L.

Mayo

Stewart R.

Hess R.

SELWYN

Mountain Time Zone

Pacific Time Zone

Stewart River

Stewart R.

Macmillan R.

Tay R.

White R.

Yukon R.

Pelly Crossing

Minto

Pelly R.

Faro

Ross R.

MTS.

Nisling R.

Carmacks

Little Salmon L.

Ross River

Pelly R.

Tungsten

South Nahanni R.

NAHANNI NATIONAL PARK RESERVE

Beaver Creek

Frances L.

Hyland R.

Coal R.

Flat R.

WRANGELL ST. ELIAS N. P.

Aishihik L.

Kluane L.

Rock R.

Beaver R.

Fort Liard

Burwash Landing

Destruction Bay

KLUANE NATIONAL PARK

ST. ELIAS MTS.

Haines Junction

L. Laberge

Teslin R.

ALASKA HWY

Whitehorse

Wolf L.

Liard R.

Watson Lake

Lower Post

Carcross

Tagish

Johnsons Crossing

Teslin

ALASKA HWY

Upper Liard

YUKON

BRITISH COLUMBIA

Teslin L.

© GeoSystems Global Corp.

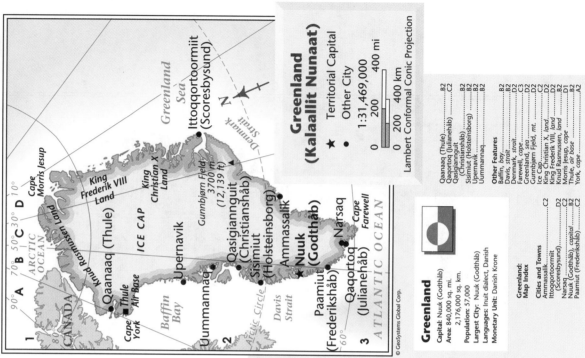

Greenland (Kalaallit Nunaat)

★ Territorial Capital
● Other City

1:31,469,000

0   200   400 km
0   200   400 mi

Lambert Conformal Conic Projection

© GeoSystems Global Corp.

Greenland

Capital: Nuuk (Godthåb)
Area: 840,000 sq. mi.
2,176,000 sq. km.
Population: 57,000
Largest City: Nuuk (Godthåb)
Languages: Inuit dialect, Danish
Monetary Unit: Danish Krone

Greenland:
Map Index

Cities and Towns
Ammassalik C2
Ittoqqortoormiit
(Scoresbysund) D2
Narsaq C2
Nuuk (Godthåb), *capital* B2
Paamiut (Frederikshåb) C2

Qaanaaq (Thule) B2
Qaqortoq (Julianehåb) C2
Qasigiannguit
(Christianshåb) D2
Sisimiut (Holsteinsborg) B2
Upernavik B2
Ummannaq B2

Other Features
Baffin, *bay* B2
Davis, *strait* B2
Denmark, *strait* C3
Farewell, *cape* D2
Greenland, *sea* D2
Gunnbjørn Field, *mt.* C2
Ice Cap C2
King Christian X, *land* D2
King Frederik VIII, *land* D1
Knud Rasmussen, *land* B2
Morris Jesup, *cape* C2
Thule, *air base* B2
York, *cape* A2

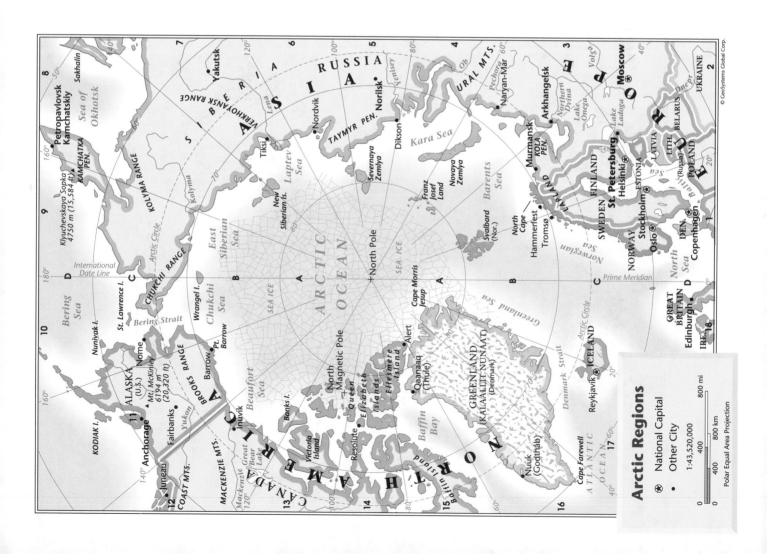

Arctic Regions

⊛ National Capital
● Other City

1:43,520,000

0   400   800 km
0   400   800 mi

Polar Equal Area Projection

© GeoSystems Global Corp.

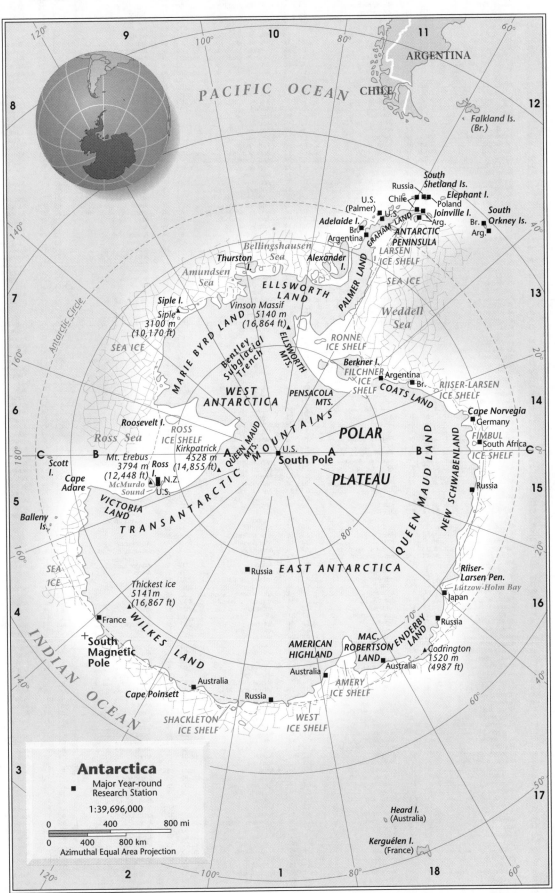

PACIFIC OCEAN

ARGENTINA

CHILE

Falkland Is.
(Br.)

Russia
South
Shetland Is.

U.S.
(Palmer)
Chile
Elephant I.

Poland

Adelaide I.
Br.
U.S.
Arg.
Joinville I.

South
Orkney Is.
Br.
Arg.

Argentina
GRAHAM LAND
ANTARCTIC
PENINSULA

Bellingshausen
Sea

Thurston
I.

Alexander
I.

LARSEN
ICE SHELF

SEA ICE

Amundsen
Sea

ELLSWORTH
LAND

PALMER LAND

Weddell
Sea

Siple I.
Siple
3100 m
(10,170 ft)

MARIE BYRD LAND

Vinson Massif
5140 m
(16,864 ft)

RONNE
ICE SHELF

SEA ICE

WEST
ANTARCTICA

Bentley
Subglacial
Trench

ELLSWORTH
MTS.

Berkner I.

FILCHNER
ICE
SHELF

COATS LAND

Argentina
Br.

RIISER-LARSEN
ICE SHELF

PENSACOLA
MTS.

Cape Norvegia
Germany

Roosevelt I.

ROSS
ICE SHELF

QUEEN MAUD MTS.

POLAR

FIMBUL
South Africa
ICE SHELF

Ross Sea

Kirkpatrick
4528 m
(14,855 ft)

U.S.
South Pole

QUEEN MAUD LAND

NEW SCHWABENLAND

Russia

Scott
I.

C   B
Mt. Erebus
3794 m
(12,448 ft)
Ross
I.
N.Z.
U.S.

A   A   C

PLATEAU

Cape
Adare
McMurdo
Sound

VICTORIA
LAND

TRANSANTARCTIC MOUNTAINS

Russia
EAST ANTARCTICA

Riiser-
Larsen Pen.
Lützow-Holm Bay

Balleny
Is.

SEA
ICE

Thickest ice
5141m
(16,867 ft)

Japan

Russia

France

South
Magnetic
Pole

WILKES LAND

AMERICAN
HIGHLAND

MAC.
ROBERTSON
LAND

ENDERBY
LAND

Codrington
1520 m
(4987 ft)

Australia

Australia

Australia

Cape Poinsett

Russia

AMERY
ICE SHELF

INDIAN
OCEAN

SHACKLETON
ICE SHELF

WEST
ICE SHELF

Heard I.
(Australia)

Kerguélen I.
(France)

Antarctic Circle

Antarctica

■ Major Year-round
Research Station

1:39,696,000

0   400   800 mi

0   400   800 km
Azimuthal Equal Area Projection

© GeoSystems Global Corp.

Key Page

A

Aachen A3 40
Aaiún, el- B1 58
Aalst C2 33
Aarau C1 35
Aare, river B1, B2 35
Aba D5 65
Abadan B3 22
Abaí E4 75
Abakaliki E4 65
Abakan D6 44
Abancay C3 77
Abaya, lake B3 60
Abbeville C1 34
Abbey B10 104
Abbotsford L6 95
Abdali B1 24
Abéché C4 59
Abemama, island ...A1 17
Abengourou E3 63
Abenrá B3 32
Abeokuta C4 65
Aberdeen ....Inset 10
Aberdeen C1 30
Aberdeen, lake H4 99
Aberdeen, S. Dak...D1 126
Aberystwyth B3 30
Abha B2 24
Abhe, lake C2 60
Abia, river C3 66
Abidjan D4 63
Abilene, Tex. D2 126
Abkhazia,
  autonomous republic A3 45
Aboisso E4 63
Abomey A4 64
Abou Deïa B5 59
Abrantes A3 36
Abruzzi C2 38
Abşeron, peninsula ..C2 45
Abu Dhabi, capital ..C2 25
Abu Kamal B2 27
Abuja, capital D3 65
Abuná, river A2 77
Acadia Valley E5 94
Acajutla A2 86
Acámbaro D4 84
Acapulco E4 84
Acarai, mts. B5 80
Acaray, river E4 75
Acarigua C2 79
Accra, capital B4 64
Achill, island A2 31
Achinsk D6 44
Achwa, river C2 61
Acklins, island C4 89
Acme D5 94
Acolman ....Inset 84
Aconcagua, mt. A3 74
Aconcagua, river ...B4 76
Aconibe C3 66
Acquaviva A1 39
Acre A2 81
Acre (Akko) B1 26
Acton E4 102
Acton Vale D6 103
Açúcar, mt. ......Inset I 81
Adamawa, massif ..B2, E5 65
Adams, lake N5 95
Adana C3 27
Adapazari B2 27
Adare, cape B5 107
Addis Ababa, capital ..C2 60
Addu, atoll A5 19
Adelaide, island ...C11 107
Adelaide, S.A.,
  capital ....C3, Inset II 14
Aden B2 25
Aden E6 94
Aden, gulf B1, C2 60
Adi Keyih B2 60
Adi Ugri B2 60
Adige, river B1 38
Adirondack, mts., N.Y. ..F1 126
Adjuntas B2 90
Admiralty, islands ..A2 15
Ado-Ekiti C4 65
Adolphustown H3 102
Adour, river B5 34
Adrar C2 58
Adrar des Iforas, massif ..D2 58
Adriatic, sea C2 38
Advocate Harbour ..C2 100
Adwa C1 60
Adygea, republic ..E4 44
Adzopé E3 63
Ægean, sea C2 51
Ærø, island C4 32
Aetna D6 94
Afadjoto, mt. C3 64
Afikpo D5 65
Afram, river B3 64
Afyon B2 27
Aga, autonomous okrug ..D7 44
Agadès B2 59
Agadir B2 57
Agartala F4 20
Agboville D4 63
Ağcabädi B2 45
Ağdam B3 45
Agen C4 34
Aginskoye D7 44
Agou, mt. B3 64
Agra C3 20
Ağri E2 27
Agrigento C3 38
Agrínion B2 51
Ağstafa A2 45
Agua Prieta C1 84
Aguada A2 90
Aguadilla A2 90
Aguadulce B2 87
Aguán, river B2 86
Aguarico, river C3 79
Aguas Blancas C2 76
Aguas Buenas C2 90

Key Page

Aguascalientes,
  state capital D3 84
Águilas F4 37
Aguilita B2 90
Agung, mt. C2 13
Agusan, river C4 12
Ahmadabad B4 20
Ahmadi, al- C2 24
Ahmic Harbour F2 102
Ahuachapán A2 86
Ahvaz B3 22
Ahwar B2 25
Aibonito C2 90
Aigáleo, mts. .....Inset 51
Ailinglaplap, island ..B2 16
Aillik B1 98
Ailuk, island B1 16
Air Force, island ...O3 99
Air Ronge E5 104
Air, mts. B2 59
Airdrie C5 94
Aishihik, lake B5 105
Aisne, river D2 34
Aiwo A2 16
Aix-en-Provence ...D5 34
Aix-les-Bains D4 34
Aíyina, island B3 51
Aizawl F4 20
Aizuwakamatsu ...C2 8
Ajaccio ....Inset I 34
Ajaria, autonomous republic ..A4 45
Ajdabiya D1 56
Ajka A2 43
Ajmer B3 20
Akanyaru, river B2 61
Akashi B3 8
Akhalkalaki B4 45
Akhaltsikhe B4 45
Akharnaí ....Inset 51
Akhelóös, river B2 51
Akhmeta C3 45
Akhuryan, river ...A2 45
Akita D2 8
Akjoujt B3 58
Aklavik A3 99
Akmola (Tselinograd) ..D1 23
Akobo, river A3 60
Akola C4 20
Akordat A2 60
Akosombo, dam ...C3 64
Akpatok, island P4 99
Akranes A2 52
Akron, Ohio E1 126
Aksaray C2 27
Aksu B1 10
Akulivik A1 101
Akure C4 65
Akurenam C3 66
Akureyri B2 52
Akuseki, island A4 8
Alabama E2 126
Alagoas E3 81
Alagoinhas E3 81
Alajuela B2 86
Alakol, lake E2 23
Alamayn, al- A1 56
Alameda H11 104
Alampur ....Inset II 20
Åland, islands B2 53
Alanya C3 27
Alarcón, reservoir ..E3 37
Alaska ....Inset I 126
Alaska, gulf, Alaska ..Inset I 126
Alaska, range, Alaska ..Inset I 126
Älät C3 45
Alaverdi B1 45
Alay, mts. B1, C3 23
Alayli Dadda B1 60
Alazani, river C4 45
Alba Iulia B2 43
Albacete F3 37
Alban E1 102
Albany, capital, N.Y. ..F1 126
Albany, Ga. E2 126
Albany, river C2 101
Albany, W.A. A3 14
Albert Nile, river ..B2 61
Albert, canal C1 33
Albert, lake B3 61
Alberton A2 100
Albi C5 34
Albina B2 80
Ålborg B1 32
Ålborg, bay C2 32
Albuquerque, cays ..Inset 88
Albuquerque, N. Mex. ..C2 126
Albury, N.S.W. ...D3 14
Alcalá de Henares ..Inset II 37
Alcañiz F2 37
Alcántara, reservoir ..C3 37
Alcázar de San Juan ..E3 37
Alcira F3 37
Alcobendas .....Inset II 37
Alcorcón ......E2, Inset II 37
Alcoy F3 37
Aldabra, islands ...A2 70
Aldan D8 44
Aldan, river D8 44
Alderney, island ..Inset II 30
Aleg B3 58
Alençon C2 34
Alert Q1 99
Alès D4 34
Alessandria B1 38
Ålesund B3 52
Aleutian islands, Alaska ..Inset I 126
Alexander A4 96
Alexander, island ..B11 107
Alexandra A4 15
Alexandria C4 43
Alexandria A1 56
Alexandria, La. L2 102
Alexandroúpolis ..C1 51
Alexis Creek L5 95

Key Page

Alexis, river C3 98
Alfios, river B3 51
Alfred L2 102
Algarrobo ....Inset 76
Algarve, region A4 36
Algeciras D4 37
Alghero B2 38
Algiers, capital B1 57
Alí Adde B2 60
Äli Bayramli B2 45
Ali-Sabieh B2 60
Aliákmon, river ...B1 51
Alibori, river B1 64
Alicante F3 37
Alice C3 71
Alice Arm H3 95
Alice Springs, N.T. ..C2 14
Alice Town B2 89
Aligarh C3 20
Alima, river C4 66
Aliwal North C3 71
Alix D5 94
Alkmaar B2 32
Allahabad D3 20
Allardville D1 97
Allen, lake B1 31
Allenford D3 102
Allentown, Pa. F1 126
Alleppey (Alappuzha) ..C7 20
Alliance A3 89
Allier, river C3 34
Alligator Pond B3 88
Alliston F3 102
Allumette, lake H2 102
Alma E3 97
Alma E3 103
Almada A3 36
Almadén D3 37
Almansa F3 37
Almaty (Alma-Ata), capital ..D2 23
Almelo D2 32
Almendra, reservoir ..C2 37
Almería E4 37
Almirante A2 87
Almonte J2 102
Alonsa B4 96
Alor Setar A1 13
Alor, island D2 13
Alotau B3 15
Alpena, Mich......E1 126
Alps, mts. 29
Alsace D2 34
Alsask A9 104
Alta E1 52
Altai, mts. B1 10
Altamira C2 81
Altamira A3 76
Altario E5 94
Altay B1 10
Altay B2 11
Altdorf C2 35
Altiplano, plateau ..A3 77
Altona C4 96
Altun, range B2 10
Aluksne D2 46
Alvinston D5 102
Alytus C2 46
Alzette, river B2 33
Am Timan C5 59
Amadjuak, lake ...O4 99
Amadora A3 36
Amagasaki B3 8
Amahai D2 13
Amakusa, islands ..A3 8
Amambay, mts. ...E3 75
Amami, island ...Inset II 8
Amapá C1 81
Amapala B3 86
Amarah, al- C2 24
Amarante B4 96
Amarillo, Tex. C2 126
Amasya C2 27
Amazon, basin B2 81
Amazon, river B2 81
Amazonas B3 79
Ambato B3 79
Ambatolampy B2 69
Ambatondrazaka ..B2 69
Amberg B4 40
Ambergris Cay, island ..C2 85
Ambergris, cay D4 89
Amberley D3 102
Ambon D2 13
Ambositra B3 69
Ambre, cape C3 18
Ambrym, island ...C3 18
Amdanga ....Inset II 20
Ameca D3 84
Ameland, island ...C1 32
Amersfoort C2 32
Amery Ice Shelf, glacier ..C18 107
Amherst C2 100
Amherstburg B5 102
Amiens C2 34
Amindivi, islands ..B6 20
Amirante, islands ..B2 70
Amisk E5 94
Amisk, lake H6 104
Amlamé B3 64
Amman, capital ...A2 26
Ammassalik C2 106
Ammersee, lake ...B4 40
Amos A4 101
Ampanihy A3 69
Amparai C4 19
Amqui J3 103
Amran A1 25
Amravati C4 20
Amritsar B2 20
Amsterdam, capital ..B2 32
Amstetten D2 39
Amu Darya, river ..B1, D2 22
Amund Ringnes, island ..J1 99
Amundsen, gulf ...C2 99
Amundsen, sea B9 107
Amur, river D8 44
Amyun A1 26

Key Page

Ana María, gulf ...D2 88
Anabar C1 16
Anaco D2 79
Anadyr C10 44
Anadyr, gulf C11 44
Anahim Lake K5 95
Anáhuac D2 84
Añasco A2 90
Añasco, beach A2 90
Anatahan, island ..C5 18
Anchorage, Alaska ..Inset I 126
Ancona C2 38
Ancud B7 76
Ancud, gulf B7 76
Andalusia D4 37
Andaman, islands ..F6 20
Andaman, sea B3 12
Anderlecht C2 33
Anderson, river ...C3 99
Andes, mts. 73
Andheri ....Inset I 20
Andizhan D2 23
Andoany B1 69
Andong C4 9
Andorra la Vella, capital ..A3 89
Andreas, cape C1 27
Ándros, island A3 89
Ándros, island C3 51
Androka A3 69
Andros, island B3 64
Anegada, island ...B3 90
Anelghowhat C5 18
Anetan B1 16
Aneto, mt. G1 37
Angara, river D6 44
Angarsk D7 44
Angaur, island A4 17
Angel, falls D2 79
Angeles B3 12
Ångermanälven, river ..C2 53
Angers B3 34
Angikuni, lake H4 99
Angkor Thom, ruins ..B2 11
Angkor Wat, ruins ..B2 11
Anglesey, island ...B3 30
Angoche C3 68
Angol B6 76
Angola F3 102
Angoulême C4 34
Anholt, island C2 32
Anhui E2 10
Anibare B2 16
Añisoc C3 66
Anju J5 103
Ankang D2 10
Ankara, capital ...C2 27
Ankaratra, mts. ...B2 69
Ankobra, river A4 64
Ann Arbor, Mich. ..E1 126
Anna Regina B2 80
Annaba B1 57
Annagpurna, mt. ..C2 19
Annandale C2 100
Annapolis Royal ...B3 100
Annapolis, capital, Md. ..F2 126
Annapurna, mt. ...C2 19
Annecy D4 34
Anse Boileau ......Inset 70
Anse Royale ......Inset 70
Anse-à-Galets C2 89
Anshan F1 10
Ansongo D2 58
Antalaha C1 69
Antalya B3 27
Antalya, gulf B3 27
Antananarivo, capital ..B2 69
Antarctic, peninsula ..C12 107
Antequera D4 37
Anti-Atlas, ranges ..B2 57
Anti-Lebanon, mts. ..B1 26
Anticosti, island ...D4 101
Antigonish F2 100
Antigua C5 85
Antigua, island ...D4 90
Antioch (Antakya) ..D3 27
Antofagasta B2 76
Antrim, mts. A2 30
Antsirabe B2 69
Antsiranana B1 69
Antsohihy B1 69
Antwerp C1 33
Anuradhapura B3 19
Anxi E2 10
Anyang E2 10
Anyos B2 36
Aoa C1 18
Aoba, island B2 18
Aomori D1 8
Aoral, mt. C3 11
Aosta A1 38
Aozou B2 59
Apa, river D3 75
Apaporis, river ...C4 78
Apatity B3 44
Apatou A1 80
Apeldoorn C2 32
Apennines, range ..B1 38
Apetina B3 80
Api, mt. A2 19
Apia, capital A4 18
Apo, volcano C5 12
Apolima, island ...A3 18
Apolima, strait ...B2 18
Apoteri B3 80
Appalachian, mts. ..E2 126
Apple River B2 100
Apsley G3 102
Apulia D2 38
Apure, river C2 79
Apurímac, river ...C3 77
Apuseni, mts. B2 43
Aqaba, gulf ...A3, B3 26

Key Page

Aqabah, al- A3 26
Aqtau B2 23
Aqtobe B1 23
Aquileia C1 38
Aquitaine B4 34
Ara B2 20
Arabah, al-, river ..A2, B2 26
Arabian, desert B2 56
Arabian, sea ....A5, Inset I 20
Aracaju E3 81
Arachon B4 34
Arad A2 43
Aradah B3 25
Aragats, mt. B2 45
Aragón F2 37
Araguaia, river ...C3 81
Arak B3 22
Arakabesan, island ..B3 17
Arakan Yoma, mts. ..B2 12
Aral A2 23
Aral, sea A2, B2 23
Aran, island B2 31
Aranda de Duero ..E2 37
Aranjuez E2 37
Aranyaprathet C3 12
Arapey Grande, river ..B1 75
Ararat B3 45
Ararat (Ağri Daği), mt. ..F2 27
Aras, river E2 27
Arauca B2 78
Arauca, river C2 79
Aravalli, range B3 20
Arawa B2 15
Arba Minch B3 60
Arborfield G7 104
Arborg C4 96
Archerwill G8 104
Arcola H11 104
Arctic Bay L2 99
Arctic Red River ...B3 99
Arda, river C4 50
Ardabil B2 22
Ardara B1 31
Ardbeg E2 102
Ardennes, plateau ..D2 33
Ardennes, region ..D1 34
Arekalong, peninsula ..C2 17
Arenal, lake B2 86
Arenas, point D2 90
Arendal B4 52
Arequipa C4 77
Arezzo C2 38
Argenteuil ......Inset II 34
Argentia D5 98
Argentino, lake ...A7 74
Arges, river C3 43
Arghandab, river ..B2 22
Argonne, forest ...D2 34
Árgos B3 51
Argyle C4 96
Argyle F3 102
Århus C2 32
Ari, atoll A3 19
Ariana C1 57
Arica B1 76
Arichat F2 100
Arima A2 91
Arinsal A2 36
Aripuaná, river ...C2 81
Arish, al- B1 56
Arizona B2 126
Arkansas D2 126
Arkansas, river ...D2 126
Arkhangelsk C4 44
Arklow C2 31
Arkona D4 102
Arles D5 34
Arlit D3 59
Arlon D3 33
Armagh B3 78
Armenia, N.S.W. ..E3 14
Armidale, N.S.W. ..E3 14
Armstrong N6 95
Armstrong C2 101
Arnaud, river B2 101
Arnes C4 96
Arnhem C3 32
Arnhem Land, region ..C1 14
Arnhem, cape C1 14
Arno, river B2 38
Arnold's Cove D5 98
Arnprior J2 102
Arnsberg B3 40
Aroostook B2 97
Arorae, island A2 17
Arpa, river C2 45
Arpajon ....Inset II 34
Arqalyq C1 23
Arran, island B2 30
Arras C1 34
Arroyo C3 90
Arta B2 51
Artashat B3 45
Artemisa B1 88
Arthur E4 102
Arthur's Town B3 89
Artibonite, river ...B1 89
Artigas B1 75
Artik A2 45
Artsvashen C2 45
Artvin E2 27
Aru, islands E2 13
Arua B2 61
Aruba, island 82
Arun, river C2 19
Arusha C1 68
Aruvi, river B2 19
Aruwimi, river C1 67
Arvayheer C2 11
As Ela B2 60
Asaba C4 65
Asadabad C2 22
Asahi Dake, mt. ...Inset I 8
Asahikawa ....Inset I 8
Asama, mt. C2 8

Key Page

Asansol E4 20
Asau A2 18
Asbestos E6 103
Ascoli Piceno C2 38
Asela C3 60
Asenovgrad C3 50
Ashburton B3 15
Ashburton, river ..A2 14
Ashcroft M6 95
Ashdod B2 26
Ashern B3 96
Asheville, N.C. ...E2 126
Asheweig, river ...C2 101
Ashgabat, capital ..C3 22
Ashikaga C2 8
Ashizuri, cape B3 8
Ashmore and Cartier, islands ..B2 14
Ashqelon B2 26
Ashton A4 91
Ashuapmushuan, river ..C2 103
Asinara, island ...B2 38
Asipovichy D3 47
Asir, region B2 24
Askar B1 25
Asmara, capital ...B2 60
Asnam, el- B1 57
Aso, mt. A3 8
Asosa B2 60
Aspiring, mt. A3 15
Asprópirgos .....Inset 51
Asquith C8 104
Assab D3 60
Assal, lake B2 60
Assen D2 32
Assiniboia D11 104
Assiniboine, mt. ..P6 95
Assiniboine, river ..A4 96
Astara C3 45
Asti B1 38
Astipálaia, island ..C3 51
Astorga C1 37
Astrakhan E4 44
Asturias C1 37
Asunción, capital ..D4 75
Aswan B3 56
Aswan High, dam ..B3 56
Asyut B2 56
At-Bashy D2 23
Atacama, desert ...C2 76
Atakpamé B3 64
Ataq B2 25
Atâr B2 58
Atatürk, reservoir ..D3 27
Atbara, river B1 60
Atbarah C2 59
Atbarah, river C2 59
Atbasar C1 23
Ath C2 33
Athabasca D4 94
Athabasca, lake ...A1 104
Athabasca, river ..B4, D3, E2 104
Athens, capital ...B3, Inset 51
Athens, Ga. E2 126
Athi, river E5 61
Athlone C2 31
Áthos, mt. C1 51
Ati B4 59
Atiak C2 61
Atikameg B3 94
Atikameg Lake A2 96
Atikokan B3 101
Atitlán, lake B5 85
Atlanta, capital, Ga. ..E2 126
Atlantic City, N.J. ..F2 126
Atlas, mts. A1, B2 57
Atlin F1 95
Atlin, lake F1 95
Atrai, river B4 21
Atrak, river B2 22
Atrato, river A3 78
Attapu D4 11
Attawapiskat D2 101
Attawapiskat, river ..C2 101
Atuel, river B4 74
Atyrau B2 23
Aua C1 18
Aube, river D3 34
Auch C5 34
Auckland B2 15
Augsburg B4 40
Augusta, capital, Maine ..G1 126
Augusta, Ga. E2 126
Auki B1 16
Aulac E3 97
Aunuu, island C1 18
Auob, river C2 70
Aur, island C2 16
Aurangabad C5 20
Aurora F3 102
Ausa, river A4 96
Austin, capital, Tex. ..D2 126
Australian Alps, mts. ..D3 14
Australian Capital Territory ..D3 14
Auvergne C4 34
Auxerre C3 34
Avalon, peninsula ..E5 98
Aveiro A2 36
Avellaneda D3 74
Avellino C2 38
Aviemore B1 30
Avignon D5 34
Avila D2 37
Avilés D1 37
Avon, islands A2 18
Avonlea E10 104
Awaji B3 8
Awaji, island B3 8
Awasa C2 60
Awash, river C2 60
Awbari B2 56
Awe, lake D4 65
Awwali, river A2 26
Axel Heiberg, island ..K1 99

Name	Key	Page
Axim	A4	64
Ayacucho	C3	77
Ayagöz	E2	23
Aydin	A3	27
Ayer Chawan, *island*	A1	13
Ayer's Cliff	D6	103
Aylesbury	Inset III	30
Aylmer	E5	102
Aylmer	A6	103
Aylmer, *lake*	G4	99
Aylmer, *lake*	E6	103
Ayn, al-	C2	25
Ayoûn el-Atroûs	C3	58
Ayr	B2	30
Aytos	F3	50
Azaouâd, *region*	F2	65
Azare	A1	27
Azaz	A1	24
Azcapotzalco	Inset	84
Azerbaijan, *region*	B2	22
Azogues	B4	79
Azores, *islands*		5
Azov, *sea*	D3	47
Azraq ash-Shishan	B2	26
Azua	B2	89
Azuero, *peninsula*	B3	87

B

Name	Key	Page
Ba, *river*	B3	11
Baalbek	B1	26
Bab al-Mandab, *strait*	C1	60
Babahoyo	B3	79
Babanusah	B3	59
Babar, *island*	D2	13
Babbage, *river*	A2	105
Babda	A2	26
Babelthuap, *island*	C3	17
Babine, *lake*	J4	95
Babine, *river*	J3	95
Babruysk	D3	47
Babu Bheri	Inset II	20
Babuyan, *channel*	B2	12
Babuyan, *islands*	B2	12
Babylon, *ruins*	B2	24
Bac Lieu	A5	11
Bacabal	D2	81
Bacău	D2	43
Back, *river*	H3	99
Bačka Palanka	A2	49
Bacolod	B4	12
Bad Ems	A3	40
Bad Ischl	C3	39
Bad Kreuznach	A4	40
Bad Reichenhall	C3	37
Badajoz	H2	37
Badalona	H2	37
Badanah	B1	24
Badas	A2	13
Baddeck	G1	100
Baden	C1	35
Baden	E2	39
Badger	A3	96
Badger	D4	96
Badger	C5	98
Badou	B3	64
Bafatá	C1	62
Baffin, *bay*	L1	92
Baffin, *island*	M2	99
Baffin, *island*	Inset I	126
Baffin, *region*	N2	99
Bafilo	B2	64
Bafing, *river*	C2	62
Bafoulabé	A3	58
Bafoussam	B2	65
Baghdad, *capital*	B2	24
Baghlan	B1	22
Baglung	B2	19
Bagmati, *river*	B2	19
Bagoé, *river*	C1	63
Baguio	B2	12
Bagzane, *mt.*	B2	59
Bahawalpur	D4	21
Bahia	D3	81
Bahía Blanca	C4	74
Bahía Honda	A2	88
Bahía, *islands*	B1	86
Bahir Dar	B2	60
Bahoruco, *mts.*	A2	89
Bahr al-Arab, *river*	B3	59
Bahr al-Ghazal, *river*	C3	59
Bahr al-Jabal, *river*	C3	59
Bahr Salamat, *river*	B5	59
Bahrain, *gulf*	A2	25
Baia Mare	F1	10
Baicheng	F1	10
Baidyabati	Inset II	20
Baie Verte	C4	98
Baie-Comeau	H2	103
Baie-des-Sables	J3	103
Baie-St-Paul	F4	103
Baie-Ste-Anne	E1	97
Baie-Ste-Catherine	G3	103
Bailieboro	G3	102
Bainsville	L2	102
Bair	B2	26
Baiti	B1	16
Baja	B2	43
Baja California	A1	84
Baja California Sur	B2	84
Bajadero	B2	90
Bajo Boquete	A2	87
Bakel	C2	62
Baker Brook	A1	97
Baker Lake	J4	99
Bakersfield, Calif.	B2	126
Bakhardok	C2	22
Bakhtaran	B3	22
Bakhtiari, *region*	B3	22
Baku, *capital*	F2	102
Bala	F2	102
Bala, *lake*	B3	30
Balabac, *island*	A5	12
Balabac, *strait*	A5	12

Name	Key	Page
Balakän	B2	45
Balaklava	C4	47
Balaton, *lake*	A2	43
Balboa	C2	87
Balcarres	G10	104
Baldur	B4	96
Baldy, *mt.*	A3	96
Balearic, *islands*	G3	37
Balearic, *sea*	G2	37
Baleia, *point*	E3	81
Baleine, *river*	C2	101
Balgonie	F10	104
Balhaf	B2	25
Balho	B1	60
Bali, *island*	C2	13
Baliceaux, *island*	B3	91
Balikesir	A2	27
Balikpapan	C2	13
Balkan, *mts.*	B2	50
Balkh	B1	22
Balkhash	D2	23
Balkhash, *lake*	D2	23
Ballancourt-sur-Essonne	Inset II	34
Ballarat, Vic.	D3	14
Balleny, *islands*	C5	107
Ballerup	D3	32
Ballina	B1	31
Bally	Inset II	20
Ballymena	A2	30
Balmaceda	B8	76
Balmertown	B2	101
Balmoral	C1	97
Balmoral	E4	84
Balranald	D3	14
Balsas, *river*	A2	50
Baltic, *sea*		
Baltimore, Md.	F2	126
Baluchistan, *region*	E4	22
Balykchy	E1	23
Balzers	B2	33
Bam	D4	22
Bamako, *capital*	C3	58
Bamangachi	Inset II	20
Bambadinca	C1	62
Bamban, *river*	B2	87
Bambari	B2	66
Bamberg	B4	40
Bamenda	B2	65
Bamian	B2	22
Ban Houayxay	A1	11
Ban Phai	C2	12
Banaba, *island*	A2	17
Banana	B2	67
Banana, *islands*	A1	63
Bananga	F7	20
Banat, *region*	A3	43
Banbury	C3	30
Bancroft	H2	102
Banda Aceh	A1	13
Banda, *sea*	D2	13
Bandama Blanc, *river*	C2	63
Bandama Rouge, *river*	C2	63
Bandama, *river*	D3	63
Bandar Beheshti	E4	22
Bandar Lampung	B2	13
Bandar Seri Begawan, *capital*	B2	13
Bandar-e Abbas	D4	22
Bandar-e Anzali	B2	22
Bandar-e Bushehr	C4	22
Bandar-e Khomeyni	B3	22
Bandar-e Torkeman	C2	22
Bandeira, *mt.*	D4	81
Bandundu	B2	67
Bandung	B2	13
Banff	C5	94
Bangalore	C6	20
Bangar	C2	13
Bangassou	B3	66
Banghiang, *river*	B2	11
Bangka, *island*	B2	13
Bangkok, *capital*	B3	12
Bangor	B3	30
Bangor	B3	30
Bangor, Maine	G1	126
Bangui, *capital*	A3	66
Bangweulu, *lake*	B2	68
Bani	B2	89
Bani Suwayf	B2	56
Bani Walid	B1	56
Bani, *river*	B3	58
Baniyas	A2	27
Banja Luka	B1	48
Banjarmasin	C2	13
Banjul, *capital*	B2	62
Banks, *island*	G4	95
Banks, *island*	B3	99
Banks, *islands*	B1	18
Banks, *peninsula*	B3	15
Bann, *river*	A2	30
Bannockburn	H3	102
Bansang	D2	62
Bansbaria	Inset II	20
Banská Bystrica	B2	42
Bantry	B3	31
Bantry, *bay*	B3	31
Baoding	E2	10
Baoshan	C3	10
Baotou	E1	10
Baoulé, *river*	B3	58
Baqubah	B2	24
Baquerizo Moreno	Inset	79
Bar	A3	49
Bar-le-Duc	D2	34
Baraawe	A3	60
Barabinsk	D5	44
Baracaldo	E1	37
Barachois	M3	103
Baracoa	F3	88
Barahona	B2	89
Baraki Barak	B2	22
Barakpur	Inset II	20
Baram, *river*	B2	13
Barama, *river*	B2	80
Baranagar	Inset II	20
Baranavichy	C3	47
Barasat	Inset II	20

Name	Key	Page
Barbuda, *island*	E3	90
Barcelona	D1	79
Barcelona	H2	37
Barceloneta	B2	90
Bärdä	B2	45
Bardaï	B2	59
Bardejov	C2	42
Bareilly	C3	20
Barents, *sea*	B3	44
Bargachia	Inset II	20
Bari	D2	38
Baril, *lake*	E2	94
Barinas	B2	79
Barind, *region*	B4	21
Baris	B3	56
Barisal	D6	21
Bark, *lake*	H2	102
Barkerville	M4	95
Barkly, *tableland*	C1	14
Barletta	D2	38
Barnaul	D6	44
Barnes, *ice cap*	O3	99
Barnsley	C3	30
Barnstaple	B3	30
Barnwell	D6	94
Baro, *river*	B2	60
Barons	D6	94
Barquisimeto	C1	79
Barra, *river*	A2	30
Barrancabermeja	B2	78
Barranquilla	B2	78
Barranquitas	C2	90
Barreiro	A3	36
Barrhead	C4	94
Barrie	F3	102
Barrière	M5	95
Barrington	B4	100
Barro	B1	62
Barrouallie	B2	91
Barrow, Alaska	Inset I	126
Barrow, *river*	C2	31
Barrow-in-Furness	B2	30
Barry's Bay	H2	102
Bartang, *river*	B1	23
Bartica	A2	80
Barú, *volcano*	C1	79
Baruta	D2	11
Baruun-Urt	D2	11
Bas-Caraquet	D1	97
Basarabeasca	B2	50
Basel	B1	35
Bashi, *channel*	B1	12
Basilan	B5	12
Basilan, *island*	B5	12
Basildon	Inset III	30
Basilicata	C2	38
Baskatong, *reservoir*	A5	103
Basque Country	E1	37
Basra	C2	24
Bass Rock, *islet*	C2	30
Bass, *strait*	D3	14
Bassar	B2	64
Basse Santa Su	D2	62
Basse-Normandie	B2	34
Bassein	B3	12
Basseterre, *capital*	B2	90
Bassila	A3	64
Bastia	Inset I	
Bastogne	D2	33
Bata	B3	66
Bataan, *peninsula*	B2	88
Batabanó, *gulf*	B2	88
Batan, *islands*	B1	12
Batang	C3	10
Batang Duri	C2	13
Batangas	B2	12
Batangafo	A2	66
Batdambang	B2	11
Bate, *bay*	Inset IV	
Batéké, *plateau*	C5	66
Bath	C3	30
Bath	B2	97
Batha, *river*	C4	59
Bathsheba	B3	91
Bathurst	D1	97
Bathurst, *island*	J1	99
Batin, Wadi al-, *river*	A2	24
Batinah, al-, *region*	C1	25
Batman	E3	27
Batna	B1	57
Baton Rouge, *capital*, La.	D2	126
Batouri	B3	65
Batroun, al-	A1	26
Batteau	D2	98
Batticaloa	C4	19
Battle, *river*	A7	104
Battleford	B8	104
Batu Pahat	B2	13
Batumi	A4	45
Baubau	D2	13
Bauchi	B2	65
Bauld, *cape*	Inset II	
Bauru	D4	81
Bauru	C2	46
Bautzen	C3	40
Bavaria	B4	40
Bavarian Alps, *mts.*	B5	40
Bawiti, al-	A2	56
Bawku	B1	64
Bawlf	D5	94
Bay Bulls	E5	98
Bay de Verde	E5	98
Bay Roberts	E5	98
Bay St. Lawrence	G1	100
Bayamo	E3	88
Bayamón	C2	90
Bayamón, *river*	C2	90
Bayan Har, *range*	C2	11
Bayanhongor	C2	11
Bayda, al-	D1	56
Bayda, al-	B3	25
Baydhabo	A2	60
Bayerischer Wald, *mts.*	C4	40
Bayeux	B2	34
Bayfield	D4	102
Baygorria, *lake*	B2	75
Baykal, *lake*	D7	44

Name	Key	Page
Bayonne	B5	34
Bayport	C3	100
Bayramaly	D3	22
Bayreuth	B4	40
Bays, *lake*	F2	102
Baza	E4	37
Bazardüzü Daği, *mt.*	B2	45
Bazin, *river*	A4	103
Beachside	D4	98
Beagle, *channel*	B7	74
Bear Lake	C2	100
Bear River	B4	90
Beata, *cape*	A3	89
Beata, *island*	A3	89
Beaton	O6	95
Beau Bassin	B2	69
Beauceville	F5	103
Beaufort West	B3	71
Beaufort, *sea*	B1	105
Beaulac	E6	103
Beaumont	D4	94
Beaumont, Tex.	D2	126
Beauport	L5	103
Beaupré	F4	103
Beauséjour	C4	96
Beauvais	C2	34
Beauval	C5	104
Beaver Creek	A4	105
Beaver Harbour	E3	100
Beaver Hill, *lake*	D2	96
Beaver Mines	A6	104
Beaver, *river*	A6	104
Beaver, *river*	D5	105
Beaverton	F3	102
Bécancour	D5	103
Bečej	B2	49
Béchar	A1	57
Bedeque, *bay*	B2	100
Bedford	C3	30
Bedford	D3	100
Bedford	D6	103
Bedok	B1	13
Beechy	C10	104
Beersheba	B2	26
Behala	Inset II	20
Bei'an	F1	10
Beihai	D3	10
Beijing, *capital*	E2	10
Beinn Dearg, *mt.*	B1	30
Beira	A2	26
Beirut, *capital*	B3	36
Beja	B1	57
Béja	B1	57
Bejaïa	B1	57
Bejaïa, *gulf*	B1	57
Béjar	D2	37
Bekaa, *valley*	A2	26
Békéscsaba	C2	43
Bela	B4	91
Belair	B4	91
Belaurpada	Inset I	20
Belasica, *mts.*	C2	48
Belaya Tserkov	C2	47
Beledweyne	B3	60
Belém	D2	81
Bélep, *islands*	C2	18
Belfast	D4	20
Belford Roxo	Inset I	81
Belfort	D3	34
Belfort, *gap*	B5	20
Belgaum	B2	49
Belgrade, *capital*	B3	49
Beli Drim, *river*	B3	49
Bélinga	B1	66
Belitung, *island*	B2	13
Belize City	B2	85
Belize, *river*	B2	85
Bella Coola	J5	95
Bella Unión	B1	75
Bellary	C5	20
Bellburns	C4	98
Belle Isle, *strait*	C3	98
Belle River	C3	100
Belle, *island*	B3	34
Belle, *island*	C3	98
Belle-Anse	C2	89
Belledune	D1	97
Belleview	A4	96
Belleville	H3	102
Bellingham	L7	95
Bellingham, Wash.	A1	126
Bellingshausen, *sea*	B10	107
Bellinzona	D2	35
Bellona, *island*	A2	16
Belluno	C1	38
Bellville	A3	71
Belmont	B4	96
Belmopan, *capital*	B2	85
Belo Horizonte	D3	81
Beloeil	C6	103
Belomorsk	C3	44
Bemaraha, *plateau*	A2	69
Bemidji, Minn.	D1	126
Ben Eoin	G2	100
Ben Nevis, *mt.*	B2	30
Benavente	D1	37
Bend, Oreg.	A1	126
Bender (Tighina)	B2	50
Benderbeyla	C2	60
Bendigo, Vic.	D3	14
Benevento	C2	38
Bengal, *bay*	E2	19
Bengbu	D1	56
Benghazi	D1	56
Bengkulu	B2	13
Bengough	E11	104
Benguela	B4	70
Beni Mellal	C1	57
Beni, *river*	A2	77
Benidorm	F3	37
Benin City	C4	65
Benin, *bight*	B5	65
Benito	A3	96
Benito's Cove	B5	98
Benoni	C2	71
Benson	G11	104
Bentiaba	B4	70
Benue, *river*	E3	65

Name	Key	Page
Benxi	F1	10
Benzdorp	B3	80
Binga, *mt.*	B3	68
Bequia, *island*	B2	91
Berat	A3	49
Berbera	B1	60
Berbérati	A3	66
Berbice, *river*	B3	80
Berdoba	C4	59
Berdyansk	D3	47
Berdyche	C4	47
Berens River	C3	96
Berens, *island*	C3	96
Berens, *river*	D1	97
Beresford	D4	44
Berezniki	C2	100
Bergamo	B1	38
Bergen	A4	95
Bergen	B1	38
Bergen op Zoom	B3	32
Bergerac	C4	34
Bergisch Gladbach	A3	40
Bering, *sea*	Inset I	126
Bering, *strait*	C11	44
Berkner, *island*	B12	107
Berlin, *capital*	C2	40
Bermejo, *river*	B2	74
Bermuda, *island*		82
Bern, *capital*	B2	35
Bernburg	B3	40
Bernese Alps, *mts.*	B2	35
Bernières	K6	103
Berouna, *river*	A3	42
Berwick	C2	100
Berwick-upon-Tweed	D3	30
Besançon	D3	34
Beskid, *mts.*	D4	41
Besnard, *lake*	D5	104
Besor, *river*	B2	26
Bethanien	C4	70
Bethany	A3	71
Bethel, Alaska	Inset I	126
Bethierville	C5	103
Bethlehem	C2	71
Béticos, *mts.*	E4	37
Bétou	E2	66
Betsiamites	H3	103
Betsiamites, *river*	G2	103
Betsiboka, *river*	B2	69
Bette, *mt.*	C3	56
Beulah	A4	96
Beyla	D3	62
Beyneu	A2	23
Beyşehir, *lake*	B3	27
Béziers	C5	34
Bhadrakh	Inset II	20
Bhagalpur	E3	20
Bhairahawa	B2	19
Bhaktapur	C2	19
Bhamapur	D5	20
Bhamo	C1	12
Bhandup	Inset I	20
Bharatpur	C4	20
Bhatapara	D4	20
Bhatpara	Inset II	20
Bhavnagar	B4	20
Bhayandar	Inset I	20
Bheri, *river*	B2	19
Bhima, *river*	C5	20
Bhimpur	Inset II	20
Bhiwandi	Inset I	20
Bhopal	C4	20
Bhubaneshwar	A4	20
Bhuj	A4	20
Bhunya	B2	71
Biabou	B2	91
Biafra, *bight*	A3	65
Biak, *island*	D2	13
Biała Podlaska	F2	41
Białystok	F2	41
Biankouma	C3	63
Biarritz	B5	34
Bicaz, *reservoir*	D2	43
Biche, *lake*	E4	94
Bida	D3	65
Bié, *plateau*	C4	70
Biel	B1	35
Biel, *lake*	B1	35
Biele Karpaty, *mts.*	A2	42
Bielefeld	B2	40
Bielsko-Biała	D4	41
Bien Hoa	B4	11
Bienville, *lake*	B2	101
Big Beaver	E11	104
Big Bend	B2	71
Big Creek	L5	95
Big Fish, *river*	B1	105
Big Gull, *lake*	J3	102
Big Muddy, *lake*	F11	104
Big River	C7	104
Big Trout Lake	C2	101
Big, *island*	O4	99
Big, *river*	C8	104
Biggar	C8	104
Bignona	A3	62
Bigstone, *river*	D1	96
Bihać	A1	48
Bihar	E3	20
Bihor, *mts.*	B2	43
Bijagós, *islands*	A2	62
Bijapur	C5	20
Bijelina	B3	20
Bikaner	C3	20
Bikar, *island*	C1	16
Bikini, *island*	B1	16
Bilaspur	D4	20
Biläsuvar	C3	45
Bilauktaung, *range*	B3	12
Bilbao	E1	37
Billings, Mont.	C1	126
Billings, *reservoir*	Inset II	81
Bilma	B5	80
Biloku	B5	80
Biloxi, Miss.	E2	126
Biltine	C4	59
Bimbila	B2	64
Binche	C2	33

Name	Key	Page
Bindloss	E6	94
Bindura	B1	69
Binga, *mt.*	B3	68
Bingen	A4	40
Binscarth	A4	96
Bint Jubayl	A2	26
Bintang	B2	62
Bintimane, *mt.*	B1	63
Bío-Bío, *river*	B6	76
Bioko, *island*	A1	66
Bir Gandús	A2	58
Bîr Morgrein	C1	58
Birak	B2	56
Birao	B1	66
Biratnagar	D3	19
Birch Cliff	K5	102
Birch Hills	E7	104
Birch River	A3	96
Birch, *mts.*	D2	94
Birchy Bay	D4	98
Bird, *island*	B2	91
Birendranagar	C2	19
Birganj	C2	19
Birjand	D3	22
Birkat Qarun, *lake*	B2	56
Birkenhead	B3	30
Birkirkara	B2	36
Bîrlad	D2	43
Birmingham	C3	30
Birmingham, Ala.	E2	126
Birni Nkonni	B3	59
Birnie	B4	96
Birnin Kebbi	C1	65
Birobizhan	E8	44
Birobizhan, *autonomous oblast*	E8	44
Birtle	A4	96
Biržai	C1	46
Birzebbuga	B3	36
Biscay, *bay*	B4	34
Bishkek, *capital*	D1	23
Bishnupur	Inset II	20
Bishop's Falls	D4	98
Biskra	B1	57
Bislig	C4	12
Bismarck, *archipelago*	A2	15
Bismarck, *capital*, N. Dak.	C1	126
Bismarck, *range*	A2	15
Bismarck, *sea*	A2	15
Bismuna, *lagoon*	C1	87
Bison, *lake*	B2	94
Bissau, *capital*	B2	62
Bissett	D3	96
Bissorã	B1	62
Bistcho, *lake*	A1	94
Bistrița	C2	43
Bistrița, *river*	A1	66
Bitam	B2	48
Bitola	E2	94
Bitumount	C2	65
Biu	G2	65
Biwa, *lake*	B3	8
Biysk	D6	44
Bizard, *island*	H5	103
Bizerte	B1	57
Bjorne, *peninsula*	L1	99
Black (Da), *river*	A2	11
Black Country, *region*	C3	30
Black Lake	E1	104
Black River	B2	88
Black Tickle	D2	98
Black Volta, *river*	A2, B3	64
Black, *forest*	A4	40
Black, *hills*, S. Dak.	C1	126
Black, *lake*	E1	104
Black, *sea*		29
Blackburn	C3	30
Blackmans	B3	91
Blackpool	C3	30
Blacks Harbour	C3	97
Blackstone, *river*	B3	105
Blackville	D2	97
Blackwater, *river*	B2, C1	31
Blagoevgrad	B4	50
Blagoveshchensk	D4	44
Blagoveshchensk	D8	44
Blaine Lake	D8	104
Blainville	H5	103
Blanc, *mt.*	D4	34
Blanc, *reservoir*	C4	103
Blanc-Sablon	E3	101
Blanca, *bay*	C4	74
Blanca, *river*	B2	52
Blantyre	B3	68
Blarney	B3	31
Blatec	C2	48
Blenheim	B3	100
Blenheim	D5	102
Blida	B1	57
Bligh Water, *sound*	B2	17
Blind Bay	N6	95
Blind River	C1	102
Blitta	B2	64
Bloemfontein, *judicial capital*	C2	71
Blois	C3	34
Bloodvein, *river*	C3	96
Bloomfield	H4	102
Bloomington, Ind.	E2	126
Blossom Park	H6	102
Blow, *river*	B1	105
Blue Mountain, *peak*	C2	88
Blue Nile, *river*	C2	59
Blue Ridge	C4	94
Blue River	N5	95
Blue, *mts.*	E3	14
Blue, *mts.*	C2	88
Bluefields	C3	87
Bluenose, *lake*	C5	99
Bluffton	D4	102
Blyth	B2	30
Bo	B2	63
Bo Hai, *gulf*	E2	10
Boa Vista	B1	81
Boa Vista, *island*	D2	58
Boaco	B2	87
Bobcaygeon	G3	102

Key Page

Bobo-Dioulasso B3 64
Bocas del Toro A2 87
Bocay B1 87
Bocay, river B2 87
Bocholt A3 40
Bochum A3 40
Bodaybo D7 44
Bodo E5 94
Boda C2 52
Boende B2 67
Boggeragh, mts. B2 31
Boggy, peak D5 90
Bogor B2 13
Bogotá, capital B3 78
Bogra C4 21
Bohemia, region A3 42
Bohemian, forest A3 42
Bohemian-Moravian,
   heights B3 42
Bohol, island C4 12
Bohol, sea C4 12
Boiestown C2 97
Boileau F3 103
Bois-des-Filion H5 103
Boise, capital, Idaho B1 126
Boissevain A4 96
Boknafjord, fjord B4 52
Boksburg C2 71
Bol A4 59
Bolama B2 62
Bolands D5 90
Bole A2 64
Bolgatanga B1 64
Bolívar, mt. B2 79
Bolligen B2 35
Bolnisi C4 45
Bolobo B2 67
Bologna B1 38
Bolovens, plateau D4 11
Bolsena, lake B2 38
Bolsón de Mapimí,
   depression D2 84
Bolton C3 30
Bolton F4 102
Bolu B2 27
Bolzano B1 38
Bom Jesus da Lapa D3 81
Bombay ....B.5, Inset I 20
Bombay, harbor ....Inset I 20
Bomu, river C1 67
Bon Pays, region B2 33
Bon, cape C1 57
Bonaire, island 82
Bonao B2 89
Bonaventure L3 103
Bonaventure, river L3 103
Bonavista E5 98
Bonavista, bay E5 98
Bondo B1 67
Bondoukou E2 63
Bondy ....Inset II 34
Bongor A5 59
Bonin, islands ....Inset III 8
Bonn A3 40
Bonnet Plume, river C3 105
Bonny D5 65
Bonnyville E4 94
Bonshaw B2 100
Bonthe A2 63
Bööntsagaan, lake B2 11
Boosaaso B1 60
Boothia, gulf K2 99
Boothia, peninsula K2 99
Booué A2 66
Bor C2 49
Borås B3 53
Bordeaux B4 34
Borden B2 100
Borden C8 104
Borden, island F1 99
Borden, peninsula M2 99
Borðoy, island ....Inset 52
Borgo Maggiore B1 39
Borivli ....Inset I 20
Borjomi B4 45
Borneo, island C1 13
Bornholm, island E3 32
Bosanska Gradiška B1 48
Bosanska Krupa A1 48
Bosna, river B1 48
Boso, peninsula D3 8
Bosporus, strait B2 27
Bossangoa A2 66
Bosten, lake B1 10
Boston C3 30
Boston Bar M6 95
Boston, capital, Mass. F1 126
Boswell O6 95
Botany, bay ....Inset IV 14
Boteti, river A2 69
Botha D5 94
Bothnia, gulf B2, D2 53
Botna, river B2 50
Botoșani D2 43
Botrange, mt. E2 33
Botte Donato, mt. D3 38
Bottrop A3 40
Botwood D4 98
Bouaflé D3 63
Bouaké D3 63
Bouar A2 66
Boucherville J5 103
Bouctouche E2 97
Bougainville, island B2 15
Boughton, bay C2 100
Bougouni B3 58
Boulder, Colo. C2 126
Boulogne-Billancourt ....Inset II 34
Boulogne-sur-Mer C1 34
Bouna E2 63
Bourem D3 58
Bourg-en-Bresse D3 34
Bourges C3 34
Bourgogne C3 34
Bourke, N.S.W. D3 14
Bournemouth C4 30

Key Page

Bousso B5 59
Bow City D6 94
Bow, lake D6 94
Bow, river E6 104
Bowen, Qld. D2 14
Bowling Green, Ky. E2 126
Bowser, lake H3 95
Bowsman A3 96
Boyd's Cove D4 98
Boyne, river C2 31
Boyne B4 96
Bozeman, Mont. B1 126
Brabant Lake G4 104
Brač, island C3 48
Bracciano, lake C2 38
Bracebridge F2 102
Bradford C3 30
Braga A2 36
Bragança B2 36
Bragg Creek C6 94
Brahmanbaria E5 21
Brahmaputra, river F3 20
Bräila D3 43
Braintree ....Inset III 30
Brakpan C2 71
Bralorne L6 95
Bramalea H5 102
Brampton F4 102
Branch E5 98
Branco, river B1 81
Brandberg, mt. B2 70
Brandenburg C2 40
Brandon B4, C2 96
Brant D6 94
Brantford E4 102
Bras d'Or G1 100
Brasília, capital D3 81
Brașov C3 43
Bratislava, capital A2 42
Bratsk D7 44
Braunau C2 39
Brava, coast H2 37
Brava, island B4 58
Brazilian, highlands D3 81
Brazzaville, capital C6 66
Brčko B1 48
Brea, point B3 90
Břeclav C4 42
Brecon Beacons, mts. B3 30
Breda B3 32
Bredenbury H10 104
Bregalnica, river C2 48
Breidhafjördhur, fjord A2 52
Bremen B2 40
Bremerhaven B2 40
Brenner, pass B3 39
Brentwood ....Inset III 30
Brescia B1 38
Brest A3 47
Brest A2 34
Bretagne B2 34
Breton C4 94
Bria B2 66
Briançon D4 34
Briceni A1 50
Bridge Lake M5 95
Bridgeport, Conn. F1 126
Bridgetown B3 100
Bridgetown, capital A4 91
Bridgewater C3 100
Brienzersee, lake B2 35
Brighton C4 30
Brighton H3 102
Brikama B2 62
Brindisi D2 38
Brisbane, Qld.,
   capital ....E2, Inset III 14
Brisbane, river ....Inset III 14
Bristol C3 30
Bristol B2 97
Bristol, channel B3 30
Britannia E5 98
Britt E2 102
Brive-la-Gallarde C4 34
Brno C3 42
Broadview H10 104
Brochet C1 96
Brock, island F1 99
Brocket D6 94
Brockville K3 102
Brodfur, peninsula L2 99
Broken Hill, N.S.W. D3 14
Brokopondo B2 80
Brolin C3 30
Bromptonville E6 103
Brookdale B4 96
Brooks E6 94
Brooks range, Alaska ....Inset I 126
Broome, W.A. B1 14
Broomhill A4 96
Brossard J6 103
Brownsville, Tex. D3 126
Bruce Mines B1 102
Brugge B1 33
Brugge-Ghent, canal B1 33
Brûlé B4 94
Brunei, bay C1 13
Brunei, river B2 13
Brunswick B2 40
Brunswick, Ga. E2 126
Brunswick, peninsula B9 76
Brussels D4 102
Brussels, capital C2 33
Bryan, Tex. D2 126
Bryansk D3 44
Bsharri B1 26
Bu Craa B1 58
Bua, river B2 68
Buada A1 16
Buala A1 16
Buba B2 62
Bubanza B2 61
Bubaque B2 62
Bubiyan, island C2 24
Bucaramanga B3 78
Buchanan A3 63
Buchanan H9 104
Buchans C5 98

Key Page

Bucharest, capital D3 43
Buck Creek C4 94
Buck Lake C5 94
Buckingham A6 103
Budapest, capital B2 43
Buea A3 65
Buenaventura A4 78
Buendía, reservoir E2 37
Buene, river A2 49
Buenos Aires, capital D4 74
Buenos Aires, lake A6 74
Buffalo Narrows B5 104
Buffalo, lake D5 94
Buffalo, lake E4 99
Buffalo, N.Y. F1 126
Bug, river E2, F3 41
Bugeac, region B3 50
Bugojno B1 48
Buhayrat al-Asad, lake B1 27
Buj-Buj ....Inset II 20
Bujumbura, capital B2 61
Buka, island B2 15
Bukavu C2 67
Bukhara B3 23
Bukit Pagon, mt. C3 13
Bukit Panjang B1 13
Bukit Timah B1 13
Bükk, mts. C1 43
Bukoba B1 68
Bula B1 13
Bulawayo B2 69
Bulembu B1 71
Bulgan C2 11
Bulgaria D3 38
Bulle B2 35
Bulyea F10 104
Bumba B1 67
Bunbury, W.A. A3 14
Bundaberg, Qld. E2 14
Bungo, channel B3 8
Bunia C1 67
Bunsuru, river D1 65
Buon Me Thuot B4 11
Buqayq C1 24
Buraydah B1 24
Burco B2 60
Burdekin, river D1 14
Burdett E6 94
Burdur, lake B3 27
Burdwan E4 20
Büren B2 35
Burgas F3 50
Burgeo C5 98
Burgos E1 37
Burhanpur C4 20
Burin D5 98
Burin, peninsula D5 98
Burk's Falls F2 102
Burke, channel J5 95
Burlington F4 102
Burlington, Vt. F1 126
Burnley C3 30
Burns Lake K4 95
Burntwood, lake A1 96
Burntwood, river B1, C1, D2 96
Bururi B2 61
Bury C3 30
Bury St. Edmunds D3 30
Buryatia, republic D7 44
Bushmanland, plain A2 71
Buta C1 67
Butare B2 61
Butha-Buthe B1 71
Butte, Mont. B1 126
Buttonville K5 102
Butuan C4 12
Butwal B2 19
Buurgplaatz, mt. B1 33
Buxton C3 30
Buyant-Uhaa D3 11
Büyük Menderes, lake A3 27
Buzău D3 43
Búzi, river B4 68
Byam Martin, channel G1 99
Byam Martin, island H1 99
Byarezina, river D3 47
Byblos, ruins A1 26
Bydgoszcz C2 41
Byelaruskaya Hrada, range C3 47
Bylot, island N2 99
Bytom D3 41
Byumba C1 61

C

Ca Mau A5 11
Ca, river A2 11
Caacupé D4 75
Caaguazú E4 75
Caazapá D5 75
Cabanatuan B3 12
Cabano H4 103
Cabimas B1 79
Cabinda B1 70
Cabo Rojo A2 90
Cabora Bassa, dam B2 68
Cabora Bassa, lake B2 68
Caborca B1 84
Cabrera, island H3 37
Cabrera C1 89
Cabri B10 104
Čačak B3 49
Cache Creek M6 95
Cacheu A1 62
Cacheu, river B1 62

Key Page

Cachimbo C2 81
Cacine B2 62
Cacouna G4 103
Cadiz B4 12
Cádiz C4 37
Cádiz, gulf C4 37
Cadomin B4 94
Cadotte Lake B3 94
Caen B2 34
Caerleon C3 30
Caernarfon B3 30
Cairo, capital B1 56
Cairns, Qld. D1 14
Cairo, Ill. E2 126
Caja de Muertos, island B3 90
Cajamarca B2 77
Calabar E5 65
Calabogie J2 102
Calabozo C2 79
Calabria D3 38
Calafate A7 74
Calais B3 94
Calais B3 34
Calama C2 76
Calamian, islands A3 12
Calapan B3 12
Călărași D3 43
Calatayud F2 37
Calatrava B3 66
Calbayog C3 12
Calcutta ....E4, Inset II 20
Caldas A4 78
Caldwell, Idaho B1 126
Caledon, river A1, C2 71
Caledonia F4 102
Calgary C5 94
Cali A4 78
California B2 126
California, gulf B1 84
Callao B3 77
Calling Lake D3 94
Caltanissetta C3 38
Calvi ....Inset I 34
Calvinia A3 71
Cam Ranh B4 11
Camagüey D2 88
Camagüey, archipelago D2 88
Camberley ....Inset III 30
Cambrai C1 34
Cambrian, mts. B3 30
Cambridge D3 30
Cambridge Bay G3 99
Cambridge-Narrows D3 97
Cameron, hills B1 94
Cameron, island H1 99
Cameroon A3 65
Cameroon, mt. A3 65
Camiri B4 77
Camopi B2 80
Camopi, river B2 80
Campana, island A8 76
Campania C2 38
Campbell River K6 95
Campbellford G3 102
Campbellton A2 100
Campbellton A2 100
Campbelltown, N.S.W. ....Inset IV 14
Campbelltown, S.A. ....Inset II 14
Campbeltown B2 30
Campeche, bay F4 84
Campeche, state capital F4 84
Camper B3 96
Camperville A3 96
Campina Grande E2 81
Campinas D4 81
Campo Grande C4 81
Campobasso C2 38
Campobello, island C4 97
Campos D4 81
Campos Elísios ....Inset I 81
Camrose D4 94
Camsell Portage A1 104
Camú, river B1 89
Camuy B2 90
Can Tho A4 11
Caña Gorda, beach B3 90
Canaan B1 91
Canaima D2 79
Cananéia C2 38
Cananea B1 84
Canary, islands ....Inset I 37
Canaries A2 91
Canary, islands 55
Canaveral, cape, Fla. E3 126
Canberra, A.C.T.,
   natl. capital D3 14
Canchungo A1 62
Cancún G3 84
Candelaria C2 90
Candiac J6 103
Candle Lake E7 104
Cando B8 104
Canelles, river B3 91
Canelones B3 75
Cangamba D4 70
Cangzhou E2 10
Caniapiscau, lake C3 101
Caniapiscau, river C2 101
Çankırı C2 27
Çankuzo C2 61
Cannes D5 34
Canning C2 100
Canning, river ....Inset I 14
Canoe Narrows B5 104
Canoe, lake B5 104
Canora H9 104
Canossa B1 38

Key Page

Canouan, island B3 91
Canóvanas D2 90
Canso G2 100
Cantabria D1 37
Cantábrica, mts. C1 37
Canterbury B3 97
Canterbury D3 30
Canterbury, bight B3 15
Canterbury, plains B3 15
Canton, island B2 17
Canwood D7 104
Canyon Creek C3 94
Cao Bang B1 11
Cap-aux-Os M3 103
Cap-Chat K2 103
Cap-de-la-Madeleine D5 103
Cap-Haïtien C1 89
Cap-Pelé E2 97
Cap-St-Ignace F4 103
Cape Charles D3 98
Cape Coast B4 64
Cape Girardeau, Mo. E2 126
Cape North G1 100
Cape Race E5 98
Cape Ray B5 98
Cape St. George B5 98
Cape Tormentine E2 97
Cape Town,
   legislative capital A3 71
Cape York, peninsula D1 14
Capitán Pablo Lagerenza B1 75
Caplan L3 103
Caprara, point B2 38
Capreol D1 102
Capri, island C2 38
Capua C2 38
Caquetá, river B5 78
Car Nicobar, island F7 20
Caracas, capital C1 79
Caramoan, peninsula B3 12
Carapicuíba ....Inset II 81
Caraquet E1 97
Carberry B4 96
Carbonara, cape B3 38
Carbonear E5 98
Carbonia B3 38
Carcajou B2 94
Carcassonne C5 34
Carcross C5 105
Cardamom, mts. A3 11
Cárdenas B1 88
Cardiel, lake A6 74
Cardiff B3 30
Cardigan C2 100
Cardigan, bay B3 30
Cardigan, bay C2 100
Cardinal K3 102
Cardinal, lake B3 94
Caribbean, sea 82
Carievale A4 96
Carleton K3 103
Carleton Place J2 102
Carlingford C1 31
Carlingford, lake C1 31
Carlisle C2 30
Carlisle, bay A4 91
Carlow C2 31
Carlsbad, N. Mex. C2 126
Carlyle H11 104
Carmacks B4 105
Carman B4 96
Carmanville D4 98
Carmarthen B3 30
Carmelo A2 75
Carmel B3 71
Carnac B3 34
Carnarvon B3 71
Carnarvon G2 102
Carnarvon, W.A. A2 14
Carnduff J11 104
Carnic Alps, range C4 39
Carnsore, point C2 31
Carolina E2 81
Caroline D2 17
Caroline, island D2 17
Caroline, islands B2 15
Caron E10 104
Caroni, river D2 79
Carora C1 79
Carpathian, mts. 43
Carpentaria, gulf C1 14
Carrantuohill, mt. B3 31
Carriacou, island C1 91
Carrick-on-Shannon B2 31
Carroll A4 96
Carrot River G7 104
Carson City, capital, Nev. B2 126
Carstairs C5 94
Cartagena B2 78
Cartagena F4 37
Cartago C3 86
Carthage, ruin C1 57
Cartier D1 102
Cartwright C4 96
Cartwright C2 98
Carúpano D1 79
Carvoeiro, cape A3 36
Carway D6 94
Casa Grande, Ariz. B2 126
Casablanca ....Inset 76
Casablanca C1 57
Casamance, region B3 62
Casamance, river B3 62
Cascade ....Inset 70
Cascade, range A1 126
Cascapedia, river K3 103
Cascumpec, bay B2 100
Caserta C2 38
Cashel C3 31
Casiquiare, river C3 79
Caslan D4 94
Casper, Wyo. C1 126
Caspian, depression B2 23
Caspian, sea 7
Casselman K2 102
Cassiar H1 95
Cassiar, mts. G1 95
Castel Gandolfo C2 38
Castellón de la Plana F3 37

Key Page

Castelo Branco B3 36
Castile and León D1, E1 37
Castile-la Mancha E3 37
Castle Bruce B2 90
Castle Mountain C5 94
Castlebar B2 31
Castlegar O6 95
Castries, capital B1 91
Castro B7 76
Cat, island B3 89
Catacamas C2 86
Catalina E5 98
Catalonia G2 37
Catamarca B2 74
Catanduanes, island C3 12
Catania C3 38
Cataño C2 90
Catanzaro D3 38
Catió B2 62
Catoche, cape G3 84
Catumbela B4 70
Cauca, river B3 78
Caucasus, mts. A1, A2 45
Caungula D2 70
Caura, river C3 79
Causapscal J3 103
Căușeni B2 50
Cauto, river E3 88
Cauvery, river C6 20
Cavalla, river C3 63
Cavally, river C4 63
Cavan C2 31
Cavendish B2 100
Caviana, island D1 81
Caxito B2 70
Cayambe, mt. B3 79
Cayenne, capital B1 80
Cayer B3 96
Cayey C2 90
Cayman, trench B2 88
Cayman, islands 82
Cayon B1 90
Cazombo E2 70
Ceará E2 81
Cebollatí, river C2 75
Cebu B4 12
Cebu, island B4 12
Cedar City, Utah B2 126
Cedar Grove D1 126
Cedar Rapids, Iowa D1 126
Cedar, lake A2 96
Cedros, island A2 84
Ceduna, S.A. C3 14
Ceerigaabo B1 60
Cefalù C3 38
Ceglèd B2 43
Ceiba C2 90
Ceiba D2 90
Celada D2 90
Celaya D3 84
Celebes (Sulawesi), island D2 13
Celebes, sea D1 13
Ceram, island D2 13
Ceram, sea D2 13
Cerf, island ....Inset 70
Cernavodă E3 43
Cerro Castillo B9 76
Cerro de Pasco B3 77
Cervati, mt. C2 38
Cess, river B3 63
Cessford E6 94
Cetinje A3 49
Ceuta C5 37
Cévennes, mts. C4 34
Ceyhan, river D2 27
Chachapoyas B2 77
Chaco Boreal, region B2 75
Chad, lake A4, C3 59
Chaeryŏng, river A3 9
Chagai, hills B2 22
Chaghcharan B2 22
Chagres, river C2 87
Chaguanas A2 91
Chaitén B6 76
Chaiyaphum C3 12
Chalco ....Inset 84
Chaleur, bay D1 97
Chalna C6 21
Châlons-sur-Marne D2 34
Chambal, river C3 20
Chambéry D4 34
Chambeshi, river C2 67
Chambord D3 103
Chameleon, river A2 86
Chamonix-Mont-Blanc D4 34
Champagne Castle, mt. C2 71
Champagne-Ardenne D2 34
Champaquí, mt. C3 74
Champasak C4 11
Champerico B5 85
Champlain D5 103
Chañaral B3 76
Chança, river B3 36
Chandannagar ....Inset II 20
Chandigarh C2 20
Chandler M3 103
Chandrapur C5 20
Chang (Yangtze), river D2, E2 10
Changane, river B4 68
Changchun F1 10
Changde E3 10
Changhua B1 13
Changi B1 13
Changjiang, river B2 9
Changjin, river B2 9
Changsha E3 10

Key Page
Changuinola A2 87
Changyŏn A3 9
Changzhi E2 10
Changzhou F2 10
Channel *islands*, Calif. A2 126
Channel-Port aux Basques B5 98
Chantilly C2 34
Chao Phraya, *river* B3 12
Chapada dos Parecis, *range* C3 81
Chapala, *lake* D3 84
Chaparé, *river* A3 77
Chapleau D3 101
Chaplin D10 104
Chardzhou D2 22
Charente, *river* B4 34
Chari, *river* A5 59
Charikar B1 22
Charity B2 80
Charleroi C2 33
Charles A1 96
Charlesbourg E5, Inset 103
Charleston, *capital*, W. Va. E2 126
Charleston, S.C. F2 126
Charlestown C3 90
Charlestown A3 91
Charleville Mézières D2 34
Charleville, Qld. D2 14
Charlie Lake M3 95
Charlo C1 97
Charlotte, N.C. E2 126
Charlottetown C3 98
Charlottetown B2 100
Charlotteville B1 91
Charny E5, K6 103
Charters Towers, Qld. D2 14
Chartres C2 34
Chase N6 95
Châteauguay C6, H6 103
Châteauroux C3 34
Châtellerault C3 34
Chatfield C4 96
Chatham Inset III 30
Chatham C5 102
Chatham, *sound* G4 95
Chatkal, *river* B2 23
Chatsworth E3 102
Chattanooga, Tenn. E2 126
Chau Doc A4 11
Chaumont D2 34
Chaves B2 36
Cheb A2 42
Cheboksary D4 44
Chech'ŏn C4 9
Chechnya, republic E4 44
Cheduba, *island* B2 12
Chegutu B2 69
Cheju Inset 9
Cheju, *island* Inset 9
Cheju, *strait* Inset 9
Chek Keng Inset 10
Chelan G8 104
Cheleken A2 22
Chelif, *river* B1 57
Chelles Inset II 34
Chełm F3 41
Chelmsford D3, Inset III 30
Cheltenham C3 30
Chelyabinsk D5 44
Chelyuskin, *cape* B7 44
Chembur Inset I 20
Chemin Grenier B3 69
Chemnitz C3 40
Chenab, *river* D3 21
Chenachane A2 57
Chene Inset I 20
Chénéville A6 103
Chengde E1 10
Chengdu D2 10
Cherbourg B2 34
Cherepovets D3 44
Cherkassy C2 47
Chernigov C1 47
Chernobyl C1 47
Chernovtsi B2 47
Cherrapunji F3 20
Cherryville N6 95
Cherskiy C10 44
Cherskiy, *range* C8 44
Chesapeake, *bay* F2 126
Chesley D3 102
Chester C3 30
Chester C3 100
Chesterfield C3 30
Chesterfield Inlet K4 99
Chesterfield, *islands* A2 18
Cheticamp G1 100
Chetumal, *state capital* G4 84
Chetwynd M3 95
Cheviot, *hills* C2 30
Chevreuse Inset II 34
Cheyenne, *capital*, Wyo. C1 126
Chhukha A2 19
Chi, *river* C2 12
Chiai B2 9
Chiang Mai B2 12
Chiang Rai B2 12
Chiapa C1 76
Chiapas F4 84
Chiatura B3 45
Chiba D3 8
Chibougamau B2 103
Chibougamau, *lake* B2 103
Chicago, Ill. E1 126
Chicapa, *river* D3 70
Chichén Itzá, *ruins* G3 84
Chichester C4 30
Chichi, *island* Inset III 8
Chiclayo B2 77
Chico, *river* B6 74
Chiconcuac Inset 84
Chicoutimi E3 103
Chief, *river* L2 95
Chiem, *lake* C5 40
Chiesanuova B2 39
Chieti C2 38
Chifeng E1 10
Chignecto, *bay* C2 100
Chihuahua, *state capital* C2 84

Key Page
Chilcotin, *river* K5 95
Chile Chico B8 76
Chililabombwe B2 67
Chilko, *lake* K5 95
Chillán B6 76
Chilliwack M6 95
Chiloé, *island* B7 76
Chilpancingo, *state capital* E4 84
Chilung B1 9
Chilwa, *lake* B2, C3 68
Chimalhuacán Inset 84
Chimay C2 33
Chimborazo, *mt.* B3 79
Chimbote B2 77
Chimoio B3 68
Chin, *hills* B2 12
Chinajá C4 85
Chinandega A2 87
Chincha Alta B3 77
Chinchaga, *river* A2 94
Chinde C3 68
Chindwin, *river* B1 12
Chingola B2 67
Chingoni C2 67
Chinhae C5 9
Chinhoyi B1 69
Chiniot D3 21
Chinju C5 9
Chinko, *river* B2 66
Chioggia C1 38
Chip, *lake* C4 94
Chipata C2 67
Chipewyan Lake D3 94
Chipman D2 97
Chira, *river* A5 79
Chirchiq, *river* C2 23
Chire, *river* B3 68
Chiredzi B2 69
Chiriquí, *gulf* A3 87
Chiriquí, *lagoon* B2 87
Chirner Inset I 20
Chirripó, *mt.* C3 86
Chirripó, *river* C2 86
Chisasibi A3 101
Chisholm C4 94
Chişinău, *capital* B2 50
Chita D7 44
Chitipa B1 68
Chitose Inset I 8
Chitral D2 21
Chitré B3 87
Chittagong E6 21
Chitungwiza B1 69
Chixoy, *river* C4 85
Choa Chu Kang A1 13
Choiceland F7 104
Choiseul A3 91
Choiseul, *island* A1 16
Choisy-le Roi Inset II 34
Chojnice C2 41
Choke, *mts.* B2 60
Cholet B3 34
Cholpon-Ata E1 23
Cholula E4 84
Choluteca B3 86
Choma B3 67
Chomo Lhari, *mt.* A1 19
Chon Buri B3 12
Chone A3 79
Ch'ŏngch'ŏn, *river* A3 9
Ch'ŏngjin C2 9
Ch'ŏngju B4 9
Chŏngju A3 9
Chongqing D3 10
Chonju B5 9
Chonos, *archipelago* B7 76
Chontaleña, *mts.* B2 87
Chorzów D3 41
Choshui, *river* B2 9
Choybalsan D2 11
Christchurch B3 15
Christina, *river* E3 94
Christmas Island G2 100
Chu, *river* D1 23
Chubut, *river* A5 74
Chucunaque, *river* D2 87
Chugoku, *mts.* B3 8
Chukchi, *peninsula* C11 44
Chukchi, *range* C10 44
Chukchi, *sea* B11 44
Chukotka,
autonomous okrug C10 44
Chumphon B4 12
Chunan B1 9
Ch'unch'ŏn B4 9
Chung Hau Inset 10
Chungho B1 9
Ch'ungju B4 9
Chungli B1 9
Chungyang, *range* B2 9
Chuquicamata C2 76
Chur D2 35
Church Point A3 100
Churchbridge A4 96
Churchbridge J10 104
Churchill D1 96
Churchill Falls D3 98
Churchill, *lake* B4 104
Churchill, *river* D1 96
Churia, *mts.* B2 19
Chute-aux-Outardes H2 103
Chuuk, *islands* C2 15
Chuvashia, republic D4 44
Ciales C2 90
Cibao, *valley* A1 89
Cicia, *island* C2 17
Cidra C2 90
Ciechánow E2 41
Ciego de Ávila D2 88
Cienfuegos C2 88
Cieza F3 37
Cijara, *reservoir* D3 37
Cikobia, *island* C1 17
Cilacap B2 13
Cilician Gates, *pass* C3 27
Cimone, *mt.* B1 38
Cincinnati, Ohio E2 126
Cirebon B2 13

Key Page
Citlaltépetl, *mt.* E4 84
City View G6 102
Ciudad Acuña D2 84
Ciudad Bolívar D2 79
Ciudad Camargo C2 84
Ciudad Constitución B3 84
Ciudad del Carmen F4 84
Ciudad del Este E4 75
Ciudad Guayana D2 79
Ciudad Juárez C1 84
Ciudad Mante E3 84
Ciudad Obregón C2 84
Ciudad Real E3 37
Ciudad Rodrigo C2 37
Ciudad Valles E3 84
Ciudad Victoria,
state capital E3 84
Ciudadela H2 37
Civitavecchia B2 38
Clair A1 97
Claire, *lake* D2 94
Clandeboye C4 96
Clara C2 31
Clarenville D5 98
Clark's Harbour B4 100
Clarksville, Tenn. E2 126
Clear Creek E5 102
Clear, *cape* B3 31
Clearwater M5 95
Clearwater, *river* E3 94
Clementsport B3 100
Clermont F4 103
Clermont-Ferrand C4 34
Clervaux B1 33
Clerve, *river* B1 33
Cleveland, Ohio E1 126
Clichy Inset II 34
Clifden A2 31
Clifford E4 102
Climax B11 104
Clinton M5 95
Clinton D4 102
Clinton Colden, *lake* G4 99
Cloncurry, Qld. D2 14
Clonmel C2 31
Cloridorme M2 103
Clovis, N. Mex. C2 126
Cloyne H3 102
Cluff Lake Mine A2 104
Cluj-Napoca B2 43
Cluny D3 94
Cluny D6 94
Clutha, *river* A4 15
Clyde River B4 100
Clyde River P2 99
Clyde, *estuary* B2 30
Clyde, *river* B2 30
Clydebank B2 30
Coacalco Inset 84
Coahuila D2 84
Coal River J1 95
Coal, *river* D5 105
Coaldale D6 94
Coalspur B4 94
Coamo C2 90
Coast, *mts.* F2, J5 95
Coast, *ranges* A1, A2 126
Coaticook E6 103
Coats Land, *region* B13 107
Coats, *island* M4 99
Coatzacoalcos F4 84
Cobán C4 85
Cobden J2 102
Cóbh B3 31
Cobham, *river* D2 96
Cobija A2 77
Cobourg G4 102
Coburg B3 40
Coburg, *island* N1 99
Cocagne E2 97
Cochabamba A3 77
Cochin (Kochi) C7 20
Cochrane B8 76
Cochrane D3 101
Cochrane, *lake* B8 76
Cochrane, *river* H2 104
Cockburn Harbour D4 89
Cockburn, *island* B2 102
Coclé del Norte B2 87
Coco C2 90
Coco, *islands* B3 12
Coco, *river* A2, C1 87
Cocos, *islands* 5
Cocotitlán Inset 84
Cod, *cape*, Mass. G1 126
Codri, *region* A3 50
Codrington E2 90
Codrington, *mt.* C17 107
Cody, Wyo. C1 126
Coe Hill H3 102
Coeroeni, *river* A3 80
Coeur d'Alene, Idaho B1 126
Cogalnic, *river* B2 50
Cognac B4 34
Coiba, *island* B3 87
Coihaique B8 76
Coimbatore C6 20
Coimbra A2 36
Cojedes, *river* C2 79
Colca, *river* C4 77
Colchester D3 30
Cold Lake E4 94
Coleraine A2 30
Coles Island D3 97
Coleville A9 104
Colihaut A2 90
Colima, *state capital* D4 84
Colina Inset 76
Coll, *island* A2 30
Collaguasi C2 76
Collingwood B3 15
Collingwood E3 102
Colmar D2 34
Cologne A3 40
Colombier H3 103
Colombo, *capital* A5 19
Colón C2 87
Colón C2 88

Key Page
Colonia A2 15
Colonia B3 75
Colonia Nueva Guinea B3 87
Colonsay E9 104
Colonsay, *island* A2 30
Colorado C2 86
Colorado C2 126
Colorado Springs, Colo. C2 126
Colorado, *plateau* B2 126
Colorado, *river* B4 74
Colorado, *river* B2 126
Columbia, *capital*, S.C. E2 126
Columbia, *mts.* M4 95
Columbia, *plateau* B1 126
Columbia, *river* B1 126
Columbus, *capital*, Ohio E2 126
Columbus, Ga. E2 126
Coma Pedrosa, *mt.* A1 36
Comayagua B2 86
Comayagua, *mts.* B2 86
Combermere H2 102
Comendador A2 89
Comerío C2 90
Comilla E5 21
Comino, *island* B1 36
Cominotto, *island* B1 36
Comitán F4 84
Committee, *bay* L3 99
Communisim, *peak.* B1 23
Como B1 38
Como, *lake* B1 38
Comodoro Rivadavia B6 74
Comorin, *cape* C7 20
Comox K6 95
Compiègne C2 34
Compton E6 103
Comrat B2 50
Con Son, *islands* B5 11
Conakry, *capital* B3 62
Concepción B6 76
Concepción D3 75
Concepción del Oro D3 84
Conchalí Inset 76
Conche D4 98
Conchos, *river* C2 84
Concord, *capital*, N.H. F1 126
Concordia D3 74
Condor C5 94
Congo, *basin* D3 66
Congo, *river* D4 66
Congo, *river* B1 67
Conn, *lake* B1 31
Connecticut F1 126
Connemara, *region* B2 31
Consecon H4 102
Constance B5 40
Constance (Bodensee), *lake* D1 35
Constanța E3 43
Constantine B1 57
Constitución B5 76
Consul A11 104
Contrecoeur C6 103
Contwoyto, *lake* G3 99
Conwy B3 30
Coober Pedy, S.A. C2 14
Cook's Harbour D3 98
Cook, *mt.* B3 15
Cook, *strait* B3 15
Cookshire E6 103
Cookstown F3 102
Coos Bay, Oreg. A1 126
Copán, *ruins* A2 86
Copenhagen, *capital* D3 32
Copiapó B3 76
Copiapó, *river* B3 76
Coppename, *river* A2 80
Coppermine E3 99
Coppermine, *river* F3 99
Coquí C3 90
Coquimbo B3 76
Coral, *sea* E1 14
Corantijn, *river* A2 80
Corazón C3 90
Corbeil-Essonnes Inset II 34
Corcovado, *gulf* B7 76
Corcovado, *mt.* Inset I 81
Córdoba C3 74
Córdoba D4 37
Córdoba, *range* B3 74
Corinth B3 51
Corinth, *gulf* B2 51
Corinth, *isthmus* B3 51
Corinto A2 87
Corisco, *bay* B4 66
Corisco, *island* B4 66
Cork B3 31
Cormack C4 98
Cormoran, *reef* B2 17
Cormorant A2 96
Cormorant, *lake* A2 96
Cornellà de Llogregat G2 37
Corner Brook C5 98
Corno, *mt.* C2 38
Cornwall B2 100
Cornwall L2 102
Cornwall, *island* K1 99
Cornwallis, *island* J1 99
Coro C1 79
Coromandel, *peninsula* C2 15
Coronach E11 104
Coronado, *bay* B3 86
Coronation, *gulf* F3 99
Coronel Oviedo D4 75
Coropuna, *mt.* C4 77
Corozal B1 85
Corozal C2 90
Corpus Christi, Tex. D3 126
Corregidor, *island* B3 12
Corrib, *lake* B2 31
Corrientes D2 74
Corse Inset I 34
Corsica, *island* Inset I 34
Cortina d'Ampezzo C1 38
Cortona B2 38
Corubal, *river* D1 62
Çoruh, *river* E2 27
Çorum C2 27
Corumbá C3 81

Key Page
Corumbau, *point* E3 81
Corvallis, Oreg. A1 126
Cosenza D3 38
Coslada Inset II 37
Cosmoledo, *island group* A2 70
Cotabato C5 12
Cotentin, *peninsula* B2 34
Cotia Inset II 81
Coto Laurel B2 90
Cotonou B4 64
Cotopaxi, *mt.* B3 79
Cotswold, *hills* C3 30
Cottbus C3 40
Cotton Ground C2 90
Cotuí B1 89
Coubert Inset II 34
Couffo, *river* B4 64
Courantyne, *river* B3 80
Courland, *lagoon* A2 46
Courtenay K6 95
Courval D10 104
Coutts E6 94
Couva A2 91
Coventry C3 30
Covilhã B2 36
Cow Head C4 98
Cowan A3 96
Cowansville D6 103
Cowes C4 30
Cox's Bazar E7 21
Cox's Cove B4 98
Coyah B3 62
Coyoacán Inset 84
Cozumel, *island* G3 84
Cradock C3 71
Craigmyle D5 94
Craik E9 104
Craiova B3 43
Cranberry Portage A2 96
Cranbrook P6 95
Crane River B3 96
Crane Valley E11 104
Crapaud B2 100
Cravo Norte C3 78
Crawford Bay O6 95
Crawley Inset III 30
Crean, *lake* D6 104
Cree Lake D3 104
Cree, *river* E2 104
Cremona B1 38
Cremona C5 94
Cres, *island* B3 48
Cressday E6 94
Creston O6 95
Crete, *island* C4 51
Crete, *sea* C4 51
Créteil Inset II 34
Crewe C3 30
Crimean, *mts.* C4 47
Crimean, *peninsula* C3 47
Cristal, *mts.* A1 66
Cristóbal C2 87
Cristóbal Colón, *peak* B2 78
Crna Gora, *mts.* B3 49
Crna, *river* B2 48
Crocker, *range* D2 13
Cromer A4 96
Crooked River G8 104
Crooked, *island* C4 89
Crooked, *river* L4 95
Cross Lake C2 96
Cross, *river* E4 65
Crotone D3 38
Cruz, *cape* D3 88
Cruzeiro do Sul A2 81
Crystal City B4 96
Cu Lao Thu, *island* B4 11
Cuajimalpa Inset 84
Cuamba C2 68
Cuando, *river* D4 70
Cuango, *river* D2 70
Cuanza, *river* C3 70
Cuareim, *river* B1 75
Cuauhtémoc C2 84
Cuautitlán Inset 84
Cuautitlán Izcalli Inset 84
Cubal, *river* B4 70
Cubango, *river* D5 70
Cubatão Inset II 81
Cúcuta B3 78
Cuddalore C6 20
Cudworth E8 104
Cuenca B4 79
Cuenca E2 37
Cuernavaca, *state capital* E4 84
Cuiabá C3 81
Cuíto Cuanavale D5 70
Cuito, *river* D4 70
Cukorova, *region* C3 27
Culebra, *island* E2 90
Culebrinas, *river* A2 90
Culiacán, *state capital* C3 84
Cumaná D1 79
Cumberland K6 95
Cumberland House H7 104
Cumberland, *lake* H6 104
Cumberland, *peninsula* P3 99
Cumberland, *sound* P3 99
Cumbrian, *mts.* B2 30
Cunene, *river* B5, C4 70
Cuneo A1 38
Cupar B2 30
Cupar F10 104
Curaçao, *island* 82
Curaray, *river* C3 79
Curepipe C3 69
Curicó B4 76
Curitiba D4 81
Curral Velho D3 58
Curuzú Cuatiá D2 74
Cut Knife A8 104
Cuttack E4 20
Cuxhaven B2 40
Cuyo, *islands* B4 12
Cuyuni, *river* A2 80
Cuzco C3 77
Cyangugu A2 61
Cyclades, *islands* C3 51

Key Page
Cypress River B4 96
Czar E5 94
Częstochowa D3 41

D

Da Lat B4 11
Da Nang B3 11
Dabakala D2 63
Dabola C2 62
Dachang D3 10
Dachau B4 40
Dacotah C4 96
Dades, *river* C2 57
Dadu C4 21
Dafoe F9 104
Dagestan, republic E4 44
Dagupan B2 12
Dahlak, *archipelago* C2 60
Dahna, ad-, *desert* B1 24
Dahuk B1 24
Dajabón A1 89
Daka, *river* B2 64
Dakar, *capital* A2 62
Dakhla A2 58
Đakovica B3 49
Dalälven, *river* C2 53
Dalandzadgad C3 11
Dalhousie C1 97
Dalhousie K3 103
Dali D2 10
Dalian F2 10
Dallas C3 96
Dallas, Tex. D2 126
Dallol Bosso, *river* A3 59
Dalmatia, *region* B3 48
Daloa C3 63
Dalvík B2 52
Daly, *river* C1 14
Daman B4 20
Damanhur B1 56
Damascus, *capital* A3 27
Damaturu F2 65
Damavand, *mt.* C2 22
Damazin, ad- C3 59
Dame-Marie A2 89
Damietta B1 56
Damietta, *river* B1 56
Dammam, ad- C1 24
Dammartin-en-Goële Inset II 34
Dampier, W.A. A2 14
Damur, ad- A2 26
Danakil, *desert* C2 60
Danané B3 63
Dand A4 96
Dande, *river* B2 70
Dandeldhura A2 19
Dandong F1 10
Dangara A1 23
Dangme, *river* C2 19
Dangrek, *mts.* C3 12
Dangriga B2 85
Daniel's Harbour C4 98
Danjiangkou E2 10
Danlí B2 86
Danube, *river* 29
Danville D6 103
Danville, Va. F2 126
Dao Phu Quoc, *island* A4 11
Dapaong B1 64
Dapp D4 94
Daqing F1 10
Dar es-Salaam, *capital* C2 68
Dara A3 27
Dara B2 62
Đaravica, *mt.* B3 49
Darbhanga E3 20
Darhan C2 11
Darién, *mts.* D2 87
Dariense, *mts.* B2 87
Darjiling E3 20
Darling, *range* A3 14
Darling, *river* D3 14
Darlington C2 30
Darłowo C1 41
Darmstadt B4 40
Darnah D1 56
Darnley B2 100
Dartmoor, *plateau* B4 30
Dartmouth D3 100
Daru A2 15
Darwin, N.T., *capital* C1 14
Dashhowuz C2 22
Dasht-e Kavir, *desert* D3 22
Dasht-e Lut, *desert* D3 22
Datong E1 10
Daua, *river* F1 61
Daugavpils D3 46
Daule, *river* B3 79
Dauphin B1 96
Dauphin A3 96
Dauphin River B3 96
Dauphin, *lake* B3 96
Davao C5 12
Davao, *gulf* C5 12
Davenport, Iowa D1 126
David A2 87
Davidson D9 104
Davis Inlet E3 98
Davis, *strait* M2 92
Davos D2 35
Dawa, *river* C3 60
Dawhat as-Salwa, *bay* B3 25
Dawkah B2 25
Dawna, *range* B2 12
Dawson B3 105
Dawson Creek M3 95
Dawson, *bay* A3 96
Daymán, *river* B1 75
Dayr az-Zawr B2 27
Dayton, Ohio E2 126
Daytona Beach, Fla. E3 126
De Aar B3 71
De Quincy Village Inset 70
Dead Sea, *lake* A2 26
Dead, *sea* B2 26
Dean, *channel* J5 95

	Key	Page
Dean, river	K5	95
Dease Lake	G2	95
Death, valley, Calif.	B2	126
Deauville	C2	34
Debar	A2	48
Debden	D7	104
Debed, river	B2	45
DeBolt	A3	94
Debre Birhan	C2	60
Debre Markos	B2	60
Debrecen	C2	43
Decatur, Ill.	E2	126
Deccan, plateau	C5	20
Děčín	B2	42
Dédougou	C2	64
Dedza	B2	68
Dee, river	B3, C1	30
Deep River	H1	102
Deep, inlet	B1	98
Deepdale	A3	96
Deer Lake	C4	98
Deerfield	A4	100
Degehabur	D2	60
Dégelis	H4	103
Dehiwala-Mt. Lavinia	A5	19
Dehra Dun	C2	20
Dej	B2	43
Del Rio, Tex.	C3	126
Delacour	D5	94
Delap Cove	B3	100
Delaronde, lake	C6	104
Delaware	F2	126
Delburne	D5	94
Deleau	A4	96
Delft	B2	32
Delft, island	A2	19
Delfzijl	D1	32
Delgado	A2	86
Delhi	C3	20
Delhi	E5	102
Delicias	C2	84
Delisle	C9	104
Deloraine	A4	96
Delos, island	C3	51
Delson	J6	103
Delta Beach	B4	96
Demerara, river	B3	80
Den Helder	B2	32
Denakil, desert	C1	60
Denare Beach	H6	104
Denbigh	H2	102
Dencross	C4	96
Dender, river	B2	33
Denigomodu	A2	16
Denmark, strait	D2	106
Dennery	B2	91
Denpasar	C2	13
D'Entrecasteaux, islands	B2	15
D'Entrecasteaux, reefs	C1	18
Denver, capital, Colo.	C2	126
Denzil	A8	104
Dera Ghazi Khan	D3	21
Dera Ismail Khan	D3	21
Derby	C3	30
Derg, lake	B2	31
Derrick	B3	91
Derventa	B1	48
Derwent	E4	94
Des Moines, capital, Iowa	D1	126
Desaguadero, river	B2	74
Desaguadero, river	A3	77
Desberats	B1	102
Deschaillons	D5	103
Deschambault Lake	G6	104
Dese	C2	60
Deseado, river	B6	74
Deseronto	H3	102
Desna, river	C1	47
Desolación, island	B9	76
Desruisseau	B3	91
Dessau	C3	40
Destruction Bay	B5	105
Detmold	B3	40
Detroit, Mich.	E1	126
Deux Rivieres	G1	102
Deux-Montagnes	H5	103
Deva	B3	43
Deventer	D2	32
Devil's, island	B1	80
Devoll, river	B3	49
Devon, island	L1	99
Devonport, Tas.	D4	14
Dewberry	E4	94
Dezful	B3	22
Dháfni	Inset	51
Dhahran	C1	24
Dhaka, capital	D5	21
Dhamar	A2	25
Dhangarhi	A2	19
Dhankuta	D2	19
Dharan	D3	19
Dhaulagiri, mt.	B2	19
Dhofar, region	B3	25
Dhulagarh	Inset II	20
Dhuusamareeb	B2	60
Diadema	Inset II	81
Dialakoto	C3	62
Diamond, island	B1	91
Dibrugarh	F3	20
Diefenbaker, lake	C10	104
Diekirch	B2	33
Dien Bien Phu	A2	11
Dieppe	C2	34
Dieppe	E2	97
Dieppe Bay Town	B1	90
Diffa	C3	59
Differdange	A2	33
Digby	B3	100
Digne	D4	34
Digul, river	E2	13
Dijon	D2	34
Dikhil	B2	60
Dikson	D2	44
Dili	D2	13
Dilijan	B5	104
Dillon	B3	67
Dilolo	B3	67
Dimbokro	D3	63

	Key	Page
Dimitrovgrad	D3	50
Dimlang, mt.	F3	65
Dimona	B2	26
Dinagat, island	C4	12
Dinajpur	B3	21
Dinant	C2	33
Dinar, mt.	A2, C3	48
Dinaric Alps, mts.	A1, B3	48
Dinder, river	B1	60
Dingle	A2	31
Dingle, bay	A2	31
Dingli	B2	36
Dinsmore	C9	104
Diourbel	A2	62
Dipolog	B4	12
Dire Dawa	D2	60
Diriamba	A3	87
Dispur	F3	20
Diu	B4	20
Diuata, mts.	C4	12
Divo	D4	63
Divriği	D2	27
Diwaniyah, ad-	C2	24
Dixon Entrance, channel	F4	95
Dixonville	B3	94
Diyala, river	C2	24
Diyarbakır	E3	27
Dja, river	B3	65
Djado	C1	59
Djambala	C5	66
Djanet	B2	57
Djelfa	B1	57
Djenné	C3	58
Djerba, island	C3	57
Djibouti, capital	C2	60
Djouah, river	B1	66
Djouf, el-, desert	B1, C3	58
Djougou	A3	64
Dnepr, river	E3	47
Dnepr-Bug, canal	B3	47
Dneprodzerzhinsk	C2	47
Dnepropetrovsk	D2	47
Dnepr, river	C1	47
Dnestr, river	B2	47
Doaktown	C2	97
Doba	B5	59
Doboj	B1	48
Dobrich	F2	50
Dobruja, region	E3	43
Doctor Pedro P. Peña	A3	75
Dodecanese, islands	C3	51
Dodge City, Kans.	C2	126
Dodoma	C2	68
Dodsland	B9	104
Doetinchem	D3	32
Dogo, island	B2	8
Dogondoutchi	A3	59
Doha, capital	D3	25
Doiran, lake	C2	48
Dolbeau	D3	103
Dôle	D3	34
Dolomites, range	B1	38
Domagnano	B1	39
Domeyko, mts.	A3	76
Dominica, passage	A1	90
Dominion City	D4	96
Domont	Inset II	34
Domremy	E8	104
Domuyo, volcano	A4	74
Don Benito	D3	37
Doña Juana, mt.	C2	90
Donald Station	O5	95
Doncaster	C3	30
Dondo	B3	70
Donegal	B1	31
Donegal, bay	B1	31
Donets, basin	D2	47
Donets, river	D2	47
Dong Hoi	B3	11
Dong Nai, river	B4	11
Dongting, lake	E3	10
Dongwe, river	A2	67
Donnacona	E5	103
Dor, lake	C6	104
Dorado	C2	90
Dorchester	C4	30
Dordogne, river	C4	34
Dordrecht	B3	32
Dore Lake	C6	104
Dörgön, lake	B2	11
Dori	D1	64
Dorintosh	B8	104
Dorking	Inset III	30
Dornoch	B1	30
Dorohoi	D2	43
Dorothy	D5	94
Dorra	B1	60
Dortmund	A3	40
Dorval	H6	103
Dos Hermanas	D4	37
Dosquet	E5	103
Dosso	A3	59
Dothan, Ala.	E2	126
Douai	C1	34
Douala	A3	65
Doubs, river	A1	35
Douglas	B2	30
Douglas, channel	H4	95
Douglastown	M3	103
Dourados	C4	81
Douro, river	B2	36
Dover	D3	30
Dover, capital, Del.	F2	126
Dover, strait	D4	30
Dozen, island	B2	8
Drãa, river	A1, B2, C2	57
Draguignan	D5	34
Drake	E9	104
Drakensberg, mts.	B3, C3	71
Drava, river	A2	43
Drayton Valley	C4	94
Dresden	C3	40
Dresden	C5	102
Dreux	C2	34
Drin, river	A1	49
Drina, river	A2	49

	Key	Page
Drobeta-Turnu Severin	B3	43
Drogheda	C2	31
Drumheller	D5	94
Drummond	B2	97
Drummondville	D6	103
Dryden	B3	101
Dschang	B2	65
Duars, plain	A3	19
Duarte, mt.	B1	89
Dubăsari	B2	50
Dubawnt, lake	H4	99
Dubawnt, river	H4	99
Dubayy	C2	25
Dubbo, N.S.W.	D3	14
Dube	C3	63
Dublin, capital	C2	31
Dubrovnik	D4	48
Dubuque, Iowa	D1	126
Dubysa, river	B2	46
Duchess	E6	94
Duck Bay	A3	96
Duck Lake	D8	104
Dudelange	B2	33
Dudinka	C6	44
Dudley	C3	30
Duero, river	D2	37
Dufourspitze, mt.	B3	35
Dufrost	C4	96
Dugald	C4	96
Duisburg	A3	40
Dukhan	B3	25
Dulce	C4	86
Duluth, Minn.	D1	126
Dum-Dum	Inset II	20
Duma	A1	26
Dumaguete	B4	12
Dumbás	B3	52
Dumfries	C2	30
Dumjor	Inset II	20
Dún Laoghaire	C2	31
Dunaújváros	B2	43
Duncan	L7	95
Duncansby, cape	B1	30
Dund-Us	B2	11
Dundalk	C2	31
Dundee	C2	30
Dundee	D9	104
Dunedin	B4	15
Dunfermline	B2	30
Dungarvan	C2	31
Dunkirk (Dunkerque)	C1	34
Dunkwa	B4	64
Dunlop	B2	96
Dunnegan	F1	100
Dunnville	F5	102
Dunqulah	C1	59
Dunsinane, mt.	B2	30
Dunstable	Inset III	30
Dunster	N4	95
Duqm	C2	25
Duque de Caxias	Inset I	81
Duque de York, island	A9	76
Durance, river	D5	34
Durango, Colo.	C2	126
Durango, state capital	D3	84
Durazno	B2	75
Durban	D2	71
Durham	C2	30
Durham	E3	102
Durham, N.C.	F2	126
Durmitor, mts.	A3	49
Durrës	A2	49
Dushanbe, capital	A1	23
Düsseldorf	A3	40
Dutse	E2	65
Dyce	B2	30
Dyje, river	B4	42
Dzaoudzi, territorial capital	C2	67
Dzavhan, river	B2	11
Dzhugdzhur, range	D8	44
Dzungaria, desert basin	B1	10
Dzyarzhynskaya Hara, mt.	C3	47

E

	Key	Page
Eagle, river	B2	98
Eagle, river	B2	105
Ear Falls	B2	101
East Angus	E6	103
East Antarctica	B1	107
East Braintree	D4	96
East China, sea		7
East Coast Bays	B2	15
East Coulee	D5	94
East Frisian, islands	A2	40
East Lake Ainslie	F1	100
East London	C3	71
East Point	B2	100
East Siberian, sea	B10	44
East York	K5	102
East, cape	C2	15
Eastbourne	D4	30
Eastend	B11	104
Eastern Ghats, mts.	C6	20
Easterville	B2	96
Eastmain	A3	101
Eastmain, river	B3	101
Eastport	E5	98
Eatonia	A9	104
Eau Claire, Wis.	D1	126
Eauripik, atoll	B2	15
Ebebiyín	D2	66
Eberswalde	C2	40
Ebolowa	B3	65
Ebon, island	A4	16
Ebor	A4	96
Ebro, river	F1	37
Ecatepec	Inset	84
Echmiadzin	A2	45
Echo Bay	E3	99
Echo Bay	A1	102
Echternach	B2	33
Écija	D4	37
Ed	D4	37
Edam	C2	32
Edam	B7	104

	Key	Page
Eddies Cove	C3	98
Eddystone	B3	96
Ede	C4	65
Ede	C2	32
Edéa	B3	65
Edgerton	E5	94
Edinburgh	B2	30
Edirne	A2	27
Edmonton, capital	D4	94
Edmundston	A1	97
Edmundston	H4	103
Édouard, lake	D4	103
Edrans	B4	96
Edson	B4	94
Edward, lake	A4	61
Edwards plateau, Tex.	C2	126
Eems, river	D1	32
Éfaté, island	C3	18
Egadi, islands	C3	38
Eganville	H2	102
Eger	C2	43
Egersund	B4	52
Eglinton, island	E1	99
Egmont, bay	A2	100
Egmont, cape	A2	15
Egmont, mt.	B2	15
Eğridir, lake	B2	27
Eifel, plateau	A3	40
Eigg, island	A2	30
Eindhoven	C3	32
Einsiedeln	C1	35
Eiseb, river	D2	70
Eisenach	B3	40
Eisenhüttenstadt	C2	40
Eisleben	B3	40
Ejura	B3	64
Ekibastuz	D1	23
Ekwan, river	D2	101
El Cañuelo	C2	90
El Cerro del Aripo, mt.	A2	91
El Encanto	B5	78
El Ferrol	B1	37
El Macao	D2	89
El Paso, Tex.	C2	126
El Pital, mt.	A1	86
El Porvenir	C2	87
El Progreso	B2	86
El Seibo	C2	89
El Serrat	B1	36
El Tigre	D2	79
El Toro, mt.	D2	90
El Trebolar	Inset	76
Elat	B3	26
Elba, island	B2	38
Elbasan	B2	49
Elbe, river	B2, C3	40
Elbert mt., Colo.	C2	126
Elbląg	D1	41
Elbow	D9	104
Elburz, mts.	C2	22
Elche	F3	37
Eldon	C2	100
Eldoret	C2	61
Elephant, island	C12	107
Elephanta, island	Inset I	20
Eleuthera, island	B2	89
Elevsís	Inset	51
Elfros	C9	104
Elgin	B1	30
Elgin	A4	96
Elgin	D3	97
Elgon, mt.	D3	61
Eli Malk, island	B1	17
Elie	C4	96
Elista	E4	44
Elk	F2	41
Elk Point	E4	94
Elkford	P6	95
Elkhorn	A4	96
Elkhovo	E3	50
Elko	P6	95
Elko, Nev.	B1	126
Ellef Ringnes, island	H1	99
Ellerts de Haan, mts.	B3	80
Ellesmere, island	M1	99
Ellice, river	G3	99
Ellinikón	Inset	51
Elliot Lake	C1	101
Ellisras	C1	71
Elm Creek	C4	96
Elma	A1	96
Elmina	B4	64
Elmira	C2	100
Elmira	E4	102
Elmsdale	A2	100
Elmvale	F3	102
Elnora	D5	94
Elqui, river	B3	76
Elrose	B9	104
Elsa	C4	17
Elva	A4	96
Elvas	B3	36
Ely	D3	30
Ely, Nev.	B2	126
Embarcación	C1	74
Embarras Portage	E2	94
Embi	A2	23
Embu	D4	61
Emden	A2	40
Emerald, island	F1	99
Emerald, Qld.	D2	14
Emerson	C4	96
Emi Koussi, mt.	B1	59
Emilia-Romagna	B1	38
Emlembe, mt.	B1	71
Emmeloord	C2	32
Emmen	D2	32
Emporia, Kans.	D2	126
Encarnación	E5	75
Enchant	D6	94
Ende	D2	13
Enderbury, island	B2	17
Enderby	N6	95

	Key	Page
Enderby Land, region	C17	107
Endiang	D5	94
Enewetak, island	A1	16
Engadine, valley	D2	35
Engaño, cape	D2	89
Enggano, island	B2	13
Englee	C4	98
English, channel	C4	30
Englishtown	G1	100
Enguri, river	A3	45
Enid, Okla.	D2	126
Enilda	B3	94
Enna	C3	38
Ennadai, lake	H4	99
Ennery	C1	89
Ennis	B2	31
Ennistymon	B2	31
Enns, river	D3	39
Enriquillo, lake	A2	89
Enschede	D2	32
Ensenada	A1	84
Ensenguly	A3	22
Entebbe	C3	61
Enugu	D4	65
Épi, island	C3	18
Épinal	D2	34
Episkopi	A3	27
Epsom	Inset III	30
Equatorial, channel	A5	19
Er Rif, range	C1	57
Erciyes Daği, mt.	C2	27
Érd	B2	43
Erdenet	C2	11
Erebus, mt.	B5	107
Erenhot	E1	10
Erfurt	B3	40
Erg Chech, desert	C1	58
Erg Iguidi, desert	D1	58
Erickson	B4	96
Erie, lake	E5	102
Erie, Pa.	E1	126
Eriksdale	B4	96
Erimo, cape	Inset I	8
Erlangen	B4	40
Ermelo	C2	71
Erne	A2	30
Errigal, mt.	B1	31
Erromango, island	C4	18
Erskë	B3	49
Erzen, river	A2	49
Erzgebirge, mts.	C3	40
Erzincan	D2	27
Erzurum	E2	27
Esbjerg	B3	52
Esch-sur-Alzette	A2	33
Eschen	B1	33
Escondido, river	C2	87
Escuintla	C5	85
Escuminac	K3	103
Esfahan	C3	22
Esil	D3	98
Esker	D3	98
Eskifjördhur	C2	52
Eskilstuna	C3	53
Eskimo Point	K4	99
Eskişehir	B2	27
Esla, river	C2	37
Esmeraldas	B2	79
Espanola	D1	102
Española, island	Inset	79
Esperance, W.A.	B3	14
Espichel, cape	A3	36
Espírito Santo	D3	81
Espíritu Santo, island	B2	18
Espoo	B2	53
Esquel	A5	74
Essaouira	B2	57
Essen	B3	40
Essequibo, river	B3, B5	80
Essex	C5	102
Esslingen	B4	40
Estados, island	C7	74
Estaire	E1	102
Estany d'Engolasters, lake	B2	36
Este, point	E2	90
Esteli	A2	87
Esterhazy	H10	104
Estevan	G11	104
Esther	E5	94
Eston	B9	104
Estonia	C1	46
Estoril	A3	36
Estrela, mts.	B2	36
Esztergom	B2	43
Etchemin, river	L6	103
Ethelbert	A3	96
Ethiopia, plateau	C2	60
Etna, mt.	C3	38
Etobicoke	J5	102
Etosha, pan	C7	67
Etrechy	Inset II	34
Ettelbruck	B2	33
Ettrek	C1	22
Euboea, island	B2	51
Eugene, Oreg.	A1	126
Eugenia, point	A2	84
Euphrates, river	C2	27
Eureka, Calif.	A1	126
Eutsuk, lake	J4	95
Evandale	C3	97
Evans, river	B2	14
Evansdale	D4	61
Evansville, Ind.	E2	126
Evenkia, autonomous okrug	C6	44
Everest, mt.	C2	19
Everett, Wash.	A1	126
Everglades	E5	94
Évinayong	C3	66
Évora	B3	36
Évreux	C2	34
Évry	Inset II	34
Ewa	B1	16
Ewell	Inset III	30
Ewo	C4	66
Exeter	D4	102
Exmoor, plateau	B3	30
Extremadura	C3	37
Exuma, sound	B3	89

	Key	Page
Eyasi, lake	B1	68
Eyebrow	D10	104
Eyl	B2	60
Eyre, lake	C2	14
Eyre, peninsula	C3	14
Eysturoy, island	Inset	32

F

	Key	Page
Fabyan	E5	94
Fada	C3	59
Fadiffolu, atoll	A2	19
Faenza	B1	38
Faeroe, islands	Inset	32
Fagamalo	B1	18
Făgăraș	C3	43
Fagasa	B1	18
Fagatogo	B1	18
Fair, island	Inset I	30
Fairbanks, Alaska	Inset I	126
Fairford	B3	96
Fairmont Hot Springs	P6	95
Fairweather, mt.	D1	95
Faisalabad	D3	21
Faizabad	D3	20
Fajardo	D2	90
Fakfak	E2	13
Falciano	C1	39
Falcon Lake	D4	96
Falelatai	B2	18
Falelima	B2	18
Falémé, river	C3	62
Faleniu	B1	18
Fălești	A2	50
Falher	B3	94
Falkland, islands	C7	74
Fallujah, al-	B2	24
Falmouth	B2	88
Falmouth	B3	30
False Divi, point	D5	20
Falster, island	C4	32
Falun	C2	53
Famagusta	C2	27
Fan Sí Pan, mt.	A1	11
Fangliao	B3	9
Fanø, island	B3	32
Farafangana	B3	69
Farafenni	A2	62
Farah	A2	22
Farah, river	A2	22
Faraulep, atoll	B2	15
Farewell, island	C3	106
Farewell, cape	A3	15
Farewell, cape	C3	106
Farghona	D2	23
Fargo, N. Dak.	D1	126
Faridpur	C5	21
Farim	B1	62
Farmington	M3	95
Farmington, N. Mex.	C2	126
Farnham	Inset III	30
Faro	B3	36
Faro	C4	105
Farquhar, island group	B2	69
Farrellton	A6	103
Fashir, al-	B2	59
Fatick	A2	62
Fatoto	E2	62
Fauquier	N6	95
Faxaflói, bay	A2	52
Faxälven, river	C2	53
Faya-Largeau	B2	59
Faylakah, island	C2	24
Fayyum, al-	B2	59
Fdérik	B2	58
Fehmarn	B1	40
Fehmarn, strait	C4	32
Feira de Santana	E3	81
Feldkirch	A3	39
Felidu, atoll	A3	19
Felixstowe	D3	30
Fenelon Falls	G3	102
Fengshan	B3	9
Fengyüan	B1	9
Fens, region	D3	30
Feodosiya	D3	47
Fergana, valley	D2	23
Fergus	E4	102
Ferkéssédougou	D2	63
Ferlo, river	B2	62
Ferme-Neuve	A5	103
Fernandina, island	Inset	79
Fernie	P6	95
Ferrara	B1	38
Ferryland	E5	98
Fethiye	B3	27
Feuilles, river	B2	101
Feyzabad	C1	22
Fez	C1	57
Fianarantsoa	B3	69
Fichtelberg, mt.	C3	40
Fichtelgebirge, mts.	B4	40
Field	O5	95
Field	E1	102
Fier	A2	49
Fife, lake	E11	104
Fig Tree	C3	90
Figueira da Foz	A2	36
Figueres	H1	37
Figuig	D1	57
Filadelfia	B3	75
Filchner Ice Shelf, glacier	B12	107
Filfla, island	B3	36
Fillmore	G11	104
Fimbul Ice Shelf, glacier	B14	107
Finisterre, cape	B1	37
Finland, gulf	C3	53
Finlay, river	J2	95
Finn, river	C1	31
Finnegan	D5	94
Finnmark, plateau	E2	52
Fireside	C4	70
Firth, river	A1	105
Fish, river	C4	70
Fisher Branch	C3	96
Fisherton	C3	96

	Key	Page
Fishguard	B3	30
Fitzgerald	E1	94
Fitzroy, mt.	B8	76
Fitzroy, river	B1	14
Five Islands	C2	100
Flagstaff, Ariz.	B2	126
Flat, island	C1	69
Flatbush	C4	94
Flaxcombe	A9	104
Fleet	E5	94
Fleetwood	C3	30
Fleming	A4	96
Flensburg	B1	40
Flesherton	E3	102
Fleur de Lys	C4	98
Flevoland, polder	C2	32
Flin Flon	A2, C2	96
Flinders, range	C3	14
Flinders, river	D1	14
Flint, island	D3	17
Flint, Mich.	E1	126
Flodden Field, plain	C2	30
Florence	B2	38
Florence, S.C.	F2	126
Florenceville	B2	97
Florencia	B4	78
Flores	D3	85
Flores, island	D2	13
Flores, sea	C2	13
Floreşti	D2	50
Floriano	D4	81
Florianópolis	D4	81
Florida	B3	75
Florida	D2	88
Florida	B2	90
Florida	E3	126
Florida Keys, Fla.	E3	126
Florida, straits	B1	88
Florø	A3	52
Fly, river	A2	15
Foam Lake	G9	104
Foča	B2	48
Focşani	D3	43
Foggia	C2	38
Fogo	D4	98
Fogo, island	B4	58
Foix	C5	34
Folkestone	D3	30
Fomboni	A2	67
Fond du Lac, river	F2	104
Fond-du-Lac	C1	104
Fonseca, gulf	B3, C2	86
Fontainebleau	C2	34
Fontas	M2	95
Fontvieille	A2	35
Fonuafoʻou (Falcon), island	B3	17
Fonualei, island	C2	17
Forest	D4	102
Forestville	G3	103
Fork River	A3	96
Forli	C1	38
Formentera, island	G3	37
Formosa	D2	74
Fort Albany	D2	101
Fort Chipewyan	E2	94
Fort Collins, Colo.	C1	126
Fort Erie	G5	102
Fort Frances	B3	101
Fort Franklin	D3	99
Fort Fraser	K4	95
Fort Good Hope	C3	99
Fort Lauderdale, Fla.	E3	126
Fort Liard	D4	99
Fort MacKay	E2	94
Fort McMurray	E3	94
Fort McPherson	B3	99
Fort Myers, Fla.	E3	126
Fort Nelson	L2	95
Fort Nelson, river	L1	95
Fort Norman	C4	99
Fort Portal	B3	61
Fort Providence	E4	99
Fort Qu'Appelle	G10	104
Fort Resolution	F4	99
Fort Saskatchewan	D4	94
Fort Severn	C1	101
Fort Simpson	D4	99
Fort Smith, Ark.	D2	126
Fort Smith, region	E4	99
Fort St. James	K4	95
Fort St. John	M3	95
Fort Steele	P6	95
Fort Stockton, Tex.	C2	126
Fort Vermilion	C2	94
Fort Wayne, Ind.	E1	126
Fort William	B2	30
Fort Worth, Tex.	D2	126
Fortaleza	E2	81
Forteau	C3	98
Forth, estuary	C2	30
Forth, river	B2	30
Fortín Conde de Mirasol, fort	E2	90
Fortín Ravelo	B3	77
Fortune	D5	98
Fortune Bridge	C2	100
Fortune, bay	D5	98
Foster, river	E4	104
Fosterville	B3	97
Foumban	B2	65
Foumbouni	A1	67
Four Falls	B2	97
Foveaux, strait	A4	15
Fox Island	F2	100
Fox Lake	C2	94
Fox Valley	A10	104
Foxe, basin	N3	99
Foxe, channel	M3	99
Foxe, peninsula	N4	99
Foyle, inlet	C1	31
Foyle, river	A2	30
Foyle, river	B2	30
Foz do Iguaçu	C4	81
Frances, lake	D5	105
Franceville	B2	66
Franche-Comté	D3	34
Francis	G10	104
Francistown	B2	69
François	C5	98
François, lake	K4	95
Franconian Jura, mts.	B4	40
Frankenwald, mts.	B3	40
Frankford	H3	102
Frankfort, capital, Ky.	E2	126
Frankfurt am Main	B3	40
Frankfurt an der Oder	C2	40
Franklin, strait	J2	99
Franquelin	J2	103
Franz Josef Land, islands	A4	44
Fraser	E1	95
Fraser Lake	K4	95
Fraser, river	L5, M4	95
Fraserburgh	C1	30
Fraserdale	D2	101
Fraserwood	C4	96
Fray Bentos	A2	75
Fredericia	B3	32
Fredericton	B2	100
Fredericton Jct.	C3	97
Frederiksberg	D3	32
Frederikshavn	C1	32
Frederikstad	C4	52
Freeport	A2	89
Freeport	A3	100
Freetown	E5	90
Freetown, capital	A1	63
Freiberg	C3	40
Freiburg	A5	40
Freirina	B3	76
Fréjus	D5	34
Fremantle, W.A.	A3, Inset I	14
French River	E1	102
Frenchman, river	B11	104
Fresnillo	D3	84
Fresno, Calif.	B2	126
Fria	B2	62
Fribourg	B2	35
Friedrichshafen	B5	40
Frigate, island	C1	91
Frisches Haff, bay	D1	41
Friuli-Venezia Giulia	C4	104
Frobisher, lake	C4	104
Frog, lake	E4	94
Frome, lake	D2	14
Frontier	B11	104
Frosinone	C2	38
Fruška Gora, mts.	A2	49
Frutigen	B2	35
Frýdek-Místek	D3	42
Fua'amotu	B4	17
Fuenlabrada	Inset II	
Fuerte Olimpo	D2	75
Fuerte, river	C2	84
Fuerteventura, island	Inset I	37
Fuhayhil, al-	D2	24
Fujayrah, al-	D2	25
Fuji, mt.	C3	8
Fujian	E3	10
Fujisawa	C3	8
Fukue	A3	8
Fukue, island	A3	8
Fukui	C2	8
Fukuoka	A3	8
Fukushima	B3	8
Fukuyama	B3	8
Fulacunda	B2	62
Fuladi, mt.	B2	22
Fulda	B3	40
Fulda, river	B3	40
Fullarton	A2	91
Funabashi	D3	8
Funafuti, capital	C3	16
Funafuti, island	C3	16
Fundy, bay	A3	100
Furnas, reservoir	D4	81
Fürstenfeld	E3	39
Fürth	B4	40
Fushun	F1	10
Fushun	C4	99
Futa Jallon, plateau	B1	62
Futuna, island	C4	18
Fuxin	F1	10
Fuzhou	E3	10
Fyn, island	C3	32

G

	Key	Page
Gaalkacyo	B2	60
Gabarus	G2	100
Gabès	C3	57
Gabès, gulf	C2	57
Gaborone, capital	B3	69
Gabriel, island	C1	69
Gabrovo	D3	50
Gabú	C1	62
Gacko	B2	48
Gaeta	C2	38
Gafsa	B2	57
Gagetown	C3	97
Gagnoa	C3	63
Gagnon	C3	101
Gagra	A2	45
Gainesville, Fla.	E3	126
Gainsborough	J11	104
Gairdner, lake	C3	14
Gaizina, mt.	C2	46
Galahad	E5	94
Galana, river	A2	69
Galápagos, islands	Inset	79
Galaţi	E3	43
Galena Bay	O6	95
Galicia	C1	37
Galilee, region	B1	26
Galle	B5	19
Gallegos, river	A7	74
Gallinas, point	C1	78
Gällivare	D1	53
Galoa	B3	17
Galveston, Tex.	D3	126
Galway	B2	31
Galway, bay	A1	11
Gam, river	B2, C3, D2	62
Gambia, river	B2, C3, D2	62
Gambo	D5	98
Gamprin	B1	33
Gan, river	E3	10
Gananoque	J3	102
Gäncä	B2	45
Gander	D5	98
Gander Bay	D4	98
Gandhinagar	B4	20
Ganganagar	B3	20
Ganges, river	E3	20
Gangtok	E3	20
Gansu	C1, D2	10
Ganzhou	E3	10
Gao	D2	58
Gaoua	C3	64
Gap	D4	34
Garabil, plateau	D3	22
Garabogazköl, lake	A2	22
Garda, lake	B1	38
Garden Hill	D2	96
Garden Reach	Inset II	20
Garden, island	Inset I	14
Garden, river	A1	102
Gardenton	C4	96
Gardez	B2	22
Gardner, canal	H4	95
Gardner, island	B2	17
Garissa	A3	96
Garland	B2	96
Garmisch-Partenkirchen	B5	40
Garoowe	B2	60
Garoua	B2	65
Garry, lake	H3	99
Garson Lake	A4	104
Garulia	Inset II	20
Gary, Ind.	E1	126
Gascoyne river	A2	14
Gash, river	B2	60
Gaspé	M3	103
Gaspé, peninsula	L3	103
Gaspereau Forks	D2	97
Gatal, cape	E4	37
Gateshead	C2	30
Gatico	B2	76
Gatineau	A6	103
Gatineau Park	A6	103
Gatineau, river	A4, A5	103
Gatún, lake	C2	87
Gau, island	B3	17
Gauhati	F3	20
Gaultois	D5	98
Gävle	C2	53
Gaya	E4	20
Gaya	A3	59
Gazanjyk	B2	22
Gaza, peninsula	B2	15
Gaziantep	D3	27
Gbarnga	D3	81
Gdańsk	D1	41
Gdańsk, gulf	D1	41
Gdynia	D1	41
Géba, river	C1	62
Geelong, Vic.	D3	14
Gege	B2	71
Geidam	F1	65
Geikie, river	F3	104
Geju	C3	10
Gejiu	C3	38
Gela	C3	38
Gelibolu (Gallipoli)	A2	27
Gelsenkirchen	A3	40
Gem	D6	94
Gembloux	C2	33
Gemena	B1	67
General Eugenio A. Garay	A2	75
General Santos	C5	12
General, river	C3	86
Genesee	C4	94
Geneva	A2	35
Geneva, lake	A2	35
Genk	D2	33
Gennargentu, mts.	B2	38
Genoa	B1	38
Genoa, gulf	B1	38
Gentilly	Inset II	34
Gentofte	D3	32
George	B2	13
George Town	C2	101
George, river	D2	101
Georgetown	B2	91
Georgetown	D2	62
Georgetown	C2	100
Georgetown, capital	B2	80
Georgia	E2	126
Georgian, bay	E2	102
Gera	C3	40
Geral, range	C4	81
Gerald	A4	96
Geraldton	C3	101
Geraldton, W.A.	A2	14
Gerlachovka, mt.	A2	42
Germiston	C2	71
Gerona	H2	37
Getafe	E2, Inset II	37
Gevgelija	B3	48
Geylegphug	B3	19
Ghabah	A1	56
Ghadamis	D3	20
Ghaghara, river	D3	20
Ghanzi	A2	69
Ghardaïa	B1	57
Gharyan	B1	56
Ghat	B3	56
Ghatkopar	Inset I	20
Ghaydah, al-	C1	25
Ghazal, river	B4	59
Ghazni	B2	22
Ghent	B1	33
Ghurdaqah, al-	B2	56
Giant's Causeway, headland	A2	31
Gibraltar, strait	D5	37
Gibson, desert	B2	14
Giessen	B3	40
Gifford, river	M2	99
Gifu	C3	8
Giglio, island	B2	38
Gijón	D1	37
Gikongoro	B2	61
Gilbert Plains	A3	96
Gilbert, islands	A1	17
Gilbert, river	D1	14
Gilgit	E2	21
Gilliam	D1	96
Gillingham	D3	30
Gimie, mt.	A2	91
Gimli	C4	96
Giresun	D2	27
Gironde, river	B4	34
Gisborne	C2	15
Gisenyi	B1	61
Gitarama	B2	61
Gitega	B2	61
Giurgiu	C4	43
Giza	B2	56
Gizo	A1	16
Gjirokastër	B3	49
Gjoa Haven	J3	99
Gjøvik	C3	52
Glace Bay	H1	100
Gladstone	B4	96
Gladstone, Qld.	E2	14
Glâma, river	C3	52
Glanvillia	A2	90
Glasgow	B2	30
Glasgow, Mont.	C1	126
Glaslyn	B7	104
Glastonbury	C3	30
Gleichen	D3	100
Glen Margaret	B4	96
Glenboro	D3	96
Glencoe	D5	102
Glenella	D4	96
Glenholme	D2	100
Glenora	G2	95
Glenwood	D5	98
Glidden	A9	104
Glifádha	Inset	51
Glittertinden, mt.	B3	52
Gliwice	D3	41
Głogów	C3	41
Gloucester	C3	30
Gloucester	K2	102
Glover, reef	C3	85
Glovertown	D5	98
Gmünd	D2	39
Gnarp	C3	60
Gobabis	C2	70
Gobi, desert	D1	10
Godavari, river	C5	20
Godbout	D4	102
Goderich	D4	102
Godfrey	J3	102
Godoy Cruz	B3	74
Gods, lake	D2	96
Gogama	D3	101
Goiânia	D3	81
Goiás	D3	81
Golan Heights, occupied terr.	A3	27
Gold Coast, Qld.	E2	14
Gold River	J6	95
Golden	O5	95
Golden Lake	H2	102
Golea, el-	B2	57
Golfito	C4	86
Golmud	C2	10
Golyama Kamchiya, river	E2	50
Goma	F2	65
Gombe	F2	65
Gomera, island	Inset I	37
Gómez Palacio	C1	89
Gonaïves	B1	89
Gonâve, gulf	B1	89
Gonâve, island	B2	89
Gonder	B1	60
Gongola, river	F2	65
Goobies	E5	98
Goodlands	C2	69
Goodsoil	A6	104
Good Hope, cape	A3	71
Goose, river	C2	69
Gorakhpur	D3	20
Goražde	B2	48
Gordon, lake	E3	94
Gordondale	A3	94
Gore	B2	60
Gore Bay	C2	102
Gori	D3	45
Goris	C1	38
Gorizia	C1	38
Gorno-Altay, republic	D6	44
Gorno-Altaysk	D6	44
Goroka	A2	15
Gorontalo	D1	13
Gorzów Wielkopolski	B2	41
Gosford, N.S.W.	E3	14
Goshen	F2	100
Goslar	B3	40
Gospić	B3	48
Gosport	C4	30
Göta, canal	B3	53
Göteborg och Bohus	B3	53
Gotha	B3	40
Gotland, island	C3	53
Gotsu	B3	8
Göttingen	B2	32
Gouda	B3	40
Goudiri	C2	62
Gouin, reservoir	B3	103
Goundam	C2	58
Gouré	D2	59
Govan	E9	104
Governador Valadares	D3	81
Gowd-e Zereh, lake	A3	22
Göyçay	C4	45
Gozo, island	A1	36
Graaf-Reinet	B3	71
Gračanica	B1	48
Gracias	B2	86
Grafton, N.S.W.	E2	14
Graham Land, region	C11	107
Graham, island	F4	95
Graham, island	K1	99
Grahamstown	C3	71
Grampian, mts.	B2	30
Gran Canaria, island	Inset I	37
Gran Chaco, region	A3	75
Granada	B3	87
Granada	E4	37
Granby	D6	103
Grand Anse	B1	91
Grand Bahama, island	A2	89
Grand Bale	C2	69
Grand Bank	D5	98
Grand Bay	C1	91
Grand Bay	C3	97
Grand Bend	D4	102
Grand Bruit	B5	98
Grand Canyon, Ariz.	B2	126
Grand Centre	E4	94
Grand Cess	B3	63
Grand Erg Occidental, desert	B1	57
Grand Erg Oriental, desert	B2	57
Grand Falls	B1	97
Grand Falls-Windsor	D5	98
Grand Forks	N6	95
Grand Forks, N. Dak.	D1	126
Grand Island, Nebr.	D1	126
Grand Junction, Colo.	C2	126
Grand Manan, island	C4	97
Grand Marais	A4	96
Grand Narrows	G2	100
Grand Pré	C2	100
Grand Rapids	B2	96
Grand Rapids, Mich.	E1	126
Grand Roy	A1	80
Grand Santi	D4	89
Grand Turk, capital	D4	89
Grand Turk, island	D4	89
Grand Valley	E4	102
Grand, canal	C2	31
Grand, harbor	C2	36
Grand, lake	D2	97
Grand, lake	C4	98
Grand, river	C3	69
Grand-Etang	F1	100
Grand-Mère	D5	103
Grand-Remous	A5	103
Grande Baleine, river	A2	101
Grande de Añasco, river	A2	90
Grande de Manatí, river	C2	90
Grande de Matagalpa, river	B2	87
Grande Prairie	A3	94
Grande, bay	B7	74
Grande, range	C2	75
Grande, river	B3	77
Grande, river	D3	81
Grande, river	B3	86
Grande-Anse	D1	97
Grande-Rivière	M3	103
Grande-Vallée	M2	103
Grândola	A3	36
Grandview	A3	96
Granisle	J4	95
Grantham	C3	30
Granville Lake	A1	96
Gras, lake	A3, B2	96
Grass, river	D4	94
Grassland	D4	94
Grauspitz, mt.	B2	33
Gravelbourg	D11	104
Gravenhurst	F3	102
Gravesend	Inset III	30
Gravois, point	B3	89
Graz	D3	39
Great Abaco, island	B2	89
Great Alföld, plain	B2	14
Great Artesian, basin	D2	14
Great Australian, bight	B3	14
Great Bahama, bank	B4	89
Great Barrier, island	C2	15
Great Barrier, reef	D1	14
Great basin, Nev.	B2	126
Great Bear, lake	D3	99
Great Dividing, range	D1, D3	14
Great Exuma, island	B3	89
Great Falls	C4	96
Great Falls, Mont.	B1	126
Great Fish, river	C3	71
Great Inagua, island	C4	89
Great Indian, desert	B3	20
Great Karroo, plateau	B3	71
Great Nicobar, island	F7	20
Great Rift, valley	C2	68
Great Ruaha, river	C2	68
Great Salt, lake, Utah	B1	126
Great Sand Sea, desert	A2	56
Great Sandy, desert	B2	14
Great Scarcies, river	A1	63
Great Sea, reef	B1	17
Great Slave, lake	F4	99
Great Victoria, desert	B2	14
Great Wall of China	D2	10
Great Yarmouth	D3	30
Great Zab, river	B1	24
Great, plains	C1	126
Greater Hinggan, range	F1	10
Greater Sunda, islands	B2	13
Grébourn	B1	59
Gredos, mts.	D2	37
Greeley, Colo.	C1	126
Green Bay, Wis.	E1	126
Green Lake	C6	104
Green, islands	B2	15
Greenland, sea	B2	30
Greenock	F2	126
Greensboro, N.C.		
Greenville	B3	63
Greenville, S.C.	N6	95
Greenwood	C1	40
Greifswald	C2	32
Grenå	A4	59
Grenada, island	H10	104
Grenadines, islands	A3, B1, C1	91
Grenfell	D4	34
Grenoble	C4	96
Gretna	D3	32
Greve	C5	98
Grevenmacher	B2	33
Grey River		
Grey, range	D2	14
Greymouth	B3	15
Gribingui, river	A2	66
Griffin	G11	104
Griffith, N.S.W.	D3	14
Grijalva, river	F4	84
Grimsby	C3	30
Grimsey, island	B1	52
Grinnell, peninsula	J1	99
Griqualand East, region	C3	71
Griqualand West, region	B2	71
Griquatown	B2	71
Grise Ford	M1	99
Griswold	A4	96
Groningen	B2	80
Groningen	D1	32
Groote Eylandt, island	C1	14
Grootfontein	C1	70
Grootvloer, pan	B1	71
Gros Islet	B1	91
Gros Morne Natl. Park	C4	98
Gros-Morne	L2	103
Grosseto	B2	38
Grossglockner, mt.	C3	39
Groundbirch	M3	95
Groznyy	E4	44
Grudziądz	D2	41
Grunthal	C4	96
Guacanayabo, gulf	D3	88
Guadalajara	E2	37
Guadalajara, state capital	D3	84
Guadalcanal, island	A1	16
Guadalquivir, core		
Guadalupe, reservoir	Inset	84
Guadarrama, mts.	D2	37
Guadeloupe, island		82
Guadiana, river	C3	37
Guaíba	B4	79
Guaillabamba, river	C4	78
Guainía, river	C4	78
Guajara Mirim	B3	81
Guajira, peninsula	C1	78
Guam, island		5
Guanacaste, range	A2	86
Guanaja, island	C1	78
Guanajuato, state capital	D3	84
Guanare		
Guandu, river	Inset I	81
Guangdong	D3	10
Guangxi Zhuang	D3	10
Guangzhou	E3	10
Guánica	B3	90
Guantánamo	E3	88
Guaporé, river	A3	77
Guaqui	A3	77
Guaranda	B3	78
Guarda	C2	36
Guarujá	Inset II	81
Guarulhos	Inset II	81
Guatemala City, capital	C5	85
Guaviare, river	C4	78
Guayaguayare	A2	91
Guayama	C3	90
Guayambre, river	B2	86
Guayanilla	B2	90
Guayape, river	B2	86
Guayaquil	B4	79
Guayaquil, gulf	A4	79
Guayas, river	B4	79
Guaymas	B2	84
Guaynabo	C2	90
Guben	C3	40
Gudauta	A2	45
Gudenå, river	B2	32
Guecho	E1	37
Guéckédou	C3	62
Guelph	E4	102
Guelta Zemmur	C3	34
Guéret	E1	37
Guernica Y Luno		
Guernsey, island	Inset II	
Guerrero Negro	B2	84
Guiana, highlands	D2	79
Guiers, lake	B1	62
Guilarte, mt.	A2	90
Guildford	C3	30
Guilin	E3	10
Guimarães	A2	36
Guinea, gulf		55
Güiria	D1	79
Guiyang	D3	10
Guizhou	D3	10
Gujranwala	E3	21
Gujrat	E3	21
Gulbarga	C5	20
Gulbene	D2	46
Gulf Coastal, plain	D3	126
Gulistan		
Gull Lake	B10	104
Gull, lake	B2	94
Gulu	C2	61
Gumdag	B2	22
Gummi	C1	65
Gunisao, river	C2	96
Gunnbjørn Fjeld, mt.	D2	106
Gunton	C4	96
Guntur	D5	20
Gurabo	D2	90
Guri, reservoir	D2	79
Gusau	D1	65
Gushgy	D3	22
Gushgy, river	D3	22
Gushikawa	Inset II	8
Gustavo A. Madero	Inset	84
Güstrow	C2	40
Guysborough	F2	100
Gwadar	A3	21
Gwai, river	A2	69
Gwalior	C3	20
Gweru	B2	69
Gyda, peninsula	C3	44
Gympie, Qld.	E2	14
Gyöngyös	B2	43
Győr	A2	43
Gypsumville	B3	96
Gyumri	A2	45

Key Page

Gyzylarbat B2 22

H

Ha Giang A1 11
Ha'apai, island group.......B3 17
Haapsalu B2 46
Haarlem B2 32
Habarut C1 25
Habay A2 94
Haboro ....Inset I 8
Hachijo, island C3 8
Hachinohe D1 8
Hachioji C3 8
Haddummati, atoll A4 19
Hadejia, river E1 65
Hadera B1 26
Haderslev B3 32
Hadhramaut, district B1 25
Hadithah, al- B2 24
Haedo, range B2 75
Haeju A3 9
Hafford C8 104
Hafnarfjördhur A3 52
Hagen A3 40
Hague, cape B2 34
Haha, island ....Inset III 8
Haifa B1 26
Haifa, bay B1 26
Haikou E4 10
Hail B1 24
Hailar E1 10
Hainan D4 10
Haines Junction B5 105
Haiphong B2 11
Hairé Lao B1 62
Hajdúböszörmény C2 43
Haji Ibrahim, mt. B1 24
Hajjah A1 25
Haka B2 12
Hakodate ....D1, Inset I 8
Halab (Aleppo) A1 27
Halaib D1 59
Halba B1 26
Halberstadt B3 40
Halfmoon Bay L6 95
Haliburton G2 102
Halifax C3 30
Halifax, capital D3 100
Halil, river D4 22
Halisahar ....Inset II 20
Hall Beach M3 99
Hall, peninsula P4 99
Halla-san, mt. ....Inset 9
Hallboro B4 96
Halle C2 33
Halle B3 40
Hallingdal, valley B3 52
Halmahera, island D1 13
Halmstad B3 53
Haltiatunturi, mt B1 53
Halton Hills F4 102
Hamadan B3 22
Hamah A2 27
Hamamatsu C3 8
Hamar C3 9
Hambantota C5 19
Hamburg B2 40
Hämeenlinna B2 53
Hameln B2 40
Hamersley, range A2 14
Hamgyŏng, mts. C2 9
Hamhŭng B3 9
Hami C1 10
Hamilton C2 15
Hamilton B2 10
Hamilton F4 102
Hamilton, inlet B2 98
Hamiota A4 96
Hamm A3 40
Hammamat, al- C1 57
Hammamet, gulf C1 57
Hammerfest E1 52
Hammonds Plains D3 100
Hammondvale D3 97
Hampden C4 98
Hampstead J5 103
Hampton B2 97
Hamun-e Jaz Murian, lake ...D4 22
Hamun-e Saberi, lake A2 22
Han, river E2 10
Han, river B4 9
Hanau B3 40
Handan E2 10
Hangayn, mts. B2 11
Hangö B3 53
Hangzhou F2 10
Hanley D9 104
Hannibal, Mo. D2 126
Hannover B2 40
Hanoi, capital A2 11
Hanover D3 102
Hantzsch, river O3 99
Hanzhong D2 10
Haora ....E4, Inset II 20
Haparanda D1 53
Happy Valley-Goose Bay ..A2, E4 98
Har Us, lake B2 11
Harad C1 24
Harare, capital B1 69
Harbel A2 63
Harbin F1 10
Harbour Breton D5 98
Harbour Deep C4 98
Harbour, island B2 89
Harcourt D2 97
Hardangerfjord, fjord A3 52
Hardangervidda, plateau B3 52
Hardwood Lake H2 102
Hare Bay D5 98
Harer A2 60
Hargeysa A2 60
Hargrave A4 96
Harirud, river A2 22
Harlow ....Inset III 30
Härnösand C2 53

Key Page

Harper C3 63
Harris C9 104
Harrisburg, capital, Pa. ...F1 126
Harrogate C2 30
Harstad D2 52
Hart, ranges L3 95
Hart, river B3 105
Hartford, capital, Conn. ...F1 126
Hartland B2 97
Hartley Bay H4 95
Hartney A4 96
Harwill C3 97
Harvey C3 97
Harz, mts. B3 40
Hasa, al-, region C1 24
Hashtadan, region E3 22
Haslemere ....Inset III 30
Hasselt D2 33
Hastings C2 15
Hastings D4 30
Hastings H3 102
Hat Yai B5 12
Hatillo B2 90
Hato Mayor C2 89
Hatteras cape, N.C. F2 126
Hattiesburg, Miss. E2 126
Haugesund B4 52
Haultain, river D4 104
Haute-Normandie C2 34
Havana, capital B1 88
Havel, river C2 40
Havelock H3 102
Havířov D3 42
Havre, Mont. C1 126
Havre-St-Pierre D3 101
Hawaii ....Inset I 126
Hawaii island, Hawaii ...Inset II 126
Hawalli C2 24
Hawar, islands B2 25
Hawea, lake A3 15
Hawf C1 25
Hawick C2 30
Hawke Harbour D2 98
Hawke's Bay C4 98
Hawke, bay C2 15
Hawkesbury L2 102
Hay River 94
Hay, river A2, B1 94
Hays, river D1, D2 96
Hayma C2 25
Hayter E5 94
Hazelton J3 95
Hazleton, mts. H3 95
Hazlet B10 104
Hazm, al- A1 25
Heart's Content E5 98
Heaslip A4 96
Heath Steele C1 97
Hebei E2 10
Hebrides, sea A1 30
Hebron E3 98
Hecate, strait G4 95
Hecla C3 96
Hecla and Griper, bay F1 99
Hedley M6 95
Heerenveen C2 32
Heerlen C4 32
Hefei E2 10
Hegang G1 10
Heha, mt. B2 61
Heidelberg B4 40
Heidenheim B4 40
Heilbronn B4 40
Heilong (Amur), river F1 10
Heilongjiang F1 10
Heimaey, island A3 52
Heinsburg E4 94
Heisler D5 94
Hekla, volcano B3 52
Hel D1 41
Hellen, reef ....Inset 17
Helena, capital, Mont. ..B1 126
Helgoland, island A1 40
Hellín F3 37
Helmand, river A2 22
Helmsdale E5 94
Helsingborg B3 53
Helsingør D2 32
Helsinki, capital B2 53
Heming Lake A2 96
Henan E2 10
Henashi, cape C1 8
Hengch'un B2 9
Hengelo D2 32
Hengyang E3 10
Henley Harbour D3 98
Hensall D4 102
Henzada B3 12
Herat A2 22
Herb Lake B2 96
Herbert C10 104
Heredia B2 86
Hereford C3 30
Heriot Bay K6 95
Hermitage-Sandyville D5 98
Hermon, mt. A3 27
Hermosillo, state capital ...B2 84
Hernád, river C1 43
Herning B2 32
Herschel ....Inset II 8
Hertford D4 102
Herzliyya B1 26
Hess, river C4 105
Hesse B3 40
Hiatikulu B2 71
Hibbing, Minn. D1 126
Hicks Bay C2 15
Hidalgo E3 84
Hidalgo del Parral C2 84
Hierro, island ....Inset I 37
High Atlas, ranges B2 57
High Level B2 94

Key Page

High River D6 94
High Tatra, mts. D4 41
High Wycombe ....Inset III 30
Highrock A1 96
Highrock, lake A1 96
Higüey D2 89
Hiiumaa, island B2 46
Hijaz, al-, region A1 24
Hilda ....Inset I 94
Hildesheim B2 40
Hill Bank B2 85
Hillaby, mt. A3 91
Hillah, al- B2 24
Hillaro D3 32
Hillsborough C1 91
Hillsborough E3 97
Hillsborough, bay B2 100
Hilo, Hawaii ....Inset II 126
Hilton Beach B1 102
Hilversum C2 32
Himalayas, mts. 7
Himeji B3 8
Hinche C1 89
Hindelang B5 40
Hindu Kush, range B1 22
Hino, cape B3 8
Hinton B4 94
Hirakata B3 8
Hirakud, reservoir D4 20
Hirara ....Inset II 8
Hirmil, al- B1 26
Hirosake D1 8
Hiroshima B3 8
Hirtshals B1 32
Hisabur ....Inset II 20
Hitachi D2 8
Hixon L4 95
Hjørring B1 32
Hkakabo Razi, mt. C1 12
Ho C3 64
Ho Chi Minh City B4 11
Hoa Binh A2 11
Hobart, Tas., capital C4 14
Hobsons, bay ....Inset V 14
Hobyo B2 60
Hoceima, al- D1 57
Hodgeville D10 104
Hodgson C3 96
Hódmezővásárhely C2 43
Hoeryŏng C1 9
Hof B3 40
Höfn C2 52
Hohe Tauern, mts. C3 39
Hohhot E1 10
Hokkaido, island ......D1, Inset I 8
Hoktemberyan B2 45
Holbæk C3 32
Holden D4 94
Holdfast E10 104
Holetown A3 91
Holguín E3 88
Holhol B2 60
Holland B4 96
Holman E2 99
Holon B1 26
Holstebro B2 32
Holton C2 98
Holyhead B3 30
Holyrood E5 98
Holywood B2 30
Homathko, river K5 95
Hombori Tondo, mt. C2 58
Hombori, mts. C2 58
Homer, Alaska ....Inset I 126
Homo, bay B2 18
Homs A2 27
Homyel E3 47
Hon Gai B2 11
Hondo C3 94
Hondo, river B1 85
Honduras, gulf A1 86
Hong Kong E3 10
Hong Kong, island ....Inset 10
Hongze, lake E2 10
Honiara, capital B1 16
Honolulu, capital,
  Hawaii ....Inset II 126
Honshu, island C2 8
Hoogeveen D2 32
Hoorn C2 32
Hope M6 95
Hope Bay C2 88
Hope Valley E5 94
Hopedale A1 98
Hopedale A1 98
Hopewell Cape E3 97
Horgen C1 35
Hormigueros A2 90
Hormuz, strait D4 22
Horn, cape C9 76
Horn, cape A1 52
Hornád, river C2 42
Hornavan, lake C1 53
Hornepayne D3 101
Horsburgh, atoll A2 19
Horse, river D3 94
Horsens B3 32
Horton D3 99
Horton, river D3 99
Hospitalet H2 37
Hoste, island C9 76
Hot Springs, Ark. D2 126
Hotan A2 10
Hotchkiss B2 94
Hottah, lake E3 99
Houghton, Mich. E1 126
Houmt Souk C2 57
Houston J4 95
Houston, Tex. D3 126
Hov, river B2 11
Hove C4 30
Hoverla, mt. A2 47
Hövsgöl, lake C1 11
Howley C4 98
Hoy, island ....Inset I 30
Hradec Králové B2 42
Hrazdan B2 45
Hrazdan, river B2 45

Key Page

Hrodna A3 47
Hron, river B2 42
Hsinchu B1 9
Hsinchuang B1 9
Hsintien B1 9
Hsinying B2 9
Hua Hin B3 12
Huacho B3 77
Huai, river E2 10
Huainan E2 10
Hualien B2 9
Huallaga, river B2 77
Huambo C4 70
Huancavelica B3 77
Huancayo B3 77
Huang (Yellow), river ..D2, E2 10
Huanuco B2 77
Huapí, mts. B2 87
Huaraz B2 77
Huascarán, mt. B2 77
Hubbards C3 100
Hubei D2 10
Hubley D3 100
Hubli-Dharwar C5 20
Hudaydah, al- A2 25
Huddersfield C3 30
Hudiksvall C2 53
Hudson Bay H8 104
Hudson's Hope M3 95
Hudson, bay J3 92
Hudson, strait O4 99
Hue B3 11
Huehuetenango B4 85
Huelva C4 37
Huesca F1 37
Hufuf, al- C1 24
Hugli, river ....Inset II 20
Hugli-Chunchura ....Inset II 20
Hǜichǒn B2 9
Huila, mt. A4 78
Hǜksan Chedo, islands A5 9
Hull A6 103
Hulun, lake E1 10
Hulwan B2 56
Humacao D2 90
Humber, river D3 30
Humboldt E8 104
Humenné C2 42
Humuya, river B2 86
Húnaflói, bay A1 52
Hunan E3 10
Hunedoara B3 43h
Hŭngnam B3 9
Hünsruck, mts. A4 40
Hunter River B2 100
Huntington, W. Va. E2 126
Huntsville F2 102
Huntsville, Ala. E2 126
Hunyani, river B1 69
Huon, islands B1 18
Huon, peninsula A2 15
Huron, lake E1 126
Hussar D5 94
Hutchinson, Kans. D2 126
Hvannadalshnúkur, mt. B3 52
Hvar, island C3 48
Hvítá, river A2 52
Hwange A2 69
Hyargas, lake B2 11
Hyderabad C5 20
Hyderabad B3 21
Hyesan C2 9
Hyland Post J4 95
Hyland, river D5 105
Hylo D4 94
Hyvinkää B2 53

I

Ialomiţa, river D3 43
Ialpug, river D2 50
Iaşi D2 43
Ibadan B4 65
Ibagué B3 78
Ibar, river B3 49
Ibaraki B3 8
Ibarra B2 79
Ibb A2 25
Ibérico, mts. F2 37
Ibiza G4 37
Ibiza, island G3 37
Iboundji, mt. A2 66
Ibrahim, river A1 26
Ibri C1 25
Ica B3 77
Ica, river B2 81
Içá, river B2 81
Icacos, key D2 90
Ice Cap C2 106
Ichǒn B3 9
Ichihara D3 8
Ichikawa D3 8
Ichilo, river B3 77
Ichinomiya C3 8
Idah B4 65
Idaho B1 126
Idaho Falls, Idaho B1 126
Iddlesleigh E6 94
Idfu B3 56
Idhra, island B3 51
Idlib A2 27
Idrija B2 48
Ife C4 65
Igarka C6 44
Igloolik M3 99
Igombe, river B1 68
Iguaçu, falls C4 81
Iguaçu, river E2 74
Iguala E4 84
Iguazú, falls E4 75
Ih Bogd Uul, mt. B2 11
Ihosy B3 69
Ilan B1 9
Ilagan C1 17
Ilaisalmi C2 53
Ishigaki, island ......Inset I 8
Ishikari, river ......Inset I 8
Ishim D5 44

Key Page

Ijuw C2 16
Ikaría, island C3 51
Ikeja B4 65
Ikela B2 67
Iki, island A3 8
Ikorodu B4 65
Ila C3 65
Ilam D3 19
Ilam B3 22
Île-à-la-Crosse C5 104
Île-de-France C2 34
Ilebo B2 67
Ilesha C4 65
Ilford D1 96
Ilford J6 102
Ilhéus E3 81
Ili, river D2 23
Iligan C4 12
Illampu, mt. A3 77
Illapel B4 76
Illimani, mt. A3 77
Illinois E1 126
Ilo C4 77
Iloilo B4 12
Ilorin C3 65
Imatra C2 53
Imbarié ....Inset I 81
Imbéry B2 90
Imi D3 60
Imjin, river A2 9
Imilli A2 58
Imperatriz D2 81
Imperial E9 104
Imperial Mills E4 94
Imperial, river B6 76
Impfondo A2 66
Imphal F4 20
Inari, lake C1 53
Incheon B4 9
Incles, river C1 36
Indalsälven, river B2 53
Indian Bay D4 96
Indian Brook G1 100
Indian Cabins B1 94
Indian Harbour D3 100
Indian Head G10 104
Indiana E2 126
Indianapolis, capital, Ind. ..E2 126
Indigirka, river C9 44
Indispensable, reefs B2 16
Indore C4 20
Indus, river C4, E2 21
Ingleside K3 102
Ingolstadt B4 40
Ingonish G1 100
Ingonish Beach G1 100
Ingushetia, republic E4 44
Inhambane B5 68
Inhomirim ....Inset I 81
Inland, sea B3 8
Inn, river B3, C2 39
Inner Hebrides, islands A2 30
Inner Mongolia E1 10
Innisfail D5 94
Innisfil F3 102
Innsbruck B3 39
Inta C5 44
Interlaken B2 35
International Falls, Minn. ..D1 126
Inthanon, mt. A2 12
Inukjuak A2 101
Inuvik B3 99
Inuvik, region C3 99
Inwood C4 96
Inyangani, mt. C2 69
Ioánnina B2 51
Ionian, islands A2 51
Ionian, sea A2 51
Iori, river C4 45
Iowa D1 126
Ipel', river ....Inset I 81
Ipiíba ....Inset I 81
Ipoh B2 13
Ipoly, river B1 43
Ipswich D3 30
Iqaluit (Frobisher Bay) P4 99
Iquique B2 76
Iquitos C1 77
Iracoubo B1 80
Iráklion C4 51
Iranshahr E4 22
Irapuato D3 84
Irazú, volcano C3 86
Irbe, strait A3 46
Irbid A1 26
Irbil B1 24
Iri B5 9
Irian Jaya, region E2 13
Iringa C2 68
Iriomote, island ....Inset II 8
Iriona C2 86
Irish, sea B3 30
Irkutsk D7 44
Iron Bridge B1 102
Iron Gate Reservoir B3 43
Iroquois Falls D3 101
Irrawaddy, river B2 12
Irtysh, river D5 44
Irvine D1 23
Irun D2 56
Isangel C4 18
Isar, river C4 40
Ischia, island C2 38
Isère, river D4 34
Isernia C2 38
Iseyin B4 65
Isherton B4 80
Ishigaki, island ......Inset I 8
Ishikari, river ......Inset I 8
Ishim D5 44

Key Page

Ishim, river C1 23
Ishinomaki D2 8
Ishinomaki, bay D2 8
Ishizuchi, mt. B3 8
Isiro C1 67
Iskenderun D3 27
Iskur, river C2 50
Islamabad, capital D3 21
Island Lake D2 96
Island Lake D2 96
Islay, island A2 30
Isle aux Morts B5 98
Islington J6 102
Ismailiyah, al- B1 56
Isoka C2 67
Iwaki C4 65
Isparta B3 27
Istanbul B2 27
Istria, peninsula A2 48
Izmir A2 27
Izmit B2 27
Itabira D3 81
Itabuna E3 81
Itaipu ....Inset I 81
Itaipú, reservoir E4 75
Itajaí D4 81
Itanagar F3 20
Itapecerica da Serra ...Inset II 81
Itapeva ....Inset II 81
Itaquaquecetuba ....Inset II 81
Iténez, river B2 77
Itháki, island B2 51
Ittoqqortoormiit
  (Scoresbysund) D2 106
Ituna G9 104
Ivalo C1 53
Ivano-Frankivsk A2 47
Ivanovo D3 44
Ivindo, river B1 66
Ivujivik A1 101
Iwaki D2 8
Iwakuni B3 8
Iwo C4 65
Iwo Jima, island ......Inset III 8
Ixelles C2 33
Ixtapa D4 84
Ixtapaluca ....Inset 84
Izabal, lake E4 85
Izhevsk D4 44
Izki C1 25
Izmir A3 27
Iztacalco ....Inset 84
Iztapalapa ....Inset 84
Izu, islands C3 8
Izu, peninsula C3 8
Izuhara A3 8

J

Jabal al-Akhdar, al-, mts. ...C1 25
Jabal al-Uwaynat, mt. B3 56
Jabal an-Nabi Shuayb, mt. ..A1 25
Jabal an-Nusayriyah, mts. ...A2 27
Jabal Katrinah, mt. B2 56
Jabal Ramm, mt. A3 26
Jabal Tuwayq, mts. B2 24
Jabal Zuqar, island A2 25
Jabalpur C4 20
Jaboatão E2 81
Jacare-Acanga C2 81
Jackhead C3 96
Jackson's Arm C4 98
Jackson, capital, Miss. D2 126
Jackson, port ....Inset IV 14
Jackson, Wyo. B1 126
Jacksonville, Fla. E2 126
Jacmel C2 89
Jacques-Cartier, river E4 103
Jacquet River C1 97
Jadabpur ....Inset II 20
Jadida, el- B1 57
Jaén E4 37
Jaffna B2 19
Jafr, al- B2 26
Jagdalpur D5 20
Jaghbub, al- D2 56
Jahrah, al- B2 24
Jaipur B3 21
Jaipurhat B3 21
Jajce B1 48
Jakarta, capital B2 13
Jakobstad B2 53
Jakupica, mts. B2 48
Jalal-Abad C2 23
Jalalabad C2 22
Jalapa Enríquez,
  state capital E4 84
Jalingo F3 65
Jalisco D4 84
Jalu D2 56
Jaluit, island B2 16
Jamaame A3 60
Jamalpur C4 21
Jambi B2 13
James, bay J3 92
Jammu B2 20
Jamnagar B4 20
Jampur ....Inset II 20
Jämsä C2 53
Jamshedpur E4 20
Jamuna, river C4 21
Jan Lake H6 104
Jan Mayen, island 5
Janai A1 90
Janakpur C3 19
Janeville D1 97
Jangy-Bazar B2 23
Japan, sea 8
Japanese Alps, mts. C3 8
Japeri ....Inset II 81
Japurá, river B2 81
Jarama, river A1 26
Jarash A1 26
Jari, river C2 81
Jarvie D4 94
Jarvis E5 102
Jask D4 22
Jastrebac, mts. B3 49

K

	Key	Page
Jászberény	B2	43
Java, *island*	C2	13
Java, *sea*	C2	13
Javari, *river*	A2	81
Jawf, al-	A1	24
Jawf, al-	D3	56
Jawhar	B3	60
Jaya, *mt.*	E2	13
Jayapura	F2	13
Jayuya	B2	90
Jazirah, al-, *region*	B1	27
Jazzin	A2	26
Jebba	C3	65
Jebel Toubkal, *mt.*	C2	57
Jeddore, *lake*	D5	98
Jefferson City, *capital*, Mo.	D2	126
Jejuí-Guazú, *river*	D4	75
Jejur	Inset II	20
Jekabpils	C2	46
Jelenia Góra	B3	41
Jelgava	B2	46
Jemseg	C3	97
Jena	B3	40
Jengish Chokusu, *mt.*	G1	23
Jenner	E6	94
Jenpeg	B2	96
Jérémie	A2	89
Jerez de la Frontera	C4	37
Jersey, *island*	Inset II	13
Jerudong	B2	13
Jerusalem, *capital*	B2	26
Jesenice	B2	48
Jessore	C5	21
Jésus, *island*	J5	103
Jetait	A1	96
Jhang Sadar	D3	21
Jhansi	C3	20
Jhelum	D3	21
Jhelum, *river*	D3	21
Ji'an	E3	10
Jiamusi	G1	10
Jiangsu	E2	10
Jiangxi	E3	10
Jiddah	A2	24
Jiddah, *island*	A1	25
Jihlava	B3	42
Jilib	A3	60
Jilin	F1	10
Jilin	F1	10
Jima	B3	60
Jimaní	A2	89
Jiménez	D2	84
Jinan	E2	10
Jingdezhen	E3	10
Jining	E2	10
Jinja	C3	61
Jinotega	B2	87
Jinotepe	A3	87
Jinsha (Yangtze), *river*	C2	10
Jinzhou	F1	10
Jipijapa	A3	79
Jir Paraná	B3	81
Jirgatol	B1	23
Jiu, *river*	B3	43
Jiujiang	E3	10
Jixi	G1	10
Jizan	B2	24
Jizzakh	C2	23
João Pessoa	E2	81
Jobos	C3	90
Jodhpur	B3	20
Joe Batt's Arm	D4	98
Joensuu	C2	53
Joetsu	C2	8
Joggins	C2	100
Johannesburg	C2	71
John D'or Prairie	C2	94
Johnsons Crossing	C5	105
Johor Baharu	B2	13
Johor, *strait*	B1	13
Joinville	D4	81
Joinville, *island*	C12	107
Joka	Inset II	20
Joliet, Ill.	E1	126
Joliette	C5	103
Jolo	B5	12
Jolo, *island*	B5	12
Jonava	C2	46
Jones, *sound*	L1	99
Jonesboro, Ark.	D2	126
Jong, *river*	A2	63
Jönköping	B3	53
Jonquière	E3	103
Joplin, Mo.	D2	126
Jordan, *river*	A2	26
Jos	E3	65
Jos, *plateau*	E2	65
Jotunheimen, *mts.*	B3	52
Jou	B4	63
Joussard	C3	94
Juan de Fuca, *strait*	L7	95
Juana Díaz	B2	90
Juàzeiro	D2	81
Juàzeiro do Norte	E2	81
Juba	C4	59
Juba, *river*	A3	60
Jubayl	A1	26
Jubayl, al-	C1	24
Jubilee, *lake*	D5	98
Júcar, *river*	F3	37
Juchitán de Zaragoza	F4	84
Judique	F2	100
Juigalpa	B2	87
Juiz de Fora	D4	81
Juliaca	C4	77
Julian Alps, *mts.*	A2	48
Juliana Top, *mt.*	A3	80
Jullundur	C2	20
Jumayliyah, al-	C2	25
Jumla	B2	19
Junagadh	B4	20
Junaynah, al-	D2	90
Juncos	D2	90
Jundiaí	D4	81
Juneau, *capital*, Alaska	Inset I	126
Jungfrau, *mt.*	B2	35
Juniper	B2	97
Juniyah	A2	26

	Key	Page
Juozapines, *mt.*	C2	46
Jura, *island*	B2	30
Jura, *mts.*	A2	35
Jurbarkas	B2	46
Jurmala	B2	46
Jurong	A1	13
Juruá, *river*	B2	81
Juruena, *river*	C3	81
Jutiapa	D5	85
Juticalpa	B2	86
Jutland, *peninsula*	B3	32
Juventud, *island*	B2	88
Jvari	B3	45
Južna, *river*	B3	49
Jwaneng	B3	69
Jyväskylä	C2	53

K

	Key	Page
K2 (Godwin Austen), *mt.*	A2	10
Ka Dake	B2	71
Ka, *river*	C2	65
Kabale	B1	63
Kabale	A4	61
Kabalo	B2	67
Kabardino-Balkaria, *republic*	E4	44
Kabelebo, *river*	A2	80
Kabompo, *river*	A2	67
Kabul, *capital*	B2	22
Kabul, *river*	B2	22
Kabwe	B2	67
Kachovka	C3	47
Kadavu, *island*	B3	17
Kadei, *river*	A3	66
Kadoma	B2	69
Kaduna	D2	65
Kaduna, *river*	D2	65
Kaduqli	B3	59
Kaédi	B3	58
Kaélé	B1	65
Kaeo	B2	15
Kaesŏng	B4	9
Kafan	D3	45
Kaffrine	B2	62
Kafr ad-Dawwar	B1	56
Kafu, *river*	B3	61
Kafue	B2	67
Kafue, *river*	B2	67
Kaga Bandoro	A2	66
Kagawong	C2	102
Kagera, *river*	B4, C1, C2	61
Kagitumba	C1	61
Kagoshima	A4	8
Kahayan, *river*	C2	13
Kahemba	A3	67
Kahnawake	H6	103
Kahntah	M2	95
Kahoolawe *island*, Hawaii	Inset II	126
Kai, *islands*	E2	13
Kaieteur, *falls*	B3	80
Kaifeng	E2	10
Kaikoura	B3	15
Kailahun	C3	62
Kailahun	B1	63
Kainji, *lake*	B2	65
Kaiserslautern	A4	40
Kaitaia	B1	15
Kajaani	C2	53
Kakamega	A2	63
Kakata	A2	63
Kakeroma, *island*	Inset II	8
Kakhovka, *reservoir*	C3	47
Kakinada	D5	20
Kaladar	H3	102
Kalahari, *desert*	A2	69
Kalámai	B3	51
Kalamáki	Inset	51
Kálbácár	B2	45
Kalemie	C2	67
Kalgoorlie, W.A.	B3	14
Kali	C1	62
Kali, *river*	B2	19
Kalimantan, *region*	C2	13
Kaliningrad	D3	44
Kalixälven, *river*	D1	53
Kallithéa	Inset	51
Kalmar	C3	53
Kalmykia, *republic*	E4	44
Kalpeni, *island*	B7	20
Kalu, *river*	B5	19
Kalundborg	C3	32
Kalutara	A5	19
Kalwa	Inset I	20
Kamakwie	A1	62
Kaman	Inset I	20
Kamaran, *island*	A1	25
Kamarhati	A1	63
Kambia	A1	62
Kamchatka, *peninsula*	D10	44
Kamchiya, *river*	F2	50
Kamensk-Uralsky	D5	44
Kamet, *mt.*	C2	20
Kamina	C3	67
Kaminak, *lake*	J4	99
Kamloops	M6	95
Kamo	C2	45
Kampala, *capital*	C3	61
Kampong Cham	D4	11
Kampong Chhnang	C3	11
Kampong Saom	B5	11
Kampong Thum	C3	11
Kampot	C5	11
Kamsack	J9	104
Kamsar	A2	62
Kamui, *cape*	Inset I	8
Kananga	C2	67
Kanazawa	C2	8
Kanchenjunga, *mt.*	C2	19
Kanchipuram	C6	20
Kanchrapara	Inset II	20
Kandi	B2	64
Kandy	B4	19
Kane, *basin*	P1	99
Kangaroo, *island*	C3	14

	Key	Page
Kangen, *river*	C3	59
Kanggye	B2	9
Kanghwa, *bay*	A4	9
Kangiqsualujjuaq	C2	101
Kangiqsujuaq	B1	101
Kangirsuk	C4	9
Kangnŭng	C4	9
Kangshan	B2	9
Kankan	D2	62
Kanko	E1	65
Kanpur	D3	20
Kansaripara	Inset II	20
Kansas	D2	126
Kansas City, Kans.	D2	126
Kansas City, Mo.	D2	126
Kansay	A1	23
Kansk	D6	44
Kanté	B2	64
Kanuku, *mts.*	B4	80
Kanye	B3	69
Kaoko Veld, *mts.*	A1	70
Kaolack	A2	62
Kaoma	B2	67
Kaop'ing, *river*	D3	39
Kapfenberg	A2	13
Kapingamarangi, *atoll*	D2	101
Kapiskau, *river*	D3	101
Kaposvár	A2	43
Kapuskasing	D3	101
Kara, *sea*	B5	44
Kara-Kum, *canal*	D3	22
Kara-Kum, *desert*	C2	22
Kara-Say	C2	23
Karabakh, *canal*	B2	45
Karachay-Cherkessia, *republic*	E4	44
Karachi	C5	21
Karaj	C2	22
Karak, al-	A2	26
Karakol	F1	23
Karakoram, *range*	C1	20
Karasburg	C4	70
Karawanken, *range*	D4	39
Karbala	B2	24
Karcag	C2	43
Kardiva, *channel*	A2	19
Kárdla	B1	46
Karelia, *republic*	C3	44
Kariba	B1	69
Kariba, *lake*	A1	69
Karibib	B2	70
Karisimbi, *mt.*	B1	61
Karkar, *island*	A2	15
Karkinit, *bay*	C3	47
Karlovac	B2	48
Karlovy Vary	A2	42
Karlskrona	C3	53
Karlsruhe	B4	40
Karlstad	B3	53
Karnali, *river*	B2	19
Karnaphuli, *reservoir*	F6	21
Karnaphuli, *river*	E6	21
Karonga	C1	27
Karpas, *peninsula*	C1	27
Kárpathos, *island*	C4	51
Kars	E2	27
Kartala, *mt.*	A1	67
Kartung	B2	62
Karun, *river*	B3	22
Karuzi	C2	61
Karvina	D3	42
Kasai, *river*	C2	67
Kasama	B1	67
Kasane	B1	69
Kasba, *lake*	H4	99
Kashan	C3	22
Kashi	A2	10
Kashiwa	D3	8
Kasinathpur	Inset II	20
Kaslo	O6	95
Kassala	B3	40
Kassel	B3	40
Kasserine	C2	57
Kastamonu	C2	27
Kastoría	B1	51
Kastrup	D3	32
Kasugai	C3	8
Kasungu	B2	68
Katagum, *river*	E2	65
Katanga, *plateau*	C2	67
Kateríni	B1	51
Katherine, N.T.	C1	14
Kathgodam	C2	20
Kathiawar, *peninsula*	B4	20
Kathmandu, *capital*	C2	19
Katowice	D3	41
Katrine, *lake*	B2	30
Katsina	D1	65
Kattegat, *strait*	C2	32
Katun-Namada	D1	65
Kaua'i *island*, Hawaii	Inset II	126
Kaufbeuren	B5	40
Kaukau Veld, *region*	A2	70
Kaunas	B2	46
Kaura-Namoda	D1	65
Kavadarci	C2	48
Kavajë	A2	49
Kavála	B1	51
Kavaratti, *island*	B6	20
Kavieng	B2	15
Kavir-e Namak, *desert*	D3	22
Kaw	B1	80
Kawagoe	C3	8
Kawaguchi	C3	8
Kawasaki	C3	8
Kawhia	B2	15
Kawthaung	C4	12
Kayangel, *islands*	A1	58
Kayes	A3	80
Kayser, *mts.*	A3	80
Kayseri	C2	27
Kazakh Upland, *region*	C2	23
Kazan	D4	44

	Key	Page
Kazanlŭk	D3	50
Kazincbarcika	C1	43
Kearney	F2	102
Kearney, Nebr.	D1	126
Keban, *reservoir*	D2	27
Kebili	B3	57
Kebir, *river*	B1	26
Kebnekaise, *mt.*	C1	53
Kechika, *river*	J2	95
Kecskemét	B2	43
Kédainiai	B1	97
Kédgwick	B1	97
Kediri	C2	13
Kédougou	C3	62
Keele, *river*	C4	99
Keeley, *lake*	B6	104
Keetmanshoop	C4	70
Keewatin, *region*	J4	99
Kef, el-	B1	57
Kefallinía, *island*	B2	51
Keflavík	A3	52
Keg River	B2	94
Keila	C1	46
Kékes, *mt.*	C2	43
Kelang	A2	13
Kelani, *river*	B4	19
Kelliher	G9	104
Kelowna	N6	95
Kelsey	C1	96
Keluang	B2	13
Kelvington	G8	104
Kemano	J4	95
Kemerovo	D6	44
Kemi	B1	53
Kemijärvi	C1	53
Kemijoki, *river*	C1	53
Kemnay	A4	96
Kempenland, *region*	D1	33
Kemps Bay	B3	89
Kempt, *lake*	B4	103
Kempten	B5	40
Kemptville	K2	102
Kenaston	D9	104
Kendal	C2	30
Kendari	D2	13
Keng Tung	C2	12
Kenilworth	C3	30
Kenitra	C1	57
Kennetcook	D2	100
Keno	B4	105
Kenora	B3	101
Kensington	A4	100
Kenton	A4	96
Kentucky	E2	126
Kentville	C2	100
Kenville	A3	96
Kenya	D4	61
Keokradong, *mt.*	F7	21
Kerang Nyatan	B5	94
Keratsínion	Inset	51
Kerch	D3	47
Kerch, *strait*	D3	47
Keremeos	N6	95
Keren	B2	60
Kerewan	B2	62
Kerguelen, *islands*	C4	61
Kerinci, *mt.*	B2	13
Kerkennah, *islands*	D3	22
Kerki	A2	51
Kérkira	A2	51
Kérkira, *island*	A2	51
Kerman	D2	22
Kerman, *region*	D4	22
Kérouané	D3	62
Kerrobert	A9	104
Kerulen, *river*	D2	11
Keszthely	A2	43
Keta	C4	64
Ketchikan, Alaska	Inset I	126
Key Lake Mine	E3	104
Key West, Fla.	E3	126
Keyano	B3	101
Khabarovsk	E8	44
Khabur, *river*	B1	27
Khakassia, *republic*	D6	44
Khalándrion	Inset	51
Khalkidhikí, *peninsula*	B1	51
Khalkís	B2	51
Khaluf	C2	25
Khambhât, *gulf*	B4	20
Khamis Mushayt	B2	24
Khan-Tengri, *mt.*	E2	23
Khanaqin	C2	24
Khaniá	B4	51
Khanka, *lake*	G1	10
Khantia-Mansia, *autonomous okrug*	C5	44
Khanty-Mansiysk	C5	44
Kharagpur	E4	20
Kharg, *island*	C4	22
Kharijah, al-	B2	56
Kharijah, *oasis*	B2	56
Kharj, al-	B1	24
Kharkov	D1	47
Khartoum North	C2	59
Khartoum, *capital*	C2	59
Khashm al-Qirbah	C2	59
Khashuri	B4	45
Khasi, *hills*	F3	20
Khaskovo	D4	50
Khatanga	B7	44
Khawr, al-	D2	25
Kherson	C3	47
Khíos, *island*	C2	51
Khiran, al-	C3	24
Khmelnytskyy	B2	47
Khojak, *pass*	C3	21
Khon Kaen	C2	12
Khor Angar	C1	60
Khorasan, *region*	D2	22
Khorat, *plateau*	C2	12
Khorixas	B2	70
Khorramabad	B3	22
Khorramshahr	B3	22
Khorugh	B2	23

	Key	Page
Khouribga	C1	57
Khowst	B2	22
Khudzhand	A1	23
Khujayli	A2	23
Khulna	C6	21
Khums, al-	B1	56
Khuriya Muriya, *islands*	C3	25
Khuzdar	C4	21
Khuzestan, *region*	B3	22
Khvoy	D2	22
Khyber, *pass*	C2	21
Kibungo	B2	61
Kibuye	A2	48
Kičevo	A2	48
Kidal	D2	58
Kidderminster	C3	30
Kiel	B1	40
Kiel, *bay*	B1	40
Kiev, *capital*	C1	47
Kiev, *reservoir*	C1	47
Kiffa	C3	58
Kifisiá	Inset	51
Kifissós, *river*	B2	51
Kigali, *capital*	B1	61
Kigoma	A1	68
Kii, *channel*	B3	8
Kii, *peninsula*	B3	8
Kikinda	B2	49
Kikkertavak, *island*	B2	98
Kikwit	B2	67
Kilchu	C2	9
Kildare	C2	31
Kilimanjaro, *mt.*	C1	68
Kilinochchi	B2	19
Kilkee	B2	31
Kilkenny	C2	31
Killala, *bay*	B1	31
Killaloe	H2	102
Killarney	B2	31
Killarney	B4	96
Killarney	D1	102
Killarney Lake	E5	94
Killdeer	D11	104
Killeen, Tex.	D2	126
Kilmarnock	B2	30
Kilombero, *river*	C2	68
Kilwa Kivinje	C2	68
Kimbe	B2	15
Kimberley	O6	95
Kimberley	B1	14
Kimberley	E3	102
Kimberley, *plateau*	B1	14
Kimch'aek	C2	9
Kimchŏn	B2	9
Kinabalu, *mt.*	D1	13
Kinabatangan, *river*	D2	13
Kinbasket, *lake*	B5	94
Kinbasket, *lake*	O5	95
Kincaid	C11	104
Kincardine	D3	102
Kindersley	A9	104
Kindia	B2	62
Kindu	C2	67
King Leopold, *range*	B1	14
King William, *island*	J3	99
King's Cove	E5	98
King's Landing	B3	97
King's Lynn	D3	30
King's Point	C4	98
Kingcome Inlet	H5	95
Kingman, Ariz.	C3	100
Kingston	C3	100
Kingston	J3	102
Kingston upon Hull	C3	30
Kingston upon Thames	Inset II	30
Kingston, *capital*	C3	88
Kingstown, *capital*	B2	91
Kingsville	F2	100
Kingsville	C5	102
Kinistino	E8	104
Kinkala	C6	66
Kinkora	B2	100
Kinloss	D3	102
Kinmount	G3	102
Kinnairds, *cape*	C1	30
Kinosota	B4	96
Kinsarvik	B3	52
Kinsella	E5	94
Kinshasa, *capital*	A2	67
Kinyeti, *mt.*	C4	59
Kioa, *island*	G1	102
Kiosk	C1	102
Kipengere, *range*	B2	68
Kipling	H10	104
Kirakira	B2	16
Kirensk	D7	44
Kırıkkale	C2	27
Kiritimati (Christmas), *island*	D1	17
Kirkcaldy	B2	30
Kirkenes	F2	52
Kirkfield	G3	102
Kirkland Lake	D3	101
Kirkpatrick, *mt.*	A5	107
Kirkuk	B1	24
Kirkwall	Inset I	30
Kirovakan	B2	45
Kirovograd	C2	47
Kirşehir	C2	27
Kirthar, *range*	C4	21
Kiruna	C1	53
Kisangani	C1	67
Kishi	B3	65
Kiskitto, *lake*	B2	96
Kiskőrei-víztároló, *lake*	C2	43
Kiskunhalas	B2	43
Kismayo	A3	60
Kissidougou	C3	62
Kissing, *lake*	C4	61
Kita	B3	58
Kitakami, *river*	D2	8
Kitakyushu	A3	8
Kitale	C3	61
Kitami	Inset I	8

	Key	Page
Kitami, *mts.*	Inset I	8
Kitchener	E4	102
Kitgum	C2	61
Kithira, *island*	B3	51
Kitikmeot, *region*	G3	99
Kitimat	H4	95
Kitwanga	H3	95
Kitwe	B2	67
Kivi, *river*	C2	53
Kivu, *lake*	B1	61
Kizil Irmak, *river*	C2	27
Kjølen, *mts.*	C1	53
Kladno	B2	42
Klagenfurt	D4	39
Klaipėda	A2	46
Klamath Falls, Oreg.	A1	126
Klarälven, *river*	B2	53
Klatovy	A2	42
Kleinburg	J5	102
Klemtu	H5	95
Kleve	A3	40
Kloulklubed	B3	17
Kluane, *lake*	B5	105
Knee, *lake*	D1	96
Knight, *inlet*	K6	95
Knockboy, *mt.*	B3	31
Knokke	B1	33
Knoxville, Tenn.	E2	126
Ko Chang, *island*	C3	12
Ko Kut, *island*	C4	12
Ko Phangan, *island*	B4	12
Ko Samui, *island*	B4	12
Ko Tarutao, *island*	B5	12
Kobe	C3	8
Koblenz	A3	40
Kobuleti	A4	45
Kočani	C2	48
Kočevje	B3	48
Kochi	B3	8
Kodiak, Alaska	Inset I	126
Kofarnihon, *river*	A2	23
Köflach	D3	39
Koforidua	B3	64
Kofu	C3	8
Køge	D3	32
Kohima	F3	20
Kohtla-Järve	D1	46
Koindu	B1	63
Koje-do, *island*	C5	9
Kokkina	A1	27
Kokkola	B2	53
Kokshetau	C1	23
Kola	A4	96
Kola, *peninsula*	C3	44
Kolari	B1	53
Kolda	B3	62
Kolding	B3	32
Kolhapur	B5	20
Kolín	B2	42
Kolobrzeg	B1	41
Kolpashevo	D6	44
Kolshet	Inset I	20
Kolumadulu, *atoll*	A3	19
Kolwezi	C3	67
Kolyma, *range*	C10	44
Kolyma, *river*	C9	44
Kolyma, *river*	—	—
Komadugu Gana, *river*	F2	65
Komadugu Yobe, *river*	F1	65
Komárno	B3	42
Komárom	B2	43
Komati, *river*	B2	71
Komatsu	C2	8
Komi, *republic*	C4	44
Komoé, *river*	E3	63
Komotiní	C1	51
Komsomolsk-na-Amure	D8	44
Konar, *river*	B1	22
Konduz	B1	22
Konduz, *river*	C2	18
Koné	D4	11
Kong, *river*	C2	12
Konibodom	B1	23
Konin	C2	41
Konnagar	Inset II	20
Konotop	C1	47
Kontagora	C2	65
Kontum	B3	11
Konya	C3	27
Kootenay, *lake*	O6	95
Kootenay, *river*	P6	95
Kopaonik, *mts.*	B3	49
Kópavogur	A2	52
Koper	A2	48
Kopet, *mts.*	B2, D2	22
Koprivnica	C2	48
Korab, *mt.*	A1	48
Korab, *mt.*	A2	48
Korçë	B3	49
Korčula, *island*	C4	48
Korea, *bay*	A3	9
Korea, *strait*	C5	9
Korhogo	D2	63
Koriyama	D2	8
Korla	B1	10
Koro	B4	59
Koro, *channel*	B2	17
Koro, *sea*	B2	17
Koror, *capital*	B3	17
Koror, *island*	B3	17
Körös, *river*	C2	43
Korosten	B1	47
Kortrijk	B2	33
Koryak, *range*	C10	44
Koryakia, *autonomous okrug*	C10	44
Kosŏng	C3	9
Kos, *island*	D3	51
Kosciusko, *mt.*	D3	14
Koshigaya	C3	8
Koshiki, *islands*	A4	8
Košice	C2	42
Kosovo, *autonomous province*	B3	49
Kosrae	D2	15
Kossol, *passage*	C2	17
Kossol, *reef*	Inset I	17
Kossou, *lake*	D3	63

Name	Key	Page
Koszalin	C1	41
Kota	C3	20
Kota Baharu	B1	13
Kota Kinabalu	D2	13
Kotcho, *lake*	M1	95
Kotka	C2	53
Kotlas	C4	44
Kotor, *gulf*	A3	49
Kotovsk	B2	47
Kotto, *river*	B2	66
Kouchibouguac	D2	97
Koudougou	C2	64
Koula-Moutou	B2	66
Koulikoro	B3	58
Koulountou, *river*	C3	62
Koumac	C2	18
Koungheul	B2	62
Kourou	B1	80
Kouroussa	D2	62
Kousséri	B1	65
Koutiala	B3	58
Kouto	C2	63
Kouvola	C2	53
Kovel	A1	47
Kowŏn	B3	9
Kowloon	Inset	10
Kowt-e Ashrow	B2	22
Kozáni	B1	51
Kozhikode	C6	20
Kozloduy	B2	50
Kozu, *island*	C3	8
Kožuf, *mts.*	C2	48
Kpalimé	C3	64
Kpandu	C3	64
Kpémé	B3	64
Kra, *isthmus*	B4	12
Kracheh	E3	11
Kragujevac	B2	49
Krakatau, *island*	B2	13
Kraków	D3	41
Kraljevo	B3	49
Kramatorsk	D2	47
Kranj	B2	48
Kranji	B1	13
Krasnodar	E3	44
Krasnoyarsk	D6	44
Krefeld	A3	40
Kremenchug	C2	47
Kretinga	A2	46
Kribi	A3	65
Krishna, *river*	C5	20
Kristiansand	B4	52
Kristianstad	B3	53
Kristiansund	B3	52
Kristinehamn	B3	53
Krivoy Rog	C2	47
Krk, *island*	B2	48
Krka, *river*	B2	48
Krong Kaoh Kong	A4	11
Kroonstad	C2	71
Krosnow	E4	41
Krško	C3	48
Krugersdorp	C2	71
Krujë	A2	49
Kruševac	B3	49
Kruševo	B2	48
Krychaw	E3	47
Kuala Abang	B2	13
Kuala Belait	A2	13
Kuala Lumpur, *capital*	A2	13
Kuala Terengganu	B2	13
Kuantan	B2	13
Kuching	C2	13
Kuchino, *island*	A4	8
Kudymkar	D4	44
Kufstein	C3	39
Kuito	C4	70
Kukës	B1	49
Kul, *river*	D4	22
Kula Kangri, *mt.*	B1	19
Kuldiga	A2	46
Kulmbach	B3	40
Kulob	A2	23
Kulpawn, *river*	B1	64
Kum, *river*	B4	9
Kumamoto	A3	8
Kumanovo	B1	48
Kumasi	B3	64
Kume, *island*	Inset II	8
Kumo	F2	65
Kunda	D1	46
Kunene, *river*	A1	70
Kunlun, *mts.*	B2	10
Kunming	D3	10
Kunsan	B5	9
Kuntaur	D2	62
Kuopio	C2	53
Kupa, *river*	C2	48
Kupang	D3	13
Kür, *river*	A2, C2	45
Kür-Aras, *lowland*	C2	45
Kura, *river*	E2	27
Kurashiki	B3	8
Kuraymah	C1	59
Kürdzhali	D4	50
Kure	B3	8
Kuressaare	B2	46
Kurgan	D5	44
Kuril, *islands*	E9	44
Kurinwás, *river*	B2	87
Kurla	Inset I	20
Kurnool	C5	20
Kuršénai	B1	46
Kursk	D3	44
Kuru, *river*	C2	10
Kuruman	B2	71
Kurume	A3	8
Kurunegala	B4	19
Kushiro	Inset I	8
Kushtia	C5	21
Kusti	C2	59
Kut, al-	C2	24
Kütahya	B2	27
Kutch, *gulf*	A4	20
Kutno	D2	41
Kuujjuaq	C2	101

Name	Key	Page
Kuujjuarapik	A2	101
Kuwait, *bay*	B2	24
Kuwait, *capital*	B2	24
Kwa, *river*	B2	67
Kwahu, *plateau*	B3	64
Kwajalein, *island*	B2	16
Kwangju	B5	9
Kwango, *river*	B2	67
Kwekwe	B2	69
Kyaukpyu	B2	12
Kyle	B10	104
Kyle of Lochalsh	B1	30
Kyoga, *lake*	C3	61
Kyŏngju	C5	9
Kyoto	B3	8
Kyrenia	B1	27
Kyrenia, *range*	B1	27
Kyushu, *island*	A3	8
Kyustendil	A3	50
Kyzyl	D6	44
Kyzyl-Kyya	C2	23
Kyzyl-Suu, *river*	C3	23
Kyzylkum, *desert*	B2	23

L

Name	Key	Page
La Asunción	D1	79
La Baie	F3	103
La Broquerie	C4	96
La Ceiba	B2	86
La Coma, *river*	B1	36
La Conception	B5	103
La Condamine	B1	35
La Coruña	B1	37
La Crete	B2	94
La Croix Maingot	A2	91
La Crosse, Wis.	D1	126
La Cruz	A1	86
La Digue, *island*	C1	70
La Doré	D3	103
La Esperanza	A2	86
La Goulette	C1	57
La Grande, *river*	B3	101
La Guadeloupe	F6	103
La Guaira Maiquetía	C1	79
La Have	C3	100
La Laguna	Inset I	37
La Libertad	A4	79
La Libertad	C3	85
La Loche	A4	104
La Louvière	C2	33
La Malbaie	F4	103
La Martre	K2	103
La Martre, *lake*	E4	99
La Montaña, *region*	C2	77
La Oroya	B3	77
La Palma	C2	87
La Palma, *island*	Inset I	37
La Paz	B2	86
La Paz, *capital*	A3	77
La Paz, *state capital*	B3	84
La Pérouse	B1	96
La Pérouse, *strait*	Inset I	8
La Plaine	B3	90
La Plata	D4	74
La Plata, *river*	C2	90
La Plonge, *lake*	C5	104
La Pocatière	F4	103
La Prairie	J6	103
La Rioja	B2	74
La Rioja	E1	37
La Rochelle	B3	34
La Roda	E3	37
La Romana	D2	89
La Ronge	E5	104
La Ronge, *lake*	E6	104
La Rosita	B2	87
La Salle	C4	96
La Salle	J6	103
La Scie	D4	98
La Serena	B3	76
La Spezia	B1	38
La Tortuga, *island*	C1	79
La Tuque	D4	103
La Unión	B7	76
La Unión	C2	86
La Vega	B1	89
La Virtud	A2	86
La-Roche-sur-Yon	B3	34
Labasa	A2	17
Labé	B2	62
Labe (Elbe), *river*	B2	42
Labelle	C3	100
Laberge, *lake*	B5	105
Labi	A3	13
Laborec, *river*	C2	42
Laborie	B3	91
Labrador City	D3	98
Labrieville	G2	103
Labu	C2	13
Labuan, *island*	D2	13
Laç	A2	49
Lac du Bonnet	C4	96
Lac La Biche	E4	94
Lac La Hache	M5	95
Lac Mégantic	F6	103
Lac-aux-Sables	D5	103
Lac-Bouchette	D3	103
Lac-des-Aigles	H4	103
Lac-des-Îles	A5	103
Lac-Édouard	D4	103
Lac-Etchemin	F5	103
Lac-Nominingue	A5	103
Lac-Saguay	A5	103
Laccadive, *islands*	B6	20
Lachenaie	J5	103
Lachine	H6	103
Lachute	B6	103
Lacombe	D5	94
Ladhiqiyah, al- (Latakia)	A2	27
Ladysmith	C2	71
Ladywood	C4	96
Lae	A2	15
Lae, *island*	B2	16
Laem, *mt.*	B3	12

Name	Key	Page
Læsø, *island*	C1	32
Lafayette, La.	D2	126
Lafia	E3	65
Lafleche	D11	104
Lafond	E4	94
Laghouat	B1	57
Lagodekhi	D4	45
Lagos	B4	65
Lagos	A4	36
Laguna de Bay, *lake*	B3	12
Lahave, *river*	C3	100
Lahij	A2	25
Lahn, *river*	B3	40
Lahore	E3	21
Lahti	C2	53
Laï	B5	59
Lairg	B1	30
Lajas	A2	90
Lajes	C4	81
Lakatoro	B3	18
Lake Alma	F11	104
Lake Charlotte	E3	100
Lake Edward	B2	97
Lake Harbour	O4	99
Lake Lenore	F8	104
Lake St. Peter	G2	102
Lake, *district*	B2	30
Lakeba, *island*	C3	17
Lakeba, *passage*	C3	17
Lakefield	G3	102
Lakelse Lake	H4	95
Lakhpat	A4	20
Laki, *volcano*	B2	52
Lakselv	F1	52
Lalitpur	C2	19
Lamaline	D5	98
Lamap	B3	18
Lambaréné	A2	66
Lambton	E6	103
Lamèque	E1	97
Lamèque, *island*	E1	97
Lami	B3	17
Lamía	B2	51
Lammermuir, *hills*	C2	30
Lamon, *bay*	B3	12
Lampa	Inset	76
Lampang	B2	12
Lampeter	B3	30
Lampman	H11	104
Lamu	F5	61
Lan, *island*	B2	9
Lanai island, Hawaii	Inset II	126
Lanark	J2	102
Lancaster	C2	30
Lancaster	L2	102
Land's End, *promontory*	B4	30
Lander, Wyo.	C1	126
Landes, *region*	B5	34
Landis	B8	104
Landshut	C4	40
Lang Son	B2	11
Langeburg, *mts.*	B3	71
Langeland, *island*	C4	32
Langenburg	J10	104
Langham	D8	104
Langkawi, *island*	A1	13
Langley	L6	95
Langruth	B4	96
Langstaff	K5	102
Langton	E5	102
Languedoc-Roussillon	C5	34
Lanigan	E9	104
Lanín, *volcano*	A4	74
Länkäran	C3	45
L'Annonciation	B5	103
Lansdowne	J3	102
Lansdowne House	C2	101
L'Anse-à-Valleau	M2	103
L'Anse-au-Loup	C3	98
L'Anse-aux-Gascons	M3	103
L'Anse-St-Jean	F3	103
Lansing, *capital, Mich.*	E1	126
Lantau, *island*	Inset	10
Lanús	D3	74
Lanzarote, *island*	Inset I	37
Lanzhou	D2	10
Lao Cai	A1	11
Laoag	B2	12
Laoang	C3	12
Laon	C2	34
Lapithos	B1	27
Lapland, *region*	B1	53
Lappeenranta	C2	53
Laptev, *sea*	B8	44
L'Aquila	C2	38
Larache	C1	57
Laramie, Wyo.	C1	126
Laredo, Tex.	D3	126
Lares	B2	90
Larestan, *region*	D4	22
Large, *island*	C1	91
Lárisa	B2	51
Lark Harbour	B4	98
Larkana	C4	21
Larkhall	C4	96
Larnaca	B2	27
Larne	C2	31
Larochette	B2	33
Larrys River	F2	100
Larsen Ice Shelf, *glacier*	C12	107
Las Cruces, N. Mex.	C2	126
Las Minas, *mt.*	B2	86
Las Palmas	Inset I	37
Las Piedras	D2	90
Las Piedras	B3	75
Las Tablas	B3	87
Las Tunas	E3	88
Las Vegas, N. Mex.	C1	126
Las Vegas, Nev.	B2	126
L'Ascension	B5	103
Lashburn	A7	104
Lashio	C2	12
Lashkar Gah	A2	22
Last Mountain, *lake*	E9	104
Latacunga	B3	79
Late, *island*	C2	17
Latina	C2	38

Name	Key	Page
Latium	C2	38
Lau, *island group*	C2	17
Laucala, *island*	C2	17
Laudat	B3	90
Lauder	A4	96
Launceston	B4	30
Launceston, Tas.	D4	14
Laurie River	A1	96
Laurier	B4	96
Lausanne	A2	35
Lautoka	A2	17
Laval	A2	35
Laval	C6, J5	103
Lavenham	B4	96
Lavoy	E4	94
Lavumisa	B3	71
Lawa, *river*	A2, B2	80
Lawn	D5	98
Lawrence Station	B3	97
Lawton, Okla.	D2	126
Layland	B4	96
Layou, *river*	B3	90
Lázaro Cárdenas	D4	84
Le Bic	H3	103
Le Creusot	D3	34
Le Havre	C2	34
Le Mans	C2	34
Le Puy	C4	34
Leader	A10	104
Leading Tickles	D4	98
Leaf Rapids	D1	96
Leamington	C5	102
l'Eau Claire, *lake*	B2	101
Lebanon, *mts.*	B1	26
Lebombo, *mts.*	C2, D1	71
Lebu	B6	76
Lecce	D2	38
Lech	B3	39
Lech, *river*	B4	40
Leduc	D4	94
Lee, *river*	B3	31
Leeds	C3	30
Leeton	Inset II	14
Leeuwarden	C1	32
Leeuwin, *cape*	A3	14
Leeward Group	B3	58
Lefka	A1	27
Lefkoniko	B1	27
Leganés	Inset II	37
Legazpi	B3	12
Legnica	C3	41
Leicester	C3	30
Leichhardt, *river*	D1	14
Leiden	B2	32
Leie, *river*	B3	33
Leikanger	B3	52
Leipzig	C3	40
Leiria	A3	36
Leitrim	H6	102
Leixões	A2	36
Lékéti, *mts.*	C5	66
Léloma	B2	62
Lelystad	C2	32
Lema, *river*	A1, B2	80
Lena, *river*	C8	44
Leninsk	C2	23
Lenghu	C2	10
Lengoué, *river*	C3	66
Lenore	A4	96
Lens	C1	34
Lensk	C7	44
Léo	B3	64
Leoben	D3	39
Léogâne	C2	89
León	D3	84
León	D1	37
Leone	B2	18
Leova	B2	50
Leoville	C7	104
Lepontine Alps, *mts.*	C2	35
Lepreau	C3	97
Lepsi	D2	23
Leribe	B1	71
Lérida	G10	104
Lerwick	Inset I	30
Les Cayes	C2	89
Les Éboulements	F4	103
Les Escaldes	B2	36
Les Escoumins	G3	103
Les Islets-Caribou	J2	103
Les Méchins	K3	103
Les Tantes, *island*	B1	91
Les Ulis	Inset II	34
Leskovac	B3	49
Lesosibirsk	D6	44
Lesser Caucasus, *mts.*	A2, B4	45
Lesser Hinggan, *range*	F1	10
Lesser Slave, *lake*	C3	94
Lesser Sunda, *islands*	C2	13
Lestrock	G9	104
Lésvos, *island*	C3	51
Leszno	C3	41
Lethbridge	D6	94
Lethbridge	E5	98
Lethem	B4	80
Letlhakeng	B3	69
Leticia	C6	78
Letterkenny	C1	31
Levallois-Perret	Inset II	34
Leveque, *cape*	B1	14
Leverkusen	A3	40
Levice	B2	42
Lévis	E5, L6	103
Levittown	D4	90
Lewes	D4	30
Lewisporte	D4	98
Lewiston, Idaho	B1	126
Lewiston, Maine	F1	126
Lexington, Ky.	E2	126
Leyte, *island*	C4	12
Lhasa	C3	10
Lhuntshi	C2	19
Lianyungang	E2	10
Liao, *river*	F1	10
Liaoning	F1	10

Name	Key	Page
Liaoyang	F1	10
Liaoyuan	F1	10
Liard River	J1	95
Liard, *river*	K1	95
Libau	C4	96
Liberec	B2	42
Liberia	A2	86
Libono	B1	71
Libreville, *capital*	A1	66
Libyan, *desert*	A2, D2	56
Lichfield	C3	30
Lichinga	B2	68
Lida	B3	47
Liège	D2	33
Lieksa	D2	53
Lienz	C4	39
Liepāja	A2	46
Lièvre, *river*	A5	103
Lifford	C1	31
Lifou, *island*	D2	18
Lifuka, *island*	C3	17
Liguria	B1	38
Ligurian, *sea*	B2	38
Lihir, *group*	B2	15
Likasi	C3	67
Likiep, *island*	B1	16
Lille	C1	34
Lille, *strait*	B3	32
Lillehammer	C3	52
Lillooet	M6	95
Lillooet, *river*	L6	95
Lilongwe, *capital*	B2	68
Lima, *capital*	B3	77
Lima, *river*	A2	36
Limassol	B2	27
Limbazi	C2	46
Limbe	A3	65
Limbourg	D2	33
Limburg	B2	31
Limerick	B2	31
Limfjorden, *channel*	B2	32
Límnos, *island*	C2	51
Limoges	C4	34
Limón	C3	86
Limousin	C4	34
Limpopo, *river*	C1	71
Linares	B5	76
Linares	E3	84
Linares	E3	37
Lincoln, *capital, Nebr.*	D1	126
Lindau	B5	40
Lindbergh	E4	94
Linden	B3	80
Linden	D2	100
Lindi	C2	68
Lindsay	G3	102
Line, *islands*	D1	17
Lingayen, *gulf*	B2	12
Lingga, *island*	B2	13
Lingshi	B2	19
Linguère	B2	62
Linköping	C3	53
Linhe	D1	10
Linnhe, *lake*	B2	30
Linvanti, *river*	A1	69
Linwood	F2	100
Linz	D2	39
Lion, *gulf*	D5	34
Lionel Town	B3	88
Lions Head	D3	102
Lipari, *islands*	C3	38
Lipetsk	D4	44
Lipova	A2	43
Lippstadt	B3	40
Lipton	G10	104
Liptovský Mikuláš	B2	42
Lira	C2	61
Lisala	B1	67
Lisbon, *capital*	A3	36
Lischansk	D2	47
L'Isle-Adam	Inset II	34
L'Isle-Verte	G3	103
Lismore, N.S.W.	E2	14
Listowel	E4	102
Litani, *river*	B2	26
Litani, *river*	A2, B3	80
Little Alföld, *plain*	A2	43
Little Andaman, *island*	F6	20
Little Bay	B5	98
Little Bras d'Or	G1	100
Little Current	D2	102
Little Fort	M5	95
Little Grand Rapids	D3	96
Little Inagua, *island*	C4	89
Little Rock, *capital, Ark.*	D2	126
Little Salmon, *lake*	C4	105
Little Scarcies, *river*	A1	63
Little Seldom	D4	98
Little Smoky, *river*	A4	94
Little St. Bernard, *pass*	D4	34
Little Zab, *river*	B1	24
Liuzhou	D3	10
Liverpool	C3	30
Liverpool	C3	100
Liverpool, *bay*	B3	30
Livingstone	B2	67
Livno	B2	48
Livorno	B2	38
Ljubljana, *capital*	B2	48
Ljusnälven, *river*	C2	53
Llallagua	A3	77
Llandrindod Wells	C2	30
Llanos, *plain*	C2	79
Llanos, *prairie*	C1	89
Llanquihue, *lake*	B7	76
Lleyn, *peninsula*	B3	30
Llorts	B1	36
Lloyd, *river*	B3	104
Lloydminster	E4	94
Lloydminster	A7	104
Lloyds, *river*	C5	98
Llullaillaco, *volcano*	B1	74
Lo Wu	Inset	10
Lo, *river*	A1	11
Loa, *river*	B2	76
Lobamba	B2	71
Lobatse	B3	69

Name	Key	Page
Lobaye, *river*	A2	66
Lobito	B4	70
Locarno	C2	35
Lockeport	B4	100
Lockport	C4	96
Lod (Lydda)	B2	26
Lodja	B2	67
Lodwar	C2	61
Łódź	D3	41
Loei	B2	12
Loess, *plateau*	D2	10
Lofoten, *islands*	C2	52
Logan, *river*	Inset III	14
Logan, Utah	B1	126
Logone, *river*	A5	59
Logroño	E1	37
Loi-kaw	C2	12
Loire, *river*	C3	34
Loíza	D2	90
Loja	B4	79
Loja	D4	37
Lokka, *reservoir*	C1	53
Lokoja	D4	65
Lokossa	A4	64
Lola	B3	59
Lolland, *island*	C4	32
Loma	B2	50
Lomami, *river*	C2	67
Lomas de Zamora	D4	74
Lomawai	A3	17
Lombardy	B1	38
Lombardy	J3	102
Lombok, *island*	C2	13
Lomé, *capital*	B3	64
Lomond, *lake*	B2	30
Łomża	F2	41
London	D5	102
London, *capital*	C3, Inset III	30
Londonderry	A2	30
Londrina	C4	81
Lone Butte	M5	95
Long Beach, Calif.	B2	126
Long island, N.Y.	F1	126
Long Lake	C3	101
Long Range, *mts.*	B5, C4	98
Long Xuyen	A4	11
Long, *island*	C3	89
Longford	C3	31
Longlac	C3	101
Longreach, Qld.	D2	14
Longueuil	J5	103
Longview, Tex.	D2	126
Loon Lake	C3	94
Loon Lake	A6	104
Loop Head, *cape*	B3	31
Lop Buri	B3	12
Lop, *lake*	C1	10
Lorca	F4	37
Loreburn	D9	104
Lorengau	A2	15
Loreto	B2	84
Lorette	C4	96
Loretteville	K5	103
Lorient	B3	34
L'Original	L2	102
Lorne, *estuary*	A2	30
Lorraine	D2	34
Lorraine	H5	103
Los Andes	B4	76
Los Ángeles	B6	76
Los Angeles, Calif.	B2	126
Los Chiles	B1	86
Los Mochis	C2	84
Los Reyes	Inset	84
Los Teques	C1	79
Lot, *river*	C4	34
Louang Namtha	A1	11
Loubomo	B6	66
Louga	A2	62
Lough Erne, *lake*	A2	30
Loughborough, *lake*	J3	102
Lougheed, *island*	G1	99
Louisbourg	H2	100
Louisdale	F2	100
Louiseville	D5	103
Louisiade, *archipelago*	B3	15
Louisiana	D2	126
Louisville, Ky.	E2	126
Lourdes	B5	34
Louri	C2	19
Louvain	C2	33
Louvres	Inset II	34
Lovech	C2	50
Lovell Village	B3	91
Lovettville	B4	96
Lowe Farm	C4	96
Lower Arrow, *lake*	N6	95
Lower Debert	D2	100
Lower Five Islands	C2	100
Lower Hutt	B3	15
Lower Montague	C2	100
Lower Post	H1	95
Lower Saxony	B2	40
Lower Tunguska, *river*	C6	44
Lower Woods Harbour	B4	100
Lowestoft	D3	30
Loyada	C2	60
Loyoro	D2	61
Loyalty, *islands*	C2	18
Lualaba, *river*	C2	67
Luanda, *capital*	B2	70
Luang Prabang	B2	11
Luang Prabang, *range*	A3	11
Luang, *mt.*	B4	12
Luangwa, *river*	C3	67
Luanshya	B2	67
Luapula, *river*	B2, C2	67
Luau	E3	70
Luba	A1	66
Lubango	B5	70
Lubbock, Tex.	C2	126
Lübeck	B2	40
Lubicon, *lake*	C3	94
Lublin	F3	41
Lubumbashi	C3	67
Lucapa	D2	70
Lucca	B2	38

Key	Page
Lucea	A2 88
Lucena	B3 12
Lucena	D4 37
Lučenec	B2 42
Lucern, *lake*	C2 35
Lucerne	C1 35
Lucie, *river*	A3 80
Luckenwalde	C2 40
Lucknow	D3 20
Lucknow	D4 102
Lucky Lake	C9 104
Luda Kamchiya, *river*	E3 50
Lüderitz	B4 70
Ludhiana	E2 50
Ludogorie, *region*	E2 50
Ludwigsburg	B4 40
Ludwigshafen am Rhein	B4 40
Luena	D3 70
Lugano	C3 35
Lugano, *lake*	C3 35
Lugansk	D2 47
Luganville	B2 18
Lugenda, *river*	C2 68
Lugo	C1 37
Lugoj	A3 43
Lukuga, *river*	C2 67
Luleå	D1 53
Luleälven, *river*	D1 53
Lumphat	F2 11
Lumsden	E4 98
Lumsden	F10 104
Lumut	A2 13
Lund	B3 53
Lund	K6 95
Lundar	B4 96
Lundazi	C2 67
Lundi, *river*	B2 69
Lüneburg	B2 40
Lünen	A3 40
Lunenburg	C3 100
Lunga, *river*	B2 67
Lungwebungu, *river*	A1 63
Lunsar	A1 63
Luoyang	E2 10
Lupeni	B3 43
Luperón	B1 89
Luquillo	D2 90
Luremo	C2 70
Lúrio, *river*	C2 68
Lusaka, *capital*	B3 67
Lusambo	B2 67
Luseland	A8 104
Lushnjë	A3 49
Lusutfu, *river*	B2 71
Luton	C3 30
Lutsk	B1 47
Lützow-Holm, *bay*	C16 107
Luuq	A3 60
Luvua, *river*	B1, C2 67
Luwegu, *river*	C2 68
Luxembourg, *capital*	B2 33
Luxor	B2 56
Luzarches	Inset II 34
Luzhou	D3 10
Luzon, *island*	B3 12
Luzon, *strait*	B2 12
Lviv	A2 47
Lyddal	B1 96
Lyme, *bay*	C4 30
Lynn Lake	C1 96
Lyon	D4 34
Lytton	M6 95

M

Key	Page
Ma, *river*	A2 11
Maan	A2 26
Maas, *river*	C3, D3 32
Maastricht	C4 32
Mabaruma	B1 80
Maberly	J3 102
Mabou	F1 100
Mac Tier	F2 102
MacAlpine, *lake*	H3 99
Macapá	C1 81
Macas	B4 79
Macau	7
Maccan	C2 100
Macdonnell, *ranges*	C2 14
Maceió	E2 81
Macenta	D3 62
Macerata	C2 38
Macfarlane, *river*	C2 104
Macgregor	B4 96
Machakos	D4 61
Machala	B4 79
Machida	C3 8
Machupicchu, *ruins*	C3 77
MacKay, *lake*	F4 99
Mackay, Qld.	D2 14
Mackenzie	L3 95
Mackenzie King, *island*	F1 99
Mackenzie, *bay*	B1 105
Mackenzie, *mts.*	C4 99
Mackenzie, *river*	B3, D4 99
Mackey	H1 102
Macklin	A8 104
Maclean, *strait*	G1 99
Macmillan, *river*	C4 105
Mâcon	D3 34
Macon, Ga.	E2 126
Madaba	A2 26
Madan	C4 50
Madang	A2 15
Madawaska	G2 102
Madden	C5 94
Madeira, *island*	A2 57
Madeira, *river*	B2 81
Madhumati, *river*	C5 21
Madhupur Tract, *region*	D4 21
Madinat ath-Thawrah	B2 27
Madison, *capital*, Wis.	E1 126
Madiun	C2 13
Madoc	H3 102
Madras	D6 20
Madre de Dios, *island*	A9 76
Madre de Dios, *river*	A2, C3 77
Madrid, *capital*	E2, Inset II 37
Madriu, *river*	B3 36
Madura, *island*	C2 13
Madurai	C7 20
Maebashi	C2 8
Maestra, *mts.*	D3 88
Maéwo, *island*	C2 18
Mafeteng	A2 71
Mafia, *island*	C2 68
Mafikeng	C2 71
Mafra	A3 36
Magadalena de Kino	B1 84
Magadan	D9 44
Magburaka	B1 63
Magdagachi	D8 44
Magdalena	B2 77
Magdalena Contreras	Inset 84
Magdalena, *island*	B7 76
Magdalena, *river*	B3 78
Magdeburg	B2 40
Magelang	C2 13
Magellan, *strait*	B9 76
Maggiore, *lake*	B1 38
Magnetawan	F2 102
Magnitogorsk	D4 44
Magog	D6 103
Mahabharat, *range*	C2 20
Mahajamba, *river*	B2 69
Mahajanga	B2 69
Mahalapye	B2 69
Mahallah al-Kubra, al-	B1 56
Mahanadi, *river*	D4 20
Mahaska	C4 94
Mahbas, al-	C1 58
Mahdia	B3 80
Mahé	C2 57
Mahé, *island*	C1, Inset 70
Mahébourg	C3 69
Mahilyow	E3 47
Mahim, *bay*	Inset I 20
Mahón	J3 37
Mai-Ndombe, *lake*	B2 67
Maidstone	D3 30
Maidstone	A7 104
Maiduguri	G2 65
Main Brook	C3 98
Main, *river*	B4 40
Main-à-Dieu	H1 100
Main-Danube, *canal*	B4 40
Maine	G1 126
Mainland, *island*	Inset I 30
Maintirano	A2 69
Mainz	B4 40
Maio, *island*	C3 58
Maipo, *river*	B4, Inset 76
Maipú	Inset 76
Maisí, *cape*	F3 88
Maisons-Laffitte	Inset II 34
Maitland Bridge	B3 100
Maíz, *islands*	C2 87
Maizuru	B3 8
Majardah, *river*	B1 57
Majé	Inset I 87
Majorca, *island*	H3 37
Majuro, *capital*	C2 16
Majuro, *island*	C2 16
Makamba	B3 61
Makassar, *strait*	C2 13
Makeni	B1 63
Makeyevka	D2 47
Makhachkala	E4 44
Makhaleng, *river*	A2 71
Makin, *island*	A1 17
Makkovik	B1 98
Makokou	B1 66
Makona, *river*	A1 63
Makoua	C4 66
Makran Coast, *range*	B5 21
Makung	A2 9
Makurdi	E4 65
Malabar, *coast*	B6 20
Malabo, *capital*	A1 66
Malacca, *strait*	A1, A2 13
Malad	Inset I 20
Maladzyechna	C2 47
Málaga	D4 37
Malagarasi, *river*	B1 68
Malaita, *island*	A1 16
Malakal	C3 59
Malakula, *island*	B3 18
Malang	C2 13
Malanje	C3 70
Malanville	B2 64
Mälaren, *lake*	C3 53
Malatya	D2 27
Malay, *peninsula*	A1 13
Malbaie, *river*	F4 103
Malbun	B2 33
Malcolm, *island*	A1 19
Malden, *island*	D2 17
Male Karpaty, *mts.*	A2 42
Male, *atoll*	A2 19
Male, *capital*	A2 19
Maleb	E6 94
Malegaon	B4 20
Mali Rajinac, *mt.*	B3 48
Malindi	F5 61
Mallaig	B1 30
Mallow	B2 31
Malmberget	D1 53
Malmédy	E2 33
Malmö	B3 53
Maloelap, *island*	C2 16
Malombe, *lake*	C2 68
Maloti, *mts.*	B2 71
Malta, *island*	B2 36
Malta, *capital*	B3 70
Maltahöhe	B3 70
Malton	J5 102
Mamári	B2 62
Mamawi, *lake*	E2 94
Mambéré, *river*	A2 66
Mamburao	B2 12
Mamiña	C2 76
Mamoré, *river*	B2 81
Mamou	A2 62
Mamry, *lake*	E1 41
Mamtalah, al-	B2 25
Mamuno	A2 69
Man	C3 63
Mana	B1 80
Mana, *river*	B1 80
Manado	D1 13
Managua, *capital*	A2 87
Managua, *lake*	A2 87
Manakara	B3 69
Manama, *capital*	B1 25
Manatí	B2 90
Manaus	B2 81
Manawan, *lake*	G5 104
Manbij	A1 27
Manchester	C3 30
Manchester, N.H.	F1 126
Manchurian, *plain*	F1 10
Mand, *river*	C4 22
Mandalay	C2 12
Mandalgov	C2 11
Mandara, *mts.*	B1 65
Mandaue	B4 12
Mandeville	B2 88
Mandurah, W.A.	A3 14
Manfredonia	C2 38
Manga, *region*	C2 59
Mangalore	B6 20
Mango	B1 64
Mangoky, *river*	A3 69
Manicouagan, *reservoir*	C3 101
Manicouagan Deux, *reservoir*	H2 103
Manigotagan	C3 96
Manila, *bay*	B3 12
Manila, *capital*	B3 12
Manisa	A2 27
Manito, *lake*	A8 104
Manitoba, *lake*	B3, B4, D2 96
Manitou	B4 96
Manitoulin, *island*	C2 102
Manitowaning	D2 102
Manitouwadge	C3 102
Maniwaki	A5 103
Manizales	B3 78
Mankato, Minn.	D1 126
Mankayane	B2 71
Mankota	C11 104
Mankulam	B2 19
Mannar, *gulf*	C7 20
Mannar, *island*	C7 20
Mannheim	B4 40
Manning	B3 94
Mannville	E4 94
Mano, *river*	A2, B2, B2 63
Manokwari	E2 13
Manono	C2 67
Manono, *island*	B2 18
Manor Park	H5 102
Manori, *point*	Inset I 20
Manouane	B4 103
Manp̄o	B2 9
Mansa	B2 67
Mansa Konko	B2 67
Mansel, *island*	M4 99
Manson Creek	K3 95
Mansurah, al-	B1 56
Manta	A3 79
Manta, *bay*	A3 79
Mantiqueira, *range*	D4 81
Mantua (Mantova)	B1 38
Manu, *island*	A2 15
Manus, *island*	A2 15
Manyara, *lake*	C1 68
Manzanillo	D3 88
Manzanillo	D4 84
Manzini	B2 71
Mao	A1 89
Mao	A4 59
Maple	J5 102
Maple Creek	A11 104
Maputo, *capital*	B5 68
Maquela do Zombo	C2 70
Mar Chiquita, *lake*	C3 74
Mar del Plata	D4 74
Mar, *range*	D4 81
Mara, *river*	C4 61
Maraba	D2 81
Maracaibo	B1 79
Maracaibo, *lake*	B2 79
Maracay	C1 79
Maradi	B3 59
Marajó, *island*	D2 81
Marakei, *island*	A1 17
Maramasike, *island*	B1 16
Maranhão	D2 81
Marano, *river*	C1 39
Marañón, *river*	B1, B2 77
Maras	D3 27
Marathon	C3 101
Marbella	D4 37
Marburg	B3 40
Marcelin	D8 104
Marche	C2 38
Marchena, *island*	Inset 79
Mardan	D2 21
Mardin	E3 27
Maré, *island*	D2 18
Maremma, *region*	B2 38
Margaree Forks	F1 100
Margaret, *lake*	C2 94
Margarita, *island*	D1 79
Margate	D3 30
Margherita, *peak*	A3 61
Mari El, *republic*	D4 44
Maria	L3 103
Maria, *islands*	B3 91
Mariana	D3 81
Marianao	B1 88
Marianas, *islands*	C3 84
Marías, *islands*	C3 84
Marib	B2 25
Maribor	C2 48
Marie Byrd Land, *region*	B8 107
Marie-Reine	B3 94
Mariehamn (Maarianhamina)	A2 53
Mariental	C3 70
Marigot	B2 90
Marijampolė	A2 46
Marinduque, *island*	B3 12
Marino	C2 18
Marion Bridge	G2 100
Maripasoula	A2 80
Mariscal Estigarribia	B3 75
Maritime Alps, *range*	D4 34
Maritsa, *river*	D3 50
Mariupol	D3 47
Marj 'Uyun	A2 26
Marj, al-	D1 56
Marka	A3 60
Markham	F4, K5 102
Markham, *river*	A2 15
Markstay	E1 102
Marl	A3 40
Marmara, *sea*	B2 27
Marmora	H3 102
Marne, *river*	C2, Inset II 34
Marneuli	C4 45
Maromokotro, *mt.*	B1 69
Marondera	B2 69
Maroni, *river*	A1 80
Maros	C2 43
Maroua	B1 65
Marovoay	B2 69
Marowijne, *river*	B2 80
Marquette, Mich.	E1 126
Marquis	B2 91
Marrakech	B2 57
Marsa al-Burayqah	C1 56
Marsabit	E2 61
Marsala	C3 38
Marsaxlokk, *bay*	C3 36
Marsden	A8 104
Marseille	D5 34
Marsh Harbour	B2 89
Marsoui	L2 103
Marten River	F1 102
Martensville	D8 104
Martin	D2 42
Martinique, *island*	82
Martins River	C3 100
Martorell	D2 92
Martuni	C2 45
Mary	C3 22
Mary's Harbour	D3 98
Maryborough, Qld.	E2 14
Maryfield	A4 96
Maryfield	J11 104
Maryland	F2 126
Marystown	D5 98
Masada, *ruins*	B2 26
Masai, *steppe*	C1 68
Masaka	B4 61
Masan	C5 9
Masaya	A3 87
Masbate	B3 12
Masbate, *island*	C6 103
Mascouche	C3 100
Maseru, *capital*	A2 71
Masfut	D2 25
Mashhad	D2 22
Masindi	B3 61
Masirah, *gulf*	C2 25
Masirah, *island*	C2 25
Mask, *river*	B2 31
Maskall	B2 85
Masqat, *capital*	C1 25
Massachusetts	F1 126
Massacre	B3 90
Massawa	B2 60
Massenya	B5 59
Masset	F4 95
Massey	C1 102
Massif Central, *plateau*	C4 34
Massif des Bongos, *range*	B2 66
Massy	Inset II 34
Masuda	A3 8
Masvingo	B2 69
Mat, *river*	B2 49
Matadi	A2 67
Matagalpa	B2 87
Matagami	A4 101
Matale	B4 19
Matam	C2 62
Matane	J3 103
Matanzas	B1 88
Matara	C2 19
Mataram	C2 13
Matautu	H2 37
Matawin, *river*	C5 103
Matehuala	D3 84
Matelot	A2 91
Matera	D2 38
Mathura	C3 20
Matlock	C3 30
Mato Grosso	C3 81
Mato Grosso do Sul	C4 81
Mato Grosso, *plateau*	C3 81
Matosinhos	A2 36
Matrah	C1 25
Matruh	A1 56
Matsoku, *river*	B2 71
Matsue	B3 8
Matsumoto	C2 8
Matsuyama	B3 8
Mattawa	G1 102
Mattawin, *river*	C5 103
Matterhorn, *mt.*	B3 35
Matthew Town	C4 89
Matthews Ridge	A2 80
Mauá	Inset II 81
Maui, *island*, Hawaii	Inset II 126
Maule, *river*	B5 76
Maun	A1 69
Maunturk, *mts.*	B2 31
Mauna Loa, *mt.*, Hawaii	Inset II 126
Maunabo	D2 90
Mauren	B1 33
Maurepas	Inset II 34
Mavinga	D5 70
May Pen	A3 85
Maya, *mts.*	B2 85
Mayaguana, *island*	C4 89
Mayaguana, *passage*	C4 89
Mayagüez	A2 90
Maydi	A1 25
Mayfair	C7 104
Maymont	C8 104
Maymyo	C2 12
Maynooth	H2 102
Mayo	B4 105
Mayo, *lake*	C4 105
Mayombé, *massif*	B5 66
Mayon, *volcano*	B3 12
Mayotte, *island*	C2 67
Mayreau, *island*	A4 91
Mayumba	A2 66
Mazabuka	B3 67
Mazandaran, *region*	B2 22
Mazar-e Sharif	B1 22
Mazaruni, *river*	A2 80
Mazatenango	C3 84
Mazatlán	C3 84
Mažeikiai	A1 46
Mazoe, *river*	B1 69
Mazyr	D3 47
Mbabane, *capital*	B2 71
Mbahiakro	D3 63
Mbaké	A2 62
Mbala	C1 67
Mbale	D3 61
Mbalmayo	B3 65
Mbandaka	B2 67
M'banza Congo	A2 70
Mbanza-Ngungu	A2 67
Mbarara	B4 61
Mbemkuru, *river*	C3 68
M'Beni	A1 67
Mbéré, *river*	B2 65
Mbeya	B2 68
Mbini	C3 66
Mbini, *river*	C3 66
Mboro, *river*	D2 66
Mboune	B2 62
Mbour	A2 62
Mbuji-Mayi	B2 67
Mbulzane, *river*	B2 71
Mbuluzi, *river*	B2 71
McAdam	B3 97
McAllen, Tex.	D3 126
McBride	M4 95
McCallum	C5 98
McCreary	A4 96
McDame	H1 95
McGee	B9 104
McKerrow	D1 102
McKinley *mt.*, Alaska	Inset I 126
McLeese Lake	L5 95
McLeod Lake	L4 95
McLeod Valley	C4 94
M'Clintock, *channel*	H2 99
M'Clure, *strait*	D2 99
McLure	L5 95
McMurdo, *sound*	B5 107
McRae	E8 104
Meacham	E8 104
Meadow Lake	B6 104
Meadow Portage	B3 96
Meaford	E3 102
Mealy, *mts.*	A3 98
Meander River	B1 94
Mecca	A2 24
Mechelen	C1 33
Mecklenburg, *bay*	B1 40
Mecklenburg-Western Pomerania	C2 40
Mecsek, *mts.*	B2 43
Medan	A1 13
Medellín	B3 78
Medford, Oreg.	A1 126
Medgidia	E3 43
Media,s	C2 43
Medicine Hat	E6 94
Medika	A4 96
Medina	A1 24
Medina del Campo	D2 37
Medit	B2 13
Mediterranean, *sea*	29
Medley	E4 94
Medora	A5 96
Meductic	B3 97
Meelpaeg, *lake*	C5 98
Meerut	C3 20
Meghna, *river*	D5 21
Meghri	D4 45
Meighen, *island*	J1 99
Meiktila	B2 12
Meissen	C3 40
Mejicanos	A2 86
Mékambo	B1 66
Mekele	C1 60
Meknès	C1 57
Mekong, *delta*	B5 11
Mekong, *river*	A1, A4, C4, D3 11
Mékrou, *river*	D2 64
Melaka	B2 13
Melbourne, Fla.	E3 126
Melbourne, Vic., *capital*	D3 14
Meldrum Bay	B2 102
Meleb	C3 96
Melekeok	C3 17
Mélèzes, *river*	B2 101
Melfi	C2 38
Melfort	E3 102
Melilla	A4 57
Melipilla	Inset 76
Melita	D3 47
Melitopol	D3 47
Mellieha	B2 36
Mellieha, *bay*	B2 36
Melo	C2 75
Melrose	E2 100
Melun	Inset II 34
Melville	H10 104
Melville, *island*	C1 14
Melville, *island*	F1 99
Melville, *lake*	B2 98
Melville, *peninsula*	M3 99
Memmingen	B5 40
Memphis, Tenn.	D2 126
Memphrémagog, *lake*	D6 103
Menai, *strait*	B3 30
Ménaka	D3 58
Mende	C4 34
Mendoza	B3 74
Menemen	B3 16
Menihek	D3 98
Mennecy	Inset II 34
Menominee, *islands*	A2 13
Menongue	C4 70
Mentawai, *islands*	A2 13
Menzel Bourguiba	B1 57
Meppel	D2 32
Mequinenza, *lake*	F2 37
Merano	B1 38
Merauke	F2 13
Mercedario, *mt*	B3 74
Mercedes	A2 75
Mergui	C3 12
Mergui, *archipelago*	C4 12
Mérida	C3 37
Mérida	B2 79
Mérida, *mts.*	B2 79
Mérida, *state capital*	G3 84
Meridian, Miss.	E2 126
Merigomish	E2 100
Merin, *lagoon*	D2 75
Merkys, *river*	C2 46
Meron, *mt.*	B1 26
Merredin, W.A.	A3 14
Merrick, *mt.*	A3 96
Merridale	A3 96
Merritt	M6 95
Mersch	B2 33
Mersey, *river*	C3 30
Mersin	C3 27
Merthyr Tydfil	B3 30
Meru	D3 61
Merume, *mts.*	A2 80
Mesaoria, *plain*	B1 27
Meseta, *plateau*	D3 37
Mesolóngion	B2 51
Mesopotamia, *region*	B2 24
Messina	C3 38
Messina, *strait*	C3 38
Mesta, *river*	B4 50
Meta Incognita, *peninsula*	P4 99
Meta, *river*	C3 78
Métabetchouan	E3 103
Metcalfe	K2 102
Meteghan	A3 100
Methariskaw	ES 94
Métis-sur-Mer	J3 103
Metiskow	ES 94
Metz	D2 34
Meulan	Inset II 34
Meuse, *river*	D2 33
Mexiana, *island*	D1 81
Mexicali, *state capital*	A1 84
Mexico City, *national capital*	E4, Inset 84
Mexico, *gulf*	82
Meymaneh	A1 22
Meyungs	B3 17
Mgwavuma, *river*	B3 71
Mhlume	B2 71
Miami	B4 96
Miami, Fla.	E3 126
Mianwali	D3 21
Miaoli	B1 9
Mica Creek	N5 95
Michalovce	C2 42
Miches	C2 89
Michigan	E1 126
Michigan, *lake*	E1 126
Michoacán	D4 84
Mico, *river*	B3 91
Micoud	G11 104
Midale	G11 104
Middelburg	C3 71
Middelburg	A3 32
Middle Andaman, *island*	F6 20
Middle Arm	C4 98
Middle Atlas, *ranges*	C1 57
Middle Lake	E8 104
Middle Musquodoboit	D2 100
Middlebro	D4 96
Middlesbrough	C2 30
Middleton	B3 100
Midi-Pyrénées	C5 34
Midland	F3 102
Midland, Tex.	C3 126
Midlands, *region*	C3 30
Miercurea Ciuc	C2 43
Mieres	D1 37
Mikkeli	C2 53
Mikkwa, *river*	C2 94
Mikomeseng	C2 66
Míkonos, *island*	C3 51
Mikura, *island*	C3 8
Miladummadulu, *atoll*	A1 19
Milagro	B4 79
Milan	C9 104
Milden	D3 14
Milford Haven	B3 30
Milford Sound	A3 15
Milh, *lake*	B2 24
Milk, *river*	E6 99
Mill Bay	K5 102
Mill Village	C3 100
Miller Lake	D2 102
Millet	D4 94
Milliken	K5 102
Milltown	D5 98
Millville	B2 97
Milne, *bay*	B3 15

Name	Key	Page
Milo	D6	94
Milo, river	D3	62
Mílos, island	C3	51
Milton	B2	100
Milton	F4	102
Milverton	E4	102
Milwaukee, Wis.	E1	126
Mimico	J6	102
Miminegash	A2	100
Mina Baranis	C3	56
Mina Salman	B1	25
Minami, island	Inset III	8
Minas	C3	75
Minas Gerais	D3	81
Minas, channel	C2	100
Minatitlán	F4	84
Minch, strait	B1	30
Mindanao, island	C5	12
Mindelo	B2	58
Mindemoya	C2	102
Minden	B3	102
Mindoro, island	B3	12
Mindoro, strait	B3	12
Miner's Bay	G3	102
Miner, river	B3	105
Mingäçevir	B2	45
Mingäçevir, reservoir	B2	45
Minho, river	A1	36
Minicoy, island	B7	20
Minija, river	A2	46
Miniota	A4	96
Minitonas	A3	96
Mink Creek	A3	96
Minna	D3	65
Minneapolis, Minn.	D1	126
Minnedosa	B4	96
Minnesota	D1	126
Miño, river	C1	37
Minorca, island	H2	37
Minot, N. Dak.	C1	126
Minsk, capital	C3	47
Minto	B4	96
Minto	C2	97
Minto	B4	105
Minto, lake	B2	101
Minton	F11	104
Minya, al-	B2	56
Miquelon, island	M4	92
Mira	H1	100
Mirabel	B6	103
Mirador Nacional, mt.	C3	75
Miraflores	B4	78
Miragoâne	B2	89
Miramichi	D1	97
Miramichi, bay	E1	97
Miranda de Ebro	E1	37
Mirbat	B3	25
Mirebalais	C2	89
Miri	D2	13
Mirnyy	C7	44
Mirpur Khas	C5	21
Mirror	D5	94
Miscou, island	E1	97
Miscouche	B2	100
Misere	Inset	70
Misery, mt.	B1	90
Miskolc	C1	43
Misool, island	E2	13
Missinipe	F5	104
Mississauga	F4, J6	102
Mississippi	D2	126
Mississippi, lake	J2	102
Mississippi, river	D1	126
Missoula, Mont.	B1	126
Missouri	D2	126
Missouri, river	D1	126
Mistassini	D1	103
Mistassini	D3	103
Mistassini	B3	101
Mistassini, river	D2	103
Mistatim	G8	104
Mistelbach	E2	39
Misurata	C1	56
Mitchell	D4	102
Mitchell, mt., N.C.	E2	126
Mitchell, river	D1	14
Mitchinamécus, lake	A4	103
Mitilíni	C2	51
Mito	D2	8
Mitsamiouli	A1	67
Mittelland, canal	B2	40
Mitú	C4	78
Mitumba, mts.	C2	67
Mitzic	A1	66
Miyake, island	C3	8
Miyako	D2	8
Miyako, island	Inset II	8
Miyakonojo	A4	8
Miyazaki	A4	8
Mizen Head, cape	B3	31
Mizo, hills	F4	20
Mizpe Ramon	B2	26
Mjøsa, lake	C3	52
Mkondvo, river	B2	71
Mliba	B2	71
Mmabatho	C2	71
Mo	C2	52
Moa, island	D2	13
Moa, river	B2	63
Moab, Utah	C2	126
Moala, island group	B3	17
Moanda	B2	66
Moba	C2	67
Mobaye	B3	66
Mobile, Ala.	E2	126
Moca	B1	89
Moca	A2	90
Moçambique	D2	68
Mocha, (Mukha, al-)	A2	25
Mocímboa da Praia	D1	68
Môco, mt.	C4	70
Mocoa	A4	78
Modena	B1	38
Moengo	B2	80
Moers	A3	40
Mogadishu, capital	C3	60
Mogami, river	D2	8
Mogi das Cruzes	Inset II	81
Mogilev Podolskiy	B2	47
Mogocha	D7	44
Mogotón, mt.	A2	87
Mohács	B2	43
Mohales Hoek	A3	71
Mohammedia	C1	57
Moher, cliffs	B2	31
Mojave, desert, Calif.	B2	126
Mojos	A2	77
Mokhotlong	C2	71
Mokolo	B1	65
Mokpb	B5	9
Mold	B3	30
Moldavia, region	D2	43
Molde	B3	52
Moldoveanu, mt.	D3	43
Molepolole	B3	69
Molise	C2	38
Mollendo	C4	77
Molokai island, Hawaii	Inset II	126
Molopo, river	B2	71
Moloundou	C3	65
Molson, lake	C2	96
Molucca, sea	D2	13
Moluccas, islands	D2	13
Mombasa	E5	61
Mombetsu	Inset I	8
Mon Repos	B2	91
Møn, island	D4	32
Mona, passage	D2	89
Monaco, capital	B1	35
Monaghan	C1	31
Monastery	F2	100
Monastir	C2	57
Mönchengladbach	A3	40
Monclova	D2	84
Moncton	E2	97
Mondego, cape	A2	36
Mondego, river	A2	36
Monforte	C1	37
Mongo	B4	59
Mongolian, plateau	C2	11
Mongomo	D3	66
Mongu	A3	67
Monitor	E5	94
Monjolo	Inset I	81
Monkey Bay	B2	68
Mono, river	A4, B2	64
Monopoli	D2	38
Monrovia, capital	A2	63
Mons	B2	33
Mont-Carmel	G4	103
Mont-Joli	H3	103
Mont-Laurier	A5	103
Mont-Royal	J5	103
Mont-Saint-Michel	B2	34
Mont-St-Pierre	L2	103
Mont-Tremblant-Village	B5	103
Montague	C2	100
Montalto, mt.	C3	38
Montana	B2	50
Montana	B1	126
Montargis	C2	34
Montauban	C4	34
Monte Carlo	B1	35
Monte Cristi	A1	89
Monte Plata	C2	89
Montebello	B6	103
Montecristo, island	B2	38
Montegiardino	B2	39
Montego Bay	B2	88
Montélimar	D4	34
Montellno, river	C3	75
Montenegro, republic	A3	49
Montepulciano	B2	38
Monterey, Calif.	A2	126
Montería	B2	78
Montero	B3	77
Monterrey, state capital	D2	84
Montes Claros	D3	81
Montevideo, capital	B3	75
Montgomery, capital, Ala.	E2	126
Montluçon	C3	34
Montmagny	F5	103
Montmartre	G10	104
Montpelier, capital, Vt.	F1	126
Montpellier	C5	34
Montréal, island	J5	103
Montreal, lake	E6	104
Montreal, river	E6	104
Montreuil	Inset II	34
Montreux	A2	35
Montrose	C2	30
Monywa	B2	12
Monza	B1	38
Moore Park	B4	96
Moose Factory	D2	101
Moose Jaw	E10	104
Moose Lake	A2	96
Moose, river	D2	101
Moosehorn	B3	96
Moosomin	J10	104
Moosonee	D2	101
Mopti	C3	58
Moquegua	C4	77
Moradabad	C3	20
Morant Bay	C3	88
Moratuwa	B2	63
Morava, river	A2, C3	42
Morava, river	B3	49
Moravia, region	C3	42
Moray, estuary	B1	30
Morden	B4	96
Mordovia, republic	E4	44
Moree, N.S.W.	D2	14
Morehead	A2	15
Morelia, state capital	D4	84
Morell	C2	100
Morelos	E4	84
Morena, mts.	D3	37
Moresby, island	F5	95
Moreton, bay	Inset III	14
Morgan City, La.	D3	126
Morges	A2	35
Morghab, river	A1	22
Morghob	B1	23
Morghob, river	B1	23
Morice, lake	J4	95
Moricetown	J3	95
Morija	A2	71
Morinville	D4	94
Morioka	D2	8
Morlaix	B2	34
Morne Diablotin, mt.	B2	90
Moro, gulf	B5	12
Moro	A2	63
Morogoro	C2	68
Morombe	A3	69
Morón	D2	88
Mörön	C2	11
Morón de la Frontera	D4	37
Morondava	A3	69
Moroni, national capital	A1	67
Morotai, island	D1	13
Moroto	D2	61
Morpeth	D5	102
Morphou	A1	27
Morris	D5	94
Morris	C4	96
Morrisburg	K3	102
Mors, island	B2	32
Morse	C10	104
Mortlach	D10	104
Mortlock, islands	C2	15
Moruga	A2	91
Morvan	A4	40
Mosel, river	A4	40
Moshi	C1	68
Mosjøen	C2	52
Mosquitos, coast	C3	87
Moss	C4	52
Mossbank	E11	104
Mossel Bay	B3	71
Mossendjo	B5	66
Mossleigh	D6	94
Mossy, river	F6	104
Most	A2	42
Mostaganem	B1	57
Mostar	B2	48
Móstoles	Inset II	37
Mosul	B1	24
Motagua, river	D4	85
Motherwell	B2	30
Mouila	A2	66
Mould Bay	E1	99
Moule à Chique, cape	B3	91
Moulins	C3	12
Moulmein	C3	12
Moulouya, river	D1	57
Moundou	B5	59
Mount Carmel	A2	100
Mount Gambier, S.A.	D3	14
Mount Hagen	A2	15
Mount Isa, Qld.	C2	14
Mt. Stewart	C2	100
Mountain Park	B5	94
Moura	B3	36
Mourne, mts.	A2	30
Mouscron	B2	33
Moussa Ali, mt.	B1	60
Mouths of the Danube, delta	E3	43
Mouths of the Ganges, delta	C7	21
Mouths of the Indus, delta	C5	21
Moyale	C2	61
Moyamba	A1	63
Moyie	P6	95
Moyobamba	B2	77
Moyowosi, river	B1	68
Mozambique, channel	22	69
Mozzoro	E2	81
Mpanda	B2	68
Mpika	C2	67
Mpoko, river	A2	66
Mporokoso	C1	67
Mqinvartsveri, mt.	C3	45
M'Ramani	B2	67
Mtkvari, river	C4	45
Mtshketa	C4	45
Mtwara	D3	68
Muang Khammouan	C3	11
Muang Không	C4	11
Muang Khôngxédôn	C4	11
Muang Paklay	A2	11
Muang Pakxan	B2	11
Muang Vangviang	B2	11
Muang Xaignabouri	A2	11
Muang Xay	A1	11
Muang Xépôn	D3	11
Muang Xon	B1	11
Muar	B2	13
Muara	C1	13
Mubende	B3	61
Mubi	G2	65
Muchinga, mts.	C2	67
Mudanjiang	F1	10
Mudawwarah, al-	B3	26
Mufulira	B2	67
Muğla	B3	27
Muharraq, al-, island	B1	25
Mühlhausen	B3	40
Mui Bai Bung, point	A5	11
Mukalla, al-	B2	25
Muko, island	Inset III	8
Mukumbura, al-	A3	19
Mulde, river	C3	40
Mulhacén, mt.	E4	37
Mülheim an der Ruhr	A3	40
Mulhouse	D3	34
Mull, island	A2	30
Mullaittivu	B2	19
Mullingar	C2	31
Multan	D3	21
Mulund	Inset I	20
Mulvihill	B4	96
Mumbai	Inset I	20
Mumbwa	B3	67
Mun, river	C3	12
Muna, island	D2	13
Munamägi, mt.	D3	46
Muncho Lake	K2	95
Munich	B4	40
Munsan	B4	9
Münster	A3	40
Munster, province	B2	31
Muonio	B1	53
Muonioälven, river	D1	53
Muoniojoki, river	B1	53
Mur, river	D3	39
Mura, river	C2	48
Muramvya	B2	61
Murat, river	E2	27
Murchison, river	A2	14
Murcia	F4	37
Murdochville	L3	103
Mureş, river	B2	43
Murgab, river	D3	22
Muriel, lake	E4	94
Murilo, atoll	C2	15
Müritz, lake	C2	40
Murmansk	C3	44
Muroran	D1, Inset I	8
Muroto, cape	B3	8
Murray Harbour	C3	100
Murray River	C2	100
Murray, harbour	C2	100
Murray, lake	A2	15
Murray, river	D3	14
Murray, river	C1	14
Murrumbidgee, river	D3	14
Murska Sobota	D2	48
Mürz, river	D3	39
Murzuq	B2	56
Muş	E2	27
Müša, river	B1	46
Musala, mt.	B3	50
Musan	C1	9
Musgrave Harbour	E4	98
Musgrave, ranges	C2	14
Musgravetown	E5	98
Mushin	B4	65
Muskeg River	A4	94
Muskegon, Mich.	E1	126
Muskogee, Okla.	D2	126
Muskoka, lake	F2	102
Muskwa, ranges	J2	95
Musoma	B1	68
Musquodoboit Harbour	D3	100
Mussau, island	A2	15
Mustang	B2	19
Mustique, island	B3	91
Mustvee	D2	46
Musu-dan, point	C2	9
Mut	A2	56
Mutare	C2	69
Mutsamudu	A2	67
Mutsu	D1	8
Muyinga	C1	61
Muyun Kum, desert	C2	23
Muzaffarabad	D2	21
Muynoq	A2	23
Mwali (Mohéli), island	A2	67
Mwanza	B1	68
Mwene-Ditu	B2	67
Mweru, lake	B1, C3	67
Mwinilunga	A2	67
My Tho	B4	11
Myingyan	B2	12
Myitkyina	C1	12
Mymensingh	D4	21
Myrnam	E4	94
Mysore	C6	20
Mzimba	B2	68
Mzuzu	B2	68

N

Name	Key	Page
N'dalatando	B3	70
N'Djamena, capital	A4	59
N'zeto	B2	70
Naas	C2	31
Nabatiyah at-Tahta, an-	A2	26
Naberezhnyye Chelny	D4	44
Nabeul	C1	57
Nabk, al-	A2	27
Nabouwalu	B2	17
Nacala	D2	68
Nacaome	B3	86
Nackawic	B3	97
Nadi	A2	17
Nadi, bay	A2	17
Nadur	B1	36
Naduri	B2	17
Næstved	C3	32
Nafud, an-, desert	B1	24
Nag Hammadi	B2	56
Naga	B3	12
Naga, hills	F3	20
Nagano	C2	8
Nagaoka	C2	8
Nagarote	A2	87
Nagasaki	A3	8
Nagoya	C2	8
Nagpur	C4	20
Nagua	C1	89
Naguabo	D2	90
Nagykanizsa	A2	43
Naha	Inset II	8
Nahanni, river	C4	99
Nahariyya	B1	26
Naicam	F8	104
Naihati	Inset II	20
Nain	E3	98
Nairobi, capital	D4	61
Najaf, an-	B2	24
Najd, region	B1	24
Najin	D1	9
Najran	B2	24
Nakadori, island	A4	8
Nakano, island	A4	8
Nakfa	B1	60
Nakhichevan	A3	45
Nakhodka	E8	44
Nakhon Phanom	C2	12
Nakhon Ratchasima	C2	12
Nakhon Sawan	B3	12
Nakhon Si Thammarat	B4	12
Nakina	C2	101
Nakodu	B2	17
Nakskov	C4	32
Naktong, river	C5	9
Nakuru	D4	61
Nakusp	O6	95
Nal, river	B4	21
Nalikul	Inset II	39
Nam Dinh	B2	11
Nam Ngum, reservoir	B2	11
Nam Tok	B3	12
Namangan	D2	23
Namew, lake	H6	104
Namib, desert	A1, B3	70
Namibe	B5	70
Namoluk, atoll	C2	15
Namonuito, atoll	C2	15
Nampb	A3	9
Nampa	B3	94
Nampula	C2	68
Namsos	C3	52
Namu, island	B2	16
Namuli, highlands	C2	68
Namur	C2	33
Namur, lake	D2	94
Namwala	B3	67
Nan	B2	12
Nan Ling, mts.	E3	10
Nan, river	B2	12
Nanaimo	L6	95
Nanchang	E3	10
Nanchong	D2	10
Nancy	D2	34
Nanda Devi, mt.	C2	20
Nanded	C5	20
Nanga Parbat, mt.	E2	21
Nanga-Eboko	B3	65
Nangi	Inset II	20
Nangnim-sanmaek, mts.	B3	9
Nanjing	E2	10
Nanning	D3	10
Nanole	Inset I	20
Nantbu	B2	9
Nanterre	Inset II	34
Nantes	B3	34
Nanticoke	E5	102
Nanumanga, island	B2	16
Nanumea, island	B2	16
Nanyang	E2	10
Nao, cape	G3	37
Napadogan	C2	97
Napaktulik, lake	F3	99
Napanee	J3	102
Napier	C2	15
Naples	C2	38
Naples, bay	C2	38
Napo, river	B3	8
Nara	C2	8
Nara, canal	C4	21
Narathiwat	B5	12
Narayanganj	D5	21
Narayani, river	B2	19
Narbonne	C5	34
Narcisse	C4	96
Nares, strait	O1	99
Narew, river	E2	41
Narmada, river	C4	20
Narok	C4	61
Narrogin, W.A.	A3	14
Narrows, strait	B4	94
Narsaq	C2	106
Narva	E1	46
Narva, river	D1	46
Naryan-Mar	C4	44
Naryn	E2	23
Naryn, river	E2	23
Nashshash, an-	C3	25
Nashville, capital, Tenn.	E2	126
Nashwaak Bridge	C2	97
Näsi, lake	B2	53
Nasik	B4	20
Nasiriyah, an-	C2	24
Nass, river	H3	95
Nassau, capital	B2	89
Nasser, lake	B3	56
Nata	B2	69
Natal	E2	81
Natalkuz, lake	K4	95
Natashquan	D3	101
Natitingou	A2	64
Natron, lake	C1	68
Natuna Besar, island	B1	13
Naucalpan de Juárez	Inset	84
Naujoji Akmenė	B1	46
Naumburg	B3	40
Navabad	A1	23
Navarino, island	C9	76
Navarra	F1	37
Navojoa	C2	84
Navua	B3	17
Navua, river	A3	17
Nawabshah	C4	21
Nawoiy	C2	23
Náxos, island	C3	51
Nayarit	B3	84
Nazareth	B1	26
Nazca	C3	77
Naze	Inset II	8
Nazko	L5	95
Nazret	C2	60
Nchelenge	B1	67
Ndélé	B2	66
Ndendé	A2	66
Ndjolé	A2	66
Ndola	B2	67
Néa Liósia	Inset	51
Neagh, lake	A2	30
Neápolis	B3	51
Nebitdag	A2	22
Nebligan, mt.	B1	81
Nebraska	D1	126
Neckar, river	B4	40
Necochea	D4	74
Neder Rijn, river	C3	32
Nee Soon	B1	13
Needles	N6	95
Neepawa	B4	96
Nefta	A3	57
Negele	C3	60
Negev, region	B2	26
Negombo	A4	19
Negra, lagoon	D2	75
Negra, point	A2	77
Negril	A2	88
Negro, river	B2	74
Negro, river	B2	81
Negro, river	C2	75
Negros, island	B4	12
Neguac	D1	97
Neiafu	C2	17
Neiba	A2	89
Neiba, mts.	A2	89
Neijiang	D3	10
Neil Harbour	G1	100
Neilburg	A8	104
Neisse, river	C3	40
Neiva	B4	78
Nekemte	B2	60
Nellore	C6	20
Nelson	B3	15
Nelson	O6	95
Nelson Forks	L1	95
Nelson House	B1	96
Nelson, river	C1, D1	96
Nelspruit	D2	71
Néma	D3	58
Nemeiben, lake	E5	104
Nemunas, river	C2	46
Nemuro	Inset I	8
Nemuro, strait	Inset I	8
Nenagh	B2	31
Nendo, island	C2	16
Nenetsia, autonomous okrug	C4	44
Nepalganj	B2	19
Nepean	G6, K2	102
Nepisiguit, river	C1	97
Neretva, river	B2	48
Neris, river	C2	46
Ness, lake	B1	30
Nesselrode, mt.	E1	95
Nestaocano, river	C2	103
Netanya	B1	26
Nettilling, lake	O3	99
Netzahualcóyotl	Inset	84
Neubrandenburg	C2	40
Neuchâtel	A2	35
Neuchâtel, lake	A2	35
Neudorf	G10	104
Neufchâteau	D3	33
Neumünster	B1	40
Neunkirchen	A4	40
Neuquén	B4	74
Neusiedler, lake	E3	39
Neuss	A3	40
Neustadt	A2	85
Neustrelitz	C2	40
Nevada	B2	126
Nevada, mts.	E4	37
Nevers	C3	34
Neves	B4	63
Nevėžis, river	B2	46
Nevis, island	C3	90
Nevşehir	Inset I	81
Nevis	C4	90
New Amsterdam	C2	80
New Brigden	E5	94
New Britain, island	B2	15
New Caledonia, island	C2	14
New Carlisle	L4	103
New Delhi, capital	C3	20
New Denver	O6	95
New England, range	E3	14
New Ferolle	C4	98
New Fish Creek	B3	94
New Georgia Group, islands	A1	15
New Glasgow	E2	100
New Guinea, island	A2	15
New Hamburg	E4	102
New Hampshire	F1	126
New Hanover, island	B2	15
New Haven, Conn.	F1	126
New Ireland, island	B2	15
New Jersey	F1	126
New Kowloon	Inset	10
New Liskeard	E3	101
New Mexico	C2	126
New Minas	C2	100
New Orleans, La.	D3	126
New Plymouth	B2	15
New Providence, island	B3	89
New Richmond	L3	103
New Ross	C3	100
New Sandy Bay	B1	91
New Schwabenland, region	B16	107
New Siberian, islands	B9	44
New South Wales	D3	14
New Territories, island	Inset	10
New Waterford	G1	100
New Waterway, channel	B3	32
New York	F1	126
New York, N.Y.	F1	126
New, river	C4	80
New, river	B1	85
Newark, N.J.	F1	126
Newboro	J3	102
Newcastle	C2	90
Newcastle	C2	71
Newcastle upon Tyne	C2	30
Newcastle, N.S.W.	E3	14
Newcastle-under-Lyme	C3	30
Newdale	A4	96
Newell, lake	E6	94
Newman, W.A.	A2	14
Newmarket	F3	102
Newmarket	D3	102
Newport News, Va.	F2	126
Newquay	B4	30
Newry	A2	30
Newtown St. Boswells	C2	30
Neyagawa	B3	8
Neyshabur	D2	22
Ngami, lake	A2	69
Ngaoundéré	B2	65
Ngara	B1	68
Ngaramasch	B4	17

	Key	Page
Ngauruhoe, mt.	C2	15
Ngerkeel	B3	17
Ngemelis, islands	B3	17
Ngermechau	C2	17
Ngetbong	C2	17
Ngiro, river	D3	61
Ngoc Linh, mt.	B3	11
Ngonini	B1	71
Ngorongoro, crater	C1	68
Ngounié, river	A2	66
Ngozi	B1	61
Nguigmi	C3	59
Ngulu, atoll	A2	15
Nguru	F1	65
Ngwempisi, river	A2	71
Nha Trang	B4	11
Nhlangano	B3	71
Niagara Falls	F4	102
Niagara-on-the-Lake	F4	102
Niagassola	D1	62
Niamey, capital	A3	59
Niamtougou	B2	64
Niari, river	B5	66
Nias, island	A1	13
Nibok	B2	16
Nicaragua, lake	B3	87
Nice	D5	34
Nicholls' Town	A2	89
Nickerie, river	A2	80
Nicobar, islands	F7	20
Nicola	M6	95
Nicolet	D5	103
Nicosia, capital	B1	27
Nicoya, gulf	B3	86
Nictau	B1	97
Nidže, mts.	B3	48
Niedere Tauern, range	D3	39
Niefang	C3	66
Nienburg	B2	40
Niéri Ko, river	C2	62
Nieuw Amsterdam	B2	80
Nieuw Nickerie	A2	80
Nigadoo	D1	97
Niğde	C3	27
Niger, delta	C5	65
Niger, river	B3	58
Nii, island	C3	8
Niigata	C2	8
Niihama	B3	8
Niihau, island, Hawaii	Inset II	126
Nijmegen	C3	32
Nikaia	Inset	
Nikki	B3	64
Nikko	C2	8
Nikolayev	C3	47
Nikolayevsk-na-Amure	D9	44
Nikopol	C2	47
Nikšić	A3	49
Nikunau, island	A2	17
Nilandu, atoll	A3	19
Nile, river	B2	56
Nilgiri, hills	C6	20
Nilópolis	Inset I	81
Nimba, mt.	B3	63
Nimba, mts.	B2	63
Nîmes	D5	34
Nine Mile River	D2	100
Ninette	A4	96
Ninga	B4	96
Ningbo	F3	10
Ningxia Hui	D2	10
Ninigo, group	A2	15
Niono	B3	58
Nioro du Rip	B3	62
Nioro du Sahel	B2	58
Niort	B3	34
Nipawin	F7	104
Nipigon	C3	101
Nipigon, lake	C3	101
Nipissing	F1	102
Nipissing, lake	F1	102
Niš	B3	49
Nišava, river	C3	49
Nishino, island	Inset III	8
Nishinomiya	B3	8
Nisling, river	B4	105
Niterói	D4, Inset I	81
Nitra	B2	42
Niuafo'ou, island	B1	17
Niuatoputapu, island	C1	17
Niulakita, island	C4	16
Niutao, island	B2	16
Niverville	C4	96
Nizamabad	C5	20
Nizhnevartovsk	C5	44
Nizhny Novgorod	D4	44
Nizhny Tagil	D4	44
Njazidja (Grande Comore), island	A1	67
Njombe, river	B2	68
Nkawkaw	B3	64
Nkhata Bay	B2	68
Nkhotakota	B2	68
Nkongsamba	A2	65
Noakhali	E6	21
Nobeoka	A3	8
Noel	D2	100
Nogales	B1	84
Nogales, Ariz.	B2	126
Nojima, cape	D3	8
Nok Kundi	B4	21
Nokaneng	A1	69
Nokomis	E9	104
Nola	A3	66
Nome, Alaska	Inset I	126
Nonacho, lake	G4	99
Nong Khai	C2	12
Nonsan	B4	9
Nonthaburi	B3	12
Nootka, island	J6	95
Norak	A1	23
Nord-Ostsee, canal	B1	40
Nord-Pas-de-Calais	C1	34
Nordenham	B2	40
Nordhausen	B3	40
Nordhorn	A2	40
Nordvik	B7	44
Norfolk	D5	94

	Key	Page
Norfolk, Va.	F2	126
Norilsk	C6	44
Norland	G3	102
Normandin	D3	103
Norquay	H9	104
Norra Storfjället, mt.	C1	53
Norris Arm	D4	98
Norris Point	C4	98
Norrköping	C3	53
Norte, key	E2	90
N. Albanian Alps, mts.	A1, B3	49
North Andaman, island	F6	20
North Battleford	B8	104
North Bay	F1	102
North Cape	B1	100
North Carolina	F2	10
North China, plain	B1	36
North Comino, channel	B1	36
North Dakota	C1	126
North Downs, hills	C3	30
North Frisian, islands	B4	32
North Holland, canal	B2	32
North Magnetic Pole	B13	106
North Malosmadulu, atoll	A2	19
N. Moose, lake	B2	96
North Ossetia, republic	E4	44
North Platte, Nebr.	C1	126
North Portal	H11	104
North Rhine-Westphalia	A3	40
North Rustico	B2	100
North Saskatchewan, river	D8	104
North Sea, canal	B2	32
North Shields	C2	30
North Siberian, lowland	B6	44
North Star	B3	94
North Taranaki, bight	B2	15
N. Thompson, river	N5	95
North Uist, island	A1	30
North Wabasca, lake	D3	94
North West River	A2	98
North West, cape	A2	14
North York	K5	102
North, cape	F1	52
North, channel	A2	30
North, channel	B1	102
North, channel	B2	15
North, river	B2	98
North, sea		29
Northallerton	C2	30
Northampton	C3	30
Northeast, polder	C2	32
Northeim	B3	40
Northern Divina, river	C4	44
Northern European, plain	B2	40
Northern Sporades, islands	B2	51
Northern Territory	C2	14
Northgate	H11	104
Northumberland, strait	B3, D2	100
Northwest Gander, river	D5	98
Norton	D3	97
Norvegia, cape	B14	107
Norway House	C2	96
Norwegian, bay	K1	99
Norwegian, sea	A2	52
Norwich	D3	30
Norwich	E4	102
Nossob, river	C3	70
Nosy Be, island	B1	69
Nosy Sainte Marie, island	B2	69
Noteć, river	C2, D2	41
Noto, peninsula	C2	8
Notre Dame de Lourdes	B4	96
Notre Dame Junction	D4	98
Notre Dame, bay	D4	98
Notre-Dame	E2	97
Notre-Dame-de-la-Merci	B5	103
Notre-Dame-de-la-Salette	A6	103
Notre-Dame-de-Lorette	D2	103
Notre-Dame-du-Bon-Conseil	D5	103
Notre-Dame-du-Lac	H4	103
Notre-Dame-du-Laus	A5	103
Nottingham	C3	30
Nottingham, island	N4	99
Nouadhibou	A2	58
Nouakchott, capital	A3	58
Nouméa, capital	C4	18
Nouvelle	K3	103
Nova Gorica	A3	48
Nova Iguaçu	Inset I	81
Novara	B1	38
Novaya Zemlya, islands	B4	44
Nové Zamky	B3	42
Novgorod	D3	44
Novi Pazar	B3	49
Novi Sad	A2	49
Novo Mesto	C3	48
Novokuznetsk	D6	44
Novosibirsk	D6	44
Novra	A3	96
Nowshak, mt.	D2	21
Nowy Sącz	E4	41
Nsanje	C3	68
Nsawam	B4	64
Nsok	D3	66
Nsoko	B3	71
Nsukka	D4	65
Ntem, river	C3	65
Nu'ulua, island	B2	18
Nu'utele, island	B2	18
Nuba, mts.	B2	59
Nubian, desert	C1	59
Nueltin, lake	J4	99
Nueva Casas Grandes	C1	84
Nueva Gerona	B2	88
Nueva Loja	C2	79
Nueva Ocotepeque	A2	86
Nueva Palmira	A3	75
Nueva Rosita	D2	84
Nueva San Salvador	D2	88
Nuevitas	D2	88
Nuevo Laredo	E2	84
Nuevo León	D2	84
Nuevo Rocafuerte	D3	79
Nuguria, islands	B2	15
Nuhud, an-	B2	59
Nui, island	B2	16
Nuku'alofa, capital	B4	17

	Key	Page
Nukufetau, island	C2	16
Nukulaelae, island	C3	16
Nukuoro, atoll	C2	15
Nukus	A2	23
Nullarbor, plain	B3	14
Numazu	C3	8
Ñuñoa	Inset	76
Nuoro	B2	38
Nuremberg	B4	40
Nutak	E3	98
Nuuk (Godthåb), capital	B2	106
Nuuuli	B1	18
Nuwara Eliya	B5	19
Nyaake	C3	63
Nyaba, river	B2	61
Nyala	B2	59
Nyanga, river	A2	66
Nyanza	B2	61
Nyasa (Malawi), lake	B2, B3	68
Nyborg	C3	32
Nyeri	D4	61
Nyetane, river	B2	71
Nyika, plateau	B2	68
Nyíregyháza	C2	43
Nykøbing	C4	32
Nyoman, river	B3	47
Nyong, river	B3	65
Nysa	C3	41
Nzérékoré	D4	62
Nzi, river	D3	63
Nzoia, river	C3	61
Nzwani (Anjouan), island	B2	67

O

	Key	Page
O'Leary	A2	100
Oahu, island, Hawaii	Inset II	126
Oak Lake	A4	96
Oak Point	C4	96
Oak Point	C3	97
Oak River	A4	96
Oakland, Calif.	A2	126
Oakner	A4	96
Oakview	B3	96
Oakville	C4	96
Oakville	F4	102
Oamaru	B4	15
Oaxaca, state capital	E4	84
Ob, river	C5	44
Oban	B4	30
Oberammergau	B5	40
Oberhausen	A3	40
Oberpfälzer Wald, mts.	D2	13
Obi, island	D2	13
Obihiro	Inset I	
Obo	C2	66
Obock	C2	60
Obskaya	B3	64
Occidental, mts.	B2, C4	77
Ocean Falls	J5	95
Ochamchire	A3	45
Ochil, hills	B2	30
Ocho Rios	B2	88
Ocoa, bay	B2	89
Ocotal	A2	87
Ocotlán	D3	84
Oda	C1	8
Odei, river	C1	96
Odemira	A4	36
Odense	C3	32
Odense, fjord	C3	32
Odenwald, forest	B4	40
Oder, river	B2, C3	40
Oderhaff, lake	C2	40
Odessa	C2	126
Odessa, Tex.	C2	126
Odienné	A3	63
Oelemari, river	B3	80
Oenpelli	C1	14
Offa	C3	65
Offenbach	B3	40
Ofu, island	A1	18
Ogaden, region	D3	60
Ogbomosho	C3	65
Ogden, Utah	B1	126
Ogema	F11	104
Ogilvie, mts.	B3	105
Oglio, river	B1	38
Ogoki, river	C2	101
Ogooué, river	A2	66
Ogosta, river	B2	50
Ograżden, mts.	C2	48
Ogre	C2	46
Ogun, river	C3	65
Ohio	B2	126
Ohio, river	E2	126
Ohonua	C4	17
Ohrid	A2	48
Ohrid, lake	B2	49
Øibenik	B3	48
Oise, river	C2, Inset II	34
Oistins	B5	91
Oita	A3	8
Ojinaga	D2	84
Ojos del Salado, mt.	B4	44
Oka, river	D4	44
Okahandja	B2	70
Okakarara	C2	70
Okanagan Falls	N6	95
Okanagan, lake	N6	95
Okara	D3	21
Okavango, basin	A1	69
Okavango, river	A1	69
Okayama	B3	8
Okazaki	C3	8
Okeechobee, lake, Fla.	E3	126
Okene	D4	65
Okha	D9	44
Okha	D2	21
Okhotsk	D9	44
Okhotsk, sea	D9	44
Oki, islands	B2	8
Okinawa, island	Inset II	8
Okino Erabu, island	Inset II	8
Oklahoma	D2	126

	Key	Page
Oklahoma City, capital, Okla.	D2	126
Okondja	B2	66
Okotoks	C6	94
Okushiri, island	C1, Inset I	8
Okwa, river	A2	69
Ólafsvík	A2	52
Olanchito	B2	86
Öland, island	C3	53
Olavarría	C4	74
Olbia	B2	38
Old Brahmaputra, river	C4	21
Old Crow	B2	105
Old Perlican	E5	98
Old Road	D5	90
Old Road Town	A2	90
Old Wives, lake	D10	104
Oldenburg	B2	40
Oldham	C3	30
Oldman, river	D6	94
Olds	C5	94
Olekma, river	C7	44
Olenek, river	B4	44
Oléron, island	B4	34
Olgilvie, river	B3	105
Ölgiy	A2	11
Olifants, river	A3, C1	71
Olinda	E2	81
Oliver	N6	95
Ollagüe, volcano	C2	76
Ollei	C2	17
Olmaliq	C2	23
Olomouc	C3	42
Olongapo	B3	12
Olosega, island	A1	18
Olsztyn	E2	41
Olt, river	C3	43
Oltenița	D3	43
Olympia, capital, Wash.	A1	126
Olympus, mt., Wash.	A1	126
Olympus, mt.	A2	27
Olympus, mt.	B1	51
Omagh	B2	30
Omaha, beach	Inset II	34
Omaha, Nebr.	D1	126
Oman, gulf	C1, D2	25
Omaruru	B2	70
Omatako, river	C1	70
Omboué	A2	66
Omdurman	C2	59
Omemee	G3	102
Ometepe, island	B3	87
Omineca, mts.	J2	95
Omineca, river	K3	95
Omiya	C3	8
Omo, river	B3	60
Omsk	D5	44
Omuta	A3	8
Onanole	B4	96
Ondame	B2	62
Ondangwa	B1	70
Ondava, river	C2	42
Ondjiva	C5	70
Ondo	C4	65
Öndörhaan	D2	11
Onefour	E6	94
Onega, lake	C3	44
Oneşti	D2	43
Ongjin	A4	9
Ongole	C5	20
Onilahy, river	A3	69
Onion Lake	A7	104
Onitsha	D4	65
Ono, island	B3	17
Onon, river	D2	11
Onota, island	A2	17
Onsŏng	C1	9
Ontario, lake	K4	92
Ontong Java, island	A1	16
Oostende	A1	33
Oostende-Brugge, canal	B1	33
Oosterschelde, channel	A3	32
Ootsa, lake	J4	95
Opava	G2	102
Opeongo, lake	C3	41
Opole	A2	36
Oporto (Porto)	C4	66
Opuwo	A1	70
Oqsu, river	C2	23
Oradea	A2	43
Oral	B1	23
Oran	A1	57
Orange Walk	B1	85
Orange, N.S.W.	D3	14
Orange, river	A3, B2	71
Orangeville	E4	102
Oranienburg	B3	40
Oranjemund	B4	70
Orapa	B2	69
Ordino	B2	36
Ordu	D2	27
Örebro	C3	53
Oregon	A1	126
Orellana, lake	D3	37
Orenburg	D4	44
Orense	C1	37
Øresund, sound	D3	32
Órganos, mts.	A2	88
Órgãos, range	Inset I	81
Orhei	B2	50
Orhon, river	C2	11
Oriental, mts.	B2, C3	89
Oriental, range	C3	89
Orillia	F3	102
Orinoco, river	C3, D2	79
Orion	E6	94
Oristano	B3	38
Orizaba	E4	84
Orkney, islands	Inset I	30
Orlando, Fla.	E3	126
Orléans	C3	34
Orléans, island	F5, L5	103
Ormoc	C4	12
Orne, river	B2	34
Örnsköldsvik	C2	53
Orocué	C3	78
Oromocto	C3	97
Oron	E5	65

	Key	Page
Orontes, river	A2	27
Orosháza	C2	43
Orrefors	C3	53
Orsha	E2	47
Orsk	D4	44
Ortegal, cape	C1	37
Orumiyeh (Urmia)	A2	22
Oruro	A3	77
Oryakhovo	B2	50
Os, river	A3	36
Osaka	B3	8
Osasco	Inset I	81
Osh	C2	23
Oshakati	B1	70
Oshawa	G4	102
Oshima, peninsula	D1, Inset I	8
Oshogbo	C4	65
Osijek	D2	48
Osilinka, river	K3	95
Öskemen (Ust-Kamenogorsk)	E1	23
Oslo, capital	C3	52
Oslofjord, fjord	C4	52
Osnabrück	B2	40
Osorno	B7	76
Osoyoos	N6	95
Oss	C3	32
Osse, river	C4	65
Osterdälälven, river	B2	53
Östersund	B2	53
Ostrava	D3	42
Ostrołęka	E2	41
Osum, river	B3	49
Osum, islands	A4	8
Osumi, peninsula	A4	8
Osumi, strait	A4	8
Ošům, river	C3	50
Otaru	Inset I	8
Otavalo	B2	79
Otavi	C1	70
Oti, river	B1, C2	64
Otjiwarongo	B2	70
Otranto	D2	38
Otranto, strait	A3	49
Otsu	B3	8
Ottawa	K4	102
Ottawa, river	G1, G5 H5, K2	102
Otterlo	C2	32
Ötztal Alps, range	B4	39
Ou, mts.	D2	8
Ou, river	B1	11
Ouadane	C2	58
Ouagadougou, capital	D2	64
Ouahigouya	C2	64
Ouaka, river	B2	66
Ouanary	C1	80
Ouara, river	C2	66
Ouarzazate	B1	57
Oudtshoorn	B3	71
Ouémé, river	B3	64
Ouesso	D3	66
Ouezzane	C1	57
Ouham, river	A2	66
Ouidah	B4	64
Oujda	D1	57
Oulu	C1	53
Oulu, lake	C2	53
Oulujoki, river	C2	53
Oum er-Rbia, river	C1	57
Ounasjoki, river	C1	53
Oungre	G11	104
Our, river	B1	33
Ourthe, river	D2	33
Ouse, river	C2, D3	30
Outarde, river	H2	103
Outer Hebrides, islands	A1	30
Outjo	C9	104
Outlook	C9	104
Ouvéa, island	C2	18
Ovalau, island	B2	17
Ovalle	A4	76
Overflakkee, island	A2	96
Overflowing River	A2	96
Oviedo	A3	89
Oviedo	D1	37
Owando	C4	66
Owen Sound	E3	102
Owen Stanley, range	A2	15
Owendo	A1	66
Owensboro, Ky.	E2	126
Owerri	C3	30
Oxbow	H11	104
Oxford	C3	30
Oxford	D2	100
Oxford House	D1, D2	96
Oxford, lake	D2	96
Oyapock, river	B2	80
Oyem	A1	66
Oyo	B4	65
Ozama, river	B2	89
Ozark, plateau	D2	126
Özd	C1	43
Özgön	C2	23
Ozoir-la-Ferrière	Inset II	34
Ozurgeti	A4	45

P

	Key	Page
Pa-an	C3	12
Paamiut (Frederikshåb)	C2	106
Pabna	C4	21
Pacaraima, mts.	D3	79
Pacasmayo	B2	77
Pachuca, state capital	E3	84
Padang	B2	13
Paddle Prairie	B2	94
Paderborn	B3	40
Padma, river	D5	21
Padua (Padova)	B1	38
Paektu-san, mt.	C2	9
Pagadian	B5	12
Pago Pago, capital	Inset	18
Pahang, river	Inset	51
Paianía	Inset	51
Päijänne, lake	C2	53
Paint, lake	B1	96

	Key	Page
Paisley	B2	30
Paita	A2	77
Pakaraima, mts.	A3	80
Pakowki, lake	E6	94
Paks	B2	43
Pakse	C4	11
Pala	A5	59
Palaiseau	Inset II	34
Palana	D10	44
Palanga	A2	46
Palangkaraya	C2	13
Palapye	...	5
Palau	B2	48
Palembang	B2	13
Palencia	D1	37
Palermo	C3	38
Palestine	D3	81
Palikir, capital	C2	15
Palk, strait	C7	20
Palliser, cape	C3	15
Palma, island	A4	91
Palma	H3	37
Palmanova	B2	38
Palmerston	C3	15
Palmerston North	A4	78
Palmira	A4	78
Palmyra, ruins	B2	27
Palos, cape	F4	37
Palu	C2	13
Pamirs, mts.	B2	23
Pamirs, region	A2	10
Pampas, plain	C4	74
Pamplemousses	C2	69
Pamplona	F1	37
Panagyurishte	C3	50
Panaji	B5	20
Panama, canal	C2	87
Panamá, capital	C2	87
Panay, gulf	B4	12
Panay, island	B4	12
Pančevo	B2	49
Panch'iao	B1	9
Pandan, strait	A2	13
Pandaruan, river	C2	13
Panevėžys	C2	46
Pangani, river	C1	68
Pangkalpinang	B2	13
Pangnirtung	P3	
Panihati	Inset II	20
Panj	A2	23
Panj, river	B2	23
Panjakent	A1	23
Panjgur	B4	21
P'anmunjŏm	B4	9
Pantanal, lowland	C4	81
Pantelleria, island	C3	38
Pánuco, river	E3	84
Papagayo, gulf	A2	86
Paphos	A2	27
Papua, gulf	A2	15
Paquetville	D1	97
Pará	C2	81
Pará, river	A7	104
Paradise Hill	A7	104
Paradise River	C2	98
Paraguaí, river	C3	81
Paraguarí	D4	75
Paraguay, river	C2, C5	75
Paraíba	E2	81
Parakou	B3	64
Paramaribo, capital	B2	80
Paraná	C3	74
Paraná	C4	81
Paraná, river	D2	74
Paranaguá	B2	81
Paranam	B2	80
Pardubice	C2	42
Parent	B4	103
Parepare	C2	13
Paria, gulf	D1	79
Parima, range	B1	81
Paris, capital	C2, Inset II	34
Paris	E4	102
Parkhill	D4	102
Parkland	D6	94
Parksville	K6	95
Parma	B1	38
Parnaíba	D2	81
Parnaíba, river	D2	81
Pärnu	C2	46
Pärnu, river	C2	46
Paro	A2	19
Paropamisus, range	A2	22
Páros, island	C3	51
Parral	B6	76
Parrsboro	C2	100
Parry	D2	99
Parry Sound	F3	102
Parry, channel	J2	99
Parsnip, river	L4	95
Parson's Pond	C2	98
Pas de la Casa	C2	36
Pasadena	C2	98
Pasfield, lake	E2	104
Pasión, river	C3	85
Paso de los Toros	B2	75
Paso de Palmar, lake	B2	75
Passau	C4	40
Passero, cape	C3	38
Passo Fundo	C4	81
Pastavy	B1	47
Pastaza, river	B1	77
Pastillo	C3	90
Pasto	A4	78
Patagonia, region	B6	74
Patavilca	B3	79
Paterson, N.J.	F1	126
Patía, river	A4	78
Patiala	C2	20
Patillas	C2	90
Patna	E3	20
Patos, lagoon	C5	81

Name	Key	Page
Pátrai	B2	51
Patricia	E6	94
Pattani	B5	12
Patuakhali	D6	21
Patuca, mts.	C2	86
Patuca, river	C2	86
Pau	B5	34
Pauingassi	D3	96
Paulatuk	D3	99
Paulaya, river	C2	86
Paulo Afonso	E2	81
Pavaiai	B2	18
Pavia	B1	38
Pavilosta	A2	46
Pavlodar	D1	23
Paxbán	C2	85
Payar	B2	62
Paye	Inset I	20
Payne, lake	B2	101
Paynton	B7	104
Pays De La Loire	B3	34
Paysandú	A2	75
Paz, river	C6	85
Pazardzhik	C3	50
Peace Point	D1	94
Peace River	C2	94
Peace, river	A3, C2	94
Peachland	N6	95
Pebane	C3	68
Peć	B3	49
Pechora	C4	44
Pechora, river	C4	44
Pécs	B2	43
Pedernales	A2	89
Pedja, river	D2	46
Pedra Açú, mt.	Inset I	81
Pedra Lume	D2	58
Pedro Juan Caballero	E3	75
Pedro Santana	A1	89
Peebles	H10	104
Peel, river	B3, C2	105
Peerless Lake	C3	94
Pegasus, bay	B3	15
Pegu	C3	12
Peipus, lake	D2	46
Pekalongan	B2	13
Pekanbaru	B1	13
Pelee, island	C6	102
Peleliu, island	B4	17
Peleng, island	D2	13
Pelican Narrows	H5	104
Pelican Portage	D3	94
Pelican Rapids	A3	96
Pelican, lake	G5	104
Pelkan, lake	A3	96
Pelly	J9	104
Pelly Bay	L3	99
Pelly Crossing	B4	105
Pelly, river	C4, C5	105
Pelotas	C5	81
Pematangsiantar	A1	13
Pemba	D2	68
Pemba, island	C2	68
Pemberton	L6	95
Pembina, river	B4	94
Pembina, river	B4	96
Pembroke	B3	30
Pembroke	H2	102
Penas, gulf	B8	76
Pendé, river	A2	66
Pendleton, Oreg.	B1	126
Penetanguishene	F3	102
P'enghu (Pescadores), islands	A2	9
Peniche	A3	36
Peninsular Malaysia, region	B2	13
Pennant	B10	104
Pennine Alps, mts.	B2	35
Pennines, mts.	C2	30
Pennsylvania	F1	126
Penonomé	B2	87
Penrith	C2	30
Pensacola, Fla.	E2	126
Pensacola, mts.	A11	107
Pentecost, island	C2	18
Penticton	N6	95
Peñuelas	B2	90
Penza	D4	44
Penzance	B4	30
Penzhihua	D3	10
Peoria, Ill.	E1	126
Perak, river	A2	13
Percé	M3	103
Perdue	C8	104
Pereira	B3	78
Péribonca, river	B3	101
Péribonka	D3	103
Périgueux	C4	34
Perim, island	A2	25
Peristéri	Inset	51
Perlas, archipelago	C2	87
Perlas, lagoon	C2	87
Perm	D4	44
Permyakia, autonomous okrug	D4	44
Pernambuco	E2	81
Pernik	B3	50
Perpignan	C5	34
Perrot, island	G6	103
Perth	J3	102
Perth	B2	30
Perth, W.A., capital,	A3, Inset I	14
Perth-Andover	B2	97
Perugia	B2	38
Pervomaysk	C2	47
Pesaro	C2	38
Pescadores, channel	A2	9
Pescara	C2	38
Peshawar	C2	21
Peshkopi	B2	49
Petah Tiqwa	B1	26
Petare	C1	79
Petauke	C2	67
Petawawa	H2	102
Petén-Itzá, lake	D3	85
Peterborough	C3	30
Peterborough	G3	102
Peterhead	C1	30
Petersfield	C4	96
Petit Canouan, island	C1	91
Petit Martinique, island	C1	91
Petit Mustique, island	B3	91
Petit St. Vincent, island	A4	91
Petit-Rocher	D1	97
Petitcodiac	D3	97
Petite Riviere	C3	100
Petlura	A3	96
Petra, ruins	A2	26
Petrich	B4	50
Petrila	B3	43
Petrolia	C5	102
Petrólina	D2	81
Petropavl	C1	23
Petropavlovsk-Kamchatskiy	D9	44
Petrópolis	D4, Inset I	81
Petroşani	A3	43
Petrozavodsk	C3	44
Pevek	C10	44
Peyia	A2	27
Pforzheim	B4	40
Phan Rang	B4	11
Phan Thiet	B4	11
Phatthalung	B5	12
Phayao	B2	12
Phetchabun	B2	12
Phetchabun, range	B3	12
Phetchaburi	B2	12
Phichit	B2	12
Philadelphia, Pa.	F2	126
Philippine, sea	C3	12
Philippine, sea	D2	17
Phitsanulok	B2	12
Phnom Penh, capital	C4	11
Phnum Tbeng Meanchey	C2	11
Phoenix, capital, Ariz.	B2	126
Phoenix, island	B2	17
Phoenix, islands	B2	17
Phôngsali	B1	11
Phou Bia, mt.	B2	11
Phra Nakhon Si Ayutthaya	B2	12
Phuket	B5	12
Phumi Samraong	B1	11
Phuntsholing	A3	19
Piapot	A10	104
Piatra Neamţ	D2	43
Piauí	D2	81
Piave, river	C1	38
Pibor Post	C3	59
Pic de la Selle, mt.	D2	89
Picardie	C2	34
Pickle Lake	B2	101
Pico do Cano, volcano	B4	58
Picton	H3	102
Pictou	E2	100
Pidurutalagala, mt.	B4	19
Piedmont	A1	38
Piedra Sola	B2	75
Piedras Negras	D2	84
Pielinen, lake	C2	53
Pierceland	A6	104
Pierre, capital, S. Dak.	C1	126
Pierrefonds	G5	103
Pierreville	A2	91
Piešťany	A2	42
Pietermaritzburg	D2	71
Pietersburg	C1	71
Piggs Peak	B1	71
Pikangikum	B2	101
Pikes peak, Colo.	C2	126
Pikwitonei	C1	96
Piła	C2	41
Pilar	C5	75
Pilar	B4	77
Pilaya, river	E3	77
Pilcomayo, river	B3, C4	75
Pilica, river	E3	41
Pilibhit	B3	51
Pilot Butte	F10	104
Pilot Mound	B4	96
Pinang, island	A2	13
Pinar del Río	A2	88
Pinawa	D4	96
Pine, mts.	B2	51
Pine Bluff, Ark.	D2	126
Pine Dock	C3	96
Pine Falls	C4	96
Pine Point	F4	99
Pine River	A3	96
Pinehouse Lake	D5	104
Pines, island	D2	18
Ping, river	B2	12
P'ingtung	B2	9
Piniós, river	B2	51
Pink Mountain	L2	95
Pink, river	F4	104
Pinsk	C3	47
Piotrków Trybunalski	D3	41
Pipmuacan, reservoir	F2	103
Piracicaba	D4	81
Pirada	C1	62
Piraiévs	B3, Inset	51
Pirmasens	A4	40
Pirot	C3	49
Pirris, river	B3	86
Pisa	B2	38
Pisagua	B1	76
Pisco	B3	77
Pistoia	B2	38
Piteşti	C3	43
Pitlochry	B2	30
Pitseng	B2	71
Pitt, island	H4	95
Pittsburgh, Pa.	E1	126
Piura	A2	77
Placentia	D5	98
Placentia, bay	D5	98
Placenza	B1	38
Placetas	C2	88
Planken	B1	33
Plantagenet	K2	102
Plasencia	C2	37
Plaster Rock	B2	97
Plata, Río de la, estuary	D3	74
Plata, river	B3	75
Plauen	C3	40
Playgreen, lake	B2	96
Pleasant Bay	G1	100
Pleiku	B4	11
Plenty, bay	C2	15
Plessisville	E5	103
Pleven	C2	50
Plevna	J3	102
Plibo	C3	63
Pljevlja	A3	49
Ploče	C3	48
Plock	D2	41
Ploieşti	D3	43
Plovdiv	C3	50
Plum Coulee	C4	96
Plumas	B4	96
Plymouth	B1	91
Plymouth	B4	30
Plzeň	A2	42
Po, river	A1, B1	38
Poá	Inset II	81
Pobé	B4	64
Pocatello, Idaho	B1	126
Podgorica	A3	49
Pogradec	B3	49
P'ohang	C4	9
Pohnpei, island	D2	15
Poinsett, cape	C2	107
Point Fortin	A2	91
Point Leamington	D4	98
Point Pedro	C1	19
Point Prim	B2	100
Point, lake	F3	99
Pointe au Baril	E2	102
Pointe du Bois	D4	96
Pointe Michel	B3	90
Pointe Sapin	E2	97
Pointe-a-la-Croix	K3	103
Pointe-Claire	H6	103
Pointe-des-Monts	J2	103
Pointe-Lebel	H2	103
Pointe-Noire	A6	66
Pointe-Verte	D1	97
Poisson Blanc, reservoir	A6	103
Poissy	Inset II	34
Poitiers	C3	34
Poitou-Charentes	C3	34
Pokemouche	E1	97
Pokhara	B2	19
Polar, plateau	A14	107
Polba	Inset II	20
Polonnaruwa	C4	19
Polotsk	D2	47
Poltava	C2	47
Poltimore	A6	103
Pomeranian, bay	C1	40
Ponce	B2	90
Pond Cove	C3	98
Pond Inlet	N2	99
Pondicherry	C6	20
Ponferrada	C1	37
Ponoka	D5	94
Pont Cassé	B3	90
Pont-Rouge	E5	103
Pontchartrain	Inset II	34
Ponteix	C11	104
Pontevedra	B1	37
Pontianak	B2	13
Pontic, mts.	D2	27
Pontine, islands	C2	38
Pontine, marshes	C2	38
Pontoise	Inset II	34
Ponton	B2	96
Poole	C4	30
Poopó, lake	A3	77
Popayán	A4	78
Poperinge	A2	33
Poplar River	C3	96
Popomanaseu, mt.	B1	16
Popondetta	A2	15
Poprad	D2	42
Porcupine Plain	G8	104
Porcupine, river	B2	105
Pori	B2	53
Port Alberni	K6	95
Port Antonio	C2	88
Port au Choix	C4	98
Port au Port	B5	98
Port Augusta, S.A.	C3	14
Port Bickerton	F2	100
Port Blair	F6	20
Port Blandford	D5	98
Port Bruce	E5	102
Port Burwell	D3	98
Port Burwell	E5	102
Port Clements	F4	95
Port Colborne	F5	102
Port Coquitlam	L6	95
Port Dufferin	E3	100
Port Elgin	E3	97
Port Elgin	D3	102
Port Elizabeth	B2	91
Port Elizabeth	C3	71
Port Franks	D4	102
Port George	B2	100
Port Glaud	Inset	70
Port Harcourt	D5	65
Port Hardy	J6	95
Port Hawkesbury	F2	100
Port Hedland, W.A.	A2	14
Port Hood	F1	100
Port Hope	G4	102
Port Hope Simpson	C3	98
Port Laoise	C2	31
Port Lincoln, S.A.	C3	14
Port Loko	A1	63
Port Louis, capital	B2	69
Port Macquarie, N.S.W.	E3	14
Port Maria	C2	88
Port McNeill	J6	95
Port Moody	L6	95
Port Morant	C3	88
Port Moresby, capital	A2	15
Port Mouton	C4	100
Port Nolloth	A2	71
Port of Spain, capital	A2	91
Port Perry	G3	102
Port Phillip, bay	Inset V	14
Port Pirie, S.A.	C3	14
Port Renfrew	K7	95
Port Rowan	E5	102
Port Said	B1	56
Port Saunders	C4	98
Port Stanley	D5	102
Port Sudan	D1	59
Port Talbot	B3	30
Port-au-Prince, bay	C2	89
Port-au-Prince, capital	C2	89
Port-Cartier	C3	101
Port-de-Paix	C1	89
Port-Gentil	A2	66
Port-Salut	B2	89
Portadown	A2	30
Portage	A2	100
Portage la Prairie	B4, D2	96
Portalegre	B3	36
Porter, lake	C4	104
Porters Lake	D3	100
Porth Edward	D3	71
Portimão	A4	36
Portland	A2	91
Portland Creek	C4	98
Portland, bight	B8	88
Portland, inlet	G4	95
Portland, Maine	F1	126
Portland, Oreg.	A1	126
Portneuf, river	G3	103
Pôrto Alegre	B4	63
Pórto Alegre	C5	81
Pôrto Inglês	C3	58
Pôrto Velho	B2	81
Porto-Novo, capital	B4	64
Porto-Vecchio	Inset I	34
Portobelo	C2	87
Portoviejo	A3	79
Portree	A1	30
Portsmouth	C4	30
Portsmouth	A2	90
Portsmouth, Va.	F2	126
Porvenir	B9	76
Posadas	D2	74
Poste	C3	69
Postojna	B3	48
Postville	B2	98
Potaro, river	B3	80
Potenza	C2	38
Poti	A3	45
Potiskum	F2	65
Potnarvin	C4	18
Potosí	A3	77
Potrerillos	C3	76
Potsdam	C2	40
Pottuvil	C5	19
Pouch Cove	E5	98
Poutasi	C3	18
Pouthisat	B3	11
Považská Bystrica	B2	42
Povungnituk	A1	101
Powassan	F1	102
Powell River	K6	95
Powerview	C4	96
Poyang, lake	E3	10
Poza Rica	E3	84
Požarevac	B2	49
Poznań	C2	41
Pozo Colorado	C3	75
Pra, river	B4	64
Prachuap Khiri Khan	B4	12
Prague, capital	B2	42
Praia, capital	C4	58
Praslin	B2	91
Praslin, island	C1	70
Prato	B2	38
Prawda	D4	96
Preeceville	H9	104
Prelate	A10	104
Preparis, island	B3	12
Přerov	C2	42
Prescott	K3	102
Prescott, Ariz.	B2	126
Presidencia Roque Sáenz Peña	C2	74
Prešov	C2	42
Prespa, lake	B3	48
Presque Isle, Maine	G1	126
Prestea	A4	64
Preston	C3	30
Pretoria, administrative capital	C2	71
Préveza	B2	51
Prey Veng	C4	11
Priboj	A3	49
Priddis	C6	94
Prievidza	B2	42
Prijedor	A1	48
Prilep	B3	48
Priluki	C1	47
Primorsko	F3	50
Primrose, lake	A6	104
Prince Albert	E7	104
Prince Albert, hills	L3	99
Prince Albert, peninsula	G1	99
Prince Charles, island	N3	99
Prince George	L4	95
Prince of Wales, island	J2	95
Prince Patrick, island	E1	99
Prince Regent, inlet	K2	99
Prince Rupert	G4	95
Princes Town	A2	91
Princess Harbour	C3	96
Princess Margriet, canal	C1	32
Princess Royal, island	M6	95
Princeton	M6	95
Princeville	E5	103
Príncipe, island	C1	63
Prinzapolka	C2	87
Prinzapolka, river	B2	87
Pripyats, marshes	C4	47
Pripyats, river	C3	47
Priština	B3	49
Privas	D4	34
Prizren	B3	49
Progresso	B1	85
Prokopyevsk	D6	44
Prokuplje	B3	49
Prome	B2	12
Prophet River	L2	95
Prostĕjov	B2	42
Provence-Alpes-Côte-d'Azur	D4	34
Providence Bay	C2	102
Providence, capital, R.I.	F1	126
Providencia, island	Inset	78
Providenciales, island	C11	44
Provideniya	C11	44
Provo, Utah	B1	126
Pru, river	B3	64
Prut, river	D2	43
Przemyśl	F4	41
Psel, river	C2	47
Pskov	D3	44
Pskov, lake	D3	46
Ptsich, river	D3	47
Ptuj	C2	48
Pu'apu'a	B2	18
Pubnico	B4	100
Pucallpa	C2	77
Puck	D1	41
Puebla, state capital	E4	84
Pueblo, Colo.	C2	126
Puente Alto	Inset	76
Puerca, point	D2	90
Puerto Aisén	B8	76
Puerto Armuelles	A2	87
Puerto Ayacucho	C2	79
Puerto Bahía	C2	75
Puerto Barrios	E4	85
Puerto Bolívar	B4	79
Puerto Cabello	C1	79
Puerto Cabezas	C1	87
Puerto Carreño	D3	78
Puerto Cisnes	B7	76
Puerto Cortés	B2	86
Puerto Deseado	C6	74
Puerto Escondido	E4	84
Puerto Inírida	D4	78
Puerto Jiménez	C2	86
Puerto Leguízamo	B5	78
Puerto Lempira	D2	86
Puerto Maldonado	D3	77
Puerto Montt	B7	76
Puerto Natales	B9	76
Puerto Peñasco	B1	84
Puerto Pinasco	D3	75
Puerto Plata	B1	89
Puerto Princesa	A4	12
Puerto Quepos	B3	86
Puerto Real	A2	90
Puerto Sandino	A2	87
Puerto Santa Cruz	B9	74
Puerto Suárez	C3	77
Puerto Vallarta	C3	84
Puerto Varas	B7	76
Puerto Williams	C9	76
Puertollano	D3	37
Puglia	C2	38
Pugwash	D2	100
Pujehun	B2	63
Pukatawagan	A1	96
Pukch'ŏng	C2	9
Pukë	A1	49
Pula	A3	48
Pulangi, river	B4	12
Puławy	E3	41
Pulo Anna, island	Inset	17
Pulusuk, island	B2	15
Puná, island	A4	79
Punakha	A2	19
Pune	B4	20
Punggol	B1	13
Punta, mt.	B2	90
Punta Arenas	B9	76
Punta del Este	C5	75
Punta Gorda	B3	85
Punta Santiago	D2	90
Puntarenas	B2	86
Punto Fijo	B1	79
Purari, river	A2	15
Purbeck's Cove	C4	98
Purus, river	B2	81
Pusan	C5	9
Putao	C1	12
Putgarden	B1	40
Puttalam	A3	19
Putumayo, river	B5	78
Puysegur, point	A4	15
P'yandzh, river	B1	23
P'yŏnggang	B3	9
P'yŏngsŏng	B3	9
P'yŏngsan	B3	9
P'yŏngyang, capital	A3	9
Pyrenees, range	C5	34
Qaanaaq (Thule)	B2	106
Qachas Nek	B3	71
Qadarif, al-	C2	59
Qaidam, basin	C2	10
Qalat	B2	22
Qalat Bishah	C2	24
Qaleh-ye Now	A2	22
Qaleh-ye Panjeh	C2	22
Qamea, island	C2	17
Qamishli, al-	B1	27
Qandahar	B2	22
Qaqortoq (Julianehåb)	B2	106
Qaraghandy (Karaganda)	D2	23
Qardho	B2	60
Qareh, river	B3	22
Qarokul, lake	B1	23
Qarshi	C3	23
Qaryah ash-Sharqiyah, al-	B1	56
Qasigiannguit (Christianshåb)	B2	106
Qasr as-Sabiyah	C2	24
Qatranah, al-	A2	26
Qatrun, al-	B3	56
Qattarah, depression	A2	56
Qayrawan, al-	C2	57
Qayyarah, al-	B1	24
Qazvin	D2	22
Qelelevu, island	C2	17
Qeshm, island	D4	22
Qilian, range	C2	10
Qin Ling, mts.	B2	10
Qina	B2	56
Qingdao	F2	10
Qinghai	C2	10
Qinghai, lake	C2	10
Qinhuangdao	E2	10
Qiqihar	F1	10
Qiryat Gat	B2	26
Qiryat Shemona	B1	26
Qishn	C1	25
Qom	C3	22
Qormi	B2	36
Qostanay	C1	23
Qu'Appelle	G10	104
Qu'Appelle, river	D10	104
Quang Ngai	B3	11
Quantaq	C1	101
Quanzhou	E3	10
Quatre Bornes	B3	69
Quba	C2	45
Qubayyat, al-	B1	26
Québec, capital	E5, L6	103
Quebo	C2	62
Quebradillas	B2	90
Queen Charlotte	F4	95
Queen Charlotte, islands	G4	95
Queen Charlotte, sound	H5	95
Queen Charlotte, strait	H5	95
Queen Elizabeth, islands	H1	99
Queen Maud Land, region	B16	107
Queen Maud, gulf	H3	99
Queen Maud, mts.	A5	107
Queen Maude, gulf	H3	99
Queensland	D2	14
Queenstown	B1	13
Queenstown	A3	15
Queenstown	C3	71
Queenstown, Tas.	D4	14
Queguay Grande, river	B2	75
Queimados	Inset I	81
Quelimane	C3	68
Quellón	B7	76
Queluz	A3	36
Querétaro, state capital	D3	84
Quesnel	L5	95
Quesnel, lake	M5	95
Quetta	C3	21
Quetzaltenango	B5	85
Quevedo	B3	79
Quezon City	B3	12
Qui Nhon	B4	11
Quibala	C2	66
Quibdó	A3	78
Quilchena	M6	95
Quill Lake	F8	104
Quill, lakes	F8	104
Quillota	B4	76
Quilpué	Inset	76
Quimbele	A2	66
Quimper	A2	34
Quinhámel	A2	62
Quintana Roo	G4	84
Quispamsis	D3	97
Quito, capital	B3	79
Qunaytirah, al-	A2	26
Qunfudhah, al-	B2	24
Qunghirot	A2	23
Quqon	D2	23
Qurghonteppa	A2	23
Qurnat as-Sawda, mt.	B1	26
Quthing	A3	71
Qyzylorda	C2	23

R

Name	Key	Page
Raahe	B2	53
Raanes, peninsula	L1	99
Raba	C2	13
Rába, river	A2	43
Rabat	B2	36
Rabat, capital	C1	57
Rabaul	B2	15
Rabbit Lake	C7	104
Rabbit Lake Mine	G2	104
Rabi, island	C2	17
Rach Gia	A4	11
Rachidia, er-	C2	57
Racine, Wis.	E1	126
Rădăuţi	C2	43
Radium Hot Springs	O6	95
Radom	E3	41
Radviliškis	B2	46
Radville	F11	104
Rae	E4	99
Rafha	B1	24
Rafter	A1	96
Ragged, point	C3	91
Ragueneau	H2	103
Ragusa	C3	38
Rahimyar Khan	D4	21
Rainbow Lake	A2	94
Rainier mt., Wash.	A1	126
Raipur	D4	20
Rajang, river	C3	19
Rajbiraj	C3	19
Rajkot	B4	20
Rajpur	Inset II	20
Rajshahi	B4	21
Raleigh, capital, N.C.	F2	126
Ralik, island chain	A1	16
Rama	B2	87

	Key	Page
Ramadi, ar-	B2	24
Ramanbati	Inset II	20
Ramat Gan	B1	26
Ramea	C5	98
Ramla	B2	26
Ramon, *mt.*	B2	26
Ramree, *island*	B2	12
Ramtha, ar-	B1	26
Ramu	F2	61
Ramu, *river*	A2	15
Rancagua	B4	76
Rance, *river*	B2	34
Ranchi	E4	20
Randa	B2	60
Randers	C2	32
Randonopolis	C3	81
Ranfurly	E4	94
Rangamati	F6	21
Ranger Lake	B1	102
Rangitikei, *river*	C2	15
Rangoon, *capital*	C3	12
Rangpur	C3	21
Ranong	B4	12
Rapel, *river*	B4	76
Rapid City	A4	96
Rapid City, S. Dak.	C1	126
Rapla	C1	46
Rapti, *river*	B2	19
Raqqah, ar-	B2	27
Ras al-Khafji	C1	24
Ras al-Khaymah	C2	25
Ras an-Naqb	A2	26
Ras Dashen, *mt.*	C1	60
Ras Musandam, *cape*	C1	25
Ras Tanura	C1	24
Rasa, *point*	C5	74
Rashayya	A2	26
Rasht	B2	22
Ratak, *island chain*	B1	16
Ratchaburi	B3	12
Rathlin, *island*	A2	30
Ratingen	A3	40
Ratnapura	B5	19
Raukumara, *range*	C2	15
Rauma	B2	53
Raurkela	D4	20
Raut, *river*	B2	50
Ravenna	C1	38
Ravensburg	B5	40
Ravi, *river*	D3	21
Rawa, *river*	B4	80
Rawalpindi	D3	21
Rawdatayn, ar-	B2	24
Rawdon	D2	100
Rawson	B5	74
Raymore	F9	104
Rayong	B3	12
Rayside-Balfour	D1	102
Raz, *point*	A3	34
Razelm, *lake*	E3	43
Razgrad	E2	50
Ré, *island*	B3	34
Reading	C3	30
Rebun, *island*	Inset I	8
Rechytsa	E3	47
Recife	E2	81
Recklinghausen	A3	40
Reconquista	D2	74
Red (Hong), *river*	A2	11
Red Bay	C3	98
Red Deer	D5	94
Red Deer, *lake*	A2	96
Red Deer, *river*	D5, E6	94
Red Indian, *lake*	C5	98
Red Rose	C3	96
Red Sucker, *lake*	E2	96
Red Volta, *river*	B1, D3	64
Red Willow	D5	94
Red, *river*	C4	96
Red, *river*	Inset II	24
Red, *river*	D2	126
Red, *sea*	A1	24
Redange	A2	33
Redbridge	F1	102
Redding, Calif.	A1	126
Redonda, *island*	A6	90
Redstone	L5	95
Redvers	A4	96
Redvers	J11	104
Ree, *lake*	B2	31
Reed, *lake*	A2	96
Regensburg	C4	40
Reggio di Calabria	C3	38
Reggio nell'Emilia	B1	38
Reghin	C2	43
Regina	F10	104
Régina	B1	80
Registan, *region*	A2	22
Rehoboth	C3	70
Rehovot	B2	26
Reigate	Inset III	30
Reims	D2	34
Reina Adelaida, *archipelago*	B9	76
Reindeer, *island*	C3	96
Reindeer, *lake*	H3	104
Reindeer, *river*	G4	104
Reinosa	D1	37
Reliance	G4	99
Remagen	A3	40
Remich	B2	33
Rémire	B1	80
Remscheid	A3	40
Rencontre East	D5	98
Renfrew	J2	102
Rennell, *island*	B2	16
Rennes	B2	34
Rennie	D4	96
Reno, Nev.	B2	126
Renous	D2	97
Repentigny	K5	103
Reserve	H8	104
Resistencia	D2	74
Reşiţa	A3	43
Resolute	J2	99
Resolution, *island*	P4	99
Restigouche, *river*	B1	97
Restoule	F1	102
Réunion, *island*		55

	Key	Page
Reus	G2	37
Reuss, *river*	C2	35
Reutlingen	B4	40
Revelstoke	N6	95
Reventazón, *river*	C3	86
Revillagigedo, *islands*	B4	84
Rexdale	J5	102
Rexton	E2	97
Rey, *island*	C2	87
Reykjavik	B3	96
Reykjavík, *capital*	A2	52
Reynosa	E2	84
Rezekne	D2	46
Reznas, *lake*	D2	46
Rhaetian Alps, *mts.*	D2	35
Rharsa, *salt marsh*	A2	57
Rhine, *canal*	B1, B2	33
Rhine, *river*	A3, A4	40
Rhineland-Palatinate	A4	40
Rhode Island	F1	126
Rhodes	D3	51
Rhodes, *island*	D3	51
Rhodope, *mts.*	C4	50
Rhondda	B3	30
Rhône, *river*	D4	34
Rhône-Alpes	D4	34
Rhum, *island*	A1	30
Riaba	A1	66
Ribe	B3	32
Ribeira Brava	B2	58
Ribeira Grande	A1	58
Ribeirão Pires	Inset II	81
Ribeirão Prêto	D4	81
Riberalta	A2	77
Ribniţa	B2	50
Rice, *lake*	G3	102
Richard, *lake*	C1	104
Richards Bay	D2	71
Richards Landing	A1	102
Richardson, *mts.*	B1	105
Richardson, *river*	E2	94
Richelieu, *river*	C6	103
Richer	C4	96
Richibucto	E2	97
Richmond	L6	95
Richmond	D6	103
Richmond Hill	F4, K5	102
Richmond Park	D4	94
Richmond, *capital, Va.*	F2	126
Ricobayo, *reservoir*	D2	37
Rida	A2	25
Rideau, *lake*	J3	102
Rideau, *river*	H6	102
Riesa	C3	40
Rieti	C2	38
Riga, *capital*	C2	46
Riga, *gulf*	B2, B3	46
Rigolet	B2	98
Riiser-Larsen Ice Shelf, *glacier*	B14	107
Riiser-Larsen, *peninsula*	C16	107
Rijeka	B2	48
Rila, *mts.*	B3	50
Rîmnicu Vîlcea	C3	43
Rimini	C1	38
Rimouski	H3	103
Rincón, *bay*	C3	90
Rincón del Bonete, *lake*	B2	75
Ringkøbing	B2	32
Río Blanco	B2	87
Río Branco	B2	81
Rio Claro	A2	91
Río Cuarto	C3	74
Rio de Janeiro	D4, Inset I	81
Río Gallegos	B7	74
Río Grande	C5	81
Río Grande	D2	90
Río Grande	A2	87
Rio Grande (Río Bravo), *river*	D2	84
Rio Grande do Norte	E2	81
Rio Grande do Sul	C4	81
Rio Verde	C3	81
Riobamba	B3	79
Ríohacha	B2	78
Rioni, *river*	B3	45
Riou, *lake*	D1	104
Rîşcani	A2	50
Rishiri, *island*	Inset I	8
Rishra	Inset II	20
Riske Creek	L5	95
Ritchies, *archipelago*	F6	20
Rivas	B3	87
River Cess	B3	63
River Hills	C4	96
River John	D2	100
Rivera	C1	75
Rivercrest	C4	96
Riverhurst	D10	104
Rivers	A4	96
Rivers Inlet	J5	95
Riverside, Calif.	B2	126
Riverside-Albert	E3	97
Riverton	C3	96
Riverview	E2	97
Rivière Bleue	G4	103
Rivière du Loup	G4	101
Rivière du Rempart	C2	69
Rivière Noire, *mt.*	B3	69
Rivière-à-Pierre	E5	103
Rivière-au-Renard	M3	103
Rivière-aux-Rats	D4	103
Rivière-du-Loup	E1	97
Rivière-du-Portage	D5	103
Rivière-Matawin	D5	103
Rivière-Ste-Marguerite	G3	103
Rivière-Verte	A1	97
Riyadh, *capital*	B1	24
Riyaq	B2	26
Roanne	D3	34
Roanoke, Va.	F2	126
Roatán	B1	86
Roatán, *island*	B1	86
Robertsport	A2	63
Roberval	C4	101
Robinsonville	C1	97
Roblin	A3	96

	Key	Page
Roboré	C3	77
Robson, *mt.*	N4	95
Roca, *cape*	A3	36
Rocanville	J10	104
Rochdale	C3	30
Rochefort	B4	34
Rochester	D4	94
Rochester, Minn.	D1	126
Rochester, N.Y.	F1	126
Rock Island	D6	103
Rock, *river*	D5	105
Rockcliffe Park	H5	102
Rockford, Ill.	E1	126
Rockglen	E11	104
Rockhampton, Qld.	E2	14
Rockland	K2	102
Rocky Harbour	C4	98
Rocky Island, *lake*	B1	102
Rocky Mountain House	C5	94
Rocky, *mts.*		82
Rockyford	D5	94
Roddickton	C4	98
Rodez	C4	34
Rodney	D5	102
Roermond	D3	32
Roeselare	B2	33
Rogersville	D2	97
Roi, *island*	B2	16
Roi Et	C2	12
Rojo, *cape*	A3	90
Rokel, *river*	A1	63
Roland	C4	96
Rolling Hills	E6	94
Rollo, *bay*	C2	100
Rolphton	H1	102
Roma	A2	71
Roma, Qld.	D2	14
Roman	D2	43
Roma, *capital*	C2	38
Rømø, *island*	B3	32
Roncador, *cay*	Inset	78
Roncador, *range*	C3	81
Ronde, *island*	B1	91
Rondônia	B3	81
Rongelap, *island*	B1	16
Rongerik, *island*	B1	16
Ronne Ice Shelf, *glacier*	B11	107
Roodeport	C2	71
Roosevelt, *island*	B6	107
Roper, *river*	C1	14
Roraima	B1	81
Roraima, *mt.*	A3	80
Rosa, *mt.*	A1	38
Rosalie	B3	90
Rosalind	D5	94
Rosario	C3	74
Roscelare	B2	33
Roscommon	B2	31
Roscrea	C2	31
Rose Belle	C3	69
Rose Blanche	B5	98
Rose Hill	B2	69
Rose Valley	G8	104
Roseau, *capital*	B3	90
Roseau, *river*	B4	96
Rosebud	D5	94
Rosemary	D6	94
Rosenfeld	C4	96
Rosenheim	C5	40
Rosenort	C4	96
Rosetown	B9	104
Rosetta	B1	56
Roskilde	D3	32
Ross Ice Shelf, *glacier*	A6	107
Ross River	C5	105
Ross, *island*	B5	107
Ross, *river*	C4	105
Ross, *sea*	B6	107
Rossburn	A4	96
Rosseau, *lake*	F2	102
Rossel, *island*	B3	15
Rossendale	B4	96
Rossland	O6	95
Rosslare	C2	31
Rosso	B3	58
Rosthern	D8	104
Rostock	C1	40
Rostov-na-Donu	E3	44
Roswell, N. Mex.	C2	126
Rothesay	D3	97
Rothesay	D3	97
Rotorua	C2	15
Rotterdam	B3	32
Roubaix	C1	34
Rouen	C2	34
Rouleau	F10	104
Round Lake Centre	H2	102
Round, *island*	D1	69
Round, *pond*	C5	98
Routhwaite	B4	96
Rouyn-Noranda	A4	101
Rovaniemi	C1	53
Rovigo	B1	38
Rovno	B1	47
Rovuma, *river*	C1	68
Rowley	D5	94
Roxas	B4	12
Royal, *canal*	C2	31
Ruacana, *falls*	B2	70
Ruahine, *range*	C2	15
Ruapehu, *mt.*	C2	15
Rub al-Khali (Empty Quarter), *desert*	C2	24
Rubtsovsk	D6	44
Ruda Śląska	D3	41
Rudnyy	C1	23
Rufiji, *river*	C2	68
Rügen, *island*	C1	40
Ruggell	B1	33
Ruhengeri	B1	61
Ruhr, *river*	B3	40
Ruhwa, *river*	B2	61
Rukwa, *lake*	B2	68

	Key	Page
Rum, *cay*	C3	89
Rumbek	B3	59
Runaway Bay	B2	88
Rundu	Inset	76
Rungue	Inset	76
Rungwa, *river*	B2	68
Rupel, *river*	C1	33
Ruse	D2	50
Russell	A4	96
Rustavi	C4	45
Rutana	B2	61
Rutbah, ar-	B2	24
Rutherglen	F1	102
Rutland	N6	95
Ruvubu, *river*	C2	61
Ruvuma, *river*	C2	68
Ruways, ar-	B2, C1	25
Ruwenzori, *range*	B3	61
Ruyigi	C2	61
Ruzizi, *river*	A1, A2	61
Ružomberok	B2	42
Rwanda		61
Rweru, *lake*	C2	61
Ryazan	D3	44
Rybnik	D3	41
Ryotsu	C2	8
St. Helens	C3	30
Rysy, *mt.*	E4	41
Ryukyu, *islands*	A4, Inset II	8
Rzeszów	F3	41

S

	Key	Page
's Hertogenbosch	C3	32
Saale, *river*	B3	40
Saar, *river*	A4	40
Saarbrücken	A4	40
Saaremaa, *island*	B2	46
Saarland	A4	40
Sab Abar	A3	27
Šabac	A2	49
Sabadell	H2	37
Sabana de la Mar	C1	89
Sabana Grande	B2	90
Sabaneta	A1	89
Sabha	B2	56
Sable *cape*, Fla.	E3	126
Sable River	B4	100
Sabzevar	D2	22
Sachigo, *river*	B2	101
Sackville	E3	97
Sacramento, *capital, Calif.*	A2	126
Sadah	A1	25
Sado, *island*	C2	8
Sado, *river*	A3	36
Safata, *bay*	C3	18
Safed Koh, *range*	D3	21
Safi	B1	57
Safotu	B1	18
Saga	A3	8
Sagaing	B2	12
Sagami, *bay*	C3	8
Sagamihara	C3	8
Saginaw, Mich.	E1	126
Sagua la Grande	C2	88
Saguenay, *river*	F3	103
Sagunto	F3	37
Sahara, *desert*		55
Saharanpur Panipat	C3	20
Şahbuz	A3	45
Sahel, *region*		55
Sahiwal	D3	21
Sai Kung	Inset	10
Saidpur	B3	21
Saimaa, *lake*	C2	53
St. Adolphe	C4	96
St. Alban's	D5	98
St. Albans	C3, Inset III	30
St. Albert	D4	94
St-Alexis-des-Monts	C5	103
St-Ambroise	E3	103
St. Ambroise	B4	96
St.-André	B1	97
St-André	G4	103
St. Andrews	C2	30
St. Andrews	B3	97
St-Angèle-de-Mérici	J3	103
St. Ann's Bay	B2	88
St. Anne, *island*	Inset	70
St. Anthony	D3	98
St. Antoine	C6	103
St-Apollinaire	E5	103
St-Augustin	E3	101
St. Augustine	A2	91
St. Augustine, Fla.	E3	126
St. Austell	B4	30
St. Barbe	C3	98
St.-Basile	A1	97
St. Bernard's	D5	98
St-Brendan's	E5	98
St. Bride's	D5	98
Saint-Brieuc	B2	34
St. Brieux	F8	104
St-Bruno	E3	103
St-Camille-de-Lellis	F5	103
St. Catharines	F4	102
St. Catherine's	E5	98
St. Catherine, *mt.*	B2	91
St-Charles, *lake*	K5	103
St. Clair, *lake*	C5	102
St. Clair, *river*	C5	102
St. Claude	B4	96
Saint-Cloud	Inset II	34
St. Cloud, Minn.	D1	126
St-Côme	C5	103
St-Constant	J6	103
St. Croix	B3	97
St-Cyprien	H4	103
St. David-de-Falardeau	E3	103
St. David's	B2	91
St. David's	B3	30
Saint-Denis	Inset II	34
St-Dizier	D2	34
St-Donat	B5	103
St. Edward	B2	100
St. Eleanors	B2	100
St. Elias, *mts.*	A5	105
St. Elias, *mt.*	B1	80
Saint-Élie	B1	80
St-Émile	K5	103

	Key	Page
Saint-Étienne	D4	34
St. Eustache	C4	96
St-Eustache	H5	103
St-Fabien	H3	103
St-Fabien-de-Panet	F5	103
St-Félicien	D3	103
St-Félix-d'Otis	F3	103
St-François, *lake*	E6	103
St-François, *river*	D5	103
St.-Gédéon	F6	103
St. George	C3	97
St. George's	B5	98
St. George's, *bay*	B5	98
St. George's, *capital*	A2	91
St. George's, *channel*	B2	15
St. George's, *channel*	C3	31
St. George, Utah	B1	126
St. Georges, *bay*	F2	100
St-Georges	F5	103
Saint-Georges	C2	80
St-Germain	G4	103
Saint-Germain-en-Laye	Inset II	34
St. Gotthard, *pass*	C2	35
St. Gotthard, *tunnel*	C2	35
St. Helens	C3	30
St-Henri-de-Taillon	E3	103
St-Hubert	H5	103
St-Hyacinthe	D6	103
St.-Isidore	D1	97
St-Jacques	A1	97
St-Jacques-de-Leeds	E5	103
St-Jean, *lake*	D3	103
St. Jean Baptiste	C4	96
St-Jean-Chrysostome	L6	103
St-Jean-de-Matha	C5	103
St-Jean-Port-Joli	F4	103
St-Jean-sur-Richelieu	C6	103
St-Jérôme	B6	103
St. John	C3	97
St. John, *river*	B2	97
St. John's	E5	98
St. John's, *capital*	D5	90
Saint Joseph	A3	90
St. Joseph	E2	97
St. Joseph, *island*	B1	102
St. Joseph, Mo.	D2	126
St-Joseph-de-Beauce	F5	103
St. Kitts (St. Christopher), *island*	B2	90
St. Labre	C4	96
St-Lambert	J5	103
St. Laurent	C4	96
St-Laurent	J5	103
Saint-Laurent du Maroni	A1	80
St. Lawrence	D5	98
St. Lawrence, *cape*	G1	100
St. Lawrence, *gulf*	L4	92
St. Lawrence, *river*	K4	92
St.-Lazare	A4	96
St-Leonard	J5	103
St. Léonard	B1	97
St. Lewis	D3	98
St. Lewis, *river*	C3	98
Saint-Lô	B2	34
St. Louis	A2	100
St. Louis	E8	104
St. Louis, Mo.	D2	126
St-Louis, *lake*	H6	103
St.-Louis-de-Kent	E2	97
Saint Lucia, *channel*	B1	91
St-Ludger	D5	98
St-Ludger-de-Milot	E3	103
St. Malo	C4	96
St. Malo	E6	103
Saint-Malo	B2	34
Saint-Malo, *gulf*	B2	34
Saint-Marc	C1	89
St-Marc-du-Lac-Long	H4	103
St. Marcel	F5	103
St-Marcellin	H3	103
St. Margarets	D2	97
St. Martin	B3	96
St. Martin, *lake*	B2	96
St. Martins	D3	97
St. Mary's	D4	102
St. Mary's	E5	98
St-Maurice, *river*	C3	98
St-Michel	F5	103
St-Michel-des-Saints	C5	103
St.-Milaire	A1	97
St. Moritz	D2	35
Saint-Nazaire	B3	34
St-Nicolas	E5	103
St-Pacôme	F5	103
St-Pamphile	G5	103
St. Paul	E4	94
St. Paul, *capital, Minn.*	D1	126
St. Paul, *island*	A2	63
St. Paul, *river*	C3	98
St. Paul's	A1	90
Saint Paul's, *bay*	B2	36
St. Peters	G2	100
St. Peters	C2	100
St. Peters, *bay*	C2	100
St. Peters, *island*	B2	100
St. Petersburg	D3	44
St. Petersburg, Fla.	E3	126
St-Philémon	F5	103
St. Pierre, *island*	M4	92
St. Pierre-Jolys	C4	96
St.-Quentin	B1	97
St-Raphaël	F5	103
St-Rédempteur	K6	103
St-Rémi-d'Amherst	B5	103
St-Romuald	L6	103
St. Shotts	E5	98
St. Siméon	G4	103
St. Stephen	B3	97
St. Thomas	D5	102
St-Tite-des-Caps	F4	103
Saint-Tropez	D5	34
St-Vallier	F5	103
Saint Vincent, *passage*	B4	91
St. Vincent, *gulf*	Inset II	14
St. Vincent, *island*	B2	91

	Key	Page
St. Walburg	A7	104
St-Zacharie	F5	103
Ste-Agathe-des-Monts	B5	103
Ste-Amélie	B4	96
Ste-Anne-des-Monts	K2	103
Ste-Anne-du-Lac	A5	103
Ste-Apolline	F5	103
Ste-Claire	F5	103
Ste-Croix	E5	103
Ste-Eulalie	D5	103
Ste-Foy	E5, K6	103
Ste-Luce	H3	103
Ste-Marie	E5	103
Ste-Monique	A5	103
Ste-Rose-du-Nord	F3	103
Ste-Thérèse	E5	103
Ste-Véronique	A5	103
Ste. Agathe	C4	96
Ste. Anne	C4	96
Ste. Rose du Lac	A3	96
Ste.-Anne-de-Madawaska	A1	97
Saintes	B4	34
Sajama, *mt.*	A3	71
Sak, *river*	B3	71
Sakai	B3	8
Sakarya, *river*	B2	27
Sakhalin, *island*	I4	44
Sakishima, *islands*	Inset II	8
Sakon Nakhon	C2	12
Sal Rei	B2	58
Sal, *island*	D2	58
Sala'ilua	A1	18
Salaberry-de-Valleyfield	B6	103
Salacgriva	C2	46
Salado, *river*	B3, C2	74
Salaga	C2	64
Salahiyah	A2	27
Salal	B2	59
Salalah	B3	25
Salamá	C4	85
Salamanca	D2	37
Salamís, *island*	Inset	51
Salar de Uyuni, *salt flat*	A4	77
Salaverry	B1	89
Salcedo	C1	89
Saldanha	A3	71
Saldus	B2	46
Salé	C1	57
Salekhard	C5	44
Salelologa	A1	18
Salem	C6	20
Salem, *capital, Oreg.*	A1	126
Salerno	C3	38
Salerno, *gulf*	C2	38
Salford	C3	30
Salgótarján	B1	43
Salibia	B1	90
Salihorsk	C3	47
Salima	B2	68
Salina Cruz	E4	84
Salina, Kans.	D2	126
Salinas	C3	90
Salinas, *point*	A2	90
Salisbury	C3	30
Salisbury, *island*	N4	99
Salluit	A1	101
Sallum, as-	A1	56
Sally's Cove	C4	98
Salmon Arm	N6	95
Salmon River	A3	100
Salmon, Idaho	B1	126
Salmon, *river*	L4	95
Salo	B2	53
Salonta	A2	43
Saloum, *river*	B2	62
Salt Lake City, *capital, Utah*	B1	126
Salt Water, *lake*	Inset II	20
Salt, as-	A2	26
Salt, *cay*	D4	89
Salta	B1	74
Saltcoats	H9	104
Saltery Bay	K6	95
Saltillo, *state capital*	D2	84
Salto	B1	75
Salto del Guairá	E4	75
Salut, *islands*	B1	80
Salvador	E3	81
Salween, *river*	C2	10
Salyan	C3	45
Salzach, *river*	C3	39
Salzburg	C3	39
Salzburg Alps, *range*	C3	39
Salzgitter	B2	40
Samaná	C1	89
Samaná, *bay*	C1	89
Samaná, *cape*	C1	89
Samana, *cay*	C3	89
Samangan	B1	22
Samar, *island*	C4	12
Samar, *sea*	C4	12
Samara	D4	44
Samarian, *hills*	B1	26
Samarinda	C2	13
Samarqand	C2	23
Samarra	B2	24
Samawah, as-	C2	24
Sambalpur	D4	20
Sambre, *river*	C2	33
Samch'ŏk	C4	9
Samina, *river*	B2	33
Samokov	B3	50
Sámos, *island*	C1	51
Samothráki, *island*	C1	51
Samsø, *strait*	C3	32
Samsonvale, *lake*	Inset III	14
Samsun	B1	27
Samtredia	B3	45
Samur, *river*	D3	45
San	C3	58
San Andrés, *island*	Inset	78
San Angelo, Tex.	C2	126
San Antonio	B4, Inset	75
San Antonio	A3	85
San Antonio	C2	90

Name	Key	Page
San Antonio Oeste	B5	74
San Antonio, cape	D4	74
San Antonio	A2	88
San Antonio, Tex.	D3	126
San Baudilio de Llobregat	G2	37
San Bernardino, Calif.	C4	96
San Bernardo	Inset	76
San Blas, mts.	C2	87
San Borja	A2	77
San Carlos	B4	12
San Carlos	C3	75
San Carlos	B3	87
San Carlos de Bariloche	A5	74
San Carlos, river	B2	86
San Clara	A3	96
San Cristóbal	B2	77
San Cristóbal	B2	79
San Cristóbal de las Casas	F4	84
San Cristóbal	B2	16
San Cristóbal, island	Inset	79
San Diego, Calif.	B2	126
San Felipe	D4	78
San Felipe	B1	84
San Félix	B3	76
San Fernando	B2	12
San Fernando	C4	70
San Fernando	B4	76
San Fernando	A2	91
San Fernando de Apure	C2	79
San Francique	A2	91
San Francisco	C3	74
San Francisco	B2	86
San Francisco de Macorís	B1	89
San Francisco, Calif.	A2	126
San Germán	A2	90
San Gimignano	B2	38
San Ignacio	B3	77
San Ignacio	A2	85
San Isidro	D2	90
San Jorge, gulf	B6	74
San José	B3	75
San José	C6	85
San José de Chiquitos	B3	77
San José de las Matas	A1	89
San José del Guaviare	B4	78
San Jose, Calif.	A2	126
San José, capital	B3	86
San José, river	B2	75
San Juan	B3	74
San Juan	B4	77
San Juan	A2	89
San Juan, capital	C2	90
San Juan, passage	D2	90
San Juan Bautista	D5	75
San Juan de Los Morros	C2	79
San Juan del Norte	C3	87
San Juan del Norte, bay	C3	87
San Juan del Sur	B3	87
San Juan, river	A3	78
San Juan, river	B3	87
San Lorenzo	D4	75
San Lorenzo	B2	79
San Lorenzo	B3	86
San Lorenzo	D2	90
San Lorenzo, cape	A3	79
San Lucas	C3	84
San Lucas, cape	B3	84
San Luis	B3	74
San Luis	D3	85
San Luis Potosí, state capital	D3	84
San Luis Río Colorado	B1	84
San Luis, lake	B2	77
San Marino, capital	B1	39
San Marino, river	A1	39
San Martín, lake	A6	74
San Matías	C3	77
San Matías, gulf	C5	74
San Miguel	B2	86
San Miguel de Tucumán	B2	74
San Miguelito	C2	87
San Nicolás	C3	74
San Pablo	B3	12
San Pablo, river	B3	77
San Pawl il-Bahar	B2	36
San Pedro	C4	63
San Pédro	C4	63
San Pedro de Atacama	C2	76
San Pedro de las Colonias	D2	84
San Pedro de Macorís	C2	89
San Pedro Sula	A2	86
San Pedro, river	C2	85
San Pietro, island	B3	38
San Rafael	B3	74
San Remo	A2	38
San Salvador de Jujuy	B1	74
San Salvador, capital	A2	86
San Salvador, island	Inset	79
San Salvador, island	C3	89
San Salvador, river	A2	75
San Sebastián	F1	37
San Sebastián	B2	90
San Severo	C2	38
San Valentín, mt.	B8	76
San Vicente	B2	86
San Vito, cape	C3	38
San, river	E2	11
San, river	F3	41
Sana, capital	A1	25
Sanaga, river	B2	65
Sanandaj	B2	22
Sanaw	C1	25
Sancti Spíritus	C2	88
Sand, river	E3	94
Sandakan	D2	13
Sanday, island	Inset I	30
Sandilands	C4	96
Sandougou, river	B3	62
Sandoy, island	Inset	32
Sandspit	G4	95
Sandur	Inset	32
Sandwich, bay	C2	98
Sandy Bay	H5	104
Sandy Cove	A3	100
Sandy Lake	D3	94
Sandy Lake	A4	96
Sandy Lake	B2	101
Sandy Point	B2	89
Sandy Point Town	A1	90
Sandy, island	B2	18
Sandy, island	B2	91
Sandy, lake	C4	98
Sanford	C4	96
Sangha, river	D2	66
Sangmélima	B3	65
Sangre Grande	A2	91
Sangro, river	C2	38
Sangudo	C4	94
Sankosh, river	B2	19
Sankrail	Inset II	20
Sankt Gallen	D1	35
Sankt Pölten	D2	39
Sankuru, river	C2	67
Sannar	C2	59
Sanski Most	A1	48
Sant Julià de Lòria	A3	36
Sant'Antioco, island	B3	38
Santa Ana	A2	77
Santa Ana	B2	86
Santa Ana, range	C1	75
Santa Ana, volcano	A2	86
Santa Bárbara	B2	86
Santa Barbara, Calif.	B2	126
Santa Catarina	B1	81
Santa Clara	C2	88
Santa Coloma de Gramanet	H2	37
Santa Cruz	B3	77
Santa Cruz de Tenerife	Inset I	37
Santa Cruz, island	Inset	79
Santa Cruz, islands	C2	16
Santa Cruz, river	A7	74
Santa Elena de Uairen	D3	79
Santa Elena, point	A4	79
Santa Fe	C3	74
Santa Fe, N. Mex.	C2	126
Santa Inés	Inset	76
Santa Inés, island	B9	76
Santa Isabel	C3	90
Santa Isabel, island	A1	16
Santa Isabel, peak	A1	66
Santa Lucía, river	B3	75
Santa Lucía, island	B2	58
Santa Maria	D2	58
Santa Maria	J3	103
Santa Maria di Leuca, cape	D3	38
Santa Maria, island	B2	18
Santa María, island	Inset	79
Santa Marta	B2	78
Santa Rita	B2	86
Santa Rosa	C4	74
Santa Rosa	B4	79
Santa Rosa de Copán	A2	86
Santa Rosa del Palmar	B3	77
Santa Rosalía	B2	84
Santana do Livramento	C5	81
Santander	E1	37
Santarém	A3	36
Santarém	C2	81
Santiago	B2	87
Santiago	B1	89
Santiago de Compostela	B1	37
Santiago de Cuba	E3	88
Santiago del Estero	C2	74
Santiago, capital	B4, Inset	76
Santiago, river	A2	89
Santo André	Inset II	81
Santo Antão, island	A1	58
Santo Domingo	B2	90
Santo Domingo de los Colorados	B3	79
Santo Domingo, capital	C2	89
Santo Tomás de Castilla	E4	85
Santos	D4, Inset II	81
Sanyati, river	B1	69
São Bernardo do Campo	Inset II	81
São Caetano do Sul	Inset II	81
São Domingos	A1	62
São Filipe	B4	58
São Francisco, river	D3	81
São Gonçalo	Inset I	81
São João de Meriti	Inset II	81
São José do Rio Prêto	D4	81
São Luís	D2	81
São Nicolau, island	B3	58
São Paulo	D4, Inset II	81
São Tiago, island	C3	58
São Tomé, capital	B2	63
São Tomé, island	B4	63
São Tomé, mt.	B4	63
São Vicente, cape	A4	36
São Vicente	Inset II	81
Saona, island	D2	89
Saône, river	D3	34
Sapele	C5	65
Sapitwa, mt.	B3	68
Sapporo	Inset I	8
Sar, passage	B3	17
Sar-e Pol	B1	22
Sara Buri	B3	12
Saragossa	F2	37
Sarajevo, capital	B2	48
Saramacca, river	B2	80
Sarandë	A4	49
Saransk	D4	44
Sarapiquí river	B2	86
Sarasota, Fla.	E3	126
Saratov	D4	44
Saravan	D2	11
Sarawak, state	C2	13
Saraya	B3	62
Sarbhang	B3	19
Sarcelles	Inset II	34
Sarda, river	A2	19
Sardinia, island	B2	38
Sargodha	D3	21
Sarh	B5	59
Sari	C2	22
Sariwŏn	A3	9
Sarjektjakko	C1	53
Sarnia	C5	102
Saronic, gulf	Inset	51
Šar Planina, mts.	B3	49
Sarstoon, river	A4	85
Sarstún, river	D4	85
Sary Tash	C3	23
Sarygamysh Koli, lake	B2	22
Saryshaghan	D2	23
Sasamungga	A1	16
Sasaram	D4	20
Sasebo	A3	8
Saskatchewan, river	G3	92
Saskatoon	D8	104
Sassandra	C4	63
Sassandra, river	C2, C4	63
Sassari	B2	38
Sassnitz	C1	40
Satpura, range	C4	20
Satsuma, peninsula	A4	8
Sattahip	B3	12
Satu Mare	B2	43
Sauble Beach	D3	102
Saudhárkrókur	B2	52
Saül	B2	80
Sault Ste. Marie	A1	102
Sault Ste. Marie, Mich.	E1	126
Sault-au-Mouton	G3	103
Saumur	B3	34
Saurimo	D3	70
Sauteurs	B2	91
Savá	B2	86
Savai'i, island	A2	18
Savalou	A3	64
Savan, island	B3	91
Savannah, Ga.	E2	126
Savannakhet	C3	11
Savé	B2	64
Savigny-sur-Orge	Inset II	34
Savissivik	B2	48
Savona	B1	38
Savonlinna	C2	53
Savu, sea	D2	13
Sawda, mt.	B2	24
Sawhaj	B2	56
Sawqirah	C2	25
Sawqirah, bay	C2	25
Saxony	C3	40
Saxony-Anhalt	B3	40
Sayabec	J3	103
Sayan, mts.	D6	44
Sayhut	C1	25
Sayward	K6	95
Sázava, river	B3	42
Scafell Pike, mt.	B2	30
Scarborough	C2	30
Scarborough	C2	91
Scarborough	F4, L5	102
Schaan	B2	33
Schaerbeek	C2	33
Schaffhausen	C1	35
Schefferville	D3	98
Schefferville	C3	101
Schelde, river	B2	33
Schellenberg	B1	33
Scheveningen	B2	32
Schiedam	B3	32
Schiermonnikoog, island	D1	32
Schleswig	B1	40
Schleswig-Holstein	B2	40
Schouwen, island	A3	32
Schreiber	C3	101
Schuler	E6	94
Schwäbisch Gmünd	B4	40
Schwedt	C2	40
Schweinfurt	B3	40
Schwerin	B2	40
Schweriner, lake	B2	40
Schwyz	C1	35
Scilly, islands	A4	30
Scone	B2	30
Sconser	A1	30
Scotstown	E6	103
Scotswood	A3	94
Scott, island	C5	107
Scottsbluff, Nebr.	C1	126
Scugog, lake	G3	102
Scunthorpe	C3	30
Scutari, lake	A1, A3	49
Sczcecinek	C2	41
Seal Cove	C4	98
Seal, river	D1	96
Searchmont	A1	102
Seattle, Wash.	A1	126
Seawell	C4	91
Sebdero, river	C1	57
Sebright	F3	102
Sechura, desert	A2	77
Seda, river	B3	36
Sedalia	E5	94
Sedan	D2	34
Sédhiou	B3	62
Sedley	F10	104
Seeley's Bay	J3	102
Sefadu	B1	63
Segbana	B2	64
Ségou	B2	64
Segovia	D2	37
Séguéla	C3	63
Segura, river	E3	37
Seinäjoki	B2	53
Seine, river	C2, Inset II	34
Sekake	B2	71
Sekondi-Takoradi	B4	64
Selebi-Phikwe	C2	69
Selenge Mörön, river	C2	11
Sélibaby	B3	62
Selínia	Inset	51
Selkirk	C4	96
Selvas, region	B2	81
Selwyn, river	A3	49
Semara	A1	58
Semarang	B2	13
Sembawang	B1	13
Semeru, mt.	C2	13
Semey (Semipalatinsk)	E1	23
Semmering, pass	D3	39
Semois, river	D3	33
Sempach	C1	35
Sen, river	D2	11
Senaki	B3	45
Sendai	B2	8
Senegal, river	B1, C2	62
Senkaku, islands	Inset II	8
Senmonorom	F3	11
Senne, river	C2	33
Senneterre	A4	101
Senta	B2	49
Seoul, capital	B4	9
Sept-Îles	C3	101
Septentrional, range	A1	89
Serangoon	B1	13
Serbia, republic	B2	49
Seremban	A2	13
Serenje	C2	67
Sergipe	E3	81
Seria	A2	13
Serov	D5	44
Serowe	B2	69
Serpent, island	D1	69
Sérrai	B1	51
Serranilla, bank	Inset	88
Serravalle	B1	39
Serrekunda	C2	62
Serule	B2	69
Sese, islands	C4	61
Sesheke	A3	67
Seti, river	A2	19
Sétif	B1	57
Settat	C1	57
Setúbal	A3	36
Setúbal, bay	A3	36
Sevan, lake	C2	45
Sevastopol	C4	47
Seven Persons	E6	94
Seven Sisters Falls	C4	96
Severn, river	C3	30
Severn, river	B2	101
Severnaya Zemlya, islands	A6	44
Seville	D4	37
Sevran	Inset II	34
Sèvres	Inset II	34
Sewa, river	B2	63
Seward, Alaska	Inset I	126
Sfax	C2	57
Sfîntu Gheorghe	C3	43
Sha Tin	Inset	10
Shaanxi	D2	10
Shabwah	B1	25
Shache	A2	10
Shackleton Ice Shelf, glacier	C2	107
Shahr-e Kord	C3	22
Shaki	B3	65
Shalqar	B2	23
Sham, ash-	D1	25
Shamattawa	E2	96
Shamgong	B2	19
Shan, plateau	C2	12
Shanchung	B1	9
Shandong	E2	10
Shangani, river	A2	69
Shanghai	F2	10
Shannon	B2	31
Shannon, river	B2	31
Shantou	E3	10
Shanxi	E2	10
Shanxi	F3	10
Shaoguan	E3	10
Shaoxing	F3	10
Shaoyang	E3	10
Sharbot Lake	J3	102
Sharjah	C2	25
Shashe, river	C2	69
Shashi	E2	10
Shatt al-Arab, river	C2	24
Shaunavon	B11	104
Shawinigan	D5	103
Sheberghan	B1	22
Shediac	E2	97
Sheet Harbour	E3	100
Sheffield	C3	30
Sheguianda	D2	102
Sheho	G9	104
Shek Pik	Inset	10
Shelburne	B4	100
Shelburne	E3	102
Shelikhov, gulf	C9	44
Shell Lake	C7	104
Shellbrook	D7	104
Shelter Bay	N6	95
Shëngjin	A2	49
Shenyang	F1	10
Sherbro, island	A2	63
Sherbrooke	E6	103
Sheridan, Wyo.	C1	126
Sherridon	A1	96
Sherwood Park	D4	94
Shetland, islands	Inset I	30
Sheva	Inset I	20
Shewa Gimira	B3	60
Shibar, pass	B2	22
Shibin al-Kawm	B1	56
Shijiazhuang	E2	10
Shikarpur	C4	21
Shikoku, island	B3	8
Shillong	F3	20
Shimizu	C3	8
Shimonoseki	A3	8
Shimonoseki, strait	A3	8
Shinano, river	C2	8
Shinas	C1	25
Shindand	A2	22
Shinyanga	B1	68
Shiono, cape	B3	8
Ship Cove	D3	98
Shippagan	E1	97
Shirane, mt.	C3	8
Shiraz	C4	22
Shire, river	B3	68
Shiretoko, cape	Inset I	8
Shizuoka	C3	8
Shkhara, mt.	B3	45
Shkodër	A1	49
Shkumbin, river	A2	49
Shoal Lake	A4	96
Sholapur	C5	20
Shostka	C1	47
Shreveport, La.	D2	126
Shrewsbury	C3	30
Shrirampur	Inset II	20
Shubenacadie	D2	100
Shubra al-Khaymah	B1	56
Shumen	E2	50
Shurugwi	B2	69
Shwebo	B2	12
Shymkent (Chimkent)	C2	23
Siahan, range	B4	21
Sialkot	E3	21
Siargao, island	C4	12
Šiauliai	B2	46
Sibbald	E5	94
Siberia, region	C7	44
Siberut, island	A2	13
Sibiti	B5	66
Sibiu	C3	43
Sibu	C2	13
Sibuyan, island	B3	12
Sibuyan, sea	B3	12
Sicamous	N6	95
Sichuan	D2	10
Sicily, island	C3	38
Sicily, strait	B3	38
Sico, river	C2	86
Sicuani	C3	77
Sidi bel Abbès	A1	57
Sidi Bou Zid	B2	57
Sidlaw, hills	B2	30
Sidney	L7	95
Sidney	B2	96
Sidon (Sayda)	A2	26
Sidra, gulf	C1	56
Sidvokodvo	B2	71
Siedlce	F2	41
Siegen	B3	40
Siemiang	E1	11
Siemreab	B2	11
Siena	C2	38
Sieradz	D3	41
Sierra de Cayey, mts.	C2	90
Sierra de Loquillo, mts.	D2	90
Sierra Madre, mts.	B2	12
Sierra Madre, mts.	C5	85
Sierra Nevada de Santa Marta, mts.	B2	78
Sierra Nevada, mts., Calif.	A2	126
Sifton	A3	96
Siggiewi	B2	36
Sighetul Marmației	B2	43
Sighișoara	C2	43
Siglufjördhur	B1	52
Siguatepeque	B2	86
Siguiri	D2	62
Siirt	E3	27
Sikanni Chief	L2	95
Sikasso	B3	58
Sikhote Alin, range	E8	44
Sikkim (state)	E3	20
Šilalė	B2	46
Silay	B4	12
Silesia, region	C3	41
Silet	B2	57
Silgarhi	B2	19
Silhouette, island	C1	70
Siliana	B1	57
Silifke	C3	27
Silisili, mt.	B2	18
Silistra	F1	50
Silkeborg	B2	32
Sillery	K6	103
Šilutė	A2	46
Silvassa	B4	20
Silver	C4	96
Silver City, N. Mex.	C2	126
Sima	B2	67
Simcoe, lake	E4	101
Simeulue, island	A1	13
Simferopol	C4	47
Simikot	B1	19
Simla	C2	20
Simon, lake	A6	103
Simonette, river	A4	94
Simonhouse	A2	96
Simpson, desert	C2	14
Sinai, peninsula	B2	56
Sinaloa	C3	84
Sincelejo	B2	78
Sinclair	A4	96
Sinclair Mills	M4	95
Sindhuli Garhi	C2	19
Siné, river	B2	62
Sines	A4	36
Singapore, capital	B1	13
Singapore, island	B1	13
Singapore, strait	B2	13
Singen	B5	40
Singida	C1	68
Singur	Inset II	20
Sinoe	C2	27
Sinpo	C2	9
Sint-Niklaas	C1	33
Sint-Truiden	D2	33
Sinŭiju	A2	9
Sió, river	B2	43
Siófok	B2	43
Sion	B2	35
Sioux City, Iowa	D1	126
Sioux Falls, S. Dak.	D1	126
Sioux Lookout	B2	101
Sipaliwini	A3	80
Siparia	A2	91
Siping	F1	10
Sipiwesk, lake	C1	96
Siple, mt.	B8	107
Sirajganj	C4	21
Sirba, river	D2	64
Siret	D2	43
Siret, river	D2	43
Sirjan	D4	22
Sisak	C1	48
Sisian	D3	45
Sisimiut (Holsteinsborg)	B2	106
Sisophon	B2	11
Siteki	B2	71
Sitka, Alaska	Inset I	126
Sittang, river	C2	12
Sittard	C4	32
Sittwe	A2	12
Siuna	B2	87
Sivas	D2	27
Siwah	A2	56
Sixaola, river	C3	86
Sjælland, island	C3	32
Skagen	C1	32
Skagerrak, strait	A3	53
Skåne, region	B3	53
Skaw, cape	C1	32
Skead	E1	102
Skeena, mts.	H3	95
Skeena, river	H4	95
Skeleton, coast	A1	70
Skellefteå	D2	53
Skellefteälven, river	C1	53
Skien	B4	52
Skierniewice	E3	41
Skikda	B1	57
Skíros, island	C2	51
Skive	B2	32
Skjern, river	B3	32
Skookumchuck	P6	95
Skopje, capital	B2	48
Skovorodino	D8	44
Skownan	A3	96
Skye, island	A1	30
Slagelse	C2	32
Slaná, river	C3	42
Slatina	C3	43
Slave Lake	C3	94
Slave, river	F2	92
Slavonia, region	C2	48
Slavonska Požega	C2	48
Slavonski Brod	D2	48
Sliema	C2	36
Slieve Donard, mt.	B2	31
Sligo	B1	31
Sliven	E3	50
Slobozia	D3	43
Slough	Inset III	30
Slovenskérudohorie, mts.	C2	42
Sluch', river	B1	47
Słupsk	C1	41
Småland, region	B3	53
Smallwood, reservoir	D3	98
Smeaton	F7	104
Smederevo	B2	49
Smilovichi	D2	47
Smiltene	C2	46
Smith River	J1	95
Smithers	J4	95
Smithers Landing	J3	95
Smiths Cove	B3	100
Smiths Falls	J3	102
Smithville	F4	102
Smoky, river	A3, A4	94
Smolensk	D3	44
Smolevichi	D2	47
Smolyan	C4	50
Smoothstone, lake	D6	104
Smoothstone, river	D6	104
Snake, river	C3	105
Snake, river	B1	126
Snaring	A4	94
Sneek	C1	32
Snežka, mt.	B2	42
Śniardwy, lake	F2	41
Snow Lake	A2	96
Snowdon, mt.	B3	30
Snowdrift	F4	99
Snowflake	B4	96
Snug Harbour	E3	11
Snuol	E3	11
Soan-kundo, islands	B5	9
Sobaek, mts.	B5	9
Sobat, river	C3	59
Sobradinho, reservoir	D3	81
Sobral	D2	81
Soc Trang	A5	11
Sochi	E3	44
Socompa	C2	76
Socorro, N. Mex.	C2	126
Socotra, island	C2	25
Söderhamn	C2	53
Sofia, capital	B3	50
Sofiya	B3	69
Sognafjord, fjord	B3	52
Soissons	C2	34
Söjosŏn, bay	A3	9
Sokch'o	C3	9
Sokodé	B2	64
Sokoto	C1	65
Sokoto, plains	C1	65
Sokoto, river	C1	65
Sol, coast	D4	37
Sola	B1	18
Soldeu	B1	36
Solihull	C3	30
Solo	B2	13
Solomon, sea	B2	15
Solosolo	C2	18
Solway, estuary	B2	30
Solwezi	B2	67
Sombe, beach	E2	90
Sombor	A2	49
Sombra	C5	102
Somerset	A4	96
Somerset, island	K2	92
Somes, river	B2	43
Somme, river	C2	34
Somoto	A2	87
Son La	A2	11
Son, river	D4	20
Sondrio	B1	38
Sønderborg	B4	32
Songea	C3	68
Songhua, river	F1	10

	Key	Page
Songkhla	B5	12
Songköl	D2	23
Sŏngnam	B4	9
Songnim	A3	9
Songwe, river	B1	68
Sonora	B1	84
Sonsonate	A2	86
Sonsoral, island	Inset	17
Sooke	L7	95
Sopron	A2	43
Sor, river	B3	36
Sorel	C5	103
Soria	E2	37
Sørøya	C3	32
Soroca	B1	50
Sorocaba	D4	81
Sorong	E2	13
Soroti	C3	61
Sorraia, river	A3	36
Sorrento	C2	38
Sosnowiec	D3	41
Soso, bay	B3	17
Sota, river	B2	64
Sotk	C2	45
Sotouboua	B2	64
Soubré	C4	63
Soufrière	B4	90
Soufrière	A2	91
Soufrière, mt.	A1	91
Soufrière	B1	91
Soufrière, volcano	A2	91
Souillac	C4	69
Soungrougrou, river	B3	62
Sources, mt.	B1	71
Souris	A4	96
Souris	C2	100
Souris, river	G11	104
Sous, plain	B2	57
Sous, river	B2	57
Sousse	C2	57
Sousúa	B1	89
South Andaman, island	F6	20
S. Aulatsivik, island	E3	98
South Australia	C2	14
South Baymouth	C2	102
South Bend, Ind.	E1	126
South Branch	B5	98
South Brook	C4	98
South Carolina	E2	126
South China, sea	E4, Inset	10
South Corona, channel	B2	36
South Dakota	C1	126
South Downs, hills	C3	30
South Dum-Dum	Inset II	20
South Georgia, island		4
S. Gut St.-Anns	G1	100
South Henik, lake	J4	99
S. Indian Lake	D1	96
South Magnetic Pole	C3	107
South Male, atoll	A3	19
South Malosmadulu, atoll	A2	19
South Milford	B3	100
S. Moose, lake	B2	96
South Orkney, islands	C12	107
South Ossetia, region	B3	45
South Pole	A17	107
South Rawdon	D3	100
South River	F2	102
South Ronaldsay, island	Inset I	30
South Saskatchewan, river	D8	104
South Shetland, islands	C12	107
South Shields	C2	30
South Taranaki, bight	B2	15
South Uist, island	A1	30
South West, cape	A4	15
South, island	A3	15
Southampton	C4	30
Southampton	D3	102
Southampton, island	L4	99
Southend	G4	104
Southend-on-Sea	D3	30
Southern Alps, mts.	A3	15
Southern Bug, river	B2	47
Southern Uplands, mts.	B2	30
Southland, plains	A4	15
Southport	C3	30
Southport	B2	100
Sovetskaya Gavan	E9	44
Soweto	C2	71
Soya, point	Inset I	8
Soyapango	A2	86
Soyo	B2	70
Sozh, river	E3	47
Spa	D2	33
Spandau	C1	102
Spanish	C1	102
Spanish Town	C3	88
Sparta	B3	51
Spartanburg, S.C.	E2	126
Spartivento, cape	D3	38
Sparwood	P6	95
Speightstown	A2	91
Spence Bay	K3	99
Spencer, gulf	C3	14
Spences Bridge	M6	95
Sperrin, mts.	A2	30
Spessart, mts.	B4	40
Spey, river	B1	30
Speyer	B4	40
Spiritwood	C7	104
Spišská Nová Ves	C2	42
Spithead, channel	C4	30
Split	C3	48
Split Lake	D1	96
Splügen, pass	D2	35
Spokane, Wash.	B1	126
Spoleto	C2	38
Sprague	C1	102
Sprague	D4	96
Spree, river	C3	40
Spring Bay	C2	102
Spring Coulee	D6	94
Spring Hall	A2	91
Springbok	A2	71
Springdale	A2	98
Springfield, capital, Ill.	E2	126
Springfield, Mass.	F1	126
Springfield, Mo.	D2	126
Springhill	C2	100

	Key	Page
Springs	C2	71
Springside	H9	104
Springstein	C4	96
Springwater	B9	104
Spruce Grove	D4	94
Spy Hill	J10	104
Squamish	L6	95
Square Islands	D3	98
Sre Ambel	B4	11
Srebrenica	C1	48
Sredna Gora, mts.	C3	50
Sremska Mitrovica	A2	49
Sreng, river	B2	11
Srinagar	B2	20
Stafford	C3	30
Stand Off	D6	94
Standard	D5	94
Stanley	C2	97
Stanmore	E5	94
Stanovoy, range	D8	44
Star City	F8	104
Stara Zagora	D3	50
Starbuck	C4	96
Starbuck, island	D2	17
Starnberg, lake	B5	40
Start, point	B4	30
Staubbach, falls	B2	35
Stavanger	B4	52
Stavropol	E4	44
Stayner	E3	102
Stead	C4	96
Steen River	B1	94
Stefanson, island	G2	99
Steinbach	C4	96
Steinkjer	C3	52
Stellarton	E2	100
Stellenbosch	A3	71
Stendal	B2	40
Stepanavan	A2	45
Stephenville	B5	98
Stettler	D5	94
Stevenage	Inset III	30
Stevenson, lake	C2	96
Stewart River	B4	105
Stewart, island	B4	15
Stewart, river	B4, C3	105
Stewiacke	D2	100
Steyr	D2	39
Stikine	G3	95
Stikine, river	G2	95
Stirling	B2	30
Stirling	H3	102
Štip	C2	49
Stockerau	E2	39
Stockholm, capital	C3	53
Stoeng Treng	D2	11
Stoke-on-Trent	C3	30
Stonecliffe	H1	102
Stoneham	E4	103
Stonewall	C4	96
Stoney Point	C5	102
Stony Mountain	C4	96
Stony Plain	D4	94
Stony Rapids	E1	104
Storå, river	B2	32
Storavan, lake	C1	53
Store, strait	C3	32
Storkerson, peninsula	G2	99
Stornoway	A1	30
Stornoway	E6	103
Storsjön, lake	B2	53
Storthoaks	A4	96
Stoughton	G11	104
Strakonice	A3	42
Stralsund	C1	40
Strangford	B2	30
Stranraer	B2	30
Strasbourg	D2	34
Strasbourg	F9	104
Stratford	D4	102
Stratford	E6	103
Stratford-upon-Avon	C3	30
Strathclair	A4	96
Strathlorne	F1	100
Strathnaver	L4	95
Strathroy	D5	102
Straubing	C4	40
Streymoy, island	Inset	32
Stromboli, island	C3	38
Stronsay, island	Inset I	30
Struer	A2	48
Struma, river	A3	50
Strumica	C2	48
Stryama, river	C3	50
Stuart, lake	K4	95
Stubbs	B2	91
Stuie	J5	95
Sturgeon	C2	100
Sturgeon Falls	D3	101
Sturgis	H9	104
Stuttgart	B4	40
Subotica	A1	49
Suceava	D2	43
Suchiate, river	A5	85
Sucre, capital	A3	77
Sudbury	E1	102
Sudd, region	B3	59
Suddie	B2	80
Sudeten, mts.	B3	41
Sudirman, range	E2	13
Suduroy, island	Inset	32
Sue, river	B3	59
Suez	B2	56
Suez, canal	B1	56
Suez, gulf	B2	56
Sugandha	Inset II	20
Suhar	C1	25
Sühbaatar	C1	11
Suhl	B3	40
Suir, river	C2	31
Suita	B3	8
Sukabumi	B2	13
Sukhnah, as-	B2	27
Sukhothai	B2	12
Sukhumi	A3	45
Sukkur	C4	21

	Key	Page
Sula, islands	D2	13
Sulaiman, range	C4	21
Sulaybikhat, as-	B2	24
Sulaymaniyah, as-	C1	24
Sulayyil, as-	B2	24
Sulima	B2	63
Sullana	A1	77
Sullivan, lake	E5	94
Sulu, archipelago	B5	12
Sulu, sea	A4	12
Sülüktü	A3	23
Sumatra, island	B2	13
Šumava, mts.	A3	42
Sumba, island	D2	13
Sumbar, river	B2	22
Sumbawa, island	C2	13
Sumbawanga	B2	68
Sumbe	B3	70
Summerford	D4	98
Summerland	N6	95
Summerside	B2	100
Summerville	E5	98
Summit Lake	K2	95
Summit Lake	L4	95
Šumperk	C3	42
Sumqayit	C2	45
Sumy	C1	47
Sun City	C2	71
Sun Kosi, river	C2	19
Sunch'ŏn	B5	9
Sundarbans, region	C7	21
Sunderland	C2	30
Sunderland	F3	102
Sundi	C1	63
Sundown	C4	96
Sundridge	F2	102
Sundsvall	C2	53
Sunnynook	E5	94
Sunset House	B3	94
Sunyani	A3	64
Sup'ung, reservoir	A2	9
Superior, Wis.	D1	126
Sur	C1	25
Sur (Tyre)	A2	26
Surab	C4	21
Surabaya	C2	13
Surakarta	C2	13
Surat	B4	20
Surat Thani	B4	12
Sûre, river	A2, B2	33
Surgut	C5	44
Surigao	C4	12
Surin	C3	12
Suriname, river	B3	80
Surkhob, river	B1	23
Surma, river	E3	21
Surprise	F1	95
Surt	C1	56
Surtsey, island	A3	52
Surud Ad, mt.	B1	60
Sussex	D3	97
Susuman	C9	44
Sutlej, river	D4	21
Sutton West	F3	102
Suva, capital	B3	17
Suvadiva, atoll	A4	19
Suwałki	F1	41
Suwanose, island	A4	8
Suwar, as-	B2	27
Suwayda, as-	A3	27
Suwŏn	B4	9
Suzano	Inset II	81
Suzhou	F2	10
Svalbard, islands		5
Svay Rieng	D4	11
Svendborg	C3	32
Šventoji, river	C2	46
Svetozarevo	B3	49
Svishtov	D2	50
Svitavy	C3	42
Svobodnyy	D8	44
Swabian Jura, mts.	B4	40
Swains, island	A1	18
Swakopmund	B2	70
Swan Hills	C4	94
Swan Lake	B4	96
Swan River	A3	96
Swan, lake	A3	96
Swan, river	Inset I	14
Swansea	B3	30
Swift Current	D5	98
Swift Current	C10	104
Swindon	C3	30
Świnoujście	B2	41
Swords	C2	31
Sydney	G1	100
Sydney	B2	17
Sydney, N.S.W., capital	E3, Inset IV	14
Syktyvkar	C4	44
Sylhet	E4	21
Syracuse (Siracusa)	C3	38
Syracuse, N.Y.	F1	126
Syrdarya, river	A1, C2	23
Syrian, desert	B1	26
Szczecin	B2	41
Szeged	C2	43
Székesfehérvár	B2	43
Szekszárd	B2	43
Szentes	C2	43
Szolnok	C2	43
Szombathely	A2	43

T

	Key	Page
Taabo, lake	D3	63
Tabar, islands	B2	15
Tabasará, mts.	B2	87
Tabasco	F4	84
Tablebala	A2	57
Tablas, island	B3	12
Tabligbo	B3	64
Taboão da Serra	Inset II	81

	Key	Page
Tábor	B3	42
Tabora	B2	68
Tabou	C4	63
Tabriz	B2	22
Tabuaeran, island	D1	17
Tabuk	A1	24
Tabusintac	D1	97
Tabwemasana, mt.	B2	18
Tacaná, volcano	A4	85
Tacloban	C4	12
Tacna	C4	77
Tacoma, Wash.	A1	126
Tacuarembó	C1	75
Tacuarembó	C1	75
Tacuarí, river	D2	75
Tadjoura	B2	60
Tadmur	B2	27
Tadoussac	G3	103
Taebaek-Sanmaek, mts.	C3	9
Taedong, river	B3	9
Taegu	C5	9
Taejŏn	B4	9
Tafahi, island	C1	17
Tafilah, at-	A2	26
Taga	C1	18
Taganrog, gulf	D3	47
Tagish	C5	105
Tagish, lake	C5	95
Tagula, island	B3	15
Tagus, river	D3	37
Tahan, mt.	B2	13
Tahat, mt.	B2	57
Tahoua	B3	59
Tai, lake	F2	10
Tai'an	E2	10
T'aichung	B1	9
Taif, at-	B2	24
T'ainan	B1	9
Taipei, capital	B1	9
Taitao, peninsula	A8	76
T'aitung	B2	9
Taiwan, strait	E3	10
Taiyuan	E2	10
Taizz	A2	25
Tajumulco, volcano	B4	85
Tak	B2	12
Taka, island	B1	16
Takamaka	A4	8
Takamatsu	B3	8
Takara, island	A4	8
Takatsuki	B3	8
Takev	C5	11
Takikawa	C1	8
Takla Makan, desert	B2	10
Takla, lake	K3	95
Takua Pa	B4	12
Takutu, river	A4	80
Talagante	Inset	76
Talak, region	B2	59
Talamanca, range	C3	86
Talara	A1	77
Talas	C1	23
Talaud, islands	D1	13
Talavera de la Reina	D3	37
Talca	B5	76
Talcahuano	B6	76
Taldyqorghan	D2	23
Talish, mts.	C3	45
Tall Afar	B1	24
Tallahassee, capital, Fla.	E2	126
Tallinn, capital	C1	46
Taloqan	B1	22
Talsi	B2	46
Taltal	A3	76
Taltson, river	F4	99
Tamale	B2	64
Tamanrasset	B3	57
Tamarin	B3	69
Tamaulipas	E3	84
Tambacounda	C3	62
Tambo, river	C3, C4?	77
Tâmega, river	B2	36
Tampa, Fla.	E3	126
Tampere	B2	53
Tampico	E3	84
Tampines	B1	13
Tampok, river	B2	80
Tamsagbulag	D2	11
Tamu	B1	12
Tamworth, N.S.W.	E3	14
Tan-Tan	B2	57
Tana, lake	B1	60
Tana, river	F4	61
Tana, river	F1	52
Tanabe	B3	8
Tanchŏn	C2	9
Tandil	D4	74
Tanega, island	A4	8
Tanen, range	B2	12
Tanezrouft, mts.	A2	57
Tanga	C2	68
Tanga, islands	B2	15
Tangail	C4	21
Tanganyika, lake	A2	68
Tanggula, range	C2	10
Tangier	C1	57
Tangier	E3	100
Tangshan	E2	10
Tanimbar, islands	E2	13
Tanjungpinang	B1	13
Tanna, island	C4	18
Tano, river	A3	64
Tanshui	B1	9
Tanta	B1	56
Taongi, island	B1	16
Taoudenni	C1	58
T'aoyüan	B1	9
Tapa	C1	46
Tapachula	F5	84
Tapajós, river	C2	81
Tapanahoni, river	B3	80
Tapeta	B2	63
Taquari, river	C3	81
Tara	D5	44
Tara, river	A3	49
Taraba, river	F3	65
Tarakan	C1	13
Taranto	D2	38

	Key	Page
Taranto, gulf	D2	38
Tarapoto	B2	77
Tararua, range	C3	15
Tarat	B2	57
Tarawa, capital	A1	17
Tarbes	C5	34
Taree, N.S.W.	E3	14
Tarif	B2	25
Tarija	B4	77
Tarim, river	B1	10
Tarin Kowt	B2	22
Tarnobrzeg	E3	41
Tarnów	E3	41
Taroudant	C2	57
Tarrafal	C3	58
Tarragona	G2	37
Tarrasa	G2	37
Tarsus	C3	27
Tartu	D2	46
Tartus	A2	27
Tarvo	B3	77
Taseko, lake	L5	95
Tash Kömür	C2	23
Tashigang	C2	19
Tashir	B1	45
Tashkent, capital	C2	23
Tasikmalaya	B2	13
Tasman, bay	B3	15
Tasman, sea	E3	14
Tasmania	D4	14
Tata	C2	57
Tatabánya	B2	43
Tatamagouche	D2	100
Tataouine	C3	57
Tatar, strait	D9	44
Tatarstan, republic	D4	44
Tathlina, lake	E4	99
Tatla Lake	K5	95
Tatlayoko Lake	K5	95
Tatra, range	B2	42
Tau	A1	18
Taumaruni	C2	15
Taunggyi	C2	12
Taunton	C3	30
Taunus, mts.	B3	40
Taupo	C2	15
Taupo, lake	C2	15
Tauragé	B2	46
Tauranga	C2	15
Taureau, reservoir	C5	103
Taurus, mts.	B3	27
Tauu, island	A1	15
Tavan Bogd Uul, mt.	A2	11
Taverny	Inset II	34
Taveuni, island	C2	17
Tavoy	C3	12
Tavoy, point	C3	12
Tawau	D3	13
Tawi Tawi, island	A5	12
Tay, estuary	C2	30
Tay, river	B2	30
Tay, river	C4	105
Taymouth	C2	97
Taymyr, peninsula	B6	44
Taymyria, autonomous okrug	B6	44
Taza	C1	57
Tazin, lake	A1	104
Tazin, river	B1	104
Tbilisi, capital	C4	45
Tchamba	B2	64
Tchaourou	B3	64
Tchentlo, lake	K3	95
Tchibanga	A2	66
Te Anau	A4	15
Tebicuary, river	D5	75
Tecomán	D4	84
Tecuci	D3	43
Tedzhen	C3	22
Tedzhen, river	C3	22
Tees, river	C2	30
Teeswater	D3	102
Tefé	B2	81
Tegal	B2	13
Tegucigalpa, capital	B2	86
Tehek, lake	J4	99
Tehkummah	D2	102
Tehran, capital	B2	22
Tehuacán	E4	84
Tehuantepec, gulf	E4	84
Tehuantepec, isthmus	F4	84
Teifi, river	B3	30
Tekapo, lake	B3	15
Tekeze, river	B1	60
Tekirdağ	A2	27
Tel Aviv-Jaffa	B1	26
Tela	B2	86
Telavi	C4	45
Telde	Inset I	37
Telegraph Creek	G2	95
Teles Pires, river	C2	81
Telford	C3	30
Telkwa	J4	95
Telok Anson	B2	13
Telšiai	B2	46
Tema	B2	64
Temagami, lake	E1	102
Temburong, river	D1	13
Temirtau	C1	23
Tempisque, river	B6	76
Temuco	B6	76
Téna Kourou, mt.	B3	64
Ténéré, desert	C2	59
Tenerife, island	Inset I	37
Tengiz, lake	C1	23
Tenkodogo	C3	64
Tennant Creek, N.T.	C1	14
Tennessee	E2	126
Tennessee, river	E2	126
Tenojoki, river	C1	53
Tenryu, river	C3	8
Teotihuacán	Inset	84

	Key	Page
Tepexpan	Inset	84
Tepic, state capital	D3	84
Téra	A3	59
Terai, region	A2, C3	19
Teraina, island	D1	17
Teramo	C2	38
Teresina	D2	81
Tereul	F2	37
Termez	C3	23
Termoli	C2	38
Ternate	D1	13
Terni	C2	38
Ternopil	B2	47
Terrace	H4	95
Terre Haute, Ind.	E2	126
Terrebonne	J5	103
Terreiro Velho	C1	63
Terrenceville	D5	98
Terschelling, island	C1	32
Teseney	A2	60
Teshio, river	Inset I	8
Tesiyn, river	B2	11
Teslić	B1	48
Teslin	C5	105
Teslin, lake	C5	105
Teslin, river	C5	105
Tessalit	D1	58
Tessaoua	B3	59
Testa del Gargano, point	D2	38
Tete	B3	68
Tête Jaune Cache	N5	95
Tétouan	C1	57
Tetovo	A1	48
Teulada, cape	A3	38
Teulon	C4	96
Tewkesbury	C3	30
Texarkana, Tex.	D2	126
Texas	D2	126
Texcoco	Inset	84
Texel, island	B1	32
Teyateyaneng	A2	71
Tezoyuca	Inset	84
Tezzeron, lake	K4	95
Thaba-Tseka	B2	71
Thabana Ntlenyana, mt.	C2	71
Thai Nguyen	A2	11
Thailand, gulf	B4, C4	12
Thames, river	C3, Inset III	30
Thames, river	D5	102
Thamesville	C4	102
Thane	Inset I	20
Thanh Hoa	A2	11
Thanjavur	C6	20
Thar, desert	B4	20
Thásos	C1	51
Thásos, island	C1	51
The Crane	C4	91
The Hague	B2	32
The Ovens	C3	100
The Pas	A2, C2	96
Thedford	D4	102
Thekulthili, lake	F4	99
Thelon, river	H4, J4	99
Theodore	H9	104
Thessalon	B1	102
Thessaloníki	B1	51
Thetford	D3	30
Thetford Mines	E5	103
Thicket	C4	91
Thicket Portage	C1	96
Thiès	A2	62
Thika	D4	61
Thimphu, capital	A2	19
Thingvellir	A2	52
Thio	B2	18
Thisted	B2	32
Thlewiaza, river	J4	99
Tholen, island	B3	32
Thomaston Corner	B3	97
Thompson	C1, D2	96
Thompson, river	M6	95
Thong Hoe	A1	13
Thornhild	E2	94
Thornhill	K5	102
Thorold	F4	102
Thrace, region	D4	50
Thracian, plain	C3	50
Three Kings, islands	B1	15
Thule, air base	B2	106
Thun	B2	35
Thunder Bay	C3	101
Thunersee, lake	B2	35
Thuringia	B3	40
Thuringian, forest	B3	40
Thurso	B1	30
Thurston, island	B9	107
Ti'avea	D2	18
Ti-n-Zaouâtene	B2	57
Tiáhuac	Inset	84
Tianjin	E2	10
Tibati	B2	65
Tiber, river	C2	38
Tiberias (Galilee), lake	A1, B1	26
Tibesti, massif	B2	59
Tibet (Xizang)	B2	10
Tibet, plateau	B2	10
Tiburón, island	B2	84
Tichit	C3	58
Tichla	C3	58
Ticino, river	C2	35
Tidaholm	C1	97
Tidjikdja	C3	58
Tierra del Fuego, island	C9	76
Tieté, river	Inset II	81
Tignish	A2	100
Tigre	B1	77
Tigris, river	B1	24
Tijuana	A1	84
Tikal	B2	85
Tikrit	B2	24
Tiksi	B8	44
Tiladummati, atoll	A1	19
Tilbury	C5	102
Tillabéry	A3	59

	Key	Page
Tilley	E6	94
Tillsonburg	E5	102
Tilomonte	C2	76
Tilston	A4	96
Timaru	B3	15
Timbuktu	C2	58
Timgad, *ruins*	B1	57
Timișoara	A3	43
Timmins	D3	101
Timor, *island*	D2	13
Timor, *sea*	B1	14
Tindouf	A2	57
Tingo María	B2	77
Tinkissa, *river*	C2	62
Tio	C2	60
Tipitapa, *river*	A2	87
Tipperary	B2	31
Tiranë, *capital*	A2	49
Tiraspol	B2	50
Tiree, *island*	A2	30
Tîrgoviște	C3	43
Tîrgu Jiu	B3	43
Tîrgu-Mureș	C2	43
Tîrgu Neamț	D2	43
Tîrgu Ocna	D2	43
Tirich Mir, *mt.*	D2	21
Tirso, *river*	B2	38
Tiruchchirappalli	C6	20
Tisa, *river*	B2	49
Tisdale	F8	104
Tista, *river*	C2	21
Tisza, *river*	C2	43
Titagarh	Inset II	20
Titano, *mt.*	B1	39
Titicaca, *lake*	A3, D4	77
Titov Veles	B2	48
Titova Mitrovica	B3	49
Tivaouane	A2	62
Tiverton	B4	30
Tiverton	D3	102
Tivoli	B2	91
Tiznit	B2	57
Tlaipan	Inset	84
Tlalnepantla	Inset	84
Tlaxcala, *state capital*	E4	84
Tlemcen	A1	57
Toa Payoh	B1	13
Toad River	K2	95
Toamasina	B2	69
Toba Kakar, *range*	C3	21
Tobago, *cays*	A4	91
Tobago, *island*	B1	91
Tobermory	D2	102
Tobi, *island*	Inset	17
Tobin, *lake*	G7	104
Tobol, *river*	C1	23
Tobolsk	D5	44
Tobruk	D1	56
Tocantins	D3	81
Tocantins, *river*	D2	81
Toco	B2	91
Tocopilla	B2	76
Tofino	K6	95
Tofua, *island*	B3	17
Tokachi, *river*	Inset I	8
Tokaj	C1	43
Tokara, *islands*	A4	8
Tokat	D2	27
Tŏkchŏk-kundo, *islands*	A4	9
Tokmok	D1	23
Tokorozawa	C3	8
Toktogul	C2	23
Toku, *island*	C2	17
Tokuno, *island*	Inset II	8
Tokushima	B3	8
Tokuyama	A3	8
Tokyo, *capital*	C3	8
Tôlanaro	B3	69
Toledo	D3	37
Toledo, *mts.*	D3	37
Toledo, Ohio	E1	126
Toliara	A3	69
Tolima, *mt.*	B3	78
Tolland	E4	94
Toltén, *river*	B6	76
Toluca, *state capital*	E4	84
Tolyatti	D4	44
Tom Price, W.A.	A2	14
Tomahawk	C4	94
Tomakomai	Inset I	8
Tomanivi, *mt.*	B2	17
Tombua	B5	70
Tomé	B6	76
Tomelloso	E3	37
Tomiko, *lake*	F1	102
Tompkins	B10	104
Tomsk	D6	44
Tonalá	F4	84
Tonbridge	Inset III	30
Tone, *river*	C2	8
Tongariro, *mt.*	C2	15
Tongatapu, *island*	B4	17
Tonghua	F1	10
Tongjosŏn, *bay*	B3	9
Tongliao	F1	10
Tongsa	B2	19
Tongsa, *river*	B2	19
Tonkin, *gulf*	B2	11
Tonle Sap, *lake*	B2,C3	11
Tonle Sap, *river*	B2	11
Toowoomba, Qld.	E2	14
Topeka, Kans.	D2	126
Topley Landing	J4	95
Torbay	B4	30
Torbay	E5	98
Torghay, *plateau*	C1	23
Tormes, *river*	D2	37
Torneälven, *river*	D1	53
Torngat, *mts.*	D3	98
Tornio	B1	53
Torniojoki, *river*	B1	53
Toronto, *capital*	F4, K5	102
Tororo	D3	61
Torquay	G11	104
Torre del Greco	C2	38
Torrejón de Ardoz	Inset II	37
Torrelavega	D1	37
Torrens, *lake*	C2	14
Torrens, *river*	Inset II	14
Torrente	F3	37
Torreón	D2	84
Torres, *islands*	B1	18
Torres, *strait*	D1	14
Torrington	D5	94
Tórshavn	Inset	32
Tortosa	G2	37
Tortosa, *cape*	G2	37
Tortuga, *island*	C1	89
Toruń	D2	41
Tõrva	C2	46
Tory Hill	G3	102
Tosa, *bay*	B3	8
Totness	A2	80
Tottori	B3	8
Touggourt	B1	57
Tougué	C2	62
Toulaman, *river*	B2	90
Touliu	B2	9
Toulon	D5	34
Toulouse	C5	34
Toungoo	C2	12
Toura, *mts.*	C2	63
Tourcoing	C1	34
Tournai	B2	33
Tours	C3	34
Toussoro, *mt.*	B2	66
Toutes Aides	B3	96
Tovuz	A2	45
Towada, *lake*	D1	8
Townsville, Qld.	D1	14
Toxkan, *river*	E2	23
Toyama	C2	8
Toyama, *bay*	C2	8
Toyohashi	C3	8
Toyonaka	B3	8
Toyota	C3	8
Tozeur	B3	57
Tqvarcheli	A3	45
Trabzon	D2	27
Tracadie-Sheila	E1	97
Tracy	C3	97
Tracy	C5	103
Trafalgar	E2	100
Trail	O6	95
Tralee	B2	31
Trang	B5	12
Transantarctic, *mts.*	B4	107
Transylvanian Alps, *mts.*	C3	43
Trapani	C3	38
Trasimeno, *lake*	C2	38
Trat	C3	12
Traun, *river*	D2	39
Traverse City, Mich.	E1	126
Trebinje	B2	48
Treherne	B4	96
Treinta y Tres	C2	75
Trembleur, *lake*	K4	95
Trenche, *river*	C3	103
Trenčín	B2	42
Trent, *river*	C3	30
Trentino-Alto Adige	B1	38
Trento	B1	38
Trenton	E2	100
Trenton	H3	102
Trenton, *capital*, N.J.	F1	126
Trepassey	E5	98
Tres Puntas, *cape*	B6	74
Treska, *river*	B2	48
Treviso	C1	38
Trier	A4	40
Triesen	B2	33
Triesenberg	B2	33
Trieste	C1	38
Trieste, *gulf*	A3	48
Triglav, *mt.*	A2	48
Trikala	B2	51
Trim	C2	31
Trincomalee	C3	19
Trinidad	B2	77
Trinidad	B2	75
Trinidad	C2	88
Trinidad, *island*	A2	91
Trinidad, *mts.*	C2	88
Trinity East	E5	98
Trinity, *bay*	E5	98
Triolet	C2	69
Tripoli (Tarabulus)	A1	26
Tripoli, *capital*	B1	56
Tripolitania, *region*	B1	56
Triton	D4	98
Trivandrum (Thiruvananthapuram)	C7	20
Trnava	A2	42
Trobriand, *islands*	B2	15
Trois-Pistoles	G3	103
Trois-Rivières	D5	103
Troisvierges	B1	33
Trollhättan	B3	53
Trombay	Inset I	20
Tromsø	D2	52
Trondheim	C3	52
Trondheimsfjord, *fjord*	B3	52
Trongisvágur	Inset	32
Troödos, *mts.*	A2	27
Trossachs	F11	104
Trout Creek	F1	102
Trout Lake	C3	94
Trout River	B4	98
Trout, *lake*	D4	99
Trout, *lake*	B2	101
Trouville	C2	34
Trowbridge	C3	30
Troyes	D2	34
Trujillo	B2	77
Trujillo	B2	79
Trujillo	B2	86
Trujillo Alto	C2	90
Truro	B4	30
Truro	D2	100
Trutch	L2	95
Trutnov	B2	42
Tsaratanana, *mts.*	B1	69
Tsavo	E5	61
Tsedike, *river*	B3	71
Tsengwen, *river*	B2	9
Tsetserleg	C2	11
Tsévié	B3	64
Tshabong	A3	69
Tshane	A3	69
Tshaneni	B1	71
Tshikapa	B2	67
Tshuapa, *river*	B2	67
Tsiribihina, *river*	B2	69
Tsiroanomandidy	B2	69
Tsiteli-Tsqaro	D4	45
Tskhinvali	B3	45
Tsnori	C4	45
Tsu, *island*	A3	8
Tsuen Wan	Inset	10
Tsugaru, *strait*	D1, Inset I	8
Tsumeb	C1	70
Tsumkwe	D1	70
Tsuruga	C3	8
Tsuruoka	C2	8
Tuam	B2	31
Tuas	A1	13
Tuasivi	B2	18
Tubarão	D4	81
Tübingen	B4	40
Tubmanburg	A2	63
Tucson, Ariz.	B2	126
Tucumcari, N. Mex.	C2	126
Tucupita	D2	79
Tucuruí, *reservoir*	D2	81
Tuen Mun	Inset	10
Tugela, *river*	D2	71
Tuguegarao	B2	12
Tuira, *river*	D2	87
Tuktoyaktuk	B3	99
Tukums	B2	46
Tula	D3	44
Tula, *ruins*	D3	84
Tulcán	C2	79
Tulcea	E3	43
Tullamore	C2	31
Tulsa, Okla.	D2	126
Tulsequah	F2	95
Tulsipur	B2	19
Tultitlán	Inset	84
Tulun	D7	44
Tuma, *river*	B2	87
Tumaco	A4	78
Tumba, *lake*	B2	67
Tumbes	A1	77
Tumbler Ridge	M3	95
Tumen, *river*	C1	9
Tumuc-Humac, *mts.*	A2, B3	80
Tumucumaque, *range*	C1	81
Tunbridge Wells	D3	30
Tundzha, *river*	E3	50
Tungsten	C4	99
Tunis, *capital*	C1	57
Tunis, *gulf*	C1	57
Tunja	B3	78
Tupelo, Miss.	E2	126
Tupiza	A4	77
Tupungato, *mt.*	B3	74
Tur, at-	B2	56
Tura	C7	44
Turan, *lowland*	A2	23
Turayf	A1	24
Turbo	A2	78
Turda	B2	43
Turfan, *depression*	C1	10
Türgovishte	E2	50
Türi	C2	46
Turin	A1	38
Turin	D6	94
Turkana (Rudolf), *lake*	D2	61
Turkeston, *mts.*	A1	23
Turks and Caicos Islands	D4	89
Turks, *islands*	D4	89
Turku	B2	53
Turkwel, *river*	C2	61
Turnberry	A2	96
Turnbull	B2	96
Turneffe, *islands*	C2	85
Turnhout	C1	33
Turnor Lake	B4	104
Turnu Măgurele	C4	43
Turquino, *mt.*	E3	88
Tursunzoda	A1	23
Turtle, *lake*	B7	104
Turtleford	B7	104
Tuscaloosa, Ala.	E2	126
Tuscany	B2	38
Tusket	B4	100
Tuticorin	C7	20
Tutong	B2	13
Tutong, *river*	B2	13
Tutuila, *island*	Al, C2	18
Tuul, *river*	C2	11
Tuva, republic	D6	44
Tuxtla Gutiérrez, *state capital*	F4	84
Tuy Hoa	B4	11
Tuya, *lake*	G1	95
Tuz, *lake*	C2	27
Tuzla	B1	48
Tweed	H3	102
Tweed, *river*	C2	30
Twillingate	D4	98
Twin Butte	D6	94
Twin Falls, Idaho	B1	126
Two Creeks	A4	96
Tychy	D3	41
Tynda	D8	44
Tyndall	C4	96
Tyne Valley	B2	100
Tyne, *river*	C2	30
Tyrrhenian, *sea*	B2	38
Tyumen	D5	44
Tywi, *river*	B3	30

U

	Key	Page
Uaboe	B1	16
Ubangi, *river*	B1	67
Ubayyid, al-	C2	59
Ube	A3	8
Úbeda	E3	37
Úbeda	E3	37
Uberaba	D3	81
Uberlândia	D3	81
Ubin, *island*	B1	13
Ubon Ratchathani	C3	12
Ucayali, *river*	C2	77
Uccle	C2	33
Uchiura, *bay*	Inset I	8
Uchquduq	B2	23
Ucluelet	K7	95
Udaipur	B4	20
Uddevalla	B3	53
Uddjaur, *lake*	C1	53
Udine	C1	38
Udmurtia, republic	D4	44
Udon Thani	C2	12
Udu, *point*	C2	17
Uele, *river*	C1	67
Uelzen	B2	40
Ufa	D4	44
Uga, *river*	B2	70
Ugalla, *river*	B2	68
Uíge	C2	70
Uitenhage	C3	71
Ujae, *island*	B2	16
Ujelang, *island*	A2	16
Ujjain	C4	20
Ujung Pandang	C2	13
Ukhta	C4	44
Ukmergė	C2	46
Ulaan-Uul	C2	11
Ulaangom	B2	11
Ulan Bator, *capital*	C2	11
Ulan-Ude	D7	44
Ulansuhai, *lake*	D1	10
Ulchin	C4	9
Ulhas, *river*	Inset I	20
Uliastay	B2	11
Ulithi, *atoll*	B2	15
Ullŭng-do, *island*	D4	9
Ullapool	B1	30
Ulm	B4	40
Ulsan	C5	9
Ulster, *province*	C1	31
Ulu Dağ (Mt. Olympus), *mt.*	B2	27
Ulúa, *river*	B2	86
Ulubaria	Inset II	20
Uluru (Ayers Rock)	C2	14
Uman	C2	47
Umbeluzi, *river*	B2	71
Umboi, *island*	A2	15
Umbria	C2	38
Umeå	D2	53
Umeälven, *river*	C2	53
Umm al-Qaywayn	C2	25
Umm Bab	B3	25
Umm Qasr	C2	24
Umm Said (Musayid)	D4	25
Umniati, *river*	B2	69
Umtata	C3	71
Umuahia	D5	65
Umzingwani, *river*	B2	69
Una, *river*	A1	48
Unayzah	B1	24
Ungava, *bay*	L3	92
Ungheni	A2	50
Unión	C2	76
Union, *island*	A4	91
Unity	A8	104
Unst, *island*	Inset I	30
Upemba, *lake*	C3	67
Upernavik	B2	106
Upington	B2	71
Upolu, *island*	C2	18
Upper Arrow, *lake*	O6	95
Upper Liard	D5	105
Upper Lough Erne, *lake*	A	30
Upper Musquodoboit	E2	100
Upper Ohio	B4	100
Uppsala	C3	53
Ural, *mts.*	D4	44
Ural, *river*	B2	23
Uran	Inset I	20
Uranium City	B1	104
Urawa	C3	8
Urgench	B2	23
Urmia, *lake*	B2	22
Uroševac	B3	49
Uruapan	D4	84
Urubamba, *river*	C3	77
Uruguai, *river*	C4	81
Uruguay, *river*	D3	74
Urukthapel, *island*	B3	17
Ürümqi	B1	10
Usak	B2	27
Ushuaia	B7	74
Usk, *river*	C3	30
Üsküdar	B2	27
Usmas, *lake*	B2	46
Ussuri, *river*	E8	44
Ussuriysk	E8	44
Ust-Ilimsk	D7	44
Ust-Kamchatsk	D10	44
Ust-Kut	D7	44
Ust-Orda, autonomous okrug	D7	44
Ust-Ordynskiy	D7	44
Uster	C1	35
Ústí nad Labem	B2	42
Ustica, *island*	C3	38
Ustka	C1	41
Ustyurt, *plateau*	A2, B2	23
Usulután	B2	86
Usumacinta, *river*	F4	84
Utah	B2	126
Utah, beach	B2	34
Utan	Inset I	20
Utena	C2	46
Utikuma, *lake*	C3	94
Utila, *island*	B1	86
Utrecht	C2	32
Utsunomiya	C2	8
Uttaradit	B2	12
Utuado	B2	90
Utupua, *island*	C2	16
Uummannaq	B2	106
Uvira	C2	67
Uvs, *lake*	B1	11
Uwajima	B3	8
Uwaynat, al-	B2	56
Uyo	D5	65
Uyuni	A4	77
Uzhhorod	A2	47
Užice	A3	49

V

	Key	Page
Vaal, *reservoir*	C2	71
Vaal, *river*	B2	71
Vaalserberg, *mt.*	D4	32
Vaasa	B2	53
Vác	B2	43
Vache, *island*	B2	89
Vadodara	B4	20
Vadsø	F1	52
Vaduz, *capital*	B2	33
Vágar, *island*	Inset	32
Váh, *river*	A2	42
Vahsh, *river*	A1	23
Vaitupu, *island*	C2	16
Vakhan, *region*	C1	22
Val Comeau	E1	97
Val Marie	C11	104
Val-d'Or	A4	101
Val-des-Bois	A6	103
Valcourt	D6	103
Valdecaño	D2	37
Valdepeñas	E3	37
Valdés, *peninsula*	C5	74
Valdivia	B6	76
Valemount	N5	95
Valença	A1	36
Valence	D4	34
Valencia	C1	79
Valencia	F3	37
Valencia, *gulf*	G3	37
Valenciennes	C1	34
Valera	B2	79
Valga	D3	46
Valira d'Orient, *river*	B2	36
Valira, *river*	B2	36
Valjevo	A2	49
Valka	C2	46
Valladolid	G3	84
Valladolid	D2	37
Valle d'Aosta	A1	38
Valledupar	B2	78
Vallenar	B3	76
Valletta, *capital*	C2	36
Valley, *river*	A3	96
Valmiera	C2	46
Valparaíso	B4, Inset	76
Van	E2	27
Van, *lake*	E2	27
Vancouver	L6	95
Vancouver, *island*	J6	95
Vanderhoof	K4	95
Vänern, *lake*	B3	53
Vanguard	C11	104
Vanier	H5	102
Vanier	L5	103
Vanikolo, *islands*	C2	16
Vanimo	A2	15
Vannes	B3	34
Vanrhynsdorp	A3	71
Vanscoy	D8	104
Vansittart, *island*	M3	99
Vantaa	B2	53
Vanua Balavu, *island*	C2	17
Vanua Lava, *island*	B1	18
Vanua Levu, *island*	B2	17
Varanasi	D3	20
Varaždin	C2	48
Vardar, *river*	C2	48
Varde, *river*	B3	32
Vardenis	C2	45
Varkaus	C2	53
Varna	F2	50
Vasai	Inset I	20
Vasai, *creek*	Inset I	20
Vaslui	D2	43
Vassar	D4	96
Västerås	C3	53
Vatnajökull, *ice cap*	B2	52
Vättern, *lake*	B3	53
Vatu Lele, *island*	A3	17
Vaudreuil	C6	103
Vaupés, *river*	B4	78
Vava'u, *island*	C2	17
Vavenby	N5	95
Vavuniya	B3	19
Vawkavysk	B3	47
Växjö	B3	53
Vayk	C3	45
Vega	C4	94
Vega Alta	C2	90
Vega Baja	C2	90
Vegreville	D4	94
Veimandu, *channel*	A3	19
Vejle	B3	32
Velika Morava, *river*	B2	49
Veliki, *canal*	A2	49
Veliko Tŭrnovo	D2	50
Vélingara	B2	62
Vélingara	B3	62
Vella Lavella, *island*	A1	16
Vellore	C6	20
Veneto	B1	38
Venezuela, *gulf*	B1	79
Venice	C1	38
Venice, *gulf*	C1	38
Venlo	D3	32
Venta, *river*	B1	46
Ventimiglia	A2	38
Ventspils	A2	46
Veracruz	E4	84
Vercelli	B1	38
Verde, *river*	C3	75
Verdun	D2	34
Verdun	J6	103
Vereeniging	C2	71
Verkhoyansk	C8	44
Verkhoyansk, *range*	C8	44
Vermillion, *river*	C4	103
Vermont	F1	126
Vernal, Utah	C1	126
Verner	E1	102
Vernon	N6	95
Vernon Bridge	C2	100
Vernon River	C2	100
Véroia	B1	51
Verona	B1	38
Verona	J3	102
Versailles	C2, Inset II	34
Vert, *cape*	A2	62
Verviers	D2	33
Vesoul	D3	34
Vesterålen, *islands*	C2	52
Vestmanna	Inset	32
Vestmannaeyjar	A3	52
Vesuvius, *volcano*	C2	38
Veszprém	A2	43
Vetauua, *island*	C1	17
Viana do Castelo	A2	36
Vianden	B2	33
Vibank	G10	104
Viborg	B2	32
Vicenza	B1	38
Vich	H2	37
Vichada, *river*	C3	78
Vichy	C3	34
Victoria	D3	14
Victoria	B6	76
Victoria	A1	36
Victoria	B2	100
Victoria Beach	C4	96
Victoria Beach	B3	100
Victoria Land, *region*	B5	107
Victoria Nile, *river*	C3	61
Victoria, *capital*	Inset	70
Victoria, *capital*	L7	95
Victoria, *falls*	B3	67
Victoria, *island*	F2	99
Victoria, *lake*	B4, C4	61
Victoria, *peak*	B3	85
Victoria, *river*	C1	14
Victoria, Tex.	D3	126
Victoriaville	E5	103
Vidin	A2	50
Viedma	C5	74
Viedma, *lake*	A6	74
Vieille Case	A1	90
Vienna, *capital*	E2	39
Vienne, *river*	C3	34
Vientiane, *capital*	B3	11
Vieques	D2	90
Vieques, *island*	E2	90
Vieques, *passage*	D2	90
Vieques, *sound*	E2	90
Vierzon	C3	34
Viet Tri	A2	11
Vieux Fort	B3	91
Vigan	B2	12
Vignemale, *mt.*	B5	34
Vigo	B1	37
Vijayawada	D5	20
Vijosë, *river*	A3	49
Vila do Conde	A2	36
Vila Nova de Gaia	A2	36
Vila Real	B2	36
Vila Real de Santo Antonio	B4	36
Vila, *capital*	C3	18
Vilaine, *river*	B3	34
Vilanculos	B4	68
Vilcabamba, *mts.*	C3	77
Viljandi	C2	46
Vilkaviškis	B2	46
Villa Ahumada	C1	84
Villa Hayes	D4	75
Villa María	C3	74
Villa Obregón	Inset	84
Villach	C4	39
Villahermosa, *state capital*	F4	84
Villalba	C2	90
Villarreal de los Infantes	F3	37
Villarrica	D4	75
Villavicencio	B3	78
Villazón	A4	77
Ville-Marie	A4	101
Villeneuve-Saint-Georges	Inset II	34
Villeroy	E5	103
Vilnius, *capital*	C2	46
Vilyuy, *river*	C7	44
Vilyuysk	C8	44
Viña del Mar	B4, Inset	76
Vincennes	Inset II	34
Vincente de Carvalho	Inset II	81
Vinces, *river*	B3	79
Vindelälven, *river*	C2	53
Vindhya, *range*	C4	20
Vinh	A2	11
Vinnitsa	B2	47
Vinson Massif, *mt.*	B10	107
Virden	A4	96
Virgin, *river*	C3	104
Virgin, *islands*		82
Virginia	F2	126
Virtsu	B2	46
Virunga, *mts.*	B1	61
Visayan, *islands*	B4	12
Visayan, *sea*	B4	12
Visby	C3	53
Viscount Melville, *sound*	F2	99
Viseu	B2	36
Vishakhapatnam	D5	20
Vista	A4	96
Vista Hermosa	B4	78
Vistula, *river*	D2, E3	41
Vita	C4	96
Viterbo	C2	38
Viti Levu, *island*	A2	17
Vitoria	E1	37
Vitória	D4	81
Vitória da Conquista	D3	81
Vitsyebsk	E2	47
Vivian	C4	96
Vizcaíno, *desert*	B2	84
Vlaardingen	B3	32
Vladivostok	E8	44
Vlieland, *island*	B1	32
Vlissingen	A3	32
Vlorë	A3	49
Vltava, *river*	B3	42
Vöcklabruck	C2	39
Voinjama	B1	63

Key Page

Vojvodina,
  autonomous province....A2 49
Volcano, islands ....Inset III 8
Volga, river....E4 44
Volgograd....E4 44
Vologda....D3 44
Vólos....B2 51
Volta Redonda....D4 81
Volta, lake....C3 64
Volta, river....C3 64
Vonda....D8 104
Vorkuta....C5 44
Voronezh....D3 44
Vorotan, river....C3 45
Vorskla, river....C1 47
Võrts Järv, lake....D2 46
Võru....D3 46
Vosges, mts....D2 34
Vostok, island....D3 17
Vranje....B3 49
Vratsa....B2 50
Vrbas....A2 49
Vrbas, river....B1 48
Vršac....B2 49
Vryburg....B2 71
Vukovar....D2 48
Vunaniu, bay....A3 17
Vung Tau-Con Dao....B4 11
Vunisea....B3 17
Vyatka....D4 44

W

Wa....A1 64
Waal, river....C3 32
Wabag....A2 15
Wabamun, lake....C4 94
Wabana....E5 98
Wabasca, river....C2 94
Wabe Gestro, river....C3 60
Wabe Shebele, river....D3 60
Wabowden....B2 96
Wabush....D4 98
Waco, Tex....D2 126
Wad Madani....C2 59
Waddan....C2 56
Waddenzee, sound....C1 32
Waddington, mt....K5 95
Wadena....G9 104
Wadi al-Malik, river....B2 59
Wadi as-Sirhan, depression....B2 26
Wadi Halfa....C1 59
Wafrah, al-....B3 24
Wagga Wagga, N.S.W....D3 14
Waigeo, island....E2 13
Waikato, river....C2 15
Waimamaku....B2 15
Waingapu....D2 13
Wairau, river....B3 15
Waitaki, river....B3 15
Wajh, al-....A1 24
Wajir....F3 61
Wakasa, bay....B3 8
Wakaw....E8 104
Wakayama....B3 8
Wakefield....C3 30
Wakkanai....Inset I 8
Wakomata, lake....B1 102
Wakrah, al-....D3 25
Walachia, region....B3 43
Wałbrzych....C3 41
Walcheren, island....A3 32
Walden....D1 102
Waldersee....B4 96
Waldheim....D8 104
Walensee, lake....D1 35
Walkerton....D3 102
Wallace....D2 100
Wallaceburg....C5 102
Walsall....C3 30
Walton....C2 100
Walton....D4 102
Walvis Bay....B2 70
Wami, river....C2 68
Wanaka, lake....A3 15
Wanapitei, lake....E1 102
Wandering River....D3 94
Wando....B5 9
Wanganui....C2 15
Wanham....A3 94
Wapawekka, lake....F5 104
Wapiti, river....A4 94
Wapawsik....B1 96
Warangal....C5 20
Warbah, island....C1 24
Wardlow....E6 94
Ware....K2 95
Warman....D8 104
Warner....D6 94
Warren....C4 96
Warren....E1 102
Warren Landing....C2 96
Warri....C5 65
Warrington....C3 30
Warrnambool, Vic....D3 14
Warsaw, capital....E2 41
Warta, river....B2, C2 41
Warwick....C3 30
Wasa....P6 95
Wasaga Beach....F3 102
Wasagaming....B4 96
Washago....F3 102
Wash, bay....D3 30
Washington....A1 126
Washington, cape....A3 17
Washington, capital, D.C....F2 126
Waskada....A4 96
Waskaganish....A3 101
Waskesiu Lake....D7 104
Waspam....C1 87
Water Valley....C5 94
Water, cays....A3 89
Waterbury, lake....F2 104
Waterford....C2 31
Waterhen, lake....B3 96
Waterloo....E4 102

Key Page

Waterloo....D6 103
Watertown, N.Y....F1 126
Watford....Inset III 8
Watford....D5 102
Wathaman, lake....G3 104
Watrous....E9 104
Watsa....C1 67
Watson....F8 104
Watson Lake....D5 105
Wau....A2 15
Waw....B3 59
Wawa....D3 101
Wawa, river....B1 87
Wawanesa....B4 96
Weagamow Lake....B2 101
Webbwood....D1 102
Webequie....C2 101
Webi Shabeelle, river....B3 60
Weddell, sea....B12 107
Wedgeport....A4 100
Weert....C3 32
Wei, river....D2 10
Weiden....C4 40
Weifang....E2 10
Weimar....B3 40
Weipa, Qld....D1 14
Weitzel, lake....D3 104
Wekusko....B2 96
Wekusko, lake....B2 96
Weldiya....C2 60
Welkom....C2 71
Wellington....A2 100
Wellington, capital....B3 15
Wellington, island....A8 76
Wels....C2 39
Welsford....C3 97
Welshpool....B3 30
Welwyn....A4 96
Wembere, river....B1 68
Wenchi....A3 64
Weno....C2 15
Weno, island....C2 15
Wenshan....D3 10
Wentworth....D2 100
Wenzhou....F3 10
Werder....D3 60
Werra, river....B3 40
Weser, river....B2 40
Wesley....B2 90
Wesleyville....E4 98
West Antarctica....A8 107
West Devon....A2 100
West Frisian, islands....B1 32
West Ice Shelf, glacier....C1 107
West Palm Beach, Fla....E3 126
West Point....A2 100
West Road, river....K4 95
West Siberian, plain....C5 44
West St. Modeste....C3 98
West Virginia....E2 126
Westbank....N6 95
Westbourne....B4 96
Western Australia....B2 14
Western Dvina, river....C2 46
Western Ghats, mts....B5 20
Western, channel....C5 9
Westerschelde, channel....A3 32
Westfield....C3 97
Westlock....D4 94
Westminster....Inset III 8
Weston....J5 102
Westport....B3 15
Westport....B2 31
Westport....J3 102
Westray, island....Inset I 8
Wetar, island....D2 13
Wetaskiwin....D5 94
Wete....C1 68
Wetzlar....B3 40
Wewak....A1 15
Wexford....C2 31
Weyakwin....E6 104
Weyburn....G11 104
Weymouth....A3 100
Whakatane....C2 15
Whale Cove....K4 99
Whaletown....K6 95
Whangarei....B2 15
Wheatland....A4 96
Wheatley....C5 102
Wheeling, W. Va....E1 126
Whistler....L6 95
Whitbourne....E5 98
Whitby....G4 102
White Fox....F7 104
White Lake....J2 102
White Nile, river....C3 59
White Rock....L6 95
White Sands....C3 100
White Volta, river....B1, D2 64
White, bay....C4 98
White, island....L3 99
White, river....A4 105
White, sea....C3 44
Whitecourt....C4 94
Whitefish Falls....D1 102
Whitehaven....A1 102
Whitehaven....B2 30
Whitehorse....C5 105
Whitelaw....A3 94
Whiteman, range....A2 15
Whitemouth....D4 96
Whitestone, river....B3 105
Whitewood....H10 104
Whitney....G2 102
Wholdaia, lake....H4 99
Whyalla, S.A....C3 14
Whycocomagh....F2 100
Wiarton....D3 102
Wichita Falls, Tex....D2 126
Wichita, Kans....D2 126
Wick....B1 30
Wicklow....C2 31
Wicklow Head, cape....D2 31
Wicklow, mts....C2 31

Key Page

Wiener Neustadt....E3 39
Wieprz, river....F3 41
Wiesbaden....B3 40
Wigan....C3 30
Wight, island....C4 30
Wilberforce....G2 102
Wilge, river....C2 71
Wilhelm, mt....A2 15
Wilhelmina, canal....B3 32
Wilhelmina, mts....A2 80
Wilhelmshaven....B2 40
Wilkes Land, region....C3 107
Wilkie....B8 104
Williams Harbour....D3 98
Williams Lake....L5 95
Williamsport....C4 98
Williston....K3 95
Willow Bunch....E11 104
Willow Creek....A11 104
Willowbunch, lake....E11 104
Wilmington, Del....F2 126
Wilmington, N.C....B3 126
Wilmot....B3 100
Wiltondale....C4 98
Wiltz....A2 33
Wimbledon....Inset III 8
Winchester....C3 30
Winchester....K2 102
Wind, river....B3 105
Windermere....O6 95
Windermere....F2 102
Windfall....B4 94
Windhoek, capital....C2 70
Windsor....Inset III 8
Windsor....D3 100
Windsor....C5 102
Windsor....D6 103
Windward Group....B2 58
Windward, islands....B4 91
Windward, passage....F3 88
Winefred, lake....E3 94
Winfield....N6 95
Wingham....D4 102
Winisk....C1 101
Winisk, lake....C2 101
Winisk, river....C2 101
Winkler....C4 96
Winneba....B4 64
Winnemucca, Nev....B1 126
Winnipeg....C4, D2 96
Winnipeg Beach....C4 96
Winnipeg, lake....B3, C4, D2 96
Winnipeg, river....D4 96
Winnipegosis....B3 96
Winnipegosis, lake....A3 96
Winslow, Ariz....B2 126
Winston-Salem, N.C....A1 24
Winter Harbour....H6 95
Winterthur....C1 35
Wisconsin....D1 126
Wismar....B2 40
Witless Bay....E5 98
Witten....A3 40
Wittenberg....C3 40
Wittenberge....B2 40
Witten....A3 40
Witu, island....A2 15
Wiwili....B2 87
Władysławowo....D1 41
Włocławek....D2 41
Wodzisław Śląski....D3 41
Woking....A3 94
Wolf, lake....C5 105
Wolfsberg....D4 39
Wolfsburg....B2 40
Wolfville....C2 100
Wollaston Lake....G2 104
Wollaston, lake....H2 104
Wollaston, peninsula....E3 99
Wollongong, N.S.W....E3 14
Wolseley....G10 104
Wolverhampton....C3 30
Wong, river....A2 19
Wŏnju....B4 9
Wonowon....M3 95
Wŏnsan....B3 9
Wood Islands....C3 100
Woodbridge....J5 102
Woodlands....B1 13
Woodlands....C4 96
Woodlark (Muyua), island....B4 15
Woodnorth....A4 96
Woodridge....C4 96
Woods, lake....B3 101
Woodstock....A2 100
Woodstock....C4 102
Woody Point....C4 98
Woomera, S.A....C3 14
Worcester....C3 30
Worcester....A3 71
Worcester, Mass....F1 126
Worms....B4 40
Wotho, island....B1 16
Wotje, island....B2 16
Wrangel, island....B10 44
Wrath, cape....B1 30
Wreck Cove....D5 98
Wrentham....D6 94
Wrigley....D4 99
Wrocław....C3 41
Wuhai....D2 10
Wuhan....E2 10
Wuhu....E2 10
Wukari....E4 65
Wum....B2 65
Wuppertal....B3 40
Würzburg....B4 40
Wutivi, mt....B1 63
Wuwei....D2 10
Wuxi....F2 10
Wuzhong....D2 10
Wuzhou....E3 10
Wyndham, W.A....B1 14
Wynyard....F9 104
Wyoming....C1 126

Key Page

X

Xaçmaz....C2 45
Xai-Xai....B5 68
Xam Nua....C1 11
Xangongo....C5 70
Xankändi....B3 45
Xánthi....C1 51
Xau, lake....B2 69
Xi'an....D2 10
Xi, river....E3 10
Xiamen....E3 10
Xiangfan....E2 10
Xiangkhoang....B2 11
Xiangtan....E3 10
Xigaze....B3 10
Xingu, river....C3 81
Xining....D2 10
Xinjiang Uygur....B1 10
Xinxiang....E2 10
Xinyang....E2 10
Xochimilco....Inset 84
Xuddur....A3 60
Xuzhou....E2 10

Y

Ya'an....D2 10
Yablonovyy, range....D7 44
Yabucoa....D2 90
Yacuiba....B4 77
Yafran....B1 56
Yaguarí, river....C1 75
Yaguarón, river....D2 75
Yahk....O6 95
Yakima, Wash....A1 126
Yaku, island....A4 8
Yakutia (Sakha), republic....C8 44
Yakutsk....C8 44
Yala....B5 12
Yale....M6 95
Yalinga....B2 66
Yalta....C4 47
Yalu, river....B2 9
Yamagata....D2 8
Yamaguchi....A3 8
Yamal, peninsula....C5 44
Yamalia,
  autonomous okrug....C5 44
Yambio....B4 59
Yambol....E3 50
Yamoussoukro, capital....D3 63
Yampi, sound....B1 14
Yamuna, river....C3 20
Yan, river....B3 19
Yanbu al-Bahr....A2 24
Yangambi....C1 67
Yangdŏk....B3 9
Yangquan....E2 10
Yangtze, river....C2, D2 10
Yangzhou....E2 10
Yanji....F1 10
Yantai....F2 10
Yantra, river....D2 50
Yao....B3 8
Yaoundé, capital....B3 65
Yap, islands....A2 15
Yapen, island....E2 13
Yaque del Norte, river....A1 89
Yaque del Sur, river....A2 89
Yaqui, river....C2 84
Yare, river....D3 30
Yaren, capital....B16 16
Yariga, mt....C2 8
Yarmouth....A4 100
Yaroslavl....D3 44
Yasawa, island group....A2 17
Yasuj....C3 22
Yata, river....A2 77
Yates....B4 94
Yauco....B2 90
Yavarí, river....C1 77
Yaviza....D2 87
Yazd....C3 22
Yazd, region....C3 22
Ybbs, river....D2 39
Ye....C3 12
Yeboah....C3 30
Yecla....F3 37
Yeguas, point....D2 90
Yekaterinburg....D5 44
Yekepa....B2 63
Yell, island....Inset I 30
Yellow Grass....F11 104
Yellow, sea....F2 10
Yellowknife, capital....F4 99
Yen Bai....A2 11
Yendi....B2 64
Yeovil....C4 30
Yerevan, capital....B2 45
Yeşilhırmak, river....D2 27
Yeu, island....B3 34
Yevlax....B2 45
Yevpatoriya....C3 47
Yi, river....C2 75
Yialousa....C1 27
Yibin....D3 10
Yichang....E2 10
Yichun....F1 10
Yinchuan....D2 10
Yingkou....F1 10
Yining....B1 10
Yin Shan, mts....E1 10
Ylikitka, lake....C1 53
Ylivieska....B2 53
Yoboki....B2 60
Yogyakarta....C2 13
Yojoa, lake....B2 86
Yokkaichi....C3 8
Yokohama....C3 8
Yokosuka....C3 8
Yola....G3 65
Yom, river....B2 12
Yomou....D4 62

Key Page

Yonago....B3 8
Yonaguni, island....Inset II 8
Yŏnggu....C4 9
Yonne, river....C2 34
Yopal....B3 78
York....B2 100
York....C3 30
York....K5 102
York Factory....E1 96
York, cape....D1 14
Yorkton....H9 104
Yoro....B2 86
Yoron, island....Inset II 8
Yoshino, river....B3 8
Yoshkar-Ola....D4 44
Yōsu....B5 9
Yotvata....B3 26
Youghal....C3 31
Young....E9 104
Youngs Cove....D2 97
Ypané, river....D3 75
Ypoá, lake....D4 75
Ypres....A2 33
Yssyk-Köl, lake....E1 23
Yú Shan, mt....B2 10
Yuan, river....D3 10
Yubari....Inset I 8
Yucatán, channel....A2 88
Yucatán, peninsula....G4 84
Yuen Long....Inset 10
Yueyang....E3 10
Yukon, river....D2 92
Yuma, Ariz....B2 126
Yumen....C2 10
Yuna, river....B2 89
Yundum....B2 62
Yungas, region....A3 77
Yungho....B1 9
Yunnan....C3 10
Yurimaguas....B2 77
Yuscarán....B3 86
Yushu....C2 10
Yuzhno-Sakhalinsk....E9 44
Yverdon....A2 35

Z

Zaanstad....B2 32
Zabbar....C2 36
Zabid....A2 25
Zabol....E3 22
Zabrze....D3 41
Zacapa....D5 85
Zacatecas, state capital....D3 84
Zacatecoluca....B2 86
Zadar....B3 48
Zafra....C3 37
Zagazig....B1 56
Zaghouan....C1 57
Zagreb, capital....B2 48
Zagros, mts....B3 22
Zahedan....E4 22
Zahlah....A2 26
Zaječar....C3 49
Zákinthos, island....B3 51
Zakopane....D4 41
Zala, river....A2 43
Zalaegerszeg....A2 43
Zalău....A2 43
Zambales, mts....B3 12
Zambezi....A2 67
Zambezi, river....A3, B3 67
Zamboanga....B5 12
Zamboanga, peninsula....B5 12
Zamora....D2 37
Zamora....B5 79
Zamora, river....B4 79
Zamość....F3 41
Zanderij....B2 80
Zanjan....B2 22
Zanzibar....C2 68
Zao, mt....D2 8
Zapandna Morava, river....B3 49
Zapatera, island....B3 87
Zaporozhye....D2 47
Zaqatala....B2 45
Zarafobod....A1 23
Zarafshon....B2 23
Zaranj....A2 22
Zareh Sharan....B2 22
Zarqa, az-....B1 26
Zarzis....C3 57
Zavidovići....B1 48
Zaysan....E2 23
Zaysan, lake....E2 23
Zebbug....A1 36
Zeebrugge....B1 33
Zefat....B1 26
Zenica....B1 48
Zeravshan, mts....A1 23
Zeravshan, river....A1, B2 23
Zermatt....B2 35
Zestaponi....B3 45
Zevulun, plain....B1 26
Zêzere, river....A3 36
Zhambyl (Dzhambul)....D2 23
Zhangjiakou....E1 10
Zhangye....D2 10
Zhanjiang....E3 10
Zhejiang....E3 10
Zhelaniya, cape....B5 44
Zhengzhou....E2 10
Zhenjiang....E2 10
Zhezqazghan....B2 23
Zhitomir....B1 47
Zhlobin....D3 47
Zhob, river....C3 21
Zhoda....C4 96
Zhongba....D3 10
Zhuzhou....E3 10
Zibo....E2 10
Zielona Góra....B3 41
Zigong....D3 10
Ziguinchor....A3 62
Žilina....B2 42

Key Page

Zillah....C2 56
Zillertal Alps, range....B3 39
Zima, lake....A2 94
Zinder....B3 59
Zion....C3 90
Zittau....C3 40
Ziway, lake....C3 60
Zlatibor, mts....A3 49
Zlín....C3 42
Znojmo....C4 42
Zomba....C3 68
Zonguldak....B2 27
Zorzor....B2 63
Zouar....B2 58
Zouïrât....B2 58
Zrenjanin....B2 49
Zug....C1 35
Zugdidi....A3 45
Zugspitze, mt....B5 40
Zuid-Willemsvaart, canal....C3 32
Zújar, reservoir....D3 37
Zululand, region....D2 71
Zunyi....D3 10
Zürich....C1 35
Zürichsee, lake....C1 35
Zurrieq....B2 36
Zuwarah....B1 56
Zvishavane....B2 69
Zvolen....C3 42
Zvornik....C1 48
Zwedru....B2 63
Zwickau....C3 40
Zwolle....D2 32
Zyryanka....C9 44

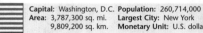

Capital: Washington, D.C. **Population:** 260,714,000
Area: 3,787,300 sq. mi. **Largest City:** New York
9,809,200 sq. km. **Monetary Unit:** U.S. dollar

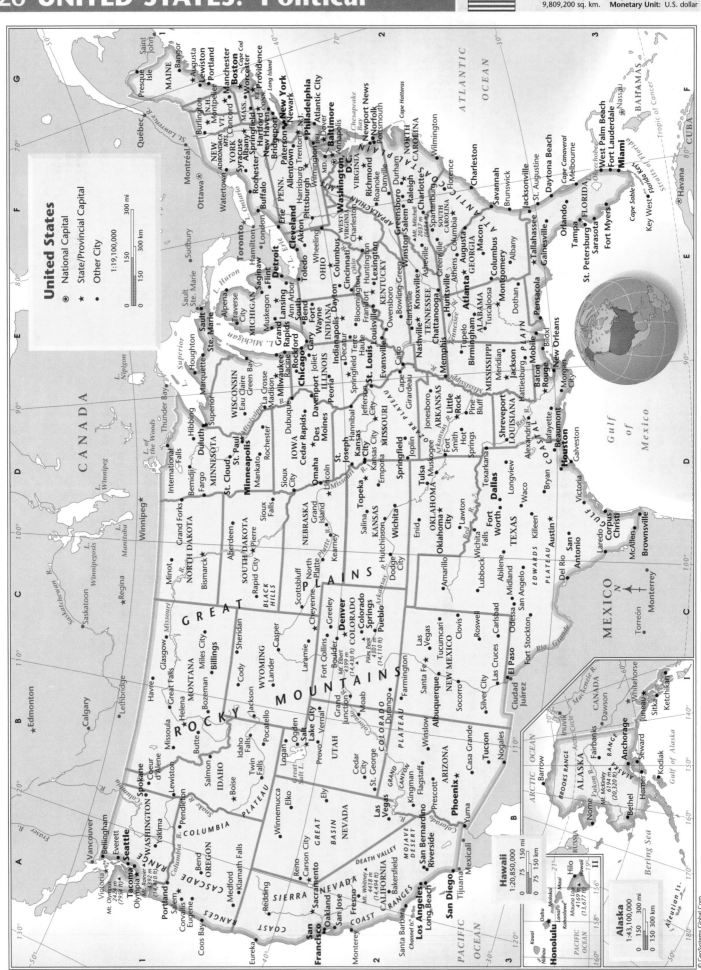

United States

⊛ National Capital
★ State/Provincial Capital
• Other City

1:19,100,000

0   150   300 mi
0   150   300 km

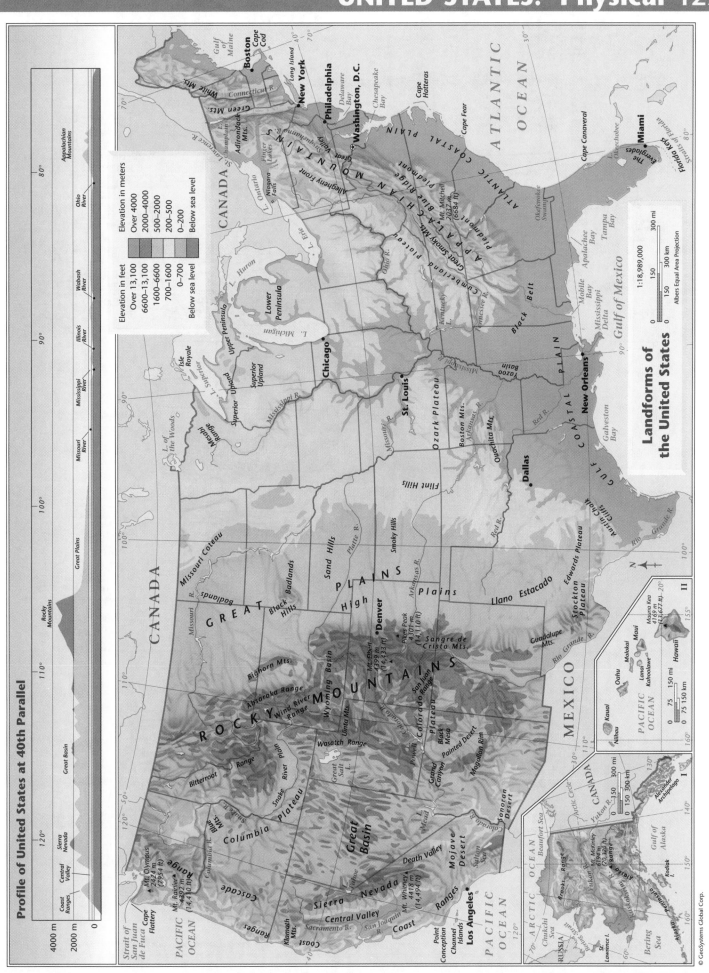

Profile of United States at 40th Parallel

4000 m
2000 m
0

Coast Ranges — Cape Flattery — Strait of San Juan de Fuca

Central Valley — Sierra Nevada — Great Basin — Rocky Mountains — Great Plains — Missouri River — Mississippi River — Illinois River — Wabash River — Ohio River — Appalachian Mountains

120° 110° 100° 90° 80°

Elevation in meters
Over 4000
2000–4000
500–2000
200–500
0–200
Below sea level

Elevation in feet
Over 13,100
6600–13,100
1600–6600
700–1600
0–700
Below sea level

Landforms of the United States

1:18,989,000

0   150   300 mi

0   150   300 km

Albers Equal Area Projection

© GeoSystems Global Corp.

Capital: Montgomery **Population:** 4,187,000
Area: 52,400 sq. mi. **Largest City:** Birmingham
135,800 sq. km.

TENNESSEE

ALABAMA

MISSISSIPPI

GEORGIA

FLORIDA

GULF OF MEXICO

Alabama

★ State Capital   ── Limited Access Highway
• County Seat   ── Other Major Road

1:2,443,000

0   25   50 mi
0 25 50 75 km

Albers Equal Area Projection

© GeoSystems Global Corp.

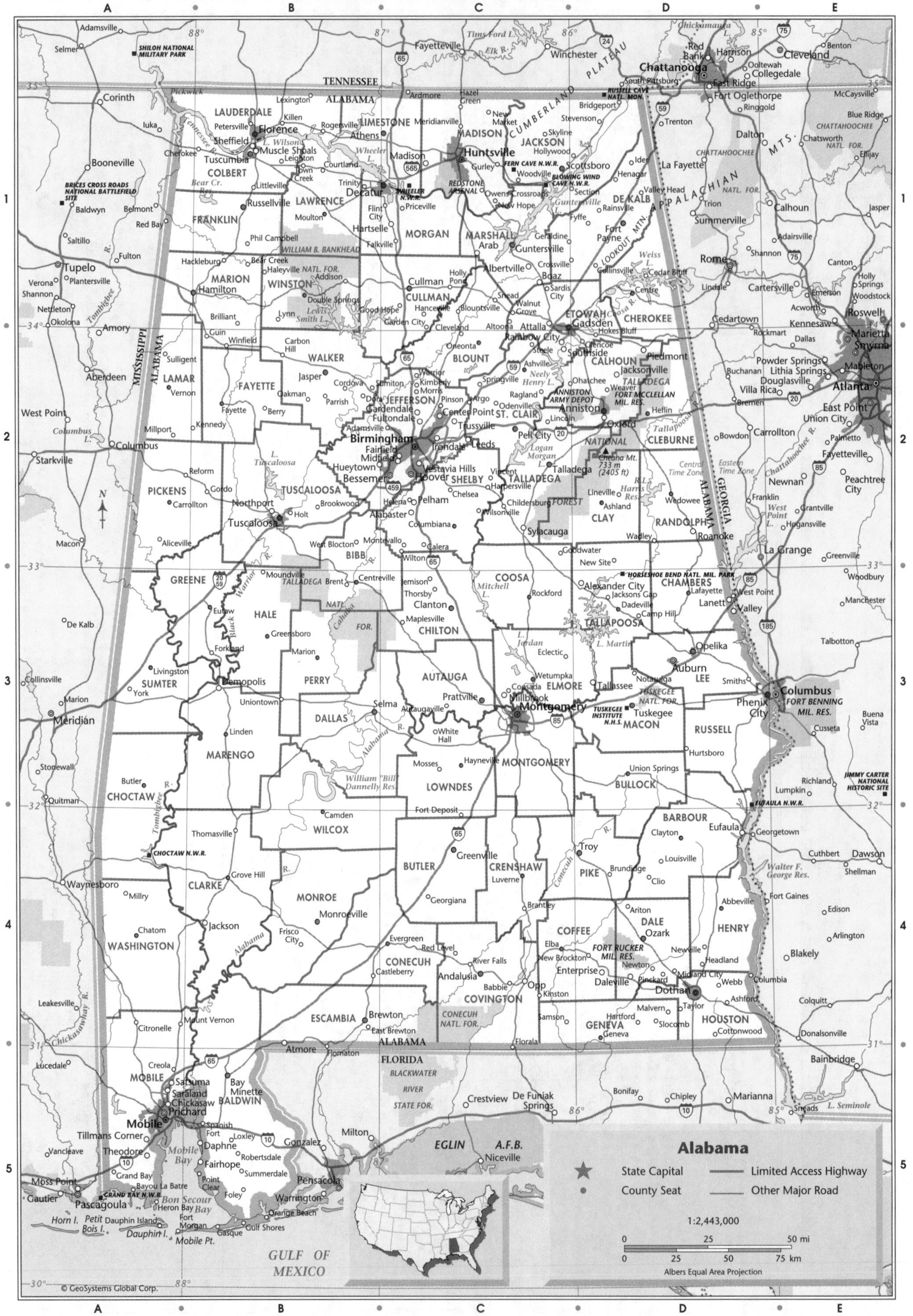

Capital: Juneau
Area: 656,400 sq. mi.
1,700,000 sq. km.
Population: 599,000
Largest City: Anchorage

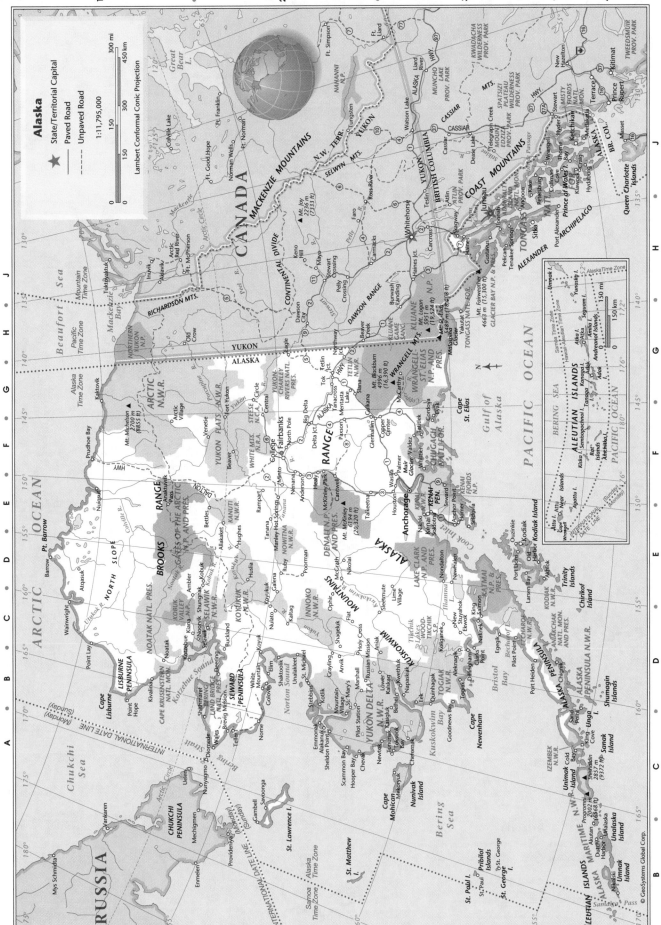

Alaska

★ State/Territorial Capital
— Paved Road
--- Unpaved Road

1:11,795,000

Lambert Conformal Conic Projection

Capital: Phoenix
Area: 114,000 sq. mi.
295,300 sq. km.
Population: 3,936,000
Largest City: Phoenix

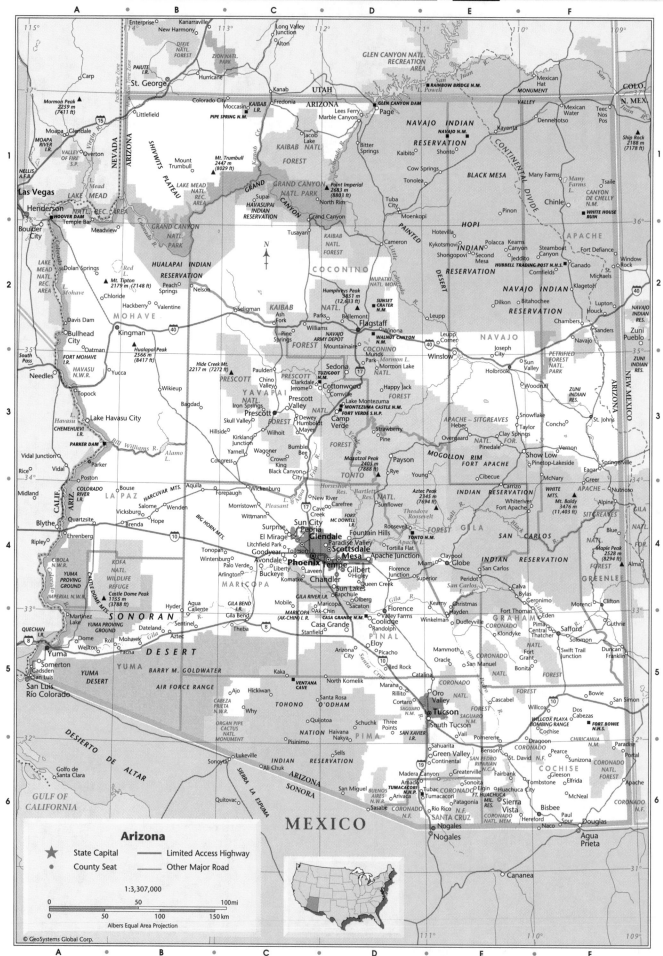

Arizona

★ State Capital — Limited Access Highway
• County Seat — Other Major Road

1:3,307,000

0   50   100mi
0   50   100   150 km

Albers Equal Area Projection

© GeoSystems Global Corp.

Capital: Little Rock
Area: 53,200 sq. mi.
137,700 sq. km.
Population: 2,424,000
Largest City: Little Rock

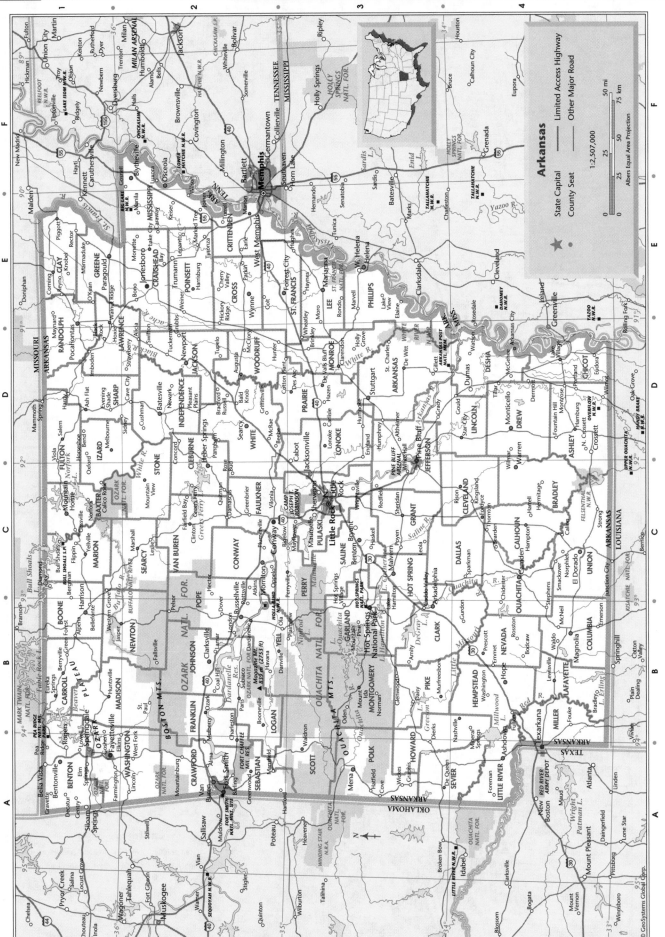

Arkansas

Limited Access Highway
Other Major Road

State Capital
County Seat

1:2,507,000

0   25   50 mi
0   25   50   75 km

Albers Equal Area Projection

© GeoSystems Global Corp.

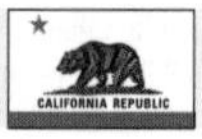
CALIFORNIA REPUBLIC

Capital: Sacramento
Area: 163,700 sq. mi.
424,000 sq. km.
Population: 31,211,000
Largest City: Los Angeles

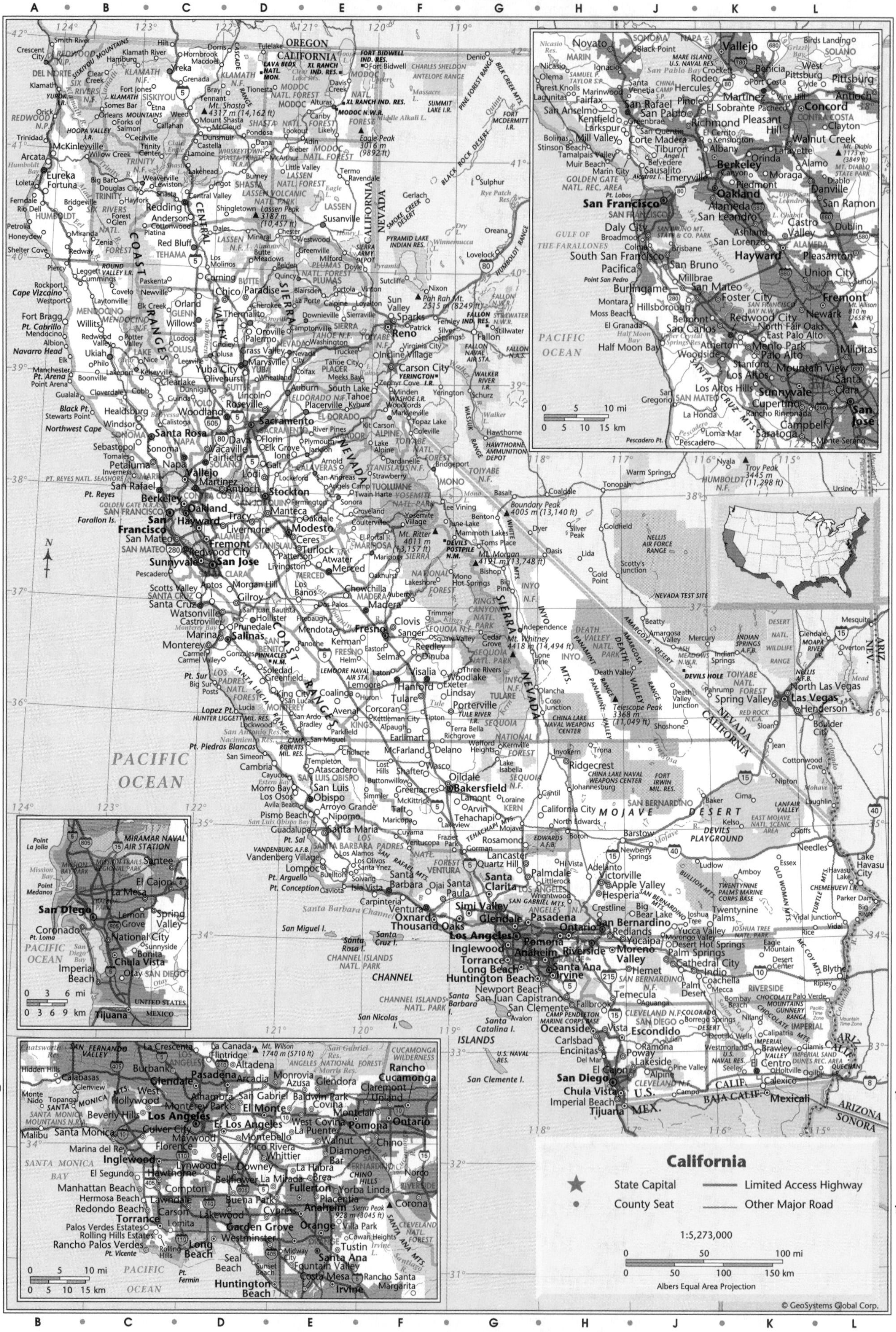
California
State Capital
County Seat
Limited Access Highway
Other Major Road
1:5,273,000
0 50 100 mi
0 50 100 150 km
Albers Equal Area Projection
© GeoSystems Global Corp.
PACIFIC OCEAN
MOJAVE DESERT
OREGON
CALIFORNIA
NEVADA
ARIZONA
SONORA
BAJA CALIF.
U.S.
MEX.

Capital: Denver
Area: 104,100 sq. mi.
269,600 sq. km.
Population: 3,566,000
Largest City: Denver

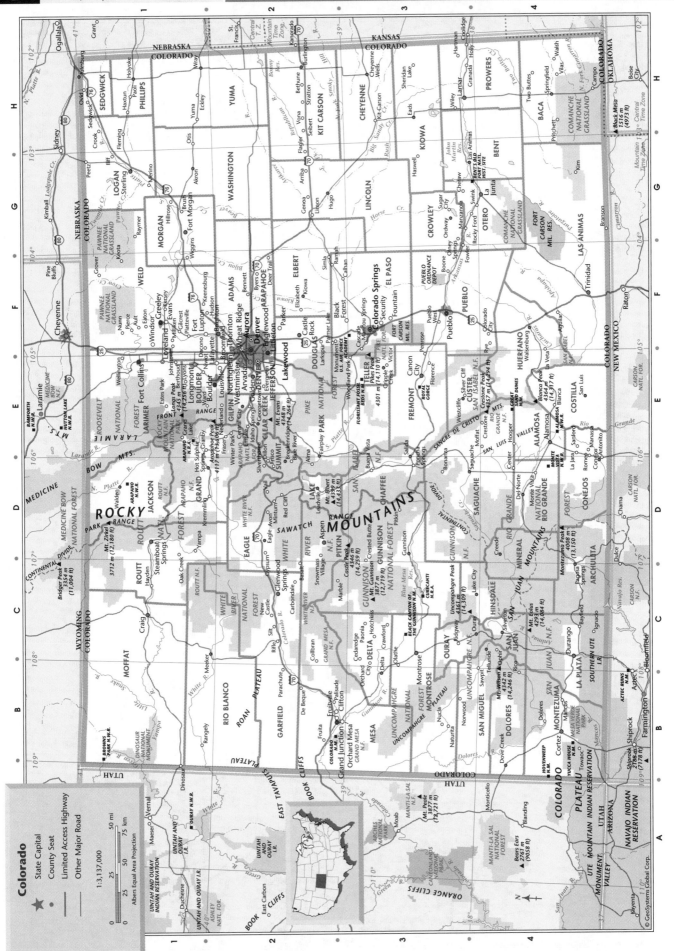

Colorado

★ State Capital
• County Seat
— Limited Access Highway
— Other Major Road

1:3,137,000

0   25   50 mi
0 25 50 75 km

Albers Equal Area Projection

© GeoSystems Global Corp.

Capital: Hartford   **Population:** 3,277,000
Area: 5,500 sq. mi.   **Largest City:** Hartford
14,400 sq. km.

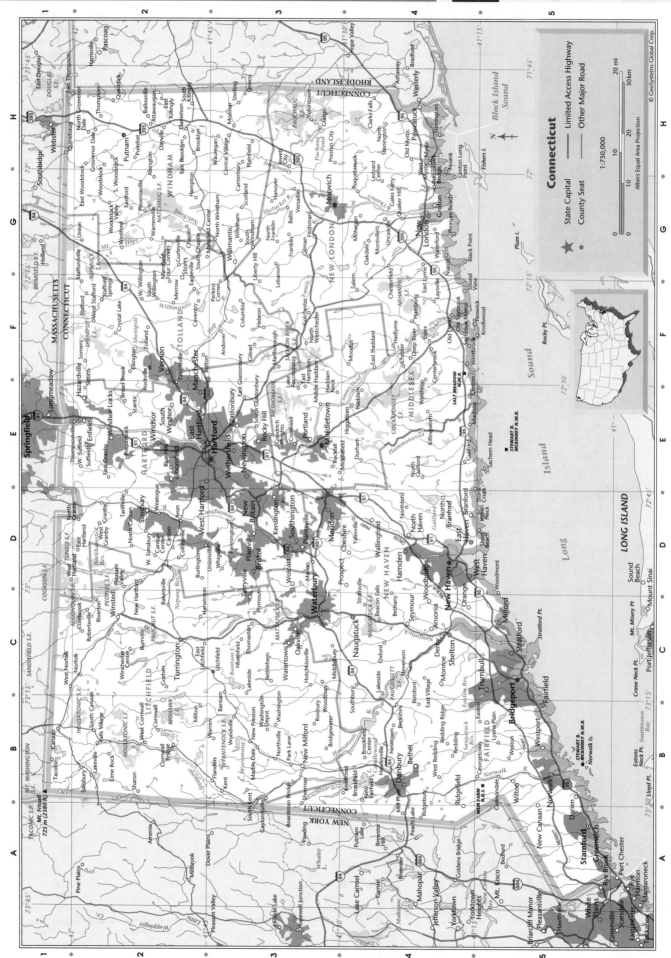

Capital: Dover
Area: 2,500 sq. mi.
6,400 sq. km.
Population: 700,000
Largest City: Wilmington

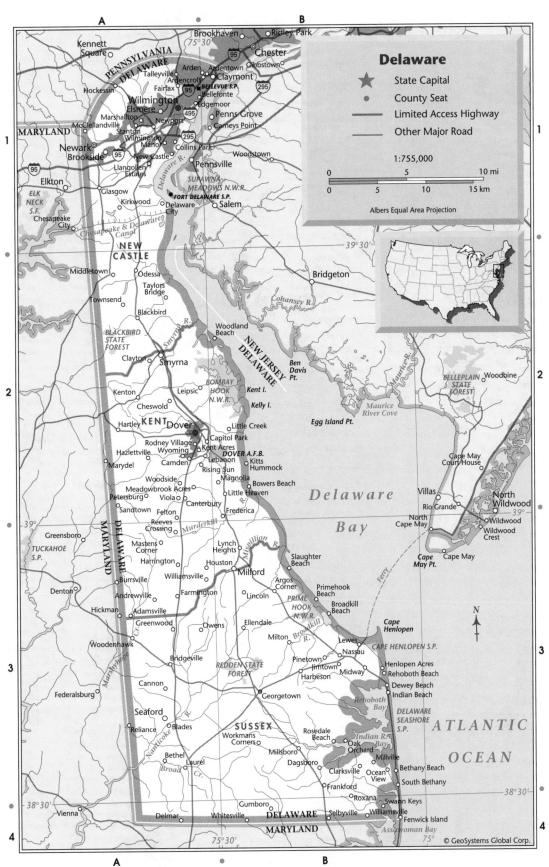

Delaware

★ State Capital

● County Seat

━━ Limited Access Highway

── Other Major Road

1:755,000

| 0 | | 5 | | 10 mi |
| 0 | 5 | 10 | 15 km |

Albers Equal Area Projection

© GeoSystems Global Corp.

Capital: Tallahassee
Area: 65,800 sq. mi.
170,300 sq. km.
Population: 13,679,000
Largest City: Miami

Florida

★ State Capital
• County Seat
— Limited Access Highway
— Other Major Road

1:3,135,000

0 — 25 — 50 mi
0 — 25 — 50 — 75 km
Albers Equal Area Projection

Capital: Atlanta
Area: 59,400 sq. mi.
153,900 sq. km.
Population: 6,917,000
Largest City: Atlanta

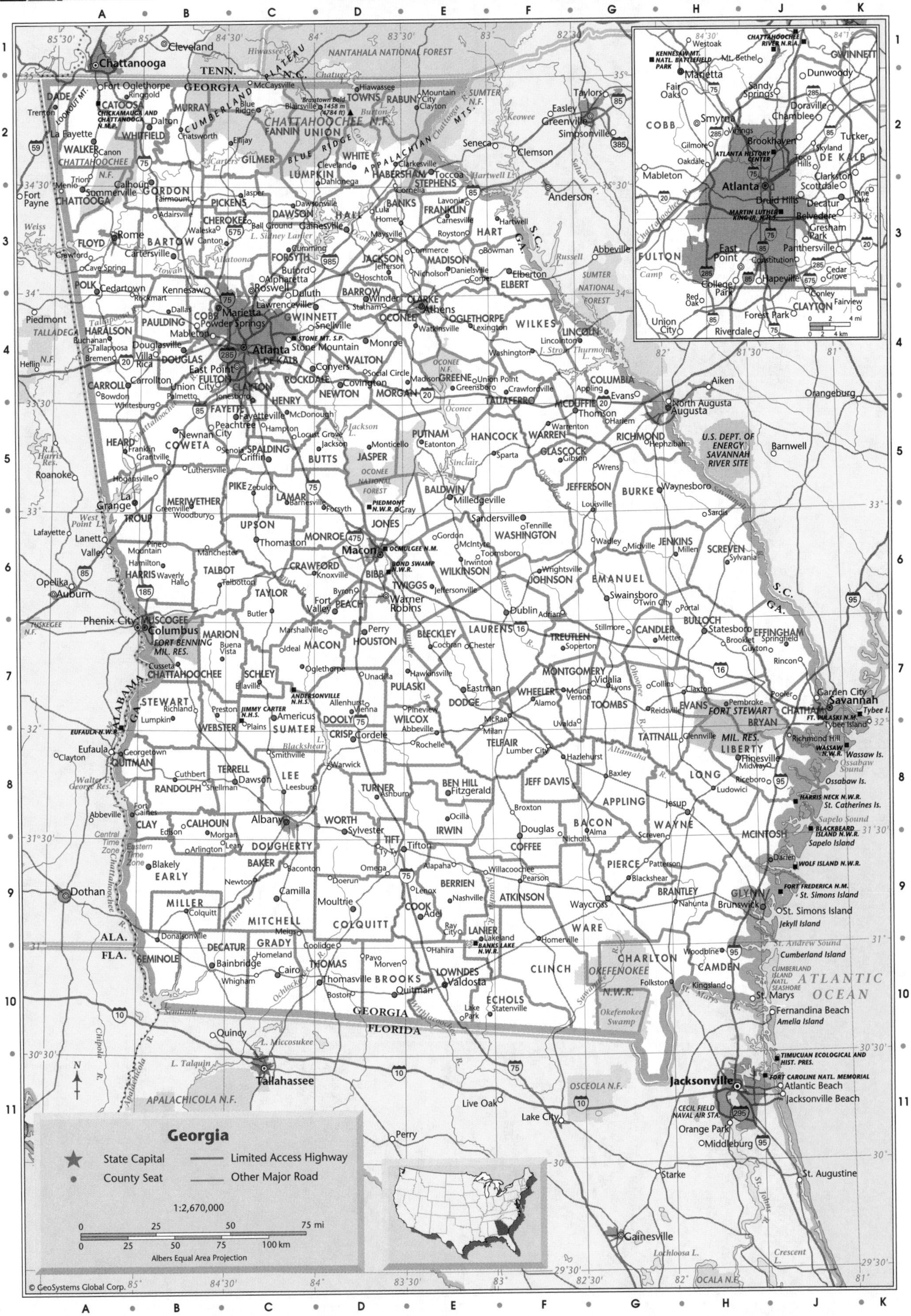

Georgia

★ State Capital
● County Seat
— Limited Access Highway
— Other Major Road

1:2,670,000

0   25   50   75 mi
0   25 50 75 100 km

Albers Equal Area Projection

© GeoSystems Global Corp.

Capital: Honolulu
Area: 10,900 sq. mi. 28,300 sq. km.
Population: 1,172,000
Largest City: Honolulu

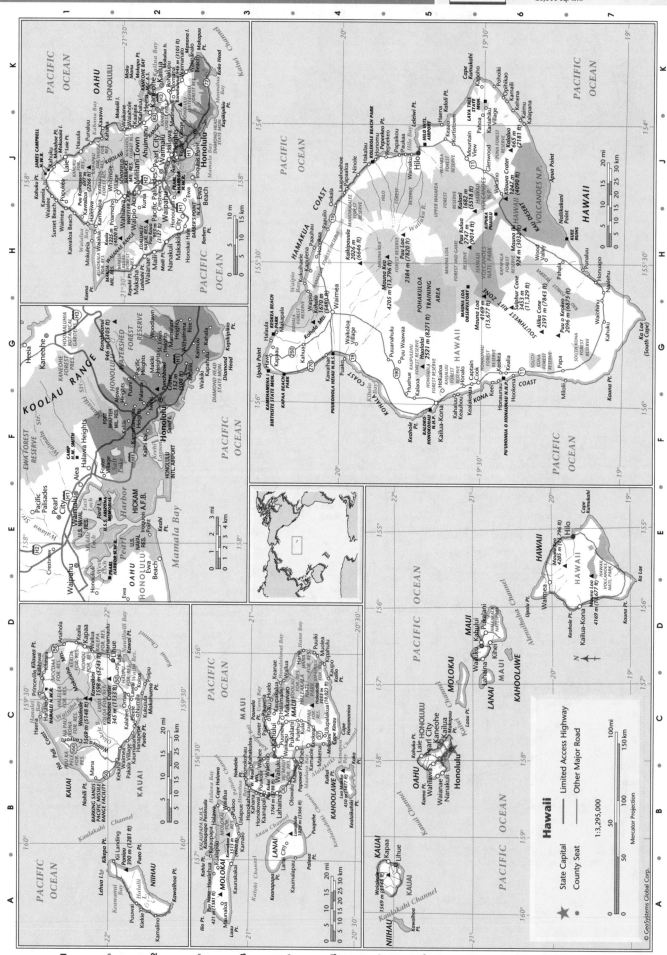

Capital: Boise
Area: 83,600 sq. mi.
216,500 sq. km.
Population: 1,099,000
Largest City: Boise

Idaho

★ State Capital
◉ County Seat
━━━ Limited Access Highway
━━━ Other Major Road

1:3,295,000

0 — 50 — 100mi
0 — 50 — 100 — 150 km

Albers Equal Area Projection

© GeoSystems Global Corp.

CAN.
U.S.
B.C.
MONTANA
WASH.
ORE.
OREGON
IDAHO
NEVADA
UTAH
WYOMING

Trail, Porthill, Eastport, Moyie Springs, Bonners Ferry, Naples, Nordman, Coolin, Samuels, Elmira, Kootenai, Sandpoint, Priest River, Dover, Sagle, Hope, Laclede, Clark Fork, Cocolalla, Careywood, Blanchard, Lakeview, Spirit Lake, Athol, Rathdrum, Hayden, Spokane, Post Falls, Coeur d'Alene, Opportunity, Cheney, Worley, Harrison, Rose Lake, Pinehurst, Kingston, Kellogg, Osburn, Burke, Mullan, Wallace, Murray, St. Maries, Calder, Avery, Plummer, Santa, Emida, Fernwood, Clarkia, Potlatch, Harvard, Viola, Deary, Bovill, Elk River, Moscow, Troy, Helmer, Kendrick, Genesee, Southwick, Headquarters, Ahsahka, Grangemont, Pierce, Clarkston, Lewiston, Peck, Gifford, Orofino, Greer, Weippe, Reubens, Winchester, Nezperce, Craigmont, Ferdinand, Kamiah, Stites, Kooskia, Lowell, Waha, Cottonwood, Harpster, Fenn, Grangeville, Golden, Elk City, Red River Hot Springs, White Bird, Orogrande, Lucile, Dixie, Riggins, Shoup, North Fork, Pollock, Burgdorf, Warren, Salmon, Carmen, Baker, Cuprum, Big Creek, Yellow Pine, Cobalt, Tendoy, Leadore, Patterson, New Meadows, McCall, Council, Fruitvale, Cambridge, Mesa, Indian Valley, Lake Fork, Donnelly, Cascade, Warm Lake, Challis, May, Ellis, Midvale, Weiser, Smiths Ferry, Stanley, Sunbeam, Clayton, Humphrey, Kilgore, Spencer, Dubois, Island Park, Cambridge, Ontario, Payette, Fruitland, New Plymouth, Letha, Sweet, Garden Valley, Lowman, Banks, Placerville, Horseshoe Bend, Idaho City, Atlanta, Rocky Bar, Mackay, Leslie, Darlington, Howe, Moore, Terreton, Mud Lake, Hamer, Sugar City, Rexburg, Ashton, Chester, Warm River, Newdale, Tetonia, Driggs, Victor, Caldwell, Notus, Middleton, Star, Eagle, Garden City, Boise, Nampa, Kuna, Bowmont, Melba, Orchard, Marsing, Murphy, Reynolds, Silver City, Oreana, Grand View, Bruneau, Featherville, Prairie, Pine, Mayfield, Mountain Home, Hill City, Corral, Fairfield, Picabo, Carey, Bellevue, Gannett, Hailey, Ketchum, Sun Valley, Arco, Atomic City, Idaho Falls, Ammon, Iona, Ucon, Rigby, Menan, Roberts, Thornton, Rexburg, Tetonia, Felt, Ririe, Swan Valley, Irwin, Jackson, King Hill, Glenns Ferry, Hammett, Gooding, Wendell, Hagerman, Bliss, Richfield, Shoshone, Dietrich, Jerome, Eden, Hazelton, Paul, Rupert, Acequia, Minidoka, Declo, Burley, Albion, Oakley, Malta, Sublett, Buist, Almo, Bridge, Stone, Woodruff, Malad City, Samaria, Holbrook, Curlew, Rockland, Arbon, Pauline, Robin, Arimo, Downey, Virginia, McCammon, Lava Hot Springs, Bancroft, Grace, Soda Springs, Conda, Henry, Wayan, Freedom, Thatcher, Swanlake, Oxford, Clifton, Dayton, Weston, Preston, Franklin, Georgetown, Bennington, Montpelier, Paris, Bloomington, St. Charles, Ovid, Dingle, Fish Haven, Castleford, Buhl, Filer, Twin Falls, Murtaugh, Kimberly, Hollister, Rogerson, Three Creek, Roseworth, Grasmere, Riddle

Castleford, Buhl, Filer, Twin Falls, Hansen, Kimberly, Rock Creek

Mt. Cleveland 3190 m (10,466 ft)
Lolo Peak 2786 m (9139 ft)
Warren Peak 3189 m (10,464 ft)
Granite Peak 3228 m (10,590 ft)
Sacajawea Peak 2998 m (9839 ft)
Scott Peak 3473 m (11,393 ft)
Castle Peak 3601 m (11,815 ft)
Borah Peak 3859 m (12,662 ft)
Ryan Peak 3595 m (11,795 ft)
Hyndman Peak 3660 m (12,009 ft)
Grand Teton 4280 m (13,770 ft)
Cache Peak 3151 m (10,339 ft)

KANIKSU NATIONAL FOREST, KOOTENAI NATIONAL FOREST, BOUNDARY, BONNER, COLVILLE NATL. FOREST, SELKIRK MTS., KOOTENAI NATIONAL FOREST, COEUR D'ALENE NATIONAL FOREST, LOLO NATIONAL FOREST, SHOSHONE, BENEWAH, LATAH, ST. JOE NATIONAL FOREST, CLEARWATER NATIONAL FOREST, NEZ PERCE, LEWIS, IDAHO, CLEARWATER N.F., NEZ PERCE NATIONAL FOREST, BITTERROOT NATIONAL FOREST, SALMON NATIONAL FOREST, PAYETTE NATIONAL FOREST, ADAMS, VALLEY, CHALLIS NATIONAL FOREST, LEMHI, CUSTER, BUTTE, CLARK, FREMONT, MADISON, TETON, JEFFERSON, BONNEVILLE, BINGHAM, CARIBOU, BANNOCK, POWER, CASSIA, TWIN FALLS, MINIDOKA, JEROME, LINCOLN, GOODING, CAMAS, BLAINE, ELMORE, BOISE NATIONAL FOREST, SAWTOOTH NATIONAL FOREST, ADA, CANYON, GEM, PAYETTE, WASHINGTON, OWYHEE, ONEIDA, FRANKLIN, BEAR LAKE, CARIBOU NATIONAL FOREST, TARGHEE NATIONAL FOREST, BEAVERHEAD NATIONAL FOREST, YELLOWSTONE NATIONAL PARK, GRAND TETON NATIONAL PARK, SAWTOOTH NATIONAL RECREATION AREA, HELLS CANYON NATIONAL RECREATION AREA, CRATERS OF THE MOON NATL. MON., CITY OF ROCKS NATL. RES.

Spokane, Pullman, Clarkston, Lewiston, Missoula, Helena, Anaconda, Butte, Bozeman, Livingston, Pocatello, Chubbuck, Blackfoot, Ontario

Snake River, Salmon River, Clearwater River, Payette River, Bear River, Bruneau River, Owyhee River, Lochsa R., Selway R., Lemhi R., Clark Fork, Kootenai R., Pend Oreille R.

Pend Oreille L., Coeur d'Alene L., Dworshak Res., Cascade Res., Palisades Res., American Falls Res., Bear Lake

Capital: Springfield
Area: 57,900 sq. mi.
150,000 sq. km.
Population: 11,697,000
Largest City: Chicago

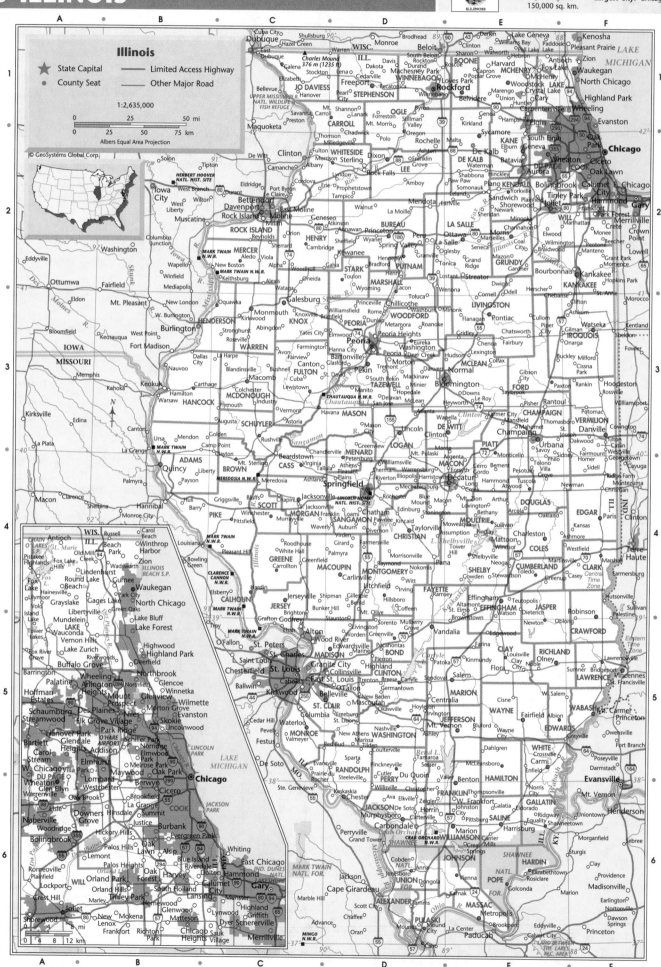

Illinois

★ State Capital
● County Seat

▬▬▬ Limited Access Highway
▬▬ Other Major Road

1:2,635,000

0   25   50 mi
0   25   50   75 km
Albers Equal Area Projection

© GeoSystems Global Corp.

Capital: Indianapolis
Area: 36,400 sq. mi.
94,300 sq. km.
Population: 5,713,000
Largest City: Indianapolis

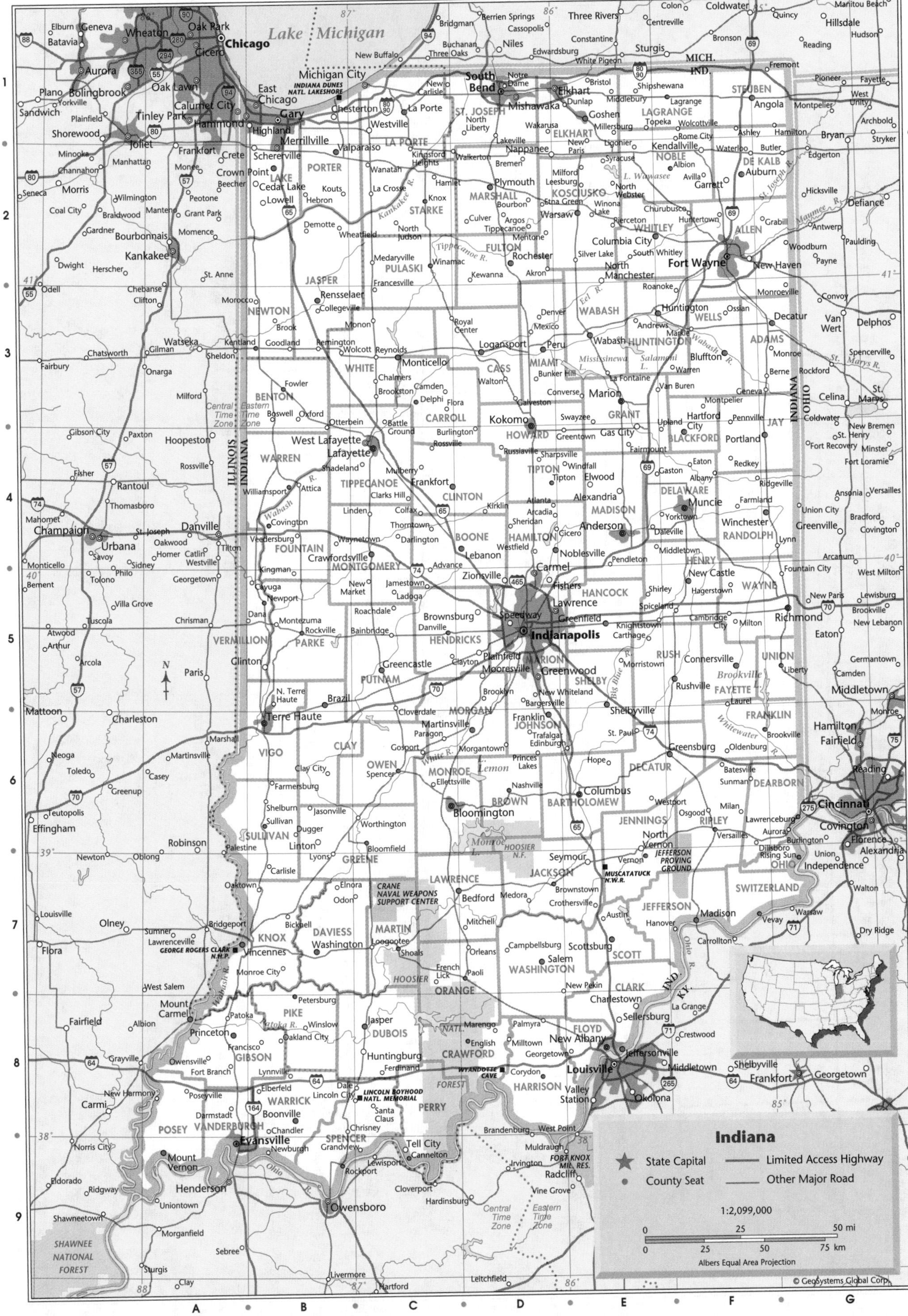

Lake Michigan

MICH.
IND.

ILLINOIS
OHIO
KY.
IND.

Central Time Zone
Eastern Time Zone

Counties / regions:
LAKE, PORTER, LA PORTE, ST. JOSEPH, ELKHART, LAGRANGE, STEUBEN, NEWTON, JASPER, STARKE, MARSHALL, KOSCIUSKO, NOBLE, DE KALB, BENTON, WHITE, PULASKI, FULTON, WHITLEY, ALLEN, WARREN, TIPPECANOE, CARROLL, CASS, MIAMI, WABASH, HUNTINGTON, WELLS, ADAMS, FOUNTAIN, MONTGOMERY, CLINTON, HOWARD, GRANT, BLACKFORD, JAY, TIPTON, DELAWARE, MADISON, RANDOLPH, BOONE, HAMILTON, HENRY, WAYNE, VERMILLION, PARKE, PUTNAM, HENDRICKS, MARION, HANCOCK, RUSH, FAYETTE, UNION, VIGO, CLAY, OWEN, MORGAN, JOHNSON, SHELBY, FRANKLIN, SULLIVAN, GREENE, MONROE, BROWN, BARTHOLOMEW, DECATUR, RIPLEY, DEARBORN, OHIO, KNOX, DAVIESS, MARTIN, LAWRENCE, JACKSON, JENNINGS, JEFFERSON, SWITZERLAND, WASHINGTON, SCOTT, CLARK, PIKE, DUBOIS, ORANGE, CRAWFORD, FLOYD, HARRISON, GIBSON, WARRICK, PERRY, SPENCER, POSEY, VANDERBURGH

Major cities and towns:
Chicago, Gary, Hammond, East Chicago, Calumet City, Oak Lawn, Oak Park, Cicero, Wheaton, Aurora, Joliet, Michigan City, South Bend, Mishawaka, Elkhart, Goshen, La Porte, Valparaiso, Merrillville, Crown Point, Schererville, Highland, Plymouth, Warsaw, Columbia City, Fort Wayne, New Haven, Decatur, Huntington, Wabash, Peru, Logansport, Rochester, Angola, Kendallville, Auburn, Garrett, Rensselaer, Monticello, Delphi, Kokomo, Marion, Hartford City, Portland, Lafayette, West Lafayette, Frankfort, Crawfordsville, Lebanon, Noblesville, Carmel, Fishers, Anderson, Muncie, Winchester, Richmond, New Castle, Terre Haute, Brazil, Greencastle, Danville, Plainfield, Speedway, Indianapolis, Greenwood, Greenfield, Shelbyville, Connersville, Rushville, Bloomington, Columbus, Martinsville, Franklin, Nashville, Greensburg, Batesville, Cincinnati, Covington, Lawrenceburg, Vincennes, Washington, Bedford, Seymour, North Vernon, Madison, Salem, Scottsburg, Charlestown, Jeffersonville, New Albany, Louisville, Corydon, Jasper, Huntingburg, Paoli, English, Princeton, Boonville, Evansville, Mount Vernon, Tell City, Cannelton, Henderson, Owensboro

Landmarks:
INDIANA DUNES NATL. LAKESHORE, GEORGE ROGERS CLARK N.H.P., CRANE NAVAL WEAPONS SUPPORT CENTER, MUSCATATUCK N.W.R., JEFFERSON PROVING GROUND, HOOSIER N.F., WYANDOTTE CAVE, LINCOLN BOYHOOD NATL. MEMORIAL, FORT KNOX MIL. RES., SHAWNEE NATIONAL FOREST

Indiana
★ State Capital — Limited Access Highway
● County Seat — Other Major Road

1:2,099,000

0 — 25 — 50 mi
0 — 25 — 50 — 75 km

Albers Equal Area Projection

© Geosystems Global Corp.

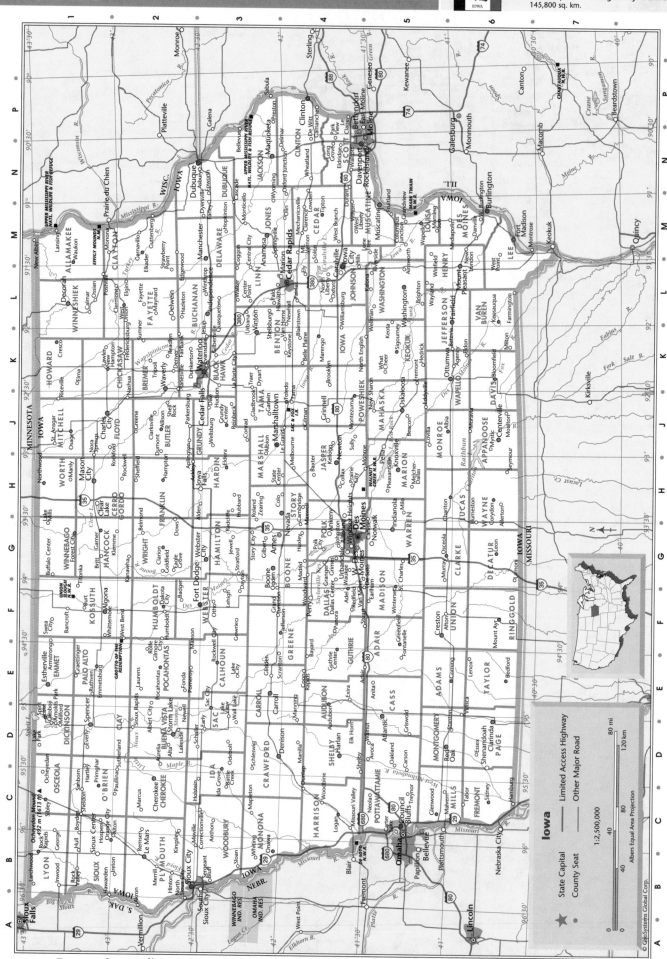

Capital: Des Moines
Area: 56,300 sq. mi.
145,800 sq. km.
Population: 2,814,000
Largest City: Des Moines

Iowa

1:2,500,000

Albers Equal Area Projection

State Capital
County Seat

Limited Access Highway
Other Major Road

©GeoSystems Global Corp.

Capital: Topeka
Area: 82,300 sq. mi.
213,100 sq. km.
Population: 2,531,000
Largest City: Wichita

KANSAS

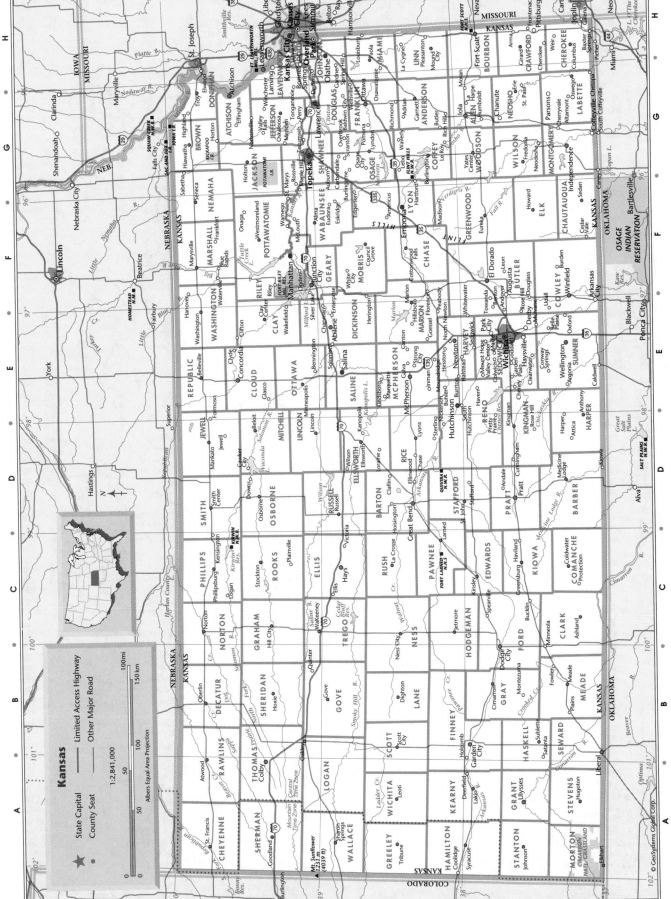

Kansas

Limited Access Highway
Other Major Road

★ State Capital
● County Seat

1:2,841,000

Albers Equal Area Projection

© GeoSystems Global Corp.

Capital: Frankfort
Area: 40,400 sq. mi.
104,700 sq. km.
Population: 3,789,000
Largest City: Louisville

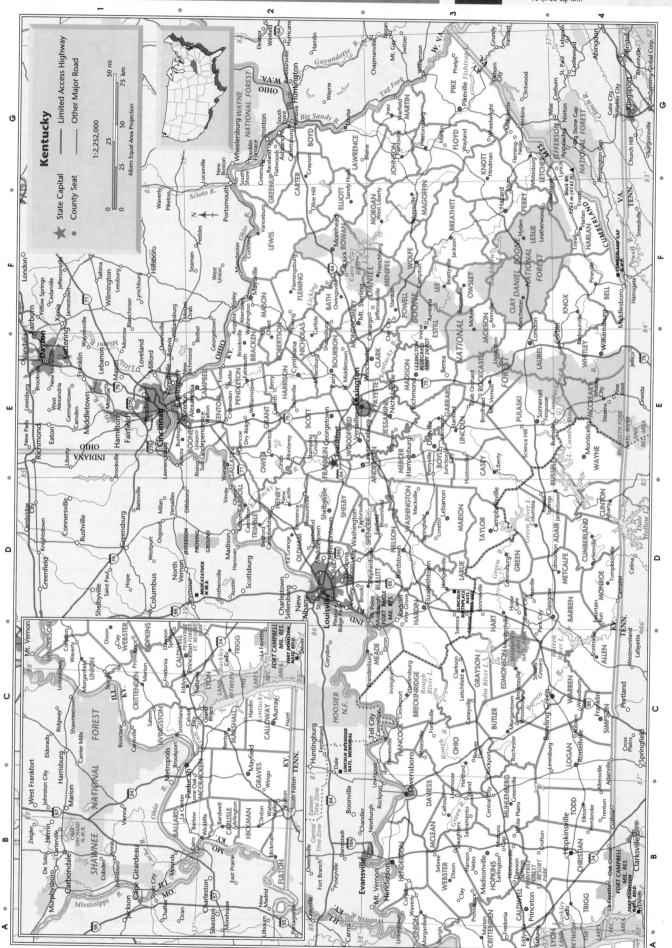

Capital: Baton Rouge
Area: 51,800 sq. mi.
134,300 sq. km.
Population: 4,295,000
Largest City: New Orleans

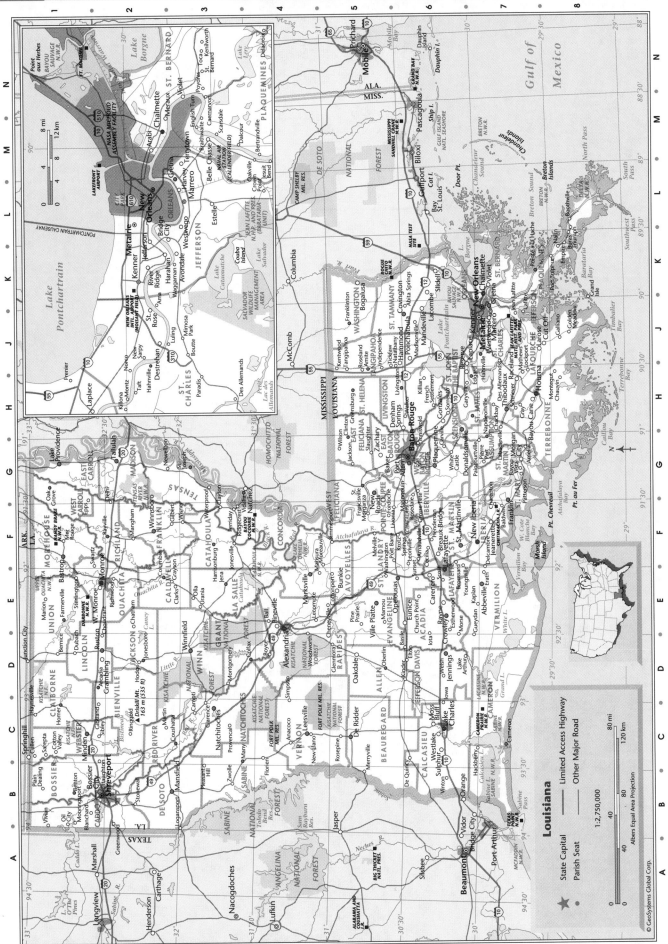

Capital: Augusta	**Population:** 1,239,000
Area: 35,400 sq. mi.	**Largest City:** Portland
91,700 sq. km.	

Maine

★ State/Provincial Capital
● County Seat
▬ Limited Access Highway
═ Other Major Road

1:2,074,000

0	25	50 mi
0	25	50	75 km

Albers Equal Area Projection

© GeoSystems Global Corp.

Counties: AROOSTOOK, PISCATAQUIS, PENOBSCOT, SOMERSET, FRANKLIN, OXFORD, WASHINGTON, HANCOCK, WALDO, KENNEBEC, ANDROSCOGGIN, KNOX, LINCOLN, SAGADAHOC, CUMBERLAND, YORK

Regions / features: LAURENTIDES PROVINCIAL RESERVE, APPALACHIAN MOUNTAINS, ALLAGASH WILDERNESS WATERWAY, BAXTER STATE PARK, WHITE MTS., WHITE MTN. NATL. FOR., ACADIA NATL. PARK, FRONTENAC PROV. PARK, MT. CARLETON PROV. PARK, CANADA, U.S., QUEBEC, MAINE, NEW BRUNSWICK, GULF OF MAINE, ATLANTIC OCEAN

Mt. Katahdin 1606 m (5268 ft)
White Cap Mt. 1111 m (3644 ft)
Snow Mt. 1204 m (3948 ft)
Sugarloaf Mt. 1291 m (4237 ft)
Saddleback Mt. 1255 m (4116 ft)

Capital: Annapolis
Area: 12,400 sq. mi.
32,100 sq. km.
Population: 4,965,000
Largest City: Baltimore

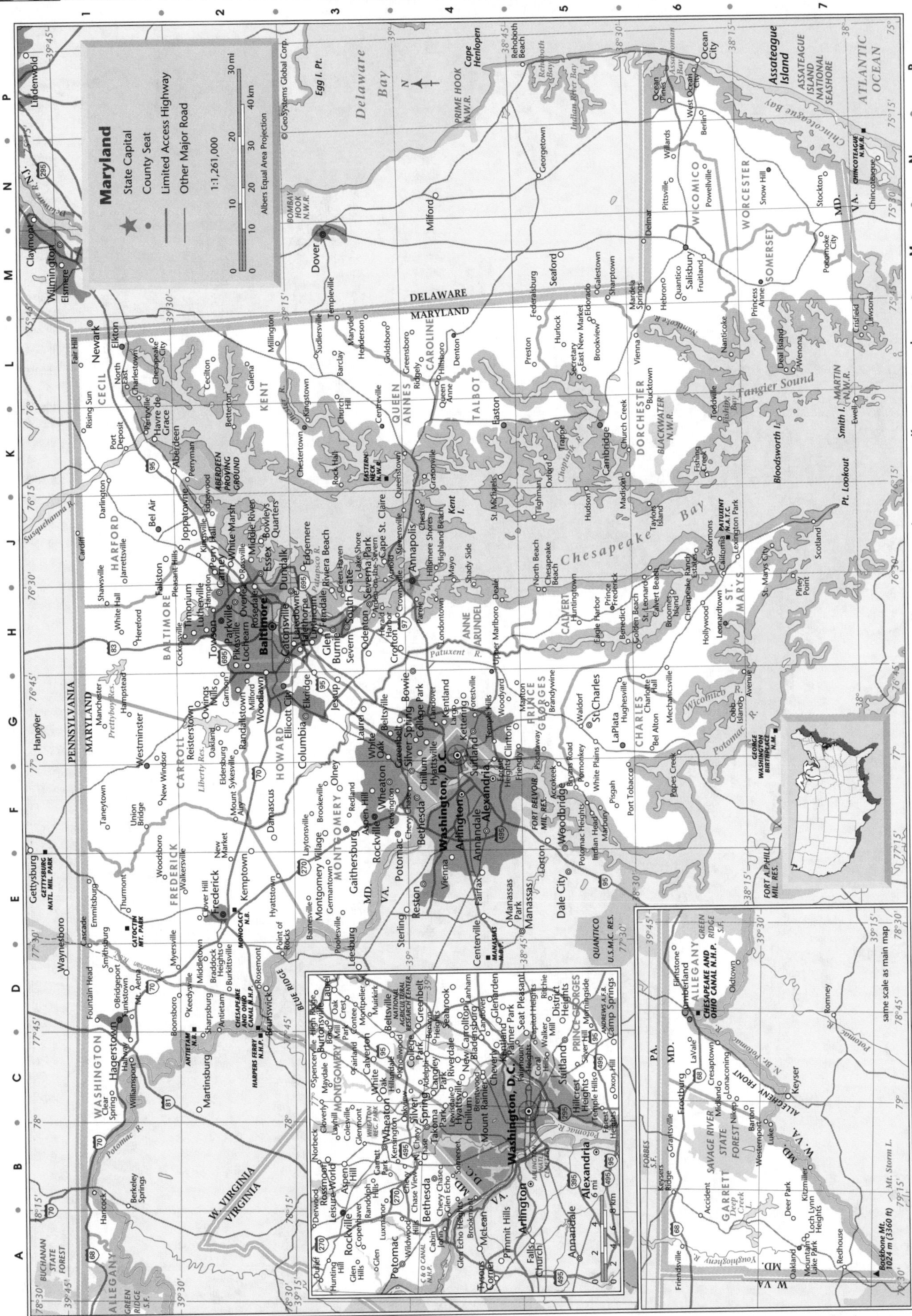

Maryland

★ State Capital
• County Seat
— Limited Access Highway
— Other Major Road

1:1,261,000

Albers Equal Area Projection

GeoSystems Global Corp.

30 mi
40 km

PENNSYLVANIA

DELAWARE
MARYLAND

WEST VIRGINIA
W. VIRGINIA
VIRGINIA

Chesapeake Bay

Delaware Bay

ATLANTIC OCEAN

Assateague Island
ASSATEAGUE ISLAND NATIONAL SEASHORE

Chincoteague Bay

Washington, D.C.

Baltimore

Annapolis

Backbone Mt. 1024 m (3360 ft)

same scale as main map

Counties: ALLEGANY, GARRETT, WASHINGTON, FREDERICK, CARROLL, HOWARD, MONTGOMERY, BALTIMORE, HARFORD, CECIL, KENT, QUEEN ANNES, TALBOT, CAROLINE, DORCHESTER, WICOMICO, WORCESTER, SOMERSET, ANNE ARUNDEL, PRINCE GEORGES, CALVERT, CHARLES, ST. MARYS

Capital: Boston
Area: 10,600 sq. mi.
27,300 sq. km.
Population: 6,012,000
Largest City: Boston

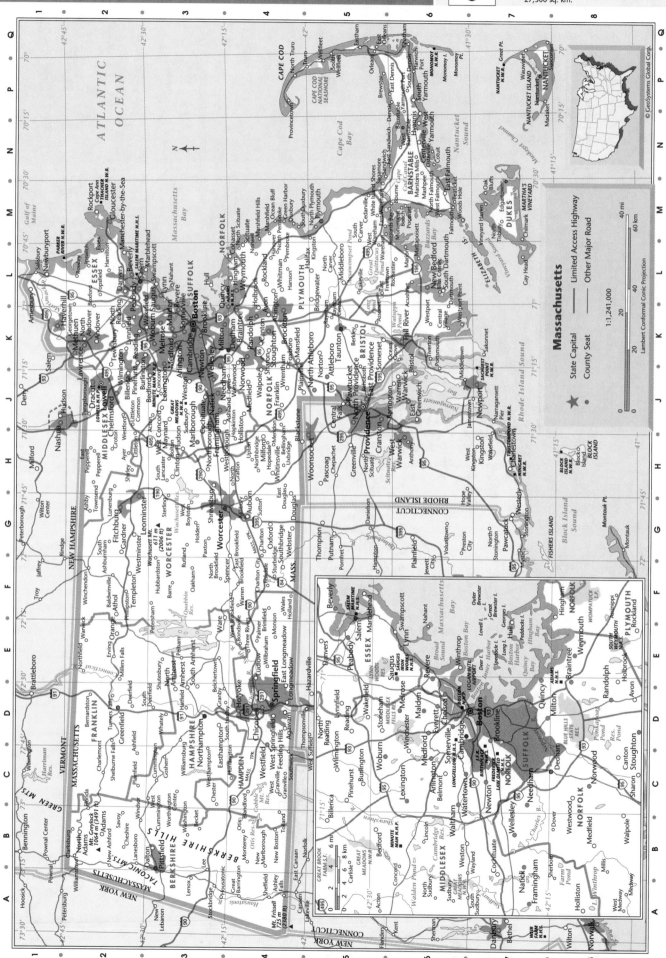

Massachusetts

★ State Capital
• County Seat

⎯⎯ Limited Access Highway
⎯⎯ Other Major Road

1:1,241,000

Lambert Conformal Conic Projection

© GeoSystems Global Corp.

Capital: Lansing
Area: 96,700 sq. mi.
250,500 sq. km.
Population: 9,478,000
Largest City: Detroit

Michigan

★ State Capital
● County Seat
▬ Limited Access Highway
— Other Major Road

1:3,205,000

0   50   100 mi
0   50   100   150 km
Albers Equal Area Projection

© GeoSystems Global Corp.

Inset (upper left): same scale as main map — Central Time Zone / Eastern Time Zone — Apostle Islands Natl. Lakeshore — Lake Superior — APOSTLE ISLANDS — Outer I. — Madeline I. — Silver City — Ontonagon — Government Peak 564 m (1850 ft) — ONTONAGON — White Pine — PORCUPINE MTS. WILDERNESS S.P. — OTTAWA N.F. — Ewen — Birch — Connorville — Merriweather — Wakefield — Bessemer — Hurley — Ironwood — Montreal — BAD RIVER I.R. — MICH. — WIS. — Presque Isle — GOGEBIC — Marenisco — Turtle Flambeau Flowage — NORTHERN HIGHLAND AMERICAN LEGION S.F. — Manitowish Waters — Manitowish — Butternut — Lac du Flambeau — LAC DU FLAMBEAU I.R. — Eagle River — Park Falls — Minocqua — CHEQUAMEGON N.F. — Lake Gogebic

Regions & Features (main map)
LAKE SUPERIOR · ISLE ROYALE · ISLE ROYALE NATL. PARK · KEWEENAW PENINSULA · HURON MTS. · BARAGA · MARQUETTE · IRON · DICKINSON · NICOLET NATIONAL FOREST · MENOMINEE · HIAWATHA NATIONAL FOREST · ALGER · SCHOOLCRAFT · DELTA · LUCE · MACKINAC · CHIPPEWA · EMMET · CHARLEVOIX · ANTRIM · OTSEGO · MONTMORENCY · ALPENA · PRESQUE ISLE · CHEBOYGAN · LEELANAU · BENZIE · GRAND TRAVERSE · KALKASKA · CRAWFORD · OSCODA · ALCONA · IOSCO · OGEMAW · ROSCOMMON · MISSAUKEE · WEXFORD · MANISTEE · MASON · LAKE · OSCEOLA · CLARE · GLADWIN · ARENAC · BAY · MIDLAND · ISABELLA · MECOSTA · NEWAYGO · OCEANA · MUSKEGON · MONTCALM · GRATIOT · SAGINAW · TUSCOLA · HURON · SANILAC · LAPEER · GENESEE · SHIAWASSEE · CLINTON · IONIA · KENT · OTTAWA · ALLEGAN · BARRY · EATON · INGHAM · LIVINGSTON · OAKLAND · MACOMB · WAYNE · WASHTENAW · JACKSON · CALHOUN · KALAMAZOO · VAN BUREN · BERRIEN · CASS · ST. JOSEPH · BRANCH · HILLSDALE · LENAWEE · MONROE

LAKE MICHIGAN · LAKE HURON · LAKE ERIE · GREEN BAY · SAGINAW BAY · Straits of Mackinac

Cities and towns
Thunder Bay · Eagle River · Hancock · Houghton · L'Anse · Ishpeming · Negaunee · Marquette · Munising · Newberry · Sault Ste. Marie · Elliot Lake · Crystal Falls · Iron Mountain · Norway · Kingsford · Niagara · Escanaba · Gladstone · Manistique · Garden · St. Ignace · Cheboygan · Petoskey · Charlevoix · Boyne City · Gaylord · Atlanta · Alpena · Traverse City · Bellaire · Kalkaska · Grayling · Mio · Harrisville · Cadillac · Lake City · Houghton Lake · Roscommon · West Branch · Tawas City · East Tawas · Standish · Manistee · Ludingon · Baldwin · Reed City · Harrison · Gladwin · Bad Axe · Big Rapids · Mt. Pleasant · Midland · Bay City · Caro · Sandusky · Fremont · White Cloud · Stanton · Ithaca · Alma · St. Louis · Shields · Saginaw · Carrollton · Bridgeport · Frankenmuth · Vassar · Hart · Muskegon · Muskegon Hts. · Norton Shores · Whitehall · Grand Haven · Greenville · Belding · Owosso · Flushing · Mt. Morris · Flint · Burton · Grand Blanc · Lapeer · Imlay City · Marysville · Port Huron · Sarnia · Grand Rapids · Wyoming · Kentwood · Walker · Jenison · Hudsonville · Zeeland · Holland · Allendale · Lowell · Ionia · Portland · De Witt · St. Johns · Lansing · E. Lansing · Okemos · Williamston · Howell · Brighton · Fowlerville · Milford · Wixom · Pontiac · Holly · Fenton · Oxford · Romeo · New Baltimore · Wallaceburg · Allegan · Wayland · Hastings · Charlotte · Eaton Rapids · Mason · Holt · South Haven · Kalamazoo · Battle Creek · Marshall · Albion · Jackson · Chelsea · Ann Arbor · Ypsilanti · Saline · Milan · Flat Rock · Benton Harbor · St. Joseph · Paw Paw · Portage · Three Rivers · Dowagiac · Cassopolis · Sturgis · Coldwater · Hillsdale · Hudson · Adrian · Tecumseh · Dundee · Monroe · Temperance · Lambertville · Toledo · Buchanan · Niles · Centreville

Detroit area inset (lower left)
Rochester Hills · Pontiac · Utica · Chesterfield · Troy · Sterling Heights · Mount Clemens · Fraser · Warren · Roseville · St. Clair Shores · Clawson · Madison Hts. · Center Line · Eastpointe · Grosse Pointe Woods · Grosse Pointe Shores · Grosse Pointe Farms · Farmington Hills · Beverly Hills · Royal Oak · Berkley · Huntington Woods · Oak Park · Ferndale · Hazel Park · Hamtramck · Highland Park · Harper Woods · Grosse Pointe · Detroit · Windsor · Dearborn · Dearborn Hts. · Garden City · Westland · Livonia · Southfield · Inkster · Melvindale · River Rouge · Ecorse · Lincoln Park · Wyandotte · Southgate · Taylor · Allen Park · Romulus · Wayne · Tecumseh · St. Clair Beach

Chicago area inset (lower left, continued)
Lake Zurich · Highland Park · Carpentersville · Wheeling · Elgin · Evanston · De Kalb · Batavia · Aurora · Cicero · Oak Park · Chicago · Waterman · Sandwich · Bollingbrook · Joliet · Calumet City · Hammond · Gary · East Chicago · Michigan City · South Bend · Mishawaka · Elkhart · Goshen · La Porte · Westville · INDIANA

Wisconsin / western edge
Shawano · New London · Oneida I.R. · Green Bay · De Pere · Howard · Appleton · Kaukauna · Neenah · Oshkosh · Berlin · Ripon · Omro · Chilton · Two Rivers · Manitowoc · Sturgeon Bay · DOOR PENINSULA · Marinette · Menominee · Peshtigo · STOCKBRIDGE I.R. · MENOMINEE INDIAN RES. · POTAWATOMI I.R. · SOKAOGON CHIPPEWA I.R. · Crandon

INDIANA · OHIO · ONTARIO · CANADA · U.S. · LAKE ERIE · CAN. · U.S. · Perrys Victory and Int. Peace Mem. · OTTAWA N.W.R.

Capital: St. Paul
Area: 86,900 sq. mi. / 225,200 sq. km.
Population: 4,517,000
Largest City: Minneapolis

Minnesota

★ State Capital
• County Seat
— Limited Access Highway
— Other Major Road

1:2,773,000

0   40   80 mi
0   40   80   120 km
Albers Equal Area Projection

MANITOBA
MINNESOTA
MAN. ONT.
Whitemouth L.
Lake of the Woods
Rainy R.
Fort Frances
International Falls
QUETICO PROV. PARK
CAN. / U.S.
ONT. MINN.

KITTSON
ROSEAU
LAKE OF THE WOODS
RED LAKE INDIAN RES.
KOOCHICHING
ST. LOUIS
SUPERIOR NATIONAL FOREST
VERMILION RANGE
LAKE FOREST
COOK

Hallock
Roseau
Greenbush
Warroad
Baudette
Littlefork

MARSHALL
Karlstad
Stephen
Argyle
Warren
Thief River Falls
PENNINGTON
BELTRAMI
Ponemah
Upper Red L.
Lower Red L.
Redby
Blackduck
CHIPPEWA NATIONAL FOREST
ITASCA
MESABI RANGE
Ely
Tower
Babbitt

East Grand Forks
Grand Forks
Crookston
RED LAKE
Red Lake Falls
McIntosh
Fosston
POLK
Clearbrook
Bagley
Bemidji
LEECH LAKE
Cass Lake
Deer River
Grand Rapids
Keewatin
Nashwauk
Hibbing
Chisholm
Virginia
Eveleth
Aurora
Mountain Iron
Buhl
Marble
Bovey
Silver Bay

NORMAN
MAHNOMEN
WHITE EARTH I.R.
CLAY
BECKER
HUBBARD
CASS
AITKIN
CARLTON
Two Harbors
Lake Superior

Halstad
Ada
Twin Valley
Ulen
Mahnomen
ITASCA S.P.
Floodwood
Hermantown
Proctor
Duluth
Superior
Cloquet
Carlton

Fargo
Moorhead
West Fargo
Dilworth
Glyndon
Hawley
Lake Park
Detroit Lakes
Frazee
TAMARAC N.W.R.
Park Rapids
WADENA
Menahga
Pine River
Emily
Cross Lake
Nisswa
Crosby
Aitkin
Moose Lake
RICE LAKE N.W.R.
FOND DU LAC I.R.

WILKIN
OTTER TAIL
TODD
CROW WING
MILLE LACS
KANABEC
PINE

Breckenridge
Wahpeton
Fergus Falls
Battle Lake
Henning
New York Mills
Wadena
Verndale
Staples
Parkers Prairie
Bertha
Eagle Bend
Clarissa
Browerville
CAMP RIPLEY MIL. RES.
Brainerd
Baxter
East Gull Lake
Lake Shore
Deerwood
Randall
Pierz
Little Falls
Isle
Onamia
MILLE LACS I.R.
Sandstone
Hinckley
Mora
Ogilvie
Milaca
Pine City
Rock Creek
Braham

GRANT
DOUGLAS
MORRISON
BENTON
ISANTI
CHISAGO
Mille Lacs L.

Elbow Lake
Hoffman
Evansville
Alexandria
Osakis
Long Prairie
Royalton
Rice
STEVENS
POPE
STEARNS
Holdingford
Melrose
Freeport
Albany
Avon
Sauk Rapids
Sartell
St. Joseph
Waite Park
St. Cloud
Cold Spring
Richmond
Rockville
Princeton
Cambridge
Isanti
Harris
North Branch
E. Bethel
Forest Lake
Wyoming

Morris
Chokio
Starbuck
Glenwood
Hancock
Brooten
Belgrade
Paynesville
Watkins
Kimball
Becker
Big Lake
Elk River
Monticello
Zimmerman

BIG STONE
SWIFT
KANDIYOHI
MEEKER
WRIGHT
ANOKA
HENNEPIN
RAMSEY
WASHINGTON

Ortonville
Clinton
Appleton
Kerkhoven
Spicer
New London
Willmar
Kandiyohi
Raymond
Atwater
Litchfield
Cokato
Howard Lake
Buffalo
St. Michael
Albertville
Ramsey
Coon Rapids
Maple Grove
Plymouth
Minneapolis
St. Paul
Stillwater
Bayport

Milbank
BIG STONE N.W.R.
Madison
Montevideo
Clara City
Dawson
Granite Falls
Sacred Heart
Renville
Olivia
Bird Island
Hector
Danube
Prinsburg
Cosmos
Winsted
Lester Prairie
Mound
Orono
Edina
Bloomington
Chanhassen
Chaska
Burnsville
Hastings

LAC QUI PARLE
CHIPPEWA
YELLOW MEDICINE
RENVILLE
McLEOD
CARVER
SCOTT
DAKOTA

Canby
Clarkfield
Cottonwood
Minneota
Ivanhoe
Hendricks
Redwood Falls
Morgan
Wabasso
Winthrop
Gibbon
Gaylord
Arlington
Young America
Brownton
Glencoe
Belle Plaine
Jordan
Shakopee
Prior Lake
Lakeville
Farmington
Cannon Falls
Red Wing
Northfield

LINCOLN
LYON
REDWOOD
BROWN
NICOLLET
SIBLEY
LE SUEUR
RICE
GOODHUE
WABASHA

Brookings
Tyler
Lake Benton
Balaton
Tracy
Walnut Grove
Lamberton
Springfield
Sleepy Eye
New Ulm
St. Peter
Le Sueur
Montgomery
Le Center
Cleveland
Kasota
Waterville
Morristown
Faribault
Kenyon
Wanamingo
Zumbrota
Pine Island
Wabasha
Whitehall
Osseo

PIPESTONE
MURRAY
COTTONWOOD
WATONWAN
BLUE EARTH
WASECA
STEELE
DODGE
OLMSTED
WINONA

FLANDREAU I.R.
Pipestone
PIPESTONE N.M.
Jasper
Edgerton
Slayton
Fulda
Westbrook
Mountain Lake
Butterfield
St. James
Madelia
Truman
Mankato
North Mankato
Lake Crystal
Good Thunder
Mapleton
Minnesota Lake
Wells
New Richland
Blooming Prairie
Owatonna
Medford
Janesville
Waseca
Waldorf
West Concord
Mantorville
Dodge Center
Kasson
Hayfield
Rochester
Goodview
Stockton
Lewiston
St. Charles
Eyota
Winona
La Crescent

ROCK
NOBLES
JACKSON
MARTIN
FARIBAULT
FREEBORN
MOWER
FILLMORE
HOUSTON

Sioux Falls
Luverne
Hills
Adrian
Ellsworth
Worthington
Brewster
Lakefield
Jackson
Sherburn
Fairmont
Welcome
Trimont
Winnebago
Blue Earth
Alden
Clarks Grove
Albert Lea
Austin
Adams
Lyle
Grand Meadow
Stewartville
Spring Valley
Chatfield
Preston
Rushford
Houston
Caledonia
Harmony
Spring Grove
Mabel
La Crosse

WISCONSIN
IOWA
Mississippi R.

© GeoSystems Global Corp.

Capital: Jackson
Area: 48,400 sq. mi.
125,400 sq. km.
Population: 2,643,000
Largest City: Jackson

A   B   C   D   E

TENN.
MISS.

Memphis
Germantown
Collierville
Forrest City
Southaven
Olive Branch
Horn Lake
Walnut
Corinth
DE SOTO
Byhalia
Ashland
Kossuth
Burnsville
Iuka
Florence
Marianna
Hernando
Holly Springs
Falkner
Rienzi
Woodall Mtn. 246 m (806 ft)
Sheffield
Tuscumbia
Coldwater
MARSHALL
SPRINGS BENTON
Blue Mountain
Jumpertown
TISHOMINGO
Russellville
West Helena
Senatobia
Potts Camp
Dumas
RIDGE
Paden
Tishomingo
Big Springs L.
Helena
TATE
Hickory Flat
Myrtle
PRENTISS
Belmont
Stuttgart
Como
Abbeville
NATIONAL
New Albany
Baldwyn
Guntown
Marietta
Friars Point
Crenshaw
UNION
Blue Springs
Saltillo
Golden
Red Bay
Tunica
Sardis
Oxford
FOREST
Sherman
ITAWAMBA
Coahoma
Sledge
PANOLA
LAFAYETTE
Ecru
Thaxton
Mantachie
Fulton
Clarksdale
Falcon
SARDIS L.
Taylor
Toccopola
Pontotoc
Verona
Plantersville
Tremont
Lyon
Marks
Batesville
PONTOTOC
Netleton
Algoma
TUPELO N.B.S.
Tupelo
Crowder
Pope
Water Valley
New Houlka
Shannon
Smithville
Hamilton
Duncan
Tutwiler
COAHOMA
QUITMAN
Enid L.
TOMBIGBEE
Okolona
Amory
Hatley
Alligator
Oakland
YALOBUSHA
Coffeeville
Pittsboro
Houston
N.F.
Shelby
Sumner
Charleston
Bruce
Vardaman
CHICKASAW
Aberdeen
Gunnison
Webb
TALLAHATCHIE
HOLLY
Slate Spring
Calhoun City
Derma
Woodland
MONROE
Winstonville
Glendora
Grenada L.
CALHOUN
Mantee
Rosedale
Merigold
Grenada
Mathiston
WEBSTER
CLAY
Caledonia
BOLIVAR
Drew
Renova
Duck Hill
Walthall
Maben
West Point
Columbus L.
Beulah
Pace
Ruleville
GRENADA
Eupora
Starkville
Columbus
Cleveland
Boyle
DAHOMEY N.W.R.
Doddsville
MONTGOMERY
CARROLL
Winona
Mathiston
OKTIBBEHA
Benoit
Schlater
LEFLORE
Carrollton
Kilmichael
CHOCTAW
Artesia
LOWNDES
Shaw
Sunflower
Greenwood
Vaiden
French Camp
Ackerman
Crawford
Aliceville L.
Indianola
Itta Bena
Sidon
Weir
N.F.
Brooksville
Tuscaloosa
Greenville
Metcalfe
Moorhead
McCool
NOXUBEE N.W.R.
Leland
SUNFLOWER
MATTHEWS BRAKE N.W.R.
Cruger
WEST
Louisville
Macon
Arcola
Inverness
Bola
MORGAN BRAKE N.W.R.
Lexington
ATTALA
Ethel
NOXUBEE
Hollandale
Belzoni
Tchula
Durant
WINSTON
Noxapater
Shuqualak
WASHINGTON
HUMPHREYS
Sidon
HOLMES
Goodman
Anguilla
Silver City
HILLSIDE N.W.H.
Eden
Pickens
Scooba
OVERFLOW N.W.R.
Louise
Rolling Fork
DELTA
Yazoo City
MISS. CHOCTAW I.R.
Philadelphia
De Kalb
Mayersville
Cary
N.F.
Carthage
NESHOBA
KEMPER
Crossett
SHARKEY
PANTHER SWAMP N.W.R.
YAZOO
LEAKE
MERIDIAN N.A.S.
HANDY BRAKE N.W.R.
Lake Providence
Satartia
MADISON
Lena
Walnut Grove
Union
Okatibbee L.
POVERTY POINT N.M.
Bentonia
Canton
Sebastopol
Demopolis
ISSAQUENA
Flora
Conehatta
Collinsville
Tallulah
WARREN
Ross Barnett Res.
Decatur
Marion
Bastrop
VICKSBURG N.M.P.
Madison
Ridgeland
SCOTT
NEWTON
Meridian
TENSAS RIVER N.W.R..
Vicksburg
Clinton
Forest
LAUDERDALE
Winnsboro
Edwards
Jackson
Lake
Chunky
Raymond
Pearl
Brandon
Newton
Hickory
Quitman
Learned
Richland
RANKIN
Enterprise
Stonewall
Utica
Florence
Polkville
Montrose
CLARKE
Terry
Puckett
Louin
Pachuta
Port Gibson
Raleigh
Paulding
CLAIBORNE
Crystal Springs
D'Lo
Braxton
Sylvarena
Shubuta
Georgetown
Mendenhall
SMITH
Bay Springs
COPIAH
Hazlehurst
SIMPSON
Magee
Mize
JASPER
Heidelberg
Jackson
JEFFERSON
Beauregard
Wesson
PINE
Taylorsville
Sandersville
WAYNE
Fayette
HILLS
New Augusta
Soso
Laurel
Waynesboro
ADAMS
Natchez
Meadville
Mount Olive
COVINGTON
JONES
DE SOTO
ST. CATHERINE CREEK N.W.R.
Roxie
Bude
LINCOLN
Collins
Ellisville
NATIONAL
State Line
BAYOU COCODRIE N.W.R.
HOMOCHITTO
LAWRENCE
Seminary
Sumrall
FOREST
NATCHEZ N.H.P.
Summit
MARION
Petal
Richton
Crosby
NATIONAL
Columbia
Hattiesburg
PERRY
GREENE
LAKE OPHELIA N.W.R.
Gloster
FOREST
LAMAR
Beaumont
Leakesville
FRANKLIN
McComb
Purvis
CAMP SHELBY
McLain
WILKINSON
Liberty
Magnolia
FORREST MIL. RES.
Jackson
Woodville
AMITE
Tylertown
GEORGE
Saraland
Centreville
PIKE
Osyka
WALTHALL
Lumberton
Lucedale
Prichard
MISSISSIPPI
LOUISIANA
Poplarville
Wiggins
STONE
Mobile
MISSISSIPPI
ALABAMA
Bogalusa
PEARL RIVER
NATIONAL
Tillmans Corner
Daphne
Fairhope
BOGUE CHITTO N.W.R.
Picayune
JACKSON
FOREST
Vancleave
Mobile Bay
HANCOCK
HARRISON
D'Iberville
Ocean Springs
Moss Point
Pascagoula
GRAND BAY N.W.R.
Lacombe
Lyman
MISS. SANDHILL CRANE N.W.R.
Theodore
Diamondhead
Gulfport
Biloxi
Gautier
Kiln
Long Beach
Mississippi Sound
Horn I.
Petit Bois I.
Dauphin I.
Waveland
Pass Christian
Bay St. Louis
Pearlington
Ship I.
Cat I.
GULF ISLAND NATL. SEASHORE
Mobile Pt.
Slidell
BAYOU SAUVAGE N.W.R.
Grand I.
Chandeleur Sound
BRETON N.W.R.
Gulf of Mexico
Kenner
New Orleans
Chalmette
Lake Borgne
Lake Pontchartrain

Mississippi

★ State Capital — Limited Access Highway
● County Seat — Other Major Road

1:2,386,000

0   40   80 mi
0   40   80   120 km

© GeoSystems Global Corp.

Capital: Jefferson City
Area: 69,700 sq. mi.
180,500 sq. km.
Population: 5,234,000
Largest City: St. Louis

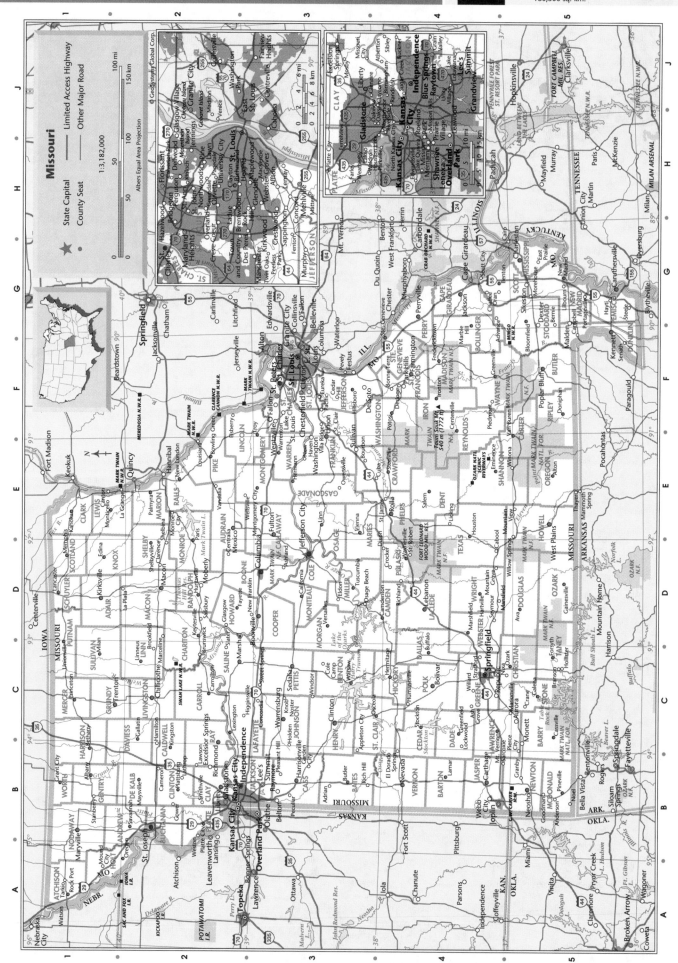

MONTANA
Capital: Helena
Area: 147,000 sq. mi.
380,800 sq. km.
Population: 839,000
Largest City: Billings

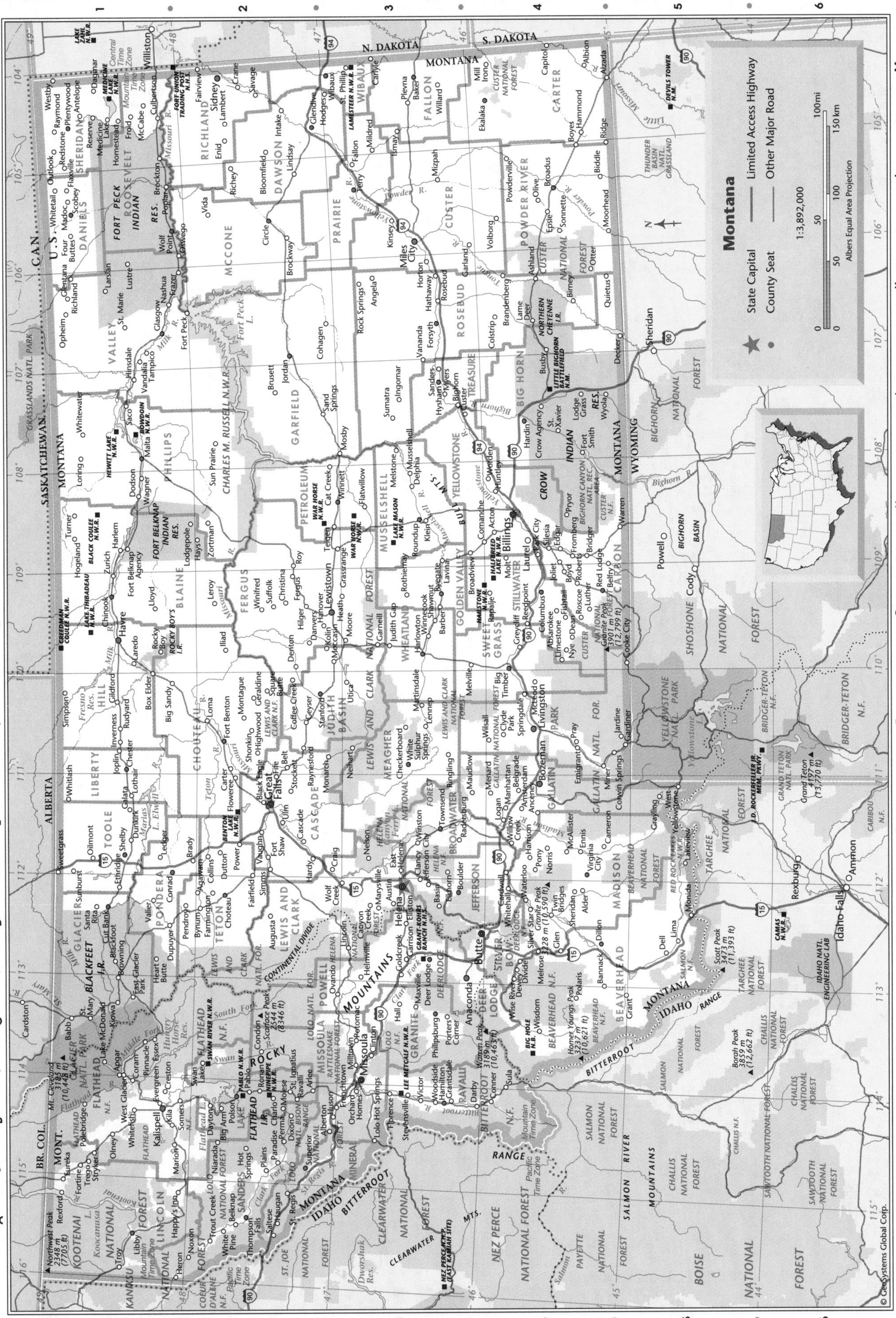

Montana

Limited Access Highway
Other Major Road

★ State Capital
• County Seat

1:3,892,000

Albers Equal Area Projection

N. DAKOTA   S. DAKOTA
MONTANA
CAN.
U.S.
SASKATCHEWAN
ALBERTA
BR. COL.
MONT.
IDAHO
WYOMING

DANIELS   SHERIDAN   ROOSEVELT   RICHLAND   WIBAUX
DAWSON   PRAIRIE   FALLON   CARTER
VALLEY   MCCONE   CUSTER   POWDER RIVER
PHILLIPS   GARFIELD   ROSEBUD   BIG HORN
BLAINE   PETROLEUM   MUSSELSHELL   TREASURE   CROW
HILL   CHOUTEAU   FERGUS   GOLDEN VALLEY   YELLOWSTONE   CARBON
LIBERTY   TOOLE   TETON   JUDITH BASIN   WHEATLAND   SWEET GRASS   STILLWATER   PARK
GLACIER   PONDERA   CASCADE   MEAGHER   GALLATIN
LEWIS AND CLARK   BROADWATER   JEFFERSON   MADISON
FLATHEAD   LAKE   MISSOULA   POWELL   GRANITE   DEER LODGE   SILVER BOW   BEAVERHEAD
LINCOLN   SANDERS   MINERAL   RAVALLI

Helena
Billings
Great Falls
Missoula
Butte
Bozeman
Miles City
Glendive

FORT PECK INDIAN RES.
FORT BELKNAP INDIAN RES.
BLACKFEET I.R.
FLATHEAD INDIAN RES.
NORTHERN CHEYENNE I.R.
CROW INDIAN RES.
ROCKY BOY'S I.R.

CHARLES M. RUSSELL N.W.R.
YELLOWSTONE NATIONAL PARK
GLACIER NATIONAL PARK
GRASSLANDS NATL. PARK
FORT UNION TRADING N.H.S.

LEWIS AND CLARK NATIONAL FOREST
GALLATIN NATIONAL FOREST
CUSTER NATIONAL FOREST
BEAVERHEAD NATIONAL FOREST
BITTERROOT NATIONAL FOREST
LOLO NATIONAL FOREST
KOOTENAI NATIONAL FOREST
FLATHEAD NATIONAL FOREST
HELENA NATIONAL FOREST
DEERLODGE NATIONAL FOREST

BITTERROOT RANGE
CONTINENTAL DIVIDE

Northwest Peak 2348 m (7705 ft)
Mt. Cleveland 3185 m (10,448 ft)
Granite Peak 3901 m (12,799 ft)
Scott Peak 3473 m (11,393 ft)
Grand Teton 4197 m (13,770 ft)

© Geosystems Global Corp.

Capital: Lincoln
Area: 77,400 sq. mi.
200,300 sq. km.
Population: 1,607,000
Largest City: Omaha

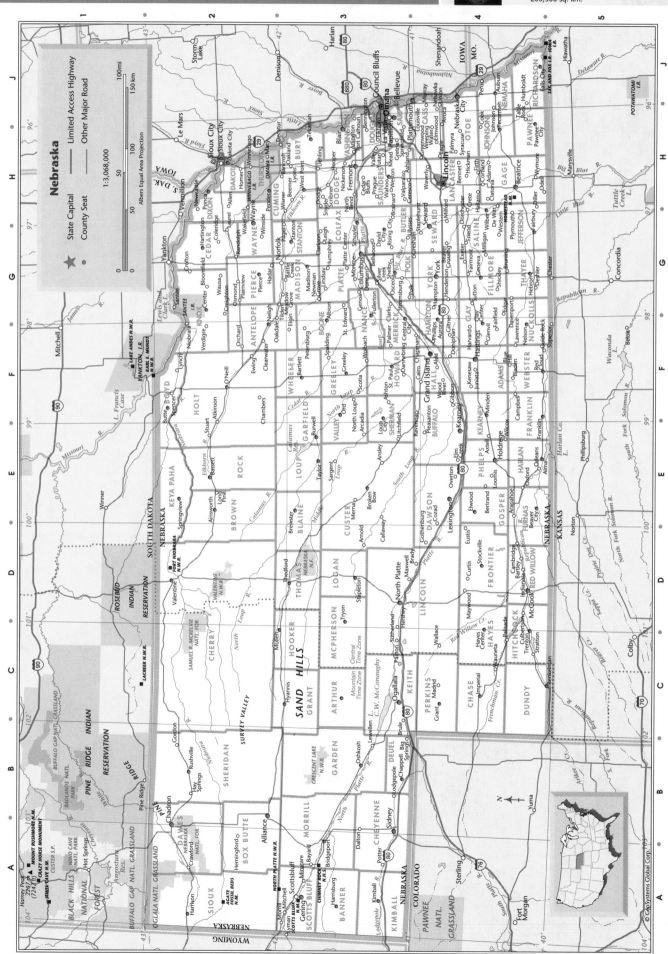

Nebraska

Limited Access Highway
Other Major Road

★ State Capital
• County Seat

1:3,068,000

Albers Equal Area Projection

© GeoSystems Global Corp. 103

Capital: Carson City
Area: 110,600 sq. mi.
286,400 sq. km.
Population: 1,389,000
Largest City: Las Vegas

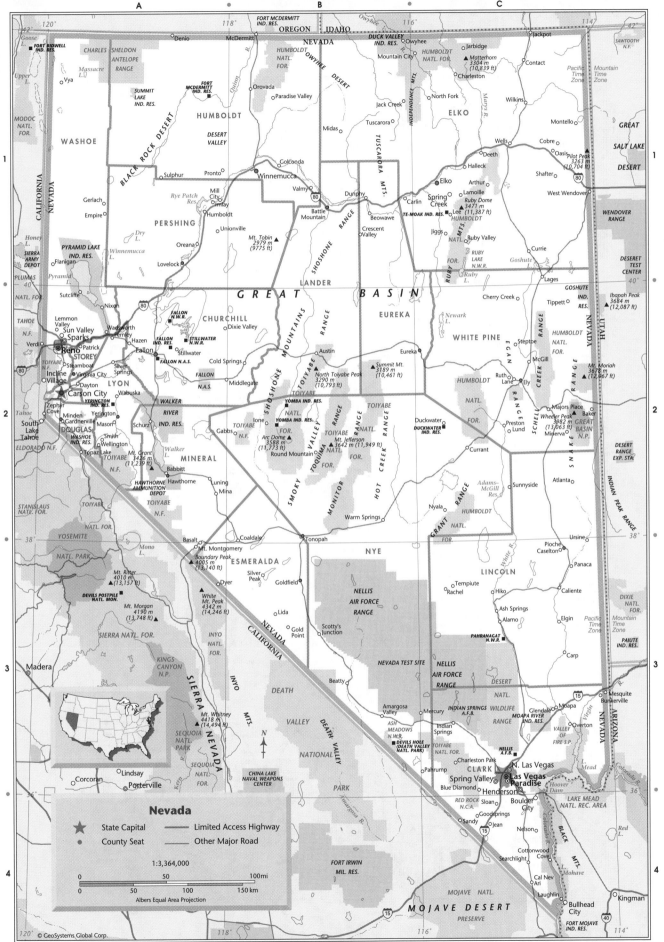

Nevada

★ State Capital
● County Seat
━━━ Limited Access Highway
─── Other Major Road

1:3,364,000

0   50   100mi
0   50   100   150 km

Albers Equal Area Projection

© GeoSystems Global Corp.

Capital: Concord
Area: 9,400 sq. mi.
24,200 sq. km.
Population: 1,125,000
Largest City: Manchester

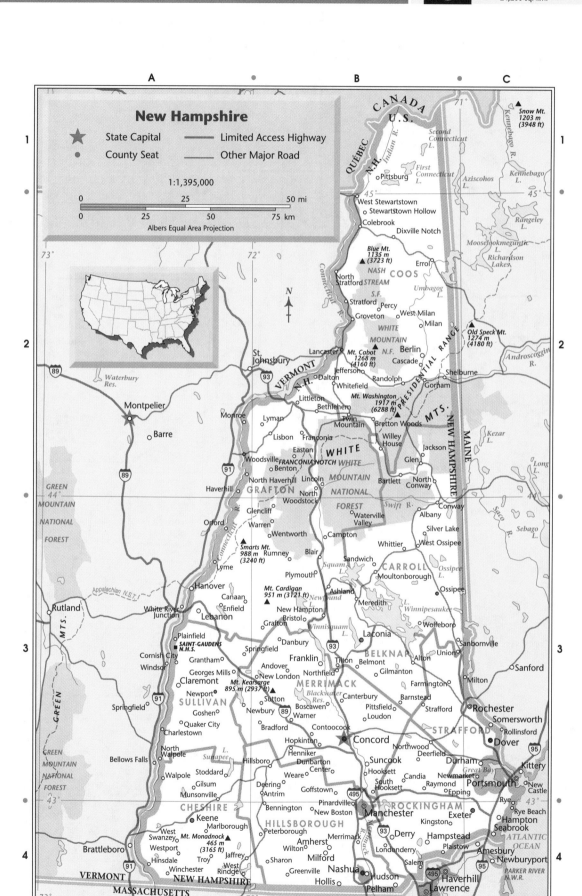

New Hampshire

★ State Capital
● County Seat

━━━ Limited Access Highway
━━━ Other Major Road

1:1,395,000

| 0 | 25 | 50 mi |
| 0 | 25 | 50 | 75 km |

Albers Equal Area Projection

© GeoSystems Global Corp

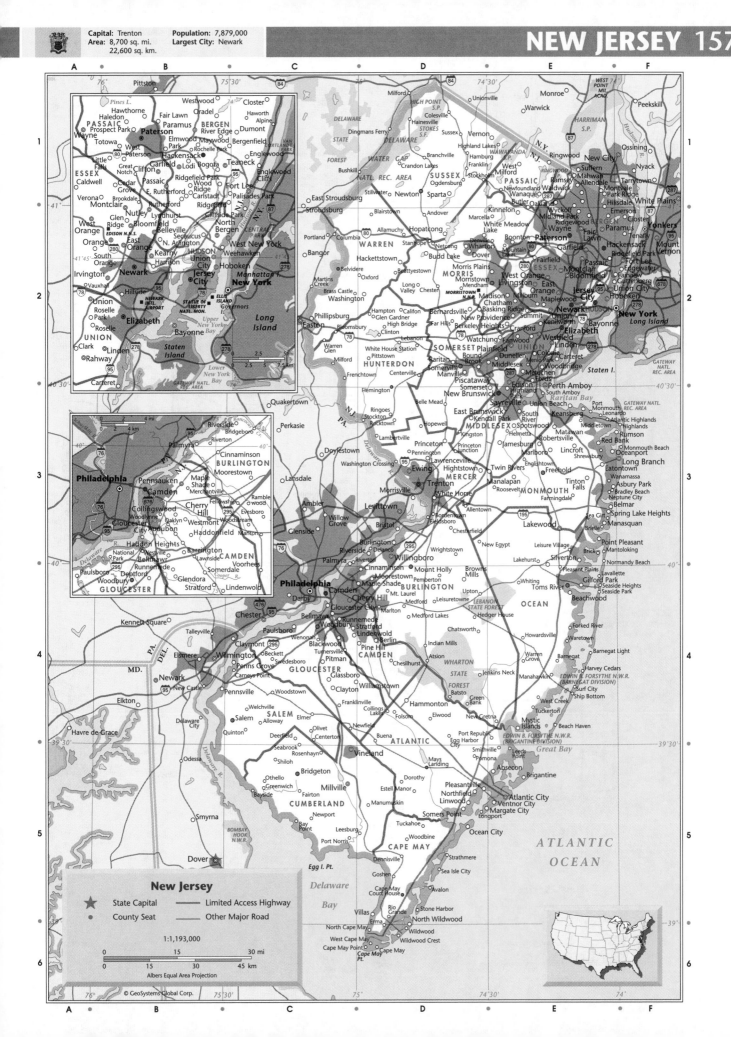

Capital: Trenton
Area: 8,700 sq. mi.
22,600 sq. km.
Population: 7,879,000
Largest City: Newark

New Jersey

★ State Capital
• County Seat

Limited Access Highway
Other Major Road

1:1,193,000

0   15   30 mi
0   15   30   45 km
Albers Equal Area Projection

© GeoSystems Global Corp.

Capital: Santa Fe
Area: 121,600 sq. mi. 314,900 sq. km.
Population: 1,616,000
Largest City: Albuquerque

New Mexico

★ State Capital
• County Seat
— Limited Access Highway
— Other Major Road

1:3,409,000

0   50   100mi
0   50   100   150 km

Albers Equal Area Projection

© GeoSystems Global Corp.

Surrounding regions and states
UTAH, ARIZ., COLORADO, OKLA., TEXAS, U.S. MEXICO, CHIHUAHUA

Selected places and features
Hovenweep N.M., Cortez, Durango, Rio Grande, Monte Vista N.W.R., National Peak 4008 m (13,150 ft), Alamosa N.W.R., Alamosa, Trinidad, Fort Carson Mil. Res., Comanche Natl. Grassland

Yucca House N.A.M., Mesa Verde Natl. Park, Ute Mountain I.R., San Juan National Forest, Capulin Volcano N.M., Folsom, Des Moines, Capulin

Beklabito, Shiprock, Shiprock 2188 m (7178 ft), La Plata, Cedar Hill, Flora Vista, Waterflow, Aztec, Blanco, Turley, Dulce, New Mexico, San Miguel, Amalia, Raton, Grenville, Mt. Dora, Clayton

Farmington, Kirtland, Bloomfield, Aztec Ruins N.M., Chama, Brazos, Cerro, Questa, Wheeler Peak 4011 m (13,161 ft), Eagle Nest, Cimarron, Ute Park, Maxwell N.W.R., Maxwell, Sofia, Farley, Gladstone, Colfax

Navajo Indian Res., Sanostee, Burnham, Newcomb, Blanco Trading Post, Gobernador, La Puente, Las Nutrias, Tres Piedras, Amarilla, Cebolla, Canon Plaza, Baldy Mt. 3792 m (12,442 ft), Angel Fire, Miami, Springer, Abbott, Miami, Union

Toadlena, Sheep Springs, Gavilan, Lindrith, Llaves, El Vado, Cerro Vista 3639 m (11,939 ft), Holman, Cleveland, Mora, Fort Union, Buena Vista, Ocate, Levy, Wagon Mound, Roy, Solano, Harding, Mosquero

Canyon de Chelly Natl. Mon., Crystal, Naschitti, White Rock, Lake Valley, Chaco Culture N.H.S., Counselor, Regina, Gallina, Youngsville, Abiquiu, Velarde, Chimayo, San Juan, Espanola, Pojoaque, Tesuque, Cowles, La Cueva, Sapello, Watrous, Sabinoso, Maes, Sanchez, Nara Visa, Amistad

Navajo, Tohatchi, Coyote Canyon, Standing Rock, Pueblo Pintado, Star Lake, Torreon, Cuba, Santa Clara Pueblo, Los Alamos, White Rock, Bandelier N.M., Santa Fe, Las Vegas, Las Vegas N.W.R., Romeroville, Trujillo, Tremintina, Variadero, Logan, Conchas Dam

Mexican Springs, Window Rock, Yah-Tah-Hey, Seven Lakes, Hospah, Jemez Ind. Res., Zia Ind. Res., Jemez, San Ysidro, Cochiti, La Cienega, Glorieta, Pecos, Lower Colonias, O.N. San Ysidro, Los Montoyas, Rencona, Sena, Villanueva, San Miguel, Montoya, Tucumcari

Gallup, McGaffey, Church Rock, Coolidge, Thoreau, Prewitt, Ambrosia Lake, San Mateo, Cubero, Laguna, San Felipe Pueblo, Santo Domingo Pueblo, Galisteo, Lamy, San Jose, Ribera, Conchas L., Quay, San Jon

Manuelito, Navajo I.R., Zuni Pueblo, Black Rock, El Morro, Mt. Taylor 3445 m (11,301 ft), Milan, Grants, Corrales, Rio Rancho, Bernalillo, Petroglyph Natl. Mon., Canoncito I.R., Alameda, Albuquerque, Edgewood, Stanley, Clines Corners, Santa Rosa, Montoya, Guadalupe, Pastura, Puerto de Luna, McAlister, House, Field, Curry, Melrose, Clovis, Texico

Zuni Indian Res., Ojo Caliente, Ramah Navajo I.R., San Rafael, McCartys, Acoma Pueblo, Isleta Indian Res., Los Padillas, Miera, Escabosa, Chilili, Moriarty, McIntosh, Pintada, Dahlia, Colonias, Cuervo, Jordan, Ragland, Grady, Cannon A.F.B., Floyd

Cibola Natl. For., Bluewater, El Malpais Natl. Cons. Area, Acoma Indian Res., Cebollita Peak 2671 m (8762 ft), Valencia, Los Chavez, Bosque Farms, Tajique, Torreon, Manzano, Willard, Encino, Vaughn, Yeso, Taiban, Tolar, Roosevelt, Portales, Grulla N.W.R.

Fence Lake, El Morro, Belen, Jarales, Turn, Veguita, Punta, Mountainair, Duran, Cedarvale, Cibola Natl. Forest, Corona, Ramon, Elida, Dora, Causey, Llano, Milnesand

Quemado, Omega, Alegres Mt. 3122 m (10,244 ft), Red Hill, Pie Town, Datil, Magdalena, Alamo, Alamo Band Navajo I.R., Abeytas, Bernardo, La Joya, San Acacia, Polvadera, Lemitar, Escondida, Socorro, Gran Quivira, Salinas Pueblo Missions N.M., Gallinas Peak 2626 m (8615 ft), De Baca, Fort Sumner, Sunner L., Ancho, White Oaks, Kenna

Catron, Luna, Apache Creek, Cruzville, Reserve, Lower San Francisco Plaza, S. Baldy Peak 3287 m (10,783 ft), Luis Lopez, San Antonio, Bingham, Clauch, Carrizozo, Lincoln, Capitan, Arabela, Elkins, Chaves

Apache-Sitgreaves Natl. For., Aragon, Old Horse Springs, Mt. Withington 3083 m (10,115 ft), Bosque del Apache N.W.R., Nogal, Fort Stanton, Lincoln, Bitter Lake N.W.R., Pecos, Caprock, Estacado

Gila National Forest, Whitewater Baldy 3319 m (10,890 ft), Alma, Monticello, Chloride, Cuchillo, Truth or Consequences, Oscuro, Three Rivers, Sierra Blanca 3651 m (11,977 ft), Bent, Alto, San Patricio, Hondo, Riverside, Roswell, Midway, Plains, Tatum

Pleasanton, Cliff Dwellings N.M., Mule Creek, Buckhorn, Cliff, Gila, Reeds Peak 3051 m (10,011 ft), Hillsboro, Las Palomas, Caballo Res., Sierra, Alamogordo, Mescalero Apache Indian Res., Mescalero, Cloudcroft, Flying H, Dexter, Greenfield, Hagerman, Lake Arthur, Lovington

Silver City, Pinos Altos, Mangas Springs, Central, San Lorenzo, San Juan, Bayard, Hurley, Dwyer, Arroyo, Derry, Garfield, Salem, Rincon, La Luz, High Rolls, Mayhill, Weed, Elk, Dunken, Hope, Atoka, Loco Hills, Humble City, Hobbs, Nadine

Grant, Whitewater Baldy, Burro Peak 2449 m (8033 ft), White Signal, Nutt, Cooke's Peak 2563 m (8408 ft), Radium Springs, Dona Ana, Holloman A.F.B., White Sands Natl. Mon., Sacramento, Timberon, Pinon, Seven Rivers, Lakewood, Eddy, Artesia, Riverside, Maljamar, Lea, Eunice

Virden, Redrock, Lordsburg, Cotton City, Deming, Sunshine, Dona Ana, Fairacres, Las Cruces, University Park, Mesilla, Organ, Orogrande, Otero, Guadalupe National Forest, Carlsbad, Carlsbad Caverns Natl. Park, Loving, Malaga, Jal

Separ, Luna, Hachita, Columbus, New Mexico, Anthony, Sunland Park, El Paso, Ciudad Juarez, San Miguel, Vado, Berino, Chamberino, La Union, Vinton, Chaparral, Whites City, Black River Village, Otis

Animas, Rodeo, Cloverdale, Coronado National Forest, Hidalgo, Playas L., Mountain Time Zone, Central Time Zone, Chihuahua, Hueco Mts., Socorro, Fabens, Guadalupe, Sierra Blanca 2100 m (6890 ft)

Guadalupe Mts. Natl. Park, Guadalupe Peak 2667 m (8751 ft), Salt Basin, Kermit, Pecos, Mt. Livermore 2501 m (8206 ft), Fort Davis N.H.S., Alpine

Counties
SAN JUAN, RIO ARRIBA, TAOS, COLFAX, UNION, MCKINLEY, SANDOVAL, LOS ALAMOS, SANTA FE, MORA, HARDING, CIBOLA, BERNALILLO, SAN MIGUEL, QUAY, VALENCIA, TORRANCE, GUADALUPE, CURRY, CATRON, SOCORRO, LINCOLN, DE BACA, ROOSEVELT, CHAVES, SIERRA, OTERO, EDDY, LEA, GRANT, LUNA, DONA ANA, HIDALGO

Capital: Albany
Area: 54,700 sq. mi.
141,100 sq. km.
Population: 18,197,000
Largest City: New York

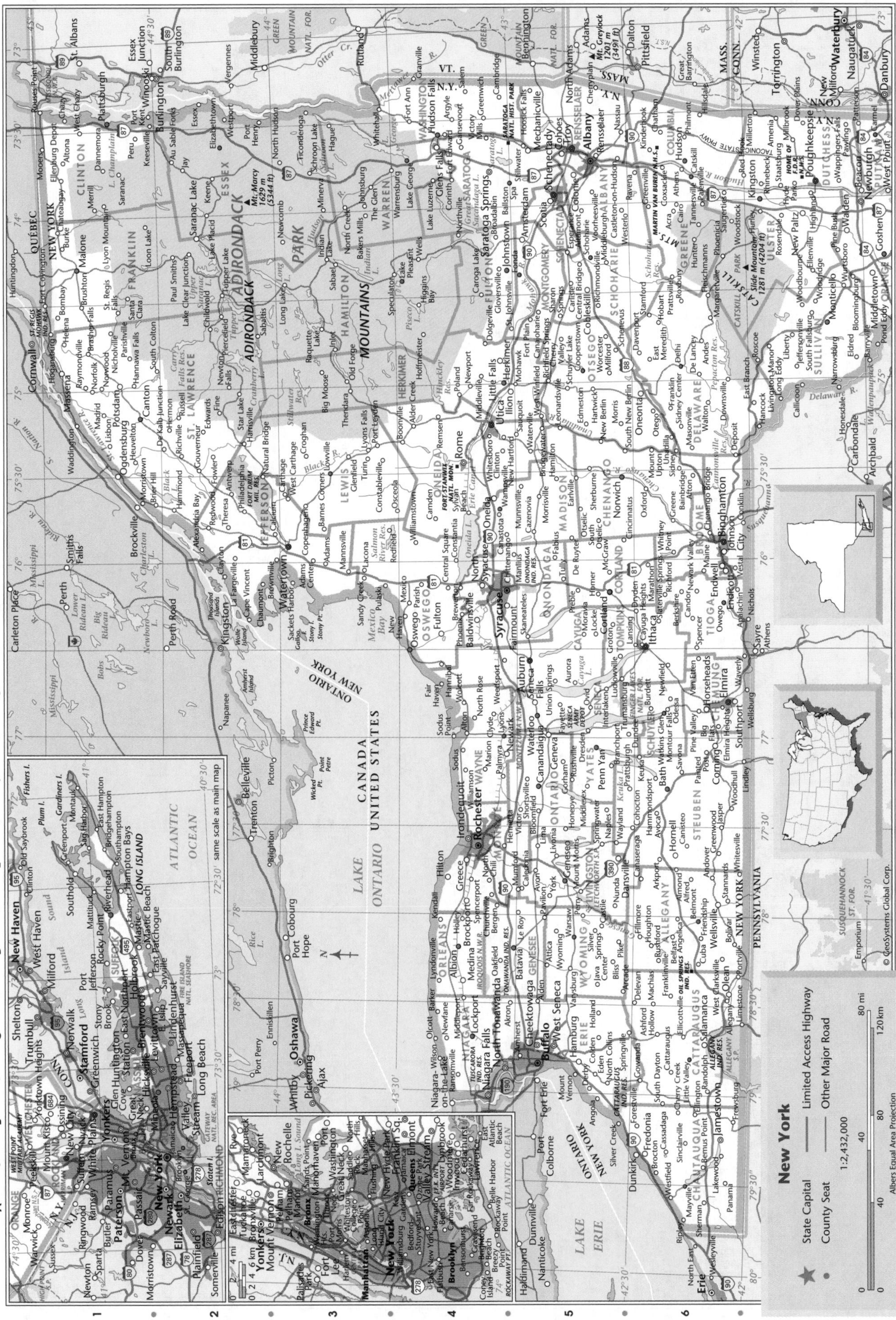

New York

1:2,432,000

Albers Equal Area Projection

★	State Capital
•	County Seat
——	Limited Access Highway
——	Other Major Road

0   40   80 mi
0   40   80   120km

same scale as main map

© GeoSystems Global Corp.

(Map of New York State with surrounding areas including Québec, Ontario, Lake Ontario, Lake Erie, Canada, United States, Vermont, Massachusetts, Connecticut, New Jersey, Pennsylvania, and the Atlantic Ocean.)

Major labeled features and places include:

ADIRONDACK PARK, ADIRONDACK MOUNTAINS, Mt. Marcy (1629 m / 5344 ft), CATSKILL MTS., Slide Mountain (1281 m / 4204 ft), Mt. Greylock (1064 m / 3491 ft), CLINTON, FRANKLIN, ST. LAWRENCE, ESSEX, HAMILTON, WARREN, WASHINGTON, HERKIMER, LEWIS, JEFFERSON, OSWEGO, ONEIDA, MADISON, ONONDAGA, CAYUGA, WAYNE, ORLEANS, GENESEE, WYOMING, LIVINGSTON, ONTARIO, YATES, SENECA, SCHUYLER, STEUBEN, ALLEGANY, CATTARAUGUS, CHAUTAUQUA, ERIE, NIAGARA, CORTLAND, TOMPKINS, TIOGA, BROOME, CHENANGO, OTSEGO, DELAWARE, SCHOHARIE, MONTGOMERY, FULTON, SARATOGA, RENSSELAER, COLUMBIA, GREENE, ULSTER, SULLIVAN, ORANGE, DUTCHESS, PUTNAM, WESTCHESTER, ROCKLAND, NASSAU, SUFFOCK, LONG ISLAND

Cities: Albany, New York, Buffalo, Rochester, Syracuse, Utica, Rome, Binghamton, Elmira, Ithaca, Jamestown, Niagara Falls, Watertown, Plattsburgh, Saratoga Springs, Schenectady, Troy, Poughkeepsie, Newburgh, Kingston, Yonkers, White Plains, New Rochelle, Mount Vernon

Water features: LAKE ONTARIO, LAKE ERIE, Lake Champlain, Lake George, Oneida Lake, Finger Lakes (Seneca L., Cayuga L., Keuka L., Canandaigua L., Owasco L.), Great Sacandaga L., Hudson R., Mohawk R., Delaware R., Susquehanna R., St. Lawrence R., Niagara R., ATLANTIC OCEAN

(Inset maps: Long Island / New York City metropolitan area detail; United States locator map; New York State locator map.)

Capital: Raleigh
Area: 53,800 sq. mi.
139,400 sq. km.
Population: 6,945,000
Largest City: Charlotte

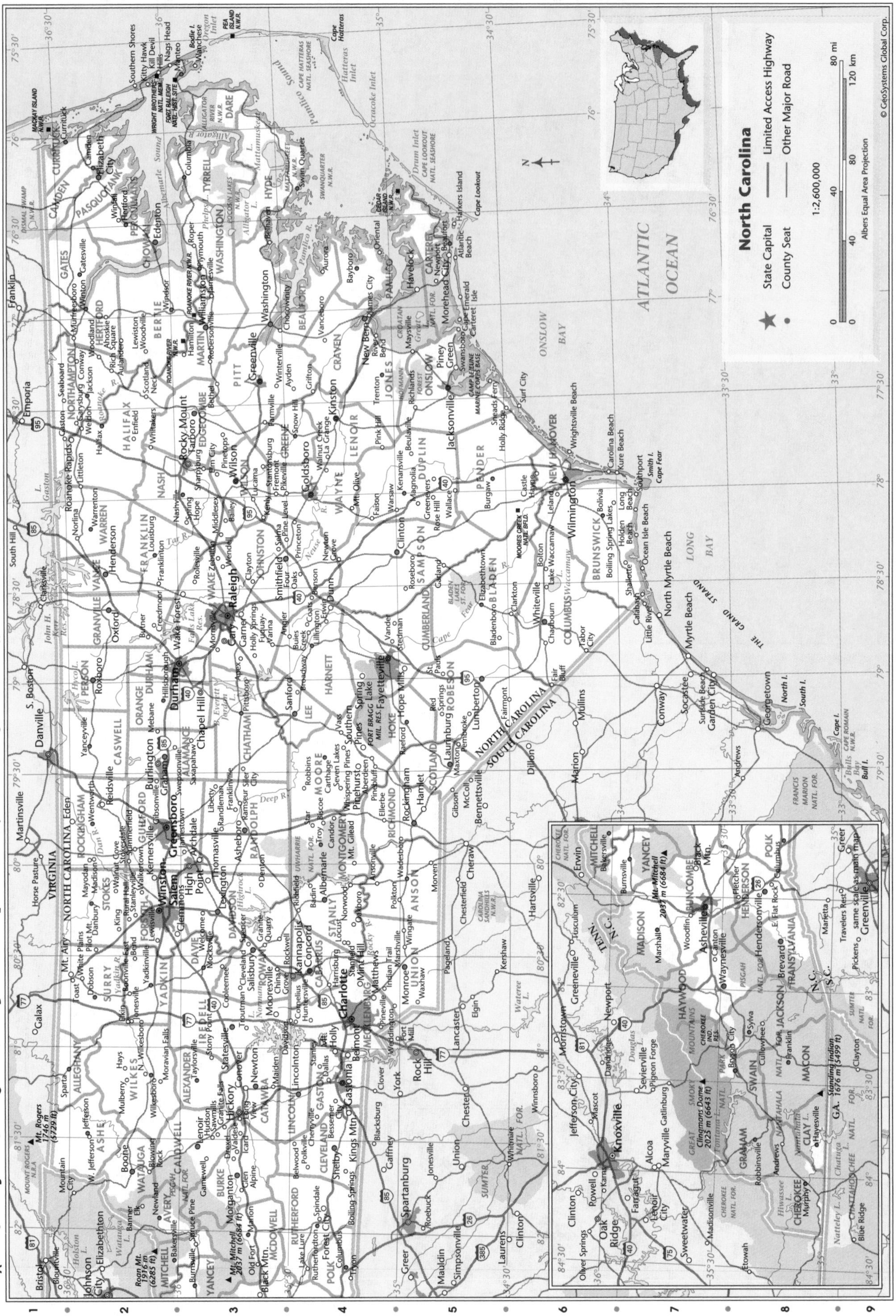

North Carolina

Limited Access Highway
Other Major Road

★ State Capital
• County Seat

1:2,600,000

0   40   80 mi
0   40   80   120 km

Albers Equal Area Projection

© GeoSystems Global Corp.

ATLANTIC OCEAN

VIRGINIA

SOUTH CAROLINA

TENN.

GEORGIA

Capital: Bismarck
Area: 70,700 sq. mi.
183,100 sq. km.
Population: 635,000
Largest City: Fargo

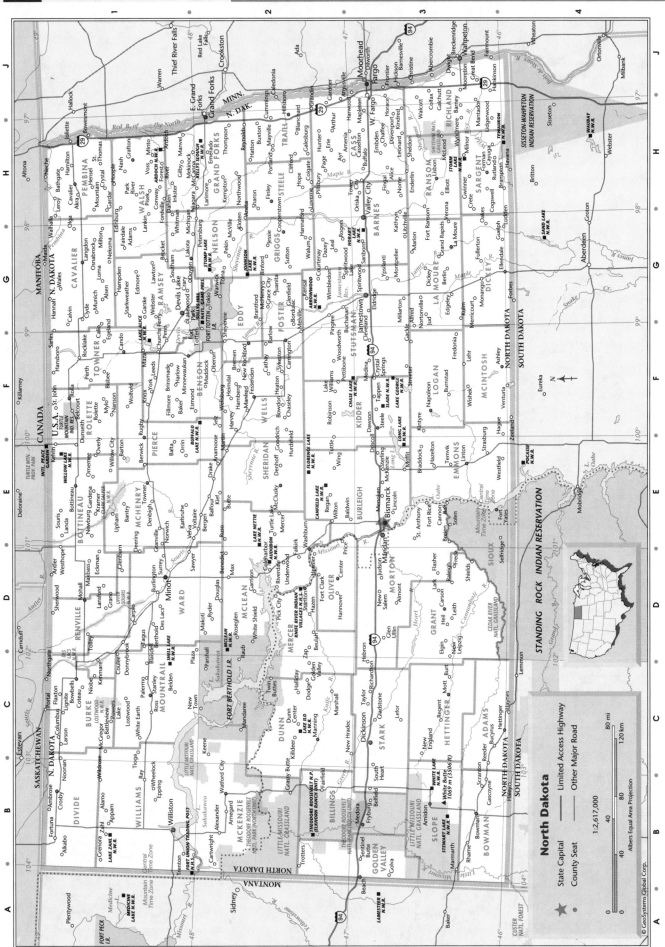

North Dakota

State Capital ★
County Seat •

Limited Access Highway
Other Major Road

1:2,617,000

| 0 | 40 | 80 mi |
| 0 | 40 | 80 | 120 km |

Albers Equal Area Projection

© GeoSystems Global Corp.

Capital: Columbus
Area: 44,800 sq. mi.
116,100 sq. km.
Population: 11,091,000
Largest City: Columbus

Ohio

★ State Capital
● County Seat
── Limited Access Highway
── Other Major Road

1:2,131,000

0 ——— 30 ——— 60 mi
0 —— 30 —— 60 —— 90 km
Albers Equal Area Projection

© GeoSystems Global Corp.

Capital: Oklahoma City   **Population:** 3,231,000
Area: 69,900 sq. mi.   **Largest City:** Oklahoma City
181,000 sq. km.

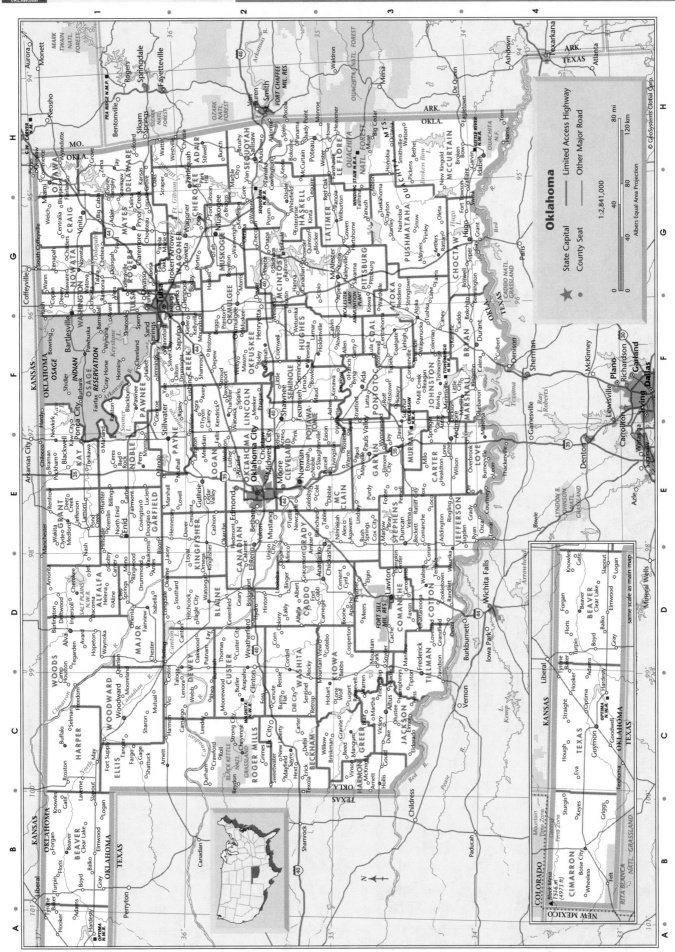

Capital: Salem
Area: 98,400 sq. mi.
254,800 sq. km.
Population: 3,032,000
Largest City: Portland

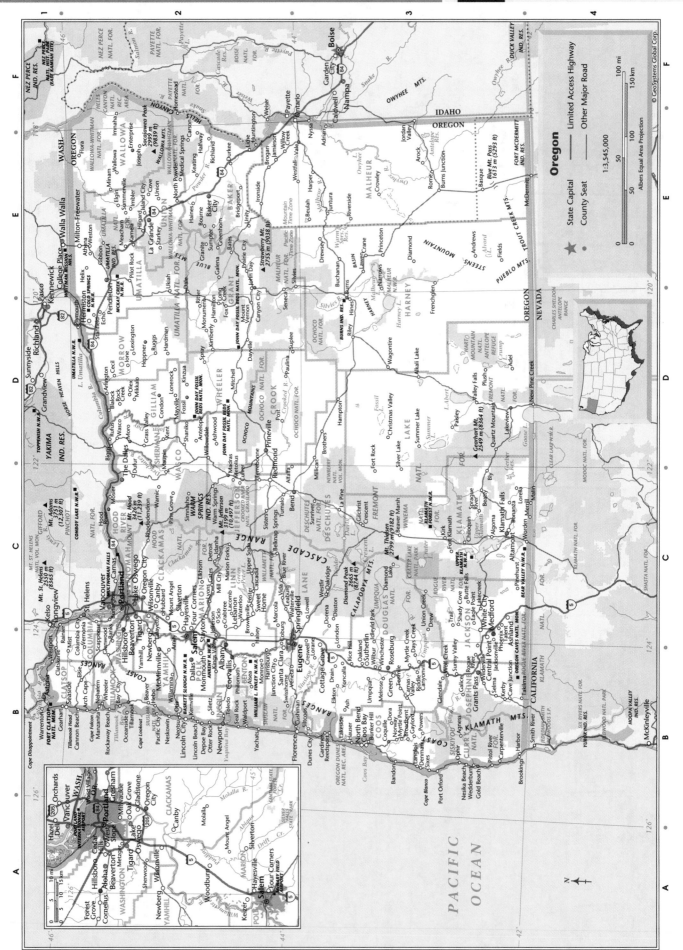

Capital: Harrisburg
Area: 45,300 sq. mi.
117,300 sq. km.
Population: 12,048,000
Largest City: Philadelphia

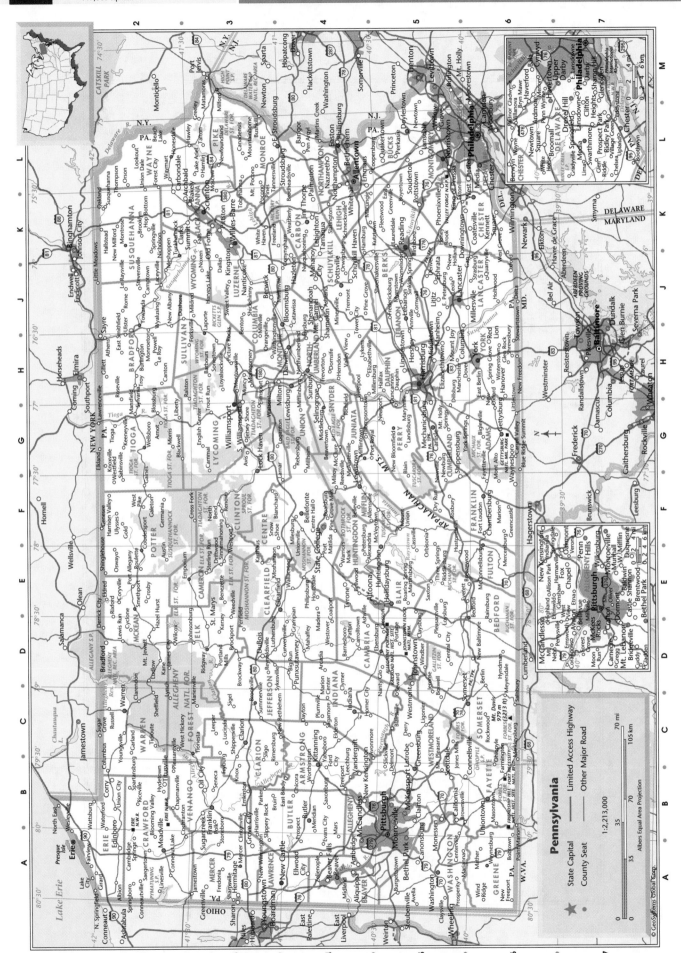

Pennsylvania

★ State Capital
• County Seat

— Limited Access Highway
— Other Major Road

1:2,213,000

Albers Equal Area Projection

© GeoSystems Global Corp.

Capital: Providence
Area: 1,500 sq. mi.
4,000 sq. km.
Population: 1,000,000
Largest City: Providence

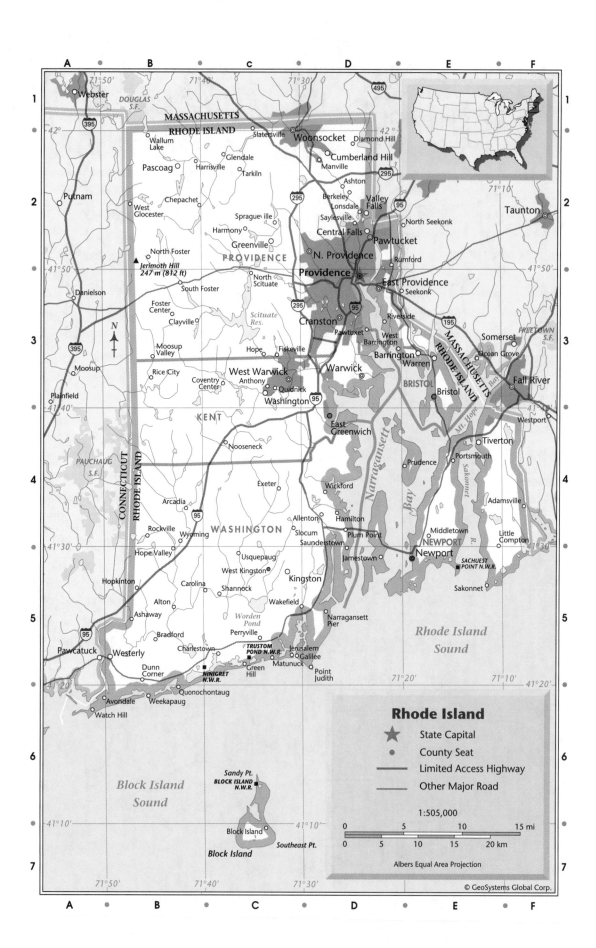

Webster

DOUGLAS
S.F.

71°50'
71°40'
71°30'

MASSACHUSETTS
RHODE ISLAND

Slatersville

Woonsocket
Diamond Hill

42°

Cumberland Hill
Manville

Wallum
Lake

Glendale

Pascoag
Harrisville
Tarkiln

Ashton

Putnam

Chepachet

West
Glocester

Spragueville

Berkeley
Lonsdale
Saylesville

Valley
Falls

North Seekonk

Taunton

Harmony

Central Falls

Greenville

Pawtucket

PROVIDENCE

N. Providence

North Foster

Jerimoth Hill
247 m (812 ft)

North
Scituate

Providence

Rumford

East Providence

71°10'

Danielson

South Foster

Seekonk

Foster
Center

Scituate
Res.

Riverside

Somerset

FREETOWN
S.F.

Clayville

Cranston

Pawtuxet
West
Barrington

MASSACHUSETTS
RHODE ISLAND

Ocean Grove

Moosup

Moosup
Valley

Hope
Fiskeville

Warwick

Barrington
Warren

Fall River

Rice City

West Warwick

BRISTOL

Bristol

PAUCHAUG
S.F.

Plainfield

Coventry
Center
Anthony
Quidnick

Washington

East
Greenwich

Westport

KENT

Nooseneck

CONNECTICUT
RHODE ISLAND

Narragansett

Prudence
Portsmouth

Tiverton

Exeter

Wickford

Adamsville

Arcadia

Allenton
Hamilton

Bay

Sakonnet R.

Rockville
Wyoming

WASHINGTON

Slocum
Saunderstown

Plum Point

Middletown

Little
Compton

Hope Valley

Usquepaug

Jamestown

NEWPORT
Newport

SACHUEST
POINT N.W.R.

Hopkinton

West Kingston

Kingston

Carolina
Shannock

Sakonnet

Alton

Wakefield

Ashaway

Worden
Pond

Narragansett
Pier

Rhode Island
Sound

Bradford

Perryville

Pawcatuck
Westerly

Charlestown

TRUSTOM
POND N.W.R.

Green
Hill

Jerusalem
Galilee

Matunuck

Point
Judith

Dunn
Corner

NINIGRET
N.W.R.

Avondale
Weekapaug

Quonochontaug

Watch Hill

Block Island
Sound

Sandy Pt.
BLOCK ISLAND
N.W.R.

Rhode Island

★ State Capital

• County Seat

Limited Access Highway

Other Major Road

1:505,000

0   5   10   15 mi

0   5   10   15   20 km

Block Island

Block Island
Southeast Pt.

Albers Equal Area Projection

© GeoSystems Global Corp.

71°50'
71°40'
71°30'

Capital: Columbia
Area: 32,000 sq. mi.
      82,900 sq. km.
Population: 3,643,000
Largest City: Columbia

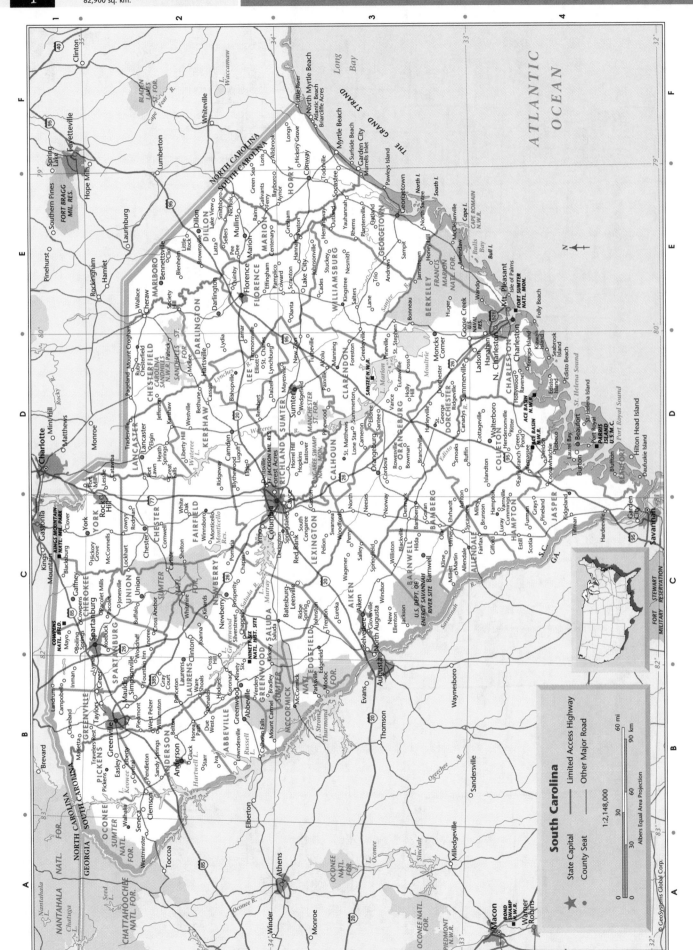

South Carolina

Limited Access Highway
Other Major Road

★ State Capital
● County Seat

1:2,148,000

0   30   60 mi
0   30   60   90 km

Albers Equal Area Projection

© GeoSystems Global Corp.

Capital: Pierre
Area: 77,100 sq. mi.
199,700 sq. km.
Population: 715,000
Largest City: Sioux Falls

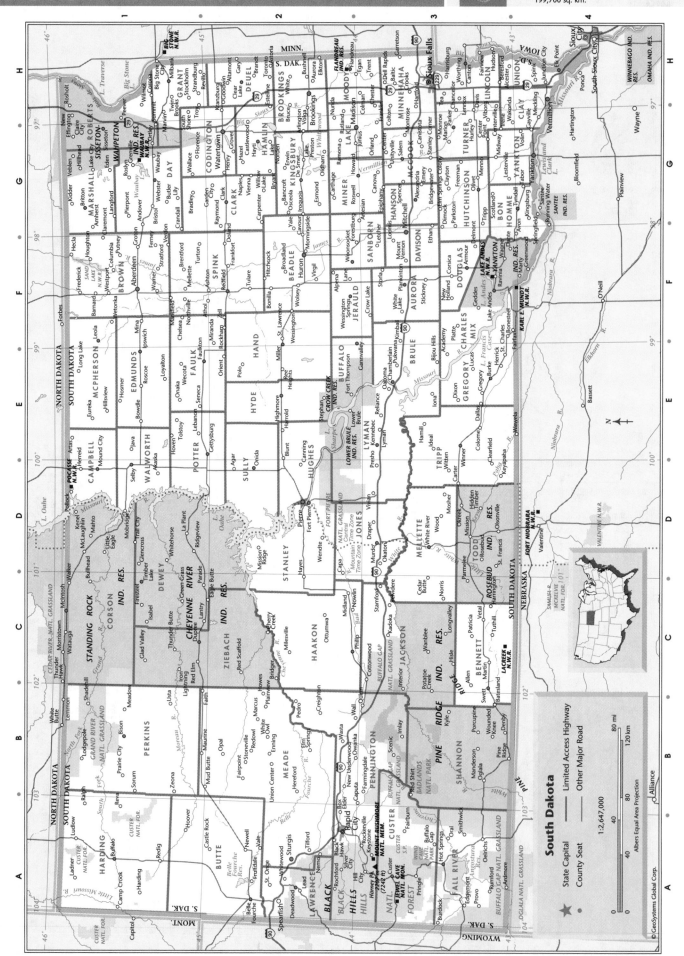

South Dakota

State Capital ★

County Seat •

Limited Access Highway

Other Major Road

1:2,647,000

Albers Equal Area Projection

©GeoSystems Global Corp.

Capital: Nashville **Population:** 5,099,000
Area: 42,100 sq. mi. **Largest City:** Memphis
109,200 sq. km.

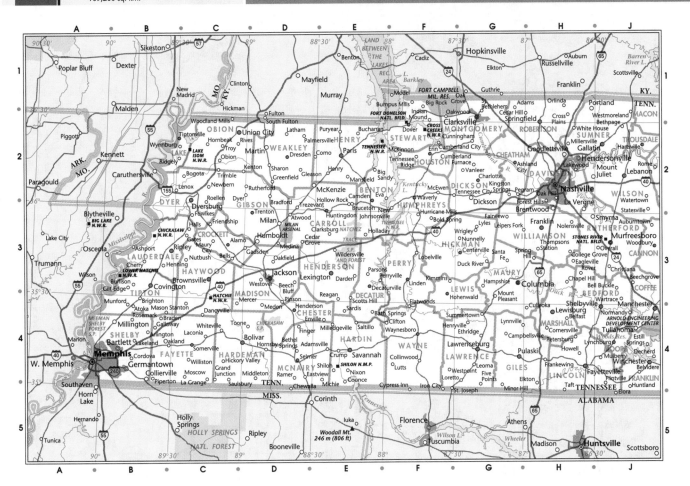

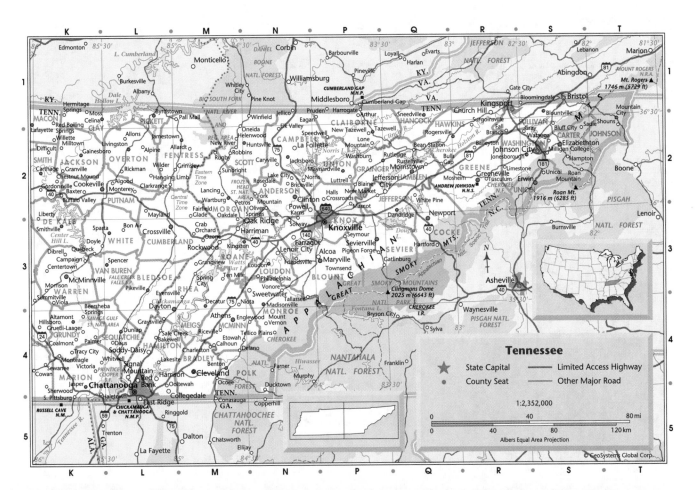

Tennessee

★ State Capital ── Limited Access Highway

● County Seat ── Other Major Road

1:2,352,000

0	40	80 mi

0	40	80	120 km

Albers Equal Area Projection

© GeoSystems Global Corp.

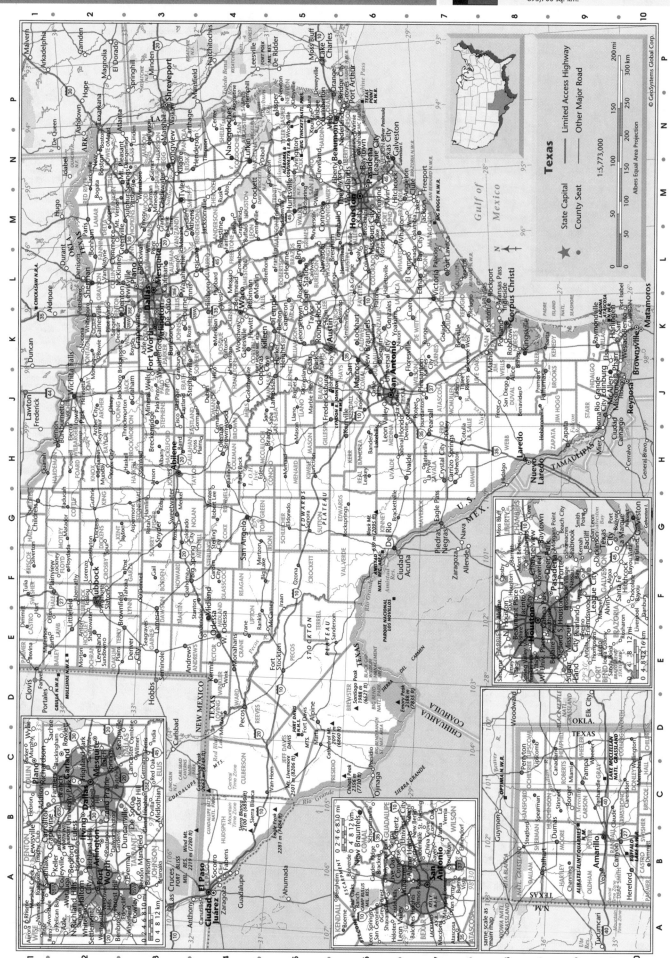

Capital: Austin
Area: 268,600 sq. mi.
695,700 sq. km.
Population: 18,031,000
Largest City: Houston

Texas
1:5,773,000

★ State Capital
● County Seat

Limited Access Highway
Other Major Road

© GeoSystems Global Corp.

Gulf of Mexico

Capital: Salt Lake City
Area: 84,900 sq. mi.
219,900 sq. km.
Population: 1,860,000
Largest City: Salt Lake City

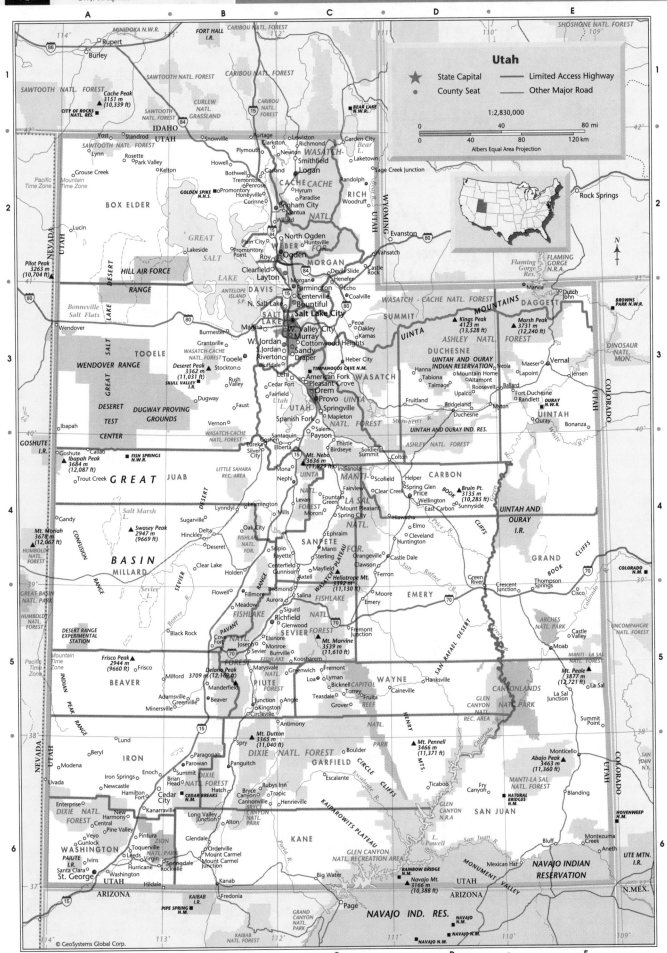

Utah

★ State Capital

● County Seat

Limited Access Highway

Other Major Road

1:2,830,000

0   40   80 mi

0   40   80   120 km

Albers Equal Area Projection

© GeoSystems Global Corp.

Capital: Montpelier
Area: 9,600 sq. mi.
24,900 sq. km.
Population: 576,000
Largest City: Burlington

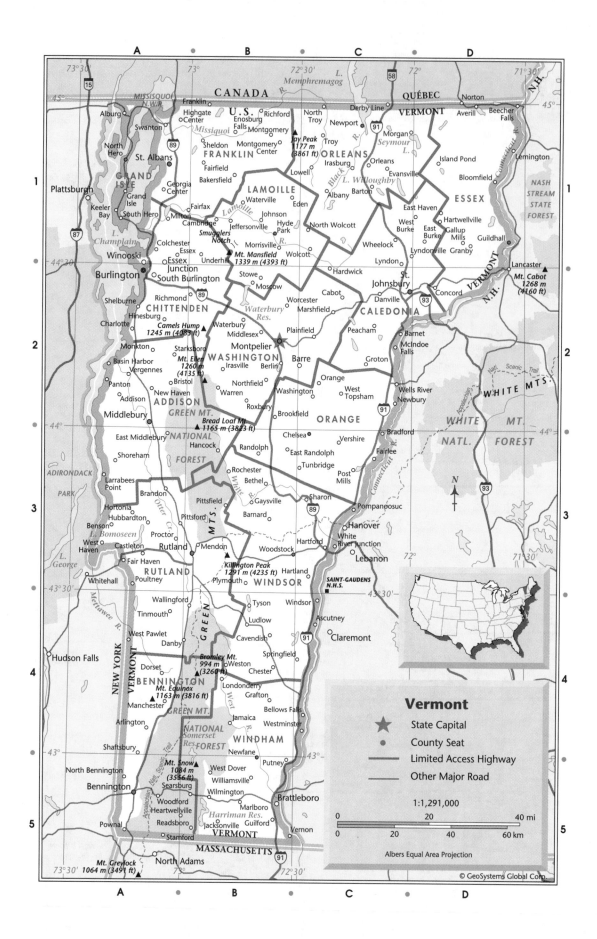

Vermont

★ State Capital

• County Seat

—— Limited Access Highway

—— Other Major Road

1:1,291,000

0   20   40 mi

0   20   40   60 km

Albers Equal Area Projection

© GeoSystems Global Corp.

Capital: Richmond
Area: 42,800 sq. mi.
110,800 sq. km.
Population: 6,491,000
Largest City: Virginia Beach

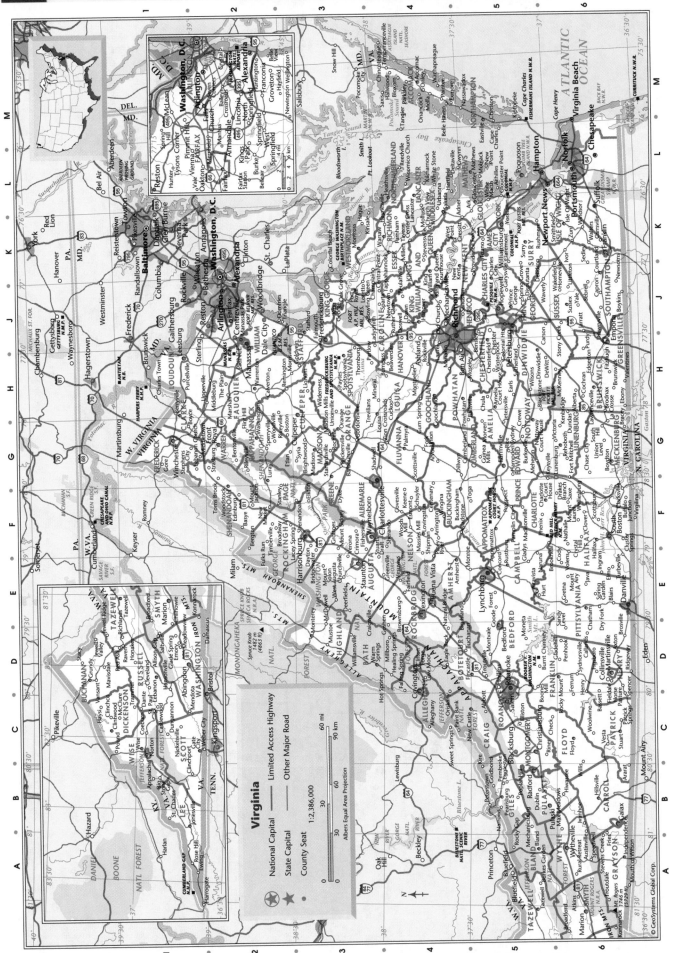

Virginia

— Limited Access Highway
— Other Major Road

★ National Capital
★ State Capital
• County Seat

1:2,386,000

Albers Equal Area Projection

© GeoSystems Global Corp.

Capital: Olympia
Area: 71,300 sq. mi.
184,700 sq. km.
Population: 5,255,000
Largest City: Seattle

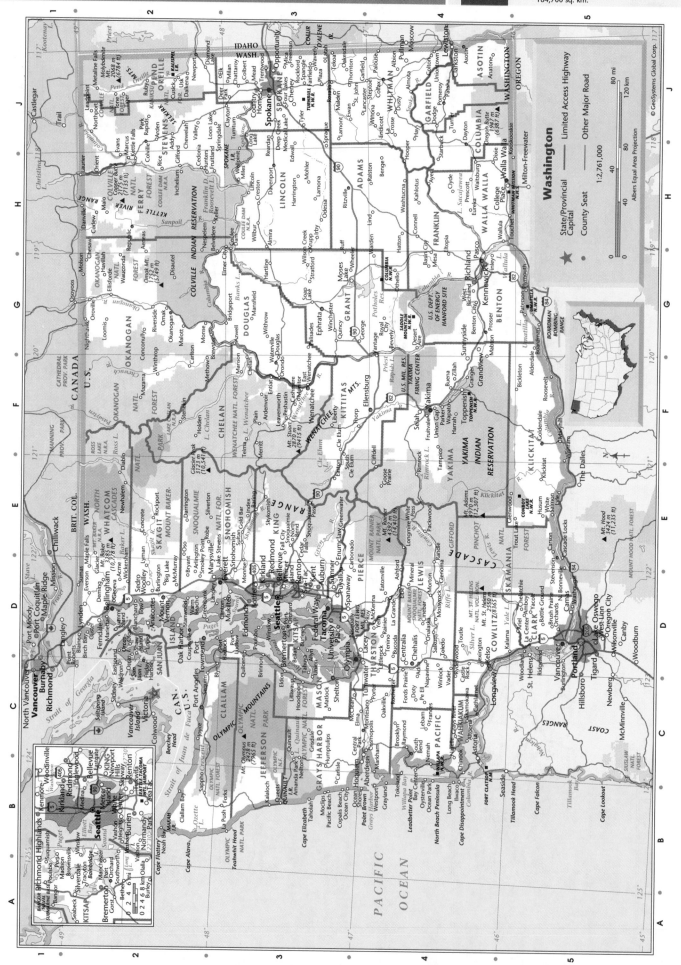

Washington

Limited Access Highway
Other Major Road

★ State/Provincial Capital
• County Seat

1:2,761,000
Albers Equal Area Projection

© GeoSystems Global Corp. 117

Capital: Charleston
Area: 24,200 sq. mi.
62,800 sq. km.
Population: 1,820,000
Largest City: Charleston

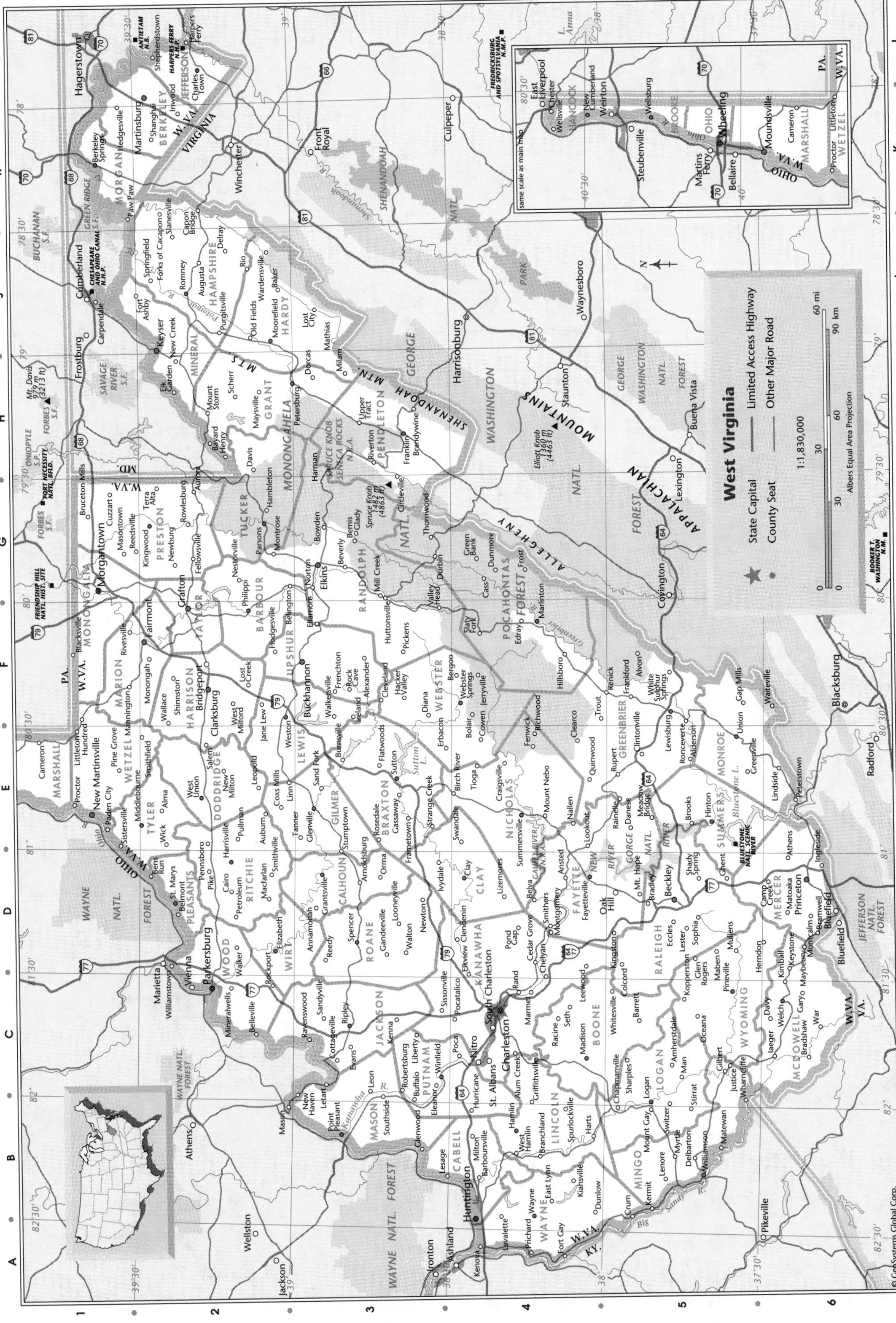

West Virginia

★ State Capital
• County Seat

—— Limited Access Highway
—— Other Major Road

1:1,830,000

0   30   60
0   30   60   90 km

Albers Equal Area Projection

N

FREDERICKSBURG AND SPOTSYLVANIA N.M.P.

BOOKER T. WASHINGTON N.M.

Counties and places (selected labels)

MARSHALL, WETZEL, MONONGALIA, PRESTON, MARION, TAYLOR, BARBOUR, TUCKER, GRANT, MINERAL, HAMPSHIRE, HARDY, PENDLETON, RANDOLPH, UPSHUR, LEWIS, HARRISON, DODDRIDGE, TYLER, PLEASANTS, WOOD, WIRT, RITCHIE, GILMER, CALHOUN, BRAXTON, WEBSTER, POCAHONTAS, NICHOLAS, CLAY, ROANE, JACKSON, MASON, PUTNAM, CABELL, WAYNE, LINCOLN, BOONE, LOGAN, MINGO, WYOMING, McDOWELL, MERCER, RALEIGH, FAYETTE, SUMMERS, MONROE, GREENBRIER, KANAWHA, BERKELEY, MORGAN, JEFFERSON

Charleston, South Charleston, Huntington, Parkersburg, Wheeling, Morgantown, Martinsburg, Beckley, Bluefield, Clarksburg, Fairmont, Weirton, Lewisburg, Elkins, Princeton, Moundsville

MONONGAHELA NAT'L FOREST, GEORGE WASHINGTON NAT'L FOREST, JEFFERSON NAT'L FOREST, WAYNE NAT'L FOREST

Ohio River, Kanawha River, New River, Gauley River, Greenbrier River, Shenandoah River, Potomac River, Big Sandy River

HARPERS FERRY N.H.P., ANTIETAM N.B., CHESAPEAKE AND OHIO CANAL N.H.P., FRIENDSHIP HILL NAT'L HIST. SITE, FORT NECESSITY NAT'L BTLFD., NEW RIVER GORGE NAT'L RIVER, BLUESTONE NAT'L SCENIC RIVER, GAULEY RIVER N.R.A., SPRUCE KNOB–SENECA ROCKS N.R.A.

Spruce Knob (4,863 ft.), Mt. Davis (3,213 ft.), Elliott Knob (4,463 ft.)

© GeoSystems Global Corp.

Capital: Madison
Area: 65,500 sq. mi.
169,600 sq. km.
Population: 5,038,000
Largest City: Milwaukee

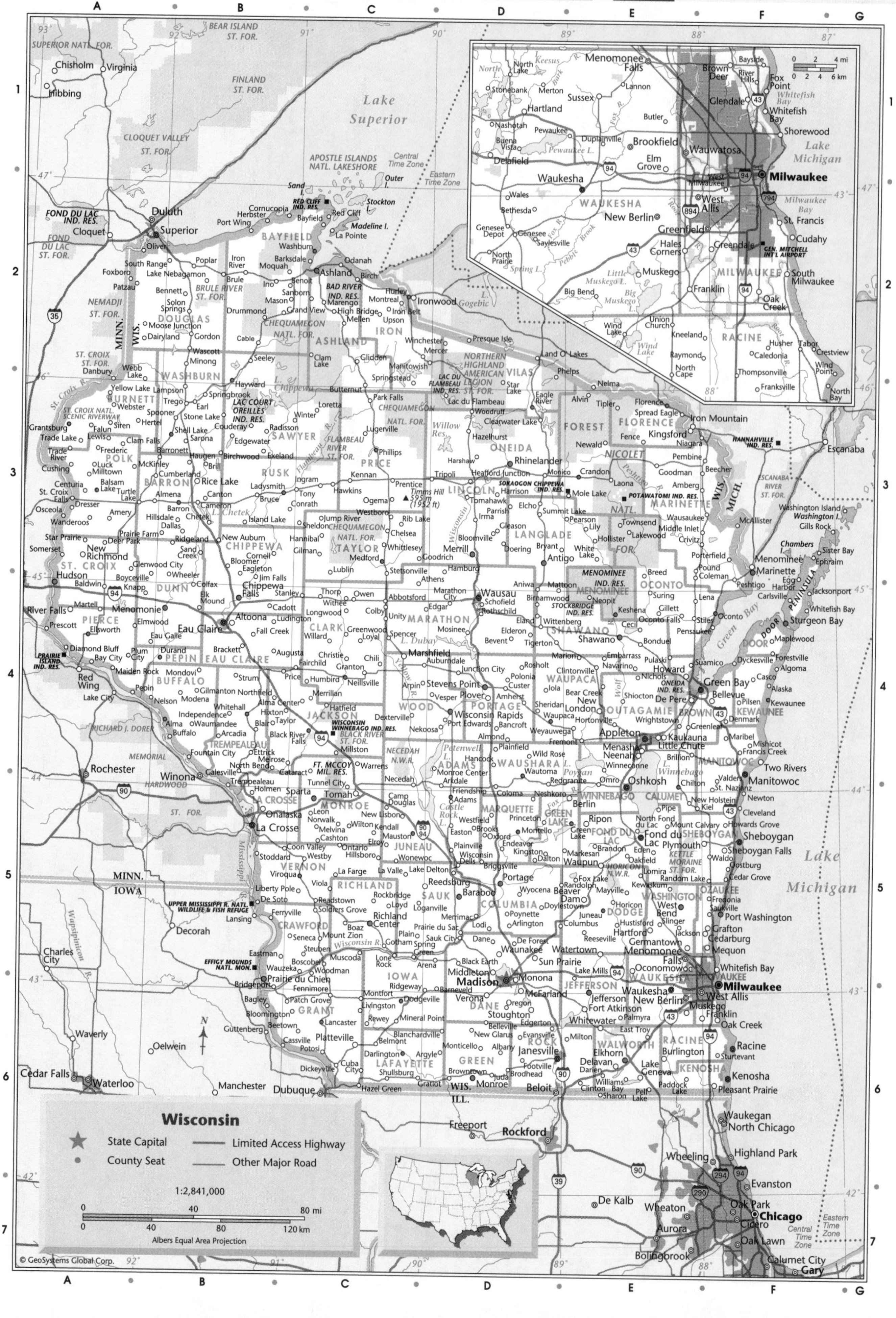

WISCONSIN
1848

Wisconsin

★ State Capital
• County Seat

— Limited Access Highway
— Other Major Road

1:2,841,000

0   40   80 mi
0   40   80   120 km
Albers Equal Area Projection

© GeoSystems Global Corp.

0   2   4 mi
0 2 4 6 km

Capital: Cheyenne
Area: 97,800 sq. mi.
253,300 sq. km.
Population: 470,000
Largest City: Cheyenne

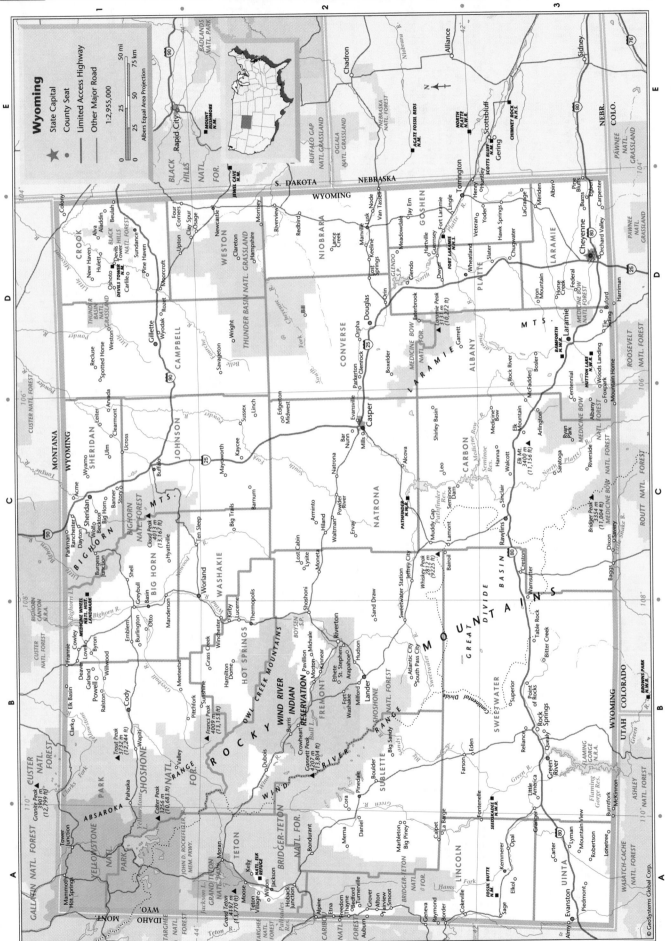

Wyoming

★ State Capital
● County Seat
— Limited Access Highway
— Other Major Road

1:2,955,000

50 mi
75 km

Albers Equal Area Projection

Abbreviations
N.H.P. ... National Historical Park
N.H.S. ... National Historic Site
N.M. ... National Monument
N.P. ... National Park
N.R.A. ... National Recreation Area

Alabama ... page 128

Cities and Towns — Key
Abbeville D4
Adamsville C2
Alabaster C2
Albertville C1
Alexander City D3
Aliceville A2
Andalusia C4
Anniston D2
Arab C1
Ashford D4
Ashland D2
Ashville C2
Athens C1
Atmore B4
Attalla C1
Auburn D3
Bay Minette B5
Bayou La Batre A5
Bessemer C2
Birmingham C2
Blountsville C1
Boaz C1
Brent B3
Brewton B4
Bridgeport D1
Brundidge D4
Butler A3
Calera C2
Camden B4
Camp Hill D3
Carbon Hill B2
Carrollton A2
Center Point C2
Centre D1
Centreville B3
Chatom A4
Chelsea C2
Cherokee B1
Chickasaw A5
Childersburg C2
Citronelle A4
Clanton C3
Clayton D4
Clio D4
Collinsville D1
Columbiana C2
Cordova B2
Cottonwood D4
Creola A5
Crossville D1
Cullman C1
Dadeville D3
Daleville D4
Daphne B5
Decatur C1
Demopolis B3
Dora B2
Dothan D4
Double Springs B1
East Brewton B4
Elba C4
Enterprise C4
Eufaula D4
Eutaw B3
Evergreen C4
Fairfield C2
Fairhope B5
Falkville C1
Fayette B2
Flomaton B4
Florala C4
Florence B1
Foley B5
Fort Morgan A5
Fort Payne D1
Frisco City B4
Fultondale C2
Gadsden C1
Gardendale C2
Gasque B5
Geneva D4
Georgiana C4
Glencoe D2
Good Hope C1
Goodwater C2
Gordo B2
Grand Bay A5
Greensboro B3
Greenville C4
Grove Hill B4
Guin B2
Gulf Shores B5
Guntersville C1
Haleyville B1
Hamilton B1
Hanceville C1
Hartford D4
Hartselle C1
Hayneville C3
Hazel Green C1
Headland D4
Heflin D2
Helena C2
Henagar D1
Heron Bay A5
Hokes Bluff D2
Holt B2
Hoover C2
Hueytown B2
Huntsville C1
Irondale C2
Jackson B4
Jacksonville D2
Jasper B2
Jemison C3
Lafayette D3
Lanett D3
Leeds C2
Lincoln C2
Linden B3
Lineville D2
Livingston A3
Luverne C4
Madison C1
Marion B3
Meridianville C1
Midfield C2
Midland City D4
Millbrook C3
Mobile A5
Monroeville B4
Montevallo C2
Montgomery, *capital* C3
Moulton B1
Moundville B3
Muscle Shoals B1
New Hope C1
Newton D4
Northport B2
Oneonta C2
Opelika D3
Opp C4
Orange Beach B5
Oxford D2
Ozark D4
Parrish B2
Pelham C2
Pell City C2
Petersville B1
Phenix City D3
Phil Campbell B1
Piedmont D2
Pinson C2
Point Clear B5
Prattville C3
Priceville C1
Prichard A5
Ragland C2
Rainbow City C2
Rainsville D1
Reform A2
Roanoke D2
Robertsdale B5
Rockford C3
Russellville B1
Samson C4
Saraland A5
Sardis City C1
Satsuma A5
Scottsboro C1
Selma B3
Sheffield B1
Slocomb D4
Smiths D3
Southside C2
Spanish Fort B5
Springville C2
Stevenson D1
Sulligent A2
Sumiton B2
Sylacauga C2
Talladega C2
Tallassee D3
Taylor D4
Theodore A5
Thomasville B4
Thorsby C3
Tillmans Corner A5
Town Creek B1
Trinity B1
Troy D4
Trussville C2
Tuscaloosa B2
Tuscumbia B1
Tuskegee D3
Union Springs D3
Uniontown B3
Valley D3
Vernon A2
Vestavia Hills C2
Vincent C2
Warrior C2
Weaver D2
Wedowee D2
West Blocton B2
Wetumpka C3
Winfield B2
York A3

Other Features
Alabama, *river* B4
Appalachian, *mts.* D1
Bear Creek, *reservoir* B1
Black Warrior, *river* B3
Bon Secour, *bay* B5
Cahaba, *river* B3
Cheaha, *mt.* D2
Conecuh, *river* C4
Coosa, *river* D1
Dauphin, *island* A5
Guntersville, *lake* C1
Jordan, *lake* C3
Lewis Smith, *lake* B1
Logan Morgan, *lake* C2
Lookout, *mt.* D1
Martin, *lake* D3
Mitchell, *lake* C3
Mobile, *bay* A5
Neely Henry, *lake* C2
Pickwick, *lake* A1
R.L. Harris, *reservoir* D2
Russell Cave Natl. Monument D1
Tallapoosa, *river* D2
Tennessee, *river* A1
Tombigbee, *river* A4
Tuscaloosa, *lake* B2
Tuskegee Institute Natl. Hist. Site D3
Weiss, *lake* D1
Wheeler, *lake* C1
William "Bill" Dannelly, *reservoir* B3
Wilson, *lake* B1

Alaska ... page 129

Cities and Towns
Adak Inset
Anchorage F2
Barrow D1
Bethel C2
Big Delta F2
College F2
Cordova F2
Craig J3
Delta Jct. F2
Dillingham D3
Fairbanks F2
Haines H3
Homer E3
Juneau, *capital* J3
Kenai E2
Ketchikan J3
Kodiak E3
Kotzebue C1
McKinley Park F2
Metlakatla J3
Nikiski E2
Nome B2
North Pole F2
Palmer F2
Petersburg J3
Prudhoe Bay F1
Seward F2
Sitka H3
Skagway H3
Soldotna E2
Talkeetna E2
Tok G2
Unalaska B4
Valdez F2
Wasilla F2
Whittier F2
Wrangell J3

Other Features
Adak, *island* Inset
Admiralty Island Natl. Monument J3
Agattu, *island* Inset
Alaska, *gulf* F3
Alaska, *peninsula* C3
Alaska, *range* E2
Aleutian, *islands* A4, Inset
Alexander, *archipelago* H3
Amchitka, *island* Inset
Amlia, *island* Inset
Andreanof, *islands* Inset
Aniakchak N.M. and Preserve D3
Atka, *island* Inset
Attu, *island* Inset
Barrow, *point* D1
Beaufort, *sea* H1
Becharof, *lake* D3
Bering, *sea* B3
Bering, *strait* B2
Blackburn, *mt.* G2
Bristol, *bay* C3
Brooks, *range* D1
Cape Krusenstern N.M. C1
Chirikof, *island* D3
Chukchi, *sea* A1
Colville, *river* E1
Cook, *inlet* E3
Copper, *river* G2
Denali Natl. Park and Preserve E2
Fairweather, *mt.* H3
Gates of the Arctic N.P. and Preserve E1
Glacier Bay N.P. and Preserve H3
Iliamna, *lake* D3
Inside Passage, *waterway* J3
Kanaga, *island* Inset
Katmai Natl. Park and Preserve D3
Kenai, *peninsula* E2
Kenai Fjords Natl. Park F3
Kiska, *island* Inset
Kobuk, *river* D1
Kobuk Valley Natl. Park D1
Kodiak, *island* E3
Kotzebue, *sound* C1
Koyukuk, *river* D1
Kuskokwim, *bay* C3
Kuskokwim, *mts.* D2
Kuskokwim, *river* D2
Lake Clark Natl. Park and Preserve E2
Lisburne, *cape* B1
Lisburne, *peninsula* C1
Logan, *mt.* G2
Lynn, *canal* J3
McKinley, *mt.* E2
Malaspina, *glacier* G3
Michelson, *mt.* G1
Mohican, *cape* B2
Muir, *glacier* F2
Near, *islands* Inset
Noatak, *river* D1
Norton, *sound* C2
Nunivak, *island* B3
Porcupine, *river* G1
Pribilof, *islands* B3
Prince of Wales, *island* J3
Progromni, *volcano* C4
Rat, *islands* Inset
St. Elias, *mt.* G2
St. George, *island* B3
St. Lawrence, *island* A2
St. Matthew, *island* A2
St. Paul, *island* A3
Samalga, *pass* B4
Sanak, *island* C4
Seguam, *island* Inset
Semisopochnoi, *island* Inset
Seward, *peninsula* C1
Shishaldin, *volcano* C4
Shumagin, *islands* D4
Stikine, *river* J3
Tanaga, *island* F3
Tanana, *river* E2
Tikchik, *lakes* D2
Trinity, *islands* E3
Umnak, *island* Inset
Unalaska, *island* B4
Unga, *island* C3
Unimak, *island* C4
Utukok, *river* C1
White Mts. Natl. Rec. Area F1
Wrangell, *mts.* G2
Wrangell-St. Elias N.P. and Preserve G2
Yukon, *river* D2
Yukon-Charley Rivers Natl. Preserve G2
Yunaska, *island* Inset

Arizona ... page 130

Cities and Towns
Ajo C5
Apache Junction D4
Avondale C4
Bagdad B3
Benson E6
Bisbee F6
Bitahochee E2
Buckeye C4
Bullhead City A2
Camp Verde D3
Carefree D4
Casa Grande D5
Catalina E5
Cave Creek D4
Chandler D4
Chinle F1
Chino Valley C3
Cibecue E3
Clarkdale C3
Claypool E4
Clifton F4
Colorado City C1
Coolidge D5
Cornville D3
Cow Springs E1
Crown King C3
Douglas F6
Dudleyville E5
Eagar F3
El Mirage C4
Eloy D5
Flagstaff D2
Florence D4
Fort Defiance F2
Fountain Hills D4
Ganado F2
Geronimo E4
Gila Bend C5
Gilbert D4
Globe E4
Goodyear C4
Grand Canyon C1
Greaterville E6
Green Valley E6
Guthrie F5
Happy Jack D3
Holbrook E3
Huachuca City E6
Kayenta E1
Kearny E4
Kingman A2
Kirkland Junction C3
Lake Havasu City A3
Lake Montezuma D3
Litchfield Park C4
Mammoth E5
Many Farms F1
Marana D5
Mesa D4
Miami E4
Nogales E6
Oracle E5
Oro Valley E5
Page D1
Paradise Valley D4
Parker A3
Payson D3
Peoria C4
Phoenix, *capital* C4
Pima F5
Pinetop-Lakeside F3
Prescott C3
Prescott Valley C3
Quartzsite A4
Queen Creek D4
Randolph D5
Sacaton D4
Safford F5
Sahuarita E6
St. David E6
St. Johns F3
San Carlos E4
Sanders F2
San Manuel E5
Scottsdale D4
Sedona D3
Sells D6
Show Low E3
Sierra Vista E6
Snowflake E3
Somerton A5
South Tucson E5
Springerville F3
Sun City C4
Sun Lakes D4
Superior D4
Surprise C4
Taylor E3
Tempe D4
Thatcher F5
Three Points D5
Tolleson C4
Tombstone E6
Tuba City D1
Tucson E5
Whiteriver F4
Wickenburg C4
Willcox F5
Williams C2
Window Rock F2
Winslow E2
Yuma A5

Other Features
Agua Fria, *river* C4
Alamo, *lake* B3
Apache, *lake* D4
Aztec Peak, *mt.* E4
Baldy, *mt.* F4
Bartlett, *reservoir* D4
Big Horn, *mts.* B4
Bill Williams, *river* A3
Black, *mesa* E1
Black, *river* E4
Canyon De Chelly N.M. F1
Casa Grande Natl. Monument D5
Castle Dome, *mts.* A4
Castle Dome Peak, *mt.* A4
Chiricahua Natl. Monument F6
Colorado, *river* B2, D1
Coronado Natl. Mem. E6
Gila, *river* B5, D4, F4
Glen Canyon, *dam* D1
Glen Canyon Natl. Rec. Area D1
Grand, *canyon* C1
Grand Canyon Natl. Park B2, C1
Harcuvar, *mts.* B4
Havasu, *lake* A3
Hide Creek, *mt.* C3
Hoover, *dam* A1
Hopi Indian Res. E2
Horseshoe, *reservoir* D4
Hualapai, *mt.* B2
Hubbell Trading Post N.H.S. F2
Humphreys Peak, *mt.* D2
Lake Mead Natl. Rec. Area B1
Little Colorado, *river* D2
Many Farms, *lake* F1
Maple Peak, *mt.* F4
Mazatzal Peak, *mt.* D3
Mohave, *lake* A2
Montezuma Castle N.M. D3
Monument, *valley* F1
Mormon, *lake* D3
Navajo Indian Res. E1, E2
Navajo Natl. Monument E1
Organ Pipe Cactus N.M. C5
Painted, *desert* D2
Parker, *dam* A3
Petrified Forest Natl. Park F3
Pipe Spring Natl. Monument C1
Pleasant, *lake* C4
Point Imperial, *mt.* D1
Powell, *lake* D1
Red, *lake* B2
Saguaro Natl. Monument E5
Salt, *river* E4
San Carlos, *lake* E4
San Pedro, *river* E5
Santa Cruz, *river* D5
Sonoran, *desert* B5
Sunset Crater Natl. Monument D2
Theodore Roosevelt, *lake* D4
Tipton, *mt.* A2
Tonto Natl. Monument D4
Trumbull, *mt.* B1
Tumacacori Natl Hist. Park D6
Tuzigoot Natl. Monument C3
Ventana, *cave* C5
Verde, *river* D3
Virgin, *river* A1
Walnut Canyon Natl. Monument D2
White, *mts.* F4
White House, *ruin* F1
Wupatki Natl. Monument D2
Yuma, *desert* A5

Arkansas ... page 131

Cities and Towns
Alicia D2
Alma A2
Arkadelphia B3
Arkansas City D4
Ashdown A4
Ash Flat D1
Atkins C2
Augusta D2
Bald Knob D2
Barling A2
Batesville D2
Bay E2
Beebe D2
Bella Vista A1
Benton C3
Bentonville A1
Berryville B1
Blytheville F2
Bodcaw B4
Booneville B2
Brinkley D3
Bryant C3
Bull Shoals C1
Cabot D3
Camden C4
Caraway E2
Carlisle D3
Cave City D2
Charleston A2
Clarendon D3
Clarksville B2
Clinton C2
Conway C2
Corning E1
Crossett D4
Daisy B3
Damascus C2
Danville B2
Dardanelle B2
De Queen A3
Dermott D4
Des Arc D3
De Valls Bluff D3
De Witt D3
Dierks A3
Dumas D4
Earle E2
El Dorado C4
England D3
Eudora D4
Eureka Springs B1
Fairfield Bay C2
Fallsville B2
Farmington A1
Fayetteville A1
Fordyce C4
Foreman A4
Forrest City E2
Fort Smith A2
Fountain Hill D4
Gentry A1
Glenwood B3
Gosnell F2
Gould D4
Gravette A1
Greenbrier C2
Green Forest B1
Greenwood A2
Griffithville D2
Gurdon B4
Hamburg D4
Hampton C4
Harrisburg E2
Harrison B1
Haskell C3
Hatfield A3
Hazen D3
Heber Springs C2
Helena E3
Hope B4
Horseshoe Bend D1
Hot Springs National Park B3
Hot Springs Village B3
Hoxie E1
Hughes E3
Hunter D2
Huntsville B1
Jacksonville C3
Jasper B1
Jonesboro E2
Lake City E2
Lake Hamilton B3
Lake Village D4
Lepanto E2
Lewisville B4
Lincoln A2
Little Rock, *capital* C3
Lonoke D3
Luxora F2
McCrory D2
McGehee D4
McNeil B4
McRae D2
Magnolia B4
Malvern C3
Manila E2
Marianna E3
Marion E2
Marked Tree E2
Marshall C2
Marvell E3
Maumelle C3
Mayflower C3
Melbourne D1
Mena A3
Monticello D4
Morrilton C2
Mountain Home C1
Mountain View C2
Mount Ida B3
Mulberry A2
Murfreesboro B3
Nashville B4
Newport D2
North Crossett D4
North Little Rock C3
Oden B3
Osceola F2
Ozark B2
Paragould E1
Paris B2
Parkin E2
Pea Ridge A1
Pelsor B2
Perryville C2
Piggott E1
Pine Bluff D3
Pocahontas E1
Prescott B4
Rector E1
Rison C4
Rogers A1
Rose Bud C2
Russell D2
Russellville B2
St. Charles D3
St. Paul B2
Salem D1
Searcy D2
Sheridan C3
Sherwood C3
Siloam Springs A1
Smackover C4
Springdale A1
Springhill B4
Star City D4
Stuttgart D3
Texarkana A4
Tillar D4
Trumann E2
Tuckerman D2
Tupelo D2
Van Buren A2
Waldo B4
Waldron A3
Walnut Ridge E1
Warren C4
Washington B4
West Fork A2
West Helena E3
West Memphis E2
White Hall C3
Wynne E2
Yellville C1

Other Features
Arkansas, *river* D3
Arkansas Post Natl. Mem. D3
Beaver, *lake* B1
Black, *river* D2
Boston, *mts.* B2
Buffalo, *river* B1
Buffalo Natl. River C2
Bull Shoals, *lake* C1
Cache, *river* E2
Catherine, *lake* C3
Dardanelle, *reservoir* B2
DeGray, *lake* B3
Erling, *lake* B4
Fort Smith Natl. Hist Site A2
Greers Ferry, *lake* C2
Greeson, *lake* B3
Hamilton, *lake* B3
Hot Springs Natl. Park B3
Little Missouri, *river* B4
Magazine, *mt.* B2
Maumelle, *lake* C3
Millwood, *lake* B4
Mississippi, *river* E3
Nimrod, *lake* B3
Norfork, *lake* C1
Ouachita, *lake* B3
Ouachita, *mts.* A3
Ouachita, *river* B3, C4
Ozark, *plateau* B1
Pea Ridge Natl. Mil. Park A1
Red, *river* B4
St. Francis, *river* E1
Saline, *river* C3
Table Rock, *lake* B1
White, *river* C2, D3

California ... page 132

Cities and Towns
Adelanto H8
Alameda K2
Alamo L2
Albany K1
Alhambra D10
Alpine J10
Altadena D10
Alturas E1
Anaheim E11, H9
Anderson C2
Antioch D4, L1
Apple Valley H8
Aptos D5
Arcadia D10
Arcata A2
Arnold E4
Arroyo Grande E7
Arvin G7
Ashland K2
Atascadero E7
Atherton K3
Atwater E5
Auberry F5
Auburn E4
Avalon G9
Avenal E6
Azusa E10
Bakersfield G7
Baldwin Park E10
Barstow H8
Bell D10
Bellflower D11
Belmont K3
Belvedere J1
Benicia K1
Berkeley C5, K2
Beverly Hills C10
Big Bear Lake J8
Bishop G5
Black Point J1

CALIFORNIA–CONNECTICUT 179

Key
Blythe L9
Bonita C9
Boron H8
Borrego Springs J9
Brawley K10
Brea E11
Bridgeport F4
Brisbane J2
Broadmoor J2
Buellton E8
Buena Park E11
Burbank C10
Burlingame J3
Burney D2
Buttonwillow F7
Calabasas B10
Calexico K10
California City H7
Calipatria K9
Calistoga C4
Cambria D7
Campbell L4
Canyon K2
Carlsbad H9
Carmel D6
Carmel Valley D6
Carpinteria F8
Carson D11
Castroville D6
Cathedral City J9
Cayucos E7
Central Valley C2
Ceres E5
Chester D2
Chico D3
Chino F10
Chowchilla E5
Chula Vista C9, H10
Claremont F10
Clayton L1
Clearlake C4
Cloverdale B4
Clovis F6
Clyde L1
Coachella J9
Coalinga E6
Cobb C4
Colfax E3
Colusa D3
Compton D11
Concord L1
Corcoran F6
Corning C3
Corona F11
Coronado B8
Corte Madera J1
Costa Mesa E11
Cottonwood C2
Covina E10
Cowan Heights E11
Crescent City A1
Crestline H8
Crockett K1
Culver City C10
Cupertino L4
Cypress D11
Daly City J2
Danville L2
Davis D4
Delano F7
Del Mar H10
Desert Hot Springs J9
Diablo L2
Diamond Bar E10
Dinuba F6
Dos Palos E6
Downey D11
Downieville E3
Dublin L2
Dunsmuir C1
Earlimart F7
East Los Angeles D10
Easton F6
East Palo Alto K3
El Cajon C8, J10
El Centro K10
El Cerrito K1
El Granada J3
Elk Grove D4
El Monte D10
El Segundo C11
El Sobrante K1
Emeryville K2
Encinitas H9
Escondido H9
Eureka A2
Exeter F6
Fairfax H1
Fairfield D4
Fallbrook H9
Ferndale A2
Firebaugh E6
Florence D11
Florin D4
Fort Bragg B3
Fortuna A2
Foster City K3
Fountain Valley E11
Frazier Park G8
Fremont D5, L3
Fresno F6
Fullerton E11
Galt D4
Garden Grove E11
Gilroy D5
Glendale D10, G8
Glendora E10
Glenview B10
Gonzales D6
Grass Valley D3
Greenacres F7
Greenbrae J1
Greenfield D6
Greenville E2
Gridley D3
Groveland E5
Guadalupe E8
Half Moon Bay J3
Hanford F6
Hawthorne C11
Hayfork B2
Hayward C5, L2
Healdsburg C4
Hemet J9
Hercules K1
Hermosa Beach C11
Hesperia H8
Hidden Hills B10
Hillsborough J3
Hollister D6
Holtville K10

Key
Huntington Beach E11, G9
Huron E6
Ignacio J1
Imperial Beach B9, H10
Independence G6
Indio J9
Inglewood C11, G9
Ingot C2
Inyokern H7
Ione E4
Irvine E11, H9
Isla Vista F8
Jackson E4
Joshua Tree J8
Julian J9
Kelseyville C4
Kensington K1
Kentfield J1
Kerman E6
Kernville G7
Kettleman City F6
King City D6
La Canada-Flintridge D10
La Crescenta D10
Lafayette K1
La Habra E11
La Honda K4
Lake Isabella G7
Lakeport C3
Lakeside J10
Lakewood D11
La Mesa C8
La Mirada D11
Lamont G7
Lancaster G8
La Puente E10
Larkspur J1
Laton F6
Lawndale C11
Lee Vining F5
Lemon Grove C8
Lemoore F6
Lincoln D4
Lindsay F6
Littlerock H8
Livermore D5
Livingston E5
Lockeford D4
Lodi D4
Loma Mar K4
Lomita C11
Lompoc E8
Lone Pine G6
Long Beach D11, G9
Los Altos K3
Los Altos Hills K4
Los Angeles D10, G8
Los Banos E5
Los Molinos C2
Los Osos E7
Lynwood D11
McCloud C1
McFarland F7
McKinleyville A2
Madera E6
Malibu B10
Mammoth Lakes G5
Manhattan Beach C11
Manteca D5
Marina D6
Marina del Rey C11
Marin City J1
Marinwood J1
Mariposa F5
Markleeville F4
Martinez C4, K1
Marysville D3
Maywood D10
Mecca J9
Mendota E6
Menlo Park K3
Merced E5
Midway City E11
Millbrae J3
Mill Valley J1
Milpitas L3
Miranda B2
Modesto E5
Mojave G7
Monrovia E10
Montara J3
Montclair F10
Montebello D10
Monte Nido B10
Monterey D6
Monterey Park D10
Monte Sereno L4
Moraga K2
Moreno Valley H9
Morgan Hill D5
Morongo Valley J8
Morro Bay E7
Moss Beach J3
Mountain View K3
Mount Shasta C1
Muir Beach H1
Napa C4
National City C9
Needles L8
Nevada City D3
Newark L3
Newberry Springs J8
Newport Beach H9
Nicasio H1
Nice C3
Nipomo E7
Nipton K7
Norco F11
North Edwards H7
North Fair Oaks K3
Novato H1
Oakdale E5
Oakhurst F5
Oakland K2, C5
Oceanside H9
Oildale F7
Ojai E8
Olema H1
Olivehurst D3
Ontario F10, H8
Orange E11
Orinda K1
Orland C3
Oroville D3
Otay C9
Oxnard F8
Pacheco L1
Pacifica J2
Palermo D3
Palmdale G8
Palm Desert J9

Key
Palm Springs J9
Palo Alto K3
Palos Verdes Estates C11
Paradise D3
Pasadena D10, G8
Patterson D5
Petaluma C4
Pico Rivera D10
Piedmont K2
Pine Valley J10
Pinole K1
Pismo Beach E7
Pittsburg L1
Placentia E11
Placerville E4
Pleasant Hill L1
Pleasanton L2
Pomona E10, H8
Port Costa K1
Porterville G6
Portola E3
Poway H10
Prunedale D6
Quartz Hill G8
Quincy E3
Ramona J9
Rancho Cucamonga F10
Rancho Palos Verdes C11
Rancho Rinconada L4
Rancho Santa Margarita F11
Red Bluff C2
Redding C2
Redlands H8
Redondo Beach C11
Redwood City C5, K3
Reedley F6
Richgrove F7
Richmond J1
Ridgecrest H7
Rio Dell A2
Riverside H9
Rodeo K1
Rolling Hills C11
Rolling Hills Estates C11
Rosamond G8
Roseville D4
Sacramento, *capital* D4
Salinas D6
San Andreas E4
San Anselmo H1
San Bernardino H8
San Bruno J2
San Carlos K3
San Clemente H9
San Diego B8, H10
San Francisco C5, J2
San Gabriel D10
Sanger F6
San Gregorio J4
San Jose D5, L4
San Juan Bautista D6
San Juan Capistrano H9
San Leandro K2
San Lorenzo K2
San Luis Obispo E7
San Mateo C5, K3
San Pablo J1
San Quentin J1
San Rafael C5, J1
San Ramon L2
Santa Ana E11, H9
Santa Barbara F8
Santa Clara L4
Santa Clarita G8
Santa Cruz C6
Santa Maria E8
Santa Monica C10
Santa Paula F8
Santa Rosa C4
Santa Venetia J1
Santa Ynez E8
Santee C8
Saratoga L4
Sausalito J2
Scotts Valley C5
Seal Beach D11
Sebastopol C4
Selma F6
Shafter F7
Shingletown D2
Shoshone J7
Simi Valley G8
Soledad D6
Solvang E8
Sonoma C4
Sonora E5
South Lake Tahoe F4
South San Francisco J2
Spring Valley C8
Squaw Valley F6
Stanford K3
Stinson Beach H1
Stockton D5
Sunnyvale C5, L4
Sunol L3
Sunset Beach D11
Susanville E2
Taft F7
Tamalpais Valley J1
Tehachapi G7
Temecula H9
Templeton E7
Terra Bella F7
Thermalito D3
Thousand Oaks G8
Tiburon J1
Tipton F6
Topanga B10
Torrance C11, G9
Tracy D5
Truckee E3
Tulare F6
Turlock E5
Tustin E11
Twain Harte E4
Twentynine Palms J8
Ukiah B3
Union City L3
Upland F10
Vacaville D4
Vallejo C4, K1
Vandenberg Village E8
Ventucopa F8
Ventura F8
Victorville H8
Villa Park E11
Vine Hill K1
Visalia F6
Vista H9
Walnut E10
Walnut Creek L1

Key
Wasco F7
Watsonville D6
Weaverville C2
Weed C1
West Covina E10
West Hollywood C10
Westminster E11
Westmorland K9
West Pittsburg L1
Westwood E2
Wheatland D3
Whittier D10
Willits B3
Willow Creek B2
Willows C3
Windsor C4
Wofford Heights G7
Woodlake F6
Woodland D4
Woodside K3
Wrightwood H8
Yorba Linda E11
Yosemite Village F5
Yreka C1
Yuba City D3
Yucaipa H8
Yucca Valley J8
Zenia B2

Other Features

Alameda, *river* L3
Alcatraz, *island* J2
Allison, *mt.* L3
Almanor, *lake* D2
Amargosa, *range* J6
Amargosa, *river* J7
Angel, *island* J1
Balboa, *park* B8
Berryessa, *lake* C4
Boundary, *peak* G5
Bullion, *mts.* J8
Cascade, *range* D1
Central, *valley* C2
Chabot, *lake* K2
Channel, *islands* F9
Channel Islands Natl. Park E9, F9
Chatsworth, *reservoir* B10
Chino, *river* F10
Chocolate, *mts.* K9
Clair Engle, *lake* C1
Clear, *lake* C3
Clear Lake, *reservoir* D1
Coast, *ranges* C2, D6
Colorado, *desert* J9
Colorado, *river* L9
Cucamonga, *river* F11
Death, *valley* H6
Death Valley Natl. Park H6
Devils Postpile Natl. Monument F5
Diablo, *mt.* L1
Eagle, *lake* E2
Eagle, *peak* E1
Eel, *river* B2
Estero, *bay* E7
Farallon, *islands* B5
Farallones, *gulf* H1
Golden Gate Natl. Rec. Area C5, J2
Goose, *lake* E1
Grizzly, *bay* L1
Half Moon, *bay* J3
Honey, *lake* E2
Humboldt, *bay* A2
Imperial, *valley* K9
Inyo, *mts.* H6
Irvine, *lake* F11
Joshua Tree Natl. Park K8
Kern, *river* G6
Kings, *river* F6
Kings Canyon Natl. Park G5
Klamath, *mts.* B1
Klamath, *river* B1
Lanfair, *valley* K7
Lassen, *peak* D2
Lassen Volcanic Natl. Park D2
Lava Beds Natl. Monument D1
McCoy, *mts.* L9
Mad, *river* B2
Merced, *river* E5
Middle Alkali, *lake* F1
Mission, *bay* B8
Mission Bay, *park* B8
Mojave, *desert* H7
Mojave, *river* J8
Mono, *lake* G4
Monterey, *bay* D6
Morgan, *mt.* G5
Morris, *reservoir* E10
Nacimiento, *reservoir* D7
Napa, *river* K1
Nicasio, *reservoir* H1
Old Woman, *mts.* K8
Oroville, *reservoir* D3
Otay, *river* C9
Panamint, *range* H6
Panamint, *valley* H6
Pescadero, *river* J4
Pinnacles Natl. Monument D6
Point Reyes Natl. Seashore B4
Redwood Natl. Park A1
Ritter, *mt.* F5
Sacramento, *river* C3
Salton, *sea* K9
San Antonio, *reservoir* D7
San Bernardino, *mts.* H8
San Clemente, *island* G10
San Diego, *bay* B9
San Diego, *river* B8
San Fernando, *valley* B10
San Francisco, *bay* J2
San Gabriel, *mts.* G8
San Gabriel, *reservoir* E10
San Joaquin, *river* E5
San Luis Obispo, *bay* E7
San Miguel, *island* E8
San Nicolas, *island* F9
San Pablo, *bay* J1
San Rafael, *mts.* F8
Santa Ana, *mts.* F11
Santa Barbara, *channel* E8
Santa Barbara, *island* F9
Santa Catalina, *island* G9
Santa Cruz, *island* F8
Santa Cruz, *mts.* J3
Santa Lucia, *range* D6
Santa Monica, *bay* B11
Santa Monica, *mts.* B10
Santa Monica Mts. N.R.A. B10
Santa Rosa, *island* E9
Santiago, *river* F11
Sequoia Natl. Park G6
Shasta, *lake* C2

Key
Shasta, *mt.* C1
Sierra, *peak* F11
Sierra Nevada, *range* D3, G5
Siskiyou, *mts.* B1
Tahoe, *lake* E3
Tehachapi, *mts.* G8
Telescope, *peak* H6
Trinity, *river* B2
Tule, *river* F6
Turtle, *mts.* L8
Upper, *lake* E1
Upper San Leandro, *reservoir* L2
Vizcaino, *cape* B3
Whiskeytown-Shasta-Trinity N.R.A. D1
White, *mts.* G5
Whitney, *mt.* G6
Wilson, *mt.* D10
Yosemite Natl. Park F5

Colorado ....page 133

Cities and Towns

Akron G1
Alamosa E4
Arvada E2
Aspen D2
Aurora F2
Avon D2
Bennett F2
Berthoud E1
Black Forest F2
Boulder E1
Breckenridge D2
Brighton F2
Broomfield E2
Brush G1
Buena Vista D3
Burlington H2
Canon City E3
Carbondale C2
Castle Rock F2
Cedaredge C3
Center D4
Central City E2
Cheyenne Wells H3
Clifton B2
Colorado Springs F3
Conejos D4
Cortez B4
Craig C1
Crawford C3
Creede D4
Cripple Creek E3
Dacono F1
Del Norte D4
Delta B3
Denver, *capital* F2
Dinosaur A1
Dove Creek B4
Durango C4
Eads H3
Eagle D2
Eaton F1
Englewood F2
Estes Park E1
Evans F1
Evergreen E2
Fairplay E2
Florence E3
Fort Collins E1
Fort Lupton F1
Fort Morgan G1
Fountain F3
Frisco D2
Fruita B2
Fruitvale B2
Georgetown E2
Glenwood Springs C2
Golden E2
Grand Junction B2
Greeley F1
Gunnison D3
Gypsum D2
Haswell G3
Hayden C1
Holyoke H1
Hot Sulphur Springs D1
Hugo G2
Idaho Springs E2
Johnstown F1
Julesburg H1
Keota F1
Kiowa F2
Kit Carson H3
Lafayette E2
La Junta G4
Lake City C3
Lakewood E2
Lamar H3
Las Animas G3
Leadville D2
Limon G2
Littleton F2
Longmont E1
Louisville E1
Loveland E1
Manitou Springs F3
Meeker C1
Milliken F1
Monte Vista D4
Montrose C3
Niwot E1
Northglenn F2
Olathe C3
Orchard City C3
Orchard Mesa B2
Ordway G3
Ouray C3
Pagosa Springs C4
Palisade B2
Palmer Lake F2
Paonia C3
Parker F2
Platteville F1
Pritchett H4
Pueblo F3
Pueblo West F3
Rangely B1
Rifle C2
Rocky Ford G3
Saguache D3
Salida E3
San Luis E4
Security F3
Silverthorne D2
Silverton C4
Snowmass Village D2
Springfield H4
Steamboat Springs D1
Sterling G1

Key
Telluride C4
Thornton F2
Trinidad F4
Vail D2
Vilas H4
Walden D1
Walsenburg F4
Wellington E1
Westcliffe E3
Westminster E2
Wheat Ridge F2
Wiley H3
Windsor F1
Woodland Park E3
Wray H1
Yuma H1

Other Features

Animas, *river* C4
Apishapa, *river* F4
Arapahoe, *peak* E1
Arapaho Natl. Rec. Area E1
Arikaree, *river* G2
Arkansas, *river* F3
Bent's Old Fort Natl. Hist. Site G3
Black Canyon of the Gunnison Natl. Monument C3
Blanca, *peak* E4
Blue Mesa, *reservoir* C3
Bonny, *reservoir* H2
Castle, *peak* D2
Colorado, *plateau* A4
Colorado, *river* C2
Colorado Natl. Monument B2
Crestone, *peak* E4
Cucharas, *river* F4
Curecanti Natl. Rec. Area C3
Dinosaur Natl. Monument B1
Dolores, *river* B3
Elbert, *mt.* D2
Eolus, *mt.* C4
Evans, *mt.* E2
Florissant Fossil Beds N.M. E3
Front, *range* E1
Great Sand Dunes N.M. E4
Green, *river* B1
Gunnison, *mt.* C3
Gunnison, *river* B3
Hovenweep Natl. Monument B4
John Martin, *reservoir* G3
Laramie, *mts.* E1
Laramie, *river* E1
Little Snake, *river* B1
Longs, *peak* E1
Mancos, *river* B4
Medicine Bow, *mts.* D1
Mesa Verde Natl. Park B4
Montezuma, *peak* D4
North Fork Cimarron, *river* H4
North Fork Smoky Hill, *river* H2
North Platte, *river* D1
Park, *range* D1
Pikes, *peak* E3
Purgatoire, *river* G4
Rio Grande, *river* E4
Roan, *plateau* B2
Rocky, *mts.* D1
Rocky Mt. Natl. Park E1
Royal Gorge, *canyon* E3
Sangre de Cristo, *mts.* E3
San Juan, *mts.* C4
San Luis, *valley* E4
Sawatch, *range* D2
South Fork Republican, *river* G2
South Platte, *river* E2, G1
Uncompahgre, *peak* C3
U.S. Air Force Academy F3
White, *river* B1
Wilson, *mt.* B4
Yampa, *river* B1
Yucca House Natl. Monument B4
Zirkel, *mt.* D1

Connecticut ....page 134

Cities and Towns

Abington G2
Andover F3
Ansonia C4
Attawaugan H2
Avon D2
Bakersville C2
Ballouville H2
Baltic G3
Beacon Falls C4
Berkshire B4
Berlin E3
Bethany C4
Bethel B4
Bethlehem C3
Black Point G4
Bloomfield E2
Blue Hills E2
Boardman Bridge B3
Bolton F2
Botsford B4
Branford D4
Bridgeport C5
Bridgewater B3
Bristol D3
Broad Brook E2
Brookfield B4
Brookfield Center B4
Brooklyn H2
Burlington D2
Burrville C2
Cannondale B5
Canterbury H3
Canton D2
Canton Center D2
Centerbrook F4
Central Village H3
Chaplin G2
Cheshire D4
Chester F4
Chesterfield G4
Clarks Falls H4
Clinton E4
Colchester F3
Colebrook C2
Collinsville D2
Columbia F3
Cornwall B2
Cornwall Bridge B2
Coventry F2
Cromwell E3
Danbury B4
Danielson H2
Darien B5
Dayville H2

180 CONNECTICUT–GEORGIA

Key
Deep River F4
Derby C4
Durham E4
Eagleville F2
East Brooklyn H2
Eastford G2
East Glastonbury E3
East Granby E2
East Haddam F4
East Hampton E3
East Hartford E2
East Hartland D2
East Haven D4
East Killingly H2
East Litchfield C2
East Lyme G4
Easton B5
East Thompson H1
East Village C4
East Woodstock H2
Ellington F2
Enfield E2
Essex F4
Fairfield B5
Falls Village B2
Farmington D3
Fitchman G3
Flanders B3
Franklin G3
Gales Ferry G4
Gaylordsville B3
Georgetown B5
Gilead F3
Gilman G3
Glasgo H3
Glastonbury E3
Goodrich Heights E3
Goshen C2
Granby D2
Greenwich A5
Grosvenor Dale H2
Groton G4
Groton Long Point G4
Guilford E4
Gurleyville G2
Haddam E4
Haddam Neck E3
Hadlyme F4
Hamburg F4
Hamden D4
Hampton G2
Hanover G3
Hartford, *capital* E3
Harwinton C2
Hawleyville B4
Hazardville E2
Hebron F3
Higganum E4
Hotchkissville C3
Indian Neck D5
Jewett City H3
Kensington D3
Killingworth E4
Knollcrest B4
Knollwood F4
Lake Pocotopaug E3
Lakeside C3
Lakeside C4
Laysville F4
Lebanon G3
Ledyard Center G4
Liberty Hill F3
Lime Rock B2
Litchfield C3
Lyons Plain B5
Madison E4
Manchester E2
Mansfield Center G3
Mansfield Four Corners F2
Marble Dale B3
Marion D3
Meriden D3
Merrow F2
Middlebury C3
Middlefield E3
Middle Haddam E3
Middletown E3
Milford C5
Mill Plain A4
Milton B2
Mohegan G4
Monroe C4
Montville G4
Moosup H3
Mystic H4
Naugatuck C4
New Britain D3
New Canaan B5
New Fairfield B4
New Hartford D2
New Haven D4
Newington E3
New London G4
New Milford B3
Newtown B4
Niantic G4
Noank H4
Norfolk C2
North Branford D4
North Canton D2
Northfield C3
Northford D4
North Franklin G3
North Grosvenor Dale H2
North Guilford E4
North Haven D4
North Stonington H4
Northville B3
North Westchester F3
North Windham G3
Norwalk B5
Norwich G3
Oakdale G4
Oakville C3
Old Lyme F4
Old Mystic H4
Old Saybrook F4
Oneco H3
Orange C4
Oxford C4
Park Lane B3
Pawcatuck H4
Perkins Corner G2
Phoenixville G2
Plainfield H3
Plainville D3
Plantsville D3
Pleasant Valley D2
Pleasure Beach G4
Plymouth C3
Pomfret H2

Key
Poquetanuck G4
Poquonock E2
Poquonock Bridge G4
Portland E3
Preston City H3
Prospect D4
Putnam H2
Quaddick H2
Quaker Hill G4
Redding B4
Redding Ridge B4
Ridgebury A4
Ridgefield B4
Riverton C2
Robertsville C2
Rockfall E3
Rockville F2
Rocky Hill E3
Roxbury B3
Sachem Head E5
Salem F4
Salisbury B2
Scantic E2
Scitico E2
Scotland G3
Seymour C4
Sharon B2
Shelton C4
Sherman B3
Short Beach D5
Simsbury D2
Somers F2
Sound View F4
Southbury C4
South Canaan B2
South Chaplin G2
South Glastonbury E3
Southington D3
South Kent B3
South Killingly H2
South Willington F2
South Windham G3
South Windsor E2
Stafford F2
Stafford Springs F2
Staffordville F2
Stamford A5
Sterling H3
Stevenson C4
Stony Creek E4
Storrs F2
Straitsville C4
Stratford C5
Suffield E2
Taconic B1
Talcottville F2
Tariffville D2
Terryville C3
Thompson H2
Thompsonville E2
Tolland F2
Torrington C2
Trumbull C5
Uncasville G4
Union G2
Unionville D2
Vernon F2
Versailles G3
Voluntown H3
Wallingford D4
Warren B3
Warrenville G2
Washington B3
Washington Depot B3
Waterbury C3
Waterford G4
Watertown C3
Weatogue D2
Westbrook F4
West Cornwall B2
Westford G2
West Granby D2
West Hartford E2
West Hartland D1
West Haven D4
West Mystic H4
West Norfolk C1
Weston B5
Westport B5
West Redding B4
West Simsbury D2
West Stafford F2
West Suffield E2
West Willington F2
Wethersfield E3
Whigville D3
Willimantic G3
Wilton B5
Winchester Center C2
Windham G3
Windsor E2
Windsor Locks E2
Winsted C2
Winthrop F4
Wolcott D3
Woodbridge C4
Woodmont D5
Woodstock H2
Woodstock Valley G2
Woodville B3
Yalesville D4

Other Features
Appalachian Natl. Scenic Trail B2
Bantam, *lake* C3
Barkhamsted, *reservoir* D2
Candlewood, *lake* B4
Connecticut, *river* E4
Easton, *reservoir* B4
Farmington, *river* D3
Frissell, *mt.* B1
Gaillard, *lake* D4
Hammonasset, *river* E4
Hop, *river* F3
Housatonic, *river* B4
Long Island, *sound* D5
Mt. Hope, *river* G2
Natchaug, *river* G2
Naugatuck, *river* C4
Nepaug, *reservoir* D2
Norwalk, *islands* B5
Norwalk, *river* B5
Quinebaug, *river* H3
Saugatuck, *reservoir* B4
Shenipsit, *lake* F2
Shetucket, *river* G3
Thames, *river* G4
Waramaug, *lake* B3
Weir Farm Natl. Hist. Site B5
Willimantic, *river* F2
Yantic, *river* F3

Key
Delaware page 135

Cities and Towns
Adamsville A3
Andrewville A3
Argos Corner B3
Blackbird A2
Broadkill Beach B3
Brookside A1
Burrsville A3
Camden A2
Cannon A3
Canterbury A2
Capitol Park A2
Clarksville B3
Claymont B1
Collins Park A1
Delaware City A1
Dover, *capital* A2
Edgemoor A1
Elsmere A1
Fairfax A1
Georgetown B3
Glasgow A1
Gumboro B4
Harbeson B3
Harrington A3
Hartley A2
Hazlettville A2
Hickman A3
Hockessin A1
Indian Beach B3
Jimtown B3
Kirkwood A1
Kitts Hummock B2
Laurel A3
Lewes B3
Lincoln B3
Little Heaven B2
Llangollen Estates A1
Lynch Heights B3
McClellandville A1
Marshallton A1
Marydel A2
Mastens Corner A3
Middletown A2
Midway B3
Milford B3
Millsboro B3
Milton B3
Nassau B3
Newark A1
New Castle A1
Oak Orchard B3
Owens A3
Petersburg A2
Pinetown B3
Primehook Beach B3
Reeves Crossing A3
Rehoboth Beach B3
Reliance A3
Rosedale Beach B3
Roxana B3
Sandtown A2
Seaford A3
Selbyville B4
Smyrna A2
Stanton A1
Swann Keys B4
Talleyville A1
Taylors Bridge A2
Whitesville B4
Williamsville A3
Williamsville B4
Wilmington A1
Wilmington Manor A1
Woodenhawk A3
Woodland Beach B2
Workmans Corners B3

Other Features
Broadkill, *river* B3
Chesapeake & Delaware, *canal* A1
Delaware, *bay* B2
Delaware, *river* A1
Henlopen, *cape* B3
Indian River, *bay* B3
Mispillion, *river* B3
Murderkill, *river* A3
Nanticoke, *river* A3
Rehoboth, *bay* B3
Smyrna, *river* A2

Florida page 136

Cities and Towns
Alachua C2
Altamonte Springs D3
Anna Maria C4
Apalachicola A2
Apollo Beach C4
Apopka D3
Arcadia D4
Archer C2
Astor D2
Atlantic Beach D1
Auburndale D3
Aventura B3
Avon Park D4
Baldwin D1
Bal Harbour B3
Bartow D4
Bay Harbor Islands B3
Bayonet Point C3
Bee Ridge C4
Belle Glade E5
Belleview C2
Beverly Hills C3
Big Pine Key D7
Biscayne Park A3
Blountstown A1
Boca Raton E5
Bonifay C6
Bonita Springs D5
Boynton Beach E5
Bradenton C4
Brandon C4
Bristol A1
Bronson C2
Brooksville C3
Buckhead Ridge E4
Bunnell D2
Bushnell C3
Callaway C6
Cape Canaveral E3
Cape Coral D5
Carol City A3, E6
Chattahoochee A1
Chiefland C2
Chipley C6

Key
Clearwater C4
Clermont D3
Clewiston E5
Cocoa E3
Cocoa Beach E3
Coconut Grove A3
Cooper City A2
Coral Gables A3, E6
Coral Springs E5
Crawfordville A1
Crescent City D2
Crestview B6
Cross City B2
Crystal River C3
Dade City C3
Dania B2
Davie A2, E5
Daytona Beach D2
De Bary D3
Deerfield Beach E5
De Funiak Springs B6
De Land D2
Delray Beach E5
Deltona D3
Destin B6
Dunedin C3
Dunnellon C2
East Naples D5
Eastpoint A2
Edgewater E3
El Portal A3
Elfers C3
Englewood C5
Eustis D3
Fellsmere E4
Fernandina Beach D1
Flagler Beach D2
Florida City E6
Fort Lauderdale B2, E5
Fort Meade D4
Fort Myers D5
Fort Myers Beach D5
Fort Myers Villas D5
Fort Pierce E4
Fort Walton Beach B6
Frostproof D4
Gainesville C2
Gifford E4
Golden Gate D5
Gonzalez A6
Goulds E6
Greenacres City E5
Green Cove Springs D2
Gretna A1
Gulf Breeze A6
Haines City D3
Hallandale B3, E6
Havana A1
Hawthorne C2
Hialeah A3, E6
Hialeah Gardens A3
High Springs C2
Hilliard D1
Holiday C3
Holly Hill D2
Hollywood A3, E5
Holmes Beach C4
Homestead E6
Homosassa Springs C3
Hudson C3
Immokalee D5
Indian Harbour Beach E3
Indian Rocks Beach C4
Indiantown E4
Inverness C3
Jacksonville D1
Jacksonville Beach D1
Jasper C1
Jensen Beach E4
Jupiter E5
Kendall A4, E6
Key Biscayne B4
Key Largo E6
Keystone Heights C2
Key West D7
Kissimmee D3
La Belle D5
La Crosse C2
Lady Lake D3
Lake Buena Vista D3
Lake Butler C1
Lake City C1
Lakeland D3
Lake Mary D3
Lake Panasoffkee C3
Lake Wales D4
Lake Worth E5
Land O' Lakes C3
Lantana E5
Largo C4
Lauderdale Lakes A2
Lauderdale-by-the-Sea B2
Lauderhill A2
Lawtey C1
Layton E7
Leesburg D3
Live Oak C1
Longboat Key C4
Lutz C3
Lynn Haven C6
Macclenny C1
Madison B1
Marathon D7
Marco D6
Margate E5
Marianna C6
Marineland D2
Mayo B1
Merritt Island E3
Miami A3, E6
Miami Beach B3, E6
Miami Lakes A3, A5
Miami Shores A3, A5
Miami Springs A3, A5
Middleburg D1
Milton A6
Mims E3
Miramar A3, E6
Monticello B1
Moore Haven D5
Mount Dora D3
Naples D5
Naples Manor D5
Naples Park D5
Naranja E6
New Port Richey C3
New Smyrna Beach E2
Niceville B6
Noma C5
North Bay Village A3
North Fort Myers D5

Key
North Miami A3, E6
North Miami Beach A3
North Naples D5
North Port C4
Oakland Park B2, E5
Ocala C2
Ocoee D3
Okeechobee E4
Oldsmar C3
Olympia Hts. A3
Opa-Locka A3
Orange City D3
Orange Park D1
Orlando D3
Ormond Beach D2
Ormond-by-the-Sea D2
Otter Creek C2
Oviedo D3
Pace A6
Pahokee E5
Palatka D2
Palm Bay E3
Palm Beach E5
Palm Beach Gardens E5
Palm Coast D2
Palmetto C4
Palm Harbor C3
Panama City C6
Pembroke Park A3
Pembroke Pines A3
Pennsuco A3
Pensacola A6
Perrine E6
Perry B1
Pierson D2
Pine Castle D3
Plantation A2, E5
Plant City C3
Polk City D3
Pomona Park D2
Port Charlotte C5
Port Orange E2
Port St. Joe C7
Port St. Lucie E4
Port Salerno E4
Punta Gorda C5
Quincy A1
Raiford C1
Ridge Manor C3
Riverview C4
Riviera Beach E5
Rockledge E3
Royal Palm Beach E5
St. Augustine D2
St. Augustine Shores D2
St. Cloud D3
St. Petersburg C4
St. Petersburg Beach C4
San Carlos Park D5
Sanford D3
Sanibel C5
Sarasota C4
Satellite Beach E3
Sebastian E4
Sebring D4
Silver Springs C2
Sneads A1
South Miami A3
South Venice C4
Springfield C6
Spring Hill C3
Starke C2
Stuart E4
Sunrise A2
Surfside B3
Sweetwater A3, E6
Tallahassee, *capital* A1
Tamarac A2, E5
Tampa C4
Tarpon Springs C3
Tavares D3
Tavernier E6
Temple Terrace C3
Titusville E3
Treasure Island C4
Trenton C2
Umatilla D3
Venice C4
Vero Beach E4
Vilano Beach D2
Virginia Gardens A3
Warrington A6
Wauchula D4
Webster C3
Weeki Wachee C3
Welaka D2
West Melbourne E3
West Miami A3
Weston A2
West Palm Beach E5
West Pensacola A6
Westwood Lakes A3
Wildwood C3
Williston C2
Wilton Manors B2
Winter Garden D3
Winter Haven D3
Winter Park D3
Woodville A1
Yulee D1
Zephyrhills C3

Other Features
Amelia, *island* D1
Apalachee, *bay* A2
Apalachicola, *bay* A2
Apalachicola, *river* A1
Aucilla, *river* B1
Big Cypress, *swamp* D5
Biscayne, *bay* B3, E6
Biscayne Natl. Park E6
Boca Chica Key, *island* D7
Caloosahatchee, *river* D5
Canaveral, *cape* E3
Canaveral Natl. Seashore E3
Cedar Keys, *islands* B2
Charlotte, *harbor* C5
Chattahoochee, river A1
Choctawhatchee, *bay* B6
Crooked, *island* C6
De Soto Natl. Memorial C4
Deadman, *bay* B2
Dog, *island* A2
Dry Tortugas Natl. Park C7
Elliott Key, *island* E6
Escambia, *river* A5
Everglades, *swamp* A5, E6
Everglades Natl. Park E6
Fisher, *island* B3
Florida, *bay* E6
Florida, *straits* E7

Key
Florida Keys, *islands* D7
Fort Caroline Natl. Memorial D1
Fort Matanzas Natl. Monument D2
Gasparilla, *island* C5
George, *lake* D2
Gulf Islands Natl. Seashore A6
Homosassa, *bay* C3
Indian, *river* B6
Iron, *mt.* D4
Istokpoga, *lake* D4
John F. Kennedy Space Center E3
Key Biscayne, *island* B3
Key Largo, *island* E6
Kissimmee, *lake* D4
Lochloosa, *lake* D2
Marquesas Keys, *islands* C7
Mexico, *gulf* B5, B6
Ochlockonee, *river* A1
Okeechobee, *lake* E5
Okefenokee, *swamp* C1
Peace, *river* D4
Pensacola, *bay* A6
Ponce de Leon, *bay* D6
Romano, *cape* D6
Sable, *cape* D6
St. Andrews, *bay* B6
St. George, *island* A2
St. Johns, *river* D2
St. Joseph, *bay* C7
St. Marys, *river* D1
St. Vincent, *island* A2
San Blas, *cape* C7
Sands Key, *island* E6
Sanibel, *island* C5
Santa Rosa, *island* A6
Seminole, *lake* A1
Sugarloaf Key, *island* D7
Suwannee, *river* C1, C2
Talquin, *lake* A1
Tamiami, *canal* A3
Tampa, *bay* C4
Virginia Key, *island* B3
Waccasassa, *bay* C2
Withlacoochee, *river* B1
Yellow, *river* A6

Georgia page 137

Cities and Towns
Abbeville E8
Adairsville B3
Adel E9
Alamo F7
Albany C8
Alma G8
Alpharetta C3
Americus C7
Appling G4
Arlington B9
Ashburn D8
Athens E4
Atlanta, *capital* C4, J3
Augusta H5
Bainbridge B10
Barnesville C5
Baxley G8
Belvedere K3
Blackshear G9
Blairsville D2
Blakely B9
Blue Ridge C2
Boston D10
Bremen A4
Brookhaven J2
Brunswick H9
Buchanan A4
Buena Vista B7
Buford C3
Butler C6
Byron D6
Cairo C10
Calhoun B2
Camilla C9
Canton B3
Carnesville E3
Carrollton A4
Cartersville B3
Cedar Grove J3
Cedartown A3
Chamblee J2
Chatsworth B2
Clarkesville D2
Clarkston K2
Claxton H7
Clayton E2
Cleveland D2
Cochran E7
College Park H3
Colquitt B9
Columbus B7
Commerce E3
Conley J4
Constitution J3
Conyers D4
Cordele D8
Cornelia D2
Covington D4
Crawfordville F4
Cumming C3
Cusseta B7
Cuthbert B8
Dahlonega D2
Dallas B4
Dalton B2
Danielsville E3
Darien J9
Dawson C8
Dawsonville C3
Decatur K3
Donalsonville B9
Doraville K2
Douglas F8
Douglasville B4
Druid Hills J3
Dublin F6
Dunwoody J2
Eastman E7
East Point C4, H3
Eatonton E5
Elberton F3
Ellaville C7
Ellijay C2
Evans G4
Fair Oaks H2
Fairview K4
Fayetteville C5
Fitzgerald E8
Folkston G10
Forest Park J4
Forsyth D5

GEORGIA–ILLINOIS 181

Key

Fort Gaines A8
Fort Oglethorpe A2
Fort Valley D6
Franklin A5
Gainesville D3
Garden City J7
Georgetown A8
Gibson F5
Gilmore H2
Glennville H8
Gordon E6
Gray D5
Greensboro E4
Greenville B5
Gresham Park J3
Griffin C5
Hahira E10
Hamilton B6
Hampton C5
Hapeville J3
Hartwell F3
Hawkinsville E7
Hazlehurst F8
Hephzibah G5
Hiawassee D2
Hinesville H8
Hogansville B5
Homer D3
Homerville F9
Irwinton E6
Jackson D5
Jasper C3
Jefferson E3
Jeffersonville E6
Jesup H8
Jonesboro C4
Kennesaw B3
Kingsland H10
Knoxville D6
La Fayette A2
La Grange A5
Lakeland E9
Lavonia E3
Lawrenceville D4
Leesburg C8
Lexington E4
Lincolnton G4
Locust Grove C5
Louisville G5
Ludowici H8
Lumber City F8
Lumpkin B7
Lyons G7
Mableton B4, G2
McDonough C5
McIntyre E6
Macon D6
McRae F7
Madison E4
Manchester B6
Marietta B4, H1
Marshallville D7
Metter G7
Milledgeville E5
Millen H6
Monroe D4
Monticello D5
Morgan B8
Moultrie D9
Mount Vernon F7
Mt. Bethel J1
Nashville E9
Newnan B5
Newton C9
Oakdale H2
Ocilla E8
Oglethorpe C7
Panthersville K3
Peachtree City B5
Pearson F9
Pembroke H7
Perry D7
Pooler J7
Powder Springs B4
Preston B7
Quitman E10
Red Oak H4
Reidsville G7
Richland B7
Richmond Hill J8
Rincon J7
Ringgold A2
Riverdale J4
Rochelle E8
Rockmart A3
Rome A3
Roswell C3
Royston E3
Sandersville F6
Sandy Springs J2
Savannah J7
Scottdale K3
Skyland J2
Smyrna H2
Snellville D4
Social Circle D4
Soperton F7
Sparta F5
Springfield J7
St. Marys H10
St. Simons Island J9
Statenville E10
Statesboro H7
Statham D4
Stone Mountain C4
Summerville A3
Swainsboro G6
Sylvania H6
Sylvester D8
Talbotton B6
Tennille F6
Thomaston C6
Thomasville D10
Thomson G5
Tifton E9
Toccoa E2
Toco Hills J2
Trenton A2
Trion A2
Tucker K2
Tybee Island K8
Unadilla D7
Union City B4, H4
Union Point E4
Valdosta E10
Vidalia G7
Vienna D7
Villa Rica B4
Wadley G6
Warner Robins D6
Warrenton F5
Washington F4
Watkinsville E4
Waycross G9
Waynesboro G5
Westoak H1.
Winder D4
Woodbine H10
Wrens G5
Wrightsville F6
Zebulon C5

Other Features

Alapaha, *river* E9
Allatoona, *lake* B3
Altamaha, *river* G8
Andersonville Natl. Hist. Site C7
Appalachian, *mts.* D2
Blackshear, *lake* D8
Blue, *ridge* C2
Brasstown Bald, *mt.* D2
Burton, *lake* D2
Carters, *lake* B2
Chattahoochee, *river* A5, A9, G3
Chattahoochee River N.R.A. J1
Chattooga, *river* E2
Chatuge, *lake* D1
Chickamauga and Chattanooga Natl. Military Park A2
Coosa, *river* D2
Cumberland, *island* J10
Cumberland Island Natl. Seashore J10
Etowah, *river* B3
Flint, *river* C9
Fort Frederica Natl. Monument J9
Fort Pulaski Natl. Monument K7
Hartwell, *lake* F2
Jackson, *lake* D5
Jekyll, *island* J9
Jimmy Carter Natl. Hist. Site C7
J. Strom Thurmond, *lake* G4
Lookout Mt., *ridge* A2
Martin Luther King Jr. N.H.S. J3
Ocmulgee Natl. Monument D6
Ochlockonee, *river* C10
Ocmulge, *river* E7
Oconee, *lake* E5
Oconee, *river* F6
Ogeechee, *river* F5
Ohoopee, *river* G7
Okefenokee, *swamp* G10
Ossabaw, *island* J8
Russell, *lake* F3
St. Catherines, *island* J8
St. Marys, *river* H10
St. Simons, *island* J9
Sapelo, *island* J9
Savannah, *river* H5
Seminole, *lake* B10
Sidney Lanier, *lake* C3
Sinclair, *lake* E5
Stone Mt. State Park C4
Suwannee, *river* F10
Tallapoosa, *river* A4
Tybee, *island* K7
Walter F. George, *reservoir* A8
Wassaw, *island* J8
Weiss, *lake* A3
West Point, *lake* A6
Withlacoochee, *river* E10

Hawaii .... page 138

Cities and Towns

Ahuimanu J2
Aiea F1, J2
Captain Cook G6
Crestview E1, J2
Eleele C2
Ewa D2, J2
Ewa Beach E2, J3
Foster Village F1, J2
Haena C1, J5
Halawa B3
Halawa Heights F1, J2
Haleiwa H1
Hana D4
Hanamaulu D1
Hanapepe C2
Hauula J1
Heeia G1, K2
Hilo E7, J5
Holualoa G5
Honalo G5
Honokaa H4
Honolulu, *capital* C5, F2, J2
Iroquois Point E2, J2
Kaanapali B3
Kahana B3, J1
Kahului C3, D6
Kailua C5, K2
Kailua-Kona D7, F5
Kalaheo C2
Kalaoa F5
Kaneohe C5, G1, K2
Kapaa A5, D1
Kaunakakai A3
Keaau J5
Kealakekua G5
Kealia D1, G6
Kekaha B2
Kihei C4, D6
Kilauea C1
Koloa C2
Kualapuu A3
Kula C4
Lahaina B3, D6
Laie C5, J1
Lanai City B3
Lawai C2
Lihue A5, D2
Maili H2
Makaha H2
Makakilo City H2
Makawao C3
Maunawili H2
Mililani Town H2
Mokuleia H1
Mountain View J5
Nanakuli B5, H2
Pacific Palisades E1, J2
Pahala H6
Papaikou J5
Pearl City C5, E1, J2
Pepeekeo J5
Pohakupu K2
Pukalani C3, D6
Pupukea J1
Volcano J6
Waialua B3, H1
Waianae B5, H2
Waihee C3
Waikiki G3
Waikoloa Village G4
Wailua C3, D1
Wailuku C3, D6
Waimalu E1, J2
Waimanalo K2
Waimanalo Beach K2
Waimea C2, D6, H1
Waipahu E1, J2
Waipio H4
Waipio Acres J2
Whitmore Village J2

Other Features

Alenuihaha, *channel* D6
Alika Cone, *mt.* G6
Diamond Head, *point* G3
Ford, *island* E1
Haleakala, *mt.* C4
Haleakala Natl. Park C4, D6
Hamakua, *coast* H4
Hawaii, *island* E6, G5
Hawaii Volcanoes Natl. Park E7, H6
Hilo, *bay* J5
Hualalai, *mt.* G5
Kaala, *mt.* H1
Kaena, *point* B5, H1
Kahoolawe, *island* B4, D6
Kahului, *bay* C3
Kaikipauula, *mt.* H4
Kailua, *bay* K2
Kaiwi, *channel* C5, K3
Ka Lae (South Cape), *cape* D7, G7
Kalalua, *mt.* J6
Kalaupapa, *peninsula* B3
Kalaupapa Natl. Hist. Park B3
Kaloko-Honokohau Natl. Hist. Park F5
Kamakou, *mt.* B3
Kau, *desert* H6
Kauai, *channel* B5, D2
Kauai, *island* A5, B1
Kaulakahi, *channel* A5, B1
Kawaikini, *mt.* C1
Kiholo, *bay* G4
Kilauea, *crater* J6
Kilohana, *crater* C2
Kinau, *cape* C4
Kipuka Puaulu, *mt.* H6
Kohala, *coast* F5
Kohala, *mt.* G4
Kohala, *mts.* G4
Kona, *coast* F6
Konahuanui, *mt.* G2, K2
Koolau Range, *mts.* F1, J1
Kulani, *mt.* H5
Kumukahi, *cape* E7, K5
Lanai, *island* B3, C6
Lehua, *island* A1
Lua Makika, *mt.* B4
Maalaea, *bay* C4
Makaleha, *mts.* C1
Makapuu, *point* C5, K2
Mamala, *bay* E2, J3
Maui, *island* C3, D6
Mauna Iki, *mt.* H6
Mauna Kea, *mt.* E6, H5
Mauna Loa, *mt.* D7, H6
Maunalua, *bay* K3
Mokolii, *island* J2
Mokuauia, *island* J1
Mokulua, *island* K2
Moku Manu, *island* K2
Molokai, *island* A3, C5
Molokini, *island* C4
Na Pali, *coast* B1
Niihau, *island* A2, A5
Oahu, *island* B5, D2, K1
Pearl, *harbor* E2
Punchbowl, *crater* G2
Pu'uhonua O Honaunau N.H.P. G6
Puu Kainapuaa, *mt.* J1
Puu Kaua, *mt.* H2
Puukohola Heiau Natl. Hist. Site G4
Puu Kukui, *mt.* B3
Puu Kulua, *mt.* H5
Puu Loa, *mt.* H5
Puu O Keokeo, *mt.* G6
Sand, *island* F2
Sulphur Cone, *mt.* G6
U.S.S. Arizona Memorial E1
Upolu, *point* D6, G3
Waialeale, *mt.* A5, C1
Waianae Range, *mts.* H1
Wailuku, *river* H5
Waimea, *canyon* C2
West Maui, *mts.* B3

Idaho .... page 139

Cities and Towns

Aberdeen E7
American Falls E7
Ammon F6
Arco D6
Banks A5
Bellevue C6
Bennington F7
Blackfoot E6
Boise, *capital* A6
Bonners Ferry A1
Buhl C7
Burley D7
Caldwell A6
Cascade A5
Challis C5
Chubbuck E7
Coeur d'Alene A2
Council A5
Driggs F6
Dubois E5
Eagle A6
Emmett A6
Fairfield C6
Filer C7
Fish Haven F7
Fruitland A6
Fruitvale A5
Garden City A6
Garden Valley B5
Glenns Ferry B7
Gooding C7
Grangeville A4
Hailey C6
Hayden A2
Idaho City B6
Idaho Falls E6
Jerome C7
Kamiah A3
Kellogg A2
Ketchum C6
Kuna A6
Laclede A1
Lewiston A3
McCall A5
Malad City E7
May D5
Middleton A6
Montpelier F7
Moscow A3
Mountain Home B6
Murphy A6
Nampa A6
New Plymouth A6
Nezperce A3
Orofino A3
Osburn A2
Paris F7
Parma A6
Patterson D5
Pauline E7
Payette A5
Pinehurst A2
Pocatello E7
Post Falls A2
Preston F7
Priest River A1
Rathdrum A2
Rexburg F6
Rigby F6
Rupert D7
St. Anthony F6
St. Maries A2
Salmon D4
Sandpoint A1
Shelley E6
Shoshone C7
Soda Springs F7
Sugar City F6
Sun Valley C6
Thatcher F7
Twin Falls C7
Wallace B2
Weiser A5
Wendell C7

Other Features

American Falls, *reservoir* E7
Bear, *lake* F7
Bear, *river* F7
Big Lost, *river* D6
Bitterroot, *range* B3, D4
Blackfoot, *reservoir* F7
Blackfoot, *river* F6
Bruneau, *river* B7
Cache, *mt.* D7
Caribou, *range* F6
Cascade, *reservoir* A5
Castle, *mt.* C5
Clearwater, *mts.* B3
Clearwater, *river* B4
Craters of the Moon N.M. D6
Dworshak, *reservoir* A3
Grays, *lake* F6
Hagerman Fossil Beds N.M. C7
Hells, *canyon* A5
Hells Canyon Natl. Recreation Area A4
Kootenai, *river* A1
Lemhi, *river* D5
Lochsa, *river* B3
Middle Fork Salmon, *river* B5
Nez Perce N.H.P. A3, B3
North Fork Clearwater, *river* B3
Owyhee, *mts.* A6
Owyhee, *river* A6
Palisades, *reservoir* F6
Payette, *lake* A5
Payette, *river* A5
Pend Oreille, *lake* A1
Pend Oreille, *river* A1
Priest, *lake* A1
Ryan, *mt.* C6
St. Joe, *river* A2
Salmon, *river* B4
Salmon River, *mts.* C5
Sawtooth, *range* B5
Sawtooth Natl. Recreation Area C5
Scott, *mt.* E5
Snake, *river* A4
South Fork Selway, *river* B3
Teton, *river* F6
Weiser, *river* A5
Yellowstone Natl. Park F5

Illinois .... page 140

Cities and Towns

Abingdon C3
Addison B5
Albion E5
Aledo C2
Alsip B6
Altamont E4
Alton C5
Amboy D2
Anna D6
Antioch A4, E1
Arcola E4
Arlington Heights A5
Arthur E4
Ashland C4
Athens D4
Atlanta D3
Atwood E4
Auburn D4
Aurora E2
Barrington A5
Barry B4
Bartlett A5
Bartonville D3
Batavia E2
Beach Park B4
Beardstown C3
Beecher F2
Belleville D5
Belvidere E1
Bement E4
Benld D4
Benton E6
Berwyn B6
Bethany E4
Bloomington D3
Blue Island B6
Bolingbrook A6, E2
Bourbonnais F2
Braidwood E2
Breese D5
Bridgeport F5
Brighton C4
Brookfield B6
Buffalo Grove B5
Bunker Hill D4
Burbank B6
Bushnell C3
Byron D1
Cahokia C5
Cairo D6
Calumet City C6, F2
Cambridge C2
Canton C3
Capron E1
Carbondale D6
Carlinville D4
Carlyle D5
Carmi E5
Carol Stream A5
Carpentersville E1
Carrier Mills E6
Carrollton C4
Carterville D6
Carthage B3
Cary E1
Casey F4
Catlin F3
Centralia D5
Cerro Gordo E4
Champaign E3
Channahon E2
Charleston E4
Chatham D4
Chenoa E3
Chester D6
Chicago B5, F2
Chicago Heights B6
Chillicothe D3
Christopher D6
Cicero B6, F2
Clifton F3
Clinton E3
Coal City E2
Colchester C3
Collinsville D5
Columbia C5
Crest Hill A6
Crete F2
Crystal Lake E1
Cuba C3
Danville F3
Decatur E4
Deerfield B5
De Kalb E2
Delavan D3
De Soto D6
Des Plaines B5
Dixon D2
Dolton B6
Downers Grove B6
Du Quoin D5
Dwight E2
Earlville E2
East Dubuque C1
East Moline C2
East Peoria D3
East St. Louis C5
Edwardsville D5
Effingham E4
Elburn E2
Eldorado E6
Elgin E1
Elizabethtown E6
Elk Grove Village B5
Elmhurst B5
Elmwood D3
Elmwood Park B5
Erie C2
Eureka D3
Evanston B5, F1
Evergreen Park B6
Fairbury E3
Fairfield E5
Farmer City E3
Farmington C3
Fisher E3
Flora E5
Forreston D1
Forsyth E4
Fox Lake A4, E1
Fox Lake Hills A4
Fox River Grove A5
Frankfort B6, F2
Freeburg D5
Freeport D1
Fulton C2
Gages Lake B4
Galena C1
Galesburg C3
Galva C2
Geneseo C2
Geneva E2
Genoa E1
Georgetown F4
Gibson City E3
Gillespie D4
Gilman F3
Girard D4
Glen Ellyn A5
Glencoe B5
Glendale Heights A5
Glenview B5
Glenwood B6
Godfrey C5
Golconda E6
Granite City C5
Granville D2
Grayslake A4
Grayville E5
Green Oaks B4
Greenup E4
Greenville D5
Gridley E3
Gurnee B4
Hainesville A4
Hamilton B3
Hampshire E1
Hanover Park A5
Hardin C4
Harrisburg E6
Harristown D4
Harvard E1
Harvey B6
Havana C3
Hennepin D2
Henry D2
Herrin D6
Herscher E2
Heyworth E3
Hickory Hills B6
Highland D5
Highland Park B5, F1
Highwood B5
Hillsboro D4
Hinckley E2
Hinsdale B6
Hoffman Estates A5
Homer F3
Homewood B6
Hoopeston F3
Huntley E1
Island Lake A5
Jacksonville C4
Jerseyville C4
Johnston City E6
Joliet A6, E2
Jonesboro D6
Justice B6
Kankakee F2
Kaskaskia D6
Kewanee D2
Kincaid D4
Knoxville C3
Lacon D2
La Grange B6
La Harpe C3
Lake Bluff B5
Lake Forest B5
Lake Zurich A5
Lanark D1
La Salle D2
Lansing B6
Lawrenceville F5
Lemont B6
Lena D1
Le Roy E3
Lewistown C3
Lexington E3
Libertyville B5
Lilymoor A4
Lincoln D3
Lincolnwood B5
Lindenhurst A4
Lisle A6
Litchfield D4
Lockport A6
Lombard B6
Louisville E5
Loves Park D1
Lynwood C6
McHenry E1
Machesney Park D1
Mackinaw D3
McLeansboro E5
Macomb C3
Macon E4
Mahomet E3
Manhattan F2
Manito D3
Manteno F2
Marengo E1
Marion E6
Marissa D5
Marley B6
Maroa E3
Marseilles E2
Marshall F4
Mascoutah D5
Mason City D3
Matteson B6
Mattoon E4
Maywood B5
Melrose Park B5
Mendota D2
Metamora D3
Metropolis E6
Milan C2
Milford F3
Minonk D3
Minooka E2
Mokena B6
Moline C2
Momence F2
Monmouth C3
Monticello E3
Morris E2
Morrison D2
Morton D3
Morton Grove B5
Mound City D6
Mounds D6
Mount Carmel F5
Mount Carroll D1
Mount Morris D1
Mount Olive D4
Mount Prospect B5
Mount Pulaski D3
Mount Sterling C4
Mount Vernon E5
Mount Zion E4
Moweaqua D4
Mundelein A5
Murphysboro D6
Naperville A6
Nashville D5
Neoga E4
New Athens D5
New Baden D5
New Lenox B6
Newton E5
Niles B5
Nokomis D4
Normal E3
Norridge B5
Northbrook B5
North Chicago B4, F1
Northfield B5
Oak Brook B6
Oak Forest B6
Oak Lawn B6, F2
Oak Park B5, F2
Oakwood F3
Oblong F4
O'Fallon D5
Oglesby D2
Okawville D5
Old Mill Creek B4
Olney E5
Onarga F3
Oquawka C3
Oregon D1
Orion C2
Orland Hills B6
Orland Park B6
Ottawa E2
Palatine A5
Palestine F4
Palos Heights B6
Palos Hills B6
Pana D4
Paris F4
Park City B4
Park Forest F2
Park Ridge B5
Pawnee D4

Key

Paxton E3
Pecatonica D1
Pekin D3
Peoria D3
Peoria Heights D3
Peotone F2
Peru D2
Petersburg D4
Pinckneyville D5
Pittsfield C4
Plainfield A6, E2
Plano E2
Polo D2
Pontiac E3
Princeton D2
Princeville D3
Prophetstown D2
Quincy B4
Rantoul E3
Red Bud D5
Richton Park B6
Riverdale B6
Riverton D4
Riverwoods B5
Roanoke D3
Robinson F4
Rochelle D2
Rochester D4
Rock Falls D2
Rock Island C2
Rockford D1
Rockton D1
Rome D3
Romeoville A6
Roodhouse C4
Roscoe D1
Rosiclare E6
Rossville F3
Round Lake Beach A4
Rushville C3
Russell B4
St. David C3
St. Elmo E4
St. Joseph E3
St. Libory D5
Salem E5
Sandoval D5
Sandwich E2
Sauk Village C6
Savanna C1
Savoy E3
Schaumburg A5
Schiller Park B5
Seneca E2
Sesser D5
Shawneetown E6
Shelbyville E4
Sheridan D4
Sherman D4
Shorewood A6, E2
Skokie B5
Somonauk E2
South Beloit D1
South Elgin E2
South Holland B6
South Jacksonville C4
Sparta D5
Spring Valley D2
Springfield, capital D4
Staunton D4
Steeleville D5
Sterling D2
Stockland F3
Stockton C1
Streamwood A5
Streator E2
Sullivan E4
Summit B6
Sycamore E2
Taylorville D4
Teutopolis E4
Tilton F3
Tinley Park B6, F2
Toledo E4
Tolono E4
Toluca D3
Toulon D2
Tower Lakes A5
Tremont D3
Trenton D5
Tuscola E4
Urbana E3
Vandalia D5
Vernon Hills B5
Vienna E6
Villa Grove E4
Villa Park B5
Virden D4
Virginia C4
Volo A4
Wadsworth B4
Walnut D2
Wapella E3
Warren D1
Warrensburg D4
Warrenville A6
Warsaw B3
Washington D3
Waterloo C5
Watseka F3
Wauconda A5
Waukegan B4, F1
Waverly D4
Westchester B6
West Chicago A5
West Frankfort E6
Westville F3
Wheaton A6, E2
Wheeling B5, F1
White Hall C4
Wilmette B5
Wilmington E2
Winchester C4
Winnebago D1
Winnetka B5
Winthrop Harbor B4
Woodridge A6
Wood River C5
Woodstock E1
Wyoming D2
Yorkville E2
Zeigler D6
Zion B4, F1

Other Features

Carlyle, lake D5
Chautauqua, lake C3
Chicago, river B5
Clinton, lake D4
Crab Orchard, lake D6
Des Plaines, river A6, B4

Key

Du Page, river A6
Fox, lake A4
Fox, river E2
Illinois, river D3
Ind. Dunes Natl. Lakeshore C6
Kankakee, river F2
Kaskaskia, river D4
Lincoln Home Natl. Hist. Site D4
Marie, lake A4
Michigan, lake F1
O'Hare, airport B5
Ohio, river D6
Orland, lake B6
Rend, lake D5
Rock, river D2
Sangamon, river C3
Shelbyville, lake E4
Spoon, river C3
Wabash, river E6

Indiana ....page 141

Cities and Towns

Albany F4
Albion F2
Alexandria E4
Anderson E4
Angola G1
Arcadia D4
Argos D2
Atlanta D4
Attica B4
Auburn F2
Aurora G6
Austin E7
Avilla F2
Bargersville D5
Batesville F6
Bedford D7
Berne G2
Bicknell B7
Bloomfield C6
Bloomington C6
Bluffton F3
Boonville B8
Bourbon D2
Brazil B5
Bremen D2
Brookston C3
Brookville F6
Brownsburg D5
Brownstown D7
Butler G2
Cambridge City F5
Cannelton C9
Carmel D5
Chandler B8
Charlestown E8
Chesterton B1
Churubusco F2
Cicero D4
Clayton C5
Clinton B5
Cloverdale C5
Columbia City E2
Columbus E6
Connersville F5
Corydon D8
Covington B4
Crawfordsville C4
Crothersville E7
Crown Point B2
Culver D2
Dale C8
Daleville E4
Danville C5
Darmstadt A8
Decatur G3
Delphi C3
Demotte B2
Dunlap E1
East Chicago B1
Eaton F4
Edinburgh D5
Elkhart E1
Ellettsville C6
Elwood E4
English D8
Evansville A9
Fairmount E4
Farmland F4
Ferdinand C8
Fishers D5
Flora C3
Fort Branch A8
Fort Wayne F2
Fowler B3
Frankfort C4
Franklin D6
Fremont G1
French Lick C7
Galveston D3
Garrett F2
Gary B1
Gas City E4
Geneva G3
Georgetown E8
Goshen E1
Greencastle C5
Greenfield E5
Greensburg F6
Greentown E4
Greenwood D5
Hagerstown F5
Hammond A1
Hanover F7
Hartford City F4
Hebron B2
Highland B1
Hope E6
Huntertown F2
Huntingburg C8
Huntington F3
Indianapolis, capital D5
Jasonville B6
Jasper C8
Jeffersonville E8
Kendallville F1
Kentland B3
Kingsford Heights C2
Knox C2
Kokomo D4
Kouts B2
Lafayette C4
Lagrange F1
Lakeville D1
La Porte C1
Lawrence D5
Lawrenceburg G6
Lebanon D4

Key

Liberty G5
Ligonier E2
Lincoln City B8
Linton B6
Logansport D3
Loogootee C7
Lowell B2
Madison F7
Marion E3
Martinsville D6
Merrillville B2
Michigan City C1
Middlebury E1
Milan F6
Milford E2
Mishawaka D1
Mitchell D7
Monon C3
Monticello C3
Montpelier F3
Mooresville D5
Mount Vernon A9
Mulberry C4
Muncie F4
Nappanee D2
Nashville D6
New Albany E8
Newburgh B9
New Carlisle C1
New Castle F5
New Haven F2
Newport B5
New Whiteland D5
Noblesville D4
North Judson C2
North Liberty D1
North Manchester E2
North Terre Haute B5
North Vernon E6
Notre Dame D1
Oakland City B8
Odon C7
Orleans D7
Osgood F6
Ossian F3
Otterbein B3
Oxford B3
Paoli D7
Pendleton E4
Peru D3
Petersburg B8
Plainfield D5
Plymouth D2
Portland G4
Princeton A8
Redkey F4
Rensselaer B3
Richmond G5
Rising Sun G7
Rochester D2
Rockport B9
Rockville B5
Rushville F5
Salem D7
Schererville B2
Scottsburg E7
Sellersburg E8
Seymour E7
Shadeland C4
Shelbyville E5
Sheridan D4
Shoals C7
South Bend D1
South Whitley E2
Speedway D5
Spencer C6
Sullivan B6
Syracuse E2
Tell City C9
Terre Haute B6
Thorntown C4
Tippecanoe D2
Tipton D4
Union City G4
Upland F4
Valparaiso B2
Veedersburg B4
Vernon E7
Versailles F6
Vevay F7
Vincennes A7
Wabash E3
Wakarusa E1
Walkerton D2
Warsaw E2
Washington B7
Waterloo F2
Westfield D4
West Lafayette C4
Westport E6
Westville C1
Williamsport B4
Winamac C2
Winchester G4
Winona Lake E2
Woodburn G2
Worthington C6
Yorktown F4
Zionsville D5

Other Features

Big Blue, river E5
Brookville, lake F5
Eel, river E3
George Rogers Clark N.H.P. A7
Indiana Dunes Natl. Lakeshore B1
Kankakee, river C2
Lemon, lake D6
Lincoln Boyhood Natl. Memorial C8
Maumee, river B1
Michigan, lake B1
Mississinewa, lake E3
Monroe, lake D6
Ohio, river A9
Patoka, river B8
St. Joseph, river G2
Salamoni, lake E3
Tippecanoe, river A8
Wabash, river A8
Wawasee, lake E2
White, river C6
Whitewater, river F6

Iowa ....page 142

Cities and Towns

Ackley H2
Adel F4
Akron A2
Albia J5

Key

Algona F1
Allison J2
Alta D2
Altoona H4
Ames G3
Anamosa M3
Ankeny G4
Asbury N3
Atlantic D5
Audubon E4
Avoca D5
Batavia K5
Bayard E4
Bedford E6
Belle Plaine K4
Bellevue P3
Belmond G2
Bettendorf P4
Bloomfield K6
Boone G3
Brighton L5
Britt G1
Brooklyn K4
Burlington M6
Camanche N4
Carlisle G5
Carroll E4
Carter Lake C5
Cascade N3
Cedar Falls K3
Cedar Rapids L4
Center Point L4
Centerville J6
Chariton H5
Charles City J1
Cherokee C2
Clarinda D6
Clarion G2
Clarksville J2
Clear Lake H1
Clinton P4
Colfax H4
Columbus Junction M5
Coon Rapids E4
Coralville L4
Corning E6
Corydon H6
Council Bluffs C5
Cresco K1
Creston F5
Dakota City F2
Dallas Center G4
Davenport N4
Decorah L1
Denison D4
Denver K2
Des Moines, capital G4
De Witt N4
Dubuque N2
Dunlap D4
Durant N4
Dyersville M3
Eagle Grove G2
Eldora H3
Eldridge N4
Elgin L2
Elkader M2
Emmetsburg E1
Epworth N3
Estherville E1
Evansdale K3
Fairfield L6
Farley M3
Fayette L2
Forest City G1
Fort Dodge F2
Fort Madison M6
Garner G1
Gilmore City F2
Glenwood C5
Greenfield F5
Grimes G4
Grinnell J4
Grundy Center J3
Guthrie Center E4
Guttenberg M2
Hampton H2
Harlan D4
Hartley D1
Hawarden B1
Hiawatha L3
Holstein C3
Hudson K3
Hull B1
Humboldt F2
Huxley G4
Ida Grove D3
Independence L3
Indianola G5
Iowa City L4
Iowa Falls H2
Jefferson F4
Jesup K3
Johnston G4
Kalona L5
Keokuk M7
Keosauqua L6
Knoxville H5
Lake City E3
Lake Mills G1
Lake View D3
Lamoni G6
La Porte City K3
Laurens E2
Le Claire P4
Le Mars B2
Lenox E6
Leon G5
Logan C4
Lovilia J5
Madrid G4
Manchester M3
Manly H1
Manning E4
Manson E2
Mapleton D3
Maquoketa N3
Marengo K4
Marion L4
Marshalltown J3
Mason City H1
Mediapolis M5
Melcher-Dallas H5
Milford D1
Missouri Valley C4
Monona M1
Monroe H4
Montezuma J4
Monticello M3
Mount Ayr F6
Mount Pleasant L6

Key

Mount Vernon M4
Moville B3
Muscatine M5
Nashua J2
Nevada H3
New Hampton K1
New London M6
Newton H4
Nora Springs J1
North Liberty L4
Northwood H1
Norwalk G5
Oakland D5
Oelwein L2
Ogden F3
Onawa B3
Orange City B1
Osage J1
Osceola G5
Oskaloosa J5
Ottumwa K5
Park View N4
Parkersburg J2
Pella J5
Perry F4
Pleasantville H5
Pocahontas E2
Polk City G4
Postville L1
Prairie City H4
Primghar C1
Red Oak D5
Reinbeck J3
Remsen C2
Rock Rapids B1
Rock Valley B1
Rockwell City E3
Sac City E3
Sanborn C1
Sergeant Bluff B3
Sheldon C1
Shell Rock J2
Shenandoah D6
Sibley C1
Sidney C6
Sigourney K5
Sioux Center B1
Sioux City B2
Spencer D1
Spirit Lake D1
Storm Lake D2
Story City G3
Strawberry Point L2
Stuart F4
Sumner K2
Tama J4
Tipton M4
Toledo J4
Traer K3
Urbandale E4
Villisca E6
Vinton K3
Walcott N4
Wapello M5
Washington L5
Waterloo K3
Waukee G4
Waukon M1
Waverly K2
Webster City G2
West Branch M4
West Burlington M6
West Des Moines G4
West Liberty M4
West Union L2
Williamsburg K4
Wilton M4
Windsor Heights G4
Winterset F5
Woodbine C4

Other Features

Big Sioux, river A1
Boone, river G2
Cedar, river K3
Chariton, river H6
Clear, lake H1
Coralville, lake L4
Des Moines, river F3
Effigy Mounds Natl. Monument M1
Floyd, river C2
Fox, river K6
Iowa, river D2
Little Sioux, river D2
Maple, river C3
Mississippi, river M2
Missouri, river B4
Rathbun, lake J6
Red Rock, lake J5
Saylorville, reservoir G4
Skunk, river L5
Spirit, lake D1
Storm, lake D2
Turkey, river L2
Wapsipinicon, river K2
West Nishnabota, river K2

Kansas ....page 143

Cities and Towns

Abilene E3
Adrian F3
Alma F3
Andover E4
Anthony D4
Arkansas City E4
Arma H4
Ashland C4
Atchison G2
Atwood A2
Augusta E4
Baldwin City G3
Baxter Springs H4
Belle Plaine E4
Belleville E2
Beloit D2
Bonner Springs H3
Buhler D3
Burlington G3
Butler G3
Caldwell E4
Caney G4
Carbondale G3
Chanute G4
Chapman E3
Cheney D4
Cherryvale G4
Chetopa G4
Cimarron B4
Clay Center E2

Key

Clearwater E4
Clifton E2
Coffeyville G4
Colby A2
Coldwater C4
Columbus H4
Concordia E2
Conway Springs E4
Coolidge A3
Cottonwood Falls F3
Council Grove F3
Derby E4
De Soto H3
Dighton B3
Dodge City B4
Douglass E4
El Dorado E4
Elkhart A4
Ellinwood D3
Ellis C3
Ellsworth D3
Emporia F3
Erie G4
Eudora H3
Eureka F3
Florence E3
Fort Scott H4
Fredonia G4
Frontenac H4
Galena H4
Garden City B4
Gardner H3
Garnett G3
Girard H4
Goddard E4
Goodland A2
Gove B3
Great Bend C3
Greensburg C4
Halstead D4
Harper D4
Hays C3
Haysville E4
Herington E3
Hesston E3
Hiawatha G2
Hill City C2
Hillsboro E3
Hoisington D3
Holcomb B4
Holton G2
Horton G2
Howard F4
Hoxie B2
Hugoton A4
Humboldt G4
Hutchinson D3
Independence G4
Iola G4
Iuka D4
Jetmore C3
Johnson A4
Junction City F2
Kansas City H2
Kansas City H2
Kingman D4
Kinsley C3
La Crosse C3
Lakin A4
Lansing H2
Larned C3
Lawrence G3
Leavenworth H2
Leoti A3
Liberal B4
Lincoln D2
Lindsborg E3
Lorraine D3
Louisburg H3
Lyndon G3
Lyons D3
McPherson E3
Maize E4
Manhattan F2
Mankato D2
Marion E3
Marysville F2
Meade B4
Medicine Lodge D4
Minneapolis E2
Mound City H3
Moundridge E3
Mulvane E4
Neodesha G4
Ness City C3
Newton E3
North Newton E3
Norton C2
Oakley B2
Oberlin B2
Ogden F2
Olathe H3
Osage City G3
Osawatomie H3
Osborne D2
Oskaloosa G2
Oswego G4
Ottawa G3
Overland Park H3
Paola H3
Park B2
Park City E4
Parsons G4
Peabody E3
Phillipsburg C2
Pittsburg H4
Plainville C2
Pratt D4
Rich Hill G3
Rose Hill D4
Rose Hill E4
Russell D3
Sabetha G2
St. Francis A2
St. John D3
St. Marys F2
Salina E3
Scott City B3
Sedan F4
Sedgwick E3
Seneca F2
Sharon Springs A3
Silver Lake F2
Smith Center D2
South Hutchinson D3
Spring Hill H3
Stafford D4
Sterling D3
Stockton C2
Sublette A4
Syracuse A4

	Key
Tecumseh	G2
Tonganoxie	G2
Topeka, capital	G2
Towanda	F4
Tribune	A3
Troy	G2
Ulysses	A4
Valley Center	E4
Valley Falls	G2
Wakeeney	C2
Wamego	F2
Washington	E2
Waterville	F2
Wellington	E4
Wellsville	G3
Westmoreland	F2
Wichita	E4
Winfield	F4
Yates Center	G4

Other Features

	Key
Arkansas, river	A4, D3
Big Blue, river	F2
Cedar Bluff, reservoir	C3
Cheney, reservoir	E4
Chikaskia, river	D4
Cimarron, river	A4
Clinton, lake	G3
Fall, river	F4
Flint Hills	F4
Fort Larned Natl. Hist. Site	C3
Fort Scott Natl. Hist. Site	H4
Kanapolis, lake	E3
Kansas, river	F2
Kirwin, reservoir	C2
Little Blue, river	E1
Marion, river	E3
Medicine Lodge, river	D4
Melvern, lake	G3
Milford, lake	F2
Missouri, river	G2
Neosho, river	G3
North Fork Solomon, river	B2
Republican, river	D1
Saline, river	C2
Smoky Hill, river	B3
Solomon, river	D2
South Fork Republican, river	A2
Sunflower, mt.	A2
Tuttle Creek, lake	F2
Verdigris, river	F3
Waconda, lake	D2
Wilson, lake	D3

Kentucky .... page 144

Cities and Towns

	Key
Aberdeen	F2
Albany	D4
Alexandria	E2
Allensville	B4
Ashland	G2
Auburn	C4
Augusta	E2
Barbourville	F4
Bardstown	D3
Bardwell	B2
Beattyville	F3
Beaver Dam	C3
Bedford	D2
Benton	C2
Berea	E2
Berry	E2
Booneville	F3
Bowling Green	C4
Brandenburg	D2
Brooks	D2
Brooksville	E2
Brownsville	C3
Burkesville	D4
Burlington	E1
Butler	E2
Cadiz	B4, C2
Calhoun	B3
Calvert City	C2
Campbellsville	D3
Campton	F3
Carlisle	E2
Carrollton	D2
Carrsville	C1
Catlettsburg	D3
Cave City	D3
Central City	B3
Clay City	F3
Clinton	D3
Columbia	D3
Concord	F2
Corbin	E4
Corinth	E1
Covington	E1
Crestwood	D2
Cumberland	G4
Cynthiana	E2
Danville	E3
Dawson Springs	B3, C1
Dixon	B3, C1
Dry Ridge	E2
Earlington	B3
Eddyville	A3, C2
Edmonton	D3
Ekron	C3
Elizabethtown	D3
Elkton	B4
Eminence	D2
Fairfield	D3
Falmouth	E2
Flatwoods	G2
Flemingsburg	F2
Florence	E2
Foster	E2
Frankfort, capital	E2
Franklin	C4
Frenchburg	F3
Fulton	B2
Georgetown	E2
Glasgow	D3
Gratz	E2
Grayson	G2
Greensburg	D3
Greenup	G2
Guthrie	B4
Hardinsburg	C3
Harlan	F4
Harrodsburg	E3
Hartford	C3
Hawesville	C3
Hazard	F3
Henderson	B3
Hickman	B2
Hindman	G3
Hiseville	D3
Hobson	D3
Hodgenville	D3
Hopkinsville	B4
Horse Cave	D3
Hyden	F3
Independence	E2
Inez	G3
Irvine	F3
Jackson	F3
Jamestown	D4
Jeffersontown	D2
Jeffersonville	F3
Jenkins	G3
Junction City	E3
La Fayette	B4, C2
La Grange	D2
Lancaster	E3
Lawrenceburg	E2
Leatherwood	F3
Lebanon	D3
Leitchfield	C3
Lewisport	C2
Lexington	E2
Liberty	E3
Livermore	B3
Livingston	E3
London	E3
Louisa	G2
Louisville	D2
McKee	F3
Mackville	D3
Madisonville	B3
Manchester	F3
Marion	A3, C1
Mayfield	B2
Maysville	F2
Middlesboro	F4
Middletown	D2
Monterey	E2
Monticello	E4
Morehead	F2
Morganfield	B3, C1
Morgantown	C3
Mt. Olivet	F2
Mt. Sterling	F2
Mt. Vernon	E3
Mt. Washington	D2
Muldraugh	C3
Munfordville	D3
Murray	C2
Nebo	B3
New Castle	D2
Nicholasville	E3
Oak Grove	B4
Okolona	D2
Olive Hill	F2
Owensboro	B3
Owenton	E2
Owingsville	F2
Paducah	C2
Paris	E2
Patesville	C3
Phelps	G3
Pikeville	G3
Pine Knot	E4
Pineville	F4
Pleasure Ridge Park	D2
Prestonsburg	G3
Princeton	B3, C2
Providence	B3, C1
Raceland	G2
Radcliff	D3
Richmond	E3
Rochester	C3
Russell Springs	D3
Russellville	C4
St. Matthews	D2
Salyersville	F3
Sandy Hook	F2
Scottsville	C4
Sebree	B3
Shelbyville	D2
Shepherdsville	D3
Slaughters	B3
Smithland	C1
Somerset	E3
South Shore	G2
Springfield	D3
Stanford	E3
Stanton	F3
Sturgis	A3, C1
Taylorsville	D2
Tompkinsville	D4
Valley Station	D2
Vanceburg	F2
Versailles	E2
Vicco	F3
Vine Grove	D3
Walton	E2
Warsaw	E2
West Liberty	F3
Wheelwright	G3
Whitesburg	G3
Whitley City	E4
Wickliffe	B2
Williamsburg	E4
Williamstown	E2
Wilmore	E3
Winchester	E3
Woodbury	C3
Zion	B3

Other Features

	Key
Barkley, lake	B4, C2
Barren, river	C4
Barren River, lake	C4
Big Sandy, river	G2
Big South Fork Natl. River and Rec. Area	E4
Buckhorn, lake	F3
Cave Run, lake	F2
Cumberland, lake	E4
Cumberland, river	E4
Cumberland Gap Natl. Hist. Park	F4
Dale Hollow, lake	E4
Fish Trap, lake	G3
Green, river	B3, D3
Green River, lake	D3
Kentucky, lake	C2
Kentucky, river	D2, E3
Licking, river	F2
Lincoln Birthplace Natl. Hist. Site	D3
Mammoth Cave Natl. Park	C3
Nolin River, lake	C3
Ohio, river	F2
Rough, river	C3
Rough River, lake	C2
Tennessee, river	C2
Tug Fork, river	G3

Louisiana .... page 145

Cities and Towns

	Key
Abbeville	E7
Abita Springs	J6
Alexandria	E4
Ama	Inset
Amelia	G7
Amite	J5
Arabi	Inset
Arcadia	D1
Arnaudville	F6
Avondale	Inset
Baker	G5
Baldwin	F7
Ball	E4
Basile	D6
Bastrop	F1
Baton Rouge, captial	G6
Bayou Cane	H7
Bayou Vista	G7
Belle Chasse	Inset
Bentley	E3
Bernice	D1
Bertrandville	Inset
Bogalusa	K5
Bossier City	B1
Boyce	D4
Braithwaite	Inset
Breaux Bridge	F6
Bridge City	Inset
Broussard	F6
Bunkie	E5
Buras	K8
Caernarvon	C7
Cameron	C7
Carencro	E6
Carville	G6
Cecilia	F6
Chalmette	Inset, K7
Charenton	F7
Chauvin	H8
Church Point	E6
Clinton	G5
Colfax	D3
Columbia	E2
Cottonport	E5
Coushatta	C2
Covington	J6
Crowley	E6
Crown Point	Inset
Cullen	C1
Cut Off	J7
Dalcour	Inset
Delcambre	F7
Delhi	G2
Denham Springs	H5
De Quincy	C6
De Ridder	C5
Des Allemands	J7
Destrehan	Inset
Donaldsonville	H6
Edgard	H6
Elton	D6
English Turn	Inset
Erath	E7
Estelle	Inset
Eunice	E6
Farmerville	E1
Ferriday	F3
Franklin	F7
Franklinton	J5
Frenier	Inset
Galliano	J8
Garyville	H6
Glenmora	D5
Golden Meadow	J8
Gonzales	H6
Grambling	D1
Grand Isle	K8
Gray	H7
Greensburg	H5
Greenwood	B2
Gretna	Inset, J7
Gueydan	E6
Hackberry	C6
Hahnville	Inset, J7
Hammond	J5
Harahan	Inset
Harrisonburg	E2
Harvey	Inset
Haughton	C1
Haynesville	C1
Henderson	F6
Homer	C1
Houma	H7
Independence	J5
Inniswold	Inset
Iota	D6
Iowa	C6
Jackson	G5
Jeanerette	F7
Jean Lafitte	J7
Jefferson	Inset
Jena	E3
Jennings	D6
Jesuit Bend	Inset
Jonesboro	D2
Jonesville	E3
Kaplan	E6
Kenilworth	Inset
Kenner	Inset, J7
Kentwood	J5
Killona	Inset
Kinder	D6
Krotz Springs	F5
Labadieville	H7
Lacombe	K6
Lafayette	E6
Lafitte	J7
Lake Arthur	D6
Lake Charles	C6
Lake Providence	G1
Laplace	Inset, J6
Larose	J7
Lecompte	E4
Leesville	C4
Livingston	H5
Lockport	H7
Logansport	B3
Luling	Inset
Mamou	E5
Mandeville	J6
Mansfield	B3
Mansura	E5
Many	C3
Marion	E1
Marksville	E4
Marrero	Inset, J7
Melder	D4
Melville	F5
Meraux	Inset
Metairie	Inset, J7
Mimosa Park	Inset
Minden	C1
Monroe	E1
Montegut	H8
Montz	Inset
Morgan City	G7
Moss Bluff	C6
Napoleonville	G7
Natalbany	J5
Natchitoches	C3
Newellton	G2
New Iberia	F6
New Llano	C4
New Orleans	Inset, J7
New Roads	G5
New Sarpy	Inset
Norco	Inset
Oak Grove	G1
Oakdale	D5
Oakville	Inset
Oberlin	D5
Oil City	B1
Olla	E3
Opelousas	E5
Paincourtville	G6
Paradis	Inset
Patterson	G7
Plaquemine	G6
Point a la Hache	K7
Ponchatoula	J6
Port Allen	G5
Port Barre	F5
Port Sulphur	K8
Poydras	Inset
Raceland	H7
Rayne	E6
Rayville	F2
Reserve	H6
Richwood	E2
Ringgold	C2
River Ridge	Inset
Ruston	D1
St. Bernard	Inset
St. Francisville	G5
St. Joseph	G3
St. Martinville	F6
St. Rose	Inset
Scarsdale	Inset
Schriever	H7
Scott	E6
Shreveport	B2
Simmesport	F5
Slidell	K6
Springhill	C1
Stonewall	B2
Sulphur	C6
Sunset	E6
Swartz	E2
Taft	Inset
Tallulah	G2
Terrytown	Inset
Thibodaux	H7
Toca	Inset
Vidalia	G3
Ville Platte	E5
Vinton	C6
Violet	Inset, K7
Vivian	B1
Waggaman	Inset
Walker	H6
Washington	E5
Welsh	D6
Westlake	C6
West Monroe	E1
Westwego	Inset, J7
White Castle	G6
Winnfield	D3
Winnsboro	F2
Zachary	G5
Zwolle	B3

Other Features

	Key
Atchafalaya, bay	G8
Atchafalaya, river	F5
Barataria, bay	K8
Bistineau, lake	C2
Black, river	F4
Borgne, lake	Inset, K6
Breton, islands	L8
Caddo, lake	A1
Caillou, bay	G8
Calcasieu, lake	C7
Caney, lake	E2
Catahoula, lake	E3
Chandeleur, islands	M7
Driskill, mt.	C2
Grand, lake	E7
Jean Lafitte N.H.P. and Preserve	J7
Little, river	F7
Marsh, island	F7
Mississippi, river	E2
Ouachita, river	E2
Pearl, river	K5
Pontchartrain, lake	Inset, J6
Red, river	C3
Sabine, lake	B7
Sabine, river	B4
Terrebonne, bay	H8
Timbalier, bay	J8
Toledo Bend, reservoir	B4
Vermilion, bay	F7
West Cote Blanche, bay	F7
White, lake	E7

Maine .... page 146

Cities and Towns

	Key
Alfred	B5
Amherst	D4
Athens	C4
Auburn	B4
Augusta, capital	C4
Bangor	D4
Bar Harbor	D4
Bass Harbor	D4
Bath	C4
Belfast	C4
Berwick	B5
Biddeford	B5
Boothbay Harbor	C4
Brewer	D4
Bridgton	B4
Brunswick	C4
Bucksport	D4
Calais	E3
Camden	C4
Cape Elizabeth	B5
Caribou	D2
Chisholm	B4
Clinton	C4
Conway	A4
Damariscotta	C4
Dexter	C3
Dixfield	B4
Dover-Foxcroft	C3
East Millinocket	D3
Eastport	F4
Ellsworth	D4
Fairfield	C4
Falmouth	B5
Farmington	B4
Fort Fairfield	E2
Fort Kent	D1
Frankfort	D4
Franklin	D4
Freeport	B5
Frenchboro	D4
Fryeburg	B4
Gardiner	C4
Greene	B4
Hallowell	C4
Hampden	D4
Houlton	E2
Howland	D3
Kennebunk	B5
Kittery	B5
Lewiston	B4
Lincoln	D3
Lisbon Falls	B4
Livermore Falls	B4
Machias	E4
Madawaska	D1
Madison	C4
Mars Hill	E2
Mechanic Falls	B4
Mexico	B4
Milbridge	E4
Milford	D4
Millinocket	D3
Milo	D3
Norridgewock	C4
North Amity	E3
North Berwick	B5
North Conway	A4
North East Carry	C3
North Windham	B5
Norway	B4
Oakland	C4
Old Orchard Beach	B5
Old Town	D4
Orono	D4
Oxford	B4
Patten	D3
Portland	B5
Presque Isle	D2
Richmond	C4
Rockland	C4
Rumford	B4
Saco	B5
Sanford	B5
Skowhegan	C4
South Paris	B4
South Portland	B5
Springvale	B5
Thomaston	C4
Van Buren	E1
Waldoboro	C4
Waterville	C4
Westbrook	B5
Westfield	E2
Wilsons Mills	A4
Wilton	B4
Winslow	C4
Winterport	D4
Wiscasset	C4
Woodland	E3
Yarmouth	B5
York	B5

Other Features

	Key
Acadia Natl. Park	D4
Androscoggin, river	B4
Appalachian, mts.	A3
Aroostook, river	D2
au Haut, island	D4
Azischos, lake	A3
Baskahegan, lake	E3
Baxter State Park	D2
Big, lake	E3
Casco, bay	C4
Chamberlain, lake	C2
Chesuncook, lake	C2
Churchill, lake	C2
Cross, lake	E4
Deer, island	D4
Elizabeth, cape	B5
Flagstaff, lake	B3
Grand, lake	E3
Grand Matagamon, lake	D2
Grand Seboeis, lake	D2
Great Wass, island	E4
Islesboro, island	D4
Katahdin, mt.	D3
Kennebec, river	C3
Long, island	C4
Maine, gulf	C4
Matinicus, island	C4
Mattawamkeag, river	D2
Millinocket, lake	D2
Monhegan, island	C4
Moosehead, lake	C3
Mooselookmeguntic, lake	B4
Mt. Desert, island	D4
Munsungan, lake	D2
Nicatous, lake	D3
Pemadumcook, lake	C3
Penobscot, bay	D4
Penobscot, river	D3
Piscataquis, river	C3
Richardson, lakes	B4
Saco, river	B4
Saddleback, mt.	B4
St. Croix, river	E3
St. John, river	C2
Sebago, lake	B5
Sebec, lake	C3
Seboeis, lake	D3
Seboomook, lake	C3
Snow, mt.	B3
Sugarloaf, mt.	B3
Swans, island	D4
Telos, lake	C2
Umbagog, lake	A4
Vinalhaven, island	D4
West Grand, lake	E3
West Quoddy Head, peninsula	F4
White Cap, mt.	C3

Maryland .... page 147

Cities and Towns

	Key
Aberdeen	K2
Accident	A6
Accokeek	F5
Adelphi	C4
Annapolis, capital	J4
Arden-on-the-Severn	H3
Arnold	J3
Aspen Hill	B3, F3
Avenue	G7
Baltimore	H2
Bel Air	C3, G3
Beltsville	P6
Berlin	C4
Berwyn Heights	C4
Bethesda	B4, F4
Bladensburg	C4
Boonsboro	D1
Bowie	G4
Bowleys Quarters	J2
Braddock Heights	D2
Brandywine	G5
Brentwood	C4
Brunswick	D2
Bucktown	K6
Burtonsville	C3
Cabin John	A4
California	J6
Calverton	C3
Cambridge	K5
Cape St. Claire	J3
Camp Springs	D2
Carney	D1
Cascade	H2
Catonsville	H2
Centreville	K3
Chesapeake Beach	H5
Chesapeake Ranch Estates	J6
Chestertown	K3
Cheverly	C4
Chillum	C4, G4
Clinton	E2
Clover Hill	C3
Cloverly	H2
Cockeysville	C3
Colesville	C3
College Park	C4, G4
Columbia	G3
Contee	D3
Copenhaver	A3
Coral Hills	C5
Cresaptown	A3
Crisfield	L7
Crofton	H3
Crownsville	H3
Cumberland	D6
Damascus	F2
Deale	H4
Delmar	M6
Denton	L4
Derwood	A3
District Heights	D5
Dufief	A3
Dundalk	H2
Easton	K4
Edgemere	J3
Edgewood	J2
Eldersburg	G2
Elkridge	G3
Elkton	L1
Ellicott City	G2
Emmitsburg	E1
Essex	J2
Fair Hill	J1
Fallston	J1
Federalsburg	L5
Ferndale	H3
Forest Heights	B5, G4
Forestville	G4
Fountain Head	D1
Frederick	E2
Friendsville	A6
Frostburg	C6
Fruitland	M6
Gaithersburg	F3
Garrison	G2
Germantown	E3
Glen	A3
Glenarden	H3
Glen Burnie	H3
Glen Echo Heights	B4
Glen Hills	A3
Glenmont	B3
Golden Beach	H6
Grantsville	B6
Grasonville	K4
Green Haven	H3
Greenbelt	D4, G3
Greensboro	L4
Hagerstown	D1
Halfway	C1
Hampstead	G1
Hampton	H2
Hancock	B1
Havre de Grace	K1
Herald Harbor	H3
High Ridge	D3
Hillandale	C5
Hillcrest Heights	C5
Hillsmere Shores	J4
Hughesville	G5
Hunting Hill	A3
Hurlock	L5
Hyattstown	E2
Hyattsville	C4, G4
Indian Head	F5
Jarrettsville	J1
Jessup	G3
Joppatowne	J2
Kemptown	E2
Kensington	B3, F3
Kentland	D4, G4
Kettering	H4
Keysers Ridge	B6
Kingstown	K3
Kingsville	J2
Knollwood	G2
Lake Shore	J3
Landover	C4, G4
Langley Park	C4
Lanham	H3
Lansdowne	H3
LaPlata	G5
Largo	H4
Laurel	D3, G3
LaVale	L7
Lawsonia	B3
Layhill	B3
Leonardtown	H6

Key

Lewisdale C4
Lexington Park J6
Linthicum H3
Lochearn H2
Londontown H4
Lutherville H2
Luxmanor B3
Manchester G1
Marlton G4
Maydale C3
Middle River J2
Middletown D2
Milford G2
Montgomery Village F3
Montpelier D3
Mount Aetna D1
Mountain Lake Park A7
Mount Airy F2
Mount Rainier C4
Muirkirk D3
New Carrollton D4
Norbeck B3
North Chevy Chase B4
North East L1
Oak Crest D3
Oakland A7
Oakland C3
Oakview C3
Ocean City P6
Ocean Pines P6
Odenton H3
Olney F3
Overlea H2
Owings Mills G2
Oxon Hill C5
Palmer Park D4
Parkville H2
Parole H4
Perry Hall J2
Perryman K2
Perryville K1
Pikesville H2
Pleasant Hills J2
Pocomoke City M7
Poolesville E3
Potomac A3, F3
Potomac Heights F5
Preston L5
Prince Frederick H5
Princess Anne M7
Randallstown G2
Randolph Hills B3
Redhouse A7
Reisterstown G2
Rising Sun K1
Ritchie D5
Riverdale C4
Riviera Beach H3
Rock Hall K3
Rockville A3, F3
Rosedale H2
Rossmoor Leisure World B3
Rossville J2
St. Charles G5
St. Michaels K4
Salisbury M6
Seabrook D4
Seat Pleasant D5
Severn H3
Severna Park H3
Shady Side H4
Shawsville H1
Silver Hill C5
Silver Spring B4, F4
Snow Hill N7
South Gate H3
Spencerville C3
Stevensville J3
Suitland C5, G4
Sykesville G2
Takoma Park C4
Taneytown F1
Temple Hills C5, G4
Thurmont E1
Timonium H2
Towson H2
Upper Marlboro H4
Waldorf G5
Walker Mill D5
Walkersville E2
Westernport B7
Westminster F1
West Ocean City P6
Wheaton B3, F3
White Marsh J2
White Oak C3, G3
White Plains G5
Wildwood Hills A3
Williamsport C1
Woodlawn G2
Woodyard G4

Other Features
Allegheny Front, *mt. ridge* C7
Antietam Natl. Battlefield D2
Appalachian Natl. Scenic Trail D2
Assateague Island Natl. Seashore P7
Assawoman, *bay* P6
Backbone, *mt.* A7
Chesapeake, *bay* J5
Chesapeake and Ohio Canal N.H.P. A4, D2
Chester, *river* K3
Chincoteague, *bay* N7
Choptank, *river* K5
Deep Creek, *lake* A6
Liberty, *reservoir* G2
North Branch Potomac, *river* C7
Nanticoke, *river* L6
Patapsco, *river* H3
Patuxent, *river* H4
Potomac, *river* G6
Susquehanna, *river* J1
Wicomico, *river* G6
Youghiogheny, *river* A6

Massachusetts ....page 148

Cities and Towns
Abington L4
Acton A5, J3
Acushnet L6
Adams B2
Amesbury L1
Amherst D3
Andover K2
Arlington C6, K3
Ashby G2
Ashfield C2
Ashland J3

Key

Assinippi F8
Assonet K5
Athol F2
Attleboro J5
Auburn G4
Avon D8, K4
Ayer H2
Baldwinville F2
Barnstable N6
Becket B3
Bedford B5, J3
Belchertown E3
Bellingham J4
Belmont C6
Berkley K5
Bernardston D2
Beverly F5, L2
Billerica B5, J2
Blackstone H4
Blandford C4
Bliss Corner L6
Bolton H3
Bondsville E4
Boston, *capital* D6, K3
Boxford L2
Braintree E8, K4
Brewster P5
Bridgewater L5
Brimfield F4
Brockton K4
Brookfield F4
Brookline C7, K3
Burlington C5, K2
Buzzards Bay M5
Cambridge D6, K3
Canton C8, K4
Carlisle B5
Cedarville M5
Centerville N6
Central Village K6
Charlton G4
Charlton City G4
Chatham Q6
Chelmsford J2
Chelsea D6
Cheshire B2
Chester C3
Chicopee D4
Chilmark M7
Clarksburg B2
Clinton H3
Cochituate B7, J3
Cohasset L4
Concord B6, J3
Cotuit N6
Dalton B3
Danvers E5, L2
Dartmouth K6
Dedham C7, K4
Dennis P6
Douglas H4
Dover B8, J4
Dracut H3
Duxbury M4
East Brookfield F4
East Dennis P6
East Douglas H4
East Falmouth M6
East Freetown L5
Eastham Q5
Easthampton D3
East Longmeadow D4
East Orleans Q5
East Pepperell H2
East Wareham M5
Edgartown M7
Erving E2
Essex L2
Everett D6
Fall River K6
Falmouth M6
Feeding Hills D4
Fiskdale F4
Fitchburg G2
Florida B2
Foxboro K4
Framingham A7, J3
Franklin J4
Gardner G2
Gay Head L7
Georgetown L2
Gloucester M2
Granby D3
Granville C4
Great Barrington A4
Greenfield D2
Green Harbor M4
Halifax L5
Hamilton L2
Hanover L4
Hanson L4
Haverhill K1
Hingham F8, L4
Holbrook E8, K4
Holland F4
Holliston A8, J4
Holyoke D4
Hopedale H4
Hopkinton H4
Hubbardston G3
Hudson H3
Hull F7, L3
Huntington C4
Hyannis N6
Ipswich L2
Kingston M5
Lakeville L5
Lawrence K2
Lee B3
Lenox A3
Leominster G2
Lexington C6, K3
Lincoln B6
Littleton H2
Littleton Common J2
Longmeadow D4
Lowell J2
Ludlow E4
Lunenburg H2
Lynn E6, L3
Lynnfield D5, K2
Madaket P7
Malden D6, K3
Manchester-by-the-Sea L2
Mansfield K4
Marblehead F5, L3
Marion L6
Marlborough H3
Marshfield M4
Marshfield Hills M4
Mashpee N6

Key

Mattapoisett L6
Maynard J3
Medfield B8, J4
Medford D6, K3
Medway A8
Melrose D6, K3
Mendon H4
Methuen K2
Middleboro L5
Milford H4
Millis B8
Milton D7, K3
Monson E4
Monterey B4
Monument Beach M6
Nahant E6, L3
Nantucket Q7
Natick B7, J3
Needham C7, K3
New Ashford B2
New Bedford L6
New Boston B4
Newton C7, K3
New Marlborough B4
North Adams B2
North Amherst D3
Northampton D3
North Andover K2
North Attleboro J5
Northborough H3
Northbridge H4
North Brookfield F3
North Carver L5
North Falmouth M6
Northfield E2
North Grafton H4
North Pembroke L4
North Plymouth M5
North Reading D5, K2
North Scituate L4
North Sudbury A6
North Tisbury M7
Norton K5
Norwell L4
Norwood C8, K3
Oakham F3
Ocean Bluff M4
Ocean Grove K6
Orange E2
Orleans Q5
Osterville N6
Otis B4
Oxford G4
Palmer E4
Paxton G3
Peabody E5, L2
Pelham E3
Pembroke L4
Pepperell H2
Petersham F3
Phillipston F2
Pinehurst C5, K2
Pittsfield B3
Plainfield C2
Plainville J4
Plymouth M5
Pocasset M6
Provincetown P4
Quincy E7, K3
Randolph D8, K4
Raynham K5
Raynham Center K5
Reading D5, K2
Rehoboth K5
Revere E6, K3
Rochester L6
Rockland E8, L4
Rockport M2
Rutland G3
Sagamore M5
Salem F5, L2
Salisbury L1
Sandwich N5
Saugus E6, K3
Savoy B2
Scituate L4
Sharon C8, K4
Sheffield A4
Shelburne Falls D2
Sherborn B8
Shirley H3
Shrewsbury H3
Shutesbury E3
Somerset K5
Somerville D6, K3
South Amherst D3
Southbridge F4
South Carver M5
South Deerfield D3
South Dennis P6
South Duxbury M4
South Lancaster H3
South Sudbury A7
South Wellfleet P5
South Yarmouth P6
Spencer G4
Springfield D4
Sterling G3
Stoneham D5
Stoughton D8, K4
Sturbridge F4
Sudbury A6, J3
Sutton G4
Swampscott E6, L3
Taunton K5
Teaticket M6
Templeton F2
Tewksbury K2
Three Rivers E4
Tolland B4
Topsfield L2
Truro P5
Turners Falls D2
Tyngsborough J2
Upton H4
Uxbridge H4
Vineyard Haven M7
Wakefield D5, K2
Wales F4
Walpole C8, J4
Waltham C6, K3
Ware F3
Wareham M5
Warren E4
Warwick E2
Washington B3
Watertown C6
Wauwinet P7
Wayland B7
Webster G4

Key

Wellesley B7, J3
West Barnstable N6
Westborough H3
West Boylston G3
West Brookfield F4
West Concord J3
West Cummington C3
West Falmouth M6
Westfield D4
Westford D4
West Granville C4
Westhampton C3
West Medway A8
Westminster G2
Weston B6, J3
Westport K6
Westport Point K6
West Springfield D4
West Wareham L5
Westwood C8, K4
West Yarmouth P6
Weymouth E8, L4
Whately D3
White Island Shores M5
Whitinsville H4
Whitman L4
Wilbraham E4
Williamstown B2
Wilmington C5, K2
Winchendon F2
Winchester C6
Windsor B2
Winthrop E6
Woburn C5, K3
Worcester G3
Worthington Center C3
Wrentham J4
Yarmouth Port P6

Other Features
Adams Natl. Hist. Site E8, L4
Ann, *cape* M2
Berkshire, *hills* B4
Boston, *bay* E6
Boston, *harbor* E7
Boston Natl. Hist. Park D6
Buzzards, *bay* M6
Cape Cod, *bay* N5
Cape Cod, *canal* M5
Cape Cod Natl. Seashore P5
Charles, *river* B7
Chicopee, *river* C4
Cobble Mt., *reservoir* C4
Cod, *cape* P4
Connecticut, *river* E2
Deer, *island* E7
Elizabeth, *islands* L7
Frederick Law Olmsted N.H.S. C7
Georges, *island* E7
Greylock, *mt.* B2
Hingham, *bay* E7
Housatonic, *river* A4
J.F.K. Birthplace Natl. Hist. Site D7
Long, *island* E7
Longfellow Natl. Hist. Site D6
Lowell Natl. Hist. Park J2
Maine, *gulf* M1
Martha's Vineyard, *island* M7
Massachusetts, *bay* F6, M3
Merrimack, *river* K1
Minute Man Natl. Hist. Park B6, J3
Monomoy, *island* P6
Muskeget, *channel* N7
Nantucket, *island* P7
Neponset, *river* C7
Otis, *reservoir* B4
Peddocks, *island* E7
Quabbin, *reservoir* F3
Quincy, *bay* E7
Salem Maritime N.H.S. F5, L2
Saugus Iron Works N.H.S. E6
Shawsheen, *river* B6
Spectacle, *island* E7
Swift, *river* E4
Taconic, *mts.* A4
Wachusett, *lake* E6, K3
Wachusett, *river* G3
Walden, *pond* B6

Michigan ....page 149

Cities and Towns
Adrian E7
Albion E7
Algonac G7
Allegan D7
Allendale C7
Allen Park A7
Alma E6
Alpena F4
Ann Arbor F7
Atlanta E5
Bad Axe G6
Baldwin D6
Battle Creek D7
Bay City F6
Belding D6
Bellaire D5
Belleville F7
Benton Harbor C7
Berkley A6
Bessemer C2
Beulah D5
Beverly Hills A6
Big Rapids D6
Birmingham A6
Blissfield E8
Bloomfield Hills A6
Boyne City D4
Bridgeport F6
Brighton F7
Buchanan C8
Burton F6
Cadillac D5
Carleton F7
Caro F6
Carrollton F6
Cassopolis C8
Cedar Springs D6
Center Line B6
Centreville D8
Charlevoix D4
Charlotte E7
Cheboygan E4
Chelsea E7
Chesaning E6
Christmas C3
Clare E6
Clawson B6

Key

Clio F6
Coldwater D8
Connorville C6
Coopersville C6
Crystal Falls A3
Cutlerville D7
Davison F6
Dearborn A7, F7
Dearborn Hts. A7
Detroit B7, F7
De Witt E7
Dowagiac C8
Dundee F8
Durand F7
Eagle River A2
East Lansing E7
Eastpointe B6
East Tawas F5
Eaton Rapids E7
Ecorse C8
Escanaba B4
Essexville F6
Farmington A6
Farmington Hills A6
Fenton F7
Ferndale B6
Ferrysburg C6
Flat Rock F7
Flint F6
Flushing E7
Fowlerville E7
Frankenmuth F6
Fraser B6
Fremont D6
Garden City A7
Gaylord E5
Gladstone B4
Gladwin E6
Grand Blanc F7
Grand Haven C6
Grand Ledge E7
Grand Rapids D7
Grayling E5
Greenville D6
Grosse Pointe B7
Grosse Pointe Farms B7
Grosse Pointe Park B7
Grosse Pointe Shores B6
Grosse Pointe Woods B6
Hamtramck A6
Hancock A2
Harper Woods B7
Harrison E5
Harrisville F5
Hart C6
Hastings D7
Hazel Park B6
Highland Park B7
Hillsdale E8
Holland C7
Holly F7
Holt E7
Houghton A2
Houghton Lake E5
Howell E7
Hudson E8
Hudsonville D7
Huntington Woods A6
Huron Heights A6
Imlay City F6
Inkster A7
Ionia D7
Iron Mountain A4
Ironwood C2
Ishpeming B3
Ithaca E6
Jackson E7
Jenison D7
Kalamazoo D7
Kalkaska D5
Keego Harbor A6
Kentwood D7
Kingsford A4
Lake City D5
Lake Orion F7
Lambertville F8
Lansing, *capital* E7
Lapeer F6
Lincoln Park A7, F7
Livonia A6
Lowell D7
Ludington C5
Madison Hts. B6
Manistee C5
Manistique C4
Marenisco C2
Marine City G7
Marlette F6
Marquette B3
Marshall E7
Marysville G7
Mason E7
Melvindale A7
Menominee A4
Merriweather D2
Michigan Center E7
Midland E6
Milan F7
Milford F7
Mio E5
Monroe F8
Mount Clemens B6
Mount Morris F6
Mount Pleasant E6
Munising C3
Muskegon C6
Muskegon Hts. C6
Negaunee B3
New Baltimore G7
Newberry D3
Niles C8
North Muskegon C6
Norton Shores C6
Norway B4
Oak Park B6
Okemos E7
Ontonagon D1
Orchard Lake A6
Otsego D7
Owosso E6
Oxford F7
Paw Paw D7
Paw Paw Lake C7
Petoskey E4
Plainwell D7
Pontiac A6, F7
Portage D7
Port Huron G7
Portland E7
Rapid River C4

Key

Reed City D6
Richmond G7
River Rouge B7
Rochester Hills A6
Rockford D6
Rockwood F7
Rogers City E4
Romeo F7
Romulus F7
Roscommon E5
Roseville B6
Royal Oak B6
Saginaw F6
St. Clair G7
St. Clair Shores B6
St. Ignace E4
St. Johns E6
St. Joseph C7
St. Louis E6
Saline F7
Sandusky G6
Sault Ste. Marie E3
Shields F6
Silver City D1
Skidway Lake E5
Southfield A6
Southgate A7
South Haven C7
South Lyon F7
Sparta D6
Spring Lake C6
Standish F6
Stanton D6
Sterling Heights F7
Sturgis D8
Sylvan Lake A6
Tawas City F5
Taylor A7, F7
Tecumseh E7
Temperance F8
Three Rivers D7
Traverse City D5
Troy B6
Union Lake A6
Utica B6
Vassar F6
Wakefield C2
Waldenburg B6
Walker D7
Warren B6, F7
Wayland D7
Wayne A7
West Acres A6
West Branch E5
Westland A7
White Cloud D6
Whitehall C6
White Pine D1
Whitmore Lake F7
Williamston E7
Wixom F7
Wolf Lake C6
Wyandotte B7
Wyoming D7
Ypsilanti F7
Zeeland C7

Other Features
Arvon, *mt.* A3
Au Sable, *river* E5
Beaver, *island* D4
Big Bay De Noc, *bay* C4
Big Sable, *point* C5
Bois Blanc, *island* E4
Cass, *river* F6
Chambers, *island* B4
Detroit, *river* B7
Drummond, *island* F3
Erie, *lake* G8
Escanaba, *river* B3
Glen, *lake* D4
Gogebic, *lake* C2
Government Peak, *mt.* D1
Grand, *island* C3
Grand Traverse, *bay* D4
Green, *bay* B4
Hamlin, *lake* C5
Hammond, *bay* E4
Higgins, *lake* E5
High, *island* D4
Hog, *island* D4
Houghton, *lake* E5
Hubbard, *lake* F5
Huron, *bay* A3
Huron, *lake* G5
Huron, *mts.* A3
Indian, *lake* C3
Isle Royale, *island* A1
Isle Royale Natl. Park A2
Keweenaw, *bay* A2
Keweenaw, *peninsula* A2
Keweenaw, *point* B2
Lookout, *point* F5
Manistee, *river* D5
Manitou, *island* B2
Menominee, *river* B4
Michigamme, *reservoir* A3
Michigan, *lake* C5
North Manitou, *island* C4
Paint, *river* A3
Pictured Rocks Natl. Lakeshore C3
Porcupine, *mts.* D2
Saginaw, *bay* F6
St. Clair, *lake* G7
St. Martin, *island* B4
Sleeping Bear Dunes Natl. Lakeshore C5
South Fox, *island* D4
South Manitou, *island* C4
Straits of Mackinac E4
Sturgeon, *bay* A2
Superior, *lake* A2
Thunder, *bay* F5
Whitefish, *bay* E3
Wixom, *lake* E6

Minnesota ....page 150

Cities and Towns
Ada A3
Aitkin C5
Albany C5
Albert Lea D7
Albertville D5
Alexandria B5
Annandale C5
Anoka D5
Appleton A5
Arlington C6
Aurora E3

Minnesota (Cities and Towns)

Name	Key
Austin	E7
Babbitt	F3
Bagley	B3
Barnesville	A4
Baudette	C4
Baxter	E6
Bayport	D6
Belle Plaine	D6
Bemidji	C3
Benson	B5
Big Lake	D5
Bird Island	C6
Blooming Prairie	D7
Bloomington	D6
Blue Earth	C7
Brainerd	C4
Breckenridge	A4
Brooklyn Center	E5
Buffalo	D5
Burnsville	D6
Caledonia	F7
Cambridge	D5
Canby	A6
Cannon Falls	E6
Carlton	E4
Center City	E5
Chanhassen	D6
Chaska	D6
Chatfield	E7
Chisholm	E3
Clara City	B6
Clarks Grove	D7
Clearwater	C5
Cloquet	E4
Cokato	C5
Cold Spring	C5
Columbia Hts.	F5
Coon Rapids	D5
Corcoran	D5
Crookston	A3
Crosby	D4
Dawson	A6
Detroit Lakes	B4
Dilworth	A4
Dodge Center	E6
Duluth	E4
Eagan	F6
Eagle Lake	D6
East Bethel	D5
East Grand Forks	A3
Edina	D6
Elbow Lake	B5
Elk River	D5
Ely	F3
Evansville	B4
Eveleth	E3
Eyota	E7
Fairmont	C7
Falcon Heights	F5
Faribault	D6
Farmington	D6
Fergus Falls	A4
Foley	D5
Forest Lake	E5
Fosston	B3
Fridley	F5
Gaylord	C6
Glencoe	C6
Glenwood	B5
Golden Valley	E5
Goodview	F6
Grand Forks	A3
Grand Marais	F5
Grand Portage	F4
Grand Rapids	D3
Granite Falls	B6
Hallock	A2
Hastings	E6
Hawley	A4
Hayfield	E7
Hermantown	E3
Hibbing	E3
Hokah	F7
Hopkins	E5
Hovland	F4
Howard Lake	C5
Hutchinson	C6
International Falls	D2
Ivanhoe	A6
Jackson	B7
Janesville	D6
Jordan	D6
Kasson	E6
Kenyon	E6
La Crescent	F7
Lake Crystal	C6
Lakefield	B7
Lakeville	D6
Le Center	D6
Le Sueur	D6
Lewiston	F7
Litchfield	C5
Little Canada	F5
Little Falls	C5
Long Prairie	C5
Lonsdale	D6
Lutsen	E5
Luverne	A7
McIntosh	B3
Madelia	C6
Madison	A5
Mahnomen	B3
Mankato	D6
Mantorville	E6
Maple Grove	D5
Maple Lake	C5
Mapleton	D7
Maplewood	F5
Marshall	B6
Melrose	C5
Mendota	F6
Milaca	D5
Minneapolis	D6
Minneota	B6
Montevideo	B6
Montgomery	D6
Monticello	D5
Moorhead	A4
Mora	D5
Morris	B5
Mound	D6
Mountain Iron	E3
Mountain Lake	C7
New Hope	E5
Newport	F6
New Prague	D6
New Ulm	C6
Nisswa	C4
North Branch	E5
Northfield	D6
North Mankato	C6
North Oaks	F5
Olivia	C6
Orono	D6
Oronoco	E6
Ortonville	A5
Osakis	B5
Owatonna	D6
Park Rapids	B4
Paynesville	C5
Pelican Rapids	A4
Perham	B4
Pigeon River	F4
Pine City	E5
Pine Island	E6
Pipestone	A7
Plainview	E6
Plymouth	D5
Preston	E7
Princeton	D5
Prinsburg	B6
Prior Lake	D6
Proctor	E4
Ramsey	D5
Red Lake Falls	A3
Red Wing	E6
Redwood Falls	B6
Renville	B6
Richfield	F6
Robbinsdale	E5
Rochester	E6
Roseau	B2
Rushford	F7
St. Anthony	F5
St. Charles	E7
St. Cloud	C5
St. Francis	D5
St. James	C7
St. Joseph	C5
St. Louis Park	E5
St. Michael	D5
St. Paul, capital	D6
St. Peter	D6
Sandstone	E4
Sartell	C5
Sauk Centre	C5
Sauk Rapids	D5
Shakopee	D6
Silver Bay	F3
Slayton	B7
Sleepy Eye	C6
South St. Paul	F5
Spring Valley	E7
Springfield	C6
Staples	C4
Stewartville	E7
Stillwater	E5
Thief River Falls	A2
Tracy	B6
Truman	C7
Two Harbors	F3
Tyler	A6
Virginia	E3
Wabasha	E6
Waite Park	C5
Walker	C3
Warren	A2
Warroad	B2
Waseca	D6
Waterville	D6
Wells	D7
Wheaton	A5
White Bear Lake	F5
Willmar	B5
Windom	B7
Winnebago	C7
Winona	F6
Winsted	C6
Winthrop	C6
Worthington	B7
Wyoming	E5
Young America	D6
Zimmerman	D5
Zumbrota	E6

Other Features

Name	Key
Big Fork, river	D2
Brule, river	E4
Buffalo, river	A4
Chippewa, river	B5
Clearwater, river	B3
Cloquet, river	F3
Des Moines, river	B6
Eagle, mt.	F4
Grand Portage Natl. Monument	F4
Gull, lake	C4
Lake of the Woods, lake	C1
Leech, lake	C3
Little Fork, river	D2
Lower Red, lake	B3
Lower Whitefish, lake	C4
Mall of America	F6
Mesabi, range	D3
Mille Lacs, lake	D4
Minnesota, river	B6
Mississippi, river	C3
Mud, lake	B2
Namakan, lake	E2
Pipestone Natl. Monument	A6
Pokegama, lake	D3
Rainy, lake	C1
Red River of the North, river	A3
Root, river	E7
Rum, river	D5
St. Croix, river	E5
St. Louis, river	E3
Superior, lake	F3
Upper Red, lake	C2
Vermilion, range	F3
Voyageurs Natl. Park	D2
Winnibigoshish, lake	D3

Mississippi ....page 151

Cities and Towns

Name	Key
Aberdeen	D2
Ackerman	C2
Alligator	B1
Amory	D2
Ashland	D1
Baldwyn	D1
Bassfield	C4
Batesville	C1
Bay St. Louis	C5
Bay Springs	C4
Beauregard	B4
Belmont	D1
Belzoni	B2
Biloxi	D5
Blue Springs	D1
Booneville	D1
Brandon	C3
Braxton	C3
Brookhaven	B4
Bruce	C2
Calhoun City	C2
Canton	B3
Carrollton	C2
Carthage	C3
Centreville	A4
Charleston	B1
Clarksdale	B1
Cleveland	B2
Clinton	B3
Coahoma	B1
Coffeeville	C2
Coldwater	C1
Collins	C4
Collinsville	D3
Columbia	B4
Columbus	D2
Como	C1
Corinth	D1
Crystal Springs	B4
Decatur	C3
De Kalb	D3
Diamondhead	C5
D'Iberville	D5
Doddsville	B2
Drew	B2
Durant	C2
Eden	B3
Edwards	B3
Ellisville	C4
Eupora	C2
Falcon	B1
Falkner	D1
Fayette	A4
Flora	B3
Florence	B3
Forest	C3
Friars Point	B1
Fulton	D1
Gautier	D5
Glendora	B2
Gloster	A4
Golden	D1
Goodman	C3
Greenville	A2
Greenwood	B2
Grenada	C2
Gulfport	C5
Hattiesburg	C4
Hazlehurst	B4
Hernando	C1
Hollandale	B2
Holly Springs	C1
Horn Lake	B1
Houston	D2
Indianola	B2
Itta Bena	B2
Iuka	D1
Jackson, capital	B3
Jonestown	B1
Kiln	C5
Kosciusko	C2
Kossuth	D1
Laurel	C4
Leakesville	D4
Learned	B3
Leland	B2
Lena	C3
Lexington	B2
Liberty	B4
Long Beach	C5
Louisville	C2
Lucedale	D5
Lula	B1
Lumberton	C4
Lyman	C5
McComb	B4
McCool	C2
Macon	D2
Madison	B3
Magee	C4
Magnolia	B4
Mantee	C2
Marion	D3
Marks	B1
Mayersville	A3
Meadville	B4
Mendenhall	C4
Meridian	D3
Monticello	B4
Montrose	C3
Moorhead	B2
Morton	C3
Moss Point	D5
Mound Bayou	B2
Natchez	A4
Nettleton	D1
New Albany	D1
New Augusta	C4
Newton	C3
Ocean Springs	D5
Okolona	D1
Olive Branch	C1
Oxford	C1
Paden	D1
Pascagoula	D5
Pass Christian	C5
Paulding	C3
Pearl	B3
Pearlington	C5
Pelahatchie	C3
Petal	C4
Philadelphia	C3
Picayune	C5
Pickens	C3
Pittsboro	C2
Polkville	C3
Pontotoc	D1
Pope	C1
Poplarville	C5
Port Gibson	B4
Prentiss	C4
Purvis	C4
Quitman	D3
Raleigh	C4
Raymond	B3
Richland	B3
Ridgeland	B3
Ripley	D1
Rolling Fork	B3
Rosedale	A2
Ruleville	B2
Sallis	C2
Saltillo	D1
Sardis	C1
Satartia	B3
Seminary	C4
Senatobia	C1
Shannon	D1
Shaw	B2
Shelby	B2
Shubuta	D4
Silver Creek	B4
Slate Spring	C2
Southaven	B1
Starkville	D2
Summit	B4
Sumner	B1
Sylvarena	C3
Taylorsville	C4
Tchula	B2
Tillatoba	C2
Toccopola	C1
Tunica	B1
Tupelo	D1
Tutwiler	B1
Tylertown	B4
Union	C2
Vaiden	C2
Vancleave	D5
Verona	D1
Vicksburg	B3
Walthall	C2
Water Valley	C1
Waveland	C5
Waynesboro	D4
Wesson	B4
West	C2
West Point	D2
Wiggins	C5
Winona	C2
Woodland	C2
Woodville	A4
Yazoo City	B3

Other Features

Name	Key
Arkabutla, lake	B1
Big Black, river	B3
Big Springs, lake	D1
Big Sunflower, river	B2
Bogue Chitto, river	B4
Buttahatchee, river	D2
Cat, island	C5
Chickasawhay, river	D4
Coldwater, river	B1
Columbus, lake	D2
Enid, lake	C1
Grenada, lake	C2
Gulf Island Natl. Seashore	D5
Homochitto, river	A4
Horn, island	D5
Leaf, river	C4
Mississippi, river	A2
Mississppi, sound	D5
Natchez Natl. Hist. Park	A4
Noxubee, river	D2
Okatibbee, lake	D3
Pascagoula, river	D4
Pearl, river	C3
Petit Bois, island	D5
Pickwick, lake	D1
Pontotoc, mt. ridge	D1
Ross Barnett, reservoir	C3
Sardis, lake	C1
Ship, island	D5
Tallahatchie, river	B1
Tombigbee, river	D1
Tupelo Natl. Battlefield	D1
Vicksburg Natl. Mil. Park	B3
Woodall, mt.	D1
Yazoo, river	B2

Missouri ....page 152

Cities and Towns

Name	Key
Adrian	B3
Affton	H3
Albany	B1
Alton	E5
Anderson	B5
Appleton City	B3
Ashland	D3
Atherton	J4
Aurora	C5
Ava	D5
Barnett	D3
Belton	B3
Benton	G5
Bernie	G5
Bethany	B1
Birmingham	J4
Bloomfield	G5
Blue Springs	J4
Bolivar	C4
Bonne Terre	F4
Boonville	D3
Bowling Green	E2
Branson	C5
Brentwood	H2
Bridgeton	H2
Brookfield	C2
Buckner	J4
Buffalo	C4
Butler	B3
Cabool	D4
California	D3
Calverton Park	H2
Camdenton	D4
Cameron	B2
Campbell	F5
Canton	E1
Cape Girardeau	G4
Carrollton	C2
Carthage	B4
Caruthersville	G5
Cassville	C5
Cedar Hill	F3
Centerville	F4
Centralia	D2
Chaffee	G5
Charleston	G5
Chesterfield	H2
Chillicothe	C2
Claycomo	J4
Clayton	F3, H2
Clinton	C3
Columbia	D3
Concord	H3
Concordia	C3
Crestwood	H2
Creve Coeur	H2
Cuba	E3
Dellwood	H2
Desloge	F4
De Soto	F3
Des Peres	G2
Dexter	G5
Dixon	D3
Doniphan	F5
East Prairie	G5
Edina	D1
Eldon	D3
El Dorado Springs	B4
Elsberry	F2
Eminence	E4
Eureka	H3
Excelsior Springs	B2, J3
Farley	H3
Farmington	F4
Fayette	D2
Fenton	G3
Ferguson	H2
Festus	F3
Florissant	H2
Forsyth	C5
Fredericktown	F4
Fulton	D3
Gainesville	D5
Galena	C5
Gallatin	C2
Gladstone	B2, J3
Glasgow	D2
Glasgow Village	H2
Glendale	H3
Grain Valley	J4
Granby	B5
Grandview	J4
Grant City	B1
Greenfield	C4
Greenville	F4
Hamilton	C2
Hannibal	E2
Harrisonville	B3
Hartville	D4
Hayti	G5
Hazelwood	H2
Hermann	E3
Hermitage	C4
Higginsville	C2
Hillsboro	F3
Holden	C3
Hollister	C5
Houston	E4
Huntsville	D2
Independence	B2, J4
Ironton	F4
Jackson	G4
Jefferson City, capital	D3
Jennings	H2
Joplin	B4
Kahoka	E1
Kansas City	B2, H4
Kennett	F5
Keytesville	D2
Kingston	B2
Kinloch	H2
Kirksville	D1
Kirkwood	H3
Knob Noster	C3
Ladue	H2
Lake Lotawana	J4
Lake St. Louis	F3
Lamar	B4
Lancaster	D1
La Plata	D1
Lathrop	B2
Lawson	B2
Lebanon	D4
Lee's Summit	B3, J4
Lemay	H3
Lexington	C2
Liberty	B2, J3
Licking	E4
Lilbourn	G5
Linn Creek	D3
Linneus	C2
Louisiana	E2
Mackenzie	H3
Macon	D2
Malden	G5
Manchester	G3
Mansfield	D4
Maplewood	H3
Marble Hill	G4
Marceline	D2
Marionville	C5
Marshall	C2
Marshfield	D4
Maryland Heights	H2
Maryville	B1
Mattese	H3
Maysville	B2
Mehlville	H3
Memphis	D1
Mexico	E2
Milan	C1
Millard	D1
Moberly	D2
Monett	C5
Monroe City	E2
Montgomery City	E3
Monticello	E1
Mosby	J3
Mound City	A1
Mountain Grove	D4
Mountain View	E4
Mt. Vernon	C4
Murphy	G3
Neosho	B5
Nevada	B4
New Haven	E3
New London	E2
New Madrid	G5
Nixa	C4
North Kansas City	H4
Northwoods	H2
Oaks	J4
O'Fallon	F3
Olivette	H2
Oregon	A2
Osage Beach	D3
Osceola	C4
Overland	H2
Owensville	E3
Ozark	C4
Pacific	H2
Pagedale	H2
Palmyra	E2
Paris	D2
Park Hills	F4
Parkville	H4
Peculiar	B3
Peerless Park	G3
Pevely	F3
Perryville	G4
Pierce City	C5
Pine Lawn	H2
Pineville	B5
Platte City	B2, H3
Plattsburg	B2
Pleasant Hill	B3
Poplar Bluff	F5
Portageville	G5
Potosi	F4
Princeton	C1
Randolph	J4
Raymore	B3
Raytown	J4
Republic	C4
Rich Hill	B4
Richland	D4
Richmond	C2
Richmond Heights	H2
Riverside	H4
Rock Hill	H2
Rock Port	A1
Rolla	E4
St. Ann	H2
St. Charles	F3, G2
St. Clair	F3
Ste. Genevieve	F4
St. James	E3
St. John	H2
St. Joseph	B2
St. Louis	F3, H2
St. Peters	F3
St. Robert	D4
Salem	E4
Salisbury	D2
Sappington	H3
Sarcoxie	B4
Savannah	B2
Scott City	G4
Sedalia	C3
Senath	F5
Seymour	D4
Shelbina	D2
Shelbyville	D2
Shirley	F4
Sikeston	G5
Slater	C2
Smithville	B2
Springfield	C4
Stanberry	B1
Steele	G5
Steelville	E4
Stockton	C4
Stoutsville	E2
Sugar Creek	J4
Sullivan	E3
Sweet Springs	C3
Tarkio	A1
Thayer	E5
Town and Country	H2
Trenton	C1
Troy	F3
Tuscumbia	D3
Union	F3
Unionville	C1
Unity Village	J4
University City	H2
Van Buren	E5
Vandalia	E2
Versailles	D3
Vienna	E3
Villa Ridge	F3
Waldron	H3
Warrensburg	C3
Warrenton	E3
Warsaw	C3
Washington	E3
Watson	A1
Waynesville	D4
Weatherby Lake	H3
Webb City	B4
Webster Groves	H3
Wellston	H2
Wellsville	E2
Wentzville	E3
West Plains	E5
Weston	B2
Willard	C4
Willow Springs	E4
Windsor	C3

Other Features

Name	Key
Bull Shoals, lake	D5
Eleven Point, river	E5
Fox, river	E1
G.W. Carver Natl. Monument	B5
Grand, river	B1
Harry S. Truman, reservoir	C3
Lake of the Ozarks, lake	D3
Mark Twain, lake	E2
Meramec, river	E4
Mississippi, river	G4
Missouri, river	C2
Osage, river	B4, D3
Platte, river	B2
St. Francis, river	F5
Stockton, lake	C4
Table Rock, lake	C5
Taum Sauk, mt.	F4
Thomas Hill, reservoir	D2
Weldon, river	C2

Montana ....page 153

Cities and Towns

Name	Key
Anaconda	D3
Baker	M3
Belgrade	E4
Big Timber	F4
Billings	H4
Boulder	D3
Bozeman	E4
Bridger	H4
Broadus	L4
Butte	D3
Chester	F1
Chinook	G1
Choteau	D2
Circle	L2
Columbus	G4
Conrad	E1
Crow Agency	J4
Cut Bank	D1
Deer Lodge	D3
Dell	D4
Dillon	D4
East Helena	E3
Ekalaka	M4
Evergreen	B1
Forsyth	K3
Fort Benton	F2
Gardiner	F4
Glasgow	K1

	Key
Glendive	M2
Great Falls	E2
Hamilton	B3
Hardin	J4
Harlowton	G3
Hathaway	K3
Havre	G1
Helena, *capital*	D3
Kalispell	B1
Lame Deer	K4
Laurel	H4
Lewistown	G2
Libby	A1
Lincoln	D3
Livingston	F4
Lolo Hot Springs	B3
Malta	J1
Miles City	L3
Missoula	C3
Orchard Homes	B3
Philipsburg	C3
Plentywood	M1
Polson	B2
Pony	E4
Red Lodge	G4
Ronan	B2
Roundup	H3
Rudyard	F1
St. Regis	A2
Scobey	L1
Shelby	E1
Sidney	M2
Somers	B1
Stanford	F2
Superior	B2
Terry	L3
Thompson Falls	A2
Townsend	E3
West Yellowstone	E5
Whitefish	B1
Wibaux	M3
Wolf Point	L1

Other Features

	Key
Bighorn, *river*	J4
Bighorn Canyon Natl. Rec. Area	H4
Bitterroot, *river*	B3
Bull, *mts.*	H3
Canyon Ferry *lake*	E3
Clark Fork, *river*	D3
Cleveland, *mt.*	C1
Custer Battlefield Natl. Monument	J4
Elwell, *lake*	E1
Flathead, *lake*	B2
Flathead, *river*	B1
Fort Peck, *lake*	K2
Fresno, *reservoir*	F1
Glacier Natl. Park	C1
Granite Peak, *mt.*	D4
Granite Peak, *mt.*	G4
Grant-Kohrs Ranch N.H.S.	D3
Homer Youngs Peak, *mt.*	C4
Hungry Horse, *reservoir*	C1
Koocanusa, *lake*	A1
Kootenai, *river*	A1
Little Missouri, *river*	M5
Madison, *river*	E4
Marias, *river*	E1
Middle Fork, *river*	C1
Milk, *river*	D1
Missouri, *river*	G2
Musselshell, *river*	H3
Northwest Peak, *mt.*	A1
Powder, *river*	L3
Rocky, *mts.*	C2
St. Mary, *river*	C1
St. Regis, *river*	B2
Scarface Peak, *mt.*	C2
South Fork, *river*	C2
Swan, *river*	C2
Teton, *river*	E2
Tongue, *river*	K4
Warren Peak, *mt.*	C4
Yellowstone, *river*	L3
Yellowstone Natl. Park	F5

Nebraska ....page 154

Cities and Towns

	Key
Ainsworth	E2
Albion	G3
Alliance	B2
Alma	E4
Ashland	H3
Atkinson	F2
Auburn	J4
Aurora	F4
Bartlett	F3
Bassett	E2
Beatrice	H4
Beaver City	E4
Bellevue	J3
Benkelman	C4
Blair	H3
Brewster	E3
Bridgeport	A3
Broken Bow	E3
Burwell	F3
Butte	F2
Center	G2
Central City	F3
Chadron	B2
Chapman	F3
Chappell	B3
Clay Center	F4
Columbus	G3
Cozad	E4
Crete	H4
Dakota City	H2
David City	G3
Elkhorn	H3
Elwood	E4
Exeter	G4
Fairbury	G4
Falls City	J4
Franklin	F4
Fremont	H3
Fullerton	G3
Geneva	G4
Gering	A3
Gibbon	F4
Gordon	B2
Gothenburg	D4
Grand Island	F4
Grant	C4
Greeley	G3
Gretna	H3
Guide Rock	F4
Harrisburg	A3
Harrison	A2

	Key
Hartington	G2
Hastings	F4
Hayes Center	C4
Hebron	G4
Holdrege	E4
Hyannis	C3
Imperial	C4
Kearney	F4
Kimball	A3
La Vista	H3
Leigh	G3
Lexington	E4
Lincoln, *capital*	H4
Loomis	E4
Loup City	F3
McCook	D4
Madison	G3
Milford	G4
Minden	F4
Mitchell	A3
Mullen	C2
Nebraska City	J4
Neligh	F2
Nelson	F4
Norfolk	G2
North Platte	D3
Oakland	H3
Ogallala	C3
Omaha	J3
O'Neill	F2
Ord	F3
Osceola	G3
Oshkosh	B3
Papillion	H3
Pawnee City	H4
Paxton	C3
Pender	H2
Pierce	G2
Plainview	G2
Plattsmouth	J3
Plymouth	H4
Ponca	H2
Prague	H3
Ravenna	F3
Red Cloud	F4
Rushville	B2
St. Paul	F3
Schuyler	G3
Scottsbluff	A3
Seward	G4
Sidney	B3
South Sioux City	H2
Springfield	H3
Springview	F2
Stanton	G3
Stapleton	D3
Stockville	D4
Superior	F4
Sutton	G4
Syracuse	H3
Taylor	E3
Tecumseh	H3
Tekamah	H3
Thedford	D3
Trenton	C4
Tryon	D3
Valentine	D2
Valley	H3
Wahoo	H3
Waverly	H4
Wayne	H3
West Point	H3
Wilber	H4
Wisner	H4
Wymore	H4
York	G4

Other Features

	Key
Agate Fossil Beds N.M.	A2
Arikee, *river*	B5
Big Blue, *river*	G4
C.W. McConaughy, *lake*	C3
Calamus, *reservoir*	E3
Calamus, *river*	E3
Cedar, *river*	F3
Chimney Rock Natl. Hist. Site	A3
Elkhorn, *river*	E2, G3
Harlan Co., *lake*	E4
Homestead Natl. Monument	H4
Lewis and Clark, *lake*	G2
Little Blue, *river*	G4
Loup, *river*	F3
Middle Loup, *river*	D3
Missouri, *river*	J4
Niobrara, *river*	B2, E2
North Loup, *river*	C2, E3
North Platte, *river*	B3
Pine, *mt. ridge*	B3
Platte, *river*	D4, G3
Republican, *river*	D4
Sand, *hills*	C3
Scotts Bluff Natl. Monument	A3
South Fork Republican, *river*	B5
South Loup, *river*	E3

Nevada ....page 155

Cities and Towns

	Key
Alamo	C3
Battle Mountain	B1
Beatty	B3
Boulder City	C4
Carlin	B1
Carson City, *capital*	A2
Elko	C1
Ely	C2
Eureka	C2
Fallon	A2
Fernley	A2
Gardnerville	A2
Goldfield	B3
Hawthorne	A2
Henderson	C4
Incline Village	A2
Las Vegas	C4
Laughlin	C4
Lovelock	A1
McGill	C2
Mesquite	C3
Minden	A2
North Fork	C1
North Las Vegas	C4
Pahrump	B3
Paradise	C4
Pioche	C3
Reno	A2
Silver Peak	B3
Sparks	A2
Spring Creek	C1
Spring Valley	C3

	Key
Sun Valley	A2
Tonopah	B2
Virginia City	A2
Wells	C1
West Wendover	C1
Winnemucca	B1
Yerington	A2
Zephyr Cove	A2

Other Features

	Key
Arc Dome, *mt.*	B2
Black Rock, *desert*	A1
Boundary Peak, *mt.*	A3
Colorado, *river*	C4
Desert, *valley*	B1
Egan, *range*	C2
Goshute, *lake*	C1
Grant, *mts.*	C2
Grant, *range*	A2
Great Basin	B2
Great Basin Natl. Park	C2
Hoover Dam	C3
Hot Creek, *range*	B2
Independence, *mts.*	B1
Jefferson, *mt.*	B2
Lake Mead Natl. Rec. Area	C3
Marys, *river*	C1
Matterhorn, *mt.*	C1
Mead, *lake*	C3
Mohave, *lake*	C4
Monitor, *range*	B2
Moriah, *mt.*	C2
North Toiyabe Peak, *mt.*	B2
Owyhee, *desert*	B1
Owyhee, *river*	B1
Pilot Peak, *mt.*	C1
Pyramid, *lake*	A1
Quinn, *river*	B1
Ruby, *mts.*	C1
Ruby Dome, *mt.*	C1
Rye Patch, *reservoir*	A1
Schell Creek, *range*	C2
Shoshone, *mts.*	B2
Shoshone, *range*	B1
Smoky, *valley*	B2
Snake, *range*	C2
Summit, *mt.*	A2
Tahoe, *lake*	A2
Tobin, *mt.*	B1
Toiyabe, *range*	B2
Toquima, *range*	B2
Tuscarora, *mts.*	B1
Virgin, *river*	C3
Walker, *lake*	A2
Wheeler Peak, *mt.*	C2
White, *river*	C3

New Hampshire ....page 156

Cities and Towns

	Key
Albany	B3
Amherst	B4
Antrim	B3
Barnstead	B3
Bartlett	B2
Benton	B2
Berlin	B2
Blair	B3
Bradford	B3
Bretton Woods	B2
Bristol	B3
Candia	B3
Cascade	B2
Claremont	A3
Concord, *capital*	B3
Contoocook	B3
Conway	B2
Cornish City	A3
Dalton	B2
Deerfield	B3
Deering	B3
Derry	B4
Dixville Notch	B2
Dover	C3
Dunbarton Center	B3
Durham	B3
Easton	B2
Enfield	A3
Epping	B3
Exeter	C4
Farmington	B3
Franklin	B3
Gilmanton	B3
Glencliff	B2
Gorham	B2
Groveton	B2
Hampstead	B4
Hampton	C4
Hanover	A3
Haverhill	B2
Henniker	B3
Hillsboro	B3
Hinsdale	A4
Hollis	B4
Hooksett	B3
Hudson	B4
Jackson	B2
Jaffrey	A4
Jefferson	B2
Keene	A4
Laconia	B3
Lancaster	B2
Lebanon	A3
Littleton	B2
Loudon	B3
Lyman	B2
Manchester	B4
Meredith	B3
Merrimack	B4
Milan	B2
Milford	B4
Monroe	A2
Munsonville	A3
Nashua	B4
Newbury	A3
New Castle	C3
New London	B3
Newmarket	C3
Newport	A3
North Conway	B2
Northfield	B3
North Haverhill	B2
North Walpole	A3
North Woodstock	B2
Orford	A3
Ossipee	B3
Pelham	B4
Percy	B2
Peterborough	B4
Pinardville	B4

	Key
Pittsfield	B3
Plymouth	B3
Portsmouth	C3
Quaker City	A3
Randolph	B2
Raymond	B3
Rochester	C3
Rumney	B3
Rye	C4
Sandwich	B3
Sharon	B4
Shelburne	B2
Silver Lake	B3
Somersworth	C3
South Hooksett	B3
Springfield	A3
Stewartstown Hollow	B2
Strafford	B3
Stratford	B2
Suncook	B3
Sutton	B3
Tilton	B3
Warner	B3
Waterville Valley	B3
Westport	A4
West Rindge	A4
West Stewartstown	B2
Whittier	B3
Willey House	B2
Winchester	A4
Wolfeboro	B3
Woodsville	A2

Other Features

	Key
Appalachian Natl. Scenic Trail	A3
Blackwater, *reservoir*	B3
Blue, *mt.*	B2
Cabot, *mt.*	B2
Cardigan, *mt.*	B3
Connecticut, *river*	A3
First Connecticut, *lake*	B1
Franconia, *notch*	B2
Great, *bay*	C3
Indian, *river*	B1
Kearsarge, *mt.*	B3
Merrimack, *river*	B4
Monadnock, *mt.*	A4
Newfound, *lake*	B3
Ossipee, *lake*	B3
Presidential, *mt. range*	B2
Saint-Gaudens Natl. Hist. Site	A3
Second Connecticut, *lake*	B1
Smarts, *mt.*	B3
Squam, *lake*	B3
Sunapee, *lake*	A3
Swift, *river*	B3
Umbagog, *lake*	B2
Washington, *mt.*	B2
White, *mt.*	B2
Winnipesaukee, *lake*	B3
Winnisquam, *lake*	B3

New Jersey ....page 157

Cities and Towns

	Key
Absecon	E5
Allendale	E1
Allentown	D3
Alloway	C4
Alpine	C1
Asbury Park	E3
Atlantic City	E5
Atlantic Highlands	E3
Atsion	D4
Avalon	D5
Barrington	B3
Basking Ridge	D2
Batsto	D4
Bay Point	C5
Bayonne	E2
Bayside	C5
Beachwood	E4
Beattyestown	D2
Beckett	C4
Belle Mead	D3
Belleville	E2
Bellmawr	B3, C4
Belmar	E3
Belvidere	C2
Bergenfield	B1
Berkeley Heights	E2
Berlin	D4
Bernardsville	D2
Blackwood	C4
Blairstown	D2
Bloomfield	E2
Bogota	B1
Boonton	E2
Bordentown	D3
Bound Brook	D2
Bradley Beach	E2
Brass Castle	C2
Brick	E3
Bridgeboro	C3
Bridgeton	C5
Brielle	E3
Brigantine	E5
Brookdale	B1
Browns Mills	D4
Budd Lake	D2
Buena	D4
Burlington	D3
Butler	E1
Caldwell	A1
Camden	B3, C4
Cape May	D6
Cape May Court House	D5
Carlstadt	B1
Carneys Point	C4
Carteret	B2
Carteret	E2
Cedar Grove	B1
Centerton	C4
Centerville	D2
Chatham	E2
Cherry Hill	B3, C4
Chesilhurst	D4
Chesterfield	D3
Cinnaminson	B3, D4
Clark	A2
Clayton	C4
Cliffside Park	B1
Clifton	E2
Clinton	D2
Closter	F2
Colesville	D1
Collings Lakes	D4
Collingswood	B3
Colonia	E2
Cranford	E2

	Key
Deerfield	C4
Delanco	D3
Denville	E2
Deptford	B4
Dover	D2
Dumont	C1
Dunellen	E2
East Brunswick	E3
East Orange	E2
East Rutherford	B1
Eatontown	E3
Edgewater	F2
Edison	E2
Egg Harbor City	D4
Elizabeth	E2
Elmer	C4
Elmwood Park	B1
Elwood	D4
Emerson	E2
Englewood	C1
Englewood Cliffs	C1
Englishtown	E3
Erma	D6
Estell Manor	D5
Evesboro	C3
Ewing	D3
Fair Lawn	B1, E2
Fairfield	E2
Fairton	C5
Fairview	F2
Fanwood	E2
Farmingdale	E3
Fellowship	C3
Fieldsboro	D3
Flemington	D3
Folsom	D4
Fords	E2
Forked River	E4
Fort Lee	C1
Franklin	D1
Franklinville	C4
Freehold	E3
Frenchtown	C2
Garfield	E2
Gilford Park	E4
Glassboro	C4
Glen Gardner	D2
Glen Ridge	B2
Glendora	B4
Gloucester City	B3, C4
Goshen	D5
Great Notch	B1
Green Bank	D4
Greenwich	C5
Guttenberg	F2
Hackensack	E2
Hackettstown	D2
Haddon Heights	B3
Haddonfield	B3
Hainesville	D1
Haledon	B1
Hamburg	D1
Hammonton	D4
Hampton	D2
Harrison	B2
Haworth	C1
Hawthorne	B1
Hedger House	E1
High Bridge	D2
Highland Lakes	E1
Highland Park	E3
Highlands	F3
Hightstown	D3
Hillsdale	E1
Hillside	B2
Hoboken	E2
Hopatcong	D2
Hopewell	D3
Howardsville	D4
Indian Mills	D4
Irvington	E3
Jamesburg	E3
Jenkins Neck	D4
Jersey City	E2
Keansburg	E2
Kearny	B2
Kendall Park	D3
Kenilworth	E2
Kinnelon	E2
Lakehurst	E3
Lakewood	E3
Lambertville	D3
Lavallette	E4
Lawnside	C4
Lawrenceville	D3
Leeds Point	E5
Leisure Village	E3
Leonardo	E3
Lincroft	E3
Linden	E2
Lindenwold	B4, C4
Linwood	D5
Little Falls	B1
Livingston	E2
Lodi	B1
Long Branch	F3
Long Valley	D2
Lyndhurst	B1
Madison	E2
Mahwah	E1
Manahawkin	E4
Manalapan	E3
Manasquan	E3
Manumuskin	D5
Manville	D2
Maple Shade	B3, D4
Maplewood	E2
Marcella	E2
Margate City	E5
Marlboro	E3
Marlton	C3, D4
Matawan	E3
Mays Landing	D5
Maywood	B1
Medford Lakes	D4
Mendham	E2
Menlo Park	E2
Merchantville	B3
Metuchen	E2
Middlesex	E2
Middletown	E2
Midland Park	E2
Milford	D2
Millburn	E2
Millville	C5
Monmouth Beach	F3
Montclair	E2
Montvale	E1
Moorestown	C3, D4
Morris Plains	E2

	Key
Morristown	E2
Mountain Lakes	E2
Mount Holly	D4
Mount Laurel	D4
Mystic Islands	E4
National Park	B3
Neptune City	E3
Netcong	E2
Newark	E2
New Brunswick	E3
New Egypt	D3
Newfield	C4
New Gretna	E4
Newfoundland	E1
New Providence	E2
Newton	D1
Normandy Beach	E4
North Arlington	B2
North Bergen	B2
North Cape May	D6
Northfield	D5
North Wildwood	D5
Nutley	E2
Oakland	E1
Oaklyn	B3
Ocean City	D5
Oceanport	E3
Ogdensburg	D1
Olivet	C4
Oradel	B1
Orange	E2
Othello	D5
Oxford	D2
Palisades Park	B3, C3
Palmyra	B3, C3
Paramus	B1, E2
Park Ridge	E1
Passaic	E2
Paterson	E2
Paulsboro	A4, C4
Pemberton	D4
Pennington	D3
Penns Grove	C4
Pennsauken	B3
Pennsville	B4
Perth Amboy	E2
Phillipsburg	C2
Piscataway	E2
Pine Hill	D4
Pitman	D2
Pittstown	D2
Plainfield	E2
Pleasant Plains	E4
Pleasantville	D5
Point Pleasant	E3
Pomona	D5
Port Monmouth	E2
Port Norris	C5
Princeton	D3
Princeton Junction	D3
Prospect Park	E2
Quinton	C4
Rahway	E2
Ramblewood	C3
Ramsey	E1
Raritan	D2
Red Bank	E3
Ridgefield	B2
Ridgefield Park	B1, E2
Ridgewood	E2
Ringoes	E1
Ringwood	E1
Rio Grande	D5
River Edge	B1
Riverside	C3, D3
Riverton	B3, C3
Robertsville	E3
Rochelle Park	E2
Rocktown	D3
Roselle	A2
Roselle Park	A2
Rumson	E3
Runnemede	B4, C4
Rutherford	B1
Salem	C4
Sayreville	E3
Seabrook	C5
Sea Girt	E3
Sea Isle City	D5
Seaside Heights	E4
Seaside Park	E4
Secaucus	B2
Ship Bottom	E4
Shrewsbury	E3
Silverton	E4
Smithville	E5
Somerdale	B4
Somers Point	D5
Somerset	D2
Somerville	D2
South Amboy	E3
South Orange	A2
South River	E3
Sparta	D1
Spotswood	E3
Spring Lake Heights	E3
Stanhope	D2
Stillwater	D1
Stockholm	E1
Stratford	B4, C4
Strathmere	D5
Summit	E2
Surf City	E4
Sussex	D1
Swedesboro	C4
Teaneck	B1
Tenafly	C1
Tinton Falls	E3
Toms River	E4
Totowa	B1
Trenton, *capital*	D3
Tuckahoe	D5
Tuckerton	E4
Turnersville	C4
Twin Rivers	E3
Union	E3
Union Beach	E3
Union City	E2
Upton	D4
Vauxhall	A2
Ventnor City	E5
Vernon	E1
Verona	E2
Villas	D5
Vineland	C4
Voorhees	C4
Waldwick	E1
Wanamassa	E3
Wanaque	E1
Waretown	E4
Warren Glen	C2

	Key
Warren Grove	E4
Washington	D2
Washington Crossing	D3
Watchung	E2
Wayne	A1, E2
Weehawken	B2
Welchville	C4
Wenonah	C4
Westfield	E2
Westmont	B3
West Milford	E1
West New York	C2
West Orange	E2
West Paterson	B1
Westville	B3
Westwood	B1
Wharton	D2
White Horse	D3
White House Station	D2
White Meadow Lake	D2
Whiting	D4
Wildwood	D6
Wildwood Crest	D6
Williamstown	D4
Willingboro	D3
Woodbine	D5
Woodbridge	B4, C4
Woodbury	B4, C4
Woodlynne	B3
Wood Ridge	B1
Woodstown	C4
Woodstream	C3
Wrightstown	D3
Wyckoff	E1

Other Features

	Key
Cape May, point	D6
Cooper, river	B4
Delaware, bay	C5
Delaware, river	D3
Delaware Water Gap N.R.A.	D1
Edison Natl. Hist. Site	B2
Gateway Natl. Rec. Area	E3
Great, bay	E5
Hudson, river	C2
Morristown Nat. Hist. Park	D2
Pines, river	B1
Raritan, bay	E3
Statue of Liberty N.M.	B2

New Mexico .... page 158

Cities and Towns

	Key
Acoma Pueblo	B2
Acomita	B2
Alameda	B2
Alamogordo	C3
Albuquerque	B2
Anthony	B4
Artesia	C3
Aztec	B1
Bayard	A3
Belen	B2
Bernalillo	B1
Bloomfield	B1
Bosque Farms	B2
Carlsbad	C3
Carrizozo	C3
Central	A3
Chaparral	B3
Chimayo	C1
Clayton	D1
Clovis	D2
Corrales	B2
Deming	B3
Dulce	B1
Elida	D3
Elk	C3
Elkins	C3
Espanola	B2
Estancia	B2
Eunice	D3
Fairacres	B3
Farmington	A1
Floyd	D2
Fort Sumner	C2
Gallup	A2
Grants	B2
Greenfield	C3
Hobbs	D3
Hurley	A3
Jal	D3
Jemez Pueblo	B2
Kirtland	A1
La Luz	C3
Las Cruces	B3
Las Vegas	C2
Lordsburg	A3
Los Alamos	B2
Los Chavez	B2
Los Lunas	B2
Los Padillas	B2
Lovington	D3
Lower Colonias	C2
Lower San Francisco Plaza	A3
Maxwell	C1
Mayhill	C3
Mesilla	B3
Milan	B2
Mora	C2
Moriarty	B2
Mosquero	D2
Navajo	A2
Polvadera	B2
Portales	D2
Questa	C1
Ranchos De Taos	C1
Raton	C1
Reserve	A3
Rio Rancho	B2
Roswell	C3
Ruidoso	C3
Sabinoso	C2
San Felipe Pueblo	B2
San Miguel	B1
San Miguel	B3
Santa Fe, capital	C2
Santa Rosa	C2
Santo Domingo Pueblo	B2
Shiprock	A1
Silver City	A3
Socorro	B2
Springer	C1
Sunland Park	C1
Taos	C1
Tesuque	C1
Tierra Amarilla	B1
Truth or Consequences	B3
Tucumcari	D2
Tularosa	B3
University Park	B3
Ute Park	C1
Valencia	B2
Waterflow	A1
Zuni Pueblo	A2

Other Features

	Key
Abiquiu, reservoir	B1
Alegres, mt.	A2
Aztec Ruins Natl. Monument	B1
Baldy, mt.	C1
Bandelier Natl. Monument	B2
Black, mt. range	B3
Burro, mt.	A3
Caballo, reservoir	B3
Canadian, river	C1
Capulin Volcano N.M.	D1
Carlsbad Caverns Natl. Park	C3
Cebolleta, mt.	B2
Cerro Vista, mt.	C1
Chaco Culture Natl. Hist. Site	B1
Cimarron, river	D1
Conchas, lake	C2
Continental Divide, mt. ridge	B3
Cooke's, mt.	B3
Elephant Butte, res.	B3
El Malpais Natl. Monument	B2
El Morro Natl. Monument	A2
Fort Union Natl. Monument	C2
Gallinas, mt.	C2
Gila, river	A3
Gila Cliff Dwellings N.M.	A3
Guadalupe, mts.	C3
Jornada Del Muerto	B3
Llano Estacado, plateau	D3
Navajo, reservoir	B1
Navajo Indian Res.	A1
Pecos, river	C2, C3
Pecos, plains	C3
Petroglyph Natl. Monument	B2
Playas, lake	A3
Reeds, mt.	B3
Rio Grande, river	C1
Rio Hondo, river	C3
Rio Puerco, river	B2
Salinas Pueblo Missions N.M.	B2
San Andres, mts.	B3
San Juan, river	A1
Sangre De Cristo, mts.	C1
Shiprock, mt.	A1
Sierra Blanca, mt.	C1
South Baldy, mt.	B3
Sumner, lake	C2
Taylor, mt.	B2
Wheeler, mt.	C1
White Sands Natl. Monument	B3
Whitewater Baldy, mt.	A3
Withington, mt.	B3
Zuni, mts.	A2

New York .... page 159

Cities and Towns

	Key
Adams	H3
Adams Center	H3
Akron	C4
Albany, capital	N5
Albion	D4
Alden	D5
Alfred	E6
Allegany	D6
Altamont	M5
Amsterdam	M5
Angola	B5
Arcade	D5
Astoria	A3
Athens	N6
Attica	D5
Auburn	G5
Avon	E5
Bainbridge	J6
Baldwinsville	H4
Ballston Spa	N4
Batavia	D4
Bath	F6
Beacon	N7
Bedford-Stuyvesant	A4
Belle Harbor	A4
Belmont	D6
Bensonhurst	A4
Big Flats	G6
Binghamton	J6
Bloomfield	F5
Bolivar	D6
Boonville	K4
Breezy Point	A4
Brentwood	C1
Brewerton	H4
Bridgehampton	E1
Brighton Beach	A4
Broadalbin	M4
Brockport	E4
Brocton	B6
Bronx	A3, B1
Bronxville	A2
Brooklyn	A4, B2
Buffalo	C5
Cairo	M6
Calcium	J2
Caledonia	E5
Cambridge	P4
Camden	J4
Canajoharie	L5
Canandaigua	F5
Canarsie	A4
Canastota	J4
Canisteo	E6
Canton	K1
Carmel	N7
Carthage	J3
Castleton-on-Hudson	N5
Catskill	N6
Cayuga Heights	H6
Cazenovia	J5
Cedarhurst	B4
Central Square	H4
Chatham	N6
Cheektowaga	C5
Chittenango	J5
Churchville	E4
Clayton	K4
Clinton	K4
Clyde	G4
Cobleskill	M5
Cohoes	N5
College Point	A3
Colonie	N5
Coney Island	A4
Cooperstown	L5
Corinth	N4
Corning	F6
Cortland	H5
Coxsackie	N6
Cuba	D6
Dannemora	N1
Dansville	E5
Delhi	L6
De Ruyter	J5
Deposit	K6
Dolgeville	L4
Dover Plains	N7
Dryden	H6
Dundee	G6
Dunkirk	B6
East Atlantic Beach	B4
Eastchester	A4
East Hampton	E1
East Islip	C2
East New York	A4
East Northport	C1
East Patchogue	D1
Eden	C5
Elizabethtown	N2
Ellenville	M7
Elmira	G6
Elmira Heights	G6
Elmont	B4
Endicott	H6
Endwell	H6
Fairmount	H4
Far Rockaway	B4
Fayette	G5
Fine	K2
Flatbush	A4
Flushing	A3
Fonda	M5
Fort Edward	N4
Fort Plain	L5
Franklin Sq.	B4
Franklinville	D6
Fredonia	B6
Freeport	C2
Frewsburg	B6
Friendship	D6
Fulton	H4
Geneseo	E5
Geneva	G5
Glen Cove	B1
Glens Falls	N4
Gloversville	M4
Goshen	M7
Gouverneur	K2
Gowanda	C6
Granville	P4
Gravesend	A4
Great Neck	B1
Greece	E4
Greene	J6
Greenport	E1
Greenwich	P4
Groton	H6
Hamburg	C5
Hamilton	J5
Hampton Bays	E1
Hancock	K7
Harlem	A3
Hempstead	B2
Herkimer	L4
Hicksville	C1
Highland	N7
Hilton	E4
Holbrook	C1
Holland	C5
Holley	D4
Homer	H5
Hoosick Falls	P5
Hornell	E6
Horseheads	G6
Houghton	D6
Howard Beach	A4
Hudson	N6
Hudson Falls	N4
Huntington Station	C1
Hurley	M7
Ilion	K4
Inwood	B4
Irondequoit	E4
Ithaca	H6
Jamaica	A4
Jamestown	B6
Johnson City	J6
Johnstown	M4
Keeseville	P1
Kew Gardens	A4
Kinderhook	N6
Kingston	N7
Lake George	N4
Lake Placid	M2
Lake Pleasant	M4
Lakewood	B6
Lansing	H5
Larchmont	B2
Lawrence	B4
Le Roy	D5
Levittown	C1
Liberty	L7
Lima	E5
Lindenhurst	C2
Little Falls	L4
Little Valley	C6
Livingston Manor	L7
Livonia	E5
Lockport	C4
Long Beach	B2
Long Eddy	K7
Long Island City	A3
Long Lake	M3
Loon Lake	M1
Lowville	K3
Lynbrook	B4
Lyons	G4
Malone	M1
Mamaroneck	B2
Manhasset Hills	B3
Manhattan	A3
Manlius	J4
Manorhaven	B1
Massapequa	C2
Massena	L1
Mastic	D1
Mastic Beach	D1
Mattituck	E1
Mayville	B6
Mechanicville	N5
Medina	D4
Mexico	H4
Middleburgh	M5
Middleport	D4
Middletown	M7
Millbrook	N7
Mineola	B1
Mohawk	K5
Monroe	A1
Montauk	F1
Monticello	L7
Montour Falls	G6
Moravia	H5
Mount Kisco	B1
Mount Morris	E5
Mount Vernon	B1, C5
Munnsville	J5
Nassau	N5
Newark	F4
Newburgh	M7
New City	B1
Newfane	C4
New Hartford	K4
New Hyde Park	B3
New Paltz	M7
New Rochelle	B3
New York	B2
Niagara Falls	B4
Norfolk	L1
North Collins	C5
North Hills	B3
North Syracuse	H4
North Tonawanda	B4
Norwich	J5
Norwood	L1
Nunda	E5
Nyack	B1
Oakfield	D4
Ogdensburg	K1
Olcott	C4
Olean	D6
Oneida	J4
Oneonta	K6
Ossining	B1
Oswego	H4
Owego	H6
Oxford	J6
Ozone Park	A4
Painted Post	F6
Palmyra	F4
Pawling	N7
Peekskill	B1
Pelham	A3
Pelham Manor	A3
Penn Yan	F5
Perry	D5
Peru	N1
Philadelphia	J2
Philmont	N6
Phoenix	H4
Pine Bush	M7
Plattsburgh	P1
Port Henry	P2
Port Jefferson	D1
Port Morris	A3
Port Washington	B3
Potsdam	L1
Poughkeepsie	N7
Pulaski	H3
Queens	B4
Randolph	C6
Ransomville	C4
Ravena	N6
Red Hook	N7
Rensselaer	N5
Rhinebeck	N7
Richfield Springs	L5
Riverhead	D1
Rochester	E4
Rockaway Point	A4
Rocky Point	D1
Rome	K4
Rosendale	M7
Rouses Point	P1
Rye	B3
Sackets Harbor	H3
Sag Harbor	E1
St. George	A2
St. Johnsville	L4
Salamanca	C6
Sands Point	B3
Saranac Lake	M2
Saratoga Springs	N4
Saugerties	N6
Sayville	D2
Schenectady	N5
Schoharie	M5
Scotia	N5
Seneca Falls	G5
Sherburne	K5
Shortsville	F5
Sidney	K6
Silver Creek	B5
Skaneateles	H5
Sodus	F4
Southampton	E1
South Fallsburg	L7
Southold	E1
Southport	G6
Spencerport	E4
Springville	C5
Stillwater	N5
Stony Brook	C1
Suffern	A1
Syracuse	H4
Throgs Neck	A3
Ticonderoga	P3
Troy	N5
Trumansburg	G5
Tupper Lake	M2
Unadilla	K6
Utica	K4
Valley Stream	B2
Victory Mills	N4
Voorheesville	N5
Walden	M7
Walton	K6
Wampsville	J4
Wappingers Falls	N7
Warrensburg	N4
Warsaw	D5
Warwick	A1
Waterloo	G5
Watertown	J3
Waterville	K5
Watkins Glen	G6
Waverly	G6
Wayland	E5
Weedsport	G4
Wellsville	D6
West Carthage	J3
Westfield	A6
West Point	N7
West Seneca	C5
Whitehall	P3
White Plains	B1
Whitesboro	K4
Whitestone	A3
Williamsburg	A4
Wilson	C4
Wolcott	G4
Woodmere	B4
Woodstock	M6
Yonkers	B1
Yorktown Heights	B1

Other Features

	Key
Adirondack, mts.	L2
Adirondack Park	M2
Appalachian Natl. Scenic Trail	A1
Black, lake	J2
Black, river	K3
Cannonsville, reservoir	K6
Catskill, mts.	L7
Catskill Park	L6
Cayuga, lake	G5
Champlain, lake	P1
Chenango, river	L2
Cranberry, lake	L2
Delaware, river	J4
Erie, canal	J4
Erie, lake	A5
Fire Island Natl. Seashore	D2
Fishers, island	F1
Fort Stanwix Natl. Monument	K4
Galloo, island	H3
Gardiners, island	F1
Gateway Natl. Rec. Area	B2
Genesee, river	D6
George, lake	N3
Great Sacandaga, lake	M4
Hinckley, reservoir	K4
Home of F.D.R. Natl. Hist. Site	N7
Hudson, river	M3
Indian, lake	M3
J.F.K. Int'l Airport	A4
Keuka, lake	F5
Long, island	E1
Long, lake	M3
Long Island, sound	C1
Marcy, mt.	M2
Martin Van Buren Natl. Hist. Site	N6
Mettawee, river	P4
Mohawk, river	L5
Oneida, lake	J4
Ontario, lake	E3
Pepacton, reservoir	L6
Piseco, lake	L4
St. Lawrence, river	K1
Salmon River, reservoir	J3
Saratoga, lake	N4
Saratoga Natl. Hist. Park	N4
Schoharie, reservoir	M6
Schroon, lake	N3
Slide, mt.	M7
Staten, island	A2
Stony, island	H3
Susquehanna, river	J6
Thousand, islands	H2
Tupper, lake	L2
Unadilla, river	K5
Upper Saranac, lake	M2
West Point Military Academy	A1

North Carolina .... page 160

Cities and Towns

	Key
Aberdeen	G4
Ahoskie	L2
Albemarle	E4
Andrews	C8
Angier	H3
Apex	H3
Archdale	F3
Asheboro	F3
Asheville	E7
Atlantic Beach	M5
Ayden	L4
Badin	E4
Bakersville	A2
Bayboro	M4
Beaufort	M5
Belhaven	M4
Belmont	C4
Benson	H4
Bessemer City	C4
Bethel	L3
Biscoe	F4
Black Mt.	A3
Bladenboro	H5
Blowing Rock	B2
Boiling Spring Lakes	J6
Boiling Springs	B4
Bolivia	J6
Boone	B2
Brevard	E8
Bryson City	C8
Buies Creek	H4
Burgaw	K5
Burlington	F3
Burnsville	A3
Butner	H2
Camden	N2
Canton	E7
Carolina Beach	K6
Carthage	G4
Cary	H3
Chadbourn	H6
Chapel Hill	G3
Charlotte	D4
Cherryville	C4
China Grove	D3
Clayton	H3
Clemmons	E3
Clinton	J5
Coats	H4
Columbia	N3
Columbus	A4
Concord	D4
Conover	C3
Cornelius	D4
Creedmoor	H2
Cullowhee	D8
Currituck	N2
Dallas	C4
Danbury	E2
Davidson	D4
Denton	E3
Dobson	E2
Drexel	B3
Dunn	H4
Durham	H2
E. Flat Rock	E8
Eden	F2
Edenton	M2
Elizabeth City	N2
Elizabethtown	H5
Elkin	D2
Elm City	K3
Emerald Isle	M5
Enfield	K2
Erwin	H4
Fairmont	G5
Farmville	L3
Fayetteville	H4
Fletcher	E8
Forest City	B4
Four Oaks	H4
Franklin	C8
Franklinton	H2
Fremont	K3
Fuquay-Varina	H3
Garner	H3
Gastonia	C4
Gatesville	M2
Gibsonville	F2
Goldsboro	K4
Graham	F3
Granite Falls	C3
Granite Quarry	E3
Greensboro	F2
Greenville	L3
Grifton	L3
Halifax	K2
Hamlet	F5
Harkers Island	M5
Harrisburg	D4
Havelock	M5
Hayesville	C8
Hays	C2
Henderson	H2
Hendersonville	E8
Hertford	N2
Hickory	C3
High Point	E3
Hillsborough	G2
Hope Mills	H5
Hudson	C3
Huntersville	D4
Icard	C3
Indian Trail	D4
Jackson	K2
Jacksonville	L5
Jamestown	F3
Jefferson	C2
Jonesville	D2
Kannapolis	D4
Kenansville	K5
Kenly	J3
Kernersville	F2
Kill Devil Hills	P2
King	E2
Kings Mt.	C4
Kinston	K4
Kitty Hawk	P2
La Grange	K4
Laurinburg	G5
Leland	J6
Lenoir	B3
Lewisville	E2
Lexington	E3
Liberty	F3
Lillington	H4
Lincolnton	C4
Locust	D4
Long Beach	J7
Long View	C3
Louisburg	J2
Lumberton	G5
Madison	F2
Maiden	C3
Manteo	P3
Marion	A3
Marshall	E7
Marshville	E5
Matthews	D4
Maxton	G5
Mayodan	F2
Mebane	G2
Mint Hill	D4
Mocksville	D3
Monroe	D4
Mooresville	D3
Moravian Falls	C2
Morehead City	M5
Morganton	B3
Mt. Airy	D2
Mt. Gilead	F4
Mt. Holly	D4
Mt. Olive	J4
Mulberry	C2
Murfreesboro	L2
Murphy	B8
Nags Head	P3
Nashville	K3
New Bern	L4
Newland	B2
Newport	M5
Newton	C3
Norwood	E4
North Wilkesboro	C2
Oxford	H2
Pembroke	G5
Pinehurst	G4
Pinetops	K3
Pineville	D4
Piney Green	L5
Pittsboro	G3
Plymouth	M3
Polkville	B4
Raeford	G5
Raleigh, capital	H3
Randleman	F3
Red Springs	G5
Reidsville	F2
River Bend	L4
Roanoke Rapids	K2
Robbinsville	C8
Robersonville	L3
Rockingham	F5
Rockwell	E3
Rocky Mount	K3
Rolesville	H3
Rose Hill	K5
Roseboro	H5
Roxboro	H2
Rural Hall	E2
Rutherfordton	B4
Salisbury	E3
Sanford	G4
Sawmills	C3
Scotland Neck	L2
Selma	J3
Seven Lakes	G4
Sharpsburg	K3
Shelby	B4
Siler City	G3
Smithfield	J3

Key
Sneads Ferry ... L5
Snow Hill ... K4
Southern Pines ... G4
Southern Shores ... P2
Southport ... J7
Sparta ... C1
Spencer ... E3
Spindale ... B4
Spring Lake ... H4
Spruce Pine ... A3
St. Pauls ... H5
Stanley ... C4
Stanleyville ... E2
Statesville ... D3
Stokesdale ... F2
Stony Point ... C3
Summerfield ... F2
Swan Quarter ... N4
Sylva ... D8
Tabor City ... H6
Tarboro ... K3
Taylorsville ... C3
Thomasville ... E3
Toast ... D2
Trenton ... L4
Troutman ... D3
Troy ... F4
Valdese ... B3
Wadesboro ... E5
Wake Forest ... H3
Wallace ... K5
Wanchese ... P3
Warrenton ... J2
Warsaw ... J5
Washington ... L3
Waxhaw ... D5
Waynesville ... D7
Weddington ... D4
Welcome ... E3
Weldon ... K2
Wendell ... J3
Wentworth ... F2
W. Jefferson ... C2
Whiteville ... H6
Wilkesboro ... C2
Williamston ... L3
Wilmington ... K6
Wilson ... K3
Windsor ... M2
Winfall ... N2
Wingate ... E5
Winston-Salem ... E2
Winterville ... L3
Winton ... M2
Woodfin ... E7
Wrightsville Beach ... K6
Yadkinville ... D2
Yanceyville ... G2
Zebulon ... J3

Other Features
Albemarle, *sound* ... N3
Alligator, *lake* ... N3
Alligator, *river* ... N3
B. Everett Jordan, *lake* ... G3
Bodie, *island* ... P3
Cape Fear, *river* ... H5
Cape Hatteras Natl. Seashore ... P4
Cape Lookout Natl. Seashore ... N5
Chatuga, *lake* ... C8
Clingmans Dome, *mt.* ... C7
Dan, *river* ... F2
Deep, *river* ... F3
Falls Lake, *reservoir* ... H3
Fear, *cape* ... K7
Fontana, *lake* ... C7
Fort Raleigh Natl. Hist. Site ... P3
Gaston, *lake* ... K1
Great, *lake* ... L5
Great Smoky Mts. Natl. Park ... C7
Hatteras, *cape* ... P4
Hatteras, *inlet* ... P4
Highrock, *lake* ... E3
Hiwassee, *lake* ... B8
Hyco, *lake* ... G2
John H. Kerr, *reservoir* ... H1
Lookout, *cape* ... M5
Mattamuskeat, *lake* ... N3
Mitchell, *mt.* ... A3
Nantahala, *lake* ... C8
Neuse, *river* ... J4
Norman, *lake* ... D3
Ocracoke, *inlet* ... N4
Oregon, *inlet* ... P3
Pamlico, *river* ... M4
Pamlico, *sound* ... P4
Phelps, *lake* ... N3
Roan, *mt.* ... A2
Roanoke, *river* ... K2
Rocky, *river* ... E4
Smith, *island* ... K7
Standing Indian, *mt.* ... C8
Tar, *river* ... J2
Waccamaw, *lake* ... J6
Wright Brothers Natl. Memorial ... P2
Yadkin, *river* ... D2

North Dakota ....page 161

Cities and Towns
Ashley ... F3
Beach ... A3
Belcourt ... F1
Beulah ... D2
Bismarck, *capital* ... E3
Bowman ... B3
Cando ... F1
Carrington ... F2
Casselton ... H3
Cavalier ... H1
Center ... D2
Cooperstown ... G2
Crosby ... B1
Devils Lake ... G1
Dickinson ... C3
Ellendale ... G3
Fargo ... J3
Fessenden ... F2
Finley ... H2
Forman ... H3
Fort Yates ... E3
Garrison ... D2
Grafton ... H1
Grand Forks ... H2
Harvey ... F2
Hazen ... D2
Hettinger ... C3
Hillsboro ... H2
Jamestown ... G3
Lakota ... G1

Key
La Moure ... G3
Langdon ... G1
Larimore ... H2
Linton ... E3
Lisbon ... H3
McClusky ... E2
Mandan ... E3
Mayville ... H2
Mohall ... D1
Mott ... C3
Napoleon ... F3
New Rockford ... F2
New Town ... C1
Oakes ... G3
Park River ... H1
Rolla ... F1
Rugby ... F1
Stanley ... C1
Stanton ... D2
Steele ... F3
Tioga ... C1
Towner ... E1
Valley City ... H3
Wahpeton ... J3
Washburn ... D2
Watford City ... B2
West Fargo ... J3
Williston ... B1

Other Features
Cannonball, *river* ... D3
Devils, *lake* ... G1
Fort Union Trading Post N.H.S. ... A1
Green, *river* ... B2
Heart, *river* ... D3
Intl. Peace Garden ... E1
James, *river* ... F2
Jamestown, *reservoir* ... G2
Knife, *river* ... C2
Knife River Indian Villages N.H.S. ... D2
Little Missouri, *river* ... B3
Long, *lake* ... E3
Maple, *river* ... G3, H2
Missouri, *river* ... D2
Oahe, *lake* ... E3
Pembina, *river* ... G1
Sakakawea, *lake* ... C2
Sheyenne, *river* ... E2, G2, H3
Souris, *river* ... D1
Theodore Roosevelt N.P. ... B2, B3
White Butte, *mt.* ... B3
Wild Rice, *river* ... H3

Ohio ....page 162

Cities and Towns
Aberdeen ... C8
Ada ... C4
Akron ... G3
Alliance ... H4
Ansonia ... A5
Antrim ... H5
Antwerp ... A3
Arabia ... F8
Arcanum ... A6
Archbold ... B2
Arlington ... C4
Ashland ... F4
Ashtabula ... J2
Athens ... F7
Aurora ... H3
Avon Lake ... F2
Baltimore ... E6
Barberton ... G3
Barnesville ... H6
Batavia ... B7
Bay Village ... G9
Beachwood ... J9
Bedford ... J9
Bedford Heights ... J9
Bellaire ... J5
Bellefontaine ... C5
Bellevue ... E3
Bellville ... E4
Berea ... G9
Berlin Heights ... F3
Bethel ... B8
Beverly ... G6
Blanchester ... C7
Blissfield ... G5
Blue Ash ... C9
Bluffton ... C4
Boardman ... J3
Bowling Green ... C3
Bradford ... B5
Bremen ... F6
Brewster ... G4
Bridgetown ... B9
Broadview Heights ... H10
Brook Park ... G9
Brooklyn ... H9
Brookville ... B6
Brunswick ... G3
Bryan ... A3
Bucyrus ... E4
Burton ... H3
Cadiz ... J5
Caldwell ... G6
Cambridge ... G5
Camden ... A6
Canal Fulton ... G4
Canal Winchester ... E6
Canfield ... J3
Canton ... H4
Cardington ... E5
Carey ... D4
Carrollton ... H4
Cedarville ... C6
Celina ... A4
Centerburg ... E5
Chagrin Falls ... H3
Chardon ... H2
Chesterhill ... G7
Cheviot ... B9
Chillicothe ... E7
Cincinnati ... A7
Circleville ... E6
Cleveland ... G2
Cleveland Heights ... G2
Cleves ... A9
Clyde ... E3
Coldwater ... A5
Columbiana ... J4
Columbus, *capital* ... D6
Columbus Grove ... B4
Congress ... F4
Conneaut ... J2
Cortland ... J3
Coshocton ... G5
Covington ... B5

Key
Crestline ... E4
Creston ... G4
Crooksville ... F6
Cuyahoga Falls ... H3
Dalton ... G4
Dayton ... B6
De Graff ... C5
Deer Park ... C9
Defiance ... B3
Delaware ... D5
Delhi Hills ... B9
Delphos ... B4
Delta ... C2
Deshler ... C3
Dover ... H4
Dresden ... F5
Dublin ... D5
Dunkinsville ... D8
E. Cleveland ... H8
East Liverpool ... J4
East Palestine ... J4
Eaton ... A6
Edgerton ... A3
Elida ... B4
Elyria ... F3
Euclid ... G2
Fairborn ... C6
Fairfield ... A7
Fairport Harbor ... H2
Fairview Park ... G9
Findlay ... C3
Fitchville ... F3
Forest ... C4
Forest Park ... B8
Forestville ... D8
Fort Recovery ... A5
Fort Shawnee ... B4
Fostoria ... D3
Franklin ... B6
Fredericktown ... E5
Fremont ... D3
Fresno ... G5
Gahanna ... E5
Galion ... E4
Gallipolis ... F8
Gambier ... E5
Garfield Hts. ... H9
Geneva ... J2
Genoa ... D2
Georgetown ... C8
Germantown ... B6
Gibsonburg ... D3
Grafton ... F3
Granville ... E5
Green ... G4
Green Springs ... D3
Greenfield ... D7
Greenville ... A5
Greenwich ... E3
Grove City ... D6
Hamilton ... A7
Hannibal ... J6
Harrisburg ... D6
Harrison ... A9
Heath ... F5
Hebron ... F6
Hicksville ... A3
Hillsboro ... C7
Hiram ... H3
Holgate ... B3
Hubbard ... J3
Huron ... E3
Independence ... H9
Jackson ... E8
Jackson Center ... B5
Jefferson ... J2
Jeffersonville ... C6
Johnstown ... E5
Keene ... G5
Kent ... H3
Kenton ... C4
Kettering ... B6
Kimbolton ... G5
Kirtland ... H2
Lakewood ... G9
Lancaster ... E6
Lebanon ... B7
Leipsic ... C3
Lewisburg ... A6
Lexington ... E4
Lima ... B4
Lisbon ... J4
Lodi ... G3
Logan ... F7
London ... D6
Lorain ... F3
Loudonville ... F4
Louisville ... H4
Loveland ... B7
Lucasville ... E8
Lyndhurst ... J8
McArthur ... F7
McConnelsville ... G6
Macedonia ... J10
Macksburg ... H6
Madeira ... C9
Manchester ... C8
Mansfield ... E4
Maple Hts. ... J9
Marietta ... H7
Marion ... D4
Martins Ferry ... J5
Marysville ... D5
Mason ... B7
Massillon ... G4
Maumee ... C2
Mayfield Hts. ... J9
Mechanicsburg ... C5
Medina ... G3
Mentor ... H2
Miamitown ... B9
Middleburg Heights ... G9
Middlefield ... H3
Middletown ... B6
Milan ... E3
Milford ... B7
Millersburg ... G4
Minerva ... H4
Minster ... B5
Monfort Heights ... B9
Monroe ... B7
Montgomery ... C9
Montpelier ... A2
Mount Gilead ... E4
Mount Healthy ... B9
Mount Orab ... C7
Mount Sterling ... D6
Mount Vernon ... E5
Napoleon ... B3
Nelsonville ... F7
Newark ... F5

Key
New Baltimore ... B9
New Boston ... E8
New Bremen ... B5
New Carlisle ... B6
Newcomerstown ... G5
New Concord ... G6
New Lebanon ... B6
New Lexington ... F6
New London ... F3
New Paris ... A6
New Philadelphia ... H5
New Richmond ... B8
Newtown ... C9
Niles ... J3
North Baltimore ... C3
North Canton ... H4
North College Hill ... B9
North Kingsville ... J2
North Olmsted ... G3
North Royalton ... H10
Northfield ... J9
Northridge ... C6
Norwalk ... E3
Norwood ... C9
Oak Harbor ... D2
Oak Hill ... E8
Oberlin ... F3
Olmsted Falls ... G9
Oregon ... D2
Orrville ... G4
Orwell ... J2
Otsego ... G5
Ottawa ... B3
Painesville ... H2
Parma ... G3
Parma Heights ... H9
Pataskala ... E6
Paulding ... A3
Peebles ... D8
Pepper Pike ... J9
Perrysburg ... C2
Pickerington ... E6
Piketon ... E7
Pioneer ... A2
Piqua ... B5
Plain City ... D5
Plymouth ... E4
Pomeroy ... F7
Port Clinton ... E2
Portsmouth ... E8
Powhatan Point ... J6
Ravenna ... H3
Reading ... B7
Reynoldsburg ... E6
Richmond Heights ... J8
Richwood ... D5
Ripley ... C8
Rittman ... G4
Roseville ... F6
Russells Point ... C5
Sabina ... C7
Sagamore Hills ... J9
St. Bernard ... C9
St. Clairsville ... J5
St. Henry ... A5
St. Louisville ... F5
St. Marys ... B4
St. Paris ... C5
Salem ... J4
Salineville ... J4
Sandusky ... E3
Selma ... C6
Seven Hills ... H9
Shadyside ... J6
Shaker Hts. ... J9
Sharonville ... C9
Shelby ... E4
Shreve ... F4
Sidney ... B5
Silverton ... C9
Smithville ... G4
Solon ... J9
Somerset ... F6
South Charleston ... C6
South Euclid ... J8
South Point ... E9
Springdale ... C9
Springfield ... C6
Steubenville ... J5
Strasburg ... G4
Streetsboro ... H3
Strongsville ... G3
Stryker ... B3
Sugarcreek ... G5
Sunbury ... E5
Sylvania ... C2
The Village of Indian Hill ... C9
Tiffin ... D3
Tipp City ... B6
Toledo ... C2
Troy ... B5
Twinsburg ... J10
Uhrichsville ... H5
University Hts. ... J9
Upper Sandusky ... D4
Urbana ... C5
Utica ... F5
Van Wert ... A4
Vandalia ... B6
Venedocia ... B4
Vermilion ... F3
Versailles ... B5
Wapakoneta ... B4
Warren ... J3
Warrensville Heights ... J9
Warsaw ... G5
Washington Court House ... D6
Waterville ... C2
Wauseon ... B2
Waverly ... E7
Waynesville ... B6
Wellington ... F3
Wellston ... E7
Wellsville ... J4
West Alexandria ... A6
West Jefferson ... D6
West Lafayette ... G5
West Liberty ... C5
West Milton ... B6
West Salem ... F4
West Union ... C8
West Unity ... B2
Westerville ... E5
Westlake ... G9
Weston ... C3
Wheelersburg ... E8
Wickliffe ... J8
Wilkesville ... F7
Willard ... E3
Williamsburg ... B7
Williamsport ... D6

Key
Williamsport ... E4
Wilmington ... C7
Woodsfield ... H6
Woodville ... D3
Wooster ... G4
Wyoming ... C9
Xenia ... C6
Yellow Springs ... C6
Youngstown ... J3

Other Features
Clendening, *lake* ... H5
Cuyahoga Valley N.R.A. ... H9
Erie, *lake* ... G1
Hocking, *river* ... F7
Hopewell Culture N.H.P. ... E7
James A. Garfield N.H.P. ... H2
Kelleys, *island* ... E2
Mohican, *river* ... F4
Muskingum, *river* ... G6
Ohio, *river* ... J6
Salt Fork, *lake* ... H5
Sandusky, *river* ... D3
Scioto, *river* ... D4
Senecaville, *lake* ... H6
William H. Taft Natl. Hist. Site ... C9

Oklahoma ....page 163

Cities and Towns
Ada ... F3
Agawam ... E3
Altus ... C3
Alva ... D1
Anadarko ... D2
Antlers ... G3
Apache ... D3
Arapaho ... D2
Ardmore ... E3
Arkoma ... H2
Atoka ... F3
Barnsdall ... F1
Bartlesville ... F1
Beaver ... B1
Bethel Acres ... E2
Bixby ... G2
Blackwell ... E1
Blanchard ... E2
Boise City ... B4
Bristow ... F2
Broken Arrow ... G1
Broken Bow ... H3
Buffalo ... C1
Cache ... D3
Calera ... F4
Carnegie ... D2
Catoosa ... G1
Chandler ... F2
Checotah ... G2
Chelsea ... G1
Cherokee ... D1
Cheyenne ... C2
Chickasha ... E2
Choctaw ... E2
Chouteau ... G1
Claremore ... G1
Cleveland ... F1
Clinton ... D2
Coalgate ... F3
Collinsville ... G1
Comanche ... E3
Commerce ... H1
Cordell ... D2
Corum ... D3
Coweta ... G2
Cushing ... F2
Davis ... E3
Dewey ... G1
Drumright ... F2
Durant ... F4
Eagletown ... H3
Edmond ... E2
Elk City ... C2
Enid ... E1
Eufaula ... G2
Fairfax ... F1
Fairview ... D1
Farris ... G3
Fittstown ... F3
Floris ... B1
Forgan ... B1
Fort Gibson ... G2
Frederick ... D3
Geary ... D2
Glenpool ... G2
Granite ... C3
Grove ... H1
Guthrie ... E2
Guymon ... C4
Harmon ... C1
Hartshorne ... G3
Haskell ... G2
Healdton ... E3
Heavener ... H3
Hennessey ... E1
Henryetta ... F2
Hobart ... C2
Holdenville ... F2
Hollis ... C3
Hominy ... F1
Hooker ... A1
Hugo ... G3
Idabel ... H4
Inola ... G1
Jay ... H1
Jenks ... G1
Joy ... E3
Kingfisher ... E2
Konawa ... F3
Krebs ... G3
Laverne ... C1
Lawton ... D3
Lenora ... C1
Lindsay ... E3
Locust Grove ... G1
Lone Grove ... E3
Loveland ... D3
Lovell ... E1
McAlester ... G3
McCurtain ... H2
McKnight ... C3
Madill ... F3
Mangum ... C3
Mannford ... F1
Marietta ... E4
Marlow ... E3
Medford ... E1
Midwest City ... E2
Minco ... E2
Moore ... E2

Key
Muldrow ... H2
Muskogee ... G2
Mustang ... E2
Newcastle ... E2
Newkirk ... E1
Norman ... E2
Nowata ... G1
Oakhurst ... F1
Okeene ... D1
Okemah ... F2
Oklahoma City, *capital* ... E2
Okmulgee ... G2
Owasso ... G1
Panama ... H2
Pawhuska ... F1
Pawnee ... F1
Perkins ... E2
Perry ... E1
Picher ... H1
Piedmont ... E2
Ponca City ... E1
Poteau ... H2
Prague ... F2
Pryor Creek ... G1
Purcell ... E2
Roll ... C2
Sallisaw ... H2
Sand Springs ... F1
Sapulpa ... F1
Sayre ... C2
Seminole ... F2
Shattuck ... C1
Shawnee ... F2
Skiatook ... F1
Slaughterville ... E2
Snyder ... D3
Sparks ... F2
Spiro ... H2
Stanley ... G3
Stigler ... G2
Stillwater ... E1
Stilwell ... H2
Stratford ... F3
Stroud ... F2
Sulphur ... F3
Tahlequah ... H2
Talihina ... G3
Tecumseh ... F2
Tishomingo ... F3
Tonkawa ... E1
Tulsa ... G1
Turley ... G1
Tuttle ... E2
Vian ... H2
Vinita ... G1
Wagoner ... G2
Walters ... D3
Wanette ... E3
Warner ... G2
Warren ... C3
Watonga ... D2
Watova ... G1
Waukomis ... E1
Waurika ... D3
Weatherford ... D2
Westville ... H1
Wetumka ... F2
Wewoka ... F2
Wilburton ... G3
Wilson ... E3
Woodward ... C1
Wynnewood ... E3
Yale ... F1
Yukon ... E2

Other Features
Arkansas, *river* ... F1
Black Mesa, *mt.* ... B4
Broken Bow, *lake* ... H3
Canadian, *river* ... C2
Canton, *lake* ... D1
Chickasaw Natl. Rec. Area ... E3
Cimarron, *river* ... C1
Fort Gibson, *lake* ... G1
Hugo, *lake* ... G3
Illinois , *river* ... H2
Kaw, *lake* ... F1
Keystone, *lake* ... F1
North Canadian, *river* ... C1
Oologah, *lake* ... G1
Ouachita, *mts.* ... G3
Red, *river* ... C3
Sooner, *lake* ... F1
Texoma, *lake* ... F4
Winding Stair Natl. Rec. Area ... H3

Oregon ....page 164

Cities and Towns
Albany ... B2
Aloha ... A2
Altamont ... C3
Ashland ... C3
Astoria ... B1
Baker City ... E2
Bandon ... B3
Beaverton ... A2, C2
Bend ... C2
Brookings ... B3
Brownsville ... C2
Burns ... D3
Canby ... A2, C2
Canyon City ... E2
Cedar Hills ... A2
Central Point ... C3
Clatskanie ... B1
Condon ... D2
Coos Bay ... B3
Coquille ... B3
Cornelius ... A2
Corvallis ... B2
Cottage Grove ... B3
Creswell ... B3
Crowley ... E3
Dallas ... B2
Eagle Point ... C3
Elgin ... E2
Enterprise ... E2
Eugene ... B2
Florence ... B3
Forest Grove ... A2
Fossil ... D2
Four Corners ... A2, C2
Glendale ... B3
Gold Beach ... B3
Grants Pass ... B3
Green ... B3
Gresham ... B2
Harbor ... B3
Harrisburg ... B2

OREGON–SOUTH CAROLINA 189

Key
Hayesville A2, C2
Heppner D2
Hermiston D2
Hillsboro A2, C2
Hines D3
Homestead F2
Hood River C2
Hubbard C2
Jacksonville C3
Jefferson C2
John Day E2
Junction City B2
Juntura E3
Keizer A2
Klamath Falls C3
Lafayette B2
La Grande E2
Lakecreek C3
Lake Oswego A2, C2
Lakeside B3
Lakeview D3
Lebanon C2
Lexington D2
Lincoln Beach B2
Lincoln City B2
McMinnville B2
Madras C2
Meacham E2
Medford C3
Metzger A2
Mill City C2
Milton-Freewater E2
Milwaukie A2
Molalla A2
Monument D2
Moro D2
Mount Angel A2, C2
Mount Vernon D2
Myrtle Creek B3
Myrtle Point B3
Newberg A2, C2
Newport B2
North Bend B3
Nyssa E3
Oak Grove A2
Oakridge C3
Ontario F2
Oregon City A2, C2
Pendleton E2
Philomath B2
Phoenix C3
Pilot Rock E2
Portland A2, C2
Post D2
Prineville D2
Rainier C1
Redmond C2
Reedsport B3
Riley D3
Rogue River B3
Roseburg B3
Rufus D2
St. Helens C2
Stanfield D2
Salem, *capital* A2, B2
Santa Clara B2
Scappoose C2
Seaside B2
Seneca E2
Shady Cove C3
Sherwood A2
Silverton A2, C2
Springfield C2
Stayton C2
Sunriver C3
Sutherlin B3
Sweet Home C2
Talent C3
The Dalles C2
Tigard A2, C2
Tillamook B2
Toledo B2
Umpqua B3
Union E2
Vale E3
Veneta B2
Vernonia B2
Waldport B2
Warm Springs C2
Warrenton B1
Waterloo C2
West Slope A2
White City C3
Willamina B2
Wilsonville A2, C2
Woodburn A2
Wood Village B2

Other Features
Abert, *lake* D3
Blue, *mts.* E2
Calapooya, *mts.* C3
Cascade, *range* C3
Clackamas, *river* C2
Coast, *mt. ranges* B2
Columbia, *river* D2
Coos, *bay* B3
Crater, *lake* C3
Crater Lake Natl. Park C3
Crescent, *lake* C3
Crooked, *river* D2
Davis, *lake* C3
Deschutes, *river* C2
Diamond Peak, *mt.* C3
Gearhart Mtn., *mt.* D3
Green Peter, *lake* C2
Harney, *basin* D3
Harney, *lake* D3
Hells, *canyon* F2
Hells Canyon Natl. Rec. Area F2
Hood, *mt.* C2
Jefferson, *mt.* C2
John Day, *river* C2
John Day Fossil Beds N.M. D2
Klamath, *mts.* B3
Lookout, *cape* B2
Malheur, *lake* E3
Malheur, *river* E3
Molalla, *river* B2
Multnomah, *waterfalls* C2
Ochoco, *mts.* D2
Oregon Caves Natl. Monument B3
Oregon Dunes Natl. Rec. Area B3
Owyhee, *lake* E3
Owyhee, *river* E3
Powder, *river* E2
Pudding, *river* A2
Pueblo, *mts.* E3
Rogue, *river* B3
Sacajawea Peak, *mt.* E2
Silvies, *river* D3
Siuslaw, *river* B3
Snake, *river* F2
South Umpqua, *river* B3
Steens, *mts.* E3
Strawberry Mt., *mt.* E2
Summer, *lake* D3
Thielsen, *mt.* C3
Tillamook, *bay* B2
Trout Creek, *mts.* E3
Umatilla, *lake* D2
Upper Klamath, *lake* C3
Waldo, *lake* C3
Wallowa, *mts.* E2
Willamette, *river* A2

Pennsylvania ....page 165

Cities and Towns
Albion A2
Aliquippa A4
Allensville F4
Allentown L4
Allison Park E6
Altoona E4
Ambridge A4
Annville H5
Archbald K2
Ardmore M6
Arnot G2
Ashland J4
Athens H2
Austin E2
Avalon D7
Avis G3
Bala Cynwyd M6
Baldwin E7
Bangor L4
Barnesboro D4
Beaver A4
Beaver Falls A4
Beavertown G4
Bedford E5
Bellefonte F4
Belleville F4
Bellevue D7
Bellwood E4
Berlin D6
Berwick J3
Berwyn L6
Bethel Park A5, D7
Bethlehem L4
Birdsboro K5
Blairsville C5
Blakely K3
Bloomsburg J4
Blossburg G2
Boalsburg F4
Boothwyn L7
Boswell C5
Boyertown K5
Bradford D2
Brentwood E7
Bridgeville D7
Brockport D3
Brockway D3
Brodheadsville L4
Brooklyn K2
Brookville C3
Broomall L6
Brownsville B5
Bryn Mawr L6
Burgettstown A5
Butler B4
California B5
Cambridge Springs A2
Canonsburg A5
Canton H2
Carbondale K2
Carlisle G5
Carnegie D7
Carroll Valley G6
Carrolltown D4
Castle Shannon E7
Catawissa J4
Chambersburg F6
Chelsea L7
Chester L6, L7
Clairton B5
Clarion C3
Clarks Summit K2
Claysburg E5
Clearfield E3
Clifton Heights L7
Clymer C4
Coatesville K6
Columbia H5
Connellsville B6
Conyngham J4
Coopersburg L5
Coraopolis D7
Cornwall J5
Corry B2
Coudersport E2
Crafton D7
Cresson D5
Crosby E2
Cuddy D7
Curwensville D4
Dallas K3
Danville H4
Darby M7
Delmont B5
Denver J5
Derry C5
Dillsburg G5
Dormont D7
Dover H5
Downingtown K5
Doylestown L5
Drexel Hill M7
DuBois D3
Duncannon G5
Duquesne E7
Dushore J2
East Greenville K5
East Lansdowne M7
Easton L4
East Petersburg J5
East Stroudsburg L3
Ebensburg D4
Eddystone L7
Edinboro A2
Effinwild E6
Elizabethtown H5
Elizabethville H4
Elkland G2
Ellwood City A4
Elysburg H4
Emlenton B3
Emmaus L4
Emporium E2
Emsworth D7
Ephrata J5
Erie A1
Etna E7
Evans City A4
Everett E5
Exton K5
Fayetteville F6
Fleetwood K5
Ford City B4
Forest City L2
Forest Grove D7
Forksville H2
Fox Chapel E7
Freeland K3
Freeport B4
Galeton F2
Gettysburg G6
Girard A2
Gladden D7
Gladwyne M6
Glenolden M7
Glen Riddle L7
Glen Rock H6
Gradyville L7
Greencastle F6
Greensburg B5
Greenville A3
Gregg D7
Grove City A3
Hallstead K2
Hamburg K4
Hanover H6
Harmarville E6
Harrisburg, *capital* H5
Harrisville A3
Harveys Lake J3
Haverford M6
Havertown M6
Hazel Hurst D2
Hazleton K4
Hermitage A3
Herndon H4
Hershey H5
Highland D6
Hollidaysburg E5
Homer City C4
Honesdale L2
Huntingdon E5
Hyndman D6
Indiana C4
Indianola E6
Jersey Shore G3
Jim Thorpe K4
Johnsonburg D3
Johnstown D5
Kane D2
Kennett Square K6
King of Prussia L5
Kingston K3
Kittanning B4
Kutztown K5
Lake City A1
Lancaster J5
Lansdale L5
Lansdowne M7
Laporte J3
Latrobe C5
Lebanon J5
Leechburg B4
Lehighton K4
Levittown M5
Lewisburg H4
Lewistown F4
Ligonier C5
Lima L7
Linglestown H5
Lititz J5
Littlestown G6
Lock Haven G3
Lykens H4
McCandless A4, D6
McConnellsburg E6
McKees Rocks D7
McKeesport B5
Macungie K4
Mahanoy City J4
Manchester H5
Manheim J5
Mansfield G2
Mars A4
Martinsburg E5
Marysville H5
Masontown B6
Matamoras M3
Meadville A2
Mechanicsburg G5
Media L6, L7
Mercer A3
Mercersburg F6
Meridian B4
Merion M6
Meyersdale C6
Middleburg G4
Middletown H5
Midland A4
Mifflinburg G4
Mifflintown G4
Mifflinville J3
Milford M3
Millersburg H4
Millersville J6
Millheim G4
Millvale E7
Milroy F4
Milton H3
Minersville J4
Monessen B5
Monroeville B5, F7
Mont Alto F6
Montgomery H3
Montoursville H3
Montrose K2
Moon Run D7
Moscow K3
Mt. Carmel J4
Mt. Holly Springs G5
Mount Joy H5
Mt. Lebanon D7
Mt. Nebo D6
Mt. Oliver E7
Mt. Pleasant B5
Mt. Pocono L3
Mount Union F5
Muncy H3
Munhall E7
Myerstown J5
Nanticoke J3
Nanty Glo D5
Nazareth L4
Nesquehoning K4
New Bloomfield G5
New Castle A3
New Freedom H6
New Holland J5
New Kensington B4, F6
New Oxford G6
Newport G5
Newtown M5
Newtown Square L6
Newville G5
New Wilmington A3
Norristown L5
North East B1
Northampton L4
North Springfield A1
Northumberland H4
Oakmont E7
Oil City B3
Old Forge K3
Orwigsburg J4
Oxford J6
Palmerton K4
Patton D4
Pen Argyl L4
Penn Hills F7
Penn Wynne M6
Perkasie L5
Philadelphia L6, M7
Philipsburg E4
Phoenixville K5
Picture Rocks H3
Pine Grove J4
Pittsburgh B5, E7
Pittston K3
Pleasantville B2
Pleasantville D5
Point Marion B6
Polk B3
Port Allegany E2
Port Matilda E4
Portage D5
Portland Mills D3
Pottstown K5
Pottsville J4
Powell H2
Prospect Park L7
Punxsutawney D4
Quakertown L5
Quarryville J6
Radnor L6
Rainsburg D6
Reading K5
Red Lion H6
Renovo F3
Reynoldsville D3
Ridgway D3
Ridley Park L7
Roaring Spring E5
St. Marys D3
Saxonburg B4
Sayre H2
Schnecksville K4
Schuylkill Haven J4
Scottdale B5
Scranton K3
Selinsgrove H4
Shamokin H4
Sharon A3
Sharon Hill M7
Sharpsville A3
Sheffield C2
Shenandoah J4
Shippensburg F5
Shoemakersville K5
Shrewsbury H6
Sinking Spring J5
Slatington K4
Slippery Rock A3
Smethport E2
Somerset C5
Souderton L5
South Williamsport G3
Spring Grove H6
Springdale F6
Springfield L7
State College F4
Stewartstown H6
Strasburg J6
Stroudsburg L4
Sugarcreek B3
Sunbury H4
Susquehanna K2
Swarthmore L7
Sykesville D3
Tamaqua K4
Tionesta C3
Titusville B2
Tobyhanna L3
Towanda J2
Tower City H4
Tremont J4
Trevorton H4
Troy H2
Tunkhannock K2
Tyrone E4
Union City B2
Uniontown B6
Upland L7
Valley View H4
Vandergrift B4
Verona E7
Village Green L7
Villanova L6
Warren C2
Washington A5
Waterford B2
Watsontown H3
Waymart L2
Wayne L6
Waynesboro F6
Waynesburg A6
Weatherly K4
Wellsboro G2
Wesleyville A1
West Chester K6
West Grove K6
West Mifflin E7
Westmont D5
West Pike F2
West View E7
Whitehall K4
White Horse L6
Wilcox D2
Wilkes-Barre K3
Wilkinsburg E7
Williamsport G3
Willow Grove L5
Windber D5
Womelsdorf J5
York H6
York Springs G5
Youngsville C2
Zelienople A4

Other Features
Allegheny, *reservoir* D2
Allegheny, *river* B3
Allegheny Natl. Rec. Area D2
Allegheny Portage Railroad N.H.S. D5
Appalachian, *mts.* F5
Clarion, *river* C3
Conemaugh, *river* C4
Davis, *mt.* C6
Delaware, *river* L2
Delaware Water Gap N.R.A. M3
Erie, *lake* A1
Friendship Hill Natl. Hist. Site B6
Gettysburg Natl. Mil. Park G6
Johnstown Flood Natl. Memorial D5
Juniata, *river* F5
Lehigh, *river* K3
Ohio, *river* A4
Presque Isle, *island* A1
Raystown, *lake* E5
Schuylkill, *river* K5
Susquehanna, *river* J2
Tioga, *river* G2
Valley Forge Natl. Hist. Park L5

Rhode Island ....page 166

Cities and Towns
Adamsville F4
Allenton D4
Alton B5
Anthony C3
Arcadia B4
Ashaway B5
Ashton D2
Avondale A6
Barrington E3
Berkeley D2
Bradford B5
Bristol E3
Carolina C5
Central Falls D2
Charlestown C5
Chepachet B2
Clayville B3
Coventry Center C3
Cranston D3
Cumberland Hill D2
Diamond Hill D2
Dunn Corner B5
East Greenwich D4
East Providence D3
Exeter C4
Fiskeville C3
Foster Center B3
Galilee C5
Glendale C2
Green Hill C5
Greenville C2
Hamilton D4
Harmony C2
Harrisville B2
Hope C3
Hope Valley B5
Hopkinton B5
Jamestown D5
Jerusalem C5
Kingston C5
Little Compton E4
Lonsdale D2
Matunuck C5
Middletown E4
Moosup Valley B3
Narragansett Pier D5
Newport E5
Nooseneck C4
North Foster B2
North Providence D2
North Scituate C3
Pascoag B2
Pawtucket D2
Pawtuxet D3
Perryville C5
Plum Point D4
Point Judith D5
Portsmouth E4
Providence, *capital* D3
Prudence E4
Quidnick C3
Quonochontaug B6
Rice City B3
Riverside D3
Rockville B4
Rumford D2
Sakonnet E5
Saunderstown D5
Saylesville D2
Shannock C5
Slatersville C1
Slocum C4
South Foster B3
Spragueville C2
Tarkiln C2
Tiverton E4
Usquepaug C5
Valley Falls D2
Wakefield C5
Wallum Lake B2
Warren E3
Warwick D3
Washington C3
Watch Hill A6
Weekapaug B6
West Barrington D3
Westerly B5
West Glocester B2
West Kingston C5
West Warwick C3
Woonsocket C1
Wyoming B4

Other Features
Block, *island* C7
Block Island, *sound* B6
Mt. Hope, *bay* E4
Narragansett, *bay* D4
Rhode Island, *sound* E5
Sakonnet, *river* E4
Scituate, *reservoir* C3

South Carolina ....page 167

Cities and Towns
Abbeville B2
Aiken C3
Allendale C3
Anderson B2
Andrews E3
Bamberg C3
Barnwell C3
Batesburg-Leesville C3
Beaufort D4
Belton B2
Belvedere C3
Bennettsville E2
Bishopville D2
Blacksburg C1
Blackville C3
Boiling Springs C1
Brownsville E2
Buffalo C2
Burton D4
Calhoun Falls B2
Camden D2
Cayce C3
Central B2
Charleston E4
Cheraw E2
Chester C2
Chesterfield D2
Clemson B2
Clinton C2
Clover C1
Columbia, *capital* C2
Conway E3
Cowpens C1
Darlington E2
Denmark C3
Dentsville D2
Dillon E2
Easley B2
Edgefield C3
Elgin D2
Enoree C2
Estill C4
Fairfax C4
Florence E2
Folly Beach E4
Forest Acres D2
Foreston D3
Fort Mill D1
Fountain Inn B2
Furman C4
Gaffney C1
Garden City F3
Georgetown E3
Gifford C4
Gloverville C3
Goose Creek D3
Great Falls D2
Greeleyville E3
Greenville B2
Greenwood B2
Greer B2
Hampton C4
Hanahan D4
Hardeeville C4
Harleyville D3
Hartsville D2
Hickory Grove C2
Hickory Grove F3
Hilda C3
Hilton Head Island D4
Holly Hill D3
Hollywood D4
Honea Path B2
Horrel Hill D3
Inman B1
Irmo C2
Isle of Palms E4
Jackson C3
Jefferson D2
Joanna C2
Johnsonville E3
Johnston C3
Kershaw D2
Kiawah Island D4
Kingstree E3
Kline C3
Ladson D4
Lake City E3
Lancaster D2
Landrum B1
Lane E3
Latta E2
Laurel Bay D4
Laurens B2
Lexington C3
Liberty B2
Little River F3
Little Rock E2
Loris F2
Lugoff D2
Lyman B2
Lynchburg D2
McBee D2
McClellanville E3
McCormick B3
Manning D3
Marion E2
Mauldin B2
Mayesville D3
Mayo C1
Moncks Corner D3
Mt. Pleasant E4
Mullins E2
Murrells Inlet E3
Myrtle Beach F3
Neeses C3
New Ellenton C3
Newberry C2
Nichols E2
Ninety Six B2
North Augusta C3
North Charleston E4
North Myrtle Beach F3
Norway C3
Olanta E3
Olar C3
Orangeburg D3
Pacolet C2
Pacolet Mills C2
Pageland D2
Pamplico E3
Patrick D2
Pelion C3
Pendleton B2
Pickens B2
Piedmont B2
Pinewood D3
Pomaria C2
Port Royal D4
Ravenel D4
Red Bank C3
Ridgeland D4
Ridgeville D3

	Key
Ridgeway	D2
Rock Hill	C2
Roebuck	C2
Rowesville	D3
Ruby	D2
St. George	D3
St. Matthews	D3
St. Stephen	E3
Salley	C3
Salters	E3
Saluda	C3
Santee	D3
Sellers	E2
Seneca	B2
Simpsonville	C2
Socastee	E3
Society Hill	E2
South Congaree	C3
Spartanburg	C2
Springfield	C3
Starr	B2
Stuckey	E3
Summerville	D3
Sumter	D3
Surfside Beach	F3
Swansea	C3
Sycamore	C3
Taylors	C2
Timmonsville	E2
Travelers Rest	B2
Trenton	C3
Turbeville	D3
Union	C2
Varnville	C4
Wagener	C3
Walhalla	A2
Walterboro	D4
Ware Shoals	B2
Westminster	A2
Whitmire	C2
Williamston	B2
Williston	C3
Winnsboro	C2
Woodruff	B2
Yemassee	D4
York	C2

Other Features

	Key
Bull, island	E4
Bulls, bay	E4
Cape, island	E3
Congaree Swamp N.M.	D3
Cowpens Natl. Bfld.	C1
Edisto, river	D3
Fort Sumter Natl. Monument	E4
Greenwood, lake	C2
Hartwell, lake	B2
J. Strom Thurmond, lake	B3
Keowee, lake	B2
Kings Mt. Natl. Mil. Park	C1
Long, bay	F3
Lynches, river	D2
Marion, lake	D3
Monticello, reservoir	C2
Moultrie, lake	D3
Murray, lake	C2
Ninety Six Natl. Hist. Site	B2
North, island	E3
Port Royal, sound	D4
Russell, lake	B2
St. Helena, sound	D4
Saluda, river	C2
Santee, river	E3
Savannah, river	C3
South, island	E3
The Grand Strand	F3
Wateree, lake	D2
Wateree, river	D2

South Dakota ....page 168

Cities and Towns

	Key
Aberdeen	F1
Alexandria	G3
Armour	F3
Belle Fourche	A2
Beresford	H3
Black Hawk	A2
Box Elder	A2
Britton	G1
Brookings	H2
Burke	E3
Canton	H3
Chamberlain	E3
Cherry Creek	C2
Clark	G2
Clear Lake	H2
Custer	A3
Deadwood	A2
Dell Rapids	H3
De Smet	G2
Dupree	C1
Elk Point	H4
Faulkton	E1
Flandreau	H2
Fort Pierre	D2
Freeman	G3
Gettysburg	E1
Hartford	H3
Highmore	E2
Hot Springs	A3
Howard	G2
Huron	F2
Ipswich	E1
Kadoka	C3
Lake Andes	F3
Lead	A2
Lemmon	B1
Lennox	G3
Leola	F1
Madison	G2
Martin	C3
Milbank	H1
Miller	E2
Mitchell	G3
Mobridge	D1
Murdo	D3
Onida	D2
Parker	G3
Parkston	G3
Philip	C2
Pierre, capital	D2
Pine Ridge	B3
Plankinton	F3
Platte	F3
Rapid City	A2
Redfield	F2
Rosebud	D3
Salem	G3
Selby	D1

	Key
Sioux Falls	H3
Sisseton	G1
Spearfish	A2
Sturgis	A2
Timber Lake	C1
Tyndall	G4
Vermillion	H4
Volga	H2
Wagner	F3
Watertown	G2
Webster	G1
Wessington Springs	F2
White River	D3
Winner	E3
Woonsocket	F2
Wounded Knee	B3
Yankton	G4

Other Features

	Key
Andes, lake	F3
Angostura, reservoir	A3
Bad, river	C2
Badlands Natl. Park	B3
Belle Fourche, reservoir	A2
Belle Fourche, river	A2
Big Sioux, river	G2
Big Stone, lake	H1
Black, hills	A2
Bois de Sioux, river	H1
Cheyenne, river	C2
Francis Case, lake	F3
Grand, river	C1
Harney Peak, mt.	A3
James, river	F1
Jewel Cave Natl. Monument	A3
Keya Paha, river	D3
Lewis and Clark, lake	G4
Little Missouri, river	A1
Little White, river	D3
Missouri, river	B1
Moreau, river	B1
Mount Rushmore Natl. Memorial	A3
North Fork Grand, river	B1
Oahe, lake	D2
Pine, ridge	B3
Sharpe, lake	E2
South Fork Grand, river	A1
Traverse, lake	H1
Vermillion, river	G3
Waubay, lake	G1
White, river	D3
Whitewood, river	G2
Wind Cave Natl. Park	A3

Tennessee ....page 169

Cities and Towns

	Key
Adamsville	E4
Alamo	C3
Alcoa	P3
Algood	L2
Altamont	K4
Arlington	B4
Ashland City	G2
Athens	M4
Bartlett	B4
Baxter	K2
Bells	C3
Benton	M4
Bethel Springs	D4
Bethpage	J2
Blaine	P2
Blountville	S1
Bluff City	S2
Bolivar	D4
Brentwood	H3
Bristol	S1
Brownsville	C3
Bruceton	E2
Buffalo Valley	K2
Byrdstown	L1
Camden	E2
Campaign	K3
Carthage	K2
Caryville	N2
Celina	K1
Centerville	G3
Charlotte	G2
Chattanooga	L4
Church Hill	R1
Clarksville	G1
Cleveland	M4
Clinton	N2
Collegedale	L4
Collierville	B4
Columbia	G3
Conasauga	M4
Cookeville	L2
Covington	B3
Cowan	J4
Crossville	L3
Dandridge	Q2
Dayton	L3
Decatur	M3
Decaturville	E3
Decherd	J4
Dickson	G2
Dover	F2
Dresden	D2
Dunlap	L4
Dyer	C2
Dyersburg	C2
East Ridge	L4
Elizabethton	S2
Englewood	N4
Erin	F2
Erwin	S2
Estill Springs	J4
Etowah	N4
Fairfield Glade	M2
Farragut	N3
Fayetteville	H4
Forest Hills	H2
Frankewing	H4
Franklin	H3
Gainesboro	K2
Gallatin	J2
Gatlinburg	P3
Germantown	B4
Gleason	D2
Goodlettsville	H2
Granville	L2
Graysville	L4
Greeneville	R2
Greenfield	D2
Grimsley	L2
Gruetli-Laager	K4
Halls	C3
Halls Crossroads	P2
Hampshire	G3

	Key
Harriman	M3
Hartsville	J2
Henderson	D4
Hendersonville	H2
Humboldt	D3
Huntingdon	E3
Huntsville	N2
Jacksboro	N2
Jackson	D3
Jamestown	M2
Jasper	K4
Jefferson City	Q2
Jellico	N1
Johnson City	S2
Jonesborough	S2
Karns	N3
Kenton	C2
Kingsport	R1
Kingston	M3
Kingston Springs	G2
Knoxville	P3
La Follette	N2
La Vergne	H2
Lakewood	H2
Lawrenceburg	G4
Lebanon	J2
Lenoir City	N3
Lewisburg	H4
Lexington	E3
Linden	F3
Livingston	L2
Loretto	G4
Loudon	N3
Lynchburg	J4
McEwen	F2
McKenzie	D2
McKinnon	F2
McMinnville	K3
Madisonville	N3
Manchester	J4
Martin	D2
Maryville	P3
Mascot	P2
Maynardville	P2
Medon	D3
Memphis	A4
Middleton	D4
Milan	D3
Millersville	H2
Milligan College	S2
Millington	B4
Monterey	L2
Morristown	Q2
Mosheim	R2
Mountain City	T1
Mount Juliet	H2
Mount Pleasant	G3
Munford	B4
Murfreesboro	J3
Nashville, capital	H2
Newbern	C2
New Johnsonville	F2
New Tazewell	P2
Nolensville	H3
Norris	N2
Oak Hill	H2
Oak Ridge	N2
Oliver Springs	M2
Oneida	M2
Overall	J3
Paris	E2
Parsons	E3
Pegram	G2
Pigeon Forge	P3
Pikeville	L3
Portland	H1
Powell	N2
Pulaski	H4
Reagan	E3
Red Bank	L4
Ridgely	C2
Ripley	B3
Rockwood	M3
Rogersville	R2
Rutherford	C2
Rutledge	Q2
Savannah	D4
Selmer	D4
Sevierville	P3
Sewanee	K4
Shelbyville	H3
Signal Mountain	L4
Smithville	K3
Smyrna	H3
Sneedville	Q1
Soddy-Daisy	L4
Somerville	C4
South Fulton	D2
South Pittsburg	K4
Sparta	L3
Spencer	L3
Spring City	M3
Spring Hill	H3
Springfield	H1
Stanton	C4
Surgoinsville	R2
Sweetwater	N3
Taft	H4
Tazewell	P2
Tellico Plains	N4
Tennessee Ridge	F2
Tiptonville	C2
Tracy City	K4
Trenton	D3
Trimble	C2
Tullahoma	J4
Tusculum	R2
Union City	C2
Wartburg	M2
Waverly	F2
Waynesboro	F4
Westmoreland	J1
White House	H2
White Pine	Q2
Whitwell	K4
Winchester	J4
Woodbury	J3

Other Features

	Key
Andrew Johnson Natl. Hist. Site	R2
Appalachian, mts.	
Appalachian Natl. Scenic Trail	Q3
Barkley, lake	F1
Big South Fork Natl. River and Rec. Area	M1
Center Hill, lake	K3
Cherokee, lake	P2
Chickamauga & Chattanooga Natl. Mil. Park	L5

	Key
Chickamauga, lake	M3
Clinch, river	Q2
Clingmans Dome, mt.	Q3
Cumberland, river	G2
Dale Hollow, lake	L1
Douglas, lake	Q3
Duck, river	H3
Great Smoky, mts.	P3
Great Smoky Mts. Natl. Park	Q3
Holston, river	R2
Kentucky, lake	F2
Mississippi, river	B3
Norris, lake	P2
Roan, mt.	S2
Shiloh Natl. Mil. Park	E4
Tennessee, river	E5, K5
Watts Bar, lake	M3
Woods, reservoir	J4

Texas ....page 170

Cities and Towns

	Key
Abernathy	F2
Abilene	H3
Addison	C1
Alamo Heights	B7
Albany	H3
Algoa	F9
Alice	J8
Alpine	D5
Alvin	M6
Amarillo	B9
Anahuac	N6
Anderson	M5
Andrews	E3
Angleton	M6
Anson	H3
Anthony	A3
Aransas Pass	K8
Archer City	H2
Arlington	L3
Asherton	H7
Atascosa	A7
Athens	M3
Atlanta	N2
Austin, capital	K5
Avondale	A1
Bacliff	G9
Baird	H3
Balch Springs	C2
Balcones Heights	A7
Ballinger	H4
Bandera	H6
Barrett	F8
Bastrop	K5
Batesville	H7
Bay City	M7
Bayou Vista	G10
Baytown	N5
Beaumont	N5
Beaumont Place	F8
Beaver	C8
Bedford	B2
Beeville	K7
Bellaire	E8
Bellmead	K4
Belton	K4
Benavides	J8
Benbrook	A2
Benjamin	H2
Bergheim	A6
Big Lake	F4
Big Spring	F3
Bishop	K8
Boerne	J6
Bogata	M2
Bonham	L2
Borger	C9
Boston	N2
Bovina	E1
Bowie	L2
Bracken	B6
Brackettville	G6
Brady	H4
Breckenridge	J3
Brenham	L5
Briar	A1
Bridge City	P5
Bridgeport	K2
Brookshire	M6
Brookside Village	F9
Brownfield	E2
Brownsville	K10
Brownwood	J4
Bryan	L5
Buckingham	C1
Buena Vista	B7
Buffalo	L4
Bulverde	A6
Buna	P5
Bunker Hill Village	E8
Burkburnett	J1
Burleson	A3
Burnet	K3
Caldwell	L5
Cameron	L5
Canadian	D9
Canton	M3
Canutillo	A4
Canyon	B9
Carrizo Springs	H7
Carrollton	B1
Carthage	N3
Castle Hills	A6
Cedar Hill	B3
Cedar Park	K5
Center	N4
Centerville	M4
Chandler	M3
Channelview	F8
Channing	B9
Childress	G1
Chocolate Bayou	F10
Cisco	J3
Clarendon	C10
Clarksville	M2
Claude	C9
Cleburne	K3
Cleveland	M5
Clifton	K4
Cloverleaf	F8
Clute	M6
Cockrell Hill	B2
Coldspring	M5
Coleman	H4
College Station	L5

	Key
Colleyville	A2
Colorado City	G3
Columbus	L6
Comanche	J4
Combine	D2
Commerce	L2
Conroe	M5
Converse	B6
Cooper	M2
Copperas Cove	K4
Corpus Christi	K8
Corsicana	L3
Cotulla	H7
Crane	E4
Crockett	M4
Crosby	F8
Crosbyton	F2
Crowell	H2
Crowley	A3
Crystal City	H7
Cuero	K6
Daingerfield	N2
Dalhart	B8
Dallas	L3
Dalworthington Gardens	B2
Danbury	F10
Dayton	N5
Decatur	K2
Deer Park	F8
Del Rio	G6
Denison	L2
Denton	K2
Denver City	E3
De Soto	L3
Devine	J6
Diboll	N4
Dickinson	F9
Dickens	G2
Dilley	H7
Dimmitt	E1
Dublin	J3
Dumas	B9
Duncanville	B2
Eagle Lake	L6
Eagle Pass	G7
Eastland	J3
Eden	H4
Edgecliff	A3
Edinburg	J9
Edna	L7
El Campo	L6
Eldorado	G5
El Paso	A4
Electra	J1
Elgin	K5
Elsa	J9
Emory	M3
Ennis	L3
Euless	B2
Everman	A3
Fabens	A4
Fair Oaks Ranch	A6
Fairfield	L4
Falfurrias	J8
Farmers Branch	B1
Farwell	D1
Ferris	C3
Flatonia	K6
Floresville	J6
Floydada	F2
Forest Hill	A2
Fort Davis	D5
Fort Stockton	E5
Fort Worth	K3
Franklin	L4
Fredericksburg	J5
Freeport	M7
Freer	J8
Friendswood	F9
Gail	F3
Gainesville	L2
Galena Park	F8
Galveston	N6
Ganado	L6
Garden City	F4
Garden Ridge	B6
Gardendale	E3
Garland	C2
Gatesville	K4
George West	J7
Georgetown	K5
Germann	C3
Giddings	L5
Gilmer	N3
Gladewater	N3
Glen Rose	K3
Glenn Heights	B3
Goldthwaite	J4
Goliad	K7
Gonzales	K6
Gorman	J3
Graham	J2
Granbury	K3
Grand Prairie	B2
Grand Saline	M3
Grapeland	M4
Grapevine	B1
Greenville	K3
Groesbeck	L2
Groves	P6
Groveton	M4
Guthrie	G2
Hallettsville	L6
Haltom City	A2
Hamilton	J4
Hamlin	G3
Harker Heights	K4
Harlingen	K9
Haskell	H2
Hearne	L5
Hebbronville	J8
Helotes	A6
Hemphill	P4
Hempstead	L5
Henderson	N3
Henrietta	J2
Hereford	B10
Hewitt	K4
Hico	J4
Hidalgo	J9
Highland Park	C2
Highlands	F8
Hillsboro	K3
Hitchcock	F9
Hollywood Park	A6
Hondo	H6
Houston	M6
Hubbard	L4
Huntsville	M5

	Key
Hurst	A2
Hutchins	C2
Idalou	F2
India	K8
Ingleside	K8
Iowa Park	J2
Irving	B2
Jacinto City	F8
Jacksboro	J2
Jacksonville	M4
Jasper	P5
Jayton	G2
Jefferson	N3
Jersey Village	E8
Johnson City	J5
Jourdanton	J7
Juliff	F9
Junction	H5
Karnes City	K7
Katy	M6
Kaufman	L3
Keller	A2
Kermit	D4
Kerrick	B8
Kerrville	H5
Kilgore	N3
Killeen	K4
Kingsland	J5
Kingsville	K8
Kirby	B7
Kirbyville	P5
Knox City	H2
Kountze	N5
La Grange	L6
Lake Jackson	M7
Lakehills	J6
La Marque	G9
Lamesa	F3
Lampasas	J4
Lancaster	C3
La Porte	F9
La Pryor	H7
Laredo	H8
League City	F9
Leakey	H6
Leon Springs	A6
Leon Valley	J6
Levelland	E2
Lewisville	L2
Liberty	N5
Linden	N3
Lipscomb	D8
Littlefield	E2
Live Oak	B6
Livingston	N5
Llano	J5
Lockhart	K6
Lockney	F1
Longview	N3
Lubbock	F2
Lufkin	N4
Luling	K6
Lumberton	N5
Mabank	L3
McAllen	J9
McCamey	E4
Macdona	A7
McKinney	L2
Madisonville	M5
Mangus Corner	A7
Mansfield	B3
Manvel	F9
Marble Falls	J5
Marfa	C5
Marlin	L4
Marshall	N3
Mason	H5
Matador	G1
Mathis	K8
Memphis	C10
Menard	H5
Mentone	D4
Meridian	K4
Merkel	G3
Mertzon	G4
Mesquite	C2
Mexia	L3
Miami	C9
Midland	E3
Midlothian	B3
Mineola	M3
Mineral Wells	J2
Mission	J9
Missouri City	M6
Monahans	E4
Mont Belvieu	G8
Montague	K2
Morgans Point	G8
Morton	E2
Moss Bluff	F8
Mt. Houston	F8
Mt. Pleasant	N2
Mt. Vernon	M2
Muleshoe	E1
Munday	H2
Murphy	C1
Nacogdoches	N4
Nassau Bay	F9
Navasota	L5
Nederland	N6
New Berlin	B6
New Boston	N2
New Braunfels	J6
Newton	P5
Nixon	K6
Nocona	K2
North Houston	E8
North Richland Hills	A2
Odessa	E4
Olmos Park	A7
Olney	J2
Olton	E1
Orange	P5
Ovilla	B3
Ozona	F5
Paducah	G1
Paint Rock	H4
Palacios	L7
Palestine	M4
Palo Pinto	J3
Pampa	C9
Panhandle	C9
Pantego	B2
Paris	M2
Parita	C1
Pasadena	M6
Pearland	F9
Pearsall	H7
Pecos	D4

Pelican Bay ... A2
Perryton ... C8
Pharr ... J9
Pilot Point ... L2
Pittsburg ... N2
Plains ... E2
Plainview ... F1
Plano ... L2
Pleasanton ... J7
Port Arthur ... P6
Port Bolivar ... G9
Port Isabel ... K9
Portland ... K8
Port Lavaca ... L7
Post ... F2
Poteet ... J6
Premont ... J8
Presidio ... C6
Quanah ... H1
Quitman ... M3
Ranger ... J3
Rankin ... F4
Raymondville ... K9
Red Oak ... C3
Refugio ... K7
Reno ... A2
Richardson ... C1
Richland Hills ... A2
Richmond ... M6
Rio Grande City ... J9
Roanoke ... A1
Robert Lee ... G4
Robinson ... K4
Robstown ... K8
Roby ... G3
Rockdale ... L5
Rockport ... K7
Rocksprings ... G5
Rockwall ... L3
Roma ... H9
Roscoe ... G3
Rosenberg ... M6
Rosharon ... E9
Rotan ... G3
Round Rock ... K5
Rowlett ... C2
Rusk ... M4
Sabinal ... H6
Sachse ... C1
St. Hedwig ... B7
San Angelo ... G4
San Antonio ... J6
San Augustine ... N4
San Benito ... K9
Sanderson ... E5
San Diego ... J8
Sandy Point ... E9
Sanger ... K2
San Geronimo ... A6
San Leon ... G9
San Marcos ... K6
San Saba ... J4
Sansom Park ... A2
Sarita ... K8
Satsuma ... E8
Sayers ... B7
Schertz ... B6
Schumansville ... C6
Seabrook ... F9
Seadrift ... L7
Seagoville ... C2
Seagraves ... E3
Sealy ... L6
Seguin ... K6
Selma ... B6
Seminole ... E3
Seymour ... H2
Shallowater ... E2
Shavano Park ... A6
Sherman ... L2
Shoreacres ... F9
Sierra Blanca ... B4
Silsbee ... N5
Silverton ... F1
Sinton ... K7
Slaton ... F2
Smith Point ... G9
Smithville ... K5
Snyder ... G3
Socorro ... A4
Sonora ... G5
South Houston ... F9
Southlake ... A1
Southside Place ... E8
Southton ... B7
Spearman ... C8
Spring Valley ... E8
Spur ... G2
Stafford ... E9
Stamford ... H3
Stanton ... F3
Stephenville ... J3
Sterling City ... C4
Stratford ... B8
Sugar Land ... E9
Sulphur Springs ... M2
Sundown ... E2
Sunnyvale ... C2
Sweetwater ... G3
Tahoka ... F2
Taylor ... K5
Temple ... K4
Texarkana ... N2
Texas City ... N6
The Woodlands ... M5
Thompsons ... E9
Three Rivers ... J7
Throckmorton ... H2
Tilden ... J7
Tomball ... M5
Trinity ... M5
Trophy Club ... A1
Tulia ... F1
Tyler ... M3
Universal City ... J6
University Park ... C2
Uvalde ... H6
Van Alstyne ... L2
Van Horn ... B4
Vega ... B9
Vernon ... H1
Victoria ... L7
Vidor ... N5
Von Ormy ... A7
Waco ... K4
Waskom ... N3
Watauga ... L3
Waxahachie ... L3
Weatherford ... K3
Webster ... F9
Wellington ... D10

Weslaco ... K9
West ... K4
West Columbia ... M6
West Odessa ... E4
Westover Hills ... A2
Westworth ... A2
Wharton ... L6
Wheatland ... A3
Wheeler ... D9
White Settlement ... A2
Whitesboro ... L2
Wichita Falls ... J2
Willis ... M5
Wills Point ... L3
Wilmer ... C2
Windcrest ... B6
Winnie ... N6
Winnsboro ... M3
Winters ... H4
Wolfforth ... F2
Woodville ... N5
Woodway ... K4
Wylie ... D1
Yoakum ... K6
Zapata ... H9
Zuehl ... B7

Other Features
Alibates Flint Quarries N.M. ... B9
Amistad, reservoir ... F6
Amistad Natl. Rec. Area ... G6
Balcones, escarpment ... A6
Big Bend Natl. Park ... D6
Big Thicket Natl. Preserve ... N5
Black, mt. ... C9
Canadian, river ... C9
Cathedral, mt. ... D5
Chinati Peak, mt. ... C6
Colorado, river ... J4
Davis, mts. ... C5
Dallas-Fort Worth Intl. Airport ... B2
Eagle Peak, mt. ... B5
Edwards, plateau ... G5
Emory Peak, mt. ... D6
Falcon, reservoir ... H9
Fort Davis Natl. Hist. Site ... D5
Galveston, bay ... G9
Galveston, island ... N6
Guadalupe, mts. ... C4
Guadalupe Mts. Natl. Park ... C4
Guadalupe Peak, mt. ... C4
Kemp, lake ... H2
Livermore, mt. ... C5
Livingston, lake ... M5
Lyndon B. Johnson N.H.P. ... J5
Meredith, lake ... C9
Nueces, river ... H6
O.H. Ivie, lake ... H4
Padre Island Natl. Seashore ... K8
Pecos, river ... E4
Pelican, island ... G9
Red, river ... H1
Red Bluff, lake ... D4
Rio Grande, river ... F6
Sabine, pass ... P6
Sabine, river ... P5
Sam Rayburn, reservoir ... N4
Santiago Peak, mt. ... D6
Sierra Del Carmen, mt. ... D6
Stockton, plateau ... E5
Toledo Bend, reservoir ... P4

Utah ... page 171

Cities and Towns
American Fork ... C3
Beaver ... B5
Bicknell ... C5
Blanding ... E6
Bluffdale ... C3
Bountiful ... C3
Brigham City ... C2
Castle Dale ... C4
Cedar City ... A6
Centerville ... C3
Clearfield ... B2
Coalville ... C3
Cottonwood Heights ... C3
Delta ... B4
Draper ... C3
Duchesne ... D3
East Carbon ... D4
Enoch ... A6
Ephraim ... C4
Farmington ... C3
Ferron ... C4
Fillmore ... B5
Garland ... B2
Grantsville ... B3
Gunnison ... C4
Heber City ... C3
Helper ... D4
Hildale ... A6
Huntington ... D4
Hurricane ... A6
Hyrum ... C2
Ivins ... A6
Junction ... B5
Kanab ... B6
Lapoint ... E3
Layton ... C2
Lehi ... C3
Lewiston ... C2
Loa ... C5
Logan ... C2
Long Valley Junction ... B6
Maeser ... E3
Magna ... B3
Manila ... E2
Manti ... C4
Mapleton ... C3
Moab ... E5
Monroe ... B5
Monticello ... E6
Morgan ... C2
Mount Pleasant ... C4
Murray ... C3
Myton ... D3
N. Salt Lake ... C3
Nephi ... C4
North Ogden ... C2
Ogden ... C2
Orangeville ... C4
Orem ... C3
Panguitch ... B6
Parowan ... B6
Payson ... C3
Plain City ... C2
Pleasant Grove ... C3
Price ... D4

Provo ... C3
Randolph ... C2
Richfield ... B5
Richmond ... C2
Riverton ... C3
Roosevelt ... D3
Roy ... B2
St. George ... A6
Salem ... C3
Salina ... C5
Salt Lake City, capital ... C3
Sandy ... C3
Santa Clara ... A6
Santaquin ... C4
Smithfield ... C2
South Jordan ... C3
Spanish Fork ... C3
Springville ... C3
Sugarville ... B4
Tooele ... B3
Tremonton ... B2
Vernal ... E3
Washington ... A6
Wellington ... D4
West Jordan ... C3
West Valley City ... C3
Willard ... B2

Other Features
Abajo Peak, mt. ... E6
Arches Natl. Park ... E5
Bear, lake ... C2
Bear, river ... C2
Beaver, river ... B5
Bonneville Salt Flats ... A3
Bruin Point, mt. ... D4
Bryce Canyon Natl. Park ... B6
Canyonlands Natl. Park ... E5
Capitol Reef Natl. Park ... C5
Cedar Breaks Natl. Monument ... B6
Colorado, river ... E5
Delano Peak, mt. ... B5
Deseret Peak, mt. ... B3
Dinosaur Natl. Monument ... E3
Dutton, mt. ... B5
Escalante, river ... C6
Flaming Gorge, reservoir ... E2
Flaming Gorge Natl. Rec. Area ... E2
Frisco Peak, mt. ... A5
Glen Canyon Natl. Rec. Area ... D6
Golden Spike Natl. Hist. Site ... B2
Great, basin ... A4
Great Salt, lake ... B2
Great Salt Lake, desert ... A3
Green, river ... E4
Heliotrope, mt. ... C4
Henry, mts. ... D6
Ibapah Peak, mt. ... A4
Kings Peak, mt. ... D3
Marsh Peak, mt. ... E3
Marvine, mt. ... C5
Monument, valley ... D6
Navajo, mt. ... D6
Navajo Indian Res. ... E6
Nebo, mt. ... C4
Paria, river ... C6
Pavant, range ... B5
Peale, mt. ... E5
Pennell, mt. ... D6
Powell, lake ... D6
Price, river ... D4
Rainbow Bridge Natl. Monument ... D6
Salt Marsh, lake ... A4
San Juan, river ... D6
San Rafael, river ... D4
Sevier, desert ... B4
Sevier, lake ... A5
Strawberry, river ... D3
Swasey Peak, mt. ... A4
Timpanogos Cave N.M. ... C3
Uinta, mts. ... D3
Utah, lake ... C3
Wasatch, plateau ... C5
White, river ... E3
Zion Natl. Park ... A6

Vermont ... page 172

Cities and Towns
Addison ... A2
Albany ... C1
Ascutney ... C4
Averill ... D1
Bakersfield ... B1
Barnard ... B3
Barnet ... C2
Barre ... C2
Basin Harbor ... A2
Beecher Falls ... D1
Bellows Falls ... C4
Bennington ... A5
Benson ... A3
Berlin ... B2
Bethel ... B3
Bloomfield ... D1
Bradford ... C3
Brandon ... A3
Brattleboro ... B5
Bristol ... A2
Brookfield ... B3
Burlington ... A2
Cabot ... C2
Cambridge ... B1
Castleton ... A3
Cavendish ... B4
Charlotte ... A2
Chelsea ... C3
Colchester ... A2
Concord ... D2
Danby ... A4
Danville ... C2
Dorset ... A4
East Burke ... D1
East Haven ... D1
East Middlebury ... A3
East Randolph ... B3
Eden ... B1
Enosburg Falls ... B1
Essex ... B2
Essex Junction ... A2
Evansville ... C1
Fair Haven ... A3
Fairfax ... B1
Fairfield ... B1
Fairlee ... C3
Franklin ... B1
Gallup Mills ... D2
Gaysville ... B3
Georgia Center ... A1

Grafton ... B4
Granby ... D1
Grand Isle ... A1
Groton ... C2
Guildhall ... D1
Guilford ... B5
Hancock ... B3
Hardwick ... C2
Hartford ... C3
Hartland ... C3
Hartwellville ... A5
Highgate Center ... A1
Hinesburg ... A2
Hortonia ... A3
Hubbardton ... A3
Hyde Park ... B1
Irasburg ... C1
Irasville ... B2
Jacksonville ... B5
Jamaica ... B4
Jeffersonville ... B1
Johnson ... B1
Keeler Bay ... A1
Larrabees Point ... A3
Lemington ... D1
Londonderry ... B4
Lowell ... C1
Lyndon ... C1
Lyndonville ... C1
McIndoe Falls ... C2
Marlboro ... B5
Mendon ... B3
Middlebury ... A3
Middlesex ... B2
Milton ... A1
Monkton ... A2
Montgomery ... B1
Montgomery Center ... B1
Montpelier, capital ... B2
Morgan ... C1
Morrisville ... B1
Moscow ... B2
Newbury ... C2
Newfane ... B4
New Haven ... A2
Newport ... C1
North Bennington ... A5
Northfield ... B2
North Hero ... A1
North Wolcott ... C1
Norton ... D1
Orange ... C2
Orleans ... C1
Peacham ... C2
Pittsfield ... B3
Pittsford ... A3
Plainfield ... C2
Plymouth ... B3
Pompanoosuc ... C3
Post Mills ... C3
Poultney ... A3
Pownal ... A5
Proctor ... A3
Putney ... B5
Randolph ... B3
Readsboro ... B5
Richford ... B1
Richmond ... A2
Rochester ... B3
Roxbury ... B2
Rutland ... A3
St. Albans ... A1
St. Johnsbury ... C2
Searsburg ... B5
Shaftsbury ... A4
Sharon ... C3
Shelburne ... A2
Sheldon ... B1
Shoreham ... A3
South Burlington ... A2
South Hero ... A1
Springfield ... C4
Stamford ... A5
Starksboro ... A2
Swanton ... A1
Tinmouth ... A4
Troy ... C1
Tunbridge ... C3
Tyson ... B4
Underhill ... B1
Vergennes ... A2
Vernon ... B5
Vershire ... C3
Warren ... B2
Washington ... C2
Waterbury ... B2
Waterville ... B1
Wells River ... C2
West Burke ... D1
West Dover ... B5
West Haven ... A3
Westminster ... C4
Weston ... B4
West Pawlet ... A4
West Topsham ... C3
Wheelock ... C1
White River Junction ... C3
Williamsville ... B5
Wilmington ... B5
Windsor ... C4
Winooski ... A1
Wolcott ... C1
Woodford ... A5
Woodstock ... B3
Worcester ... B2

Other Features
Appalachian Natl. Scenic Trail ... A5
Black, river ... C1
Bomoseen, lake ... A3
Bread Loaf, mt. ... B3
Bromley, mt. ... B4
Camels Hump, mt. ... B2
Champlain, lake ... A1
Connecticut, river ... C3
Ellen, mt. ... A4
Equinox, mt. ... A4
Green, mts. ... B4
Harriman, reservoir ... B5
Jay Peak, mt. ... B1
Killington Peak, mt. ... B3
Lamoille, river ... B1
Mansfield, mt. ... B1
Mettawee, river ... A3
Missisquoi, river ... B1
Seymour, lake ... C1
Smugglers Notch, pass ... B1
Snow, mt. ... B5
Somerset, reservoir ... B4

Waterbury, reservoir ... B2
West, river ... B4
White, river ... B3
Willoughby, lake ... C1

Virginia ... page 173

Cities and Towns
Abingdon ... D1
Accomac ... M4
Achilles ... L6
Alberta ... H6
Alexandria ... J2
Allison Gap ... D1
Altavista ... E5
Amelia Court House ... H5
Amherst ... E4
Annandale ... M2
Appalachia ... B1
Appomattox ... F5
Arlington ... J2
Ashland ... H4
Baileys Crossroads ... M2
Bassett ... C6
Basye ... F2
Bedford ... D5
Belleair ... L2
Belle Haven ... M4
Belle View ... M2
Bensley ... J5
Berryville ... H1
Big Stone Gap ... B1
Blacksburg ... C4
Blackstone ... G5
Bland ... A5
Bloxom ... M4
Bluefield ... A4
Bon Air ... J5
Bowling Green ... J3
Boyce ... G1
Boydton ... G6
Boykins ... J6
Bridgewater ... F3
Bristol ... D2
Brodnax ... G6
Brookneal ... F5
Brunswick ... H6
Buckingham ... F4
Buena Vista ... E4
Burke ... L2
Burkeville ... G5
Callands ... D6
Cape Charles ... L5
Castlewood ... C1
Centreville ... J2
Charles City ... J5
Charlotte Court House ... F5
Charlottesville ... F4
Chase City ... E6
Chatham ... D6
Cheriton ... L5
Chesapeake ... L6
Chester ... J5
Chesterfield ... H5
Chilhowie ... E1
Chincoteague ... M4
Christiansburg ... C4
Chula ... H5
Claremont ... K5
Clifton Forge ... D4
Clinchco ... C1
Clintwood ... C1
Coeburn ... C1
Collinsville ... D6
Colonial Beach ... K3
Colonial Hts. ... J5
Concord ... E5
Courtland ... J6
Covington ... D4
Crewe ... G5
Crimora ... F3
Crystal City ... M2
Crystal Hill ... F6
Culpeper ... G3
Cumberland ... G4
Dale City ... J2
Danville ... E6
Dendron ... J5
Dillwyn ... G4
Dinwiddie ... H5
Drakes Branch ... F6
Dublin ... B5
Dumfries ... J2
Dungannon ... C1
Eastville ... M5
Elkton ... F3
Emory ... D1
Emporia ... H6
Ewing ... A1
Fairfax ... J2
Fairfax Station ... L2
Falls Church ... M2
Falmouth ... J3
Farmville ... G5
Ferrum ... D6
Figsboro ... D6
Fincastle ... D4
Fishersville ... F3
Flint Hill ... G2
Floyd ... C6
Forest ... E5
Fort Mitchell ... G6
Franconia ... M2
Franklin ... K6
Fredericksburg ... J3
Fries ... B6
Front Royal ... G2
Galax ... B6
Gate City ... C1
Glade Spring ... D1
Gloucester ... K5
Gloucester Point ... K5
Goochland ... H4
Gordonsville ... G3
Goshen ... E4
Gretna ... D6
Grottoes ... F3
Groveton ... M2
Grundy ... D1
Halifax ... F6
Hampton ... L5
Hanover ... H4
Harrisonburg ... F3
Harrogate ... A1
Heathsville ... L4
Hollins ... D4
Hopewell ... J5
Horse Pasture ... D6
Huntington ... M2
Hurt ... E5

Independence ... A6
Isle of Wight ... K6
Jetersville ... G5
Jonesville ... B1
Kenbridge ... G6
King and Queen Courthouse ... K4
King George ... J3
Kings Park ... L2
King William ... J4
Lancaster ... L4
Lawrenceville ... H6
Lebanon ... D1
Leesburg ... H1
Lexington ... E4
Lincolnia ... M2
Louisa ... F4
Lovingston ... F4
Lunenburg ... G5
Luray ... G2
Lynchburg ... E5
McLean ... M1
Madison ... G3
Manakin ... H4
Manassas ... J2
Manassas Park ... J2
Mantua ... L2
Marion ... A6
Martinsville ... D6
Mathews ... L5
Mechanicsville ... H4
Meherrin ... G5
Millboro ... D4
Monterey ... D3
Montross ... K3
Mount Jackson ... F2
Narrows ... A5
New Castle ... C4
New Kent ... J4
New Market ... F2
Newport News ... L6
Newsoms ... J6
Norfolk ... L6
North Springfield ... M2
Norton ... C1
Nottoway Court House ... G5
Oakton ... L2
Onancock ... M4
Orange ... G3
Palmyra ... G4
Pearisburg ... B5
Petersburg ... J5
Peterstown ... A5
Pimmit Hills ... M1
Poquoson ... L5
Portsmouth ... L6
Powhatan ... H4
Prince George ... J5
Pulaski ... B5
Purcellville ... H1
Radford ... B5
Raven ... D1
Reston ... J2
Richlands ... C1
Richmond, capital ... J4
Ridgeway ... D6
Roanoke ... D5
Rocky Mount ... D6
Rustburg ... E5
Ruther Glen ... J3
Salem ... C5
Saltville ... D1
Saluda ... K4
Shenandoah ... F3
Smithfield ... K6
South Boston ... F6
South Hill ... G6
Spotsylvania ... H3
Springfield ... M2
Spring Hill ... M1
Stafford ... J3
Stanardsville ... G3
Staunton ... F3
Sterling ... J1
Stony Creek ... J6
Strasburg ... G2
Stuart ... C6
Stuarts Draft ... E3
Suffolk ... K6
Surry ... K5
Sussex ... J6
Tappahannock ... K4
Tazewell ... A5
Timberville ... F2
Triangle ... J2
Tysons Corner ... M1
Vale ... L1
Verona ... E3
Victoria ... G6
Vienna ... L1
Virginia Beach ... M6
Warm Springs ... D4
Warrenton ... H2
Warsaw ... K4
Washington ... G2
Waverly ... J5
Waynesboro ... F3
Weber City ... C1
Wellington ... M3
West Point ... K4
West Springfield ... M2
Williamsburg ... K5
Winchester ... G1
Wise ... C1
Woodbridge ... J2
Woodstock ... F2
Wytheville ... A6
Yorktown ... K5

Other Features
Allegheny, mts. ... D3
Anna, lake ... H3
Appalachian, mts. ... D3
Appomattox Court House N.H.P. ... F5
Arlington Natl. Cem. ... M1
Assateague Island Natl. Seashore ... M4
Booker T. Washington N.M. ... D5
Charles, cape ... M5
Chesapeake, bay ... L5
Colonial Natl. Hist. Park ... K5
Fredericksburg & Spotsylvania Natl. Mil. Park ... H3
Gaston, lake ... G6
George Washington Birthplace Natl. Monument ... K3
Henry, cape ... M6
Iron, mts. ... A6
James, river ... K5
John H. Kerr, reservoir ... F6
Mount Rogers Natl. Rec. Area ... A6
Potomac, river ... K3

Rappahannock, river......J3
Rogers, mt......A6
Shenandoah, mts......E3
Shenandoah, river......F3
Shenandoah Natl. Park......G2
Smith Mtn., lake......D5
York, river......K5

Washington ......page 174

Cities and Towns
Aberdeen......C4
Amboy......D5
Anacortes......D2
Arlington......D2
Asotin......J4
Auburn......D3
Bangor......A1
Battle Ground......D5
Bellingham......D2
Belvedere......H2
Benton City......G4
Bethel......A2
Birch Bay......D2
Blaine......D2
Boardman......G5
Bothell......D3
Bremerton......D3
Brewster......G2
Bridgeport......G3
Bucoda......D4
Burien......B2
Burlington......D2
Camas......D5
Cashmere......F3
Castle Rock......D4
Cathlamet......C4
Central Park......C3
Centralia......D4
Chehalis......D4
Chelan......F3
Cheney......J3
Chewelah......J2
Clarkston......J4
Cle Elum......F3
Clinton......D2
Colfax......J4
College Place......H4
Colville......J2
Connell......H4
Cosmopolis......C4
Country Homes......J3
Coupeville......D2
Davenport......H3
Dayton......J4
Deer Park......J3
Dusty......J4
Eastgate......B2
Easton......E3
Eastsound......D2
East Wenatchee......F3
Eatonville......D4
Edmonds......D3
Ellensburg......F3
Elma......C3
Elmer City......H3
Enumclaw......E3
Ephrata......G3
Everett......D2
Everson......D2
Fall City......E3
Federal Way......D3
Ferndale......D2
Fords Prairie......C4
Forks......B3
Four Lakes......J3
Friday Harbor......C2
Fruitvale......F4
Goldendale......F5
Gorst......D3
Grandview......G4
Granger......F4
Hoquiam......C3
Inglewood......C2
Kelso......D4
Kenmore......B1
Kennewick......G4
Kent......D3
Kettle Falls......H2
Kirkland......D3
Lacey......D3
La Grande......D4
Lake Stevens......D2
Leavenworth......F3
Lexington......D4
Longmire......E4
Longview......D2
Lynden......D2
Mabton......G4
McKenna......D4
McMurray......D2
Markham......C4
Marysville......D2
Medical Lake......J3
Medina......B2
Mercer Island......D3
Merritt......F3
Monroe......D3
Montesano......C4
Moses Lake......G3
Mount Vernon......D2
Mukilteo......D3
Newhalem......E2
Newport......J2
Newport Hills......B2
Normandy Park......B2
North Bend......E3
Oak Harbor......D2
Ocean Park......B4
Ocean Shores......B3
Okanogan......G2
Olalla......B2
Olympia, capital......D3
Omak......G2
Opportunity......J3
Orchards......D5
Oroville......G2
Othello......G4
Oysterville......B4
Pasco......G4
Plymouth......G5
Pomeroy......J4
Port Angeles......C2
Porter......C4
Port Hadlock......D3
Port Ludlow......D3
Port Orchard......D3
Port Townsend......D2
Poulsbo......D3
Prosser......G4

Pullman......J4
Puyallup......D3
Quincy......G3
Raymond......C4
Redmond......D3
Renton......D3
Republic......H2
Richland......G4
Richmond Highlands......B1
Ridgefield......D5
Ritzville......H3
St. John......J3
Seabeck......A2
Sea-Tac......B2
Seattle......D3
Sedro Woolley......D2
Selah......F4
Sequim......C2
Shelton......C3
Silverton......B2
Skyway......B2
Smokey Point......D2
Snohomish......D2
Snoqualmie......E3
South Bend......C4
Southworth......B2
Spanaway......D3
Spokane......J3
Stanwood......D2
Stevenson......E5
Sultan......D2
Sumas......D2
Sumner......D3
Sunnyside......F4
Suquamish......A1
Tacoma......D3
Tekoa......J3
Tenino......D4
Tiger......J2
Toppenish......F4
Tracyton......A2
Trentwood......J3
Tukwila......B2
Tumwater......D4
Union Gap......F4
University Place......D3
Vancouver......D5
Vashon......B2
Walla Walla......H4
Wapato......F4
Warden......G4
Washougal......D5
Waterville......F3
Wenatchee......F3
Westport......B4
West Richland......G4
White Center......B2
White Salmon......E5
Winslow......D3
Woodinville......B1
Woodland......D4
Yakima......F4
Yelm......D4
Zillah......F4

Other Features
Adams, mt......E4
Bainbridge, island......B2
Baker, mt......E2
Banks, lake......G3
Cascade, range......E2
Chelan, lake......F2
Chewuch, river......F2
Columbia, river......G2
Copper Butte, mt......H2
Coulee Dam Natl. Rec. Area......H2
Cowlitz, river......D4
Disappointment, cape......B4
Elliott, bay......B2
Flattery, cape......B2
Franklin D. Roosevelt, lake......H2
Glacier Peak, mt......E2
Grays, harbor......B4
Green, river......D3
Hood, canal......C3
Kettle River, range......H2
Klickitat, river......E4
Lake Chelan Natl. Rec. Area......F2
Lewis, river......E4
Mt. Baker Natl. Rec. Area......E2
Mount Rainier Natl. Park......E4
Mt. St. Helens Natl. Vol. Mon......D4
North Cascades Natl. Park......E2
Okanogan, river......G2
Olympic, mts......C3
Olympic Natl. Park......C3
Olympus, mt......C3
Omak, mt......G2
Orcas, island......D2
Oregon Butte, mt......J4
Ozette, lake......B2
Pasayten, river......F2
Pend Oreille, river......J2
Potholes, reservoir......G4
Priest Rapids, lake......G4
Puget, sound......B1, D2
Rainier, mt......D4
Riffe, lake......D4
Rimrock, lake......E4
Ross, lake......E2
Ross Lake Natl. Rec. Area......E2
Sacajawea, mt......H4
St. Helens, mt......D4
San Juan, island......C2
Sanpoil, river......H2
Selkirk, mts......J2
Skagit, river......E2
Skykomish, river......E3
Snake, river......J4
Spokane, river......H3
Strait of Juan de Fuca......B2
Stuart, mt......F3
Umatilla, lake......G5
Vashon, island......B2
Wallula, lake......H4
Washington, lake......B1
Wenatchee, lake......F3
Wenatchee, mts......F3
Wenatchee, river......F3
White, pass......E4
Whitman Mission Natl. Hist. Site......H4
Willapa, bay......B4
Yakima, river......F4
Yale, lake......D4

West Virginia ......page 175

Cities and Towns
Ansted......D4
Barboursville......B4

Beckley......D5
Belington......G2
Berkeley Springs......K1
Bluefield......D6
Bradley......D5
Bridgeport......F2
Buckhannon......F3
Charles Town......L2
Charleston, capital......C4
Chester......K4
Circleville......G3
Clarksburg......F2
Clay......D4
Clendenin......D4
Craigsville......E4
Davis......H2
East Liverpool......K4
Edray......E4
Eleanor......C3
Elizabeth......E2
Elkins......G3
Fairmont......F2
Fayetteville......D4
Fort Ashby......J2
Franklin......H3
Gary......C6
Glenville......E3
Grafton......F2
Grantsville......D3
Hamlin......B4
Harpers Ferry......L2
Harrisville......E2
Hinton......E5
Huntington......B4
Hurricane......B4
Inwood......K2
Kenova......A4
Keyser......J2
Kingwood......G2
Lewisburg......F5
Logan......C5
Madison......C4
Mannington......F1
Marlinton......F4
Marmet......C4
Martinsburg......L2
Matewan......B5
Middlebourne......E2
Milton......B4
Montgomery......D4
Moorefield......J2
Morgantown......G1
Moundsville......K6
Mt. Hope......D5
Mullens......D5
Newburg......G2
New Cumberland......K4
New Haven......C3
New Martinsville......E1
New Milton......E2
Nitro......C4
Oak Hill......D4
Oceana......C5
Orma......D3
Paden City......E1
Parkersburg......C2
Parsons......G2
Pennsboro......E2
Petersburg......H3
Peterstown......E6
Philippi......F2
Pineville......C5
Point Pleasant......B3
Princeton......D6
Rainelle......E5
Ravenswood......C3
Reedy......D3
Richwood......E4
Ripley......C3
Romney......J2
Ronceverte......E5
Rupert......E5
St. Albans......C4
St. Marys......D2
Salem......F2
Shady Spring......D5
Shepherdstown......L2
Shinnston......F2
Sistersville......E1
Slanesville......J2
South Charleston......C4
Spencer......D3
Summersville......E4
Sutton......E3
Terra Alta......G2
Union......E5
Vienna......C2
Wayne......B4
Webster Springs......F4
Weirton......K5
Welch......C6
Wellsburg......K5
Wellsville......K4
West Milford......F2
Weston......F2
West Union......E2
Wheeling......K5
White Sulphur Springs......F5
Whitesville......C5
Williamson......B5
Williamstown......D2
Winfield......C3

Other Features
Allegheny, mts......G4
Big Sandy, river......B5
Bluestone, lake......E5
Bluestone Natl. Scenic River......E5
Gauley River Natl. Rec. Area......D4
Greenbrier, river......F4
Harpers Ferry Natl. Hist. Park......L2
Kanawha, river......C3
New River Gorge Natl. River......D5
Ohio, river......E1
Potomac, river......J2
Shenandoah, mts......H4
Spruce Knob, mt......H3
Spruce Knob Seneca Rocks N.R.A......H3
Sutton, lake......E4

Wisconsin ......page 176

Cities and Towns
Abbotsford......C4
Adams......D5
Algoma......F4
Alma......B4
Altoona......B4
Amery......A3
Antigo......D3

Appleton......E4
Arcadia......B4
Ashland......C2
Augusta......B4
Baldwin......A4
Balsam Lake......A3
Baraboo......D5
Barronett......A3
Bayside......F1
Beaver Dam......E5
Belleville......D6
Bellevue......F4
Beloit......D6
Bennett......B2
Berlin......E5
Bethesda......D2
Big Bend......E2
Black River Falls......C4
Bloomer......B3
Bloomville......D3
Boscobel......C5
Breed......E3
Brillion......E4
Brodhead......D6
Brookfield......E1
Brown Deer......F1
Bryant......D3
Buena Vista......D1
Burlington......E6
Butler......E1
Cadott......B4
Cameron......B3
Canton......B3
Carlisville......F4
Cedarburg......F5
Cedar Grove......F5
Chelsea......C3
Chetek......B3
Chili......C4
Chilton......E4
Chippewa Falls......B4
Cleveland......F5
Clinton......E6
Clintonville......E4
Colby......C4
Coloma......D5
Columbus......D5
Conrath......B3
Cornell......B3
Cornucopia......B2
Crandon......E3
Crestview......F2
Cuba City......C6
Cudahy......F2
Cumberland......A3
Darlington......C6
De Forest......D5
De Pere......E4
Delafield......D1
Delavan......E6
Denmark......F4
Dodgeville......C6
Duplainville......E1
Durand......B4
Eagle River......D3
Easton......D5
East Troy......E6
Eau Claire......B4
Edgar......C4
Edgerton......D6
Elkhorn......E6
Ellsworth......A4
Elm Grove......E1
Elroy......C5
Evansville......D6
Fennimore......C6
Florence......E3
Fond du Lac......E5
Forestville......F4
Fort Atkinson......E6
Fox Lake......E5
Fox Point......F1
Fredonia......F5
Friendship......D5
Galesville......B4
Genesee......D2
Genesee Depot......D2
Germantown......E5
Gillett......E4
Glendale......F1
Grafton......F5
Green Bay......F4
Greendale......F2
Greenfield......F2
Green Lake......E5
Greenleaf......E4
Hales Corners......E2
Hamburg......D3
Harrison......E5
Hartford......E5
Hartland......D1
Hayward......B2
Hillsboro......C5
Hollister......E3
Holmen......B5
Horicon......E5
Hortonville......E4
Howard......E4
Howards Grove......F5
Hudson......A4
Hurley......C2
Husher......F2
Jackson......E5
Janesville......D6
Jefferson......E6
Juda......D6
Jump River......C3
Juneau......E5
Kaukauna......E4
Kenosha......F6
Keshena......E4
Kewaskum......E5
Kewaunee......F4
Kiel......E5
Kneeland......F2
Lac du Flambeau......D3
La Crosse......B5
Ladysmith......B3
Lake Delton......D5
Lake Geneva......E6
Lake Mills......E6
Lampson......B3
Lancaster......C6
La Pointe......C2
Little Chute......E4
Lodi......D5
Lomira......E5
Madison, capital......D5
Maiden Rock......A4
Manitowish......C2

Manitowoc......F4
Marathon City......D4
Marinette......F3
Markesan......E5
Marshfield......C4
Mason......B2
Mattoon......D3
Mauston......C5
Mayville......E5
Medford......C3
Menasha......E4
Menomonee Falls......E1
Menomonie......B4
Mequon......F1
Merrill......D3
Middleton......D5
Milton......E6
Milwaukee......F5
Mineral Point......C6
Mishicot......F4
Modena......B4
Mole Lake......E3
Mondovi......B4
Monona......D5
Montello......D5
Montfort......C6
Mosinee......D4
Muscoda......C6
Muskego......E6
Neenah......E4
Neillsville......C4
Nekoosa......D4
New Berlin......E1
New Glarus......D6
New Holstein......E5
New Lisbon......C5
New London......E4
New Richmond......A3
Newton......F5
Niagara......F3
North Fond du Lac......E5
North Lake......D1
North Prairie......E6
Oak Creek......F6
Oconto......E4
Oconto Falls......E4
Odanah......C2
Omro......E4
Onalaska......B5
Oostburg......F5
Oregon......D6
Osceola......A3
Oshkosh......E4
Paddock Lake......E6
Palmyra......E6
Park Falls......C3
Pell Lake......E6
Peshtigo......F3
Pewaukee......E1
Phillips......C3
Platteville......C6
Pleasant Prairie......F6
Plover......D4
Plymouth......F5
Polonia......D4
Portage......D5
Port Edwards......D4
Porterfield......F3
Port Washington......F5
Port Wing......B2
Poynette......D5
Prairie du Chien......B5
Prairie du Sac......D5
Prescott......A4
Princeton......D5
Pulaski......E4
Racine......F6
Randolph......E5
Random Lake......F5
Raymond......F2
Reedsburg......C5
Rhinelander......D3
Rice Lake......B3
Richland Center......C5
Ridgeway......D5
Ripon......E5
River Falls......A4
River Hills......F1
Rothschild......D4
St. Croix Falls......A3
St. Francis......F2
Sauk City......D5
Saukville......F5
Saylesville......D2
Schofield......D4
Shawano......E4
Sheboygan......F5
Sheboygan Falls......F5
Shell Lake......B3
Sherwood......E4
Slinger......E5
South Milwaukee......F2
Sparta......C5
Spencer......C4
Spooner......B3
Spread Eagle......E3
Spring Green......C5
Stanley......C4
Stevens Point......D4
Stonebank......D1
Stoughton......D6
Sturgeon Bay......F4
Sturtevant......F6
Summit Lake......D3
Sun Prairie......D5
Superior......A2
Sussex......E1
Tabor......F2
Thompsonville......C4
Thorp......C4
Tomah......C5
Tomahawk......D3
Tony......C4
Two Rivers......F4
Verona......D5
Viola......C5
Viroqua......B5
Wales......D2
Wanderoos......A3
Washburn......B2
Watertown......E5
Waukesha......E5
Waunakee......D5
Waupaca......D4
Waupun......E5
Wausau......D4
Wautoma......D5
Wauwatosa......E1
West Allis......F6
West Bend......E5

Westby......C5
West Milwaukee......F1
Weyauwega......E4
Whitehall......B4
Whitewater......E6
Williams Bay......E6
Wind Lake......E2
Wind Point......G2
Winneconne......E4
Wisconsin Dells......D5
Wisconsin Rapids......D4
Wrightstown......E4

Other Features
Apostle Islands Natl. Lakeshore......C1
Big Muskego, lake......E2
Castle Rock, lake......D5
Chetek, lake......B3
Chippewa, lake......C3
Door, peninsula......F4
Dubay, lake......D4
Flambeau, river......C3
Green, bay......F4
Madeline, island......C1
Michigan, lake......G5
Mississippi, river......B5
Outer, island......C1
Peshtigo, lake......E3
Petenwell, lake......D4
Pewaukee, lake......D1
Poygan, lake......E4
St. Croix Natl. Scenic Riverway......A2
Sand, island......C1
Spring, lake......D2
Stockton, island......C2
Superior, lake......C1
Timms Hill, mt......C3
Winnebago, lake......E4
Wisconsin, river......D3
Wolf, river......E4
Yellow, river......C4

Wyoming ......page 177

Cities and Towns
Afton......A2
Basin......B1
Boxelder......D2
Buffalo......C1
Byron......B1
Casper......C2
Cheyenne, capital......D3
Cody......B1
Cokeville......A2
Deaver......B1
Douglas......D2
Evanston......A3
Gillette......D1
Glenrock......D2
Green River......B3
Greybull......B1
Jackson......A2
Kemmerer......A3
Lander......C2
Laramie......D3
Lovell......B1
Lusk......D2
Lyman......A3
Medicine Bow......C3
Mills......C2
Newcastle......D2
Pinedale......B2
Powell......B1
Rawlins......C3
Reliance......B3
Riverton......B2
Rock Springs......B3
Saratoga......C3
Sheridan......C1
Sundance......D1
Thermopolis......C2
Torrington......D2
Wamsutter......B3
Wheatland......D2
Worland......C1

Other Features
Absaroka, range......A1
Belle Fourche, river......D1
Big Sandy, river......B2
Bighorn, lake......B1
Bighorn, mts......C1
Bighorn, river......B1
Bighorn Canyon Natl. Rec. Area......B1
Bridger Peak, mt......C3
Clarks Fork Yellowstone, river......B1
Cloud Peak, mt......C1
Colter Peak, mt......A1
Continental Divide, mt. ridge......B3
Devils Tower Natl. Monument......D1
Elk, mt......C3
Flaming Gorge, reservoir......B3
Flaming Gorge Natl. Rec. Area......B3
Fort Laramie Natl. Hist. Site......D2
Fossil Butte Natl. Monument......A3
Francs Peak, mt......B2
Gannett Peak, mt......B2
Grand Teton, mt......A2
Grand Teton Natl. Park......A2
Great Divide, basin......B3
Green, river......B3
Greybull, river......B1
Jackson, lake......A2
Laramie, mts......D3
Laramie, river......D3
Laramie Peak, mt......D2
Little Bighorn, river......C1
Little Missouri, river......D1
Little Powder, river......D1
Little Snake, river......C3
Medicine Bow, river......C3
North Platte, river......C2
Nowood, river......C1
Owl Creek, mts......B2
Pathfinder, reservoir......C2
Powder, river......D1
Rocky, mts......C3
Seminoe, reservoir......C3
South Fork Cheyenne, river......C2
South Fork Powder, river......C2
Sweetwater, river......C2
Teton, range......A2
Tongue, river......C1
Trout Peak, mt......B1
Whiskey Peak, mt......C2
Wind, river......B2
Wind River, range......B2
Yellowstone, lake......A1
Yellowstone Natl. Park......A1